BUSINESS STUDIES

Michael Barratt
Andy Mottershead

Longman

Edinburgh Gate
Harlow, Essex

Acknowledgements

The authors would like to thank the following people:

Tony Bussey who has provided extremely practical and useful advice

Emily Blount, Liz Brown, John Buckley, Emma Busi, Kim Carvey, Clive Curd, Peter Dickson, Ian Evans, Jamie Ferguson, Robin Field, Ashley Fraser, Andy Hicks, Roger Hotchkiss, Ivan Lax, Dave Mottershead, Emma Mottershead, Sheila Mottershead, Tim Mottershead, John Nichols, Julie Otter, Adam Paphitis, Robin Pocock, Hugh Ramsbotham, Ricardo Semler, Eddy Shah, John Thackray, Jason Tsai, and the A Level Business Studies students at Tettanhall College.

The authors would also like to thank the following companies:

Avecia, Black and Decker, BT, CICA, EMI, easyJet, Entanet, The Halifax, Hewlett Packard, Ishida UK, Leyland DAF, MFI, Manchester United, Nichol's Foods, PGL, The Prudential, The Radbrook Day Nursery, Royal Shrewsbury Hospital, Sainsbury's, Semco, the *Shropshire Star*, Toyota, Yates' Wine Lodge

We are grateful to the following for permission to reproduce copyright material:

Financial Times Ltd for adapted extracts from the articles 'Fresh ideas for baby's palate' by Katharine Campbell in *Financial Times* 21.1.97 and 'The future looks brighter as the Pru polishes up its image' by Christopher Brown Humes in *Financial Times* 29.6.99; Guardian News Service for an adapted extract from 'Now the customer is tyrant' by Simon Caulkin in *The Observer* 25.4.99; Independent Newspapers (UK) Ltd for an extract from 'I looked all over, but there was nothing' by Paul Rodgers in *Independent on Sunday* 6.10.96; the author Carol Kennedy for an adapted extract from *Guide to the Management Gurus* published by Century Business Books Ltd; News International Syndication for extracts from the articles 'Sting in the tail for new breed of bargain hunters' by Janet Bush in *The Times* 11.12.98, 'Iceland tries to thaw upmarket customers' by Dominic Rushe in *The Sunday Times* 23.5.99, 'Euro at three-month high against sterling' by Lea Paterson and Alasdair Murray in *The Times* 22.7.99, 'Firms are warned of eclipse liability' by Simon de Bruxelles in *The Times* 27.7.99, 'Firm fined £1.5m for Southall rail crash' in *The Times* 28.7.99 © Times Newspapers Limited 1999 and an adapted extract from 'Top Shop chain fashions internet expansion drive' by Kirstie Hamilton in *The Sunday Times* 28.3.99. © Times Newspapers Ltd 1998, 1999 and the author Ricardo Semler for an extract from *Maverick*; Which? Consumers' Association for text from *Which?* Magazine 1996.

We are also grateful to the following for permission to reproduce photographs & other copyright material:

Architectural Association page 277 (Clement Etienne), Art Directors & TRIP pages 6 top, 6 centre (H.Rogers), 25 centre (H.Rogers), 25 right (J.Stanley), 554; Bestfoods UK Ltd page 276 right; Camelot page 137 top; Trevor Clifford pages 59 right, 91, 233, 242 left, 253, 296 top, 296 bottom right, 320, 415; "The Coca-Cola" red disc icon is a registered trademark of the Coca-Cola Company and is reproduced with kind permission from the Coca-Cola Company" page 180; Colorific! pages 6 bottom (Steve Benbow). 25 left (David Levenson); Daewoo Cars page 133; Designs on Crystal page 271; Freud Communications page 241 top; Image Bank page 296 bottom left; based on material from "The Small Business Start-Up Guide" © National Westminster Bank page 18; Pictor International pages 286, 309 right; Popperfoto pages 19, 444, 467, "Sony" is a registered trademark of Sony Corporation, Japan page 20; Stone page 286 (Michael Rosenfeld), 309 left (Adri Berger), 311 (Michael Rosenfeld); Telegraph Colour Library page 279 (V.C.L), 285 (L.Lefkowitz); TESCO page 276 left; Topham Picturepoint page 225; Which? published by Consumers' Association page 59 right (photo Trevor Clifford)

Contents

Section 5: People in organisations

Section 6: Business environment

Synoptic Case Study

Introduction to the Student's Book

Dear Student,

You are probably thinking: not another Business Studies textbook! This is not just another, it's new and has been written with you in mind at all times. The book covers all the new specifications for AS and A2 to ensure that all the required concepts are covered for your particular course.

To enable you to get the most out of this particular book we would encourage you to read each unit as directed by your teacher, although your teacher may invite you to use the book in a way which most suitably addresses your own needs for getting the best grade for A level Business Studies. We therefore recommend that you attempt the questions as you progress, in order for you to ensure that you have understood the concepts. At the end of each unit there are some Points for Revision where the key terms are defined and the important points are clearly highlighted to make your revision easier and more effective. Finally there are Mini and Maxi case studies which will allow you to practise the examination technique of applying your knowledge in the context of a given situation.

At the end of each section of the book there is a series of questions to further enhance your revision and ultimate success in the examinations.

These questions include straightforward recall of knowledge and other questions that test your ability to apply your knowledge in another case study context.

All examination boards have to set a 'synoptic paper' – i.e. one that tests the entire course and we have therefore included case studies to help you to develop the skills required for the synoptic element.

We have used as many real-life businesses as possible to provide you with up to date examples that you can relate to and follow the development of the business at a future date.

Mindful of the use of IT, we are introducing a website to accompany the book which will introduce up to the minute cases to help you to be aware of events in the business world which might relate to your examination.

We have also included many references that will help you to achieve your key skills portfolio; your teacher will be aware of which units cover each particular key skill.

Both the authors are practising teachers and are therefore aware of your needs and concerns; we are both examiners and are consequently conscious of presenting the topics in such a manner as to make your task of understanding and subsequently passing the examinations that much easier, whilst at the same time attempting to ensure that you actually enjoy the subject.

Michael Barratt
Andy Mottershead

Introduction to business

Business activity

Learning objectives

Having read this unit, students will be able to

1 identify the factors involved in business activity

2 identify the sectors of an economy involved in creating wealth

3 appreciate the functions involved in business activity

4 understand the importance of added value in all parts of business

Context

The NSPCC is a charity which is run in a 'business-like' manner in that it seeks to cover its costs and then redistribute funds to various causes which improve the lives of certain children. On the other hand, the business activity of IKEA is aimed at improving the comfort and aesthetic effect of a home, while earning money for its employees and profit for its owners. Local councils are also involved in business activity, even though there is no profit involved. Whether people work in the local tourist office, organising trips to ancient monuments, or co-ordinate waste management, they are involved in business activity. The person who puts on bumpers for Honda or who sells compact discs is involved in yet another aspect of business activity.

So business activity encompasses everything a business does, from thinking about a new product to collecting an award for the most efficient factory in Britain.

What is a business?

A business is a collection of people or resources involved in providing goods or services for an end user. Money will flow into and out of a business; if the money which flows in is greater than the money which flows out, the business will make a profit and therefore has the potential to grow. If the opposite is the case, the business will need a third party to provide financial support. Business activity can take place only if there is enough money available.

What is business activity?

Julie Potter began her nursery by renting a suite of rooms within a business complex. The complex housed various professions such as accountants, lawyers and architects. She had identified several young professional women and men in the building who were having to juggle their careers with child minding and baby sitting and she immediately recognised there was a need for a nursery/child minding service close to where these people worked. She had to borrow some money to buy the toys, cookers (the children frequently stay for lunch) and decorations; in addition she put some of her own money into the business. This meant taking a risk with every last penny she had, but the potential rewards in terms of enjoyment of the job as well as profit were well worth it. She hired some staff who were qualified child minders and soon began to receive enquiries. The numbers coming to the nursery in the first couple of months were rather small, so she decided to forego decoration of the baby room in favour of an advertising campaign. The cost of running the nursery was the same for five children as it was for 15 children. The service she provided meant her customers were willing to pay more than the usual nursery rate because the children were so close to them at work; hence Julie easily made a profit. She was mindful of possible rent increases, which was a factor beyond her control. She was also aware of the fact that the parents of all but one of the 15 children worked within the building so if any of the businesses moved, demand for her nursery would fall.

This case study demonstrates a series of concepts which are a fundamental part of business activity:

- Business is about satisfying a customer
- Customers have **needs and wants** that must be satisfied by the product
- To satisfy a customer, a business must combine various different inputs (**resources**) to produce an **output** – in this case, a child's place at a nursery
- A business needs **money**, or an equivalent medium of exchange, to be able to carry out transactions with customers and suppliers
- There are different departments or **functions within a business**, all of which must be organised and planned carefully
- All decisions that are taken using part of the resources mean that the resources cannot be used in another part of the business. This concept is known as **opportunity cost**
- The owners take risks with their investment and require reward for their risk – profit
- If a business can create a product which can be sold for more than it is worth (in cost terms) then it will make a profit i.e. in order to make a profit, the business must create **added value**
- No business can ignore the fact that there are **external forces** which may either hinder or encourage success and growth

The customer

Sometimes the phrase 'the customer is king' is used to describe the customer's importance within a business. Without customers, a business ceases to exist. Businesses need to listen carefully to customers and must observe their purchasing patterns carefully; if customers change, so must the business.

Needs and wants

Customers have needs and wants which are satisfied by the product. Any individual has need of food, clothing and shelter i.e. whatever is required for everyday survival. Wants, on the other hand, are infinite; the fact

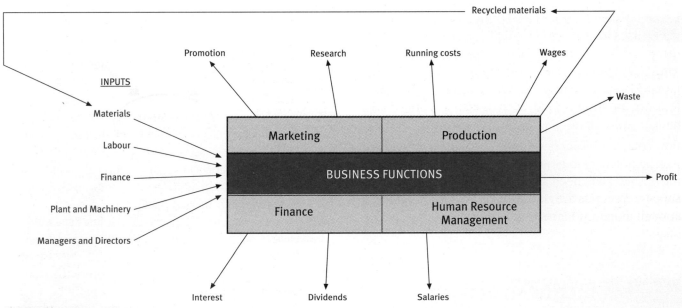

Figure 1.1 Business activity

that individuals usually want more than they can get means that people strive for greater things in life. Greater power, wealth, material possessions, even fame. It is the continual desire for more which drives the majority of business activity.

The business uses the **market** to sell to the customer. A market is much more than the town square where traders ply their products; it is a place where buyers meet sellers. A shoe shop is where the seller of shoes will meet the buyer of shoes. In certain circumstances the market is less easy to define – when shopping is carried out across the Internet, for example, the market no longer has a physical space like a shop. However, the Internet fulfils the definition of a market in that it allows buyers to meet sellers.

The final product of business can be classified as follows:

a) **fast moving consumer goods** – often referred to as fmcgs or sometimes consumer non durables – products which are sold to consumers week in, week out which are consumed only once, the majority of a family's shopping bill will be devoted to these products; if the product is used, or consumed, then in order to consume more, another product must be bought. Such products are not kept for long periods of time without being used. The consumer will use them and replace them e.g. all food products, shampoo, dog biscuits. Such products have a fast turnover in that they are used and replaced several times during a year.

b) **consumer durables** – products which are sold to consumers, but are purchased less frequently as they can be used many times e.g. washing machines, cars and carpets.

c) **capital goods** – products supplied from one business to another. A vast amount of industrial activity is between businesses. Before a consumer sees a new car, it has been through several stages of production, in different firms; then the parts are delivered to the car assembly plant to be assembled. In addition, there are companies which make the cranes, fork-lift trucks and welding machinery which allow the assembly and manufacture of industrial goods to take place.

Inputs and outputs

A business has several resources at its disposal known collectively as factors of production; it can use land, labour, capital (and materials) and managerial ability (referred to as enterprise):

Land

This refers to the actual physical assets which a business can use – sometimes the same land may be used many times by building a multi-storey building on it. Land is significant for farmers because it is used many times to grow crops and farms work hard to maintain the yield of each acre covered in crops or cattle. Land refers to any asset on, under and above the ground. A valuable resource such as oil is part of the factor of production 'land' even though it is drilled for underground.

Labour

Labour represents the skill and effort which people use at work. In return for their skill, they are paid wages or salaries.

Capital

Businesses need buildings, machinery, vehicles, shelving (for storage), fuel (to run the machines) and materials. Materials can come in the form of raw materials and components. Raw materials, such as oil or diamonds, are extracted from the ground or sea; components are also a form of capital which are used in the assembly process but are likely to be pre-manufactured by another company.

Question 1

Some businesses, such as BP Amoco or Shell, begin with raw material extraction and control the entire process of refinery, distribution and retailing.

What are the advantages and disadvantages of doing this?

[6]

Managerial ability (see page 7)

It requires entepreneurial ability (i.e. the ability to think and create) to combine the resources of a business so that the most output is produced from the least input. If these resources can be combined efficiently, it will mean that each unit of output is produced at the lowest cost.

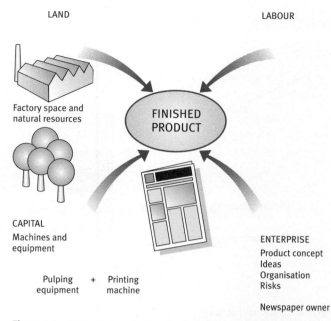
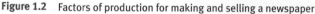

Figure 1.2 Factors of production for making and selling a newspaper

■ Money

In order to carry out transactions with suppliers of products and for customers to pay, there must be a generally accepted medium of exchange. In the middle ages, there was a barter economy, where transactions were carried out only in products e.g. three bushels of wheat for a cow. Nowadays, companies rarely carry large amounts of cash at any one time on their premises. To minimise the risk of holding large amounts of cash, they need regular visits to the bank and use companies like Securicor to do this. Money is frequently transferred through bank accounts via a computer and many customers now make most of their major purchases using a credit card or debit card.

■ Business functions

Most students may be familiar with these terms without really appreciating their role in business activity.

Question 2

a) Place in rank order the businesses in the pictures according to their need to have cash on their premises.

[3]

b) Explain why each of the above businesses requires a different amount of cash to operate effectively.

[6]

Marketing

This is likely to be the first part of business activity encountered, through advertising on television. Although there is much more to marketing than just TV advertising, billions of pounds are spent each year on producing catchy, attractive, provocative advertisements, the object of which is to entice customers to purchase the product. Marketing is much wider than advertising; it involves the process which identifies what customers want, then devises a strategy which will satisfy those wants. The main frame of the strategy is a concept called the four Ps – product, price, place (distribution) and promotion.

Production (Operations)

Production is the process whereby inputs of people, machinery and materials are converted into outputs of either finished goods or services. This could involve anything from a carpenter hand-crafting a wooden rocking horse, taking two weeks to make one unit, to a food manufacturer, such as Mars, making millions of Mars bars a year. The term operations can be interpreted in a wider sense to include all activities which are involved in day-to-day operations e.g. a solicitor's clerk has the responsibility of allocating cases, organising paperwork and ensuring the solicitors have an organised, structured day. Although this is not production in the sense of manufacturing, it is the process of operation.

Finance

In order to carry out day-to-day activity, such as buying in stock and paying people to turn up and work, a business needs finance. Alternatively, it may need to buy machinery, factories, or even an entire business; in which case it will also need finance. So financial requirements are classified according to whether they are short-term (day-to-day) or long-term. The Finance department is therefore involved in the careful planning of revenue and expenditure. Such a plan is known as a budget. Each department will be given a budget in terms of expenditure targets and, where appropriate, revenue targets. The individual budgets then build to form the budget for the entire business. Such a budget is sometimes used to persuade banks and potential investors to put money into the business.

People

All businesses involve people; very frequently the skill level, motivation and initiative of the people in the business determine its success. The Personnel or Human Resource Management departments exist to select, train, and organise the employees according to the needs of each department. If a business fails to achieve the best from its employees (who include everyone who works in the business from work-force to managers and directors) then the performance of the business may suffer.

Directors

As a business grows, the managers become more involved in the day-to-day running of the business and sometimes the longer-term perspective is ignored. The directors are responsible for considering the long-term objectives of the business and for ensuring that resources are organised carefully so that long-term objectives are achieved. Directors are also responsible for reporting to shareholders in company reports, and it is the directors, not the managers, who bear the brunt of shareholder scorn when profits are down, as well as receiving shareholders' praise when profits are up. Ironically, although directors are not known as managers, their whole job is about management!

Management

Although this is sometimes seen as a separate department, management is not a collection of individuals who sit in a suite of plush offices with cushy jobs (at least it is not meant to be!). Management is the process which includes the following responsibilities:

- Planning
- Organising
- Controlling
- Co-ordinating
- Motivating

Such responsibilities are spread across the above functions i.e. there will be individual managers in charge of each function whose job it is to ensure the process of business activity is carried out according to the various objectives the business sets itself.

Opportunity cost

'You can't have your cake and eat it!' – you may have heard this phrase before and it does apply in business. Indeed, it forms the basis of the need for decision making. If you won £10,000 on the lottery, you might be faced with the decision of what to do with the money. Suppose you considered three alternatives:

– Buying a new car
– Going on a luxury six-week cruise with your family
– Buying shares

The benefits of the first option are mobility, status and enjoyment. The second would give you a once-in-a-lifetime holiday, a temporary suntan, some photos, and some souvenirs. The third option would be risky in that the value of shares may rise and fall, although you would receive dividends from the shares and it would provide an opportunity to track the financial markets closely, watching your investment change in value.

You can choose only one of the above. If you prioritise the three options and end up wanting option 1, then 3, then 2, by going for the car and therefore not the shares you are giving up the chance to earn dividends and to watch the value of the £10,000 (hopefully) rise. This represents an opportunity cost: by choosing one alternative, you are giving up the right to benefit from the next best alternative.

Question 3

Imagine you have inherited £2,500 from a wealthy aunt. List two options you might use the money for as well as not spending it now by putting it in a high interest bank account. Decide the order of priority of your options. What benefit are you sacrificing by choosing your best option i.e. what is the opportunity cost of your decision?   [5]

In exactly the same way, a business is continually faced with the issue of opportunity cost. A business might be faced with the following alternatives:

1 purchasing a new machine which will reduce operating costs due to greater efficiency, and therefore increase profit.
2 launching an advertising campaign designed to increase awareness of its brands.

If the business chooses option 1, then the opportunity cost is the extra sales revenue which might have been earned following the advertising campaign. If the business chooses option 2, then the business loses the extra sales and profit which might have resulted from the improvement in efficiency.

Question 4

Given the above alternatives, what else might the business take into account, apart from the opportunity costs mentioned, when taking the decision whether to opt for 1 or 2?   [5]

Question 5

Watch-It has generated £2 million through the sale of one of its factories. In order to improve the efficiency of its clock-making operation, the business has moved all its production to one site. With the surplus £2 million, it can do one of three things:

1   Invest in a computerised stock control system which will mean it can save money on holding stock

2   Invest the money in the bank in a three months' notice account earning higher interest than the usual current account

3   Buy shares in one of its major suppliers

a) Identify the benefits of each of these options.   [3]

b) How would a business decide which option to choose?   [3]

c) Which do you think is the best option? Justify your choice.   [3]

d) State the opportunity cost of your decision.   [1]

■ Risk versus profit

Think of what you can do with a certain amount of money, in terms of where it is invested. Perhaps you could put it in a bank, or building society, or perhaps buy government bonds (used to finance government borrowing). You might wish to buy shares in a safe, large business like McDonald's that are likely to grow steadily; alternatively you could invest in a business

that has launched a revolutionary new computer product. Such an investment would be much riskier, but would hopefully, given the nature of the business, produce a much greater increase in profit and therefore share price.

As the risk of the investment increases, the expected return will increase.

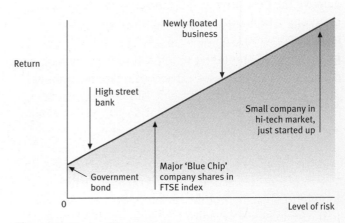

Figure 1.3   Trade-off between risk and return

An investor can invest in government stock or a bank account of a major high street bank, which will attract low levels of return, but will also be safe. Investors can then increase their risk, with shares in major companies, increasing further by investing it in new, high technology companies. In such cases, the risk levels will be extremely high, as will the potential return.

Question 6

From the following list, suggest a rank order using
(i) risk (ii) return
a) ordinary shares in a high technology company
b) building society savings account
c) the lottery
d) cash under the bed
e) ordinary shares in a major pharmaceutical company
                [7]

Briefly explain why there is a pattern when comparing answers to (i) and (ii).   [3]

■ Added value

Coca-Cola uses very simple materials in its production process. The actual product is made of carbonated water, sugar, colouring and flavouring. It is packaged in an aluminium can, with red and white ink on the side. The total cost of the labour and materials is probably less than 10 pence, although the retail price is invariably more than 35 pence. The difference between these two figures is known as added value. Every business should try to add value in everything it does. Decisions are assessed according to the amount of added value which will result. The more efficient businesses will try to remove all those processes which add costs without adding value.

Added value is normally earned in one of two ways:

– By making a production process more efficient, for example, by eliminating waste
– By encouraging customers via effective marketing to purchase a product, at a price which is greater than the cost

The end result is that the customer is willing to pay more for the product than it costs to produce one unit.

Question 7

State how the following companies add value:
Boots the Chemists
McDonald's
Boddingtons
Virgin
Gap
The Disney Shop [12]

■ External factors

In the course of business activity, a business may encounter problems which it will need to solve e.g. late supplier delivery, unskilled work-force, people leaving for jobs elsewhere. But there is also a set of forces which come from outside the business which may constrain the business or perhaps produce opportunities for growth.

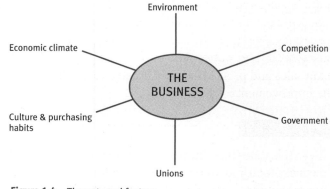

Figure 1.4 The external factors

Question 8

Explain how the external factors shown in the above diagram might **a)** help **b)** hinder a business which manufactures cycle helmets. [10]

Manufacturing versus services

Business activity can be divided into **four stages of production**, as they are known, which are used to describe and classify the nature of business activity:

Primary sector – the extraction or creation of raw materials. The primary sector is dominant in countries where there is either a wealth of raw materials or perhaps a wealth of rich, fertile land which can be used to grow crops. Animals are also a source of raw materials. Gold, silicon and coal can require complicated extraction processes, so primary industries tend to be located close to these natural supplies.

Secondary sector – once the materials have been extracted, they are turned into either part-finished goods or components, then assembled. This sector encompasses everything to do with the finished product in terms of its manufacture, apart from the extraction of raw materials.

Tertiary sector – the services which have evolved from the success of manufacturing. The service sector is responsible for a significant part of economic growth in

Britain and encompasses financial services – banks and building societies, estate agents, all retailers, solicitors, accountants, cleaners and recruitment agencies, amongst many others.

Quaternary sector – this has evolved in recent years, based on the revolution in IT. All services which are associated with IT support, from companies which allow you to browse on the Internet to those which improve and update computer technology, are involved in this sector.

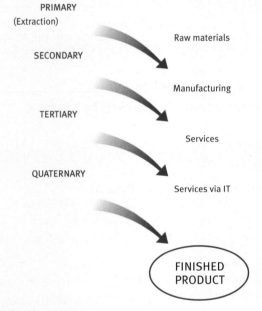

Figure 1.5   The sectors

The importance of manufacturing

Business activity depends on the amount of manufacturing within an economy; if there is no manufacturing, the activity of services must be generated from outside the economy, by importing (buying goods in from abroad). In recent years, manufacturing has declined significantly. In Britain this has been replaced by an increase in the service industry. Services can exist only if manufacturing exists e.g. loans for houses cannot be granted unless the house has been built in the first place. Shops also require the manufactured goods to sell! Although it is possible to import goods, this means that money is leaving the country – and making another country wealthier at our expense.

Question 9

Table 1   Gross value added: by industry in £million

	1989	1997	% increase
Agriculture	9097	10820	18.9
Mining and quarrying	12491	18137	45.2
Manufacturing	110407	146522	32.7
Construction	33117	36491	10.2
Service industries	283909	483072	70.2
All industries	460536	711270	54.4

Source: United Kingdom National Accounts, Office for National Statistics

a) Summarise the main changes outlined in table 1 between 1989 and 1997.   [4]

b) What are the implications for business activity of such changes?   [4]

Points for Revision

Key Terms

needs and wants	customers have needs, which are for survival (housing, food, clothing), and wants, which improve their lifestyle (e.g. bigger car, smarter clothes)
resources	factors of production (or inputs) used in the process of creating a product – land, labour, capital, management (enterprise)
output	the end product of combining all inputs
money	a medium of exchange between businesses, shareholders, suppliers and customers
business functions	the various parts of a business which combine to achieve the objectives e.g. marketing
external factors	forces over which the business has no control, which affect its activity
fast moving consumer good	a type of product which is bought frequently and once used must be purchased again e.g. washing powder
consumer durables	purchased with a view to using many times e.g. washing machine
capital goods	sold to businesses in order to help them produce a product – this could be a welding machine or raw materials
market	the place where buyer meets seller
opportunity cost	the benefit foregone of the next best alternative
added value	the process involved in making the selling price worth more than the cost
primary stage of production	extraction of raw materials
secondary	assembly and manufacture of products
tertiary	the service sector e.g. banks
quaternary	tertiary businesses associated with Information Technology

Definitions Question:
By referring to a business you know, explain the importance of any four of the above terms
(your teacher may wish to select the terms).   [5] per definition

Summary Points:

1 A business uses factors of production – land, labour, capital and managerial ability to produce its output.

2 There are several functions within business e.g. marketing, production, which must be controlled and co-ordinated if the business is to operate efficiently.

3 If a business wishes to survive and grow, it must be able to add value.

4 There are several external factors, over which the business has no control, but which affect many parts of business operations.

Mini Case Study

The Big Boot Company (BBC) manufactures a range of walking and climbing boots, which it sells through specialist mountaineering and camping shops. It used to use leather in all its products, but since the introduction of synthetic material in shoe-making, it has replaced leather boots with ones made entirely of man-made material. This has meant lower maintenance for the user and a longer life for the product. The market has divided itself into those who require boots for lightweight walking (around nature trails and woods etc.) and keener walkers who would scale the Monroes of Scotland every weekend. The marketing manager had decided on an advertising campaign to encourage more consumers to buy its walking boots, but unfortunately this would mean postponing the planned introduction of a new safety boot aimed at businesses.

1 Explain the significance of the term 'specialist' in the above case.   [3]

2 Which classification of product does the BBC sell?   [1]

3 How might the introduction of man-made material add value to the boot?   [3]

4 What are the effects on the functions of the BBC when customer needs change?   [4]

5 What are the opportunity costs of undertaking the advertising campaign?   [5]

6 From the information given, explain the relevance of risk and return to the BBC.   [4]

20

Maxi Case Study

PGL (otherwise known to customers as Parents Get Lost) is a holiday business, located in Ross-on-Wye. It is famous amongst children and teenagers for holidays which provide opportunities for adventure, activity and fun.

PGL has two types of holiday centre. The first are open from March to October. These tend to be old farmhouses and manor houses which PGL buys and converts into holiday centres with the majority of activities taking place on site. The second use boarding schools, opening for the summer season (five weeks in July and August).

The schools, which are looking to use their grounds and accommodation to greater effect, fulfil the company's requirements for accommodation for children and teenagers and grounds suitable for the activities. PGL therefore rents some of the schools' facilities – bedrooms, eating facilities, sports areas – then uses the school as a temporary 'summer' centre.

The summer centres are run by managers who are appointed on temporary contracts of six weeks to organise the entire operation and liaise with head office. The staff for the summer centres are usually students. PGL uses its own equipment and offers such activities as tennis, archery, shooting, windsurfing, fencing, motor sports, abseiling and canoeing, among many others. The investment in the equipment is significant. It frequently needs to be replaced, due to wear and tear by hundreds of children.

PGL asks for a non-refundable deposit from customers although if the booking is made within 12 weeks of the intended departure date, the full amount is required with the booking form, in one lump sum.

The cost of each holiday varies according to the type of holiday – the more exotic, such as canoeing in the Ardèche, the more expensive. Such a holiday costs nearly £400 per child. The business feels it can charge such an amount given the desire of
a) children to have a holiday of activity free from the over-protective eye of their parents, and
b) parents to buy freedom for themselves for a week!

1 Outline the evidence that the flow of money into and out of the business will not give too much cause for concern.   [3]

2 Which sector of business activity does PGL operate in?   [1]

3 Outline the differences between the customers who might use the permanent centres and those favouring the temporary centres.   [4]

4 Why might the cost of a holiday in a permanent centre be less expensive for PGL in the long term?   [3]

5 Make a list of the different groups of people who are involved directly and indirectly in operating PGL.   [3]

6 Explain how the concept of opportunity cost relates to the boarding schools' need to rent out their properties to PGL.   [4]

7 Draw a diagram to show how PGL uses inputs to create outputs.   [6]

8 Explain how PGL can exist only with the support of manufacturing industries.   [3]

9 Discuss the significance of added value for a business such as PGL.   [8]

Setting up in business

Learning objectives

Having read this unit, students will be able to

1 appreciate the reasons why people set up in business

2 understand the reasons why businesses fail

3 identify the factors which will affect the success of a business

Context

Each of the major companies to be seen on the high street, such as Virgin, the Body Shop, Woolworth and Next, began as a brainchild of just one person. Although there may have been several individuals involved at the birth of the business, the actual conception, so to speak, will have developed in the mind of one individual. Although such businesses are accepted as household names, they will all have started their lives with a significant degree of uncertainty about their future and with very little advice from others. Nowadays, advice for new firms is provided freely by banks and some management consultants have become very wealthy selling advice to new firms. To survive the first two years means that future survival is much more likely as businesses become more experienced in solving problems.

Why do people set up in business?

It is a common misconception that people start up in business with the sole view of making money. Although rags to riches stories are frequently documented in the national press and the desire for financial wealth is a driving force in a business, the actual reasons why a person sets up in business go beyond that of profit.

To fulfil a dream – such dreams may range from providing financial stability for future generations to being in charge of a modern factory.

To redistribute wealth – Anita and Gordon Roddick set up the Body Shop for several reasons, some of which are included in the unit on objectives. The prime concern was that third world countries were caught in a 'catch 22' situation because they could not persuade third world banks to lend them money. This was because of their poverty and their lack of access to a wealthy market. Despite this, the small villages and communities in Africa were capable of manufacturing popular fragrances. The Roddicks' main objective was to redistribute wealth from the first world to the third world.

To provide a service to customers – sometimes when you have suffered at the hands of unfriendly staff, or from poor quality products, perhaps you have thought of setting up a business because you feel the issue of a caring customer service is important. Seeing a customer leaving your premises satisfied with the product, and pleased to have done business with you, may be the main motivational factor. Alternatively, you may be working for a company which you feel is not providing the service in the correct manner, or is not targeting the correct market, in which case this may well motivate you to fill these gaps.

To have an interesting job – boring work tends to breed bored minds, in that there is no need to think on the job. People who have been made redundant, or who are perhaps stuck in dead end jobs, strike out on their own to provide variety and interest in their work.

To have freedom of action – if there is a dictatorial boss at work, whose autocratic approach means you never get ideas heard, or perhaps working practices are highly prescriptive; having your own business means you have only yourself to answer to. Many people start their own business because it provides an all-embracing challenge, not just to produce goods, but in terms of marketing them and financing the business.

To provide career opportunities – some groups within society have fewer career opportunities than others: women sometimes start up on their own through sheer frustration over their career prospects. Ethnic minorities may experience racial prejudice in a traditional organisation, but are willing to work hard for their livelihood, hence the massive number of small shops, usually grocers or newsagents, that open for 16 hours a day.

To fund an ambition or personal goal – a business might be started to provide funds for a hobby. Although Richard Branson has run Virgin successfully for many years, he has a wide range of spectacular hobbies, one of which has been to attempt the circumnavigation of the globe in a hot air balloon.

Question 1

Charles Marlow desperately wanted to set up in business; he was weary of working for the clothing manufacturer that had employed him since he left school and wanted to have some real responsibility and challenge in his working life. He had a strong working knowledge of the clothing market and wanted to specialise in making cardigans. Profit was also one of his motives in that he wanted to be able to fund his increasingly extravagant lifestyle. His present job did not permit this, although the 36 hour working week meant that he was able to spend a great deal of time socialising, if only he had more money! Although there were one or two competitors, he felt they were providing poor quality products at the wrong prices; his dream was to take the market by storm and develop the name of Marlow's Cardigan as synonymous with quality and value for money. With all this in mind, he walked into the director's office to hand in his resignation.

---

a) Identify the reasons why Charles wanted to start his own business.   [3]

b) Explain why he might not be able to achieve all he wants to (i.e. why his objectives might conflict with each other).   [7]

Is profit a dirty word?

Although people might have dreams that can be realised through running a business, without the financial resources to provide the foundation, the business will not survive. Business survival, therefore, implies that there is some form of financial stability. Such stability can be expressed in two fundamental, yet different, concepts:

- profit, which represents the growth of the business
- cash, which allows the business to perform many transactions between customers, suppliers, (owners), the government and the business itself.

A business therefore needs to be able to make money for two separate reasons:

1) By earning profit, a business can gain access to other funds, such as a bank loan, to fund its growth. A bank is more likely to look favourably on a profit-making business than on a loss-making one.

2) Profit means that it can reward its owners (investors) for taking the risk of investing in the business in the first place. All new and growing companies require external finance and there is a competitive market for investors' funds which are used in this manner; business owners must be able to attract such funds with promises of greater returns for those taking the risk of investment.

How are businesses born?

The mechanics of actually setting up a business are dealt with in detail in Unit 3. However, any business begins with an idea; it may not be a particularly revolutionary idea, such as running a business cleaning windows, but the driving force must come from the **entrepreneur**. Alternatively, someone may have an outlandish idea, such as inventing a wheelbarrow which moves on a ball as opposed to a wheel. Such an idea was generated by James Dyson, more famous for designing his own vacuum cleaner, which has since made him a millionaire several times over.

Organising ideas or the best way actually to start a business requires careful planning. In order to help formulate a plan on paper in more detail, a **business plan** should be drawn up. This is a detailed document, stating various stages the business must go through and various targets the business needs to achieve if it is to be successful.

The business plan provides structure and guidance to the business owner(s) so that it is possible continually to monitor and review progress. The plan can also be used to persuade other providers of capital to finance the business both as it is starting up (**seed capital**) and as it is growing (**development capital**).

Question 2

Imagine you are starting a business which requires £10,000 to begin trading. Suggest where you might try to find the sources of finance.   [6]

The business plan

The purpose of the business plan, as previously stated, is to demonstrate the particular details of a business with regard to its market and financial objectives, the details of its operation, its customer base and its financial status.

A typical business plan will contain the following:

- **Details of the business** – name, location, physical size of business etc.

- **Goals and objectives** – this may begin with a general (mission) statement of the business, what it actually intends to achieve e.g. 'Our aim is to provide quality service to customers, whilst providing meaningful, challenging work to our employees.' In more specific detail the business will then state its objectives, such as achieving a market share of 4% in the second year of operation. A more basic objective may be to operate within the limits of finance set by the bank, or to break even (ensuring that the revenue covers the costs of the business) within the first 18 months of trading.

- **Present state of the market** – this will cover the present state of the market in terms of the sales volume or revenue, location of the market and prospects for further growth.

- **Customer profile** – the intended customer will need to be targeted carefully and defined – perhaps according to levels of income, sex, location etc.

- **Competition analysis:**
  a) a significant reason for success is the ability to be better than the competitors – a detailed analysis of competitors' products and their strengths will help the business focus on trying to be better. This means the business must focus on how its own product is going to create a competitive advantage in terms of functions and features
  b) pricing policy – how the price will compare with the competitors'; given a certain level of sales and guessing the reaction of the competitors to the business's products, will break-even be achieved?
  c) promotion and advertising required – how will the business promote the product? What methods and media will it use and how much will the promotion cost?

- **Projection of sales volume and revenue in the short and long term** – these will be linked with its objectives. There will also be a statement concerning the assumptions which underpin the projection of sales e.g. assuming competitors do not react to the product with a price cut which may reduce the company's own volume of sales.

- **Present orders** – a new business will be taken much more seriously by banks if there is evidence of (new) orders.

- **Assets and required financing** – any proposed expansion will require new machinery and possibly storage space. It will also need new suppliers of raw materials. All forms of assets will require finance.

- **Staff** – what are the skills, backgrounds and ambitions of the staff? How many new staff does the business intend to employ in the near future to allow the business to meet its objectives?

- **External factors** – are interest rates rising? Perhaps the local labour force is employed by one major company which may be considering moving out of the area.

- **Ownership** – who are the owners, what is their percentage of ownership as well as the actual amount they have put in to the business and what will be the expected return to the owners?

- **Financial forecast** – this will include a projection of profit and cash flow, so that the bank can focus on particular times when extra finance may be needed.

Question 3

Tom Evans glumly surveyed the list of jobs which were advertised at the job centre. It was only three months ago that he had proudly opened his new sports shop. He had borrowed money from his parents, having spotted the advert in the local paper requesting bids for a newsagent's shop which was being sold. The price was so low, and he had always yearned to run his own sports shop, that without even researching the market, the suppliers and the customers, he had placed a deposit on the premises. He had failed to notice that the property had been on sale for nearly a year although he was in a small town with no other sports shops. This presented a real challenge for Tom; he saw himself as the saviour of this area who would bring jobs and wealth, not to mention the brand name sports clothes. He had also failed to notice that a large company which employed nearly half of the small town had just sold its factory to some property developers who were going to turn the area into large retail outlets which would result in a total of 1500 people being made redundant.

Ten weeks later, with very little trade and suppliers demanding payment, he was forced to sell his stock and property for 10% less than he had paid for it. He had also borrowed too much from his father and was not looking forward to the prospect of paying him back over the next five years!

Explain how the formulation of a business plan might have helped Tom to avoid the mistakes he made.

[10]

The Business

Name, address, legal status (*see Unit 3*), description of activities, objectives, capital structure

(i) Limited company

Shareholders	Paid up value	% of total
		100%

Partnerships and sole traders	Amount of capital	% of total
		100%

Key Personnel

Name, age, qualifications, positions held, date joined, salary ....

Premises

Size, valuation, use – existing and future, rates per annum

Plant and machinery, equipment, vehicles

a) Existing: Description   Estimated replacement date   Loan   Value

b) Future assets, needs – use, cost

Product and market

- Details of product ....
- Details of market size ....
- Major competitors ....
- Target market share in year ....
- Turnover target in year 1 ....
- Break-even figure ....
- Comments on realism of figures ......

Extent of market research

Marketing plan ....

Suppliers ....

Finance

Assets available as security

a) Business ....

b) Personal ....

Financial requirements

Amount required: ....

Provided by: • Own funds • Grants • Other sources

Bank requirements:

- Overdraft • Loan and length of time

Figure 2.1   Business plan mock-up

What are the typical problems a new business faces?

The glamour of setting up a business can frequently be the driving force, although the reality is normally somewhat different; running a business is an all-consuming affair and may require working seven days a week to get it off the ground.

Although businesses might fail (be forced to cease trading) at any point in their lives, the likelihood of business failure occurring during the first one or two years is much higher than it occurring later in its life.

Failure in the first two years tends to result from:

Lack of market research

What can seem an obvious idea to one individual may simply not appeal to the mass market. Engineers sometimes invent wonderful new gadgets which may contain some incredibly complicated circuitry, but for which there is very little demand.

Insignificance in the market-place

Lack of size sometimes leads to a lack of respectability. Smaller firms may well get paid late because the larger customers know the small business cannot afford to take them to court.

Cash flow problems

Suppliers may also be unwilling to allow long periods of credit or discounts because the business is simply not ordering enough volume from them.

Lack of skill

Putting ideas into practice needs certain characteristics ranging from technical skill to personal drive and ambition. If the entrepreneur does not have such skills, the business will not survive.

Lack of finance

This is one of the most common reasons why businesses fail. Whether the business needs money to pay suppliers, wages, or even the taxman, it will still need access to finance. Although the owner will invest as much as he/she can afford, the business will rely primarily on the bank and other external providers of money. If such financiers do not consider that the business is going to succeed, perhaps after two years of making losses, then the flow of funds will cease and the business will be forced into **liquidation** (when the assets are turned into cash and as many as possible of the bills owing are paid).

Over-expansion (overtrading)

Sometimes a business will expand too quickly, requiring more machines, more materials, more labour, without actually receiving the money from previous orders (*see Unit 34 Cash flow*). Whilst larger companies have financial resources they can fall back on, the smaller business does not have such a luxury.

Megalomania

Sometimes one business success can lead the owners to feel that whatever they produce will result in a successful venture. Sir Clive Sinclair gained his initial and formidable success as the man who anticipated the need for a pocket calculator. This led him to produce some weird and wonderful ideas. One such was the Sinclair C5 – demand for which was not researched, resulting in one of the most famous failures in corporate history.

A Sinclair C5

What are the conditions for success in business?

The best way to find an answer to this is probably to talk to various successful business people and ask the very same question. They will probably produce some of the following ideas:

- **A well designed product** – this must be exciting, interesting and one which fulfils a particular need or want, which customers are willing and able to pay for. A business will need careful and thoughtful market research to discover these customer needs.

- **Imagination** – certain products will have been created from a highly imaginative mind; the person who wanted a bank without any branches and so created First Direct, the idea of shopping through the Internet or the person who invented the idea of taking cash out of a hole in the wall are good examples in this respect. All these ideas will have been treated with suspicion at the time.

- **Tight financial control** – a budget must be drawn up and then communicated to the rest of the business as something which must be adhered to very closely. A constant focus on profit and cash flow will mean the business is most likely to be able to generate financial wealth for survival and then growth. Borrowing only when it is absolutely necessary is sometimes seen as a reason for survival, although there will be times when borrowing provides the only remaining lifeline for the business (when all other sources of finance have dried up!)

- **Motivated employees and directors** – who are willing to work hard for the success of the business and themselves.

- **An efficient production system** – which is flexible, run by highly skilled people with initiative.

- **Commitment and vision** – in order to pursue success. In his book *Against the odds*, James Dyson recounts the difficulties he faced when finding finance for his revolutionary bagless vacuum cleaner.

Question 4

Explain why each of the two companies associated with the logos above has been successful.   [6]

Points for Revision

Key Terms

entrepreneur	person who develops a business from the idea through to the birth of the business; frequently the owner as well
seed capital	money raised to fund the start of the business
development capital	money raised to fund the growth of the business
business plan	a document used to help the business organise itself to ensure good planning and control
liquidation	the legal process of turning assets into cash when a business is being wound up

Definitions Question:
By referring to a business you know, explain the importance of any two of the above terms
(your teacher may wish to select the terms).   [5] per definition

Summary Points:

1 People start up in business for a variety of reasons, only one of which is financial wealth.

2 New and small businesses face many problems at the start of their lives, particularly in the first 12–24 months.

3 Whether businesses are successful depends upon many factors, although the ability to operate within tight financial boundaries is probably the most significant reason for survival in the first two years.

Mini Case Study

A local clothes retailer close to your school has just closed down. It had tried to sell too wide a range of clothes at too wide a range of prices and had confused its customers. You have decided to focus on one of the gaps in the market that have therefore opened up, in particular, selling T-shirts which have an attractive logo on the front. One of your schoolfriends, Oliver Pickup, is a talented artist and has produced two possible designs which will be screen-printed on to white and green T-shirts. There is a supplier in Norwich willing to supply you with anything between 1,000 and 20,000 T-shirts per month at a cost of £1 per white T-shirt and £1.20 per green T-shirt. Your art teacher has agreed to let you use the screen printer in the Art department, at a cost of £500 per month and you will need to store the finished products in your garage at home for the moment. You have carried out some tentative research amongst your close school friends which reveals there is potential demand, although it is clear that the price charged will be significant in determining the final level of demand. You are not quite sure how you are going to sell the T-shirts, although your English teacher has suggested that the school magazine could be used, at a cost of £100 for a full page advertisement.

1 List the pieces of information which you think you still need in order to build a business plan. [5]

2 Using your answers to question 1, create a business plan as the basis of a presentation which you will give to the bank manager (your teacher) with a view to securing a loan to start operating the business.

You will be awarded marks for
a) realism
b) originality
c) consistency in your ideas
i.e. you would not try to sell 300,000 silk T-shirts for £1.50 each in Harrods! [15]

20

Maxi Case Study

When Alan Otter worked for a Gloucester-based fitness centre, he was not only demotivated by the personnel in the business, but for a long time had developed an ambition to run his own business. In addition, he felt there was a niche that at the time was not being served by other fitness centres. This niche market was divided into three:

- those with a psychological barrier to fitness
- those with a physical barrier to fitness
- those with a specific ailment

An opportunity arose when he saw an advert in the local small business newspaper from a professional medical centre seeking tenants within a complex of business premises that had been purpose-built next to the medical centre. The location was promising, given that it was close to an appropriate customer base, with good car parking near by. The latter was particularly important given the nature of the business. Customers normally exercised during their lunch hour or in the early evening, meaning they did not want either to pay for parking, or to be forced to park and walk a distance to the exercise centre.

He therefore began his business, Fit for Life, with capital of £45,000, almost all of which was borrowed, but not by Alan. He teamed up with a partner who was in the same position as Alan and who was keen to begin her own business – between them they were fortunate to have families who were willing to borrow the money on their behalf, acting as guarantors. The other partner was a physiotherapist, which meant that the business was immediately diversified and therefore had an alternative source of income; however, because this part of the business was based on reputation it took longer for it to make a significant contribution to profit. The advantage was that it used more or less the same customer base as the exercise business.

The business took out a 25-year lease for the 1,700 square feet on the premises, which was reviewed every five years in terms of the cost per square foot. This began at a rate of £9,000 per annum divided into 12 monthly payments. The money provided by the families went to pay for equipment and decorating the premises and they arranged a small overdraft limit of £6,000 with their bank. This was to act as a buffer zone for their expenses. The business did not suffer from a significant cash flow problem, because of the scheme it used for charging customers. Upon joining the leisure club, customers had to pay a £60 membership charge, made up of a joining fee and the first month's subscription; thereafter they paid £16 per month. The main costs were fixed costs of £1,500 per month (excluding the rent), but the partners also had to draw money from the business as a form of private income.

The marketing budget was set at £3,000. It involved some local advertising and a leaflet drop in 3,000–4,000 houses in the locality which ended up being an effective method of advertising. The business set itself the target of achieving 70% of capacity within the first year, and hit this target after only three months with 280 subscriptions, reaching capacity subscriptions after only 12 months.

1 Define: guarantors, customer base, advertising.   [6]

2 State and explain one advantage and one disadvantage of the leasing agreement in this case.   [4]

3 The pattern of subscriptions for the first three months was as follows:
Month 1 110, Month 2 200, Month 3 280. Calculate the amount of overdraft used if the owners require drawings of £1,000 each per month starting in Month 1. Your teacher will advise you on an appropriate format to use.   [10]

4 a) Calculate the capacity level that the business aimed for.   [2]

b) Given that the business had reached capacity output by 12 months, how might it have approached the objective of growth over the following years?   [5]

5 Discuss the extent to which this case study highlights the typical problems faced by new businesses.   [8]

                                                                                         $\underline{35}$

Types of business

Learning objectives

Having read this unit, students will be able to

1 distinguish between the private and public sectors within an economy

2 demonstrate an understanding of the different types of business

3 understand the significance of limited liability

4 understand how the legal structure of a business affects its decision making process

Context

If you walk down any high street, you will notice that many of the shops display their name for all to see. It may be Robinson the butcher, Brown, Macey and Brown the solicitors, a well known chain store such as Marks and Spencer plc or Hodsons Limited. All are businesses, but each with a different status in terms of how it is operated, who the owner is and how any profit is shared.

Sectors of business

Within the economy, businesses are part of either the **private sector** or the **public sector**. The distinguishing feature is the ownership. If the business is owned by firms and individuals, then it is part of the private sector. If the business is owned by the government (or the state) then it is in the public sector. One or two businesses, such as BNFL (British Nuclear Fuels Limited), are owned by the government, but are run on a private sector, profit-making basis.

Private sector

Unincorporated companies

These are companies which have two distinct characteristics:

- The **unincorporated** business does not have a separate legal identity. The owner and the business are one and the same in the eyes of the law. Consequently, if there are problems with the business, it is the owner who is sued or fined for any wrongdoing.
- If the unincorporated business is sued or goes into liquidation (when it is unable to meet all its debts), the assets of the owner e.g. his/her house can be sold to provide the cash to help meet the debts. There is no limit on the amount of assets that can be sold off to meet the debts of the business. This is called unlimited liability.

The two types of business that are unincorporated are:

- **sole traders**
- **partnerships**

Sole traders

A sole trader is a person who has total ownership of and responsibility for managing the business.

This is the most common form of business and how most businesses start their life.

Only a few procedures have to be undertaken in order to start as a sole trader. Once the name of the business has been registered with Companies House in Cardiff, it is free to start trading. Some checks will be made to ensure that the name of the business is original. The amount of capital that is required to start one's own business is not significant and is often financed from savings or a loan from the bank.

Question 1

What questions might a bank manager ask if a sole trader required a loan to start a business selling hand-made garden furniture?   [5]

The ease of setting up is also another reason why there are so many sole traders. Premises can be rented rather than paid for, which eliminates the need to find large sums of money. Labour is often provided by members of the family, who are perhaps not as expensive as employing staff, and it may be possible to obtain stock on credit. How easily stock can be purchased in this manner is dependent upon the credit-worthiness of the person involved.

The 'good' news

Any profit belongs to the owner

Total control as to how the business is operated

As it is likely that the owner will have to undertake all the tasks, buying, selling, delivery, accounts and so on, there is plenty of variety in the work

Working for oneself is highly motivating

The 'bad' news

All the tasks have to be performed by the owner, unless finance is available to pay for additional help

The hours are long, as there are insufficient funds to hire specialist staff

Unlimited liability

Difficulty of competing with larger companies

No one else taking the same risks to share ideas with

Question 2

Using the information in the table above, suggest why so many sole traders exist.   [3]

Partnerships

The legal definition of a partnership is laid out in the Partnership Act of 1890. It is when two or more people operate a business for the common goal of making a profit. The owners share the responsibility for the running of the business and any subsequent profit that may be generated.

The majority of partnerships are small businesses, often involving retailing, building or the professional services such as accountants, doctors and solicitors who have names that always seem to be similar – Nedstone, Nedstone and Nedstone!

Up to 20 partners are allowed in any one partnership (there are a few exceptions for some professional partnerships).

Having more people involved in running the business allows the partners to specialise where possible. A firm of solicitors may have several partners, with one specialising in litigation (court work), another in probate (wills), another in conveyancing (buying and selling of property) and another in possibly the most lucrative area, commercial law (company business).

Although there are few legalities for setting up a partnership, there are several rights related to this type of business.

These rights are laid out in a Deed of Partnership which can be verbal or in writing.

This will include details on the roles of the partners, stipulating:

- whether partners are 'active' (those who contribute to the actual running of the business) or '**sleeping**' (those who do not take part in the actual running of the business but contribute finance to the business)
- the amount of capital (money) each will contribute to the business
- how the profit, if any, is to be shared
- procedure for the termination of the partnership
- procedure for expanding the partnership (taking on more partners)
- whether a partner can have limited liability (although at least one partner has to have unlimited liability)
- the partnership is dissolved if one partner dies. It is normal for the existing partners to re-form immediately using the same format for the Deed of Partnership.

The 'good' news

Cheap to set up as there are no formalities to comply with

Specialisation of partners allows for greater efficiency and therefore cheaper costs

The burden of work can be shared

The potential to access more finance is greater with more owners

Better decision making due to shared knowledge and expertise

The 'bad' news

Each partner has to share the decision making and therefore has less control of the business

Each partner must share the burden of poor decisions or work of partner

Decision making may take longer and arguments may arise

Any profits are shared, irrespective of effort

Unlimited liability

Finance limited to 20 partners

Continuity may be broken on the death of a partner

Question 3

Why is it of benefit to ensure that there is a Deed of Partnership?   [4]

The major problem with both a sole trader and a partnership is the unlimited liability as a result of being unincorporated.

To overcome this problem and to allow for greater expansion by gaining greater access to finance the obvious step is to become incorporated.

Incorporation

Incorporation is the name given to the process by which a company gains its own separate legal identity. This separate identity means that the company can enter into contracts, make any legal claims and face any legal claims that are made against it in the name of the business and not in the name of the owners of the business.

Documents have to be submitted to the Registrar of Joint Stock Companies before a Certificate of Incorporation is issued. The two documents are the Memorandum of Association and the Articles of Association.

Memorandum of Association

Under the Companies Act of 1985, the details that must be included in this document are related to the purpose of the company. Other important elements of this document are:

Name, location of registered office, limited liability, nominal capital and if the company is public limited this must be clearly stated.

Articles of Association

This provides information as to the internal rules for the operation of the company. Details will include the rights of the shareholders, the frequency of company meetings, the responsibilities of the directors.

Limited liability

Because incorporated businesses have a separate legal identity, the owners of the business can be liable only for the amount of money that they have invested. In the event of liquidation, the assets of the owners cannot be used to cover the debts of the business. Limited companies are often family owned businesses that have expanded from either sole traders or partnerships which required greater access to finance in order to achieve growth. In addition, the **limited liability** provides less risk for the owners whilst allowing some control of the business to be maintained.

For example:
Ten shareholders each put in £2,000 to start a travel business offering tours to Africa. A further four shareholders each put in £15,000 and are also the directors of the business.

Unfortunately due to a lack of demand because of civil unrest, after only two years the business is wound up with debts of £150,000. Much of the debt owed is from a loan with the bank. Assets of the business are sold and raise £120,000. As a result the bank loses £30,000, but the individual shareholders lose only their original investments of either £2,000 or £15,000.

All limited companies have shareholders who own shares in the business and take a proportion of any profit made. All the shareholders are able to select the directors and chairperson at the annual general meeting (AGM) of the business.

There are two types of limited company:
- **Private Limited Companies**
- **Public Limited Companies**

Private Limited Companies (Ltd)

Under the Companies Act of 1980, limited companies must have at least two members or shareholders, although there is no upper limit.

In addition, the word 'limited' must appear in the name of the company, allowing other businesses to be aware of the type of company they are trading with.

Although shares are issued, they are not allowed to be bought and sold by members of the general public. The shares may only be sold privately.

The 'good' news

Access to capital is better than for unincorporated companies because
i) there is no limit to the number of shareholders
ii) limited liability means less risk, which in turn attracts more investors

Some control of the business is possible because the shares are sold privately

No break in continuity if a shareholder dies (shares can be sold to another by invitation)

The 'bad' news

The formation of the business requires legal documentation which is time consuming and expensive

Financial accounts have to be filed with the Registrar of Companies, and can be viewed by members of the public, including competitors

Shares cannot be sold to the general public which suggests it is harder to raise capital

Profits are distributed to shareholders and must therefore be shared

Question 4

Question 4

How would a competitor find the accounts of a rival helpful?   [3]

Question 5

What are the limitations of being a limited company in a highly competitive market?   [4]

■ Public Limited Companies (PLC)

Although there are fewer PLCs than Limited companies, they are by far the largest companies in terms of number of employees and turnover.

There has to be a minimum of two shareholders, as there does for private limited companies. However there is no maximum number of shareholders.

Several procedures have to be completed by a company 'going public'. A prospectus has to be issued and an announcement made of the intention to 'go public' to enable any member of the public to have the opportunity to invest in the company. Once a company has been 'floated', the shares of the company may be bought and sold by members of the public, pension fund managers, insurance companies, indeed anyone or any body. Owners of ordinary shares can vote (one vote per share owned) at the compulsory AGM that selects or rejects the directors.

An interesting trend has been the number of soccer clubs that have gone public, probably as a quick way to obtain additional capital. There has also been a spate of building societies that have changed from being a friendly society or mutualised company to a PLC, not just for additional capital but as a method of competing with other similar financial institutions (friendly societies are owned by their members or customers, each having a vote irrespective of the amount of money invested).

There are several advantages and disadvantages to going public and they will be dealt with in greater detail than for the other types of businesses, as PLCs represent the largest proportion of our economic activity.

The 'good' news

- **Access to finance (in the present)**
  This is the primary reason why a business will decide to go public. Stock exchanges around the world act as a market for buyers and sellers to meet. This simply makes it easier to raise money, if this is the chosen source of finance for the business. By going public, a business is inviting anyone to buy shares (a new issue) and therefore it is not restricting the ownership. This allows the business access to a much greater source of funds.

- **Access to finance (in the future)**
  If the business then decides that it requires more funds, it can either issue shares to present shareholders (known as a rights issue) or it can issue more shares to the open market (another new issue). A rights issue will be cheaper in that the business will be sending an offer to buy the shares to the present shareholders, so it will not need to spend so much money on marketing the share issue.

- **Prestige**
  The initials PLC following the name of a business add prestige. This may not impress its customers, who tend not to be too concerned with the legal structure of the business, but for the other stakeholders, such as suppliers, having a PLC on the order book of a small company can frequently be used in its own marketing.

- **Access to other forms of finance**
  A bank will look more favourably on a business which is a PLC because it is larger and therefore more stable. Bank managers look carefully for evidence of security or collateral when granting a loan. The extra security also tends to mean that the rate of interest will possibly be lower for the amount which is borrowed.

- **Reduction in gearing**
  Gearing measures the ratio of borrowed money to the amount of money raised through shares and is

calculated by borrowed money (otherwise known as debt, over equity (the value of its shares)

e.g. if borrowing = £1m and shareholders' funds are £4m, then gearing =

$$\frac{\text{£1m}}{\text{£4m}} = 25\%.$$

By raising another £1m through selling more shares, gearing then becomes

$$\frac{\text{£1m}}{\text{£5m}} = 20\%.$$

(*See Unit 38 Ratio analysis*)

The 'bad' news

■ Overall cost

The overall cost can be divided into two distinct parts:

a) the cost of launching the business on to the stock market. Selling shares is not just a question of putting one or two adverts in the financial press. In the maxi case study in Unit 40 Sources of finance the cost was around the £500,000 mark. Potential investors need gentle but assertive persuasion that the business ought to have their money in it! A prospectus will need to be printed and a merchant bank is normally hired as the underwriters – just in case the share issue fails to attract sufficient investment.

b) the cost of maintaining shareholders. Issuing shares means the business has more shareholders to manage and to communicate with. This means that the chairman or chief executive must visit the stock exchange to report on the progress of the business in terms of future plans, sales and profit. Each year, the business must also submit an interim report, which charts the progress of the business during the first six months of the year. At the end of the financial year the business then publishes its annual report which is a much more detailed account of the year, with a report by the directors, a full set of financial statements and details of future plans. It is intended to put the company in the most glowing of all lights so that shareholders will continue to be interested in the business and potential investors may consider buying shares, thus keeping the share price buoyant.

■ Dividends

These are paid on each share for as long as the share is owned and in the hands of the shareholder. Whenever new shares are issued, total dividends must increase to meet the dividends requirement on the extra shares.

Sometimes, a business will actually find the process of going public and maintaining the interest of shareholders far more onerous than the benefit of extra funds. Richard Branson, having floated Virgin in the 1980s, then bought all the shares from the shareholders some years later, following a frustrating time trying to convince the City of his ability to run a successful business.

■ Lack of control

The decision to go public is always more difficult for a family business given that it will bring outside ownership, which may reduce the amount of influence the family has over decision making. Although a business will try to ensure that the amount of share capital which has been raised means that the family's shareholding is more than 50%, this may well defeat the initial objective of raising finance.

As more shares are issued, each shareholder's percentage of ownership may fall, unless the business uses a rights issue to raise more money (*see Unit 40 Sources of finance*).

■ Threat of takeover

Trading on the open market means that anyone can buy shares. If the share price of the company falls, there is nothing to stop predator companies from buying up shares and putting in a takeover bid. Alternatively, a predator company which has a great deal of surplus cash may buy a company which is doing well, with a rising share price. It will pay a premium for the shares because it thinks that by owning the company, it will add much more value to the wealth of its own company, compared with the cost of the target business.

Question 6

Suggest why Richard Branson decided he wanted to buy back all the shares after going public.   [4]

Public sector

This sector involves businesses that are owned by or accountable to the government. In this context, the word 'government' refers to either central or local government. The majority of the capital required to operate public sector businesses is found by the government via taxation revenue. All companies within the public sector are public corporations which have incorporated status in the same way as private sector businesses. They have their own legal status and therefore can enter into contracts or be sued just like any other incorporated business.

There is a range of public corporations; the nationalised industries were examples of public corporations, but these have been privatised under a programme of **privatisation** that was started by Margaret Thatcher's governments from 1979. Some of the privatised industries are utilities such as gas, electricity and water.

The Bank of England and the BBC are also public corporations, both of which are accountable to particular government departments. The latter receives a 'grant' from the government in the form of TV licence money.

Government departments are also responsible for various 'businesses'; for example, the Department of Health is responsible for running the National Health Service.

Privatisation

This is the process that transfers ownership of public sector bodies to the private sector. As previously mentioned, the Conservative government under the leadership of Margaret Thatcher implemented a series of privatisations partly on political grounds. Privatisation included selling government businesses and deregulating certain sectors such as the bus and coach industry to allow companies to bid for the right to operate certain routes (in the belief that the majority of businesses ought to be exposed to market forces). The theory was that this would encourage efficiency and at the same time provide a useful source of finance for the government e.g. the sale of British Gas in 1986 raised approximately £6.5 billion.

Many other companies were also privatised:

Table 1

Transport:	
National Freight Company	1982
Sealink (part of British Rail)	1984
British Airways	1987
British Rail	1994
The Post Office	(forecast)
Public utilities:	
British Telecom	1984
British Gas	1986
British Water Authorities	1989
Electricity boards	1990
Electricity generators	1991
Manufacturers:	
Ferranti	1979
British Aerospace	1981
Jaguar	1984
British Leyland	1986
Rolls Royce	1987

To ensure that the privatisation process ran smoothly, barriers to entry into these markets, which had been in place to protect the nationalised industries from competition, were removed.

The 'good' news

- Likely to make the business more efficient
- Saves the government expenditure in the form of subsidies
- Efficiency may lead to either lower costs which can be passed on to the consumer or greater profits which are passed on to shareholders
- Offers the opportunity for members of the public to become shareholders in major British companies (part of the ownership culture)

The 'bad' news

- Once the sale of the business has taken place any revenue opportunities are lost: prior to privatisation BT was a profit-making business
- Selling the 'family silver' may be viewed as the sale of what belongs to the general public
- The objective to improve the efficiency of the business led to a reduction in the number of employees, thus increasing unemployment

■ Given that several of the businesses that were privatised were utilities, the government lost the ability to influence the prices of many products within the economy. All firms need fuel, heat and light, phones and transport, and any change in the price of these affects costs and consequently the prices of other goods. However, most of these costs came down following privatisation.

Question 7

Why do you think the government has not privatised
■ the Bank of England?
■ national defence?
■ the Royal Mail?
■ the police service?   [12]

Local Authority

This is another important, but often forgotten, example of public sector business. Authorities provide a wide range of services such as education, housing and social services in the community and are often one of the largest employers in any given area. The finance for these services comes from central government, which is responsible for nearly half of the revenue, from council tax, which is set and collected by the authority, from loans and from revenue from the provision of local amenities such as swimming pools and leisure centres. The latter accounts only for a very small percentage of income.

The responsibility for administering the services and collecting the revenues falls on the elected local councillors who make up the local council.

Table 2 is a summary of the different types of businesses:

Table 2

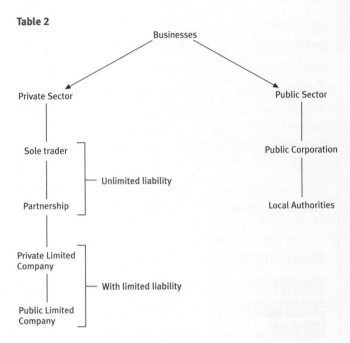

Points for Revision

Key Terms

private sector	all businesses that are owned by either individuals or groups of people referred to as shareholders
public sector	businesses that are 'owned' and organised by either local or central government
unincorporated	any business that has no separate legal identity
sole trader	a business that has one single owner
partnership	a business that is owned by between two and 20 individuals
incorporation	the process to gain a separate legal identity
limited liability	owners are liable only for the amount of money they invest in the business
Private Limited Company	a business with a separate legal identity and therefore limited liability but which cannot sell its shares to the public
Public Limited Company	a business that is able to sell its shares to the general public
privatisation	the changing of ownership from public sector to the private sector
sleeping partner	a partner who contributes financially but takes no part in the running of the business

Summary Points:

1 There are two main sectors that own companies, private and public.

2 Businesses are either unincorporated or incorporated.

3 Each type of business has a different set of rules that governs its operation in terms of number of owners and liability.

Mini Case Study

Pop-It and Sons ran a highly successful popcorn business. The company sold a range of popcorn machines and the ingredients necessary to make the popcorn, namely the popcorn seeds and the syrup. Its main customers were places of entertainment, cinemas, theatres, theme parks and leisure centres. Ron and Mary had started the business with their own capital and had built it up into a large family business.

New markets were opening up throughout the country and Ron was keen to expand into providing the catering business with larger machines and a wider range of ancillary equipment. There was a further thought in the mind of Mary who had tended to be responsible for buying in the most appropriate packaging for the popcorn. To date, she had purchased a range of boxes from a local supplier. Having visited her local fish and chip shop after finishing work late one night, she noticed a customer with a cone of chips which gave her the idea of developing this shape of container as a novelty alternative to the traditional boxes.

Ron, on hearing Mary's idea, suggested she took the idea further and at the same time found another container for the mega-size portions that were commonplace in the United States.

All their plans were worthy of development but were also expensive and although the business was potentially lucrative, cash for such investment would mean fewer foreign holidays. Ron was keen to expand the business beyond the family as a quick way of raising the needed finance. Mary was more reserved, keen to ensure her children would keep the family name of the business going for many more generations.

Ron tried to impress upon his wife that there was a growing number of competitors entering the market and consequently it was important that Pop-It and Sons invested in new ideas and was prepared to find new markets before the opposition did. Offering a complete service by providing all the equipment, materials and packaging might be the idea that would ensure the business not only survived but continued to prosper.

1 Explain the process that Ron and Mary would have to go through if they were to become a limited company.   [4]

2 State what type of business Pop-It and Sons is at present.   [2]

3 What are the main advantages and disadvantages for Pop-It if it becomes a partnership?   [4]

4 Explain the major disadvantages for Ron and Mary of becoming incorporated.   [6]

5 Why might a bank react differently to a request for a loan if the business changed its status?   [4]

Presentation

If Ron and Mary wished to compete in the popcorn business, evaluate the most appropriate type of business which would help them to achieve this objective.

20

Maxi Case Study

Government reforms cf the Health Service in the 1980s turned the provision of health care into a major financial headache for most peop e in the profession. Suddenly, targets were set in terms of financial efficiency and patient care. Costs had to be kept down, waiting lists had to be reduced and the use of assets had to be more efficient. The system now works in the following way:

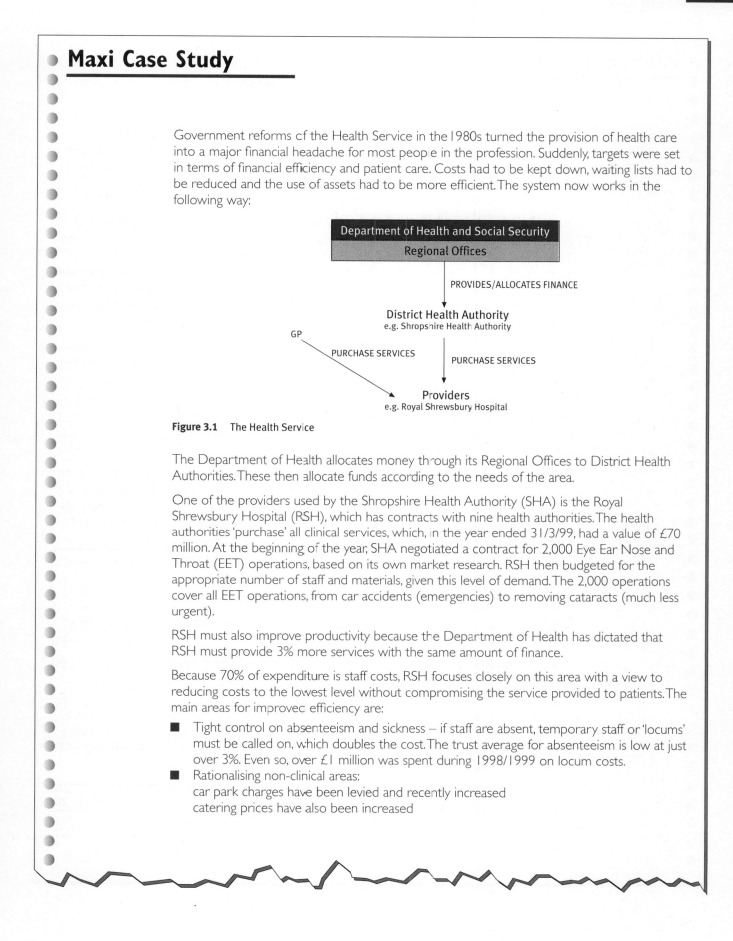

Figure 3.1   The Health Service

The Department of Health allocates money through its Regional Offices to District Health Authorities. These then allocate funds according to the needs of the area.

One of the providers used by the Shropshire Health Authority (SHA) is the Royal Shrewsbury Hospital (RSH), which has contracts with nine health authorities. The health authorities 'purchase' all clinical services, which, in the year ended 31/3/99, had a value of £70 million. At the beginning of the year, SHA negotiated a contract for 2,000 Eye Ear Nose and Throat (EET) operations, based on its own market research. RSH then budgeted for the appropriate number of staff and materials, given this level of demand. The 2,000 operations cover all EET operations, from car accidents (emergencies) to removing cataracts (much less urgent).

RSH must also improve productivity because the Department of Health has dictated that RSH must provide 3% more services with the same amount of finance.

Because 70% of expenditure is staff costs, RSH focuses closely on this area with a view to reducing costs to the lowest level without compromising the service provided to patients. The main areas for improvec efficiency are:

- Tight control on absenteeism and sickness – if staff are absent, temporary staff or 'locums' must be called on, which doubles the cost. The trust average for absenteeism is low at just over 3%. Even so, over £1 million was spent during 1998/1999 on locum costs.
- Rationalising non-clinical areas:
  car park charges have been levied and recently increased
  catering prices have also been increased

A joint venture between RSH and Birmingham's Heartland hospital has also cut costs. RSH used to buy supplies from Health Service suppliers, who were not particularly efficient. Joining with another hospital meant the two trusts could benefit from economies of scale; as a result RSH saved over £600,000 over two years.

The commercial principles extend as far as pricing; although the RSH is allowed to make some operating surplus, this rarely happens. When quoting the price of an EET operation, the RSH simply aims to break even. This involves calculating the cost of the EET department for a year, including emergency and non-urgent cases, and dividing by the budgeted number of operations. Problems occur, however, if the department fulfils its contract before the end of the year.

If an emergency EET is required, it poses an ethical dilemma for RSH. The contract states that the hospital can swap non-urgent elective cases for an emergency. Non-urgent electives are treatments on a waiting list. Treating the emergency means the waiting list rises. This, in turn, causes problems for the government's political objective of reducing waiting lists. The government therefore has a reserve fund to help reduce waiting lists. During 1998/1999, the RSH carried out 1200 extra cases by employing people out of hours, much more expensive for the government and the taxpayer.

A second problem is surplus capacity i.e. staff (and materials) have been 'employed', but there is no work to do because the contract has ended. In these cases, the money from the contract has actually paid for staff for a year, meaning that all fixed costs have been paid for. RSH can contact other health authorities and sell certain health care services at a marginal cost, just covering the cost of materials. In some cases, where material costs are low, the service can be sold at between 20 and 25% of the total cost. This may lead to more business for RSH next year, based on the understanding that the price will be at full cost.

---

1 The case study highlights a variety of business concepts which are also relevant for private sector businesses.

   Identify the evidence in the case which highlights the following business principles: break-even pricing ■ marginal cost pricing ■ productivity improvements ■ cost control ■ satisfying consumer demand ■ budgeting ■ capacity utilisation ■ hierarchy of objectives

   You may wish to ask your teacher what some of these mean.   8 × [2]

2 Use the case study to highlight the main differences between the external constraints facing a private sector business and those facing a public sector business.   [6]

3 Opinion 1 – the taxpayer: The Health Service takes up taxpayers' money; I want to see that money used in the most efficient way possible, so I applaud any attempt by the hospital to improve productivity.

   Opinion 2 – the patient: People are tired of waiting for operations; nurses' lack of morale, closure of wards and lack of bed space have meant the Health Service does not provide a thorough service. Increasing productivity by sending patients home sooner and turning overnight cases into day cases is the wrong way to operate a health care system.

   Prepare a two-minute presentation, agreeing with opinion 1 or opinion 2.   [8]

Size of business

Learning objectives

Having read this unit, students will be able to

1 identify and evaluate the various methods of measuring the size of a business

2 identify the different ways a company can grow

3 evaluate the benefits of growing in size

Context

How large is a large business? Recently, Microsoft was described as the largest company in the world; this claim was based on only one measure of size. If the chosen method were revenue or profit, Microsoft would certainly not be the largest company. If it were based on the value of its assets, or on the volume of products it sold, or even on its number of employees, it would still not be the largest company. The actual method of valuation was the number of shares and the share price. By choosing another method of valuation, another company would be the largest. Exxon, the colossal oil company, might decide to value itself based on the vast oil fields it has access to, by referring to the trillions of barrels it could produce. Certain industries might favour one particular method, and the accuracy and appropriateness of such a method is not always clear. However, all businesses usually put growth as one of their main objectives in order to reap the benefits of being larger.

Different measures of size

There are several methods of measuring the size of a business, all of which have relevance in certain circumstances.

■ Revenue – the value of products sold

This can be used by any business, although it is more frequently quoted on the news when comparing two very large businesses which compete with each other in the same market. The big food retailers such as Safeway and Asda regularly quote revenue and market share to demonstrate their size and influence in the market-place. Related to revenue is the concept of market growth – the speed of growth in one industry can be assessed only in relation to rates of growth in other industries and/or countries. Although growth is not a strict measure of size it is frequently quoted to suggest how large a business might be if future growth mirrored past growth.

■ Capital employed – the amount of money tied up in (net) assets by shareholders

This can be found by examining sets of company reports. It is more relevant for manufacturing companies or companies that deal in property, either developing it or letting it to other companies. Businesses in the service industry can appear small by this measure, but when compared to the revenue they generate, for example, they appear much more efficient because they do not have much money tied up in fixed assets (apart from a headquarters).

A derivative of this method is using a subset of assets e.g. cash. Financial companies are valued not just according to their growth, but according to their financial power. Nomura Securities, the business which bought the William Hill chain of betting shops in 1999, was once rumoured to be able to purchase the four major high street banks in Britain, with petty cash. The actual measure of size in a company of this magnitude does not matter.

■ Volume

This can be used only if volume is compared to other businesses, so that a view of relative size can be ascertained. Volume will be viewed differently by the production and marketing managers; the former will be more concerned with the actual volume whereas the marketing manager may be concerned about the value of the production as well.

■ Profit

This measure is rather crude, because it depends on the accounting policies of the company in question. It is also very difficult to make international comparisons in profit due to differences in accounting regulations. In addition, profit should be viewed in relation to revenue. Consider the following two businesses:

Firm 1: Revenue £80 billion, profit £3 billion
Firm 2: Revenue £20 billion, profit £2 billion

Firm 1 could be one of the largest companies in the world in terms of profit and revenue, but the profit in relation to revenue is much better in Firm 2. Profit alone is not necessarily a reliable measure of size because of the subjective methods of measuring profit (corresponding to accounting rules and regulations). Consideration of the profit in relation to revenue is more important.

The main reason for using profit is to assess how much the business might be worth in the future. When one business buys another, it does not always look at the value of the assets it is purchasing along with the loans and debts it might need to pay off in the short or medium term. A more accurate method of ascertaining size is the future value of profit. A business will wish to know that if it pays e.g. £5 million for another company it will be able to pay off that investment from the profit resulting from the new, larger business.

■ Number of employees

This is relatively easy to measure and allows comparisons to be made across industries as an indication both of size and whether the business is labour-intensive. A labour-intensive business tends to have a high proportion of labour costs in comparison with total costs. A recent trend in employment patterns has been the increase in the number of part-time workers. This has made labour-intensity less easy to calculate, because it is not easy to equate part-time workers with full-time workers.

Question 1

The following statistics relate to two companies which have similar revenue, profit and capital figures.

Company A: 100 employees; 35 full-time, 65 part-time
Company B: 80 employees; 48 full-time, 32 part-time.

a) What criteria might be used to calculate how many part-time workers equal one full-time worker?

[4]

b) What might be the consequences of B having a different ratio of part-time to full-time employees?

[4]

■ Market capitalisation

This is calculated by the number of shares × share price. Such a measure is one of the most frequently used for companies whose share price is quoted regularly (on the various stock exchanges around the world). As the share price rises and falls according to a variety of factors, the value of a business alters. The number of shares in circulation can be found from the company reports. The **market capitalisation** of businesses on the London Stock Exchange are quoted each day in the *Financial Times* as well. This is the measure which was hinted at in the context above; Microsoft – the world's largest company – was valued at something like £170 billion approaching the new millennium (March 1999).

When the price of a particular share falls dramatically in one day, the news headlines sometimes refer to a company losing £*x* million/billion from its value e.g. the Asian financial crisis, which was in full flow in late 1998, had a significant effect on businesses with assets and subsidiaries in the Far East. As a result, share prices fell.

When there are rapid drops in share prices, news readers will say something along the lines of 'shares tumbled today, wiping £53 billion off the value of companies'. This value is 'paper' money, in that the £53 billion is not actually going into someone else's pocket; it simply means that a share is worth less.

'London share prices fall 10% on Monday and 12% the day after.'

Companies whose share price continually falls become worried about takeover bids because this method of valuation is used when one company is bought by another. When a takeover bid is launched, the offer for the shares is likely to value the company above its present market capitalisation, in an attempt to persuade the target company's shareholders to sell the shares.

Question 2

Which method of measuring size is the most useful in the following circumstances? Justify your choice.
a) A newspaper
b) An oil producer
c) A construction company, trying to fend off a takeover bid by a predator
d) A school
e) An accountancy partnership
f) A leading manufacturer of soap powder, shampoo and other main hygiene products

6 × [3]

Question 3

Pulp-It plc is a paper-manufacturing business which is considering buying another business to increase its market share and profit. The following businesses are being considered by the board:

	Capital employed (£m)	Employees	Revenue (£m)	Profit (£m)	Issued shares	Share price
Business 1	400	300	900	100	8 million	£5.60
Business 2	150	110	600	100	4 million	£7.20

a) Calculate the market capitalisation for each of the two businesses. [2]

b) Assess the appropriateness of the various methods of calculating size when determining how much this business is worth to Pulp-It. [10]

Why is the size of a business important?

As businesses grow in size, regardless of the measure of size used, there are certain benefits that it will create for itself.

- Customers tend to be attracted to bigger names in the high street, whether they sell designer clothes or fast moving consumer goods; customers have a greater 'trust' of well known larger businesses, even if this means they charge a higher price.
- Larger companies tend to have greater status when purchasing products from a supplier; to such an extent that suppliers will concentrate the lion's share of their resources and time in ensuring that the order for the largest business (probably measured here in revenue terms) goes out first.
- Payment terms are easier to negotiate when a company is larger, especially when receiving goods from a supplier. British firms are notoriously slow at paying up, although this problem is magnified when the supplier does not have the resources to take legal proceedings against the larger customer, who may well force the supplier into liquidation by failing to pay promptly (*see Unit 62 Business Ethics*).
- Sponsorship and local community relations are easier to develop when the business is big enough and profitable enough to allocate resources. Small companies which are struggling tend not to be able to generate such a rosy glow in the eyes of the community because they are always short of resources.

Are there any advantages to being a small company?

Small companies do have distinct advantages:

Ability to change

A speed boat can turn a corner faster than an ocean cruiser; in the same way a small business is more flexible and can react to external changes more quickly. An independent tailor of suits and gentlemen's clothing can react to changes in taste much more quickly than the larger chains such as Next and Burton. The latter must organise the removal and collection of all the redundant stock throughout all their stores, whereas the tailor can effect such a change more quickly.

Attraction of the media

The press does enjoy ridiculing and criticising larger employers; this may be over excessive executive pay awards, or exploitative employers, or even the company's dealings with a country that has a poor human or animal rights record. Such attention may mean more publicity but it is more likely to produce a loss in sales, as well as the need for a public relations officer to deal with the press on a continual basis, adding to the company's costs.

Contact with the customer

Small firms who deal with local or regional markets find it easier, as a natural consequence of their size, to maintain close contact with the customer. Compare your local newsagent with the local food retailer; several visits to the former will mean that the owner gets to know your own paper order and something about you as a person – you are unlikely to enjoy the same familiarity with Lord Sainsbury!

Economies of scale

Internal

One of the major reasons businesses try to grow is to achieve **economies of scale**. Economies of scale are defined as the reduction in unit cost as output increases. Any reduction in unit cost allows the company the luxury of taking a decision on whether to reduce the price it charges (keeping the same profit margin) and sell more product or to keep the price at the same level and earn more profit per unit (*see Figure 4.1*).

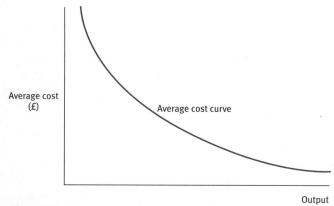

Figure 4.1   Average cost reduces as output increases

Economies of scale arise due to various factors, all connected with the issue of changing size:

■ **Technical economies of scale**
   Compare the loading capacity levels of two lorries: Lorry 1 is 3 metres by 3 metres by 8 metres, thereby giving a carrying capacity of 3 × 3 × 8 = 72 cubic metres.
   Lorry 2 has twice the dimensions – 6 × 6 × 16, which results in a carrying capacity eight times higher! If the lorry costs twice as much, it can offset the extra cost by the fact that it can carry eight times the amount (*see Figure 4.2*).

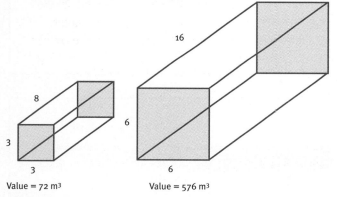

Value = 72 m³   Value = 576 m³

Figure 4.2   Twice the dimension, eight times the volume!

Another technical economy of scale occurs as a business spreads more units of output over its fixed costs.

If a business produces 10 units of output, with fixed costs of £40,000, this will result in a fixed cost per unit of

   £40,000 ÷ 10 = £4,000

If the business increases its output to 100 units, fixed cost per unit becomes

   £40,000 ÷ 100 = £400

This reduction continues until capacity (in this case 2000 units) is reached. Fixed cost per unit therefore becomes

   £40,000 ÷ 2000 = £20.

So as the business spreads the same fixed costs across more units of output, the unit cost decreases.

■ **Purchasing economies of scale**
   As a business purchases more from its suppliers, it may be possible to negotiate a bulk purchase discount. Such a discount is sometimes considered as a right, although it is only possible because the supplier is able to spread a greater number of units over the same fixed costs.

Question 4

Get-It, a retailer of household goods, was negotiating a contract with Give-It, a manufacturer of wrapping paper. Give-It had the following costs:

1000 sheets £0.30 per sheet
5000 sheets £0.22 per sheet
8000 sheets £0.16 per sheet

Prices were quoted according to how many sheets of paper were bought.

1000 sheets £0.50 per sheet
5000 sheets £0.30 per sheet
8000 sheets £0.22 per sheet

a) Which level of orders gives the greatest profit per sheet?   [1]

b) Which level of sheets would the business prefer to supply to Get-It in one order?   [2]
(Show your working for both questions).

c) Under what market circumstances would a lower price be of advantage to firms? Explain your answer.
                                                                                        [5]

■ **Technological economies of scale**
   If a business buys new machinery which is of a higher technical specification, this ought to bring benefits in terms of increased efficiency. Not only might the new machine be able to produce more quickly, but it also may produce higher quality and less wastage. Such savings are a result of technological economies of scale.

■ **Marketing economies of scale**

Companies like Nestlé become more proficient at launching new products as their experience grows. This means that launching each new product becomes less expensive because the company becomes more expert at targeting and marketing the product correctly. The brand name of Heinz, for example, is synonymous with canned food; when it launches a new brand, the business does not need to advertise the name of Heinz to build the brand. This has occurred with all the previous products, so, to customers, the new product is simply another product in a long range from Heinz. Launching therefore becomes less expensive per product.

A second way of looking at this concept is that as Heinz increases its product range, but still continues to advertise the generic brand name of Heinz, the advertising expenditure is spread across more products, therefore reducing the unit cost for advertising.

■ **Financial economies of scale**

When businesses float on the stock market, they gain prestige and status in the world of finance. This means that banks may well be more willing to lend them money than if they were a small unknown company. A large company is also a safer company, and therefore banks may well charge the business a lower rate of interest. This makes the cost of raising finance less expensive.

■ **Managerial economies of scale**

When a business starts up, there are one or two managers each responsible for a range of functions. As growth occurs, it is more likely that the business will employ specialists to run individual functions – marketing, production, finance etc. Such specialisation will mean there is greater control over each function, which is more likely to lead to lower costs.

■ **Risk-bearing economies of scale**

When profits grow and a business gains more access to finance, it can diversify into other areas of business which are not related to its core or main business. This may well reduce the risk that the business faces because it is now in two unrelated markets e.g. umbrellas and ice cream. If one business fails due to the hot weather, the other business will succeed. This economy of scale is associated with reducing the cost of losing money.

■ **Specialisation economies of scale**

This idea was introduced over 200 years ago, with the onset of the industrial revolution. Equipping one person to do several jobs is not as efficient as equipping one person to do one job. By doing the one job all the time, the individual becomes an expert and is able to devise the most efficient method of production. This application of specialisation is known as division of labour.

Question 5

Identify the economy of scale being described in the following cases:
a) buying a more efficient, more modern car
b) finding a cheaper loan because of the value of assets which can be used as collateral (security)
c) persuading suppliers to increase the delivery size by 1% at no extra cost
d) a business selling gloves diversifying into selling swimming trunks
e) splitting the production process of a television into many small jobs, with the same person doing the same job
f) employing a specialist manager (as a credit controller) to ensure that customers pay on time
g) All Saints launching a new single and all their fans going to buy the record even though they have never heard it!   [7]

Question 6

The Boeing Company has said it is considering developing a jet capable of carrying as many as 800 passengers, pitting the world's largest planemaker against Airbus Industries in the market for 'superjumbo' jets.

The company plans to either invest $3 billion to build a 550-seat version of its 747, the world's largest passenger plane, or develop an even larger jet from scratch.

Explain how Boeing is taking advantage of economies of scale.   [5]

External

As the success of one business leads to growth, employment and profit, this may well cause another business to grow. If a company which dominates one locality is successful, this may cause other tertiary sector businesses and suppliers to grow. The effect of the economy of scale is not felt within the growing major business, hence the reference to 'external'. For example, the growth of a car assembly plant benefits the supplying companies, satellite firms who build in the same area, as well as local newsagents and lunchtime snack bars. There may well be improvements in the local infrastructure. The Toyoto car plant that was built at Derby was able to persuade the local authority to build a new link road to it, hence benefiting local companies.

Effect on different functions of an increase in size

Marketing

An increase in sales volume or expansion into a new market will require more marketing resources. If the business expands into several niche markets or perhaps international markets, then more personnel will be needed to formulate the separate strategies (as opposed to selling more of the same product in the same market). This will place pressure on distribution to find new outlets or to persuade present outlets to stock more units. There may also be a requirement for new wholesalers.

Production

New machinery will be required and growth may necessitate a change in either the scale or the type of production. If demand rises, it may be required to move to a different type of production e.g. from batch to flow (*see Unit 27 Types of production*).

Finance

As businesses grow, they need money. This may sound like a paradox, because growth is meant to lead to greater profit. To a certain extent this is true, but sometimes a business may grow too quickly (overtrading) which may cause a strain on cash flow (*see Unit 34*). Finance to buy stock and new machinery is required before the money comes into the business from the extra sales revenue.

Management and Personnel

As businesses grow, the need to control and communicate effectively with employees becomes more challenging. More employees are needed, both shop floor operatives and specialist managers with greater skill levels, hence there is greater strain on the personnel department for hiring and training employees. Management needs to co-ordinate and delegate more and must therefore consider the structure of the organisation in order to enhance the efficiency of the business. When General Motors grew to such a large organisation in the 1960s the management suffered from not being able to run the business effectively and the company lost out to the better controlled Japanese companies.

Diseconomies of scale

It is not always the case that as output increases, unit costs decrease. The following reasons may cause unit cost to rise as output increases, known as **diseconomies of scale**:

- As a business gets closer to full capacity output, it may be forced to pay overtime or extra money for unsocial hours. This will add to the unit cost as the output is raised.
- If a business pushes its output to the limit, this may mean that machines are run for longer periods of time than normal. This may lead to an increase in maintenance costs per unit beyond those associated with normal output.
- If extra materials are ordered and the supplier is in the position described in either of the above points, then the supplier may be forced to charge a *higher* price, even though extra materials are required. This is particularly relevant if the order needs urgent delivery.

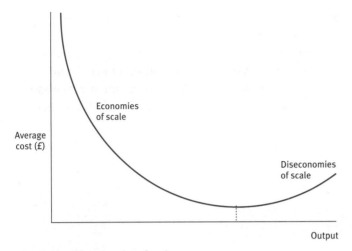

Figure 4.3   Diseconomies of scale

■ A growth in the number of personnel, customers, departments etc. may mean that co-ordination becomes very difficult. Systems need to be put into place to ensure the level of co-ordination and communication is appropriate given the increase in size. The costs of the extra co-ordination and communication can occasionally outweigh the benefits of size. This was the case in ICI before it split into ICI and Zeneca.

■ As the business employs more individuals, it is possible that the company may neglect the level of motivation of the individual, which would not happen with a smaller company in which all employees knew each other well. Control of the business becomes much harder and may require greater bureaucratic procedures (more paperwork) to ensure everything gets done (*see Unit 48 Organisational structures*).

Limitations to growth

Lack of market growth

A company might need to expand into a new market if its present market ceases to grow. BAT (British American Tobacco), one of the world's largest cigarette companies, decided to diversify into financial services in the late 1980s, buying such companies as Allied Dunbar and Eagle Star insurance; this was because there was very little prospect of growth in the tobacco market.

Lack of productive capacity

When a business reaches capacity, it may need to turn away new orders, subcontract, or prioritise present customers. Whichever choice is made, profit, customers and growth will be compromised in some way.

Lack of finance

As mentioned above, finance is needed for growth. Careful planning and negotiating with providers of finance are required to ensure cash is controlled both in the short and long term.

Lack of trained staff

This may be the cause of a sales problem, especially if the business relies on a sales-force to generate revenue. Obviously with companies that sell branded, consumer products, the advertising does most of the work. In more specialised industries, an effective sales-force is a crucial part of sales. Poor training or inappropriate selection will constrain growth.

Objectives

Some companies simply do not want to grow. If the managing director is also the owner, control and challenge from the job may be the only reasons why the business was set up in the first place; hence growth becomes highly unattractive.

Government restrictions

- When two businesses wish to unite, there may well be government interference which prevents them joining forces. The Trade and Industry Secretary stopped Rupert Murdoch's BSkyB from buying Manchester United because he felt the new company would not be in the best interest of all of its stakeholders.

- Whenever government passes a new law which means a business must change something, this hinders growth. A case in point is the minimum wage, which is having significant effects on all employees who were close to the minimum wage before the legislation was introduced. It has also threatened to dent profits.

Points for Revision

Key Terms

market capitalisation	calculated by number of shares issued × share price
internal economies of scale	benefits of reduced unit costs gained within the firm due to an increase in size
external economies of scale	benefits of reduced unit costs gained outside the firm, as a result of a firm increasing in size
diseconomies of scale	the increase in unit cost as the scale of output increases

Definitions Question:
By referring to a business you know, explain the importance of any two of the above terms (your teacher may wish to select the terms).   [5] per definition

Summary Points:

1. A business will usually try to grow in size up to a point where the benefits of further growth are outweighed by the costs.

2. The main advantage of a growth in size is known as economies of scale.

3. There are significant limitations to growth which may mean that objectives of achieving size may have to be modified.

Mini Case Study

Supermarket managers sometimes claim that the reason the first section you encounter as you walk into the shop is the fruit and vegetables is because it is not particularly valuable. Yet prices may well be 100% higher than the cost. As opposed to negotiating prices, supermarkets tend to set weekly prices for the growers, which can sometimes be lower than the prices charged by the wholesaler. Supermarkets can also change prices at short notice in response to short supply or a glut. They also dictate delivery times, packaging requirements and weights.

In turn, growers are continually searching for ways of achieving higher crop yields and fruit/vegetables which look clean, fresh and have a long shelf life. Recently, new products have been advertised as having extra flavour, such as slightly riper tomatoes. These are sold on the same shelf as other products, but are set at a higher, premium price.

Growers have reported the increased amount of trade that is now bypassing the wholesalers. Some predict that eventually supermarkets will dictate exactly what is grown, when it is grown and even how it is grown. The other disturbing fact associated with this trend is the reduction in alternative suppliers for the customer:

Butchers – supermarkets account for nearly half of all sales of red meat
Bakers – almost 75% of bread sales now go through supermarket tills
Fishmongers – Sainsbury is having to train its own fishmongers in Grimsby, given that most smaller traders have gone out of business!
Grocers and greengrocers – the number of individual outlets has declined by 25% over the past 15 years
Delicatessens – although sales are still increasing in supermarkets, the specialists are likely to survive.

Source : *Which?* March 1996

1 **Define: supermarkets, packaging.** [4]

2 **If retailers are charging 100% on cost, explain how the price relates to the cost.** [2]

3 **Explain the effect that the power of retailers is exerting on smaller businesses.** [6]

4 **One of the criticisms of UK food retailers is the level of prices in comparison with foreign retailers. Discuss this criticism in the light of the market position which the retailers enjoy.** [8]

20

Maxi Case Study

Over-capacity in the car business

Since the days of Henry Ford's dominance of the car market in the 1920s up to the present day, the car industry has continued to grow. Some companies, such as British Leyland, failed to survive the turbulent business world of the 1970s despite being government-owned. During the 1960s and 1970s, as growth in profit became more difficult to achieve due to increased competition, mainly from the Japanese, the industry turned to efficient production methods in order to create a competitive advantage. However, once all the major players in the industry had become as efficient as possible, developing a cost advantage was more difficult to achieve. In addition, car companies from south-east Asia, such as Daewoo, Samsung and Proton, have developed cheaper, more affordable alternatives for the discerning western buyer. Such car companies are part-funded by their respective governments but enjoy considerably lower labour costs. Increasing productive capacity has led to car companies aiming to use economies of scale as the main way of reducing cost, although this has unfortunately led to businesses having surplus capacity. This spare capacity occurs when the industry as a whole expands ahead of, or in anticipation of, a growth in customer demand. Such growth in capacity has meant that supply outstrips demand by some 30% i.e. car companies could cut back on their capacity levels by 30% and still meet all customer demands.

The result has been a series of joint agreements and mergers between car companies, with a view to either using capacity, or losing capacity altogether by selling off parts of a business. The other problem is the high cost of developing new vehicles: the standard response to the high cost is to either rejuvenate or relaunch old vehicles with new technology. But there are enough companies developing new models that any business which does not, stands to lose out. The main fear in the car industry is over-capacity – experts predict that by 2001, the industry may produce 23 million cars more than it can sell! In 1998 there was a spate of company mergers – e.g. Daimler-Benz, the German producer, teamed up with Chrysler.

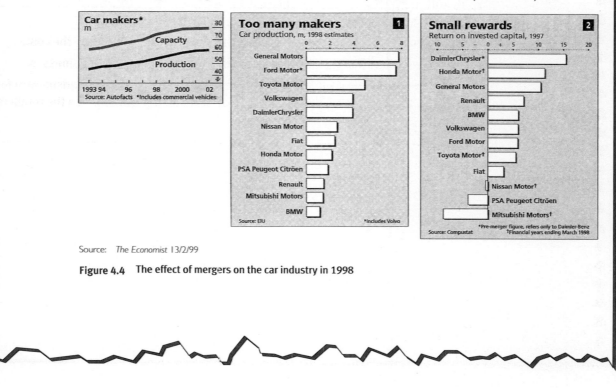

Source: *The Economist* 13/2/99

Figure 4.4   The effect of mergers on the car industry in 1998

In January 1999, Ford paid £4 billion for Volvo's car division; Volvo claimed that it needed economies of scale, allowing it to focus on buses, engines and aerospace and to acquire shares in two major truck-making businesses. Ford intended to distribute Volvos with its own cars and hoped to use Volvo's reputation for technological excellence to develop new cars, using common research platforms to save money. Renault, on the other hand, announced a joint agreement with Nissan, the debt-ridden Japanese company, to purchase a 37% stake. For Renault, the problem was not over-capacity, but rather the lack of product range. Renault was 44% owned by the French government which obviously wanted to protect one of its major companies and wealth creators. However, Renault had concentrated its major marketing effort on domestic demand in France; as the domestic market fell, profit tumbled. The expiry in 1999 of the 'gentlemen's agreement' which limited car sales from Japan was probably the main reason for teaming up with Nissan. Nissan, however, had borrowed approximately £15 billion in order to expand its productive capacity and had lost money in six of the last seven years. One estimate put 1998's losses at nearly £1 billion. The cost savings for both companies are not likely to occur until 2002, resulting mainly from purchasing economies of scale. Renault seems to have got caught between the large manufacturers who achieve economies of scale and the smaller specialist manufacturers. Although Renault wishes to expand its product range (presently only five basic models compared with Nissan's twenty-nine) this will be difficult to achieve in the near future because of the costs involved – due to Nissan's losses. They would create a company making 4.8 million cars a year, although there would be no need for such a large figure, given the level of over-capacity in the global car industry.

Source: *The Week* 6/2/99, *Financial Times* 22/3/99, *Sunday Times* 21/3/99, *The Times* 29/2/99

1 Define: cost advantage, specialist manufacturer.   [4]

2 Return on capital represents the percentage of investment which a shareholder earns in return for the investment. Comment on the conclusions which might be drawn from the charts in Figure 4.4.   [5]

3 Identify in which part of the business the purchase of Volvo cars by Ford is likely to save costs.   [5]

4 Explain how Ford might have valued Volvo, when arriving at the sum of £4 billion.   [6]

5 Discuss why size is so significant to Renault.   [10]

                                                                                              __30__

Mergers and acquisitions

Learning objectives

Having read this unit, students will be able to

1. understand the reasons for mergers

2. identify different types of mergers

3. demonstrate an understanding of the reasons for acquisitions

4. distinguish between mergers and takeovers

Context

In April 1999 business newspapers were full of articles on the proposed merger between Barclays Bank and The Royal Bank of Scotland. At that time such a merger would have made the combined business the second largest in the country and therefore more able to survive in an ever more competitive market. Are there other reasons for the merger of such companies? The press is full of companies merging, one business taking over, or acquiring another. 1998 was a boom year for merger activity: BP and Amoco, Victoria Wine and Threshers, to name but two.

Anyone knowledgeable about the history of the car industry in this country will be aware of how the number of manufacturers has fallen dramatically since the Second World War. Any article about a proposed merger, takeover or acquisition will feature a reduction in costs in the vast majority of cases. The Germans have dominated merger and acquisitions activity, Daimler Benz buying Chrysler of America, BMW purchasing Rover and Volkswagen taking over Rolls-Royce. Such are the costs involved in the design and construction of a new car today (£300 million for a new model according to R. Stead of Leeds Metropolitan University) that producing a large number of cars is essential to help reduce the fixed costs per unit.

Such grand mergers are not just the preserve of the motor industry; 1999 saw the first mention of the retail group Kingfisher proposing a merger with Asda.

Mergers, takeovers, acquisitions: what are they?

- A **merger** is when two (or occasionally more) firms combine voluntarily to form one business in an attempt to enhance their profitability, productivity or position in the market.
- A **takeover** is when one business gains control of another business for the reasons stated above. A takeover is considered to be 'hostile' if a controlling interest is bought without the consent or blessing of the management of the business which is the subject of the takeover.
- An **acquisition** is when one business gains control of part of another business. A company may be willing to sell off one of its businesses which it no longer wishes to keep or which no longer fits into its objectives for the future.

Why do businesses join together?

In a large majority of cases, reduction in costs is the reason. A combined business is able to make savings as a result of its increase in size. Growing in size can be achieved quickly by merging; there are few companies that have managed to grow without recourse to a merger, a takeover or an acquisition. The American company, Microsoft, has grown by the incredible success of its products; however this is very much the exception rather than the rule. The appropriate terminology for one of the main reasons why firms merge is to benefit from economies of scale.

Economies of scale

Huge savings can be made in marketing, production and research and development as a result of businesses joining together. In certain industries such as oil, profit margins have been falling as a result of the fall in the price of crude oil. As a consequence there has been a spate of mergers in an attempt to reduce costs. BP, with its takeover of Amoco, has become one of the largest companies in the UK. In America, Exxon and Mobil wanted to merge for similar reasons but the regulatory bodies were not so keen and investigated the likely outcome of the proposed merger, concluding that such a merger would not be in the public interest, because of the consequential market domination.

By merging, the combined business is able to spread the cost of many activities, thus reducing the unit cost. For example, spending £100 million on research and development for a new car, for a company with projected sales of 100,000, means that the unit cost for R&D will be £1,000. However after the merger, a similar venture but now with potential sales of 150,000 will reduce the unit cost to £667 (*see Table 1*).

Table 1

Research costs	Projected sales (units)	Unit costs = $\dfrac{\text{research costs}}{\text{sales}}$
£100m	100,000	£1,000
£100m	150,000	£ 667

This reduction in costs may provide a significant competitive edge, especially when other savings on marketing and production are considered (*see Unit 4 Size of business*). In addition the combined expertise may enhance the final design and ultimately the car that is produced.

Sharing the cost of investment is just one of several benefits of mergers; access or obtaining finance is another significant factor for many companies that consider a merger or takeover. Financial institutions are more likely to consider favourably a request for finance, given that the combined value of the two companies' assets is higher and therefore provides the required collateral. Once the loan is obtained, the cost, in terms of the interest to be paid, will be spread over more products, thus reducing the cost per unit. In addition, the larger business may be charged a lower interest rate because of the extra security of being larger and therefore having more assets. Similarly, the cost of purchasing raw materials is reduced as buying in bulk can be achieved. By buying more the merged companies are in a better negotiating position as the number of materials required increases.

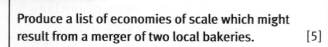

Question 1

Produce a list of economies of scale which might result from a merger of two local bakeries. [5]

Types of integration

Integration is another benefit and therefore a reason why companies merge. There are three types of integration: vertical, horizontal and conglomerate (*see Figure 5.1*).

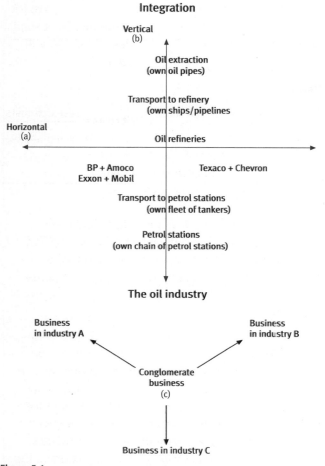

Figure 5.1 Integration of the oil industry

Horizontal integration (*see Figure 5.1a*)
This is when there is a merger between two companies that are in the same stage of production. For example, if two companies produce garden furniture, they are both involved in the secondary stage of production (manufacturing) and are producing the same product. The benefits of this type of integration are economies of scale, such as purchasing and technical economies (*see Unit 4 Size of business*). Standardisation of parts

may be possible: Peugeot-Citroen produces the same floor pan for the 106 and the AX. In addition, the combined company may be able to have a greater influence in the market or will be capable of competing with others that remain in the market.

A business may take over other businessess in an attempt to eliminate the competition. The new, larger business after the takeover will be less likely to be the victim of a takeover itself.

Vertical integration (*see Figure 5.1b*)
This is when two firms join together from different stages of production. For example, a manufacturer of garden furniture merges with a timber merchant. The benefits of such a merger are that the manufacturer now has a reliable supply of wood to produce the furniture. The wood can be delivered when required and in such a manner as to suit the needs of the manufacturer. It is also likely that profits could be increased as the wood can now be purchased at cost, without an additional increase which included the mark-up of the timber merchant. Vertical integration between a manufacturer and a retailer provides the former with a ready-made outlet for its products, thus reducing the amount of money that needs to be spent on marketing products to such outlets.

Vertical integration can be classified into 'backward' and 'forward':

■ Backward vertical integration occurs when a company joins with another from an earlier stage of production e.g. if a retailer merged with a manufacturer or a manufacturer merged with a supplier of its raw materials.

■ Forward vertical integration is e.g. when a business involved in the extraction of a raw material joins with a manufacturer.

There are a few examples of companies that are referred to as being perfectly integrated i.e. they own companies within each stage of production and thus have complete control of the whole process of distribution of their products from the extraction of the raw materials to the retail outlets that are used to satisfy the end user, namely the consumer. The best examples are the oil companies such as Shell, which has its own oilfields and tankers to transport the crude oil to its own refineries. The refined products such as petrol are then distributed to its own petrol stations using its own fleet of tankers.

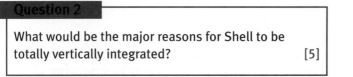

Question 2

What would be the major reasons for Shell to be totally vertically integrated?   [5]

Conglomerate integration (*see Figure 5.1c*)
This type of integration occurs when two companies join together which are not related, regardless of the stage of production they are involved in.

One of the main reasons for this type of merger is diversification. By diversifying, the business is not relying on one product or range of products and therefore reduces the risks it faces. Instead, the business will have a portfolio of products not just a range of products.

Many of the larger companies that have undertaken mergers and takeovers to take advantage of conglomerate integration are referred to as holding companies. The owner or the parent company is responsible for the objectives and long-term policy of the group of companies but allows the companies within the group to operate as separate entities. This type of integration reduces the reliance upon one type of product and therefore reduces the risk of falling foul of a downturn in a given market.

Regardless of the products sold or produced, a conglomerate business has many overheads that can be shared by the companies within the group, thus reducing costs. The trend in retailing is for outlets to sell a wider range of products and as a consequence more mergers and takeovers are occurring that allow this range of goods to be sold under one roof.

Nevertheless, the traditional conglomerate business will have a much wider range of companies, the majority of which will have no obvious connection at all.

Granada is the owner of Granada TV, Yorkshire TV and LWT, Little Chef, Travelodge, Meridian hotels and Posthouse hotels and has recently bought a 10% stake in Liverpool FC.

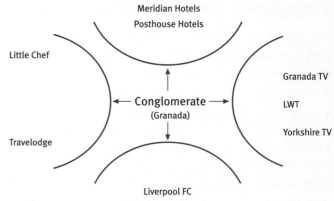

Figure 5.2   Granada the conglomerate

Question 3

An interesting quotation from the Granada annual report 1998 stated: 'We acquired a substantial shareholding in Quadrant (which owns 420 restaurants) and will bring the benefits of our business development expertise, financial support, IT systems and purchasing leverage to the joint venture'. Using the above quote state how this acquisition will benefit Granada in terms of 'purchasing leverage'.   [4]

Question 4

From the list of mergers and takeovers provided indicate the type of integration that is involved.
a) BP buying Amoco
b) Vodafone spent $62 billion buying America's AirTouch
c) Burger King is now owned by Diageo (who were formed by the merger of Grand Metropolitan and Guinness)
d) Nomura International, a Japanese investment bank, has bought many pub chains (having previously bought the William Hill chain of bookmakers)
e) Somerfield merging with Kwik Save
f) Somerfield purchasing Supermarket Direct which trades under the name of Flanagans, a retailer in the home shopping market   [6]

Globalisation and access to new markets

The growth of multinationals has increased of late as businesses attempt to take advantage not only of economies of scale or integration but of gaining access to different markets around the world.

Even whilst still negotiating the merger details with Asda, Kingfisher was involved in talks with German DIY businesses. The comments made to the press at the time (April 1999) gave no details as to the actual names of the businesses that had been approached but they did suggest that Kingfisher needed to ensure that it was involved in what was referred to as restructuring within Europe. There is no doubt that the European market will require firms to be large enough to cope with the amount of competition, which is already intense. It is a question of buy or be bought! Another example in the growth of European mergers involves Zeneca and the Swedish drug company Astra. This merger will mean that AstraZeneca will be the world's third largest drug company. An article in *The Sunday Times* (25 April 1999) suggested that firms were thinking beyond Europe and referred to a 'world order' in retailing.

Asset stripping

Some conglomerates or holding companies acquire other businesses with the sole intent of selling off the parts that will yield a profit. This process is referred to as asset stripping.

Survival

There are companies that welcome or even invite take-over bids from others, unlike hostile takeover bids which are not welcome. If a business is short of cash or afraid of being unable to compete with perhaps larger rivals, merging or being taken over can enhance the likelihood of survival. When Hanson Trust put in a bid for RHM (Rank Hovis McDougall) the target company was suspicious that Hanson would act as an asset stripper and thereby sell off its main brands e.g. Mr. Kipling's cakes. The directors of RHM invited Tomkins, more famous for its guns than cakes, to bid for RHM's shares. Shareholders of RHM were asked to accept the bid from Tomkins, even though it was sightly lower than the Hanson bid. In this case, Tomkins was referred to as a White Knight.

Synergy

By merging, the 'new' business will be more efficient and more able to dominate the market than the two separate businesses prior to the merger. Synergy follows the 'logic' of the adage of 2+2 being equal to 5. Building a brand takes a long time and is done at great expense. It is frequently quicker to purchase brands which are owned by another company. Sometimes, the individual brands are not for sale, so the entire company which makes the brands must be purchased. A particular case in point was the famous Nestlé bid, for Rowntree, in 1987, when it paid nearly £2.5 billion for Rowntree which had a book value of just over £400 million. The difference in the two figures was due to the profit which Nestlé expected to earn from owning Rowntree's famous brands e.g. Kit-Kat and Smarties.

Access to new technology

Merging can be an extremely fast way of gaining new technology. Instead of spending a significant amount of money on research and purchasing new machinery, a business can merge with a business that has already done so.

The numbers of mergers and takeovers appear to be to some degree a cyclical phenomenon. Some economists suggest that when the economy is booming and as a consequence businesses are growing there are more mergers and when the economy moves into a recession, the number of mergers and takeovers recedes.

The attitude of successive governments to the growth in the size, and therefore power, of companies has varied. There have also been occasions when governments have actively encouraged mergers in an attempt to improve international competitiveness and chances of survival in foreign markets.

The attitude of the shareholders is of interest, given the fact that the majority of shares are held not by individuals, but by pension funds and other financial institutions whose concern is the price of the shares and the dividends that may be gained. So if a business is the target of a takeover, many shareholders may be in favour because of the short-term gain rather than because of any improvements in the long-term prospects of the business.

Demergers

The benefits of mergers and takeovers have been discussed; but it is not all good news. There can be problems for a business that increases in size; organising and communicating within a large enterprise can be problematic, leading to difficulties in terms of control. Diseconomies of scale lead to an increase in the average cost of goods. If diseconomies occur, the increase in unit costs may mean that the prices the business charges are uncompetitive, leading to a decline in the number of goods sold. This in turn means that the business will be unable to reap the benefits from economies of scale such as buying in bulk and so becomes even less competitive. Alternatively, if the business decides to absorb the rise in costs as a result of the diseconomies, it may mean the level of profits is insufficient to satisfy the shareholders. Either scenario explains the reason for a **demerger**.

For example: BAT disposed of its financial services sector; Nabisco, the cereal giant, disposed of RJR, the producer of Camel cigarettes and Oreo cookies.

Points for Revision

Key Terms

merger	the combining of two businesses with the aim of improving profitability
takeover	a business gaining control of another
acquisition	a business buying a part of another business
demerger	the breaking up of a merged business into two or more separate parts
integration, vertical and horizontal	the joining of businesses in different stages of production; the joining of businesses in the same stage of production
globalisation	the growth of companies that own businesses throughout the world
conglomerate	a business that owns companies with no obvious connection

Definitions Question:
By referring to a business you know, explain the importance of any three of the above terms (your teacher may wish to select the terms).   [5] per definition

Summary Points:

1   Mergers, takeovers and acquisitions are a fast method of achieving growth for a business.

2   There is a variety of benefits for a business that undertakes a merger or a takeover.

3   There has been an increase in the number of mergers and takeovers that have been undertaken in an attempt to achieve globalisation.

Mini Case Study

In 1999 Rugby Group, the cement-maker, bought control of an Australian cement-maker. The business strategy was to concentrate on cement and in doing so to sell off its interests in other companies which were not part of its core business. These would include the sale of its joinery business to an American company called Jeld-Wen for approximately £250 million.

By doing this it was hoped that the Rugby Group would be able to raise revenue, and therefore profit, which it could use to fund a programme of acquisitions to strengthen its position as a cement-maker. Purchasing another cement business, albeit an Australian one, would provide access to any research and or technological developments that would save the Rugby Group time and money.

In addition, it was indicated that the purchase would bring about an opportunity to be involved in a wider variety of markets and consequently win contracts that the Australian business was unable to gain on its own. The 'backing' of a large and well known British cement manufacturer would be a valuable marketing tool.

1 **What type of integration occurred as a result of this takeover? Explain your answer.**   [4]

2 **By selling its non-core assets, such as the joinery business, how is the Rugby Group changing?**   [3]

3 **What will be the advantages for the Rugby Group of any further foreign acquisitions?**   [5]

4 **Discuss whether this purchase will lead to the Rugby Group gaining economies of scale.**   [8]

20

Maxi Case Study

The Ford motor company has again been busy with its cheque book in an attempt to strengthen its portfolio by buying into the car services market. Having bought Jaguar and Volvo to add to its product range, especially at the luxury end of the market, Ford has paid approximately £1 billion for Kwik-Fit, the drive-in repair business.

Kwik-Fit has 1900 outlets throughout the country, some of which are Tyre Plus centres. In addition, it has an insurance and telemarketing business that has begun to be profitable. Ford is now the proud owner of all these outlets. By purchasing Kwik-Fit, Ford has gained access to car owners who drive other makes of cars. At least one in five of Kwik-Fit's customers do not drive Ford cars. Until this purchase Ford was able to communicate with buyers of its cars only through its own dealers; now it has the opportunity to address all those on Kwik-Fit's database. Taking careful note of which car owners have just replaced their car exhausts, and so may soon be in the market for a new car, will allow Ford to target such consumers at little cost. The value of this data is difficult to estimate but in terms of the amount of time alone that it would take to collect, it is probably worth a significant amount. Ford is conscious of the changes that are in the air regarding the likely buying habits of consumers in the not so distant future. European Union regulations were due to change early in the new millennium, making it easier for a business to sell any make of car, rather than having to be tied to a dealership for one manufacturer. There are already some reports that the local supermarket will be selling cars as well as food. Ford is keen to ensure it is ready for this change in buying habits; buying a large number of outlets that are at present used to provide the consumer with new exhausts and brakes provides the means to sell other items such as cars!

Furthermore, with the emphasis very much on car manufacturers watching their prices as a result of the report by the Competition Commission, venturing into other sources of profits becomes ever more attractive.

Ford will not swallow up the name of Kwik-Fit, as it is a well known brand name that is also well liked by the consumer. Not maintaining the identity of Kwik-Fit would be throwing away much of what Ford had paid for.

---

1 Define: product range, outlets.   [4]

2 What evidence is there to suggest that this is a form of diversification?   [5]

3 Discuss whether you consider Ford's purchase of Kwik-Fit could be viewed as an example
   of vertical integration or as a form of conglomerate integration.   [6]

4 Suggest the likely savings that Ford could achieve as a result of this purchase.   [5]

5 What are the problems facing the employees of Kwik-Fit now that their employers have
   changed?   [4]

6 To what extent should Ford be concerned about diseconomies of scale?   [5]

7 Why is Ford unlikely to change the brand name of Kwik-Fit?   [4]

8 Evaluate the effect of the merger on two stakeholders of your own choosing.   [7]

40

Stakeholders

Learning objectives

Having read this unit, students will be able to

1 identify the various stakeholders that impact upon business decision making

2 identify the reasons why each stakeholder has an interest in the success of a particular business

3 recognise the problems facing a company when attempting to satisfy all stakeholders

4 analyse the circumstances when certain stakeholders are more important than others

Context

Fisons, the agricultural chemical company, continually develops new products. If it were to invent a new form of fertiliser which claimed to increase soil productivity by 10% more than any competitor's, there would be several interested parties. Not only would the shareholders and managers want to see such a product be successful, but so would the employees (production labour) because it would provide greater security in their job.

Similarly, suppliers of materials would enjoy the success of the products because it would lead to higher orders. The government would certainly be interested in the product, especially if it was sold to some of the giant farms in America, improving the country's export position as well as collecting additional tax revenue from the profits. However, the local community (if in a farming area) and environmental groups such as Friends of the Earth might well require proof that the new product would not damage the environment. Such is the significance of one product's success, that a business must increasingly pay close attention to the effect of its decisions on a wide range of individuals and institutions, not simply those on the pay roll of the business.

The stakeholder economy

Tony Blair built his election campaign of 1997 upon this catchphrase: 'the stakeholder economy'. Although it was criticised by the Conservative government as yet another of Tony Blair's soundbites, the leader of the Labour party insisted on its regular use as a way of appealing to more people (*see Figure 6.1*).

Figure 6.1   The stakeholder economy

Blair's vision was that through the lifetime of the Labour government, he would take decisions which took the entire economy into account and which would not focus on a specific group or the favoured few. In this sense, a **stakeholder** is any person, business or public sector organisation that is affected by a government decision, directly or indirectly.

Question 1

Consider the following two decisions taken by the government and identify the stakeholders involved in the decision:

a) the increase of diesel tax, making diesel similar in price to unleaded petrol   [6]

b) the change in law regarding employee share ownership programmes, such that employees can now purchase shares of the company they work for, using pre-tax income as opposed to post-tax income   [4]

In the same way, businesses have had to become more aware of the various stakeholders. In this context, a stakeholder is a person or persons or organisation that has an interest in the actions and reactions of a particular business. In this case, interest means that the actions of the business will have an effect, direct or indirect, on others. The following diagram displays the various stakeholders any business might have:

Figure 6.2   Stakeholders of a business

Stakeholders considered (in alphabetical order):

Banks – if the bank is one of the major providers of finance, the degree of success of the business may well affect the success of the bank. A bank will want to see a healthy level of cash flow and a well planned sales forecast. If the business fails, then although the bank normally has the first bite of what is owing, it may mean the bank has to take over the ownership of some of the assets and sell them off. Normally the receivers (people who are brought in to wind up a business) are called by the bank, because the bank is concerned about lack of interest payments and the probability that the company will not repay the principal sum originally lent.

Community – This includes not just the local community but also environmental groups who campaign for protection of the environment – on a scale ranging from local to global. When Tate and Lyle closed down their factory in West Everton, Liverpool some 15 years ago, well over 1,000 people were made redundant. This left a vacuum of unemployed people that has not been filled since; arguably this has led to some of the social issues which now face the area. In addition, there were several companies, in the tertiary sector, which relied on the flow of income from the main employer to support their own commercial enterprise. These will have ranged from small grocers to garages and car mechanics, all of which will have suffered following the closure of the main business. The environmental pressure groups are always seeking to ensure that nature is not disturbed by commercial activity. Recent examples of their activity have been campaigning against the Newbury by-pass as well as boarding the Brent Spa oil rig (*see Unit 62 Business ethics*) to protest against its breaking up by Shell.

Competition

Competition – if a business launches a successful product, not only will it reduce the market share for competitors, but it may also prompt competitors to copy products and emulate marketing strategies. The competition between Tesco and Sainsbury's is well documented and when one company invests in a new way of capturing customers e.g. loyalty cards, banking, pensions, the other is usually close to follow. In a similar way, the chocolate bar producers manufacture very similar products from more or less the same ingredients. Any new initiative by one company such as extra free bars or larger bars of the same price is quickly followed by competitors.

Customers

Customers – **customers** are particularly keen for the business to succeed because it will mean a continual flow of new, advanced, competitive products as well as greater choice and lower prices.

Customer loyalty depends on the individual and on the product being sold, but given that most markets are competitive, retaining customers takes up a significant amount of management time through careful marketing and research. Customers will want to know that the quality and price will be consistent wherever the purchase is made. The customer will also wish to see the same price for the same product e.g. it is particularly irritating for customers to find the same product which they bought for £1,000, marked down to £800 two weeks later.

Consumer organisations such as The Consumers' Association, which publishes *Which?* magazine in an attempt to guide the consumer to the best product in terms of value for money, seek to represent customers if they have been treated badly by companies as well as to give advice which is free and independent.

Employees and dependents – if a business is profitable, this is likely to be reflected in more pay and/or greater security along with the possibility of profit-sharing schemes. Families of employees will also reap the reward of extra benefits provided by a generous and caring employer. This is more often than not the case with Japanese companies which are renowned for their paternalistic approach to employees. Less scrupulous companies may well insist on longer hours, shorter contracts and may not reward loyalty and skill with appropriate levels of pay.

Government – a business will pay several different types of tax to the government. National insurance, income tax (paid by the employee) or sole traders and corporation tax (the tax on profits) will represent most of the tax. In addition, a petrol retailer will pay fuel duty, a publican will pay tax on alcohol (excise duty) and the majority of other companies will pay Value Added Tax. Revenue is also raised from tax on dividends and customs duties on imported goods. If a business fails, the government will not only lose tax revenue, but will also need to increase its expenditure on unemployment benefit.

Manager and directors – some of these stakeholders may well be shareholders if they have been awarded share options or may just own shares in the company they work for. The success of the company, mainly in terms of market share, profit and share price will determine the future careers of most managerial staff. Some staff will be judged by sales levels, others (perhaps production managers) by productivity levels. The higher up the executive hierarchy, the more credit each director will receive (in terms of bonuses) but the riskier the job, because failure to impress the shareholders may result in removal from office.

Retailers/wholesalers – sometimes a retailer or wholesaler (middleman) may become known for stocking a particular product, or may be the sole distributor for a particular brand. A successful manufacturer may well attribute some of the credit to the retailer and allow the business to stock more products, perhaps at a reduced cost. Manufacturers also spend a good deal of money promoting to the wholesalers and retailers, who are deemed to benefit from such promotion. If the promotion is successful and leads to greater sales, it brings in greater sales revenue to the retail outlet.

Shareholders – as the owners of the business, shareholders will be aiming to achieve two primary financial goals – some form of capital gain (where the share price increases above its purchase price) and dividends. Shareholders also take on the risk of investing in the business, in that, if the business fails, the shareholders are the last to get their money back. Consequently, they look carefully at the financial performance of the company. There are shareholders who do, however, take an 'ethical' stand when making their investment. Several shareholders sold their shares in Shell and BP following the Nigerian crisis in 1997, because of the vast oil interest in Nigeria. The extreme of this is that some shareholders invest only in 'green' companies.

Suppliers and subcontractors – one recent trend in business is to out-source, or subcontract, part of the business's activities to other companies, keeping the core or main part of the business **in-house**. As more is subcontracted, specialists in subcontracting will grow, which, in turn, will hopefully make them more efficient, which will provide further proof of the merits of subcontracting. Suppliers derive their demand from the demand by the end user e.g. the supplier of labels on tins will succeed only if Heinz and other similar companies succeed. Suppliers will also be concerned to be paid on time and their cash flow depends entirely on the major customers.

Unions – action of unions can occur regardless of the success of the business. Rather it depends on whether the employees are satisfied at the work-place. Satisfying militant unions does tend to be easier when the business has money to spend on its employees, but unions may well then bargain for even greater wage rises – such is the unpredictability of union action.

Question 2

In 1998, the consortium of 225 banks that had lent Eurotunnel well over half of its capital requirement for the Channel Tunnel became shareholders in the business. Not only had the business had further share issues, in addition to the original flotation, but the project was delayed, and there was continual insistence from the government that it was not prepared to fund any of the tunnel. The banks had lent money which was due to be repaid 60 years later, although it appeared likely that a profit was not going to be earned for some time to come. The interest charges also meant that shareholders were not paid dividends, so the banks, having granted initially an interest holiday of 18 months (the 'holiday' is a term used to describe a period when Eurotunnel do not have to pay interest on the loans), then agreed with shareholders to convert the loans into equity, otherwise know as a **debt-equity** swap. In other words the lenders of the money agreed to swap their loan for shares in the company.

a) Identify the effect on the stakeholders mentioned in the case of a debt-equity swap. [5]

b) Why did the banks give Eurotunnel an interest charge holiday? [3]

Potential for conflict

Having recognised the individual stakeholders, a business must then realise that it is almost impossible to satisfy all stakeholders all the time. As the old adage continues, it may be possible, however, to satisfy all of the stakeholders some of the time or some of the stakeholders all of the time!

Example 1: a large customer may well be given an extended credit period. The lack of cash flowing into the business may then result in a supplier not being paid on time. The business does not want to upset the larger customer, but doesn't mind upsetting the smaller supplier – here is an excellent example of market forces at work!

Example 2: company directors receiving large profit-related bonuses because they have saved money by sacking 10% of the work-force. There is clear conflict here between employees, unions and directors, and customers who feel strongly about this may well not continue to purchase from the business.

Example 3: a business decides to invest extra money in the local community at the expense of the dividend paid to shareholders. Here the shareholders may agree in principle, except when it happens to them!

Example 4: a business sponsors a charity by contributing a certain percentage of each £1 of revenue; this can be perceived as helping the community, although more cynical business observers might state that the business is using it for its own promotional ends.

Question 3

Consider the following situations, identifying the stakeholders who will be affected and explaining how they will be affected:

a) a fall in interest rates at the Cheltenham and Gloucester Building Society

b) the decision by Unilever to return £5 billion (in February 1999) to its shareholders because it could not find an appropriate use for the surplus cash (at that time)

c) the Body Shop, famous for its ethical values and modern business practices, announcing a radical 'shake-up' programme in January 1999 costing £8 million, involving unspecified redundancies, in an attempt to deal with foreign competition and falling sales $3 \times [8]$

Critics and supporters

Those in favour: the managing director at Unipart, John Neill, is a great supporter of the stakeholders theory. He believes in a close working relationship between the company, its suppliers and its employees. He encourages long-term commitment from all stakeholders in the business and with this comes a continual commitment to cut waste and therefore costs and improve quality and profitability.

Those against: it has been said that those businesses that embrace the stakeholder approach are likely to make better and more sensitive decisions for all concerned. However, there are some stern critics of the stakeholder model. Sir Stanley Kalms, the flamboyant chairman of the Dixons Group that owns a chain of high street and retail warehousing shops selling electrical goods, is one such critic. He has always seen the business world as cut-throat and without mercy; showing mercy is likely to be seen as a sign of weakness and, given the fiercely competitive markets his business operates in, he has to be equally merciless. Suppliers are kept at arm's length and given no security of contract beyond the short term – he believes the insecurity will make them fight harder. In the same way, most employees are paid a minimum basic salary and are then expected to fight hard for customer sales, on which they earn commission.

Question 4

Using your understanding of stakeholders, prepare the case for or against the stakeholder theory, with a view to making a presentation of your viewpoint to your class.   [10]

Stakeholder evaluation

Given that stakeholders will never be content with all decisions, it becomes important for the company to establish the most important stakeholder. This will vary according to the objectives of the business. Objectives represent the goals, aims and aspirations of the business. However, when a business faces a decision where one stakeholder will be more affected than the other, it must prioritise the stakeholder, given the particular situation. This in turn means the business must decide which is the most important objective to achieve.

For example: a new company sells ice-cream from vans that visit schools in order to achieve sales. The conflict here could be seen from the point of view of the owners needing the business to achieve sales (in order to generate cash flow and profit), against the ethical issue of encouraging children to eat unhealthy foods. In this case, the priority is sales revenue, due to the need for the business to survive.

Question 5

If the claim for higher wages is not met, the unions of Knit-It, a Manchester-based clothing company, intend to strike. The shareholders have criticised management for not keeping sufficiently tight control of costs and are determined to resist the unions because not to might be seen as a sign of weakness. However, a strike will upset the production schedule and the business has a delivery to make to its major customer, worth 10% of annual revenue.

In the above situation, explain the decision you would take, giving your reasons.   [8]

Points for Revision

Key Terms

stakeholders	any individual or organisation who has a stake in the success of the business
stakeholder economy	an approach taken by Tony Blair with a view to taking decisions for the benefit of all people
customer	the final user of a product and stakeholder in every business
consumer organisations	these are set up to ensure the right of the customer to quality products is not jeopardised by unscrupulous businesses
debt-equity swap	where a bank converts the money it has lent a business into shares
in-house	where a business manufactures a product itself rather than inviting a subcontractor to do it

Definitions Question:

By referring to a business you know, explain the importance of any two of the above terms (your teacher may wish to select the terms).   [5] per definition

Summary Points:

1   The stakeholder approach to business recognises that there are many people and organisations affected by business decisions.

2   A business will not always take the decision which satisfies all stakeholders and there is considerable scope for conflict.

3   Resolving such a conflict of interest requires evaluation of the stakeholders, by reference to the business objectives.

Mini Case Study

SunPower is a small, but rapidly growing, business which has developed solar panel products, designed to be installed on roof tops to catch the heat of the sun. Based in Devon, it was started by five engineers who developed the product with some cheap materials and very soon they had commissioned a plastics manufacturer to make the solar sheeting. A local electrical business was willing to make the connections and leads which would link up with the panel sheeting in order to transfer the energy into the heating system of a house.

The five engineers regularly discuss and debate issues facing the company. The latest point of contention is the marketing of the new products: Peter Clayton wants them to launch nationally and to 'clobber the docile electric and gas industry with our new product'. Oliver Parry, the founder, is keen to preserve the small, homely atmosphere in the business and go for a more gradual approach claiming that 'it would have less impact on our finances if growth was slower'. James Mason, the 'green' partner, does not care either way: 'This product will catch on because the population will see it is a more natural and environmentally friendly method of generating heat. Gone are the days of smog!'

George Rigby, the partner who actually invented this version of the product, is particularly aggrieved that the government does not recognise the product as being worthy of a patent; he recommends that the business should move to France, or even Spain, where labour costs are cheaper and the government provides financial support for companies to develop such products.

1 Identify the stakeholders in SunPower.   [4]

2 Discuss the evidence to suggest there is a conflict between the various stakeholders of SunPower.   [8]

3 In the light of the conflict between the partners, suggest who are the most important stakeholders of SunPower.   [8]

                                                                                            20

Maxi Case Study

Before July 1999, if you were boarding a ferry for either the outward or inward journey across the Channel, you were quickly told about the range of offers and opening times of the duty free shop. In the cabin of aircraft there would be a glossy magazine advertising the shop's products; air hostesses pushed their trollies up and down the aisle with a view to selling duty free goods, because a substantial part of their income was from commission based on duty free sales. All this changed with the removal of duty free shopping within the European Union from 30 June 1999. Duty free products were being sold without any tax being levied on them. When a tax is levied, the business is faced with a simple choice of either paying the tax itself or passing it on to the customer. Most businesses spread the tax between the customer and themselves. By removing the tax, the ferry companies were able to undercut the competition on land, thereby increasing the volume of sales. The alternative was to increase the price, but still be cheaper than suppliers on land, therefore increasing revenue. Alcohol tended to be one of the most popular lines in duty free shops – 24 cans of Boddingtons cost about £18.00, whereas duty free shops could sell the same amount for about £13.00.

One of the main aims of the European Union is to promote free trade. Unfortunately, duty free shopping was seen as a factor which distorted the single market in two ways:

■ by providing the transport industry with an annual subsidy of £1.4 billion. This meant that ferry companies could charge less for the journey, or they could simply earn more revenue and profit through duty free sales. This was at the cost of the taxpayer.

■ by providing the ferry companies with an unfair advantage to sell complementary products. It was estimated that companies such as Stena P&O earned about one third of total revenue from on-board sales.

The main objection to the removal of duty free sales came from the ferry companies themselves, who tried hard to persuade the public to lobby for the maintenance of duty free shopping, but Tony Blair remained in favour of its abolition, as did the German government.

The ferry companies claimed abolition would result in up to 140,000 job losses, although this figure is likely to have been an exaggeration for effect. The industries likely to be damaged were offered subsidies through the EU tax system, although such a system fails to deal with the problem of different tax rates in different EU countries – the Scotch whisky industry, for example, would much prefer drinks to be taxed at the same rate throughout the EU.

Duty free shopping actually started as a perk for those at sea to keep them supplied with cheap tobacco and alcohol, although since then the case has become much less obvious. One broadsheet observer asked. 'Where is the economic right to cut the price of a bottle of Scotch, just to face the rigours of a two-hour flight to Torremolinos?!'

Source: *The Week 27/2/99*

1 Define: commission, free trade.   [4]

2 Why was duty free shopping seen as an expense to the taxpayer?   [4]

3 a) The tax on Boddingtons beer is £5 for a case of 24 cans. What is the percentage price cut which the ferry companies can achieve by selling Boddingtons through duty free shops?   [2]

   b) What factors would have determined whether duty free shops

     i)   charged £13   [8]

     ii)   kept some for themselves by charging between £13–£18, but ensuring the price was cheaper than on land

     iii) charged £18 and used duty revenue to lower journey prices?

4 Evaluate which stakeholders would

   a)   benefit

   b)   lose out

when duty free shopping was abolished.   [12]

                                                    30

Objectives and strategy

Learning objectives

Having read this unit, students will be able to

1 appreciate the nature of objectives and mission statements

2 understand the importance of objectives in the decision making process

3 understand how objectives and strategy will differ within a business

4 appreciate the constraints upon objectives and strategies that a business may encounter

Context

The annual report of Cadbury Schweppes for 1998 stated that there were 8,374 employees. As they arrive at work each day, the employees know their job and how to do it. This is because each of the employees has a clearly defined job description which has been carefully written to ensure that the job is done in an appropriate manner.

This situation has not been achieved by accident; on the contrary, careful attention has been given to the needs of the business in order for it to operate successfully.

Each department will have certain requirements to fulfil which will have been generated from the company objectives which clearly state what the business is hoping to achieve both in the short and long term.

If Cadbury's did not have any objectives, there would be nothing for the company to work towards. The objectives determine the role of the employees within the business.

On occasions when a business is faced with a difficult decision, reference to its objectives will help in the decision making process.

Objectives provide a sense of direction for the business and its employees; the objectives can be assessed by reference to targets which in turn can be measured.

The importance of aims and objectives

One of the reasons that you are reading this, is because you are working towards an objective. That is, to achieve a pass grade for A level Business Studies. This objective is necessary in order to achieve a long-term objective of gaining a place at university or a particular job. Your short-term objectives stem from your main 'goal'. In business, this is called a mission statement.

Aims and mission statements

The mission statement sets out the purpose of the business which is communicated to all the employees and shareholders. Most mission statements refer to the values of the business as well as its main purpose. The mission statement is used to provide the framework for the running of the business and has to be communicated effectively to the employees as well as being constantly monitored to ensure it is being achieved.

The following examples from company reports show the importance of such statements:

Thistle Hotels PLC

'…creating a consistent offer for our guests to add value for our shareholders.'

MFI

'Our objective is to improve substantially the retail net margin by reducing the fixed cost base of the business.'

The Denby Group PLC

'Our primary objective is to deliver long-term growth in shareholder value by developing the Denby brand in the growing informal tableware market through our design-led strategy.'

Pilkington

'Our aim is to improve Pilkington's performance. We are transforming the company into a simpler, more focused, more efficient and lower cost glass manufacturer.'

Pizza Express PLC

'Our ongoing strategy is to maintain and improve every facet of our business…… and our objective is to sustain all our growth characteristics in the coming years.'

Diageo

'Diageo is in business to create value for our shareholders by delighting our consumers all around the world.'

Headlam Group PLC

Mission statement: 'Through its constant search for operational improvement and by providing the best possible service to both its suppliers and customers, Headlam aims to become the leading European distributor of floor coverings and home furnishings to the residential and contracts markets.'

Many of the above statements contain much that may be considered as worthy but weak on actual action. Mark Goyder* suggests that many senior managers are cynical about mission statements and that such statements are rendered less helpful because of the way in which they are prepared and introduced. To be meaningful and effective the employees have to understand their purpose and be involved in the formulation of mission statements.

Question 1

Compare the above statements from recently published annual reports and answer the following:

a) What further information would a shareholder wish to ascertain before investing in any of the companies referred to?   [4]

b) Is it possible to assess the financial value of any of the statements, noting the information given within them?   [2]

---

* in *Living Tomorrow's Company* (Gower, 1998)

Question 2

A section of Cadbury's objectives reads:

'1 to increase our earnings per share by at least 10% every year

2 to generate £150 million of free cash flow every year

3 to double the value of our shareholders' investment within four years.'

How is the statement from Cadbury's more useful than the list provided prior to Question 1?   [4]

Many of the quotes from company reports give the company's mission statement and indicate how it is to be achieved, which is a useful stepping stone to understanding the tiers or **hierarchy of objectives**.

The statement from Cadbury Schweppes says: 'Our primary objective is to grow the value of the business for our shareholders.' Everything else is geared to achieving this main aim.

Businesses have recently used objectives as an organisational tool and as a method of ensuring employees are all clear as to what is expected of them. 'Management by objectives' involves setting a series of well defined objectives that are designed to ensure each part of the business is operating in an appropriate way so as to ensure the main objective of the business is achieved.

The main aim of the business will depend upon the type of business; a newly formed sole trader may have survival as its main aim, whereas a major PLC will usually make reference to satisfying its shareholders and consequently refer to a specific target for profit. Other businesses will refer to growth; for example, achieving either a particular percentage share of the market or a certain number of sales.

Almost all businesses will have as their main aim one of the following:

- Growth
- Profit
- Survival

To achieve the main aim or major objective, a series of other objectives will need to be set; getting to university may be your ultimate objective or mission in life and as a consequence your lesser objectives to

achieve a place at university will be gaining three Bs for your A levels. How you plan to achieve these grades is another layer or hierarchy.

Objectives provide a sense of direction and unity of purpose for the business whilst providing a measurement of performance which in turn can be used as an aid to control within the business.

Unfortunately, there are occasions when the objectives for different departments within the business may conflict.

If a mission statement refers to the desire to enhance profit, an objective may have been set to cut costs. The marketing department may have an objective to develop new products, whilst the finance department has an objective to cut all department budgets.

Strategy

Strategy is defined as the way in which the objectives are achieved.

Returning to the main objectives set by a business, such as survival or growth, to satisfy shareholders, strategy will be planned to achieve:

a) a competitive advantage by low costs or
b) differentiating the product or
c) increasing productivity.

Such plans are much more geared to the short term and are often departmental. They represent the functional parts of the business. Michael Porter, a professor at the Harvard Business School*, is regarded as an expert on strategies for competitive advantage. He recommends that companies should adopt a strategy which includes:

- Selling to the most sophisticated and demanding buyers
- Seeking out buyers with the most difficult needs
- Establishing norms of exceeding the toughest regulatory hurdles or product standards
- Sourcing from the most advanced and international home-based suppliers
- Treating employees as permanent instead of using a demoralising hire-and-fire approach
- Establishing outstanding competitors as motivators.

* As referred to in *Guide to the Management Gurus*, Carol Kennedy (Century Business, 1993)

Question 3

How many of the listed strategies suggested by Michael Porter can be easily measured?   [5]

How is strategy decided upon?

Ansoff

Igor Ansoff worked for Lockheed Electronics, reaching the position of vice-president, and then left to become a professor at Carnegie, where he wrote a book called *Corporate Strategy*. Following this he spent the next 20 years researching strategic behaviour. His main thought for strategic planning was for a business to identify a competitive advantage. This ought to be coupled with analysing whether to continue with an existing product or develop a new product. This choice is considered in conjunction with the prospects for developing new markets for existing goods. His ideas can be more easily assimilated by way of a matrix.

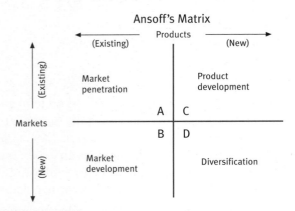

Figure 7.1   Ansoff's matrix

Figure 7.1 illustrates the options that are available to a business.

A   Market penetration requires the business to sell a greater quantity of an existing product to consumers in an existing market.
For example:
Kellogg attempted to sell more cornflakes to existing consumers by advertising the idea of eating Kellogg's Cornflakes at any time of the day, not just at breakfast.

B   Market development involves selling an existing product to new consumers.
For example:
Brylcreme, hairgel traditionally sold to the older consumer, was repackaged and advertised to the younger generation with considerable success.

C   Product development requires the business to sell a new product to existing consumers.
For example:
Walkers has launched a range of new flavours for its crisps (Cheese and Owen, for example).

D   Diversification requires the business to develop a new product to be sold to new consumers.
For example:
Mars launching a range of ice-creams.

Question 4

Using the Ansoff matrix, suggest which of A, B, C or D is the most appropriate for the following:
 i)   Lucozade launching the sports drink, Lucozade Isotonic
 ii) Nestlé launching the Kit-Kat Chunky bar   [2]

None of these decisions with regard to strategy can be made in isolation. Therefore there is a need for a business to look carefully at where its competitive advantage may lie. To do this, and thereby plan the most appropriate strategy, the marketing department may undertake a SWOT analysis.

Research into the **S**trengths
                          Weaknesses
                          Opportunities
                          Threats
will assist the company to assess the best strategy.

The strengths and weaknesses concentrate on internal factors. Cadbury Schweppes may have undertaken a SWOT analysis and reached the following conclusions:

Strengths: well-established brand names including its most famous, Cadbury's Dairy Milk; major brands in several of the chocolate market segments; a sound financial base.

Weaknesses: may be viewed as an old brand.

Opportunities: many confectionery businesses that could be acquired. New markets available, especially in eastern Europe. Other market niches to exploit following the huge success of the introduction of Favourites into the 'assortments' market.

Threats: major competitors such as Nestlé continue to expand and 'attack' Cadbury's brands; the legal and economic climate in which Cadbury's operates; health reports that highlight the dangers of eating too much chocolate; a downturn in the economy reducing the amount spent on sweets.

Task

Prepare a SWOT analysis for a well known consumer brand of your choice. [10]

Cadbury Schweppes' strategy uses a value-based management technique:

'Value-based Management is a systematic way of analysing and understanding a business, the market in which it operates, its strengths and its weaknesses as well as those of its competitors. We then seek to develop better strategies which will produce step changes in the competitive performance.......'

(Annual Report 1998)

Once the strategy is in place the final layer of objectives can be put into place, namely the **tactics** to be used to ensure the strategy is successful.

Tactics

This involves the implementation of the strategic plan on a day-to-day basis. Each part of the strategic plan must be broken down into departmental secondary objectives with targets that can be measured.

For example, Cadbury's strategy for its confectionery is based on:

'Strengthening of our key brands through marketing investment and innovation in new product development....' (Financial Statement 1998)

Therefore its tactical objectives or secondary objectives may be to:

i) Increase the marketing budget for any new lines.
ii) Attempt the launch of at least two new brands over the next financial year.

These tactical objectives ought to enhance the prospect of the strategy being a success as the tactics are the method by which the strategy is implemented.

Task

Suggest some appropriate targets for a travel agency whose strategy is to offer a better range of additional services to its customers in order to create a competitive advantage. [4]

Question 5

Suggest how your answer to the above task would differ if targets were to be set for a multinational PLC wanting to gain a wider range of consumers. [6]

Having established the various levels of objectives a simple summary is given below:

The Hierarchy of Objectives

Mission statement or Aim
(the primary objective)

Objectives that are necessary
to fulfil the mission statement

Strategy, the implementation
of the objectives

Tactics, for which targets are
set which are monitored.

Corporate culture

The way the **hierarchy of objectives** is implemented is often dependent upon the philosophy or culture of the business.

The **corporate culture** or ethos may well lead to the formulation of the business plan, which the business may use to map out its delivery of its mission statement.

The chief executive of Diageo, in the annual review, stated: 'My job is simple.

It's to make sure that everyone in this company is obsessed with delighting our consumers and creating value for our shareholders.'

He added: 'My task is to make sure that everybody in Diageo has absolute clarity on where we are heading.' Diageo is organised in such a manner as to ensure that every aspect of the business is geared to the achievement of creating value for its shareholders. This has meant establishing a common way of defining what value is and how to create it.

The whole ethos or way in which the company is run is geared to the achievement of the company objective or objectives. Goyder* suggested that 'A company's statement of its purpose should be a reflection of its personality.'

Toyota too has built a corporate culture which is used in the pursuit of its objectives and reflects its personality. The 'guiding principles' are stated as:

1 Be a company of the world
2 Serve the greater good of people everywhere by devoting attention to safety and the environment
3 Assert leadership in technology and customer satisfaction
4 Become a contributing member of the community in every nation
5 Foster a corporate culture that honours individuality while promoting teamwork
6 Pursue continuing growth through efficient global management
7 Build lasting relationships with business partners around the world

Many of the principles appear to overlap and may be just words (previously stated); mission statements can be perceived as just a series of soundbites, and no more.

Contingency plans

Unfortunately, there are occasions when external factors beyond the control of the business, if not addressed, would be either a permanent or a temporary barrier to the achievement of the aim of the business.

Having a contingency plan to 'cope' with such unforeseen situations may be included in a business plan.

An example of a contingency plan is how to cope with the threat of the millennium bug; the government launched a help service called Action 2000, in an attempt to encourage businesses to prepare themselves for any potential problems. The cost of implementing strategies to cope with the millennium bug around the world has been estimated as nearly £500 billion.

Action 2000 was not confident that all firms would have their strategies in place in time; over half of medium-sized companies at the start of 1999 had not prepared any sort of strategy at all.

The response of companies to the threat of the millennium bug was interesting to observe. Companies had already suffered problems with the bug as they attempted to prepare investment projects for 2000 and beyond. The majority of the world's airlines decided not to fly between the hours of 10 p.m. on New Year's Eve and 6 a.m. on New Year's Day, just in case there were problems with air traffic control computers. Microsoft sold a range of software 'patches' that could be used to ensure PCs did not crash.

Many businesses made contingency plans for the payment of their employees' wages and salaries. The main high street banks had plans to ensure that all branches had additional stocks of cash as it was expected that consumers would draw out of their accounts more than normal for fear of the cash dispensers not working.

Question 6

Suggest the likely contents of a contingency plan for the Channel ferry companies on the implications of a second Channel Tunnel.   [6]

Goyder* clearly states that if mission statements are to be meaningful then an 'inclusive' approach needs to be adopted by the company. This will require the company to:

■ define purpose and values
■ review key relationships
■ define success

* ibid p68

- measure and communicate performance
- reward and reinforce

In conclusion, it is evident that companies need to establish their main aims or objectives, which need to be measurable and clearly imparted to all the employees within the business.

Constraints

The setting of objectives allows the business to focus on particular areas with a view to working towards the mission statement. However, all companies face problems which prevent objectives being fulfilled and sometimes these force the business actually to change the objective. Constraints divide themselves into internal and external. The difference is that frequently a business can do something to solve the cause of the internal constraint, whereas it has to react to the external constraint.

Internal constraints

Legal structure

Frequently sole traders are unable to find the finance that they need to expand the business further. This may be due to the lack of security which sole traders offer in the event of a default on payment. Customers may also have less trust in a sole trader than in a major, famous PLC. Alternatively such a difference can work in the sole trader's favour, in that it can provide a personal service to the customer.

Time

The Stock Exchange of London, and other financial markets, have been criticised in the past for their short-term approach to business i.e. investors are looking for a quick profit before exiting from the market and putting their money elsewhere. This has led to pressure being exerted on a PLC to produce short-term profits, sometimes at the expense of long-term growth.

Geographical location

When a firm operates in several countries, it becomes difficult to co-ordinate such operations. This might be because the telecommunication system is not particularly easy to operate, or perhaps is just expensive to use. Markets, religion and cultures may be different and this may mean a separate set of objectives needs to be pursued e.g. dealing with Japanese companies takes much longer than anywhere else in the world. This is just a part of their business culture. Short-term profits in Japan, therefore, are very hard to achieve, so a longer time scale needs to be placed on the expectation of financial returns.

Conflict of interests

Whenever an individual manager or employee produces a new idea, there is likely to be some opposition to it because it causes a conflict of interests e.g. a production manager suggests that a new machine will reduce the cost of production by 10%, but that it will cost the business £250,000 to purchase. The marketing manager may be pleased that it will produce cheaper products, thereby allowing his department to earn more revenue for the business, although initially it may also mean that his marketing budget might be cut! John Adair (*see Unit 52 Leadership and management*) discussed the problem of ensuring that three separate objectives must be achieved – task, group and individual needs. Not attending to the needs of the individual may affect both group and task needs. For example, if a product manager of a business which makes soap powder has an ambition to be promoted and the business fails to recognise this, then there will be two repercussions:

- The individual will not perform the task as well, possibly resulting in a loss of market share, and
- His/her sales teams may pick up on the bad feeling and not perform as well.

Finance

Very few businesses can do everything that they want to do; there is a constraint on the availability of finance which means the business must ration itself in some respects. Perhaps a less glitzy advertising campaign which is shown on fewer occasions will be the result of a cutback in marketing, if other parts of the business are to be preferred. As a result, a sales objective may have to be refined to reflect the lack of marketing expenditure.

■ External constraints

An individual business has very little control over the external environment, which will, in turn, affect whether it can achieve its objectives. A business may well be forced to alter its objectives if an external constraint proves too significant to avoid.

Competition

The strength of competition depends on the relative size of companies e.g. in 1999, BP joined with Amoco and Texaco joined with Chevron with a view to competing more effectively against each other. As one company becomes significantly larger, the other one frequently takes similar action to wipe out any competitive advantage due to an increase in size. As a company becomes larger and therefore more influential in the market-place, one of its objectives will be to become **price leader**; this means it sets a price which becomes standard for the industry.

Government policy (local and national)

At a local level, the provision of services in the community is a primary aim for town and borough councils. When a business perhaps wishes to extend its premises in order to put new machinery in and increase capacity, planning permission can take several weeks and may ultimately be refused.

National government sets laws which can impinge on a business, such as raising VAT, therefore pushing the price of products up, making them less attractive to customers. This will affect revenue and profit according to the nature of the product. Alternatively, it might pass laws on the amount of industrial effluent which can be released into the environment, forcing a business to upgrade its production facility to minimise waste. Such an investment will add costs, but is not likely to add value.

Economic

The state of the economy may mean that plans for an expansion programme have to be delayed as the economy moves into recession. Alternatively, interest rate rises make an investment too expensive relative to the expected return.

These economic aspects are dealt with in much more detail in Section 6 Business Environment.

Ethics

In recent years businesses have had to be much more aware of ethical issues in the way they operate. Human rights records of certain countries have been significant in terms of determining where a business locates overseas, as has the issue of exploiting cheap labour. Pressure groups such as Greenpeace and Amnesty International have campaigned hard for greater awareness of such régimes in such a way that it will harm the régime's economic prosperity (*see Unit 62*).

Points for Revision

Key Terms

mission statement	the main aim or objective of the business
objective	what needs to be achieved for the aim of the business to be achieved
strategy	the implementation of objectives, the method for achieving objectives
tactics	the day-to-day procedures to fulfil the chosen strategy
hierarchy of objectives	the different levels of objectives set by the business
corporate culture	the ethos that governs the way the business operates
price leader	a company sets a price which others in the industry follow
contingency plan	a method of dealing with changes in constraints on business activity

Definitions Question:
By referring to a business you know, explain the significance of three of the above terms (your teacher may wish to select them for you).   [5] per definition

Summary Points:

1   All businesses need objectives in order to determine what they do and how they do it.

2   Within the hierarchy of objectives, a business will formulate its strategy.

3   There are several constraints, both internal and external, which hinder a business achieving its objectives.

Mini Case Study

Phil Mince is a butcher in a large northern village with a population of 8,000 which is growing rapidly. He has been concerned about the financial performance of the butcher's shop over recent years. Sales revenue has been static but with falling profit on his range of traditional products (mainly beef-based) following the BSE crisis (see *Figure 7.2*). This problem has been made worse by some customers transferring their loyalty to the local supermarket.

	1997	1998	1999
Sales revenue	£80,000	£82,000	£83,000
Profit	£25,000	£23,000	£20,000

Figure 7.2   Butcher's finances

This has led him to rethink his overall strategy in terms of increasing turnover and hence profit. As a consequence, he is thinking about extending the product range to include home-made pies, freezer products and vegetables. The property has two storeys and his wife has suggested the business could diversify, by using the space upstairs to develop a permanent site for her mobile beauty therapy business. Presently the upstairs is not used, but is costing the business money in terms of rates and maintenance.

A further option would be to establish sales at a newly opened caravan site located at a nearby beauty spot, selling barbecue food during the summer out of the back of a van.

1 Perform a brief SWOT analysis for Phil Mince's business.   [4]

2 a) Calculate profit as a percentage of sales revenue for 1997 to 1999.   [3]

  b) Briefly explain two reasons why the answers change between 1997 and 1999.   [4]

3 What problems might the business face in changing its strategy?   [5]

4 How can the Ansoff matrix be relevant to solving Phil's problem of falling profit?   [4]

20

Maxi Case Study

Hewlett Packard is a name which is synonymous with a wide range of computer products. Well over 80% of its total sales income comes from printers and scanners, with the rest coming from electronic testing equipment. The company has a global presence which reflects its degree of success in its 60-year history. The business was founded by Bill Hewlett and Dave Packard just before the Second World War. During 1940, the business had a turnover of $34,000 with three employees and eight products – by 1998, turnover had risen to $47 billion with nearly 125,000 employees and over 12,000 products. It was recently awarded the prize of America's Most Admired Computer and Office Equipment Company by *Fortune* magazine.

In 1957, the founders decided that the business, although highly successful, needed well defined goals in order to develop the company's strategy in a more detailed manner. The result of this decision was the set of Hewlett Packard (HP) objectives which the company has worked towards ever since. The objectives, taken from the HP website, have formed the basis of its strategy and have been built around the organisation's character and values.

Profit objective

To achieve sufficient profit to finance our company growth and to provide the resources we need to achieve our other corporate objectives.

Customers objective

To provide products and services of the highest quality and the greatest possible value to our customers, thereby gaining and holding their respect and loyalty.

Fields of interest

To participate in those fields of interest that build upon our technologies, competencies and customer interests, that offer opportunities for continuing growth, and that enable us to make a needed and profitable contribution.

Growth objective

To let our growth be limited only by our profits and our ability to develop and produce innovative products that satisfy real customer needs.

Our people

To help HP people share in the company's success which they make possible; to provide them with employment security based on performance; to create with them an injury-free, pleasant and inclusive work environment that values their diversity and recognizes individual contributions; and to help them gain a sense of satisfaction and accomplishment from their work.

Management

To foster initiative and creativity by allowing the individual great freedom of action in attaining well defined objectives.

Citizenship

To honour our obligations to society by being an economic, intellectual and social asset to each nation and each community in which we operate.

Table I

Recent results:

	Sales $bn	Profit $bn	Revenue per employee $	Research and Development per employee $
1993	20.3	1.2	215,200	1.8
1994	25	1.6	256,900	2
1995	31.5	2.4	314,100	2.3
1996	38.4	2.6	358,600	2.7
1997	42.9	3.1	366,900	3.1
1998	47.1	2.9	382,000	3.4

Source: Hewlett Packard website (www.hp.com)

The corporate culture of HP is known as The HP Way, which is the title of the book which employees are issued with when they join the business. This book charts the success of the company but also makes it very clear that it is the set of values and beliefs held within the organisation which forms the basis of its corporate culture. From these values come the objectives, and from the objectives comes the strategy.

There are five organisational 'values' which form the basis of the HP way.

1. Trust and respect for individuals; the belief that HP people want to do a good job and must be given the correct support and training. The business attracts capable, innovative people who are encouraged and expected to contribute enthusiastically to the business.

2. A high level of achievement and commitment; customers expect the highest quality so all employees must focus on the customer; continual improvement is therefore expected from everyone.

3. The business has integrity i.e. there is an expectation for everyone to be open and honest in order to earn trust and loyalty.

4. Objectives are achieved through teamwork; only through co-operation between different parts of the business can the best results be attained. In a sense this is another application of synergy, in that the value of the whole team is greater than the total value of the individuals working on their own.

5 Flexibility and innovation – HP employees are encouraged to produce new ideas which help HP to achieve ts objectives. It is said that one employee, who came from another large US business tc work at HP, left after three months, returning to the former business. The reason he gave was that no-one actually told him what to do!

Strategy

In order to achieve the objectives, the business employs several strategies, one of which is known as MBWA or managing by walking around, whereby leaders are seen to be actively involved in talking with employees, reserving time for impromptu discussions. Another is management by object ves which means all employees have objectives which are integrated with other employees, thereby allowing flexibility to satisfy customers. The Open Door policy is a sign to encourage employees to share their feelings, and raise the level of trust between manager and work-force. Finally, open communication promotes strong teamwork and a close relationship with the customer.

In 1999, HP decided that the business should divide into two separate parts – the computer business and the electronic testing business. The latter was the actual business which formed the start of HP and therefore the initial values and objectives were based on electronic testing. It will be interesting to see whether the values of the present HP business become equally ingrained in the two new companies.

---

1 Briefly explain each objective in the context of the business and its operations. (You might find the HP website useful for this question – www.hp.com)   **[15]**

2 To what extent do the figures in Table 1 reflect the achievement of objectives?   **[8]**

3 What other information, apart from financial data, would you require to assess whether the company has ach ieved the objectives?   **[5]**

4 What is the corporate culture of the business?   **[4]**

5 What characteristics do you think HP employees need to possess if they are going to enjoy working at HP?   **[6]**

6 The objectives of HP are written with a degree of priority in mind i.e. profit is the most important objective, citizenship the least. Discuss the significance of this order of priority for HP.   **[12]**

50

Economic theory

Learning objectives

Having read this unit, students will be able to

1 demonstrate an understanding of the relationship between demand and supply

2 understand the concept of equilibrium

3 explain the factors that affect demand and supply

4 analyse how a business may react to changes in demand and supply

5 understand the concept of markets failure

Context

Why is it that consumers are prepared to pay large sums of money to purchase a painting by Van Gogh? Why do consumers, especially teenagers, insist on paying well above the average market price for a shirt or a pair of jeans which has a very small label sewn on with the name Gap, Ralph Lauren or Levi?

Why has the price of personal computers fallen so dramatically in relation to the specification of the package of hard and software?

Why is a well known brand of baked beans much more expensive than an own-brand variety?

The answers to all of the above questions are to do with the market forces that operate. These forces are the demand for a product or service and the supply of the product or service. The interaction between demand and supply is a significant determinant of how resources are allocated in an economy (economists refer to this interaction as the price mechanism).

The role of economic theory in business

All businesses are affected by the interaction between **demand** and **supply** and to some extent are able to influence this interaction.

Watching with care how consumers react to changes in the price of goods enables the business to gauge the likely outcome of any changes in prices or circumstances that affect the demand for their product or service.

An understanding of the **market forces** that operate provides the business with a valuable insight into the behaviour of the consumer and the possible reaction of other businesses. The market forces consist of two main elements: demand and supply.

Demand

Consider the information contained in Table 1:

Table 1

Demand schedule for CDs

PRICE	DEMAND
£5	1,000,000
£8	800,000
£10	600,000
£12	400,000
£14	100,000

It is easy to see that as the price increases, the number of CDs that are demanded falls. This can be shown on a diagram (*see Figure 8.1*).

The demand line in Figure 8.1 shows the relationship between the price of a product and the level of demand, the product ('q') at a particular price ('p').

Changes in price

Any change in the price of the product leads to a change in the quantity demanded (*see Figure 8.2*).

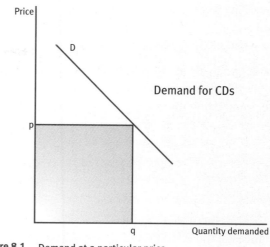

Figure 8.1   Demand at a particular price

When the price increases from £8 to £10 the quantity demanded falls from 800,000 to 600,000.

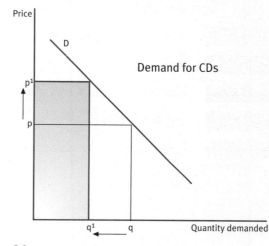

Figure 8.2   Demand when price changes

Similarly, if the price were reduced, the level of demand would increase. For any change in price, the effect on demand can be measured by the movement up or down the demand line.

The level of demand can also be affected by changes in the circumstances under which the product or service is bought. These are sometimes referred to as changes in the condition of demand and are represented on a diagram by a shift in the demand line to either the left or the right.

To gauge the actual or **effective demand** for a given product, it is important to realise that there are two main factors operating:

i) The ability to purchase (influenced by price and income)
ii) The willingness or desire (influenced by choice)

A consumer may desire to purchase a Jaguar but is unable to afford one and so cannot be included in the number demanding this car.

Changes in the condition of demand

For changes in the condition of demand, the business needs to be aware of factors other than the price of the product.

Many of the examples of changes in the condition of demand are related to the willingness to buy and the ability to buy (apart from the price) a given product or service (*see Figure 8.3*).

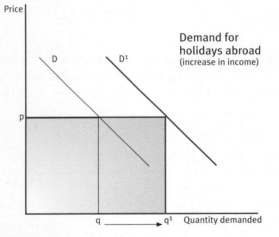

Figure 8.3 Change in the condition of demand

■ Income

In this example, which illustrates the demand for holidays abroad, an increase in the income of consumers will lead to an increase in the demand for this type of holiday. There has been a change in the condition of the market; more consumers now have a greater ability to demand holidays abroad. This leads to a new demand line to the right (D^1) and a subsequent increase in the quantity demanded (q to q^1).

Similarly, if there were a series of air traffic control strikes causing huge delays at airports, there would be

a fall in the demand for holidays abroad, as consumers would not want the problems of being left waiting at airports for hours (*see Figure 8.4*).

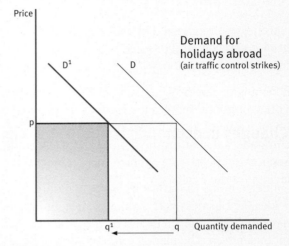

Figure 8.4 Shifting demand due to external factors

This would lead to a new demand line (D^1) being drawn to the left to show the fall in demand (q^1).

■ Advertising

Regardless of the level of income and the price of the product, the demand for a given product, such as a particular magazine, will be affected by the individual's taste and choice. If consumers are not interested in soccer they will not be tempted to purchase a soccer magazine, regardless of their ability to do so.

Consumers can be influenced to desire a product if it has been carefully advertised to appeal to a given group of consumers.

There are many other examples of changes in the condition of demand:

■ Changes in the season

A business selling ice-cream will expect demand to increase in the summer. This would lead to a new demand line to the right.

■ Changes in the population

As the population increases, there will be an increase in the demand for products which relate to the size of the population e.g. food.

■ Changes in government legislation

A business has to be aware of any changes in legislation that may affect demand for its products or services. For example, when the government changed the regulations regarding the number of tablets sold for headaches, the manufacturers had to reduce the tablets in each box or sachet. Assuming the overall demand remained constant, there would be an increase in the demand for boxes.

■ Changes in economic policy

Changes announced in the annual budget by the Chancellor of the Exchequer for taxes and grants and changes in monetary policy (*see Unit 60 Interest rates*) will affect the level of demand for certain products. Any of those products that are subjected to a change in the level of tax, such as alcohol, cigarettes and cars, will see some change in the level of demand. Changes in monetary policy that make money harder to borrow will reduce the demand for products.

The independent Monetary Policy Committee decides the base rate every month. Any changes in the base rate affect the ability of consumers to borrow and consequently demand products often bought on credit.

■ Changes in attitudes and information

Reports issued by various bodies can influence the demand for products; medical reports about genetically modified foods affected the sales of such goods almost overnight, leading to several of the main supermarket chains emptying their shelves of such products.

■ Changes in taste and fashion

Businesses involved with the manufacturing and retailing of clothes need to be conscious of the 'in-fashions' and respond accordingly. Certain products come and go very quickly (*see Unit 16 Product*). Yo-yos and South Park toys, for example, show dramatic changes in the level of demand.

■ Changes in the prices of other products

Substitutes

With so many brands available for the consumer to choose from, the demand for one product can be greatly affected by the price and advertising of another similar product. For example, the demand for Heinz soups may be influenced by the price of a similar alternative or 'substitute'. If Crosse and Blackwell soups came down in price, there could well be a fall in the demand for Heinz soups (q to q^1) as consumers switched to the cheaper substitute (*see Figure 8.5*).

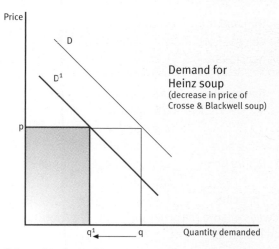

Figure 8.5   Fall in demand for Heinz soups due to price cut by competitor

There has been no change in the price of Heinz soups, but there has been a change in the condition of demand for Heinz soups, hence the new demand line to the left.

Complementary goods

Similarly, the price of one product can influence the demand for another, if the two products tend to be bought in conjunction with each other (complementary goods). For example, sales of CD players lead to sales of CDs; fish and chips, pens and ink cartridges, cars and petrol are all 'complementary goods' because they are used in conjunction with each other but do not have to be bought together. A decrease in the price of mobile phones which are sold without a rental agreement led to a large increase in the demand for the phone cards that are necessary to make calls.

Derived demand

A final example where the relationship between products can affect the demand for a given product is 'derived demand'. This occurs when automatically an increase in the demand for one product leads to an increase in the demand for another. For example, any increase in the demand for houses will automatically lead to an increase in the demand for land.

In deciding the likely changes in demand it is assumed that all other variables that affect the product in question remain constant (*ceteris paribus*).

Question 1

For the following examples, use demand curves to show the most likely change in quantity and/or price.

	Demand for:	Change:
a)	electric fans	a very hot summer
b)	revision books	it is now just prior to the A level examinations!
c)	bananas	medical report suggests that bananas help reduce heart disease
d)	Mars bars	increase in the price of Kit-Kats
e)	luxury boats	large increase in top rate of income tax
f)	Ford cars	increase in price

(Always ensure that your diagrams are carefully drawn and labelled.)   [12]

Supply

The supply line shows the relationship between the amount that a business is prepared to supply and the price (*see Figure 8.6*).

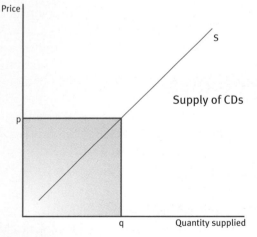

Figure 8.6   Supply at a particular price

Table 2

Supply schedule for CDs

PRICE	SUPPLY
£5	200,000
£8	400,000
£10	600,000
£12	800,000
£14	900,000

Changes in price

Again assuming that all other factors remain constant (*ceteris paribus*), the supplier will be willing to supply more products at a higher price, on the basis that the business will be making more profit.

However, if the price falls from £10 to £8, the business will be willing to supply only 400,000 CDs (*see Figure 8.7*).

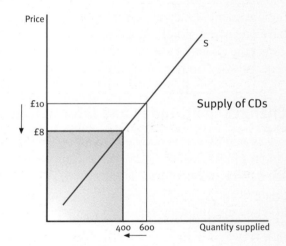

Figure 8.7   Supply when price changes

Changes in the condition of supply

There are factors that will create a change in the amount that is supplied regardless of the price that is available:

■ Changes in the productive efficiency of the business

There are several examples of this, most obviously increased efficiency due to technological progress. Using a new machine that can produce products such as video recorders at a quicker speed or at a lower cost will encourage the manufacturer to supply more (*see Figure 8.8*). This will lead to a new supply line to the right of the original (S^1 – quantity increases to q^1).

Improved production techniques, applying the concept of lean production (*see Unit 30*), will also encourage the manufacturer to supply more.

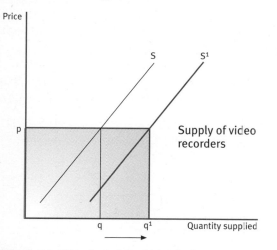

Figure 8.8 Supply rising due to improved technology

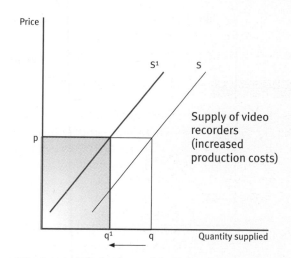

Figure 8.9 Supply dropping due to rising costs

■ Changes in the cost of production

If there are changes in the cost of production these will be reflected in the number of products the business is prepared to produce. Changes in the cost of the raw materials or labour will alter the amount the manufacturer is prepared to supply. For example, a manufacturer of cars faced with an increase in the cost of steel, assuming all other factors remain constant, will be less willing to supply cars because rising costs mean less profit (*see Figure 8.9*). There will be a new supply line to the left and a reduction in quantity supplied (q^1).

■ Government legislation

If the government introduced legislation requiring all cyclists to wear cycle helmets, the manufacturers of these products would be more likely to increase

Question 2

For the following examples, use supply curves to show the most likely change in quantity and/or price.

	Supply of:	Change:
a)	strawberries	poor weather leading to poor harvest
b)	perfume	price increases
c)	shoes	increase in the cost of leather
d)	restaurant meals	introduction of the minimum wage
e)	cola drinks	new canning machine delivered

[10]

supply. There would be a new supply line to the right and an increase in quantity supplied.

Equilibrium

Until now, the demand and supply lines have been considered in isolation; but the market reflects the behaviour of both simultaneously so there is a need to combine the two lines.

Market forces should provide a situation where the demand and supply for a given product will be equal at a given price. That point is referred to as the **equilibrium** (*see Figure 8.10*).

The equilibrium quantity (q) is the number of products that:

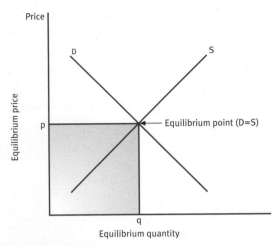

Figure 8.10   Demand and supply lines in equilibrium (also known as market clearing.)

i)   the supplier is willing to supply at the market price (p) and

ii) the consumers (demand) are willing to buy at the market price

Businesses need to be aware of the factors that may affect the price at which their products are sold. The conditions within the market for their product or products are constantly changing and therefore require careful monitoring. Demand and supply diagrams allow the business to make a useful assessment of the likely consequences of any changes within the market. Consideration of changes in the condition of demand and supply require careful attention as to which curve is affected in the first instance.

This can be seen in the following examples:

Example 1

(*See Figure 8.11*)

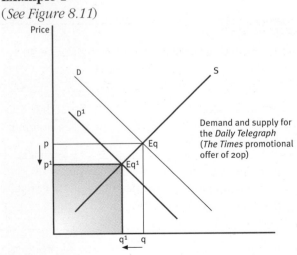

Figure 8.11   Demand and supply for the *Daily Telegraph*

If there were a promotional offer for *The Times*, it is possible to suggest the likely consequences in terms of the demand and supply. It is important to understand that the first line to be affected will be the demand for the *Daily Telegraph*. *The Times* is a substitute for the *Telegraph* and therefore consumers will switch and as a consequence demand for the *Telegraph* will fall. This is a change in the condition of demand; there has as yet been no change in the price of the *Telegraph* and therefore there will be a new demand line to the left (D^1). The consequences of this change will be:

i)   a new equilibrium point (Eq^1), and

ii) a new quantity supplied (q^1).

The change in condition of demand has affected the level of demand and as a consequence the amount supplied has fallen. The final reaction is the price falling to p^1. (To what extent the newspaper will change its price depends on a range of factors that will be discussed in Units 17 Pricing and 18 Elasticity.)

Example 2

(*See Figure 8.12*)

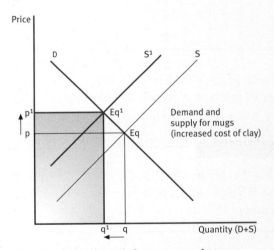

Figure 8.12   Demand and supply for mugs manufacturer

If a manufacturer of mugs is faced with an increase in the cost of clay, this increase will affect the supply of mugs in the first instance (a new supply line to the left S^1). The result of the increase in cost and change in the supply of mugs will lead to an increase in the equilibrium price and therefore a fall in the demand for the mugs (q^1). (To what extent the increase in costs will be passed on to the consumer depends on the product and the competition in the market, as explained in Units 17 Pricing and 18 Elasticity.)

Question 3

Draw a demand and supply diagram and show the likely changes for the following:

	Demand and supply for:	Change:
a)	children's bikes	massive increase in the demand for skateboards and roller blades
b)	houses	increase in the cost of land
c)	Kellogg's Cornflakes	two new rival brands enter the market
d)	tennis equipment	Greg Rusedski or Tim Henman reaches a Wimbledon final!

[12]

Equilibrium can be 'calculated' as well as drawn:

Table 3

PRICE	DEMAND	SUPPLY
£10	100	20
£12	80	40
£14	60	60
£16	40	80
£18	20	100

By looking at the demand and supply schedule for a range of prices, it is possible to see that the equilibrium price is £14 and the equilibrium quantity is 60.

Question 4

Using the demand and supply schedules for CDs (see Tables 1 and 2), what is the equilibrium price and quantity? [2]

Disequilibrium

So far, all the examples have led to a change in the condition of demand or supply and as a consequence a new equilibrium position. However, there are occasions when an equilibrium will not occur. **Disequilibrium** occurs when demand and supply are not equal at a given price.

For example, Figure 8.13 shows the equilibrium price for potatoes. If the price of potatoes was increased to p^1, this would encourage suppliers to supply more due to the attraction of more profit; but consumers might not be willing to pay this higher price. Under these circumstances there would be a surplus or glut of potatoes (excess supply over demand).

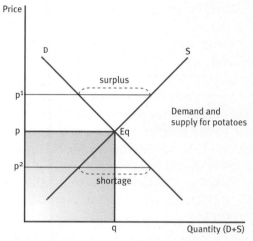

Figure 8.13   Disequilibrium

If market forces pushed the price down to p^2, consumers would be willing to buy more but the suppliers would be less willing to supply so many. This situation would result in a shortage (excess demand over supply). The extra demand may encourage the suppliers to increase their prices, given the level of demand available. Eventually, the price would be increased to a point where all the products that were supplied at that price would be bought and therefore the disequilibrium would be cleared.

Question 5

A market stall trader, Liz Brown, sold yoghurts with a shelf life of just one day. She sold each carton of yoghurt for 30p but found that by late afternoon she still had 40 left and was keen not to have to throw them away at the end of the day. Draw a diagram to show:
i) the demand and supply of yoghurts for the late afternoon, and
ii) what she ought to do in order to try and sell them all before the end of the day. [4]

Market failure

The mechanism of market forces assumes that there are no interferences or external shocks in the market.

However there are several problems with allowing market forces to determine the price and levels of demand and supply. **Market failure** is deemed to occur when either too many or too few products or services are available. If market forces were allowed to determine the price of medical care, there might well be many people who could not afford to pay for treatment. This is viewed as a failure of the market because a product or service that is considered essential is not available to all who require it. Health is often described as a 'merit' good as it is considered valuable and worthy to the extent that all consumers should be able to have access to it.

The government is one of the main 'bodies' that both interferes with market forces and attempts to rectify market failures. A maximum price is introduced for goods which the government wants to make more affordable for more people (*see Figure 8.14*).

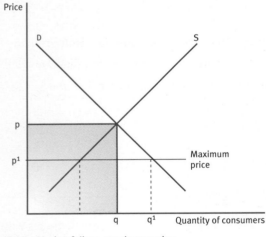

Figure 8.14   Market failure: maximum price

Introducing a maximum price (p^1) below the market equilibrium price leads to an increased number of consumers (q to q^1). To ensure the supplier is willing to supply goods at this reduced price, the government provides a subsidy for each item sold. The prescription charge is an excellent example of a product that is 'sold' at below the market price, with the pharmacist receiving a payment from the government for each prescription handled. (Some items are actually cheaper than the prescription charge.) The cost of implementing this artificial price is borne by the government and ultimately the taxpayer.

Allowing market forces to determine the level of wages within certain industries has meant that, according to the government, the wages received are in some cases too low to ensure a reasonable standard of living. As a consequence the government introduced the minimum wage. This is seen as a necessary interference in the market to 'correct' a failure (*see Figure 8.15*). The minimum wage (p^2) is above the market 'price' for labour and was initially set at £3.60 per hour for over 21s.

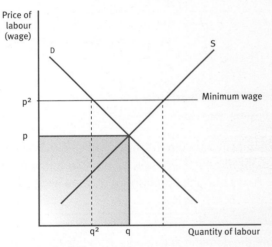

Figure 8.15   Market failure: minimum wage

The government can rectify what it considers to be market failures in the distribution of income within the economy by operating a system of **transfer payments**.

Question 6

Using Figure 8.15, suggest one possible consequence of introducing the minimum wage.   [3]

Points for Revision

Key Terms

market forces	factors that influence the price of a product (demand and supply)
demand	the number of products consumers are willing to purchase at a given price
effective demand	takes into account the willingness and ability to buy a given product or service
supply	the number of goods producers are willing to supply at a given price
equilibrium	the point where demand and supply are equal at a given price
disequilibrium	where at a given price demand and supply are not equal
market failure	when the market fails to provide or allow sufficient consumers access to merit goods
transfer payments	money paid by the government in the form of benefits (social security) to individuals who have not undertaken any economic activity
complementary substitutes	demand of these products is influenced by the price of other products

Definitions Question:
By referring to a business you know, explain the significance of three of the above terms (your teacher may wish to help you with the choice of terms).   [5] per definition

Summary Points:

1   Demand and supply can be affected by both the price and changes in the condition.

2   Market forces will allocate the goods and services within an economy according to price.

3   Market failure occurs when a product or service considered to be of merit is not accessible to all consumers.

Mini Case Study

One 2 One, one of Britain's smallest operators in the mobile phone market, announced during April 1999 that it was to alter its tariffs for pre-pay phone customers. The pre-pay market had grown significantly, with sales of 3.5 million phones. (The pre-pay market refers to those customers who purchase a mobile phone and subsequently purchase phone cards or vouchers instead of paying the usual line rental charges. These cards are put into the back of the phones in order to pay for the calls made.)

Recent estimates suggested that already one in four adults had a mobile phone and this figure would increase to one in three within the next couple of years.

One 2 One wanted to charge its pre-pay customers more, in the form of a daily charge of 50p but at the same time cut the cost of the actual calls from 40p per minute to 10p or even 2p for some off-peak calls. This daily charge would make the cost of usage similar to that of the line contract subscribers. One 2 One was keen to persuade its customers to use its mobile phones instead of fixed line BT phones. It was clear that a lot of consumers were buying pre-pay mobile phones and using them only occasionally, whilst using their fixed line phones at home for their regular calls because the call charges were so much lower.

This change in tariffs would be launched with the aid of an £8 million advertising campaign.

1 Draw a supply and demand diagram to illustrate the desired effects of the advertising campaign that was to be launched by One 2 One. [4]

2 Suggest, with the aid of a diagram, the consequences of the series of medical reports suggesting that continual use of mobile phones may be detrimental to the health of the users. [5]

3 What are the likely consequences of the change in tariffs on the sale of pre-paid mobile phones? [6]

4 If a competitor of One 2 One were to offer a similar change in call tariffs, but cut its charges to 9p or for some off-peak calls to 1p, to what extent do you think this would affect the sale of:

  i) One 2 One pre-pay phones and

  ii) The amount of calls One 2 One phone owners would be willing to make? [10]

25

Maxi Case Study

Recently the market for toys has become more competitive. It has also become harder to find a winning formula to provide the toy that all children will demand for Christmas or at any other time of the year. The doll and furry creature market has been dominated by toys such as the Barbie doll for many years. Even with numerous new outfits, accessories and revamps, the traditional favourites no longer tempt today's young children. Tastes are changing; often, the latest 'in-creature' is a popular television or cinema character who captures the imagination of children, the targeted consumers. Creatures come and go, such is the nature of the market, and yet, there are some who are challenging the one time market 'heavyweights'.

Even Mattel, the largest toy manufacturer in the world, has been struggling to maintain its dominance, underpinned by the sales of Barbie dolls and Tickle Me Elmo, which is based on a character from the successful television show, *Sesame Street*. As a result Mattel had to reduce its work-force by 10%, nearly 3,000 employees, in an attempt to ensure that profits returned to their previous levels and to satisfy one particular group of stakeholders, the shareholders.

Teletubbies are proving more than a match for the long-established Barbie and Tickle Me Elmo toys. Launched in America in 1998 after a successful debut in the UK, Teletubbies have provided Hasbro, the much smaller competitor to Mattel in the USA, with a substantial increase in profits. Hasbro, which is also the manufacturer of Tonka toys, has also had success with the Furbie, an owl-like creature with big ears, that has sold in vast numbers.

Hasbro also gained the rights to produce a range of toys to accompany the *Star Wars* film launched in May 1999. Given the amount of hype and excitement that went on prior to and after the release of the film, Hasbro were on to a winner.

In an attempt to raise the profile of Teletubbies across America, Hasbro undertook an interesting marketing ploy which involved linking with a promotional campaign of Burger King, the fast food chain.

Even with this sort of ingenious marketing, maintaining sales is not guaranteed. Just around the corner is the next craze, the 'creature' that all youngsters crave and manage to persuade their parents to go to extraordinary lengths to find in time, despite their scarcity, to place inside the Christmas stocking with a huge sigh of relief!

Kenny, Kyle, Stan and Cartman are just a few names from the *South Park* series that spring to mind. Who can judge what will be attractive to young children next?

1 Define: stakeholders, shareholders, chain, competitor.   [6]

2 Explain, with reference to market forces, the possible consequences of these 'craze toys' being so scarce.   [5]

3 Why is the price of this type of product relatively high?   [4]

4 What would be the effect of combining the launch of a new series of *Star Wars* toys with the release of the new film?   [6]

5 Why would it probably be advantageous to both Burger King and Hasbro to link the sales of fast food and Teletubbies?   [6]

6 Using a diagram, explain the concept of derived demand with reference to the fall in sales of Barbie dolls and Mattel's subsequent reduction in its number of employees.   [8]

35

Introduction to the business environment

Learning objectives

Having read this unit, students will be able to

1 realise that businesses are constrained by a variety of external influences

2 be aware that the climate within which a business operates is always changing and therefore the business must be able to adapt

3 understand the significance to a business of a particular external influence

Context

When the board of directors of McAlpine, the construction group, sits down to formulate its strategy, not only will it consider the internal factors, probably through a SWOT analysis, but it will take into account the external environment before deciding what it should aim to achieve. It must consider the demand for construction projects from customers, which will depend largely on interest rates; it might then consider the road building budget of the government and how much it is likely to receive from such a budget, if it wins a contract to build new roads. It must also look at the car-producing capacity of car manufacturers in this respect. Then it must consider the action of competitors, the reaction of pressure groups who campaign against road builders, or the unions who may be campaigning with the environmentalists (who are frequently part of the same pressure group), and perhaps European laws on standards of construction. Only when the long list of external factors has been considered, and only then, might the business look internally in order to set objectives.

The context of business

If a business could assume that, having made a decision, it would not be influenced in any way by factors outside its four walls, then decision making would be an easy task. Unfortunately, whenever a business considers a particular decision which costs money and takes time to implement, it must take into account many external factors over which it has no influence.

In the same way, a business has to face continually a range of factors which influence its success. It must therefore be capable of judging which factors are the most important and to what extent each will have an influence on the business. Finally, the business must then react in an appropriate way to survive and prosper.

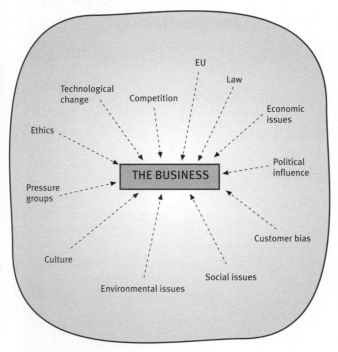

Figure 9.1   The context of business

The above diagram shows that there can be, at any one time, a multiplicity of different forces which are outside the control of the business. Even the largest companies are not immune from such influences. During 1998 and 1999, Microsoft had to undergo a lengthy and expensive legal case in America concerning anti-competitive practices. It must also compete carefully with Apple; although the latter is much smaller, the machines are reputedly more powerful and more useful in certain circumstances. Being wealthy and being run by the world's richest man means the company attracts a great deal of unwanted media attention. However, companies like Microsoft are sometimes able actually to influence other companies in their decision making; in this respect, Apple have had to react to Microsoft's immense influence over customers and its ability to persuade new and present users of computers to update their machines with the latest version of its software.

The external forces considered

In order to make remembering the external factors easier, the acronym SELECT CCEEPP can be used.

■ Social

The structure of the population has had a significant effect on the decisions made by companies. During the first part of the new century, those people born in the baby boom which followed the Second World War will have just turned 50; the bulge in the population at this age means that manufacturers, retailers and designers will have to work hard to capture this mature market. Changes in the population structure are known as **demographic trends**. These changes constitute a much more complicated shift from young to old markets.

Such individuals are wealthier, more thoughtful and careful when selecting products. This means that manufacturers will have to improve their designs and be flexible in their production to meet consumers' demands. In addition, as health care becomes more advanced, people are living longer. This means that the government must look very carefully at pensions and health care expenditure. The dependency ratio in Europe (the ratio of retired people to those of working age) has increased from 20% in 1950 to 35% today. By 2025 it will exceed 50%! Despite the baby boom of the post-War period, there are fewer young people in the population, which could mean that they earn higher wages (due to a shortage of skilled labour) – the 16–24-year-olds could therefore be fewer, but wealthier.

The other change which may well occur is that the young-old market (over 50s) will become even more influential as they receive much larger inheritances. The middle and working classes invested in home-buying following the War and the increase in house prices will be reflected in the level of money being passed on in inheritance (*see Table 1*).

Table 1   Population projections, UK

Thousands

	Projections					
	1996	2001	2006	2011	2021	2031
0–14	11,358	11,289	10,861	10,507	10,368	10,277
15–29	11,903	11,197	11,425	11,717	11,221	10,723
30–44	12,935	13,747	13,335	12,170	11,687	11,907
45–59	10,582	11,228	11,955	12,660	13,033	11,243
60–74	7,831	7,752	8,207	9,272	10,574	12,032
75+	4,193	4,406	4,504	4,602	5,361	6,640
Males	28,856	29,377	29,809	30,206	30,916	31,153
Females	29,946	30,241	30,477	30,723	31,328	31,669
Total	58,801	59,618	60,287	60,929	62,244	62,822

Sources: ONS; General Register Offices for Scotland and Northern Ireland; Government Actuary's Department, quoted in *Marketing Pocket Book 1999* (sic.), NTC Publications Ltd

Question 1

Considering all of the above, explain how the changes will affect
a)   a house builder
b)   a pharmaceuticals manufacturer
c)   a shoe retailer   [6]

■ Economic

The local, national and international economy have significant effects on individual business. The extent of the effect normally depends on how widely spread the business is across the world and how much it depends on one market/economy/product. For example, the Asian crisis of 1997 and 1998 affected many western companies who had property, manufacturing plants or customers in south-east Asia. As the crisis began to break in south-east Asia, there was a hint that a similar problem might emerge in Brazil, which caused further destabilising effects as companies tried hard to remove their investment as quickly as possible.

Question 2

The north–south divide has long been an issue with the government. The wealth of Britain tends to have been held in the south by landowners who owned the manufacturing base of the north. In recent times this difference has become more pronounced and has provided more evidence that there should be a regional policy. Unemployment, for example, was 4.4% in the south east in 1998, but 8.7% in the north east. Eddie George, the governor of the Bank of England, said in 1999 that this was a price well worth paying if inflation was kept under control. Areas such as the north east have a large manufacturing sector, high unemployment and low GDP per head, the opposite of which is the case in the south east. However, despite the problems in the north east, it is also the country's fastest growing region for financial and business services. Scotland, which voted in 1999 for its own Parliament, has a strong case for arguing for lower interest rates, given that only about half the population owns houses.

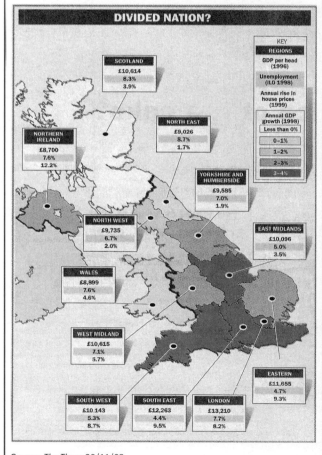

Source: *The Times* 30/11/98
Figure 9.2   North–south divide?

Discuss how the information contained in Figure 9.2 might affect the decision making of a business of your choice.   [10]

Hint: Consider the factors affecting the demand and supply for the product(s) your business sell(s).

■ Legal

When a building company wishes to convert a building from a garage into part of the living accommodation, **planning permission** will be required. If planning permission is not granted, then this results in loss of revenue for the builders. The laws on employment contracts, the Health and Safety at Work Act and the Sale of Goods Act all affect a business and a customer in several ways (*see Unit 58 Legal environment*).

■ Environment

For the past 10 years, businesses have been making new claims about how their products 'do not damage the ozone layer' or how the products are 'not tested on animals'. Even though most companies are unlikely to admit it, such claims have been made in the light of increasing consumer awareness that a business should act responsibly when it is taking decisions on what to produce and how to produce it. Companies tend to be happy to make claims that they are guardians of the environment if it means extra revenue, but not if it means extra costs. It is only since governments began to charge penalties that companies have been forced to spend money in this respect. The Environmental Protection Agency imposed a £1 billion fine on diesel truck engine makers in 1998 for violating clean air regulations.

■ Customer base

This refers to the set of customers which purchases products from companies. The problem which a business faces is the possibility of a change in the **customer base** as customers change their demands and lifestyles. This has become far more significant as markets have become more segmented and consumers' income has risen. In turn, this means the business must be flexible and react to such changes.

As the age structure of the population changes, businesses need to adapt to meet the needs of their consumers. The customer base of BT mobile phones used to be businessmen and women, but trends have changed and so has the customer base which now includes a much wider section of the population.

■ Technology

Technological change is one of the most significant, and at times, frightening aspects of our lives. The reduction in work-force in favour of machines is only one aspect of this. Businesses have been able to process much more information than ever before and technologically advanced products now have a much shorter shelf life as the speed of change increases e.g. photocopiers used to be slow at producing copies – usually about 30 per minute was considered a fast machine at the start of the 1990s. Now photocopiers are cheaper to hire, produce better quality reproductions and can create documents at a speed of nearly 100 per minute. New products are frequently being produced as the demand from customers grows for faster machines.

■ Competition

Very few businesses are without competitors. Those that face no competition are known as monopolies. When the utility industries – water, electricity, gas – were privatised during the 1980s and 1990s, initially they faced no competition, although the competitive nature of this industry has gradually been opened up, so that now electricity companies can supply gas and vice versa! Some industries are highly **concentrated**, meaning that a large part of the total market is taken up by relatively few companies. This is particularly true with food retailing – in this case six or seven large companies take up over 50% of the total market, with thousands of other companies competing for the rest. Such a market structure is known as an oligopoly. As the number of firms increases and no individual firm is able to exert control over the market, competition becomes fiercer as companies seek to outbid local and national rivals. A good example of this is the industry of fitted windows and doors; all these companies do more or less the same thing, selling just about the same products, supplied from the same manufacturer and so they have to work extremely hard to be competitive.

Question 3

Suggest five ways that double glazing companies seek to compete with each other. [5]

■ Culture

As the number of immigrants has grown over the past 40 years, there has been a need to recognise and react to the difference in cultures, but also to recognise the opportunities that such changes can provide. Different religious beliefs, ethical beliefs as well as attitudes to work have led to a change in the way we work. For example, there is now much more competition from women in the work-place who have come forward against a traditional culture which has always had the male as the breadwinner. This has fuelled the growth in child minding services and play groups along with the employment of more nannies and au pairs. In addition, companies like Land Rover are now providing crèche facilities to enable female employees to work more hours.

■ Ethics

Although it is tempting to associate this with issues such as human rights and testing products on humans and animals, business ethics is a considerably wider issue. It can involve anything from the wages it pays to whether it purchases products from countries that exploit much cheaper labour in 'sweat shop' environments. Most company reports make an issue of **corporate governance** which involves the way the business is organised, and, in particular, the way the directors run the business in a responsible manner. Ethics can also refer to the promptness of payments to suppliers and the way the business helps the community.

In the annual report of BOC (British Oxygen Group), the company states that it has more sites producing gas which are certified to ISO14001 than any other industrial gas company. Stagecoach, the transport company, set aside 0.5% of its pre-tax profits for donations to charity, demonstrating a commitment to using its wealth for worthy causes (Source: Stagecoach Annual Report, 1998).

■ Europe

The possible change in currency from the pound to the euro is probably the most important part of the influence exerted from Europe. However, this is only the tip of the iceberg. Since the Single Market was established in 1992, there have been several thousand **EC directives** over a wide range of industries. These have addressed the quality of manufacturing across the European Union as well as the need for consistent standards. This is carried out so that, for example, a plug which is taken on holiday in Portugal, France and Spain will fit the plug points in all three countries.

■ Political

The new Labour government of 1997 brought with it a change in the way politics would rule the country along with a change in political emphasis. Not only was the stakeholder state espoused by Tony Blair, but there were political objectives at the top of its agenda, such as the **minimum wage**. The effect of the minimum wage has been felt not only across those industries which used to pay below the minimum wage, but also by those industries whose work-force has been keen to maintain pay differentials which were in place before the minimum wage was introduced e.g. Business 1 pays an average of £3.20 per hour and business 2 £3.80 per hour. Both are in the same industry. The introduction of the minimum wage on April 1 1999 meant that the wage would have increased to £3.60 for business 1. This will have made the difference between the two pay rates only £0.20. There will have been a concerted effort to protect the buying power of employees in business 2 in relation to business 1, with the consequent pressure on wages to rise from £3.80 to £4.40. This would increase the costs of the business which already pays above the minimum wage, in order to maintain the wage differential.

■ Pressure groups

Pressure groups can exert a great deal of influence on the way a business operates. Unions can influence rates of pay across entire industries just as they can influence the level of inconvenience experienced by customers of a particular industry which goes on strike.

Other pressure groups such as *Which?*, the consumer affairs magazine, can bring pointed media attention to companies which have failed to provide adequate service to their customers.

Points for Revision

Key Terms

minimum wage	the minimum hourly rate which an individual can earn (initially £3.60 for non-students and £3.20 for students)
planning permission	the process of applying to the local council for permission to extend a building or change the use of a building
demographic trends	the change in the age and numbers of the population
customer base	the set of customers which forms the basis of demand for a particular product
concentrated	extent to which an industry's total sales are taken up by individual businesses
EC directives	quality guidelines for certain products
corporate governance	the directors of a business are charged with operating the business in a responsible manner

Definitions Question:
With reference to a business you know, explain the meaning of any three of the above terms (your teacher may wish to help you choose the terms).   [5] per definition

Summary Points:

1   A business must take into account various external factors when taking decisions.

2   The ability to anticipate such external factors plays a large part in the ability of the business to survive.

Mini Case Study

Oliver Wall, owner of The Big Cheese factory, was facing his biggest crisis in the company's 10-year life. Following several EU directives on the standards of manufacturing cheese as well as a Health and Safety Officer visiting the factory, the business was forced to make some harsh decisions. It had to invest in more modern machinery, but could do this only by sacking 25 employees (more than half the work-force) and reorganising the remaining employees around the new machinery. Slicers, a similar company located over 100 miles away, had been forced to close down following an outbreak of listeria (food poisoning) which had been traced back to Slicers' products. Although The Big Cheese did not make soft cheese, there was unwanted media attention on companies similar to Slicers and the Health Minister, Robin Wensleydale, had held a press conference to assert the government's commitment to ensure all cheese makers met stringent European standards. The unions were reluctant to co-operate on the issue of voluntary redundancies, preferring to rely on natural wastage in order to minimise disruption to the work-force. No matter how Oliver looked at the situation, it seemed that the only solution was to put the company up for sale and hope that he could salvage some of his initial investment.

1 Define: natural wastage, initial investment, European standards.   [6]

2 a) Explain how the government might be able to help the company in its bid to survive in the short and long term.   [4]

  b) Discuss how the other external factors mentioned in the case might affect Oliver's attempt to save the business and his investment.   [10]

                                                                                20

Maxi Case Study

Edward Rogers began life in the second-hand car trade in 1984, just as the economy was beginning to grow, following the Thatcher reforms of the early 1980s. His garage is located in a hamlet in Shropshire and the business only sells cars i.e. there are mechanics who check them and prepare them for sales, repairing them when under warranty, but Edward has deliberately not bothered with earning revenue from repairs and maintenance. Edward has found that despite a tight control of costs and a reputation of honesty and respect from his customers, sales have fluctuated.

One of the main reasons has been the increase in the number of 'out of town' supermarkets which has necessitated more car ownership. In Shrewsbury alone there have been four new supermarkets over the last 15 years, with no increase in population. As the smaller businesses have shut down, there has been an increase in the need for transport into the town. Sales of cars are also much more sensitive to the local economy than the national economy; given the large number of farmers around the hamlet, he did notice a drop in demand due to the BSE crisis. Apart from farmers, his customers come mainly from socio-economic groups C1, C2 and D, although there are a few wealthier customers from the A and B groups who visit the garage to purchase cars for their 18–21-year-old children. The interest rates do have an indirect effect. When interest rates are lower, more customers buy newer and better cars on credit. When interest rates rise again and the interest payments become higher, Edward notices a pronounced drop in the demand for products from his customers; however, this is counter-balanced as certain customers trade down with their car purchases.

He is concerned about possible Labour government plans for higher income tax, but the tax rate which is appropriate for the majority of his customers has actually decreased. He did notice a drop in volume at the time of the election in 1997, when customers were concerned about tax rises and held back their expenditure just in case the tax rate was raised.

He was affected by government legislation when the VAT rate was increased from 15% to 17.5% in that this caused his profit to fall, although he is much more worried about the trading standards on selling second-hand cars. If a car is being sold on the forecourt, it must be roadworthy – previously a car could be displayed, although not sold, with bald tyres. This means that cash flow suffers because of the need to repair the car before displaying it, although there is no guarantee of sale even after spending money on making it roadworthy.

As the level of technology built in to cars has become more complicated, this has meant there are more electrical parts to the cars and therefore fixing them is more expensive. On this issue Edward has not been affected, although his salesmen must be able to explain how the parts operate when faced with an awkward customer. The mechanics have also been made self-employed so that Edward does not have the extra costs of employing them and the responsibility of finding them work. He allows the mechanics to bring their own work into the garage and, as yet, has refused to charge them for the use of the garage. In fact, his reputation as a responsible employer goes further – in 15 years he has never actually sacked anyone and recent research earmarked him as one of the most open and honest car dealers in the county. Edward is acutely aware of the sleazy image which second-hand car dealing carries and has built his reputation upon open, honest trading.

The most significant external factor is competition; the promise of growth and profit has attracted several new competitors who are national dealers. Although Edward attracts a different type of consumer, there is always a fall in sales in the first two weeks after a competitor opens up his forecourt.

1 Define: interest rate, government legislation, warranty. [6]

2 Explain why a fall in profit might result from an increase in Value Added Tax. [6]

3 Using the SELECT CCEEPP model, highlight the external constraints which affect Edward's Cars. [15]

4 A competitor of Edward once said to him 'Ethics don't matter – once the customer has driven the car away, you move on to the next one. There are enough customers out there to sell the odd bad car.'

To what extent do you believe that ethics are important in the second-hand car market? [8]

35

'Friday afternoon'

End of section test

1 What are the four stages of production? [4]
2 Define added value. [2]
3 Explain why the concept of opportunity cost is important for a business. [3]
4 What is asset stripping? [2]
5 What is a conglomerate business? [2]
6 Give an alternative name for a conglomerate business. [1]
7 Give two examples of economies of scale. [2]
8 Why does a business aim to achieve economies of scale? [2]
9 What is meant by the term market capitalisation? [1]
10 Apart from market capitalisation, name two other methods of measuring the size of a business. [2]
11 By using a diagram, explain the meaning of diseconomies of scale. [3]
12 Why do demergers occur? [2]
13 Explain the difference between backward and forward vertical integration. [2]
14 What is the difference between a merger and an acquisition? [2]
15 What is a hostile takeover? [1]
16 What is the definition of a market? [1]
17 Describe the difference between a need and a want. [2]
18 By providing an example, define the phrase fast moving consumer good. [2]
19 Describe the relationship between risk and return. [2]
20 Explain two differences between a partnership and a sole trader. [4]
21 What is a sleeping partner? [2]
22 Give three reasons why two businesses might merge. [3]
23 What is meant by the phrase 'going public'? [1]
24 Explain the term limited liability. [2]
25 Identify one difference between a private limited company and a public limited company. [2]
26 What is a Memorandum of Association? [1]
27 Explain the difference between a private sector company and a public sector company. [2]
28 List five headings which you might find on a business plan. [5]
29 Identify two purposes of a business plan. [2]
30 What is the difference between a stakeholder and a shareholder? [2]
31 List five stakeholders (other than shareholders) of a cosmetics business. [5]
32 What is a mission statement? [2]
33 Define strategy. [2]
34 List and briefly explain four different functions of a business. [4]
35 Explain the meaning of the phrase corporate culture. [2]
36 When might a business use SWOT analysis? [4]
37 Why might a business need a hierarchy of objectives? [2]
38 List two internal constraints to a business achieving its objectives. [4]

39 List the four factors which affect demand. [4]
40 What is the name of the intersection of a
   supply and demand curve? [1]
41 Identify and explain three external factors
   which a business faces. [6]

—
100

'Friday afternoon' 1

French Courgette and Banana as well as Fish and
Fennel are dishes on the menu for a recently launched
company known as The Original Fresh Babyfood
Company. Following some basic market research,
owners Keith and Belinda Mitchell identified a need for
fresh chilled babyfood, which supermarkets failed to
provide. Two years after setting up, the business was
valued at £1.2 million, having raised £300,000 from 3i,
the venture capital company. 3i does not normally get
involved with new companies, but this seemed an
opportunity which was too good to miss. The market
for babyfood was estimated at the time to be about
£350 million per year and fresh food, a well defined
niche, worth up to £30 million per annum. The initial
objective was to achieve revenue of £1 million per
annum by the end of 1997. To persuade 3i that the
business was worth investing in, they hired a non-
executive director from Knorr soups who added a
wealth of experience. His first contribution was to
persuade the Mitchells against an aggressive marketing
campaign. Instead, they focused on activities such as
distributing menu cards to health visitors. Raising
money was always the major headache; they found
£150,000 of their own and tried to raise £100,000 from
the banks, but because the idea was not proven the
banks refused them the money.

Now the business is up and running, it has a new
objective which is to exercise greater control over
manufacturing. The size of the business now means it
can behave like a major supplier to the supermarkets
by providing marketing support. However, the Mitchells
are looking to establish a joint venture with a
manufacturer, in order to be able to compete with
supermarkets, just in case they decide to produce their
own label alternative.

Source: Fresh ideas for baby's palate, *Financial Times* 21/1/97

1 Identify the two objectives mentioned in the
  case. [2]
2 Explain why the objectives of this business
  change over time. [4]
3 Compare and contrast two methods which
  might have been used when valuing the
  business at £2.1 million. [6]
4 Discuss the pros and cons of going into a
  joint venture with a manufacturer. [8]

As the manager of 3i, prepare a presentation to
your board of directors, persuading them to lend
£300,000 to The Original Fresh Babyfood
Company.

—
20

'Friday afternoon' 2

Deltachem Ltd is a medium-sized business in a highly
competitive market that supplies chemicals to the paint
industry. The profit margins are small as a result of
intense competition which has forced prices lower. In
order to remain competitive, the business owners are
faced with the difficult decision of whether to purchase
a new filtration machine that will save the company
several thousand pounds in disposal fees. Presently
some of the waste by-products contain chemicals that
cannot just be taken to the local refuse amenity centre.
As a consequence a great deal of money is spent
employing chemists to sift the waste and drivers to
transport it to a chemical disposal company. Buying the
new machine will mean that Deltachem can treat the
waste itself and make some of the staff redundant. The
savings, although not in the short term, would be
significant due to the skill of the job. The lorry drivers,
who are all members of the Transport and General
Workers' Union (the T&G), have recently negotiated a
pay deal to compensate for the no-strike agreement
and the business is worried about the effect this might
have on costs. Local environmentalists are keen that the
waste is treated at Deltachem's site to avoid moving
hazardous waste by road and they have threatened to
run a campaign in the local paper, criticising the
business for its poor record on the environment.

However, the marketing director is keen to increase the marketing budget in order to raise the profile of the business. This is not just to pacify the local environmentalists, but, perhaps of more significance, it is an attempt to counter the negative publicity due to the redundancies. A new industrial estate has been built only 10 miles away and has already attracted two businesses that are potential customers for Deltachem. The finance director has made the situation quite clear to all the directors – there is only sufficient capital for either the new machine or an increase in the marketing budget, not both.

1 Explain the opportunity cost for Deltachem of investing in a new filtration machine. [6]

2 Suggest some of the difficulties Deltachem may face if it decides to reduce the size of the work-force due to the purchase of the new machine. [5]

3 Explain why savings will not be made in the short term. [4]

4 Explain the external pressures on the business and suggest a possible solution to each one. [5]

20

Maxi Case Study

Michael Charles founded The Creaseless Company having identified a gap in the market that no other company had attempted to satisfy. The need for more and more business travel in his job with a major oil company had necessitated endless overnight stops in hotels. Having had his luggage thrown around by the baggage crews at airports, his shirts were very frequently creased, which added to the time he had to spend at the other end of the journey preparing for his meetings. He therefore developed a product which packed into the same area as a magazine. The shirt was designed so that it packed into its own case by being folded in a certain way and the little case prevented it from being creased.

He set the business up with his wife and two business colleagues who were bored with the endless travelling and wanted to use their own experience to create something new and share in its success. Although the business began as a partnership, with each partner putting £5,000 into the business, after only six months they converted the partnership into a limited company. The attraction of limited liability, in such an unknown market, was appealing to all the partners, who all became directors in the new limited company.

Despite losses in the first year as the business was developing the product and the directors were on the road trying to gain business, there was an encouraging reaction from most retailers, especially airport shops, although because this was a niche market, and the Packed Shirt, as it was called, retailed at £50, the major clothing retailers were interested in only a few products at a time. Initially the business, by concentrating on sales, was not always meeting the delivery targets. Even though the business grew, the unit costs also grew because frequently the business had to employ short-haul couriers due to the lack of delivery facilities. Michael's other concern was that one of the larger clothes retailers might try to compete with The Creaseless Company, by using a supplier in the Far East which might well put pressure on his margins. He therefore decided to respond to these problems by expanding into retailing. The solution to this problem was to buy a company called Zenith Clothes which came up for sale following the retirement of its owner. It operated 25 small retail outlets in high-class shopping malls and airports selling relatively exclusive, branded clothing products; buying these shops meant that it could give the shirt much greater exposure and it could also widen its product range.

Although the business suffered a temporary downturn in demand over the month before and after the start of the millennium because of lack of demand for air travel, it responded with a price reduction which ensured demand ticked over during the uncertain period.

The success of the company in the first four years meant that the directors were now considering floating on the Alternative Investment Market, which would allow the company access to a much greater level of finance by being part of the Stock Exchange. However, having been part of a multinational oil company, Michael was only too aware how much their individual lives might change if The Creaseless Company decided to take such a decision.

One of the crowning moments in Michael's life was when the purchasing manager at Harrods telephoned for an order. Michael remembers smiling inwardly at the irony of the situation; not three years before he had visited Harrods to ask it to stock the product, but such was its attitude to a new business, it refused to take the shirt. Now Harrods regularly received deliveries of 1,000 shirts per month!

Source: Adapted from the *Sunday Independent* 6/10/98

1 Define: limited liability, branded.   [4]

2 Explain what each partner might have considered when making the decision to invest in the company.   [5]

3 a) Identify the factors which seemed to affect demand for the Packed Shirt.   [4]

b) Explain, by use of a diagram, the effect on costs of inefficient delivery as the business has grown.   [4]

4 Discuss the factors which the business might consider when deciding to become quoted on the Alternative Investment Market.   [8]

5 a) Briefly explain why the purchase of Zenith Clothes is known as forward vertical integration.   [3]

b) What factors might the business have considered when deciding whether to buy Zenith Clothes?   [6]

6 Identify the stakeholders involved in the decision to buy the retailer, giving a reason for their interest.   [5]

7 Using a supply and demand diagram, show the effect on the price of the shirt of

a)   a reduction in demand for air travel over the millennium period

b)   the threat of an increase in the amount of competition.   [6]

Presentation: Imagine you are Michael's business adviser at the time when he was considering going into the retail sector and that he asks you for a second opinion. Use a SWOT analysis to present your conclusion to Michael.

45

Marketing

Introduction to marketing

Learning objectives

Having read this unit, students will be able to

1 understand the need for a business to find and satisfy consumers

2 be aware of the range of marketing activities, defined as the marketing mix

3 understand the relationship between marketing and the other business activities

Context

The two most famous brands in the world are McDonald's and Coca-Cola. The names of these brands conjure up a variety of images – it might be the unique 'M' shape which greets you whenever you visit a McDonald's, or perhaps a Big Mac and medium fries. With the name Coca-Cola, you might think of energetic, youthful advertising, or the taste of the drink, or even the colour red! Both McDonald's and Coca-Cola make simple products – one is a variant on a beefburger, the other is a fizzy drink, yet both these simple brands are worth billions of pounds. More complicated, technological products can have comparatively little value because of the amount of money which has been invested in the marketing process over the lifetime of the products. Both McDonald's and Coca-Cola have placed enormous emphasis on marketing: spending money on building the image and popularity of the products in the eyes of the customer.

What is marketing?

The Chartered Institute of Marketing defines the **marketing** process as the 'identification, anticipation and satisfaction of the customer's needs, profitably'.

Marketing is frequently confused with advertising, or publicity stunts. This is far too narrow a definition, because if the product was not demanded by the customer, no amount of visibly stunning and humorous advertising would persuade consumers to purchase the product. Therefore, although advertising and publicity are a part of marketing, the process of marketing involves a much wider perspective.

Another definition of marketing is 'getting the right product to the right customers at the right price at the right time'. This suggests that marketing involves a variety of activities and that the marketing department must work towards satisfying all of the following issues:

■ Products which the customer demands
■ Pricing which the customer can afford
■ Distribution to a place where the customer will purchase the product
■ Promotion to persuade the customer to purchase in a competitive market.

Collectively, these are known as the four Ps – Product, Price, Place (distribution) and Promotion. Alternatively the four Ps can be collectively referred to as the **marketing mix**. The final point to make about the role of marketing is the need for profit. Any company can get customers to buy its products by charging very low prices (or even giving the product away) and spending heavily on advertising. The four Ps could well be used to satisfy the consumer, but if the business fails to make a profit, it will not be able to satisfy the consumer for long.

From product to market orientation

Before marketing was used to develop a **competitive advantage**, producers used to develop products that they thought would sell profitably, and then use hard-hitting advertising and a determined sales-force to generate sales. Unfortunately, this took no account of customer demand. The result was a hit-and-hope effect which meant that many companies were left with large levels of unsold stock. This approach was known as

product orientation, where the firm focused everything on the product, hoping it would fit in with customer expectations (*see Figure 11.1*).

Figure 11.1   Product orientation

There are some companies which were succcessful in using this approach. Concorde was developed as a joint project between the British and French governments in an attempt to pioneer supersonic travel; although the Concorde has a distinctive place in commercial aviation history, only 18 were actually sold! It is still in service, over 30 years after being introduced. Another example is the pocket calculator that made Sir Clive Sinclair a wealthy man; he anticipated the demand for the product and was initially highly successful until a larger, more efficient company, Casio, began to compete. Sinclair's initial success was founded on guesswork rather than hard evidence through market research, and he was lucky – but his second product, the C5, will go down in history as one of the most significant corporate failures of all time, simply due to the inventor failing to recognise the customer's needs and wants.

The alternative to this approach is known as **market orientation**, because the idea is to assess the needs of the customer through the use of market research and then develop a product which fits those needs and which can be sold at a profit (*see Figure 11.2*).

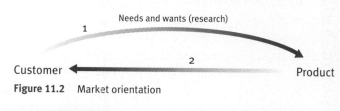

Figure 11.2   Market orientation

Question 1

To what extent do you believe that the Internet (i.e. gaining access to the World Wide Web) is a result of product or market orientation?   [6]

Growth of marketing

Only in recent corporate history has there been a greater emphasis on marketing. There are several reasons why marketing has become more significant to the success of a business:

■ Mass production

Even in the 1920s, with the development of mass production in the car industry, there was still an emphasis on production as opposed to finding out what the customer wanted. Henry Ford, famous for the phrase 'customers can have any colour as long as it is black', pioneered mass production, although he was not noted for his marketing ability. The production process was so efficient that Ford was able to reduce the price significantly due to economies of scale. In fact, he did have a perceptive marketing mind, because he realised that there was a large demand for cheap cars which appealed to the mass market. This was the **unique selling point** (USP) of the car i.e. something which distinguished the car from others.

Question 2

Identify the unique selling point(s) for the following products:
a) multi-person vehicles
b) luxury chocolates
c) mobile telephones
d) yo-yos   [8]

■ Economic growth

Following the Second World War, governments around the world invested heavily in rebuilding the infrastructure of their countries. This created a new-found wealth which meant that people earned more money and therefore had more money to spend. This meant that they were able to buy higher-quality products and companies that satisfied their demand were highly profitable. This attracted more companies into the market and so the consumer was given greater choice.

■ Competition

The attraction of new competitors also meant that simply producing exactly the same product as other companies was not enough. Competition therefore forced companies to try and differentiate themselves from each other, by developing a unique selling point. Listening carefully to customers is an essential part of developing products which the consumer wants and which are distinctive from the rest.

■ Technology

As methods of data collection and the ability to store information have become more sophisticated, businesses have been able to call on vast amounts of data with a view to anticipating purchasing habits. Products have also become more technologically advanced as has the equipment used to produce them, thereby making them cheaper, which fuels demand. Finally, if businesses are producing similar products, a frequently used USP is prompt delivery which comes from being able to find the stock of finished goods quickly and despatching them promptly to the customer. Next day delivery has therefore become commonplace. The Japanese car manufacturers were the first to ensure that prompt delivery was standard and as a result were able to capture a share of the 4x4 vehicle market before Land Rover responded with the Range Rover.

Marketing objectives

The process of marketing a product will be determined by the objectives that the business sets. The nature of the objective is likely to depend primarily on the market size and the experience of the business. A new business may have survival as its main objective and consequently the marketing objectives will be aligned to this. Gaining recognition within the market and establishing a customer base will be more significant either when the business is new or when it introduces a new product.

For an established business, an increase in market share is more likely to be the primary marketing objective and therefore the marketing will be concentrated on establishing and extending brand loyalty. Either persuading existing customers to purchase more of the product or finding new customers will be the role of the marketing department. By gaining a larger share of a particular market the business has the opportunity to benefit from economies of scale. Selling a greater quantity may enable the business to dominate the market and possibly restrict other businesses from joining the market. This enables the dominant business to operate price discrimination, charging a range of prices for the same product in different segments of the market.

It is possible for the marketing objective to be to reduce demand for a particular product or activity. Prior to the Christmas season, advertisements concentrating on warning people of the dangers of drinking and driving are funded by the government in an effort to make people more aware of this issue. Similar advertising campaigns are run in an attempt to reduce smoking.

A business may have specific product marketing objectives. A manufacturer of disposable plastic cups has to overcome the negative image of this product by highlighting its positive attributes. The marketing ought therefore to concentrate on this task by drawing the attention of the potential customer to the benefits of the plastic cups – no washing up, ideal for the children's party with no worries about damaging the family's glasses, perfect for picnics and sold in a variety of colours. Marketing is therefore able to transform negative issues into positive ones and consequently increase sales.

Summary of marketing objectives

There is a range of marketing objectives dependent upon the overall business objectives:

- building brand recognition – theme or logo
- repeat purchases – the customer buys the product on a regular basis
- gaining market leadership
- increasing market share
- market domination

Question 3

For the following products suggest an appropriate marketing objective:
a) Gap products
b) a new female magazine
c) fireworks
Explain your choice. [6]

Marketing decisions and the link with other parts of the business

Decisions on, for example, the price or the promotion strategy will need to be considered in the light of other parts of the business. In fact, when a decision is taken on any aspect of marketing, the rest of the business will be affected.

■ Production

The marketing department will need to ensure that the production department is actually able to manufacture the item according to the specifications laid down by the customer. If it cannot, it may have to subcontract from another company. It may also have to subcontract if the popularity of the product leads to sales being much greater than the rate at which the products can be produced. Cadbury underestimated the demand for Wispa when it was launched during the early 1980s, leading to a withdrawal of the product for two years while the business geared up its production to anticipated demand. Similarly, the design department must ensure the design does fit in with the customer requirements. Producing a product that is technically sound but is not aesthetically attractive may lead to a lack of interest in the product. The significance of the design will depend upon the type of product. The design features are not that important in a pencil, but the design of a house is crucial.

Finance

Marketing costs money. Not only is extensive research required before the product is launched, but the advertising may well be expensive. The finance department will be anxious to see that other departments spend within their budget, otherwise it might have to raise more money, which in turn will add to the cost of the product.

Personnel

As the sales of a product increase, the business will need to maintain customer contacts with a view to continuing the feedback or response. It will also need an increasingly competitive, 'hungry' sales-force which is ambitious. The generation of ideas also requires bright, innovative minds. The personnel department must therefore be sensitive to the demands that the company is making on its employees within the marketing department and must ensure not only that the appropriate personnel are selected for the marketing jobs but also that there is continual investment in training.

Question 4

Explain the effect on a) finance b) personnel c) production d) design for a clothing company which is intending to respond to a recent increase in demand for flared jeans.   [8]

Market aggregation

Sometimes a company will sell only one product to an entire market. Rowntree, and more recently Nestlé, have been famous for a variety of branded sweets, one of which is the Polo mint. The Polo mint was sold with one type of packaging and had one flavour – marketing such a product to a total, or aggregate, market is known as undifferentiated marketing. Following a drop in sales and the increase in popularity of its competitor's product, made by Trebor, Nestlé launched three new versions of the Polo mint and made a significant attempt to differentiate the marketing process, by targeting different customers with the wider range.

Market segmentation

This is the subdivision of a market into separate and distinct groups of customers, each having a distinct marketing mix.

As the choice available to customers has grown, so has the requirement of companies to anticipate the individual customer's needs and wants. A more detailed knowledge of the customer has led businesses to redefine the market they sell to. As they collected more information on customers, it became clear that there were different customers within the same market e.g. the market for train journeys can be subdivided according to a variety of factors. The age of the traveller, the time of travelling, the willingness of customers to pay extra for more luxurious accommodation have led rail service companies to charge a range of prices which apply to the same journey according to the individual characteristics of the company. This process of subdividing the market into separate parts and developing a product which is tailored specifically for those customers is known as market segmentation. Three examples of market segmentation are considered below:

Geographic segmentation

Businesses tend to target a particular part of the country for customers that display similar purchasing habits e.g. the drinks market. Brewers have identified the various purchasing habits of customers as distinct from each other in certain parts of the country. In Yorkshire, for example, there is much more consumption of bitter and mild than in the south, where lager is more popular. The cost of a train journey in the south east is much greater per mile travelled than that of a rural route in mid-Wales. The commuter market is much larger in the south east, and although the train companies schedule more journeys, the willingness to pay for train travel, as opposed to car travel, is very high. This helps to subsidise the less popular routes.

Demographic segmentation

A market can be divided by using characteristics of the population in terms of age, sex or income. The drinks market can be divided into the market for soft drinks, which is further subdivided into age – soft drinks can obviously be targeted at children, whereas similar flavoured drinks can be repackaged and targeted at the more sophisticated customer. The 16–24-year-old market also prefers to drink imported beer from bottles, whereas the older drinker (aged 60+) may prefer more traditional beer in pint glasses!

Travel by train is also segmented in this way: OAPs receive discounts and possibly free journeys and students can earn discounts having purchased a student rail card. One method of categorising consumers by their income is by using **socio-economic groups**. This is based on the head of each household's income and is represented by the letters A–E:

A: chairmen and chief executives of large companies, barristers, judges
B: headteachers, solicitors, accountants, doctors
C1: skilled workers – supervisors, junior managers, teachers
C2: skilled manual workers – plumbers, electricians
D: semi-skilled and unskilled manual workers – road sweepers, refuse collectors, window cleaners
E: state pensioners, casual workers, students

Another alternative is known as 'The Family Tree' where the segmentation is based on the particular stage in the consumer's life e.g. bachelor, young married, full nest, empty nest, retired. Each of these has different consumer purchasing habits. The full nest family will spend a large proportion of its income on children and their upbringing and education. The empty nest would be planning for retirement and taking holidays for two.

■ **Psychographic segmentation**
This is a more complex method of segmentation which considers the lifestyle and expectations of an individual. Various 'descriptors' are used to generate the type of person who may consider a certain product e.g. trendsetter, thrifty consumer, fashion-conscious, environmentalist. Alternatively, there have been phrases used recently to describe an entire lifestyle e.g. Yuppie, which originates from the abbreviations Y.U.P. (Young, urban, professional), or DINKY (Double Income No Kids Yet).

Question 5
Describe the likely products a Yuppie might purchase.   [4]

Question 6
Describe the possible market segmentation for a toothpaste.   [5]

Consumer profile

Sometimes a business will target particular consumers to achieve a greater market share. This is because their lifestyles suggest they are more likely to purchase the products of the business concerned e.g. a business selling screwdrivers might want to know which group of consumers undertake DIY so it can deliberately target that segment with its marketing. A **consumer profile** consists of the following:

■ consumer details, such as sex, age, income and lifestyle
■ spending details, in terms of products purchased, quantities and frequency of use

Question 7
Suggest the likely consumer profile for somebody purchasing the following:
a) cricket balls
b) glitter dust
c) factor 2 suntan lotion   [9]

Question 8
Using the following consumer profile, suggest which products would be most appropriate:
Female, 19 years of age
Socio-economic group (of family): A/B
Lives in a city
Owns a car   [5]

Points for Revision

Key Terms

marketing	identification, anticipation and satisfaction of the customer's needs, profitably
marketing mix	product, price, place and promotion – the methods used to satisfy customer needs and wants
competitive advantage	the business gaining an edge over its competitors
product orientation	emphasis on designing the product which the company hopes to sell
market orientation	emphasis on researching customer needs then designing and producing a product appropriate to meet those needs
unique selling point	an attempt to differentiate the product from competition
market aggregation	the process of aiming a product at an entire market
market segmentation	the process of splitting the market into distinct groups, with a view to targeting each specific group
socio-economic groups	a method of segmentation according to income
consumer profile	a process of identifying the lifestyle and spending habits of consumers

Definitions Question:
By referring to a business you know, explain the significance of any three of the above terms (your teacher may wish to help you with the choice).   [5] per definition

Summary Points:

1	Marketing involves identifying, anticipating and satisfying consumer needs.
2	Marketing has become more important as a result of mass production, economic growth and increased competition.
3	Marketing decisions must be compatible with other parts of the business.
4	Markets can be divided into segments, each with different characteristics.

Mini Case Study

Before 1995 the name Daewoo was almost unknown; if anyone had heard of it it was associated with poor-quality products from Korea. Since then, the phrase, 'That'll be the Daewoo' has become commonplace in television advertising and the reputation of the car is well established. This is a remarkable achievement, given that Daewoo entered an already crowded market with the consumer spoilt for choice. There were cars to match almost every consumer profile and at a range of prices to suit all purses.

The UK car market was dominated by the 'big three', Ford, Vauxhall and Rover, which accounted for over half of all sales, with no other manufacturer having more than one per cent of the market.

However, Daewoo managed to break through the one per cent barrier within the first year of launching its cars in this country.

Daewoo had decided to concentrate on its customers by providing a reliable and economical car. Its market research had indicated that many potential car customers were uncomfortable about entering a car showroom, probably as a result of the image associated with car salesmen who allegedly pressurised people into purchasing. Research showed that over 80% of customers considered the service they received from the salesmen and after sales almost as important as the car itself.

Daewoo's response was to make the experience of purchasing one of their cars a simple and pleasurable occasion. The price of the cars was fixed to avoid the pressure of having to haggle, although another significant factor was Daewoo's warranty, which was for three years and included free servicing, membership of the AA, a six-year anti-corrosion protection and a 30-day money back guarantee. To add to this impressive list of 'extras', when a service was required a courtesy car was made available to the customer. Once established in the market, Daewoo concentrated on improving the technical specifications of the car.

1 Define: consumer profile, market research.   [4]

2 Explain two of Daewoo's unique selling points.   [4]

3 What were Daewoo's marketing objectives?   [3]

4 Outline a possible consumer profile for a typical Daewoo car owner.   [4]

5 Consider some of the problems facing Daewoo's production department following a
   successful advertising campaign.   [5]

20

Maxi Case Study

Many management writers have discussed the idea of satisfying customers' needs and wants. Although the two are different, companies spend billions of pounds on market research with a view to targeting the potential customer in a more precise way. Despite the vast amount of information available on customers, finding out exactly what they require is a challenge that certain companies, such as Sainsbury's and Marks and Spencer, have found extraordinarily difficult to meet. In the spring of 1999, both companies announced heavy falls in profit largely due to their inability to listen to and respond to the customer. In a report written by the research company Business Intelligence, 50% of companies felt that their marketing communications were ineffective and 85% said that any attempt to gain customer loyalty failed.

The two extremes of marketing can be summarised by looking at the difference between the East and the West. In Russia, if there is a queue, you are advised to join it as it means a manufacturer has actually produced something, regardless of whether there is a specific need. Biros, socks, light bulbs – if it can be made and distributed then there is a market. In the prosperous West, it is the other extreme. Such is the attraction of profit, that the marketing specialists are competing with some incredibly sophisticated advertising for some rather simple products! The choice is seemingly endless, with a typical superstore stocking between 20,000 and 25,000 different lines totalling between two and four million products per store. The Internet is also adding another dimension to the marketing process as is the growing resistance to subtle, clever advertising, which seems to have lost its edge in the market-place.

Out of this turmoil there has evolved another definition of marketing known as customer-relationship marketing (CRM). Customers are much less loyal than they used to be and can afford to chop and change. It is estimated that winning over a new customer can cost up to five times as much as keeping a customer, so a new definition of marketing has evolved which is identifying, attracting and retaining the most valuable customers to sustain profitable growth.

Microsoft did this by reorganising the business around the customer, splitting itself into four new divisions which focus on the customer. Some companies now have customer call centres which are set up with the sole objective of handling complaints, inquiries and after sales service. The call centres are likely to form the basis of the future of marketing, although there is little evidence that they will work. Overcrowded telephone lines produce various strains of Vivaldi's Four Seasons as the customer is forced to wait in a 'prioritised' queue. The call centre for Green Flag ironically includes the song 'Rescue Me' although it is not always clear whether it means being rescued from a broken down car or from the phone call! Consumers also dislike the synthesised voice which asks you to press certain numbers on the key pad, depending on the service required. Although there will always be a place and function for marketing, it is unclear whether the traditional product or brand manager will still have a job in the twenty-first century, having been replaced by customer relations managers on the end of a telephone.

Adapted from an article by Simon Calkin in *The Observer*, 25/4/1999

1 Define: customer call centre, marketing communications.   [4]

2 Using the evidence in the article, outline the difference between a product-orientated approach and a market-orientated approach. Which would you rather have as
a) consumer b) producer? Explain your choice.   [6]

3 Explain the difference between the definition of marketing at the start of the unit and the definition of CRM considered in the case study.   [4]

4 What is the difference between a product and a brand?   [4]

5 How might a company research the level of loyalty of its customers?   [4]

6 Explain how the growing number of call centres may affect consumer's purchasing habits.   [5]

7 Discuss how the Internet might affect the function of marketing within a business of your choice.   [8]

35

Market research

Learning objectives

Having read this unit, students will be able to

1 understand the reasons for research

2 identify the various approaches used in the collection of data

3 select the most appropriate method of research

4 know how to analyse the data collected

Context

Walking around a shop, consumers are faced with a wide range of products carefully displayed on the shelves. If the products are not made to customer requirements, then a competitor's products will be purchased. To ensure that the customers' requirements are met, market research is undertaken. A manufacturer of crisps will undertake market research in order to ascertain the flavours, the type of packaging sought and the price at which customers are willing to purchase the crisps. Companies are constantly collecting and analysing data in an attempt to satisfy the needs of the customers and, in many cases, establish who their customers are likely to be.

What is market research?

It is the collecting, processing and interpreting of information that aids the decision making process for the marketing of goods and services.

The market in which a particular product or service is sold is always changing; fashions change, the constraints on a business change and as a consequence it is important to realise that **market research** ought to be a continual process and not just undertaken prior to the launch of a new product or brand.

Why is market research important?

Unless a business continues to research into the reaction to a given brand, it may lose sales because it has failed to anticipate a change in the tastes of consumers.

Approximately seven out of every 10 new products fail and yet there are businesses that often question the expenditure on market research. Ironically, money spent on market research may prevent a product failing and consequently save the business large sums of money in the long run. VNU, a publisher of computer journals, spent a large amount of money researching the needs of computer magazine readers. As a consequence, *Computeractive* was launched in 1998 and gained a circulation of 200,000 within its first year, according to Ian Robinson writing in *Marketing*. The main selling feature of the magazine was the simplistic language that could be understood by all possible readers and not just computer 'whiz-kids'. Research had clearly highlighted the fact that technical jargon was off-putting to many potential readers.

Tetley undertook extensive market research by asking chosen households to record their reaction to a new round tea bag. When the reaction was positive, the round bag was launched nationally. Reliable information is essential if a business is to meet the needs of its customers. Careful attention to its market research will ensure that a business is more likely to produce and promote a product that the customer is willing to purchase.

Without market research, what appears to be a great idea on paper may fail because insufficient notice has been taken of the needs of the customer. As a consequence, the idea will not be a success in the market-place. The Sinclair C5 was a classic example of an excellent idea (in the mind of the inventor) that lacked the market research to provide evidence as to how it would be perceived by consumers. There have been other classic errors, possibly due to the lack of market research:

- The brand name Nova, although successful in this country, translates as 'it won't go' in Spanish – an unfortunate name for a car!

- Renault fell foul of a similar problem, describing a model as 'pear-shaped'; unfortunately in Italy pear translates as twit.

- An advertising slogan once used successfully in this country for Pepsi Cola, 'Come Alive', translates as 'Come out of the grave' in Japanese.

- Persil ran an advertising campaign showing washing 'before and after'; such an advert would not work in Saudi Arabia because they read from right to left!

- Without research, the manufacturer of Vicks vapour rub, the decongestion treatment that is rubbed on to the chest, might not have realised that in some countries it is used as a mosquito repellent.

Research can highlight cultural differences; tea is consumed in different ways in the USA when compared with the UK. In America, consumers regularly consume tea either iced or flavoured. Flavoured tea has been available in the UK for many years but has only recently become fashionable. However drinking iced tea, whilst commonplace in the USA, has hardly made an impact in the UK.

Market research is also important in assessing the effectiveness of the marketing of the product. So businesses undertake research prior to, during and after the launch of a marketing campaign. A business is just as keen to gauge the reaction of the targeted consumer to the advertisement as it is to gauge the opinion of the consumers of the product itself.

What information is required?

Before deciding whether to launch a new product on the market, a range of information is required:

- Statistics on the size and growth or decline of the market
- Existing company sales by product, region, segment of the market (*see Unit 16 Product*)
- Degree of competition
- Existing product plan and plans for the future to ensure any new product fits with the company's product portfolio (its range of products sold)
- Government legislation and economic policy that may affect the design of the product and the likely demand for the product

The above list is quite extensive and will require a great deal of research using a variety of sources.

Quantitative Research

This type of research concentrates on the provision of facts; how many, what age, what percentage and when a product was purchased. Quantitative research provides statistical data to show, for example, how many consumers purchased mascara during a given period of time.

Qualitative Research

This type of research concentrates on the attitudes of the consumers towards a given product. For example, qualitative research provides information as to the reasons why consumers purchased the mascara.

Question 1

If a manufacturer of hair shampoo had hit upon a new anti-dandruff formula, what difficulties might the business face when attempting to collect the necessary information?   [5]

Methods of research

In addition to the information required on the market for the product in question, further research will be needed.

It is important to establish what additional information is required. In simple terms market research can also be used to collect data to establish the 'Ws'.

Who are the likely consumers?
What do they require?
Why do they require such a product?
When do they wish to purchase?
Where do they wish to purchase the product?

The sources or methods of collection can be simply divided into two categories, **desk research** and **field research**.

Desk research

This involves the collection, collation and interpretation of market data that has already been published. An alternative name for desk research is secondary data. The data has been collected by another business or body, but can be used by different businesses for differing reasons.

Table 1   The lunchbox: products consumed by food type

		Per cent of total	
Sandwiches	41.6	Fresh meat pies	17.7
Crisps, nuts & snacks	39.7	Cheese	17.6
Cold meats	36.0	Yoghurts & tub desserts	14.7
Fruit	25.3	Bread & rolls	14.4
Canned meatloaf	22.8	Salad vegetables	14.4
Biscuits	17.8	Cakes, tarts & pastries	8.4

Source: Taylor Nelson Sofres Family Food Panel, winter/spring 1998, from *Marketing Pocket Book 1999*, NTC Publications Ltd

This type of research provides valuable background information and can be used to identify trends.

This table shows the contents of lunchboxes and could be used by manufacturers of this type of food as a source of information to indicate the proportion of lunchboxes that are using their products.

Similarly, a manufacturer of lunchboxes may use the same information to assess the appropriate size of box to manufacture. The type of food consumed may influence the type of material used to manufacture the boxes, or the need to include partitions for yoghurts to protect them.

Question 2

Table 2   Something to drink?

Consumer spending (£ billion)

	1996	1997
Tea, coffee and cocoa	1.403	1.298
Soft drinks	4.249	4.259

Source: *Marketing Pocket Book 1999*, NTC Publications Ltd

a) What type of data is this?   [1]

b) Suggest who may benefit from this data.   [4]

c) What are the limitations of this type of
information?   [2]

Task

Attempt to update the information in Table 2.

Sources

There are many sources for desk research:

- Government statistics such as Annual Abstract of Statistics, Employment Gazette, Central Office of Statistics
- Competition Commission reports; Bank of England Quarterly Review and Agents Reports; European Union reports; IMF reports; CBI reports
- Newspapers and specialist magazines such as *Marketing, Marketing Weekly, Commerce*
- Company annual reports
- Data previously collected by market research businesses

Any business ought to have a wealth of information of its own at its disposal, via company records.

Question 3

List three sources of information that might be used by:
a) A supplier of office furniture considering a mail order sales drive.
b) A hotel considering converting half the hotel into a restaurant.   [6]

Benefits of desk research

Because the information has already been collected, it is relatively quick to obtain and as a consequence is also relatively inexpensive. It allows a business to gain a picture of the market from a quantitative perspective.

However, the information has not necessarily been collected specifically for one individual business and therefore may not be entirely appropriate. In addition, the information may be out-of-date and therefore less reliable.

Question 4

If you were considering the launch of a savoury snack, what desk research would you want to undertake? Justify your choice.   [10]

Field research

This is also referred to as primary data.

This type of market research involves the collection of data by a variety of techniques that will be unique to the collector and is therefore more reliable. The data collected will be information on the behaviour of consumers and their attitudes to selected products or services. Unlike desk research, which concentrates on quantities, field research provides essential information on the factors that affect consumers' choice and tastes with regard to selected products or services.

Information will also be needed to build a picture of the consumer; this picture is referred to as the 'consumer profile'.

The consumer profile should give a clear indication of gender, age, residency, income and expenditure patterns. Such information is vital if a business is to target the right type of person for a particular product. The consumer profile is likely to be based on some form of segmentation (*see Unit 16 Product*).

This is sometimes referred to as a qualitative perspective.

Question 5

Suggest the likely profile for a consumer of:
a) Holiday cruises
b) Ralph Lauren shirts   [6]

Methods of collection

The nature of the information to be collected requires different **methods of collection**. Whether the business is testing the reaction of consumers to a new product, the attitude of consumers towards different products or their awareness of adverts or products on the market influences the technique to be used.

The main techniques that are used are:

- questionnaires
- interviews
- observation
- sampling
- consumer panels

■ Questionnaires

(*This section will provide valuable information if you have to prepare coursework.*)

Questionnaires can be used to ascertain a wide range of information, from a detailed profile of a consumer's lifestyle and expenditure patterns, to a simple reaction to the meal a consumer has just eaten or a shop just visited.

The type of questions that are asked is important, as is the way in which they are asked.

If a simple answer is required such as the gender of the consumer or whether he or she has ever bought a particular brand of cereals, a closed question will be used. This type of question restricts the way in which the answer is given. For some closed questions the responses are given and just have to be ticked (*see Figure 12.1*). The tick box approach is easy to use and is therefore quick, allowing more consumers to be asked in any given period of time. Tick boxes are also helpful when it comes to the analysis of the collected data, again saving time and therefore money.

If a more detailed response is required then an open question can be used. An open question is usually asking the consumer for an explanation, often as to what it is about a product that appeals to them, or why a particular product was purchased. An open question is a better choice for ascertaining what a consumer does not like about a product. Only allowing the consumer to reply to a closed question on dislikes may mean that the real reason for their dislike of the product is missed simply because the business had not thought about such a reaction.

Question 6

Indicate whether an open or closed question is being used in the following examples:
  i Do you own a bike?
 ii Do you like cycling?
iii Why do you either like or dislike cycling?
 iv Is business studies useful? [4]

Question 7

By referring to Figure 12.1, state which (if any) are 'open' questions.
Justify your answers. [2]

Some questions may be biased because of their wording.

For example:

State why you think a Range Rover is better than a Mitsubishi.

A similar concern is the responses that are provided.

For example:

How would you describe the reliability of Rover cars?
a) Excellent
b) Very good
c) Good
d) Average
e) Below average.

The answers to the above questions on Rover cars, even assuming that each response gained exactly the same replies, could be used as part of an advertising campaign to state that 60% of those asked stated that the reliability of Rover cars was above average and only 20% suggested it was below average! Although relatively efficient in gathering a large amount of data, questionnaires assume that the person filling them in or responding orally will have understood the questions and filled them in correctly or replied 'correctly'.

Conducting a questionnaire face to face, as opposed to using a postal or self reply method, does allow for some clarification. But the manner in which the clarification is requested or indeed how the questions are asked could influence the reply if care is not taken.

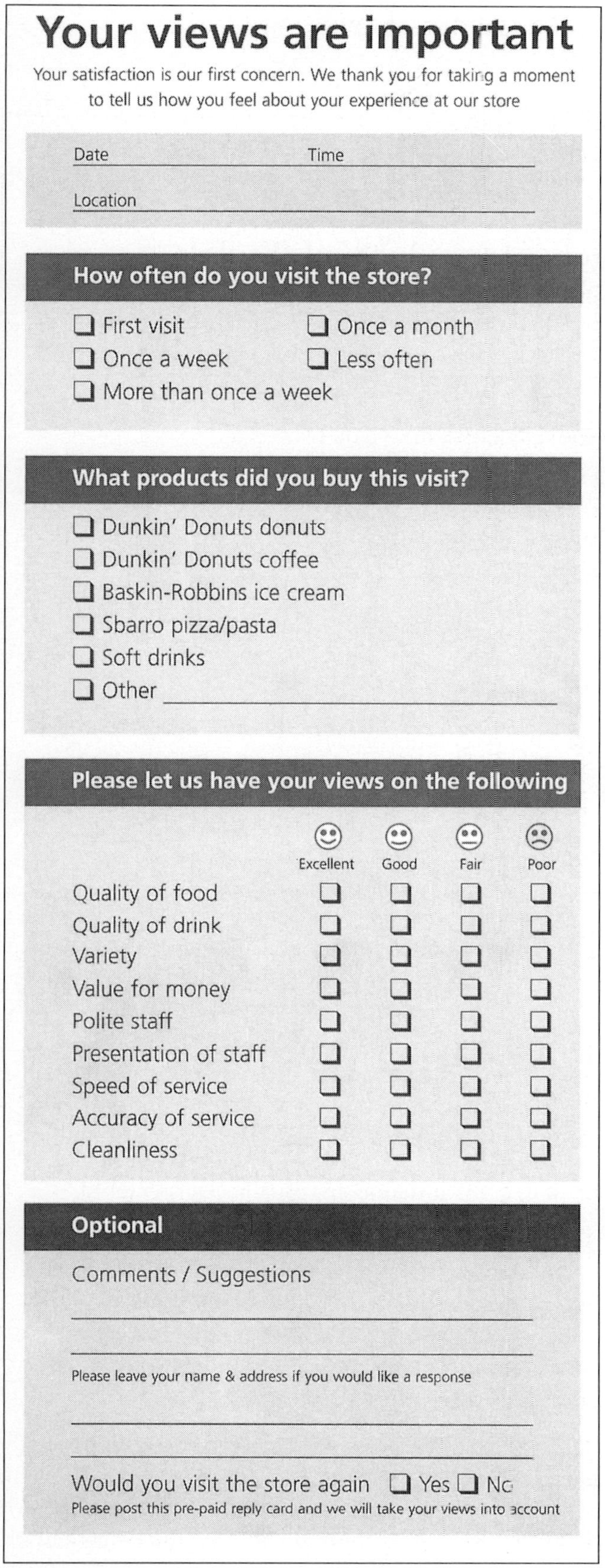

Your views are important

Your satisfaction is our first concern. We thank you for taking a moment to tell us how you feel about your experience at our store

Date _____ Time _____

Location _____

How often do you visit the store?

❑ First visit   ❑ Once a month
❑ Once a week   ❑ Less often
❑ More than once a week

What products did you buy this visit?

❑ Dunkin' Donuts donuts
❑ Dunkin' Donuts coffee
❑ Baskin-Robbins ice cream
❑ Sbarro pizza/pasta
❑ Soft drinks
❑ Other _____

Please let us have your views on the following

	Excellent	Good	Fair	Poor
Quality of food	❑	❑	❑	❑
Quality of drink	❑	❑	❑	❑
Variety	❑	❑	❑	❑
Value for money	❑	❑	❑	❑
Polite staff	❑	❑	❑	❑
Presentation of staff	❑	❑	❑	❑
Speed of service	❑	❑	❑	❑
Accuracy of service	❑	❑	❑	❑
Cleanliness	❑	❑	❑	❑

Optional

Comments / Suggestions

_____

_____

Please leave your name & address if you would like a response

_____

_____

Would you visit the store again   ❑ Yes ❑ No
Please post this pre-paid reply card and we will take your views into account

Figure 12.1   If a simple answer is required use a tick box

This is why many businesses prefer to employ trained market research experts to conduct questionnaires to ensure the replies are without influence – to enhance the reliability of the data collected.

■ Interviews

This is a method of research that allows for clarification and an opportunity to ask supplementary questions in an attempt to ensure the question is fully understood and the answer is thorough and helpful especially if consumers suddenly become reluctant to purchase a particular product. Or perhaps when their attitude towards a product appears to have changed, an interview may reveal the answers.

The interviewer can read out the questions from a questionnaire and then record the answers in an appropriate manner, thus ensuring there are fewer 'mistakes' in the recording of the responses than are likely to occur when the respondents are filling in the answers themselves. This type of interview would be classified as structured because set questions are asked in a given order.

An unstructured interview can be used either when there is no set order for the questions or no set questions. In such circumstances it is up to the trained interviewer to ascertain the information required in the informality of this type of interview. The difficulty with this type of interview is being able to analyse the replies, given the lack of structure; nevertheless, the relaxed style can be more productive in gaining the thoughts of the interviewee. Sometimes interviewers are trained in shorthand as a means of recording all the details.

Interviews are more time-consuming and consequently more expensive; the additional cost has to be traded against the fact that the information collected is likely to be more accurate.

There is, however, the possibility that many respondents are reluctant to stand and answer a large number of questions and as a consequence it may take even longer to collect a sufficient number of respondents. There is also the danger of the respondents rushing their replies as the interview progresses. Interviewers need to be experts in ensuring the attention of the respondents is maintained to elicit valid answers.

■ Interviews and questionnaires at home

To avoid some of the problems already referred to, more research is being conducted within the homes of consumers.

Data collection by phone

Initially this method of ascertaining information may appear to have all the advantages that a business requires. The interviewer incurs no travel expenses, more people can be questioned in a given period of time, it is much more cost-effective and does not cause inconvenience to the consumer who may be interrupted during their shopping.

However, many people do not like the intrusion in their home of a telephone call which requires their time and the need to answer questions, possibly in the middle of their favourite television programme. This method has, despite these reservations, grown in popularity with market research companies.

Question 8

Suggest three types of information that could be collected using telephone interviews.   [3]

Data collection by post

This is another alternative to ascertaining information from consumers or prospective consumers while they are out shopping.

This method offers the benefits of convenience for recipients of the questionnaire, as it can be answered at leisure within the comfort of their own home.

To encourage people to fill questionnaires, they are sometimes accompanied with a competition, or a free ticket in a prize draw e.g. Reader's Digest for those who fill in the form and return it within a given time period. Others, such as the National Shoppers' Survey, send the promise of several pounds worth of vouchers to be spent in local supermarkets. The majority of postal questionnaires include a Freepost envelope or a business reply service envelope to counter the problem of expecting the recipients to pay for the postage.

This type of questionnaire may well be rather longer as the pressure on time is less, but making them too long may be counterproductive as it may appear too daunting and remain blank.

■ Consumer panels

This type of research is often used to assess the reaction of a consumer either to a test product that has yet to be launched and is one of several on trial, or to a product that has yet to be launched nationwide.

For many of the consumer panels, the opinions of the consumers are collected over a period of time. A typical example is Lever Brothers, the manufacturer of washing powders which uses consumer panels to test a range of washing powders on a variety of consumers who have differing needs from a powder.

The members of the panel are asked to test the powders and comment on the powder's ability to get the clothes really clean, produce the right amount of lather and whether it smells pleasantly. A typical list of statements might be:

State whether you agree with the following descriptions:
■ Economical to use
■ Keeps colours bright
■ Works well in low temperatures
■ Dissolves easily
■ Rinses well
■ Removes stubborn stains

The replies would be returned to Lever Brothers for analysis, noting the content of each customer's replies, so that the needs of different segments can be matched with the most appropriate powder.

In order to speed up the process of analysis, scaling is often used. There are various ways in which scaling can be undertaken, the most common is attributing a mark to a given statement, usually out of 5 or 10.

Alternatively, scaling can be achieved by asking the respondent to tick a range of answers which are scaled not on the questionnaire but when the analysis is undertaken. This type of scaling usually involves answers with 'agree', 'strongly agree'; in other words, gradations of approval or disapproval.

Benefits of field research

■ It provides specific information on the behaviour of consumers and their attitudes

■ It can be collected to suit the specific needs of the business concerned

What field or primary information would you want to collect to assist you in deciding which type of savoury snack to produce and market?   [10]

Who to ask?

Collecting information from the 'right' group (or segment) of consumers is essential if a business is to gain information that will be appropriate to its needs. Breaking down consumers into groups is referred to as segmentation. Each segment of a market will have specific characteristics and consequently unique needs.

Market segmentation is the subdividing of groups of consumers who will then require a distinct marketing approach using the marketing mix.

In Figure 12.2, the brand manager of Dunkin' Donuts is trying to discover the strength of feeling with respect to the attributes listed.

Please let us have your views on the following

	Excellent	Good	Fair	Poor
Quality of food	☐	☐	☐	☐
Quality of drink	☐	☐	☐	☐
Variety	☐	☐	☐	☐
Value for money	☐	☐	☐	☐
Polite staff	☐	☐	☐	☐
Presentation of staff	☐	☐	☐	☐
Speed of service	☐	☐	☐	☐
Accuracy of service	☐	☐	☐	☐
Cleanliness	☐	☐	☐	☐

Figure 12.2   Scalling is used to speed up the process of analysis

Segmentation of toothpaste

Segment	Brand	Marketing benefit
Young children	??	Flavour
Teenagers	??	Fresh breath Kissable
Parents with young children	??	No nasty visits to the dentist No tooth decay
Parents with large family Students	??	Economical Low price

By conducting your own research, suggest the most likely brands that would be targeted at the above segments.

Samples

The validity of the research depends to a great extent on who is asked and how many are asked for their opinions.

The type of sample is crucial.

■ Stratified sampling

Stratified sampling refers to particular people who are classified in a variety of ways. Selecting all males or all females, a particular age range or a particular part of the country are obvious examples. There is little point in selecting people to interview if they do not fit in to the classification that is required. Once the group required has been selected the actual people within that group can be chosen at random (known as a stratified random sample).

More and more market research is being based on a particular segment of consumers not just according to gender or age but also by postal codes.

Geodemographic analysis links postal codes with information on the neighbourhood types, which provides a useful insight into the likely lifestyle of the consumers in that postal area.

Random sampling

If the type of research is not aimed at any particular group of consumers, then everyone has an equal chance of being selected. However there is no certainty that those who are randomly selected will be of any value to the business concerned.

If a business wanted to gauge the opinion of both men and women of all ages from all parts of the country, a random sample would not necessarily end up providing a representative sample of all those segments. The validity of the random sample can be increased by taking a large sample.

Cluster sampling

A **cluster sample** is a form of random sample but taken within a selected area. The area chosen is usually considered to be representative of the population as a whole. Swindon, in Wiltshire, is often quoted as such an area because it has a suitable balance of the population.

Quota sampling

To ensure a more representative sample, interviewing a particular number of people within a segment is preferable to a random sample. This is called a **quota sample**.

In order to gauge the attitude of teenagers to under-age drinking, a sample of 100 for each age segment would be taken.

For example:

Age segment	13–15	16–18
Gender M	50	50
F	50	50
Total	100	100

The market research team will continue until the right number of teenagers from each category has been interviewed. Any findings will therefore be more reliable than if 200 people were interviewed at random. It is possible that there could be no-one of the required age who is selected using a random sample and therefore the reliability is minimal. Quota samples are used when the characteristics of the market are known.

Question 10

A clothing company sells to men and women between the ages of 50 and 70. It is considering launching a new product and intends to ask 1,000 of the present target market their opinions of the new product. Further market characteristics are:

% of the market who are men – 60%
% of the market who are women – 40%

% of market who live in Lancashire – 50%
% of market who live in Yorkshire – 50%

% of market between 50 and 60 – 75%
% of market between 60 and 70 – 25%

1,000 men and women are approached.
a) How many will be men from Lancashire?
b) How many will be between 60 and 70 and live in Yorkshire?
c) How many women from Yorkshire are below the age of 60? [6]

Convenience sampling

If a very quick estimation of views is required and when cost is a major constraint, then conducting a sample within the area that is the most accessible at the time is described as a **convenience sample**. The reliability of this approach is dependent upon the information required. Unless the information is concerned only with people within the local area, as would be the case for a local business, its reliability is limited.

Who collects the data?

One of the dilemmas facing businesses when collecting research material is the constant battle between collecting enough information whilst ensuring the information is up to date. More information takes longer to collect and therefore costs more and will date whilst in the process of collection. Collecting less information will be quicker and therefore cheaper and will not have dated so much but it may not provide sufficient material to ensure reliability. There is no right answer to this dilemma and each business must decide what its priorities are.

The information within this unit to date has attempted to show how important up-to-date information is. Businesses are spending large sums of money in an attempt to ensure they produce the products that consumers want. It is at this point that the business has a decision to make; whether to collect the information itself (in-house) or to hire the services of a market research specialist. Much will depend upon the amount and the nature of the information required; however much will also depend upon the amount of cash the business has available to spend on obtaining the required information.

Question 11

Discuss the factors a business will consider when deciding whether to carry out market research in-house or engage an outside contractor.   [8]

Sharing information

As the cost of collecting information continues to escalate, more schemes are being undertaken whereby companies will share customer information. The companies that share the information are non-competing and therefore are no threat to each other.

Several examples of this exist already:

- **Jigsaw**, which was formed in 1997, is a consortium for information on customer needs and includes Unilever, Cadbury Schweppes and Kimberly-Clark. These companies share their database information in order to build a direct contact with appropriate consumers.

- **Let's Play Together**, formed in early 1999, is a partnership between Procter & Gamble (Pampers Playtimes) and Mattel (Fisher-Price). The partnership shares information in an attempt to build up their customer base in an effective manner. This is a unique partnership because the two companies intend to go beyond the sharing of market research data by undertaking a combined marketing campaign to launch Pampers Playtimes. This type of nappy is intended to allow the baby greater freedom of movement, which may mean the child will be able to play more easily with its Fisher-Price toys.

Is market research essential?

Certain companies, such as Amstrad, refuse to carry out any market research, because consumers do not always know what they are answering and as a result the replies may be of little value.

Akio Morita ignored consumer research indicating there was no requirement for Walkmans. He went ahead and produced the Sony Walkman.

Points for Revision

Key Terms

market research	the collection and analysis of market information to assist the business in its objective of satisfying the needs of the consumer
desk research	the collection and collation of information that is already in existence
field research	new information on the attitudes and behaviour of consumers
methods of collection	questionnaires, interviews, consumer panels and observation
stratified sample	particular set of people chosen for a sample according to e.g. age and gender
random sample	all have an equal chance of being asked, but it is unreliable
cluster sample	random sample within a particular geographical area
quota sample	set number to enhance reliability of sample
convenience sample	sample collected from an immediate area, close to the researcher

Definitions Question:

By referring to a business you know, explain the significance of three of the above terms (your teacher may wish to help you with the choice of terms).   [5] per definition

Summary Points:

1   There are two main types of research, desk and field.

2   There is a variety of methods of collecting data, each having its benefits and weaknesses.

3   Data can be collected using a range of samples, some of which are more appropriate than others.

Mini Case Study

In what appears to have been a unique piece of market research, Kellogg, the cereal manufacturer, relied upon the consumers to decide the name of one of its cereal brands.

Kellogg had decided to change the name of its popular chocolate-covered rice cereals from Coco Pops to Choco Krispies. The decision had been made when the ingredients were altered to include real chocolate in the cereal and as a consequence it was considered there was a need to reflect this in the brand name of the product.

Kellogg thought it had taken the appropriate marketing steps by naming the product to reflect the fact that real chocolate was the key feature. It was certainly unprepared for what followed.

Kellogg was inundated with complaints from loyal consumers so it decided to conduct some market research in a rather novel manner. An advertising campaign was launched, inviting consumers to register their opinions as to what the cereal ought to be called. In April 1999, a vote on the Coco issue was run for two weeks with consumers being able to vote by phone and on the web.

Over a million votes were registered, according to Kellogg, and over 90% were in favour of returning to the original name Coco Pops. Consequently, the rebranded cereals had appeared on the shelves of retail outlets by the end of May.

1 Why do you think renaming the cereal Choco Krispies was a mistake?	[3]
2 Why were a TV and web advertisement chosen to tell people about the 'vote'?	[4]
3 Which segment of the cereal market do you think this product is aimed at? (Give reasons.)	[5]
4 Discuss the factors that would need to be considered in the construction and usage of a questionnaire to ascertain whether consumers were happy with the name of the cereal.	[8]

20

Maxi Case Study

What has been described as an 'unfortunate coincidence' led to the unprecedented situation of several market research companies that specialise in the compilation of databases for lifestyles of consumers, actually issuing their questionnaires in the same month to the same consumers. September 1998 went down in the annals of market research history as the time when the nightmare scenario occurred.

The angry response of those recipients targeted by more than one questionnaire was understandable. Furthermore, the research companies were left without the normal level of responses to such questionnaires, which necessitated more having to be sent out.

A spokesman for Claritus, one of the companies involved in the 'unfortunate coincidence', indicated that this might well be another step along the road leading to the demise of this type of information-gathering. Consumers were becoming impatient and tired of aiding businesses with their thirst for information. Such information was normally used then sold on to other businesses, which would in turn ply the unfortunate customer with their own mail shots.

Quantitative research, vital to many businesses, was becoming harder to obtain. Marketing relies on data-gathering companies gaining information about the attitudes of consumers and their likes and dislikes. It is having to be more inventive in its quest to obtain knowledge from an increasingly reluctant consumer. Toyota is possibly the first car manufacturer to establish a single database for its marketing purposes and thus avoid the need to employ the data companies.

The problem has been accentuated by a growing number of companies eager to extract every morsel of information from consumers. Those whose core business is not directly involved in the collection of market data are realising that any information about consumers is a marketable commodity in itself. As a consequence these businesses, when dealing with their customers, are using their relationship to ask questions that are not necessary as part of the selling process. Even under these circumstances, such businesses are conscious that certain questions ought not to be asked too early in the buying and selling relationship. Loyal customers are more likely to be forthcoming with their agreement to divulge information that need not be asked for, but invariably is. Unfortunately, lifestyle databases are a necessary evil for consumers if the process of direct marketing is to prosper (see *Unit 19 Distribution*). Selling direct to the consumer relies heavily on knowing which consumers are willing to satisfy some of their needs in this manner. This 'catch 22' situation has created a dilemma that collators of databases have yet to resolve. Direct marketing and selling must be able to match the profile of the potential consumer with the product to be sold to prevent many wasted telephone calls or letters dropping through the letterbox.

Paul Winters of CACI, a company that specialises in geodemographic analysis, suggested that there were problems in getting both new and additional information from consumers. The latter is just as important to ensure that the database is kept up to date, given that the circumstances of individuals change constantly.

Other market research companies such as Claritus are still able to persuade their respondents to provide information a second time by rewarding them with money-off vouchers.

The consumer needs consortium called Jigsaw which consists of Cadbury Schweppes, Kimberly-Clark and Unilever has issued its respondents with a magazine with useful offers inside as a preferred means of reward. Paul Winters considers this approach better than dangling the possibility of winning a prize draw as a method of persuading consumers to respond to their endless search for knowledge.

Adapted from 'Data firms react to survey fatigue' by Ken Goften, in *Marketing*, 29/4/1999

1 Define: qualitative research, direct marketing, database.   [6]

2 What are the problems facing market research companies?   [6]

3 Comment on the likely effectiveness of Claritus's approach to gaining information.   [5]

4 Which factors are likely to affect the willingness of consumers to complete a questionnaire which is:

  i) sent through the post

  ii) issued at the retail outlet where a purchase has been made?   [8]

5 Discuss the implications for companies of getting a lower response rate to their questionnaires.   [10]

35

Presentation of data

Learning objectives

Having read this unit, students will be able to

1 use a range of presentation techniques

2 interpret data in various formats

3 evaluate a range of presentation techniques

Context

It is almost impossible to escape the constant bombardment of data that is presented to us every day of our lives. Looking through any of the broadsheet newspapers will demonstrate the sheer number of pie charts and bar charts which are used to represent data. Peter Snow, formerly a presenter on *Newsnight* (but more recently on *Tomorrow's World*), is famous for the impressive use of graphics to present the likely results on the eve of general elections. Advertisements make comparisons of the performance and the facilities that are included in a range of cars. A business will need and use all sorts of data as part of its decision making process. It is therefore important that it can be presented in a clear manner that is easy to interpret and analyse. Clearly presented data can save a business valuable time. Although information technology (IT) has enabled data to be stored more easily, the method of presentation remains crucial, if it is to be of any use.

Prior to the presentation of any type of data, certain questions need to be addressed in order to ensure the most appropriate method of presentation is used. The important questions are:

■ What is the information?
   The amount of information and its complexity will affect the method selected.

■ Who is the information for?
   The age, sex, technical expertise of the recipient will affect the method selected.

Methods of presentation

Tabulations

Table 1

	Daewoo Lanos 1.6 SX 5dr	Fiat Brava 1.6 SX 100 5dr	Peugeot 206 1.6 GLX A/C 5dr	Vauxhall Astra 1.6i Envoy A/C 5dr	Rover 200 1.4 214i 16v 5dr
RETAIL PRICE	**£10,995**	**£11,639.55**	**£10,770**	**£12,150**	**£11,920**
Delivery, Number Plates	included	£495	£500	£525	included
1 Year's Road Tax and Vehicle First Registration Fee	included	£175	£175	£175	£175
3 Years'/60,000 mile free servicing (inc. parts and labour)	included	£608.10	£438.67	£687.80	£895.13
3 Year/60,000 mile comprehensive Warranty	included	£588	£399 54k miles	£550 unlimited	£545
3 Years' roadside assistance	included	£84	£80 with warranty	with warranty	with warranty
ABS	standard	£753.18	£295	£350	£500
Passenger Airbag	standard	£274.95	£210	standard	£350
Driver Airbag	standard	standard	standard	standard	standard
Central Locking	standard	standard	standard	£300 Convenience pack	standard
Air Conditioning	standard	£307.85	standard	standard	£700
Power Steering	standard	standard	standard	standard	standard
Electric Front Windows	standard	standard	standard	Part of Convenience pack	standard
Tilt Adjustable Steering Column	standard	standard	standard	£195 Comfort pack	standard
Metallic Paint	standard	£215.03	£250	£250	£300
DAEWOOVALUE PRICE	**£10,995**	**£15,140.66**	**£13,117.67**	**£15,182.80**	**£15,385.13**
Vs Daewoo Lanos 1.6 SX 5 dr		+£4,145.66	+£2,122.67	+£4,187.80	+£4,390.13

Tabulations are an effective method of presenting data where there is a large number of variables to be shown. Although tables can be used to highlight only a few numbers, their main advantage is being able to present a lot of information in a relatively simple manner (*see Table 1*). *Which?* magazine, published by the Consumers' Association, uses tables when comparing the qualities of a number of products that have been tested. Table 1 illustrates the advantages of being able to present a great deal of information in a precise manner for the benefit of the reader who wants to be able to draw conclusions at a glance.

A simpler version of a table can be used to present information e.g. sales of a particular product, or range of products, over a stated period of time (*see Table 2*).

It is easy to glance at the table and quickly assess which size is sold most.

Table 2   Distribution of clothing sales by size

Women's dress size	Sales %
10 or less	14.9
12	25.1
14	26.9
16	18.6
18	8.3
20	3.3
22+	3.0

Source: *Marketing Pocket Book 1999*, NTC Publications Ltd

However, one of the difficulties with this type of simplified tabulation is the lack of information. The following information is not clear:

■ how many people were involved in the survey
■ where the survey was conducted
■ when the survey was conducted
■ whether the survey was carried out at the same time of the year

All the above factors need to be borne in mind when presenting such data and certainly when attempting to analyse the information.

Question 1

Using Table 3, comment on the limitations of the information provided.   [5]

Table 3   Grocery shopping habits

Grocers shopped at for regular major shopping[1]

		Per cent of all adults (18+)	
Tesco	25.8	Waitrose	2.4
Sainsbury	22.8	Netto	1.7
Asda	16.1	Gateway	1.4
Safeway	13.6	Food Giant	0.9
Kwik Save	10.6	Spar/Vivo	0.9
Iceland	6.9	Cash & Carry Warehouse	0.8
Co-op	6.3	Leo's	0.8
Somerfield	6.3	Lo-Cost	0.4
Marks & Spencer	5.8	Budgens	0.5
Morrisons	5.6	Londis	0.3
Aldi	4.1	Presto	0.3

Note: [1]Some housewives named several grocers.
Source: Target Group Index (April 1997 – March 1998), © BMRB 1998, from *Marketing Pocket Book 1999*, NTC Publications Ltd

---

The most important factor to bear in mind when using a table is to keep it simple. It is also important to ensure that sufficient information is given within the table if it is to be understood and therefore useful:

■ an appropriate title – this ensures the reader is aware of the emphasis for the table
■ a source – to provide an opportunity to judge the validity of the information
■ a date – to enable the reader to assess whether the information is still relevant
■ a key – to ensure that the figures are read correctly. Many mistakes are made when interpreting the information because

e.g. | year | sales |
|---|---|
| 1998 | 100 |
| 1999 | 120 |
| 2000 | 60 |

there is no indication as to whether the sales are the actual numbers sold, or the denomination, or whether they represent values. The information would be interpreted quite differently with slightly more, but vital information.

e.g. | year | sales revenue |
|---|---|
| 1998 | 100 |
| 1999 | 120 |
| 2000 | 60 |

or: | year | sales (£ 000s) |
|---|---|
| 1998 | 100 |
| 1999 | 120 |
| 2000 | 60 |

or: | year | sales (£ 000s) |
|---|---|
| 1998 | 100 |
| 1999 | 120 |
| 2000 | 60 |

(2000, the first 3 months only)

The above examples clearly show the need for great care when presenting tables to avoid misinterpretation.

Pie charts

The **pie chart** approach derives from portions of the edible pie rather than any particular affinity to mathematical formulae for circles!

The 'pie' represents the total of all the results and can be used to show the value of each slice or tranche.

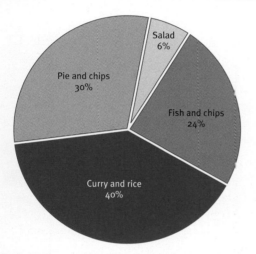

Figure 13.1   Percentage of pupils choosing different types of school dinner

This particular form of presentation is often misused. The classic mistake is to use a pie chart to show that, for example, 100% of those interviewed were female.

To display the value of each slice or portion of the pie accurately, it is necessary to calculate the proportion of the whole 'pie' represented by the individual sector or slice.

For example:

A survey of 125 teenagers' preferences for T-shirts produced the following results:

Tommy Hilfiger 27, Ted Baker 15, Nike 45, Adidas 20, Ralph Lauren 18.

The whole 'pie' represents the 125 teenagers; the proportion of the pie for Tommy Hilfiger is

$$\frac{27}{125} \times 360 = 77.76 \ (78) \text{ degrees}$$

Once the calculation has been done, the actual number of survey replies can be placed into the pie in the correct proportion.

The good news for those whose task it is to calculate the above, is that most computer software packages do this for you automatically when drawing the pie chart from **spreadsheets**.

In order for the presentation to be meaningful, it is becoming the accepted practice to arrange the answers in descending order around the pie. In general, this enables the reader to see at a glance the proportions for each response and which are the highest and the lowest.

Disneyland Paris was able to show which country visitors had travelled from to visit the theme park (*see Figure 13.2*).

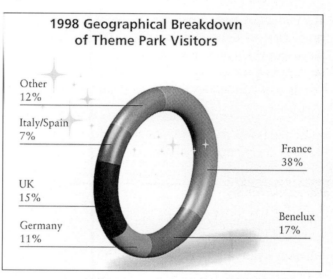

Source: Disneyland Paris

Figure 13.2   Proportions of different nationalities visiting Disneyland Paris

Even though the proportions have been calculated in a meaningful manner, the way in which the data is presented is of little value apart from the reader being able to ascertain which response was the largest or which item was mentioned the least.

Judging the percentage of replies that are very small is almost impossible and it is therefore advisable not to use pie charts when there is a large number of categories to be shown.

It is advisable to state the total number of responses collected if the reader is to be able to assimilate the information with any degree of accuracy. Looking at Figure 13.2, it is not possible to know how many people travelled from the UK to visit Disneyland Paris.

The pie chart is also of limited value if comparisons have to be made from year to year. Changing the overall size of the pie chart is of little help as the actual values are not easy to assimilate. Therefore the pie chart is of limited value and ought to be used for displaying the breakdown of data that has no more than approximately six categories.

Task 1

Calculate the rest of the responses to the T-shirt survey (on the previous page) and present them on a pie chart. (You may use a simple spreadsheet.)   [8]

The benefit of using a pie chart is that it provides a simplistic visualisation of the breakdown of data when there is only a limited number of items involved. If it is necessary to show a comparison of more than just a few items or categories then a bar chart is a better alternative.

Bar charts

This particular method of presentation is probably the most common and the most flexible to use. There are different styles of **bar charts**, vertical and horizontal.

For ease of interpretation, the better bar charts are drawn with gaps between the bars as in Figure 13.3.

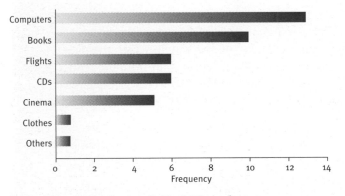

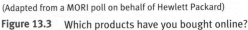
(Adapted from a MORI poll on behalf of Hewlett Packard)

Figure 13.3   Which products have you bought online?

The length of the bar is a clear indication as to which classification is the most significant. As is the case for pie charts, presenting the items in descending order enables the reader to assimilate the facts quickly. In Figure 13.3, computers, followed by books, are the most frequently purchased items via the Internet.

Comparative bar charts

Bar charts can be used to make comparisons as well as displaying simple data, as shown in Figure 13.4.

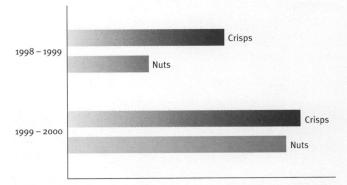

Figure 13.4   Comparing nuts/crisps sales for two consecutive years

Here a comparison is made between the level of sales for nuts and crisps for 1998–99 and 1999–2000.

The positioning of the bars allows a comparison to be made at a glance. Comparisons can be made for particular years for a certain item, or between items for a given year.

Compound or component bar charts

Another format is the **compound** or **component bar chart**. In this type, the total for a given aspect is stated by the length of the bar chart, but within the bar details of the factors that contribute to the total can be shown.

Figure 13.5 is an example of the compound or component bar chart.

It is possible to see that in 1996 the contribution of Instants to the turnover for the National Lottery was greater than in 1998. More detail can be added to this type of bar chart.

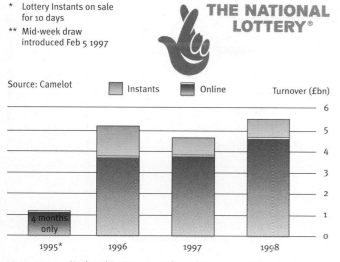

* Lottery Instants on sale
  for 10 days
** Mid-week draw
   introduced Feb 5 1997

THE NATIONAL LOTTERY®

Source: Camelot   Instants   Online   Turnover (£bn)

Figure 13.5   National Lottery scratch cards compound bar chart

Pictograms

This is another form of bar chart, where the data is presented using pictures. This is a more entertaining method of presenting data. Pictograms are frequently used in an attempt to catch the attention of the reader, who is often not an expert on the subject of interpreting data. Consequently, this method is usually easier to understand. It is often used in the press or in marketing material in an attempt to add some interest or topicality to the data.

Due to the nature of the presentation, accuracy is not the most important consideration; providing an approximation is sufficient.

For example:

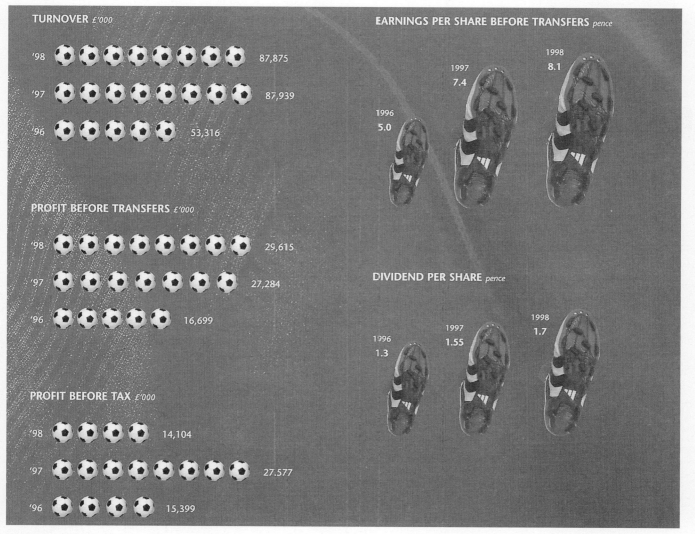

Source: Manchester United Annual Report 1998

Figure 13.6   Pictogram of Manchester United financial data

In Figure 13.6, the turnover is represented by footballs; this is topical and appropriate as part of a simple and interesting portrayal of financial data on Manchester United. However, it is impossible to measure accurately the difference in turnover between 1997 and 1998 nor the actual figures without including the numbers at the end of each line. Nevertheless, it is possible to see at a glance that the turnover actually fell slightly.

There are similar problems with the pictorial representations of the dividend per share and the earnings per share before transfers. The difference between, for example, 1996 and 1998 is exaggerated by the drawings of soccer boots. Not only has the height of the boot been increased but the width as well which may be somewhat overstating the case for the increase that has been achieved. It is apparent that looking at the pictorial representations is preferable to the 'plain' figures given on the pictogram. Using pictograms is more appropriate for reporting statistics for some businesses; figures on Disneyland Paris are presented as befits a theme park (*see Figure 13.7*).

Although this method of presenting data is not appropriate if there is a range of categories to display it has its uses when presenting data and therefore ought not to be dismissed, especially when completing coursework.

> ## Question 2
>
> You have been asked to present data for an advertisement for either:
> i) the number of people who died from smoking during the last five years for an anti-smoking campaign, or
> ii) the sales of different cakes sold at the school mini-enterprise.   [6]

Histograms

The major difference between a histogram and a bar chart is the use of the horizontal axis. For a bar chart, the axis is used only to highlight the date or the commodity that is being measured. However, for a histogram the axis is used for a separate measurement from that on the vertical axis. (The axes are interchangeable.) The histogram allows for presentation of data that covers a range rather than individual numbers. For example, a bar chart could be used to show how many people visited the cinema to see a *Star Wars* film each night. A histogram would be used to show how many people between certain ages visited the cinema.

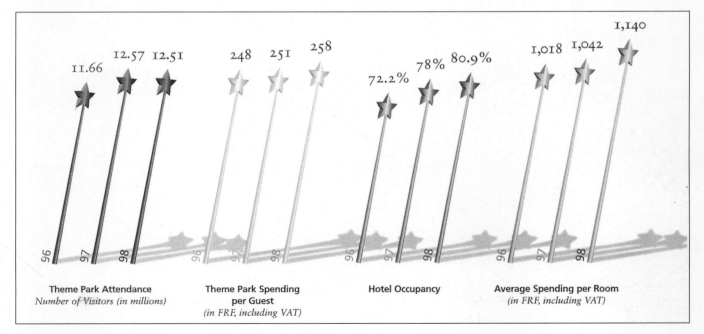

Source: Disneyland Paris

Figure 13.7   Pictogram of Disneyland Paris figures

Therefore the width of each bar may now be significant depending upon the range of ages to be highlighted.

Given the following information:
The number of people watching the *Stars* Wars film *The First Episode*.

The data is for the number of people of a certain age watching the film at a cinema in the West Midlands over a weekend.

Age range of cinema audience	Number within age range
15–18	600
19–25	450
26–35	500
36–45	700 (estimated figures)
46–65	400
66–75	150

The data can be represented using a histogram as shown in Figure 13.8:

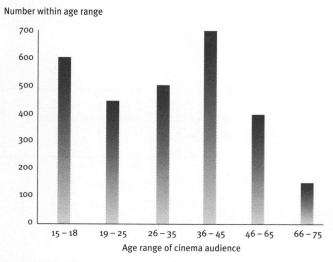

Figure 13.8   Histogram: Age range of cinema audience for *Star Wars*

Adding the frequency line at the mid-point of each age range allows the viewer to gain a clearer picture of the information at a glance. This line is known as the frequency polygon.

Line graphs

Line graphs enable two variables to be shown. The variables, whatever they are, will have some sort of relationship. One of the most obvious that has already been referred to in earlier units is a demand curve, which shows the relationship between price and the level of demand. The *Financial Times* has a section entitled 'Market at a glance', which demonstrates the benefits of line graphs. They are easy to understand and interpret quickly. The FTSE 100 index is plotted with time on the horizontal axis and the index on the vertical axis.

Comparisons can be made by using line graphs. In Figure 13.9, Sainsbury's share price is compared with the FTSE All Share index for 1998–99.

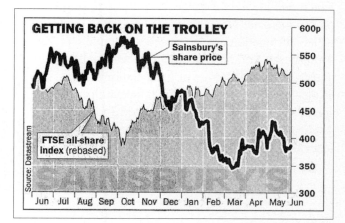

Source: *The Times* 3/6/99

Figure 13.9   Line graphs are easy to interpret quickly

Question 3

The figures below are taken from the Annual Report for BT plc, 1999.

	1995	1996	1997	1998	1999
Turnover (£ billion)	13.90	14.47	15.02	16.04	18.22
Operating profit	2.67	3.02	3.2	3.21	4.23

a) Present the information above using line graphs.
[4]

b) Comment on the change in both graphs.   [5]

Many items of economic data are presented using line graphs.

> ### Task 2
>
> Select two pieces of economic data from broadsheet newspapers and present them in
> **a)** a table
> **b)** a line graph
> Describe the information which can be interpreted from the line graph.   [6]

Spreadsheets

With greater access to PCs, more use is being made of spreadsheets as a method of presenting data. A spreadsheet is really just an IT formatted tabulation, which provides a convenient method of storing and presenting data. The table is made up of cells in which information can be placed. Depending on the sophistication of the program, the data can be transformed into a range of presentational types, such as pie charts or bar charts. The information in the spreadsheet can then be manipulated and the charts redrawn without the tedious process of doing so manually.

The dangers of presentation

Care must always be taken when looking at any form of presentation. Information can be 'distorted' to influence the way in which it will be received. Politicians are experts in presenting data to suit their needs. Companies may be tempted to enhance the growth in profits, or minimise the size of their losses.

For example, line graphs showing the rate of inflation over a period of time can be presented in two ways, both showing the same information (*see Figure 13.10*).

Line graph A might be presented by an opposition party in an attempt to suggest that there had been little improvement, whereas line graph B might be presented by a party in government wanting to show the dramatic fall while it had been in office.

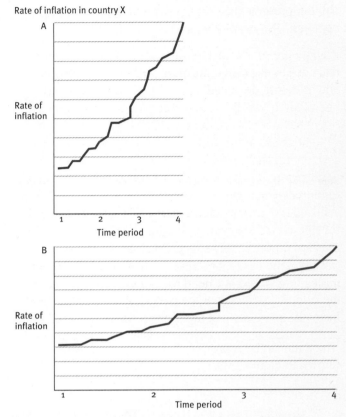

Rate of inflation in country X

Figure 13.10   Line graphs A and B presenting the same rate of inflation in two different ways

> ### Task 3
>
> Find three examples of data that has been distorted by the method of presentation.

Index numbers

Calculations and presentations

To avoid problems and allow for a comparison of data that involves, for example, financial values, **index numbers** are used.

For example:

Table 4

Year	Sales of mobile phones at The Phone Home Shop
1997	120,000
1998	130,000
1999	135,000

Table 4 presents data for the sales of mobile phones between 1997 and 1999.

If you were set the task of deciding whether the sales team at The Phone Home Shop had been successful and therefore deserved a pay rise or whether it had been failing to sell a reasonable amount and therefore ought to be replaced, there would be great difficulties straight away. Apart from the obvious omissions such as a key for the table to enable you to ascertain if the figures were for the number of phones or for the value of the sales, making any comparison between 1997 and subsequent years would be very difficult. Supposing the figures were actually the **value** of the sales over the three-year period; any suggestion that the value of the sales had increased would be premature and possibly misleading. There is a need to take into consideration the value of money over the period of time for the table. Increases in the price of the phones during the three-year period might suggest why the sales value had increased.

Index numbers convert values for different years into a value for a given year referred to as the base year. By converting all the values to a common denominator any comparisons that are made are realistic.

Using the mobile phone sales:

Year	Sales of mobile phones at The Phone Home Shop
1997	120,000
1998	130,000
1999	135,000

The sales figures can be converted to index numbers by applying the formula

$$\frac{\text{number for year 1998}}{\text{number in base year}} \times 100$$

The year to be compared with the base year is always divided by the chosen base year. In addition the base year can be assigned a value of 100 to make comparisons easier.

Therefore for an index for 1998:

$$\frac{130,000}{120,000} \times 100 = 108.3$$

The index number allows a comparison to be made between the year in question and the base year, which in this example shows an increase of 8.3%. If the figures to be compared are values rather than just numbers,

the process is still the same.

The prices below are for

year 1	year 2	year 3	year 4
60p	90p	£1.20	£1.50

Comparing year 2 with year 1 can be meaningfully accomplished by applying the formula

$$\frac{\text{price in year } x \text{ (year 2)}}{\text{price in base year (year 1)}} \times 100$$

$$\frac{90p}{60p} \times 100 = 150$$

Index numbers can be applied to a basket of items, the formula being:

$$\frac{\text{Total price of the items in year } x}{\text{Total price of the items in base year}} \times 100$$

Question 4

	1989	1999
Soft drinks		
Flavour A	15p	25p
Flavour B	12p	25p
Flavour C	30p	45p

Calculate the index for flavours A, B and C for 1999.　　　　　[4]

One of the problems of using an index for a basket of items is that it is assumed the items are of equal importance. To most customers, an increase in the cost of petrol is of greater significance than an increase in the price of light bulbs. Petrol is bought more frequently and takes up a larger proportion of customers' disposable income.

To alleviate such potential difficulties, a weighting can be used to allow for the relative importance of each item.

Sandwich	Weight	1989 Price	Total cost (weight × price) 1989	1999 Price	Total cost (weight × price) 1999
Ham	36	75p	2700p	£1.25	4500p
Beef	25	90p	2250p	£1.75	4375p
Cheese	27	60p	1620p	£1.00	2700p
Prawn	12	£1.00	1200p	£1.95	2340p
Totals			7770p		13 915p

The total cost for each item is calculated by multiplying the weighting for that item and its price. The total weighted cost for a particular year is calculated by adding the weighted costs for all the items under consideration.

To calculate the index for the above, the formula used is

$$\text{Index} = \frac{\text{Total weighted cost in year } x}{\text{Total weighted cost of base year}} \times 100$$

Therefore to calculate the weighted index for sandwiches:

$$\text{Index} = \frac{\text{Total weighted cost of 1999}}{\text{Total weighted cost of 1989}} \times 100$$

$$\text{Index} = \frac{13,915}{7770} \times 100 = 179$$

There are several examples of data that are presented on a regular basis which make use of index numbers; the FTSE and Retail Price Index are obvious examples.

Points for Revision

Key Terms

tabulations	used for the presentation of a large number of variables
spreadsheets	a method of presenting and storing a large amount of data which can be converted to one of several methods of presentation at a later date
pie charts	to represent data which can be put into several categories as a percentage of the 360 degrees of the circle
bar charts	to show the degree of importance of data according to the length of the bar
comparative bar charts	to compare data for different items for a given year
compound/ component	a bar chart which has several parts making up its total length
pictograms	an eye-catching method of presenting data in a simplistic and entertaining manner
histogram	used to present information where data takes into consideration a range of figures and frequencies using the height and width of each bar
line graph	to illustrate the relationship between variables, for example value and time
index numbers	a method to enable meaningful comparisons to be made between figures over a period of time, by 'converting' the figures to the value for a selected year

Definitions Question:
By referring to a business you know, explain the significance of three of the above terms (your teacher may wish to help you with the choice).   [5] per definition

Summary Points:

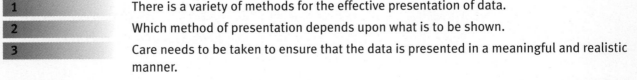

1   There is a variety of methods for the effective presentation of data.

2   Which method of presentation depends upon what is to be shown.

3   Care needs to be taken to ensure that the data is presented in a meaningful and realistic manner.

Mini Case Study

Shampoo-and-Go Ltd is a car valeting company that specialises in preparing new cars, whether imported or manufactured in this country, for the customer. Regardless of the origin of the cars, the majority have often been 'parked up' in vast car parks awaiting collection and delivery and as a consequence have collected a considerable amount of dust and dirt. The owners, Bill and Kath Sheldon, are keen to expand the business by attracting new partners and have decided to put together a brochure to show to potential partners to enable them to gain an insight into the business. Unfortunately, one of their major customers is an owner of a Rover franchise who has several showrooms but has not been selling many cars. One set of figures that Bill has obtained were for Rover sales since 1994:

	UK sales	Market share %
1994	221,380	11.58
1995	211,824	10.89
1996	198,254	9.79
1997	194,702	8.97
1998	160,323	7.13
1999*	41,057	5.01

*1st quarter only

Source: Rover Cars

Rover Cars represent approximately a third of the Sheldons' business. The other major customers are fortunately selling considerably more cars that require valeting. Japanese imports are about 40% of their business and the other car manufacturers, four in all, represent similar percentages of the business.

The other part of the business is 'bespoke tailoring' of imported cars. This involves personalising cars to meet the needs of customers who want something slightly out of the ordinary and are prepared to pay for it e.g. TV in the rear of the driver's seat. This part of the business has been growing rapidly (50% per annum) for the last three years and is now worth nearly as much as the core business.

Kath is determined to present their business in a favourable light without being untruthful, but unlike Bill wants the brochure to be a simple representation of the business that would provide anyone interested with an insight into its main features.

1 Convert the Rover sales figures into an appropriate form of presentation to be used by a member of the business who wanted to argue for an end to dealing with the Rover franchise. [5]

2 Suggest the major limitations of using the data on Rover for the decision making process on whether Shampoo-and-Go Ltd should cease dealing with the franchise. [5]

3 Using the information in the case study, select and prepare the most appropriate methods of presentations that Kath would approve of. [10]

Maxi Case Study

In 1998 Shortfellows was keen to extend its product portfolio by publishing a new magazine aimed at both male and female readers of socio-economic groups A, B and C1. The intention was to appeal to the young professional who was keen on fashion and leisure activities. In order to ascertain whether this was a viable proposition the publications company had hired the services of Mat and Kate Law.

Before starting the publications company, Kate had her own beauty therapy business and Mat had always been an entrepreneur and was the main instigator of their present business, a market research company that specialised in leisure.

Having collected the information using desk research which was presented in various formats, it was necessary to interpret their findings before making their recommendations to the publications company.

The information that Mat and Kate had collected is given below:

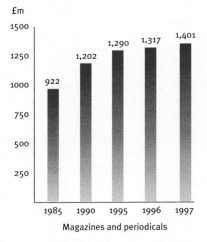

Figure 13.11   Consumer spending on magazines and periodicals

Table 5

Title	Circulation	Advertising CPT*	female (F)	male (M)
Prima	503,929	11.87	F	
Cosmopolitan	416,177	8.12	F	
New Woman	251,118	10.97	F	
Vogue	155,551	11.54	F	
FHM	551,803	4.34		M
Loaded	396,689	3.61		M
Maxim	208,445	6.55		M

Note: *CPT cost per thousand readers (£)

Source: ABC data 1997–1998

Figure 13.12 illustrates the percentage of adults who own various items of portable leisure equipment. Mat wondered whether this information might be useful to gauge the potential of a free CD or voucher for a CD as a promotional incentive for the launch of the new magazine.

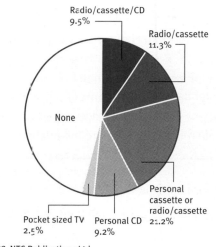

Source: *Marketing Pocket Book 1999*, NTC Publications Ltd

Figure 13.12 Percentage ownership of portable leisure equipment

Figure 13.13 was an attempt to provide data on purchases of leisure attire which, it was hoped, would give a clear indication as to the likelihood of the targeted readership being interested in articles on leisurewear.

Clothing				Percentage of adults
	Swimwear	Leotard/ Dancewear	Tracksuit/ Jogging Suit	Other Sports Clothing
Adults	24.4	3.1	14.1	14.4
Females	18.6	0.9	14.8	20.7
15–24	29.9	5.1	13.6	8.5
25–34	30.8	4.4	25.4	27.5
35–44	32.9	4.1	15.4	16.1
45–54	23.5	2.1	11.9	11.3
55+	27.9	2.0	13.6	11.4
ABC1	58.0	7.6	29.8	25.9
C2DE	57.7	6.9	38.6	31.6

Source: Target Group Index, © BMRB 1997

Figure 13.13 Purchases of leisure attire

1 With reference to Figure 13.11, and Table 5, consumer spending on purchases of magazines and periodicals, suggest how Mat and Kate ought to interpret these figures.   [4]

2 Calculate the price index for 1990 and 1997 assuming 1985 is the base year.   [4]

3 With reference to Figure 13.13, comment on the reliability of the data for Mat and Kate to use.   [6]

4 Comment on the information in Figure 13.12 (% ownership of portable leisure equipment) and highlight the limitations of this method of presentation.   [8]

5 Discuss whether Mat and Kate require any additional information in order to make a reliable recommendation to the publishing house.   [8]

30

Methods of summarising data

Learning objectives

Having read this unit, students will be able to

1. demonstrate an understanding of how to calculate the mean, median and mode of grouped and ungrouped data

2. understand the appropriateness of different measures of central tendency in different contexts

3. understand the application of standard deviation and normal distribution to certain business contexts

Context

The average household expenditure during 1997 was £16,115.79. During 1998, the average annual labour costs per employee were £35,439. The median salary in a blue chip company during 1998 was £34,690. The modal grade for the most recent Business Studies A level examination was grade C. The standard deviation of the gap on a spark plug was 0.2 mm.

Statistics and figures are used regularly in the newspapers and particularly by politicians. The terms mean and mode have separate meanings, although they are frequently confused. Being able to describe the way in which data is spread allows a more precise interpretation of the data and allows us to summarise the results in a more understandable format.

'Lies, damned lies and statistics'

Most of us have become much more aware that we live in an information age, where it is relatively easy to gain access to vast banks of information and process it in some way or other. Companies regularly buy customer databases from market research businesses which collect the data with the specific objective of selling it on to end users. Data can be used to describe spending patterns, pay awards, average pay increases and fluctuations in quality to name but a few. Unit 13 Presentation of data discussed how the data should be presented, this unit focuses on the various methods of interpretation of data, with a view to helping the decision making process.

Methods of summarising data

There are four measures of central tendency that can be used to summarise data; these are known as the **mean**, **median**, **mode** and **standard deviation**.

Measures of central tendency

The mean

The arithmetic mean is the average of all the data (*see Table 1*) and is calculated by adding up the data and dividing it by the number of observations e.g. the cost accountant of Tumbles Ltd was trying to calculate the average material cost of production. He intended to use this figure as a performance measure. If this could be reduced, profit could be increased. Data which had been provided is given in Table 1.

Table 1

	Cost per unit
Material 1	£8
Material 2	£3
Material 3	£13

He calculated the average to be $\dfrac{£8 + £3 + £13}{3} = £8$

However, he was also aware that the business used different amounts of each material (*see Table 2*).

Table 2

	Cost per unit	Amount of each material used
Material 1	£8	3
Material 2	£3	7
Material 3	£13	2

Now he could see that the cost of material 2 would have a greater influence on the overall average, because more of material 2 was used than either materials 1 or 3. In this case, he used a **weighted average**, using the quantities to show the relative importance, within the total cost, of each material.

Table 3

Cost	Amount used	Total cost
£8	3	£24
£3	7	£21
£13	2	£26

The total cost for this product is therefore £24 + £21 + £26 = £71.

However, there are 12 units of materials used, so £71/12 = £5.92.

This is known as the weighted average. The word weight is used here to demonstrate the relative importance of each item.

The following represents the annual percentage increase in the price of various items bought in a typical 'weekly basket' of shopping, along with the quantities bought.

Table 4

	Percentage increase	Quantity purchased
Bread	4%	5
Milk (litres)	2%	10
Tinned food	5%	15
Frozen food	3%	7
Eggs (doz.)	0%	1
Biscuits	2%	5
Dried food	5%	3

a) Calculate the mean increase in price for the overall basket of products.   [2]

b) Why might this calculation be of limited use?   [3]

c) Recalculate the average price increase if the change in tinned food was –5%.   [3]

Grouped data

Sometimes the data is more complicated to deal with, and needs to be organised into a more usable format before calculations can be carried out e.g. the following represents the number of working days lost through absenteeism in a year at a factory with 30 employees.

Table 5

24	26	9	15	24
26	19	11	31	17
29	23	16	20	18
30	14	13	23	19
23	12	8	5	15
16	23	26	29	15

In its present form, the mean can be calculated by adding up all the numbers and then dividing by the total number of observations.

Mean = sum x/f where x is the variable which is being measured, and f is the frequency i.e. the number of times each value of x is observed. In the above example, the **frequency** is 30.

Adding all the figures together:

Sum $x = 579$

$\dfrac{579}{30}$ = 19.3 days (never forgetting to write the units being measured)

N.B. It is possible to use some specific signs which help to abbreviate the process of writing out

$$\text{mean} = \frac{\text{sum } fx}{\text{sum } f} = \frac{\Sigma fx}{\Sigma f}$$

However, this is a rather cumbersome method of calculation, so an alternative is to use **grouped data**, placing each observation into a group. In the above example, we could use categories of five days e.g. 5–9, 10–14, etc.

Table 6

Number of days (x)	Frequency (f)
5–9	3
10–14	4
15–19	9
20–24	7
25–29	5
30–34	2

To calculate the mean from Table 6, it is necessary to use a mid-point for each group, known as an **assumed mean**. This is because the data has been grouped and therefore individual observations have been lost.

Table 7

x	f	x. ass	x. ass
5–9	3	7.5	22.5
10–14	4	12.5	50
15–19	9	17.5	157.5
20–24	7	22.5	157.5
25–29	5	27.5	137.5
30–34	2	32.5	65
			590 = Σfx. assumed

This gives a total number of absented days as 590 and not 579, hence some accuracy is lost by grouping the data. 590 is then divided by the number of observations (Σf) to give 19.67 days. Although not radically different from 19.3 days, it is still different. Grouping the data for convenience therefore might cause problems in terms of loss of accuracy.

The reference to the assumed mean is the cause of the loss of accuracy; although this data is easier to handle, when carrying out calculations, it must be assumed that each class (5–9, 10–14 etc.) has a mean, which is the mid-point. This assumes that the spread of the data across the class is even.

Question 2

The following data has been taken from a company's cost accountant:

Table 8

Wage (weekly)	Number in group
£100 – less than £110	5
£110 – less than £120	9
£120 – less than £130	15
£130 – less than £140	18
£140 – less than £150	16
£150 – less than £160	10
£160 – less than £170	6
£170 – less than £180	1

a) Calculate the estimated mean weekly wage.   [3]

b) The actual mean weekly wage is £137. Explain the difference between this and your answer to a).   [2]

Usefulness of the mean

Although the average figure gives an idea of size e.g. average wage, average amount spent, average hours spent at desk working, it can give a distorted figure because it includes all values and therefore some 'rogue' points – those which are very high or low compared with the rest of the data – can distort the mean.

Question 3

How would your answer to question 2 a) change if there was a new class of £300–310 with five people in it?   [2]

The median

The **median** is the mid-point in a range of numbers, and therefore shows the point at which 50% of the data has been covered e.g. the level of sales achieved by each salesman on a particular day, in terms of products, is:

Table 9

Number of units sold	Number of salesmen
1	1
2	3
3	5
4	4
5	3
6	3
7	1

There are 20 salesmen in this business and the median will show us what level of sales corresponds to the salesman ranked 10th in the business. This can involve ordering the data as follows:

Table 10

Sales	1 2 2 2 3 3 3 3 3 4 4 4 4 5 5 5 6 6 6 7
Observation number	1 2 3 4 5 6 7 8 9 10 11 12 13 14 15 16 17 18 19 20

Observation number 10 falls on sales units of 4, which is the median. An alternative method uses the cumulative distribution. This is calculated by using a running total of the observations.

Table 11

Number of units sold	Number of salesmen		Cumulative distribution
1	1		1
2	3	+ =	4
3	5	+ =	9
4	4	+ =	13
5	3	+ =	16
6	3	+ =	19
7	1	+ =	20

The number of salesmen selling two or fewer is 4, the number of salesmen selling three or fewer is 9, the number of salesmen selling four or fewer is 13, so the salesman ranked 10th sold 4 units. This shows that the median is four sales units.

Question 4

The following are the results of a recent examination, marked out of 20.

Table 12

Marks	Number of pupils achieving marks
10	15
11	19
12	23
13	20
14	8
15	6
16	5
17	1
18	1
19	1

a) Calculate from the above
i) the mean
ii) the median   [4]

b) How can the above results help the teacher to determine whether the test was appropriate for the year group and the ability of the year group?   [4]

The median is much more difficult to calculate when the data is grouped e.g. results from a sample of 60 stores from the same retailing company in terms of weekly revenue.

Revenue	Number of stores	Cumulative frequency
£50,000 – £100,000	10	10
£100,000 – £500,000	25	35
£500,000 – £1,000,000	18	53
£1,000,000 – £10,000,000	7	60

The median (30th observation) falls in the £100,000 – £500,000 category, although the precise figure could be anywhere between the two values, given the way the groups have been created. The crude median is the mid-point of this group, £350,000, although the assumed median (the interpolated median) can be

calculated. It is done by assuming the 25 observations are divided equally across the class width from £100,000 – £500,000 i.e. 25 observations across £400,000, meaning £16,000 per observation.

To get from 10 to 30 observations, another 20 are needed, which begin at £100,000 and leap in jumps of £16,000. 20 × £16,000 = £320,000. So the median is assumed to lie at £100,000 + £320,000 = £420,000.

The mode

The mode is the most frequent observation and can be used in a variety of applications. This is easy to calculate by straightforward observation of the data e.g. number of pupils arriving for lessons (negative means early).

Table 13

Lateness	Number of pupils
−2	4
−1	5
0	5
1	6
2	9
3	2
4	1

In this case, the most frequent period of lateness was two minutes. If the data is grouped, the mode is assumed to lie in the group which has the highest frequency. However to narrow the mode down from a group to an individual figure requires an assumption that the data is distributed around the same value. This is an unrealistic assumption, so when calculating the mode from a group, this is known as the **crude mode** e.g.

Revenue	Number of stores	Cumulative frequency
£50,000 – £100,000	10	10
£100,000 – £500,000	25	35
£500,000 – £1,000,000	18	53
£1,000,000 – £10,000,000	7	60

In this example, the modal group is £100,000 – £500,000, and the crude mode is the mid-point, £350,000.

Question 5

Crease-It manufactures shirts. The following data refers to the sizes of shirts purchased during the year 1999–2000.

Table 14

Size of collar	Number purchased
14	10000
14.5	14000
15	17000
15.5	24000
16	32000
16.5	21000
17	15000
17.5	11000
18	6000

a) Calculate the mean, median and mode for the above data.   [4]

b) How useful is each of the measures of central tendency to Crease-It?   [4]

Measures of spread

The range shows the difference between the highest and lowest value of data, although the inter-quartile range tells the reader a little more about the main part of the data. The following data relates to the diameter of a set of drinking glasses.

Table 15

Diameter	Frequency	Cumulative frequency
8 cm	6	6
8.02 cm	13	19
8.04 cm	21	40
8.06 cm	35	75
8.08 cm	17	92
8.1 cm	8	100

Plotting the data would result in the following:

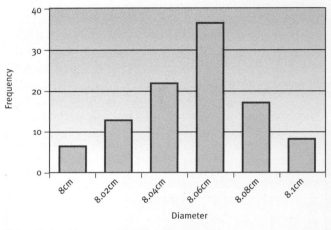

Figure 14.1   Diameter of drinking glasses

The data is grouped around the mode of 8.06 cm. Most of the data in this case is close to the mode; a method of calculating how widely spread the data is is by using the inter-quartile range. This is calculated in a similar way to the median, except, rather than using 50% of the data observed for the point of reference, 25% and 75% are used. In the above example, 25% of the data has been covered by 8.04cm and 75% of the data has been covered at 8.06 cm, therefore the inter-quartile range is 8.04 cm–8.06 cm.

The normal distribution

There is a theoretical distribution, known as the normal distribution, which can be applied to various issues in business. This is because the distribution is regular and displays certain properties:

- the mean, median and mode are the same
- the distance between the mean and the **standard deviation** will include a certain percentage of observations

The standard deviation

This represents the average distance from the mean of each observation i.e. when compared to the mean, standard deviation is a measure of how far away from this mean a particular observation/number/score/level of production is so that a comparison can be made in terms of performance i.e. whether the observation is more or less than the average.

To all intents and purposes, the standard deviation looks at the average distance of each observation from the mean. It gives an indication of how the results are clustered around the mean and therefore if there is a narrow spread of data. With a larger standard deviation, there is a wider spread.

The normal distribution therefore displays the following spread of data:

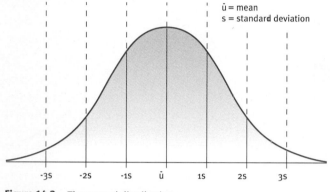

Figure 14.2   The normal distribution

Application of normal distribution

1) According to the diagram, moving from the mean by one standard deviation each way will incorporate 68% of the data, between the first and second standard deviation there will be a further 14% either side of the mean. Between the second and the third standard deviation there will be approximately 2% either side of the mean.

These figures are approximations; the actual figures are more exact – these have been rounded to the nearest percentage to make working with the normal distribution a little easier.

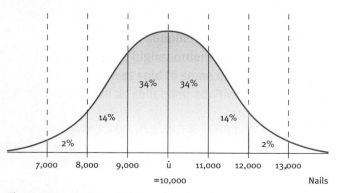
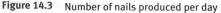

Figure 14.3   Number of nails produced per day

If, for example, the mean number of units produced per day at a nail factory was 10,000 nails and the standard deviation was 1,000 nails, and distribution was normal, then in a sample of 100 days, on 68% of occasions i.e. 68 days, there would be an output of between 9,000 and 11,000 nails produced (with 34% between 10,000 and 11,000 and another 34% between 9,000 and 10,000).

Similarly, approximately 14% of the results would be between 9,000 and 8,000 and another 14% between 11,000 and 12,000. Between 7,000 and 8,000 would be approximately 2% of all nails produced, with the same percentage between 12,000 and 13,000.

Question 6

A machine is set up to produce an average of 7,800 units per day and is operated by two people. According to the way the two operatives monitor the machine, it can produce over 8,000 units if they check the output closely and make the necessary adjustments to the settings. Sometimes, however, they do not observe the warning signs with sufficient care and output can fall below 7,800 regularly. The standard deviation of the output is 100 units and the pattern of output is normally distributed.

Over a period of 250 working days, calculate how many times the business produces
a)   over 8,000 units
b)   fewer than 7,800 units
c)   over 7,600 units
d)   between 7,800 and 8,000 units   [4]
e)   Demand is estimated to be 7,900 units per day. How often (in percentage terms) is the business likely to satisfy demand?   [2]

---

2) The second application refers to the process of collecting data from a sample and drawing conclusions about the validity of the sample e.g. just because eight out of 10 owners who expressed a preference said their cats preferred Whiskas, does this mean that this is the case for the entire population of cat owners? The problem facing every researcher is the validity and reliability of the data that has been collected. A researcher is unable to collect all possible data, because of time and cost, so a method is needed to enable conclusions to be drawn about sample data in terms of how the findings of research apply to the population.

For example, a market research company has been asked by its client, Mr Clean, to investigate the likely reaction of a change in one of the product's names. The product (known as Cleanalot) has suffered from a recent decline in sales and Mr Clean is proposing to change the name to Cleanezy. The research company asks the straightforward question to a selection of present and potential customers – would you continue to buy (or start buying) this product if the name was changed to Cleanezy? The company interviewed 1,000 people, of whom 645 said 'Yes', so we assume that the remaining 355 said 'No'.

Is such a result sufficient evidence for Mr Clean to change the name?

Historically, Mr Clean has taken the decision based on a target level of the desired response of 60%. Firstly, one needs to know the percentage of the population required by Mr Clean to convince him that a change of name is required i.e. he will decide to change the name only if he can be sure that more than 60% of the population will approve of the change. This forms the basis of the **null hypothesis** which is represented as:

Null hypothesis = 60% of the population approve of the change. If this is proven incorrect by having a result which showed that more than 60% approve, then he will change the name. We therefore need an **alternative hypothesis**: at least 60% of the population approve of the name change.

In the survey, 645 (64.5%) of the sample said yes; this does not mean that 64.5% of the population would say yes. We need to decide whether 645 is 'far enough' above 600 for us to reject the null hypothesis and accept the alternative hypothesis. For this we need to look at the normal distribution of all possible samples of size 1000.

Imagine dividing up the population into samples of 1000 people and asking the same question as above; if the null hypothesis was correct, some of the samples would give a result of more than 600 and some would give less than 600 (in practice some might be exactly 600). So if we took only one sample and 600 responded positively, then we would be no wiser as to the result for the population i.e. there would be a 50% level of certainty.

As the number responding positively increases beyond 600, we become more statistically certain that the percentage of the population agreeing with the change is at least 60%. Indeed we can investigate this with the normal distribution.

We expect 600 to be the mean result (if our hypothesis is correct) and this would be the mean result if we took many samples. The normal distribution has a certain pattern – that is, a certain range of values will lie within a given distance from the mean:

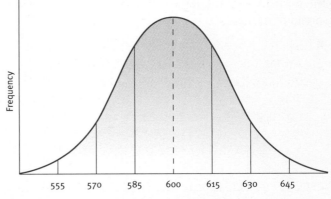

Figure 14.4   Normal distribution of sample results

The numbers refer to the standard deviations i.e. if you begin at the mean and move one standard deviation to the right and left, this will account for 68% of the results from all the samples taken. There is therefore a 68% probability that any individual result will lie between the mean + 1 standard deviation. The same applies to the mean + 2 and 3 standard deviations, with 95% and 99.9% as the equivalent probabilities.

In our example, the mean is calculated by 1000×0.6 i.e. the sample size (n) × the probability in the hypothesis (p), in other words, $n \times p$. To find the standard deviation, the formula square root ($n \times p \times q$) is used = 15.5. So if we were to take many samples, 68% of all results would be between 585 and 615.

From the hypothesis, the mean 2 standard deviations equals 600 +/– 31.

If our hypothesis is correct and if we were to take many samples we would expect about 95% of the results to be between 569 and 631. We therefore have a confidence limit of 631 to 569 where we can be reasonably sure that 95% of the means will fall. To find a sample in this interval would not be 'surprising' and we would accept the null hypothesis. However, the sample taken gives a figure of 645 which is outside this interval and is 'surprising' and we therefore reject the null hypothesis.

Warning!

There are several problems with this analysis that can be expressed under the following assumptions:

- that we are using a level of significance of 96% which is selected by the hand of the statistician. If such a level of significance changes e.g. to be 99.9%, then there is more chance of the null hypothesis being accepted

- that the sample is representative of the population's response

- that the percentage to be tested can change and if it does, this will obviously change the degree of certainty e.g. if Mr Clean said that he required 55% of the population and that he only needed to be 96% certain, a lower number replying positively in the sample would give the same result:

$n \times p = 550$

$\sqrt{(n \times p \times q)} = 16$, so 550 + (2 × 16) = 582 saying yes would fit the criteria set out by Mr Clean.

- that the population is normally distributed about the mean

Scatter diagrams

It is possible to compare two variables with a view to assessing whether there is a connection or correlation

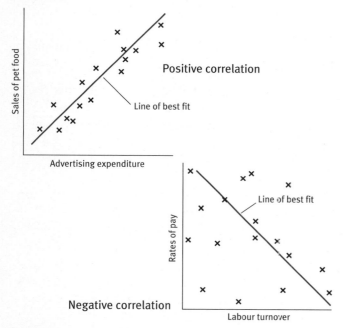

Figure 14.5   Scatter graphs

between them. This is done using a scatter graph, which plots the two variables (on two axes) and then a line of best fit can be superimposed. This establishes whether there is a positive or negative correlation as well as the strength of the correlation (strong or weak). In the first diagram in Figure 14.5, the positive correlation is very strong because the scatter graph is close to the line of best fit. This is explained by the fact that sales of pet food are highly sensitive to the amount of advertising expenditure. However, in the second diagram, the distance between the line and the points is greater, so it has a weaker, negative correlation. This is because although an increase in rates of pay encourages people to stay in a job, there are other factors which affect the level of labour turnover. The correlation, although still negative, is a weak one.

Question 7

A survey was carried out by a market research business on the likelihood of people owning a computer which has access to the Internet over the next three years. The research was commissioned by Comp-It, a company which specialises in designing and setting up websites. Comp-It decided to undergo a major marketing campaign if the results of the survey showed that 40% of the population would own a computer within the next three years. The result of the survey of 500 people was that 225 said they would definitely own one, 250 said they were unsure and the rest were undecided. Comp-It required a 95% level of confidence.

a) State the null hypothesis for Comp-It. [2]

b) Calculate the mean, given the null hypothesis. [2]

c) Calculate the standard deviation, given the null hypothesis. [2]

d) What level of certainty can Comp-It attach to the results? [3]

e) Advise Comp-It whether or not to go ahead with the major marketing campaign. State your assumptions. [6]

Points for Revision

Key Terms

mean	the average of the data
weighted average	placing more importance on certain items within the calculation due to their relative importance
median	the observation which divides the data into two equal parts by finding the mid-point
cumulative distribution	a method of calculating the mean whereby the progressive total is taken of the frequency at each class
grouped data	a method of dealing with more complicated data, which involves placing data into classes
mode	the most common observation
crude mode	the mid-point of the most common observation when the data is grouped
assumed mean	the mid-point of each class, assumed to be the mean when applying the weighting process
frequency	the number of observations in each class
standard deviation	the average distance of each observation from the mean
null hypothesis	a statement which is being tested using the normal distribution
alternative hypothesis	the claim which is opposite to the null hypothesis i.e. either the null or the alternative is correct
confidence limit	a range of data, which the business is reasonably certain can be trusted to be valid

Definitions Question:
With reference to a business you know, explain the meaning of any three of the above (your teacher may wish to help you choose the terms).   [5] per definition

Summary Points:

1 A business may use the mean, median or mode with a view to summarising data, although several assumptions are attached to their usage.

2 The standard deviation demonstrates the range of the data and the extent to which data is clustered around the mean.

3 The normal distribution can be used to assess the confidence of a particular sample as well as for the assessment of levels of output and its quality or the reliability of data such as a questionnaire.

Mini Case Study

Fire-It, a manufacturer of spark plugs, is concerned about the falling level of overall quality which has been evident in recent months. Initially it was seen as a temporary problem which was probably due to teething difficulties with the new machines it bought six months ago. The problem lies with the most important machine which determines the gap on the spark plug. If the gap is too narrow, or too wide, there will not be a spark. The number of returns from mechanics and service centres has been rising, so the business is considering implementing a new quality checking system, using an action and warning limit system. This system will trigger off responses in the employees when the gap in the spark plugs is greater than or less than a certain level. A typical production run is 10,000 spark plugs and the manufacturers insist on a tolerance level of plus or minus 1% of the desired gap. A customer has just ordered 10,000 spark plugs with a gap requirement of 2 mm and the business estimates there will be a standard deviation of 0.01mm. The cost of correcting each spark plug outside the tolerance limit is such that they will all be thrown away at a cost of £2 each. The warning and action limits are set at 1 and 2 standard deviations either side of the mean.

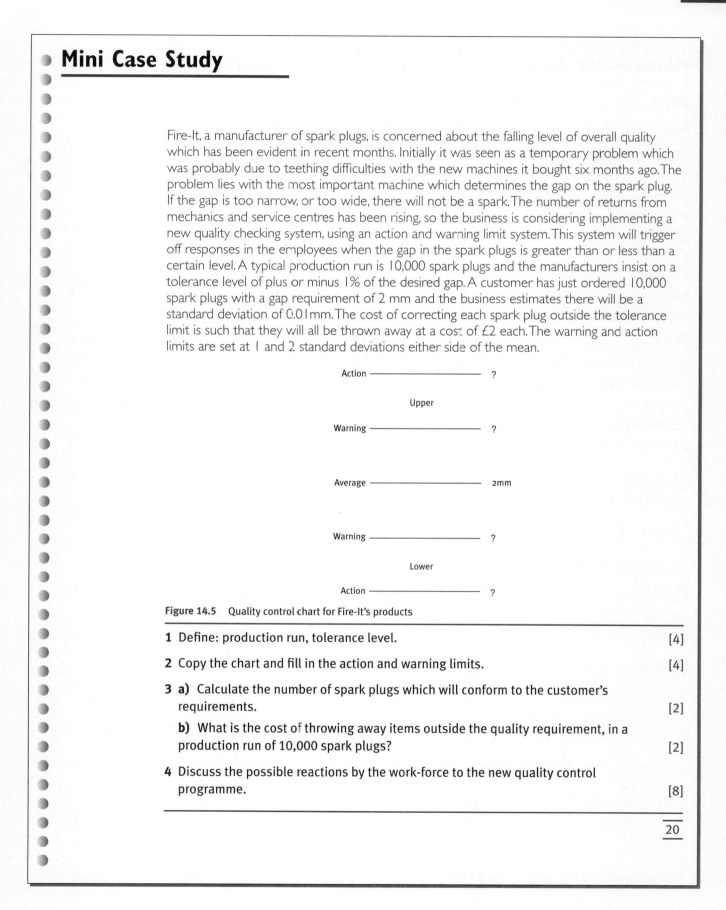

Action ————————	?
Upper	
Warning ————————	?
Average ————————	2mm
Warning ————————	?
Lower	
Action ————————	?

Figure 14.5   Quality control chart for Fire-It's products

1 Define: production run, tolerance level. [4]

2 Copy the chart and fill in the action and warning limits. [4]

3 **a)** Calculate the number of spark plugs which will conform to the customer's requirements. [2]

   b) What is the cost of throwing away items outside the quality requirement, in a production run of 10,000 spark plugs? [2]

4 Discuss the possible reactions by the work-force to the new quality control programme. [8]

$$\overline{20}$$

Maxi Case Study

Rosina Cavazza came to England in the 1980s, having spent four years training in a top Italian restaurant in Rome. She knew there was a buoyant market for take-away food in Britain. Indeed, during 1997, over 1 billion meals were purchased in fast food outlets (Source: *Marketing Pocket Book 1999*, NTC Publications Ltd). She was also aware of the growing demand for food to be supplied to businesses at lunchtime.

The rapid growth in the number of sandwich bars had led to a fax service in areas of prime business location. This was done by the sandwich bars faxing menus for the day, at 9a.m. with any order to be received by 10a.m. Delivery could then be made between 12 and 1p.m. Rosina therefore decided to set up her own small business, selling pasta dishes from a mobile kitchen located on the outskirts of Newcastle city centre. Although the mobile stand had a hatch which allowed customers to purchase goods directly, the majority of her sales were bought as take-aways, sold to businesses in batches of between three and 10. Instead of plates, she used foil dishes, calling the product Pasta in a Pot. The two types of pasta she actually sold were Ravioli and Cannelloni, which she would make fresh in the morning, before the orders came in and if they did not sell during the day, she had to throw them away because of the meat content and lack of freezer space.

Sales over the first 200-day period were:

Table 16

Sales	Number of days
60	19
65	16
70	23
75	32
80	38
85	25
90	19
95	15
100	13

Rosina was delighted with the demand for her products; the most she could make, with the cooking equipment and number of staff, was 110 and she was happy with the level of capacity utilisation during the first 200 days. However, the profit was not as much as it could have been because she had made too many to begin with and had been forced to throw away a lot of pasta, having made enough for 90 helpings per day.

The cost of cooking each portion was:
materials – tin foil with cover, plastic spoon and fork, serviette = £0.15
ingredients – flour, eggs, meat and vegetables for the filling = £1.00
cooking cost = £0.35

She sold each bowl of pasta, which was enough for a filling lunch on its own, for £3.80.

The amount of wastage was such that she decided to purchase enough food materials for 80 meals per day. Although she risked the possibility of not meeting demand for over a third of the time, the gain from not throwing food away would hopefully outweigh the problem of dissatisfied customers who would have to go elsewhere for their lunch orders.

Rosina was also thinking about introducing a new product – lasagne. She had carried out some market research, using a questionnaire sent with each invoice, offering a free meal if the questionnaire was returned fully completed. She now has 150 completed questionnaires which seem to point towards the introduction of lasagne, given that 100 were clearly in favour of the new product.

1 Referring to Table 16:

   a) Calculate, for the first 200 days, a cumulative frequency and hence the estimated median. [4]

   b) Calculate the mean level of sales for the first 200 days. [3]

   c) What is the crude mode for the data? [1]

   d) Draw a barchart from the data in Table 16. [4]

2 How can your answers in question 1 help Rosina with her decision making? [5]

3 **a)** Calculate the percentage of occasions she failed to meet demand when making 90 portions per day. [1]

   b) Calculate the amount she had to throw away. [4]

   c) Calculate the profit over the typical 200-day period if she orders enough food materials for 80 portions per day. [4]

4 Comment on the reliability of the data in Table 16 as a prediction for the future – suggest methods of improving the level of reliability of the data. [5]

5 Discuss the issue of deliberately not making enough to meet demand. [8]

6 Explain how Rosina might use the normal distribution to help her with the level of confidence she places in the results of the market research. [6]

Forecasting and decision trees

Learning objectives

Having read this unit, students will be able to

1 identify the importance of forecasting within a business

2 use a moving average forecasting technique and assess its appropriateness

3 apply probabilities to outcomes by building a decision tree

Context

Being able to predict the future accurately has been an obsession with many people throughout history. The National Lottery programme has made Mystic Meg a household name through her apparently scientifically based predictions!

The Bank of England and other financial institutions spend a great deal of time and money forecasting future values of inflation, exchange rates and share prices. The government, in its annual Budget, collects a vast amount of information in order to predict economic growth and unemployment, among other figures. When predicting the future, it is accepted that a range of possible outcomes might occur, and sometimes probabilities can be attached to different forecasts, in the same way that bets are placed on the prediction that horses will win.

The future has always been impossible to predict and yet this has not deterred businesses from forecasting a variety of different figures in an attempt, primarily, to plan ahead and be prepared for any circumstance. Given that a large amount of data can be stored and recalled easily, through the use of computers, it is not difficult to understand why the business of forecasting has become such a huge industry in recent years.

Forecasting

Importance of forecasting

Forecasting gives a business the opportunity to plan for the future as well as planning for various changes. If, for example, it is likely that the market for its products will grow at 2% per annum over the next few years, it would be sensible for a business to plan for the same level of growth. If it thinks it can gain market share from its competitors, then the prospect for growth is greater.

A business is likely to begin with a forecast of sales volume and sales revenue because this leads to such issues as labour costs, material costs, cash flow, advertising costs and the future requirement of new machinery. Sales forecasting is therefore likely to be the most important part of the forecast, although a business may try to forecast such issues as

- competitors' action
- government decisions on running the economy
- changing consumer trends and fashions

Methods of forecasting

Trying to predict the future is difficult and there are two methods used to achieve this:

- **Qualitative** – based on opinion
- **Quantitative** – based on numerical evidence

Qualitative forecasting

There are two types of qualitative methods:

a)   **consumer panels**

This is a group of individuals which meets regularly to discuss possible changes. Normally a business will have a specific objective in mind such as predicting changes in clothes styles for 16–24-year-olds. This will mean that the panel will consist of the relevant age group. It can also mean that the business produces some ideas of style and fashion for the panel members to react to, or that they are provided with an open agenda and are asked to predict based solely on their own opinions. Either way, the advantage of this method is that the group can 'bounce' ideas off each other, helping to generate discussion.

b)   **Delphi technique**

This takes the same form of open-ended prediction as a consumer panel discussion, although the difference is that there is no group discussion, rather a one-to-one between the company and the individual. The idea behind this technique is that it removes the influence of group or peer pressure (*see Unit 53 People in groups*) and arguably allows more individual ideas to come through.

Qualitative forecasting is more appropriate when the prediction and therefore the likely outcome is less certain and open to opinion. Considering your answers to question 1, the prediction for the next five days will have involved a straightforward examination of your timetable. The prediction for five years may be something you are discussing with your Head of Year or Tutor. Businesses that use qualitative forecasting do so to discover opinions on consumer reaction; the more open-ended debate is therefore useful in helping the company with its prediction over time periods well into the future. This is because predicting customers' behaviour is much more difficult in the long term, compared with the short-term numerical predictions of sales volume.

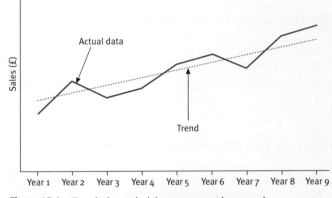

Figure 15.1   Trend: the underlying movement is upwards

Quantitative forecasting

Whilst there are several methods of forecasting data, this unit will deal with only one, which involves time series – data which covers a set period. It may be presented daily, weekly, monthly, quarterly or annually depending on what is being measured and how frequently the data is collected and collated by a particular business e.g. a retailer will compare weekly sales from one year to the next, whereas a construction company will consider annual sales levels.

Moving averages

All data can be divided into four distinct components:

■ **Trend** – this is the underlying movement of the data. There could be particular points during a year when sales are lower than previous time periods, but this could be due to the time of year. The underlying movement is therefore seen as the general movement in data (*see Figure 15.1*).

Although sales in years 3 and 7 fell compared with the year before, the 'underlying movement' (dotted line) was upwards.

■ **Cyclical variation** – this applies only to annual data. With data that stretches over several years, there may come a time when the sales of one year are lower than sales in the next, or vice versa. Cyclical variation can occur for the following reasons:

a) the trade cycle, which refers to the fluctuation in economic activity over a period of years. Companies whose product is income-elastic (*see Unit 18*) tend to pay close attention to the pattern of the trade cycle.
b) the product life cycle (*see Unit 16 Product*), which may vary from product to product – if the product with a life cycle of eight years is in decline, sales will be lower than in other years.
c) the entry of new competitors into the market-place – this can suddenly make sales fall away, or, alternatively, if a competitor leaves a market or region, sales may increase significantly.

■ **Seasonal variation** – this is based on the same principle as cyclical variation, but refers to changes in sales data within a particular year. For example, ice-cream vans will do more trade during the warmer summer and spring months than in the winter months.

■ **Random variation** – this is the part of the time series which is impossible to predict, by definition of the word random. A fire may cause a factory to need rebuilding. Faulty raw materials or even industrial sabotage may mean that an entire product range has to be recalled. Random fluctuations will not be considered in the analysis which follows.

The following data relates to sales revenue for a business selling hi-fi systems. The business wishes to predict possible sales figures for 2001. The process of forecasting divides itself up into several distinct stages, which have to be followed in strict order. For the following calculations it is assumed that random fluctuations cannot be predicted and (as stated above) that cyclical variation *or* seasonal variation will be calculated, *not both*. The data below is therefore annual data and will be forecast using a cyclical variation:

Actual data = trend + cyclical variation

Forecast data = forecast trend + forecast cyclical variation

Step 1: Identify the cycle of data

In the case below, there is a peak every fifth year (1989, 1994 and 1999) and a trough every fifth year (1992 and 1997).

Table 1   Sales for a hi-fi retailer

Column 1 Year	Column 2 Actual sales ($m)
1988	67
1989	70
1990	64
1991	61
1992	59
1993	66
1994	73
1995	69
1996	64
1997	63
1998	69
1999	75
2000	72

This means a five-period **moving average** will be used. If the data had a peak or trough every three years, then a three-period moving average would be used.

Step 2a: Calculate the (five-period) moving totals

This is done by adding the first five points of data, and writing the total in the fifth row down opposite 1992 – see Table 2.

The first five-point moving total is
67 + 70 + 64 + 61 + 59 = 321

The process of moving averages means that averages are taken from the data, thereby removing the effect of each cyclical variation. The next calculation involves dropping the figure for 1988 ($67 million) and picking up the next figure for 1993 ($66 million) then adding the five together to get 70 + 64 + 61 + 59 + 66 = 320.

This process is a bit like gauging the performance of a worker over a period of time e.g. a week and not just first thing on Monday morning. It gives a more realistic picture by smoothing out the peaks and troughs (cyclical variation).

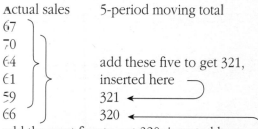

This process repeats itself until the last figure in the time series for 2000 is included. The result is:

Table 2

Column 1 Year	Column 2 Actual sales	Column 3 5-point moving total
1988	67	
1989	70	
1990	64	
1991	61	
1992	59	321
1993	66	320
1994	73	323
1995	69	328
1996	64	331
1997	63	335
1998	69	338
1999	75	340
2000	72	343

Step 2b: Calculate the five-period moving averages by dividing each five-period moving total by 5

This is inserted in the *third* row for the data, for the

following reason. The first five-point moving average is calculated based on the first five points of data; plotting an average for this data must therefore go into the middle of the range of five points.

See Figure 15.2 – a five-point moving average plots at the third point, in this case 1990. The next average plots in the following year.

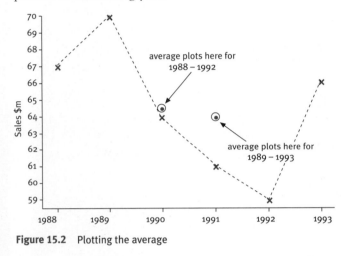

Figure 15.2   Plotting the average

The result for all the averages looks like this:

Table 3

Column 1 Year	Column 2 Actual sales	Column 3 5-point moving total	Column 4 5-point moving average
1988	67		
1989	70		
1990	64		64.2
1991	61		64
1992	59	321	64.6
1993	66	320	65.6
1994	73	323	66.2
1995	69	328	67
1996	64	331	67.6
1997	63	335	68
1998	69	338	68.6
1999	75	340	
2000	72	343	

Step 3: Calculate the cyclical variation

The reason for extracting the effect of the trend (underlying movement of data) is so that the cyclical variation can be established.

Actual = Trend + Cyclical variation

therefore

Actual – Trend = Cyclical variation

This can be calculated only for those point times where there is data for *both* actual and cyclical data.

Table 4

Column 1 Year	Column 2 Actual sales	Column 3 5-point moving total	Column 4 5-point moving average	Column 5 Cyclical variation
1988	67			
1989	70			
1990	64		64.2	– 0.2
1991	61		64	– 3
1992	59	321	64.6	– 5.6
1993	66	320	65.6	0.4
1994	73	323	66.2	6.8
1995	69	328	67	2
1996	64	331	67.6	– 3.6
1997	63	335	68	– 5
1998	69	338	68.6	0.4
1999	75	340		
2000	72	343		

It is important to note the signs as to whether the cyclical variation should be negative or positive. A negative answer means that the actual data is less than the trend i.e. during that time period, the actual data was less than the underlying movement of the data, which means a slump in sales due to the point in the cycle.

See Figure 15.3 – this is a graph showing the difference between actual sales and trend, thereby highlighting the cyclical variation.

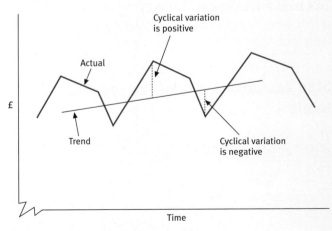

Figure 15.3   Positive and negative variation

Step 4: Calculate the average cyclical variation

This involves assigning a particular year to a particular point in the cycle, beginning with the first year of the actual data.

Table 5

Column 1 Year	Column 2 Actual sales	Column 3 5-point moving total	Column 4 5-point moving average	Column 5 Cyclical variation	Column 6 Point in cycle
1988	67				1
1989	70				2
1990	64		64.2	– 0.2	3
1991	61		64	– 3	4
1992	59	321	64.6	– 5.6	5
1993	66	320	65.6	0.4	1
1994	73	323	66.2	6.8	2
1995	69	328	67	2	3
1996	64	331	67.6	– 3.6	4
1997	63	335	68	– 5	5
1998	69	338	68.6	0.4	1
1999	75	340			2
2000	72	343			3
2001?					4

The prediction will be for 2001, which appears as point number 4 in the cycle. So the cyclical variations corresponding to point number 4 are now collected together and an average is found.

– 3 + (– 3.6) ÷ 2 = – 3.3. This is the average cyclical variation for point 4 in the cycle.

Step 5: Forecast the trend

There are two ways of doing this. The first is to draw the graph of the trend and predict, or extrapolate the line (*see Figure 15.4*).

The **extrapolation** or forecast is represented by the dotted line. Notice there are two attempts to forecast. The top line is the optimistic forecast and the bottom line is the pessimistic forecast. While never claiming to be accurate, this process represents the fact that there may be a range of possible outcomes.

The second method is to assume that the forecast of the trend will be based on the average rate of change for the entire trend i.e. by drawing a straight line which

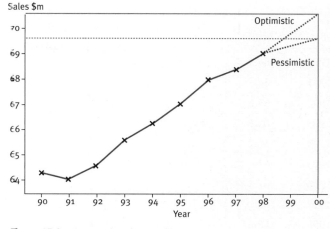

Figure 15.4 Forecasting the trend

joins the first and the last points in the trend and then continuing the line forward (*see Figure 15.5*).

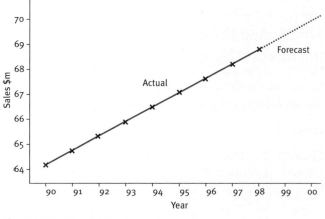

Figure 15.5 Straight-line forecast

The alternative to drawing the line is to perform a straightforward calculation, known as the 'jumps' method. Between 1990 and 1998, there are nine pieces of data and therefore eight 'jumps' between each piece of data. This means that on average, the data moves at a rate of

68.6 – 64.2 = 4.4 ÷ 8 = 0.55 per annual jump.

From 1998 to the year 2001, there are three more jumps, so the increase from the 1998 figure will be

3 × 0.55 = 1.65

Adding this on to the 1998 figure gives 68.6 + 1.65 = 70.25, which can then be used as the forecast trend. Because this technique assumes the rate of change in the past will be exactly the same in the future, there is no opportunity to calculate an optimistic and pessimistic forecast (*see Table 6*).

Table 6

Year	Actual
1990	64.2
1991	64
1992	64.6
1993	65.6
1994	66.2
1995	67
1996	67.6
1997	68
1998	68.6
1999	68.6 + 0.55 = 69.15
2000	69.15 + 0.55 = 69.7
2001	69.7 + 0.55 = 70.25

68.6 – 64. 2 = 4.4
There are eight jumps

Therefore $\frac{4.4}{8}$ = 0.55 per jump

Step 6: Add the cyclical variation to find the forecast figure

So far, the trend has been forecast. Referring back to the original time series:

Actual = Trend + Cyclical variation

The trend figure has been forecast using either of the methods described above to produce a range of forecasts between 69.7 million and 70.3 million. The final forecast is arrived at by adding the cyclical variation forecast, which is otherwise the average cyclical variation (ACV). The ACV forecast is therefore – 3.3, so the final range of forecast figures is:

optimistic 69.7 – 3.3 = $66.4 million
pessimistic 70.3 – 3.3 = $67 million.

A summary of the process is provided in Table 7.

Table 7

Step 1	identify the trend
Step 2a	calculate the moving total
Step 2b	calculate the moving average
Step 3	calculate the cyclical/seasonal variation
Step 4	calculate the average cyclical/seasonal variation
Step 5	forecast the trend using either the graphical method or the jumps method
Step 6	add the seasonal variation/cyclical variation to the forecast trend

Question 3

Sales (in 000 units) of a computer printer, originally launched in 1986.

Table 8

1986	257
1987	256
1988	280
1989	276
1990	273
1991	295
1992	293
1993	293
1994	309
1995	306
1996	304
1997	318
1998	312
1999	314

a) By using the above data, identify the trend.   [1]

b) Calculate the trend for as many years as possible.   [5]

c) Calculate the average cyclical variation for each point in the data.   [6]

d) Using either the graphical method or the 'jumps' approach, forecast the volume of sales for 2000, 2001 and 2002.   [6]

e) Outline three possible assumptions on which your forecasts are based.   [6]

Centring

The set of data overleaf was recorded by an umbrella manufacturer.

The same technique summarised above in Table 7 can be applied except when approaching the calculation of the moving average. The data has peaks and troughs every fourth quarter (in addition to the fact that the time periods used are quarters), meaning a four-point

Table 9

Year	Quarter	Actual sales (£000)
1997	1	65
	2	62
	3	41
	4	68
1998	1	67
	2	61
	3	44
	4	73
1999	1	73
	2	69
	3	45
	4	78
2000	1	75

moving average should be used. This, however, produces a curious result. The result of the first four-point moving average will not plot on a point which corresponds with actual data. Remember that the reason behind calculating the trend was so that the seasonal variation could be calculated, so the trend data must correspond with a piece of actual data (*see Figure 15.6*).

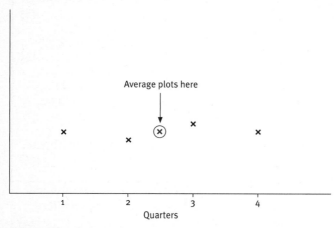

Figure 15.6   Plotting in the middle

The solution is to take a second four-point average and then take an average of the two averages! This technique applies to all moving average calculations where the number of points used is an *even* number (*see Figure 15.7*).

Figure 15.7 shows that by calculating the eight-point moving average, the first answer will correspond with the third piece of data, thereby allowing a seasonal

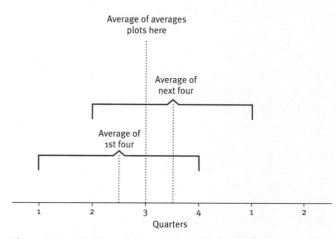

Figure 15.7   The four-point 'centred' moving average

variation to be calculated. This adds a slight complication to the number-crunching by adding an extra stage into the process. In Table 7, Step 2a divides into 2ai and 2aii.

2ai involves calculating the four-point moving total, 2aii involves the eight-point moving total.

Table 10

Year	Quarter	Actual sales (£000)	Four-point moving total
1997	1	65	
	2	62	
	3	41	
	4	68	236
1998	1	67	238
	2	61	237
	3	44	240
	4	73	245
1999	1	73	251
	2	69	259
	3	45	260
	4	78	265
2000	1	75	267

Add two consecutive four-point totals together in order to arrive at an eight-point moving total (*see Table 11*). This sum creates the total for the eight points used in the **centring** process.

Data point:	1997, qtr	1	2	3	4	
	1997, qtr		2	3	4	1998, qtr 1

There are eight points in the data which are added together to create the eight-point total.

Table 11

Year	Quarter	Actual sales (£000)	Four-point moving total	Eight-point moving total
1997	1	65		
	2	62		
	3	41		
	4	68	236	
1998	1	67	238	474
	2	61	237	475
	3	44	240	477
	4	73	245	485
1999	1	73	251	496
	2	69	259	510
	3	45	260	519
	4	78	265	525
2000	1	75	267	532

This then leads to the eight-point moving average being calculated, otherwise known as the four-point, centred moving average.

Table 12

Year	Quarter	Actual sales (£000)	Four-point moving total	Eight-point moving total	Eight-point moving average
1997	1	65			
	2	62			
	3	41			59.25
	4	68	236		59.375
1998	1	67	238	474	59.625
	2	61	237	475	60.625
	3	44	240	477	62
	4	73	245	485	63.75
1999	1	73	251	496	64.875
	2	69	259	510	65.625
	3	45	260	519	66.5
	4	78	265	525	
2000	1	75	267	532	

This data can then be manipulated in exactly the same way according to the step-by-step approach summarised in Table 7. The slightly easier part is that this now involves seasonal variations which can be identified according to quarters 1, 2, 3 and 4 and average seasonal variations can also then be calculated.

Question 4

a) Using Table 12 and the step-by-step summary in Table 7, calculate the average seasonal variation for quarters 2, 3 and 4.   [6]

b) Forecast the trend for quarters 2, 3 and 4 for 2000.   [5]

c) Forecast the actual data for 2000, quarters 2, 3 and 4.   [4]

Question 5

The following sales revenue data refers to a business which operates an amusement arcade and two restaurants in a seaside town.

Table 13

Year	Quarter	Value
1986	1	30
	2	65
	3	64
	4	35
1997	1	32
	2	70
	3	67
	4	36
1998	1	35
	2	72
	3	72
	4	37
1999	1	38
	2	78
	3	74
	4	40
2000	1	39

a) Using one of the forecasting techniques outlined above, calculate the forecast sales revenue for 2000, quarters 2 and 3.   [14]

b) Comment on the usefulness of this figure to the business.   [6]

Limitations and assumptions

■ Forecasting assumes that past information leads directly to the future. Although past information can be useful in presenting a guide to the future, because of the nature of forecasting, there can never be any guarantee. Next time you see or hear an advert for a financial product, such as a savings plan, there will always be a warning that the value of the investment can rise or fall, depending on the future!

■ The technique takes no account of changes which are outside the control of the company, such as competitive pressure, government influence in running the economy or perhaps changes in the law affecting the business and the product. All of these (and many others) can affect future predictions.

■ It also takes no account of a possible change in company objectives; perhaps a business is planning a big sales drive to increase sales volume, which would not be accounted for in the forecast. The forecast would give a starting point, however, to base the new prediction upon, if the sales push was expected to increase sales by e.g. 10%.

■ Sometimes it is the most recent information which is regarded as being the most significant. Think about the question concerning where you might be in five hours. Your answer will be based on where you are now, not where you were five hours ago! Placing greater emphasis on the more recent information is covered in a technique known as exponential smoothing, which applies a 'weight' to the more recent figures, reducing the weight the further into the past the figures relate to.

Decision trees

Decision trees are another method of aiding the decision making process. The Business Studies course you are studying is based on the decisions that are taken both in the long and the short term. With any decision, there is a possible monetary outcome or result. Due to the fact that the outcome of any decision is normally not guaranteed, there is a chance it will not happen. It is therefore possible to combine the fact that there is both a pay-off and a probability of occurrence;

in this case decision trees can be employed in order to combine the two. So there are two factors to consider for any business decision, the likely monetary 'reward' and the probability of a particular outcome occurring.

Horse racing analogy

Imagine you are considering placing a bet on three horses in the Grand National, each with the following odds:

QuickFire (a pedigree race horse with a high record of success) 5–1
Runner-Up (a horse which has always had potential, but has never made it on the day) 10–1
BadBet (a donkey from Blackpool beach ridden by a 14-stone man) 100–1

You are debating whether to put £10 on QuickFire, Runner-Up or BadBet.

Let us examine what would happen if the bet was on QuickFire. Assuming the odds were accurate, this horse has a 20% chance of winning (1 in 5). This means that if the race was run 100 times with the same horses and the same odds and the same bet, it would win on 20 occasions (i.e. 20% of the time), leading to total winnings of

$$£10 \times 5 = £50 \text{ per race}$$
$$\times 20 \text{ races} = £1000.$$

However, it would lose on 80 occasions, leading to a total loss of $80 \times £10$ (the original bet placed on the horse) = £800.

Total winnings – total losses

$$= £1000 - £800 = £200$$

Over 100 races, this is an average of £2 per race. This is the net gain of betting on this horse and is known as the '**expected value**'. It represents the average amount you would win if the bet was placed 'many' times on the same horse. This is a hypothetical scenario, but one upon which betting is based.

If the same calculation were used for a bet of £10 placed on Runner-Up and the race was run 100 times, you would win on 10 occasions (based on odds of 10–1).

Each time you would win £10 x 10 = £100, so the total winning sum would be

$$£100 \times 10 = £1000.$$

On the other hand you would lose on 90 occasions, each time losing the £10 bet:

90 × £10 = £900.

Net gain = £1000 – £900 = £100, over 100 races = £1.00 per race.

Placing £10 on BadBet would end up with a net gain of:

Wins: 1 × £1000 = £1000
Losses: 99 × £10 = £990

Net gain $= \dfrac{£10}{100} = £0.10$ per race.

The expected values for each horse are:

QuickFire	Runner-Up	BadBet
£2	£1	£0.10

A shorter method of this calculation is the **actual value** (the amount you would end up winning or losing) adjusted by the probability of winning or losing:

Table 14

WINNING

Horse	Probability	Winnings	probability of win × winnings
QuickFire	0.2	£50	£10
Runner-Up	0.1	£100	£10
BadBet	0.01	£1000	£10

Table 15

LOSING

Horse	Probability	Actual loss	probability of loss × loss
QuickFire	0.8	£10	£8
Runner-Up	0.9	£10	£9
BadBet	0.99	£10	£9.90

Taking each horse in turn, subtract the loss from the winnings

QuickFire	£10 – £8	= £2	These are the
Runner-Up	£10 – £9	= £1	expected values of
BadBet	£10 – £9.90	= £0.10	each horse.

Now we can represent this diagrammatically. A square represents a decision which is to be made, here, which horse to choose. The circle (or node) represents the risk or uncertainty and has a probability of occurrence of a decision and therefore requires a calculation.

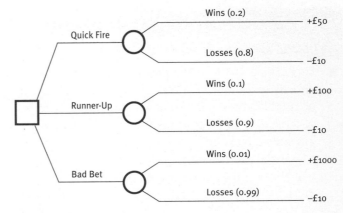

Figure 15.8   Place your bets!

Node 1 : (£50 × 0.2) + (– £10 × 0.8) = £2
Node 2 : (£100 × 0.1) + (– £10 × 0.9) = £1
Node 3 : (£1000 × 0.01) + (– £10 × 0.99) = £0.10

The decision is the one which gives us the largest net gain i.e. QuickFire. Such a decision is taken not on the actual gain or loss, but on the gain or loss adjusted by the risk or probability of this happening.

Question 6

A friend has given you a sum of money for your 18th birthday which you want to invest in shares. A local independent financial adviser suggests that you ought to consider three companies:

Techy-Co – a hi tech manufacturer
Risky-Co – a new company, selling a brand new product which is predicted to be all the rage over the next two or three years
Large-Co – a multinational conglomerate which sells to a wide range of industries

Table 16

	Chance of success	Chance of failure
Techy-Co	0.5	0.5
Risky-Co	0.3	0.7
Large-Co	0.8	0.2

	Pay-off if success	Pay-off if failure
Techy-Co	£2,000	£800
Risky-Co	£3,000	£500
Large-Co	£1,200	£900

Calculate the expected value for each of the three companies and decide on the best investment.   [6]

The business application for decision trees

A business is deciding whether or not to launch a new product. It could do some market research, costing £12,000, which would mean the chance of a successful launch would be estimated at 70%. Without market research the chance of a successful launch would be only 50%. A successful launch would earn profit of £60,000 for the business, but if it failed, only £20,000 would be earned. This information is summarised in Table 17:

Table 17

	forecast pay-off with market research		without market research
Successful launch	£60000	70%	50%
Failed launch	£20000	30%	50%

The first task is to draw a diagram (*see Figure 15.9*).

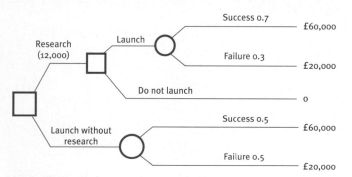

Figure 15.9   Diagram of expected values

The expected values can now be calculated:

For Node 1 (60,000 × 0.7) + (20,000 × 0.3) = £48,000
For Node 2 (60,000 × 0.5) + (20,000 × 0.5) = £40,000

The decision at square 1 is whether to launch or not. The expected value of the launch (= £48,000) is compared with that of not launching (= 0, even before the cost of the market research has been taken off).

However, to take the decision at square 2, the cost of the research is subtracted from £48,000, to give £36,000. This figure is then compared with the expected value of launching without the research = £40,000 which is clearly better, so the final decision is to launch without the research.

Mill-It is deciding how it can achieve growth. It will invest in new machinery only if there is economic growth of 2% (the probability of this occurring is 70%). If the economy grows at less than 2%, the business will not make any investment and profit will be £6m. With new investment, annual profit has a 60% chance of increasing by £30m, a 40% chance of increasing by £20m, although without the investment, the profit will increase by only £12m. The cost of financing the investment will be £10m per year. Developing the domestic market is more straightforward with an advertising campaign costing £40m. The chance of success and subsequent profits are in the table below:

Table 18

Success of advertising	High	Medium	Low
Probability	0.4	0.3	0.3
Profit	£60m	£45m	£20m

a) Copy out the following decision tree and label it using the above information. [6]

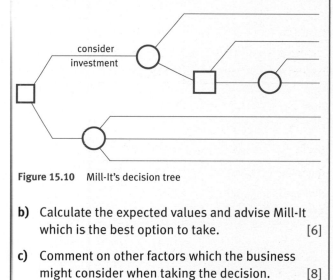

Figure 15.10   Mill-It's decision tree

b) Calculate the expected values and advise Mill-It which is the best option to take. [6]

c) Comment on other factors which the business might consider when taking the decision. [8]

Problems of using decision trees

- It is a purely quantitative technique which is designed only to allow for probability and pay-off (estimated revenue) i.e. there is no allowance for external issues which may be relevant to the decision being made

- The probabilities are extremely difficult to predict accurately, given their nature

- The forecast pay-offs are assumed to be correct, which may not be the case in reality. If both probability and forecast pay-offs are incorrect then the decision becomes as good as the information which is used

- There is no in-between value for the probability i.e. the forecast pay-off can be one of three options – successful, moderate, poor. All the probabilities must add up to one, but in reality there is a wider range of answers, each with an associated probability.

Given these problems and assumptions, what is the point of using the decision trees in the first place?

- They provide a starting point in terms of allocating probabilities and pay-offs to different decisions
- They allow all potential decisions to be viewed simultaneously
- They can therefore act as an aid to decision making and must be used in conjunction with other factors which affect the decision.

Points for Revision

Key Terms

quantitative forecasting	using a numerical technique to produce an objective figure to use for sales or cost predictions
qualitative forecasting	whereby opinions are sought and subjective ideas are suggested
panel consensus	where a group of people meet to discuss new ideas and products
Delphi technique	where individuals in a group are asked their opinion, but the group never meets
extrapolation	forecasting on a graph, by extending the trend line
random variation	change in the data due to events which cannot be predicted
trend	the underlying movement in the data
cyclical variation	the change in the data due to the point in the trade cycle
seasonal variation	the change in the data due to the change in the time of year
moving average	the process of building the calculation for the trend, in order to remove the cyclical or seasonal variation
centring	used when the trend line will not correspond to a time period when data is collected. It occurs if the cyclical movement of data occurs on an even number of points e.g. four-point, eight-point, six-point etc.
actual value	the forecast return from a particular decision
expected value	the actual value multiplied by the probability

Definitions Question:

With reference to a business you know, explain the meaning of any three of the above terms (your teacher may wish to help you choose). [5] per definition

Summary Points:

1. The moving average technique can be used to predict future values of any time series.

2. Decision trees are a method of combining probabilities with possible outcomes with a view to aiding the decision making process.

3. Both techniques do not take into account any qualitative information – there will always be a wide range of non-numerical issues which the business must consider before taking the decision based on a numerical analysis.

Mini Case Study

Forecasting

Stephen Snail was preparing for his annual report to the shareholders of the distribution company he ran, known as Load Ltd. Although it was still a relatively small business compared with Eddie Stobart and other haulage companies, he felt that there was potential in the market-place for a regional transport company which delivered to retailers and wholesalers. Being located in Stoke-on-Trent, the business transported pottery initially using two small vans. Quickly the number of vans grew until there were six Luton vans and a 3-tonne lorry. He was trying to forecast sales, given the recent growth in the market, and he knew that if he could persuade the shareholders that capacity would be reached very soon and that new vans were needed, then the business would be in a strong position to be able to supply transport to the market. Demand depended entirely on the pottery market, which was not certain to grow, but he felt that with the new computer business that had set up nearby he could use the spare capacity in the lorries to transport for them. Volume figures over the past 11 years (the entire life of the business) were as follows:

Table 19

Sales volume for Load Ltd

1989	21000 units
1990	24000 units
1991	29000 units
1992	34000 units
1993	31000 units
1994	32000 units
1995	37000 units
1996	41000 units
1997	45000 units
1998	43000 units
1999	44000 units
2000	48000 units

Figure 15.11   Sales volume for Load Ltd

1 Using a five-point moving average, predict sales levels for 2001 and 2002.   [6]

2 As a shareholder, explain to Stephen what other pieces of information you would wish to consider before giving him permission to invest in new vehicles.   [7]

3 What are the advantages and disadvantages to Load Ltd of being significantly smaller than Eddie Stobart and other haulage companies?   [7]

20

Mini Case Study

Decision trees

Shade-It Ltd is a British company which makes lights and lampshade equipment. Recently sales have been falling in the domestic and European markets as manufacturers from the Far East have adopted a policy of market penetration with a view to taking market share away from the British manufacturer. They have done this successfully, therefore Shade-It is now considering the best way to react in an effort to achieve its new objective of penetrating the market in Pacific Rim countries, such as Malaysia and Singapore. Three options have been put forward:

1   Buy a business in Singapore which is in exactly the same industry as Shade-It.

2   Establish a joint venture with another company in south-east Asia with a view to using its present distribution channels and marketing contacts.

3   Employ an agent who will act on behalf of Shade-It in order to sell products in the south-east Asia region.

The forecast pay-offs and probabilities of each option are as follows:

Table 20

	Agent	Buy company	Joint venture
Probability of success	0.8	0.75	0.65
Probability of failure	0.2	0.25	0.35
Forecast pay-off with success	400000	600000	400000
Forecast pay-off with failure	− 60000	− 140000	50000

1 Draw the decision trees for the above problem and label it showing probabilities and forecast pay-offs clearly.   [6]

2 Calculate the expected value for each option and advise the business as to the best option.   [6]

3 Discuss other factors which the business might consider when taking the decision.   [8]

20

Maxi Case Study

Stellar-Q is a large, multinational business which manufactures a variety of clothes which are then sold to retailers and wholesalers around the world. The business mass-produces millions of items each year, which are distributed to over 120 countries. The bulk of the revenue is earned during the winter months because of the reputation for quality winter clothes which the business has developed over many years of careful marketing. The business has grown through a series of acquisitions and owns several production plants, all of which are located in the European Union.

One of its plants, based in Scotland, has been experiencing an increase in wage costs over the past four years; details are contained in Table 21:

Table 21

		Labour costs £m	Trend £m
1996	1	2.1	
	2	2.1	
	3	2.2	2.325
	4	2.8	2.3875
1997	1	2.3	2.45
	2	2.4	2.5125
	3	2.4	2.575
	4	3.1	2.6125
1998	1	2.5	2.65
	2	2.5	2.7125
	3	2.6	2.7875
	4	3.4	2.875
1999	1	2.8	2.9625
	2	2.9	3.0375
	3	2.9	3.1125
	4	3.7	3.1875
2000	1	3.1	
	2	3.2	

In 1996, sales which were generated by the Scottish business were £60 million and by 1999, this had increased to £70 million. The business normally takes on extra labour during the third quarter as it gears itself up for the intensive winter selling period which starts in October and lasts until late February. Its main cloth supplier has just announced that it is closing down that side of the business in order to develop its clothing accessories side, which means Stellar-Q must find another supplier quickly, otherwise it may not be able to meet its sales target for the coming winter without subcontracting. John Nettle, the purchasing director, has identified two suppliers it could use.

Supplier 1 – a large European manufacturer that has offered to supply the required quantity, although it has quoted the price in euros, for an initial delivery, costing Stellar-Q 220,000 euros. The business is based in Spain and is able to take advantage of lower labour costs, although the distance to travel from Spain to Scotland may mean the transport costs either affect the final costs for Stellar-Q or reduce profit for the supplier.

The recent fluctuation in the euro has led John Nettle to produce a range of possible currency exchange values, with associated probability, based on previous observation.

Exchange rate   Probability
1 euro = £0.66   0.22
1 euro = £0.70   0.6
1 euro = £0.62   0.18

Supplier 2 – located less than 200 miles away, this is a new business which has expanded rapidly and is seeking an order to fulfil its capacity. The bid is for £152,000 which John thinks is a competitive offer. The firm does not have a good reputation for prompt delivery, and has tended to achieve growth through highly competitive prices rather than through high standards of customer service. John thinks he will be able to convince the managing director of the importance of a reliable supplier and will be looking for a long-term commitment from the supplier that wins the contract.

1 Define: acquisitions, sales target.   [4]

2 What evidence is there in the case study to suggest that the business is justified in its concern about labour costs?   [4]

3 a) Referring to Table 21, show how the trend figure for 1997 quarter 1 has been calculated.   [4]

   b) Explain briefly why the data in this time series has to be centred.   [3]

   c) Using the data provided in Table 21, forecast labour costs for quarters 3 and 4 for 2000.   [8]

4 a) Calculate the various forecast pay-offs, in pounds sterling, for supplier 1.   [3]

   b) Represent this problem on a decision tree, showing forecast pay-offs and probabilities clearly.   [4]

   c) Calculate the expected values and advise Stellar-Q which supplier to use.   [4]

   d) Discuss the other factors which the business should consider before making a final decision.   [8]

5 The managing director of Stellar-Q has been quoted as saying: 'I find all this forecasting and probability analysis a waste of time; business is about going on gut instinct – applying a technique to a real-life business decision means there is no opportunity for sensible, thoughtful judgement.'

   To what extent do you think that decision trees are of limited value in the decision making process?   [8]

                                                                                                          50

Product

Learning objectives

Having read this unit, students will be able to

1 identify the significance of the product in the marketing mix

2 understand how the product life cycle and the Boston matrix can help a business with its decisions on the product portfolio

3 appreciate the importance of new product development for long-term business success

Context

What does the name Hoover mean to you? Your initial reaction may well be that a Hoover (the product) is a Hoover (the brand)! Such an obvious statement is the result of decades of successful marketing, so that the product and the brand mean the same thing. Consider other famous names such as Levis, Swatch, Rolls-Royce, McDonald's. What is brought to mind when these names are mentioned ought to be the product with which each one is associated. In terms of marketing, it is the product that is designed to meet consumer needs; the other parts of the marketing mix are used to make the product attractive and to ensure it is positioned in the market correctly. Products also go through a life cycle which means that at times, sales might grow slowly, or the product may not be well known.

What is the definition of a product?

A product is anything that fulfils a customer's need(s). A product can either be a good (which is tangible, such as a pen) or a service which is provided (hiring a car, having a haircut). A product also usually has two other aspects to it: the first is that it has some form of aesthetic value attached to it, in that it is pleasing to the eye; the second is that it can be produced at a cost which is (hopefully) less than the price it can be sold for (*see Unit 26 Value analysis*).

Successful products

Depending on the industry, for every successful product that becomes a household name, there are literally tens of thousands of failures. Those that become household items are so commonplace and accepted by society that it is hard to imagine what life was like before they were invented.

The following are four inventions from the 20th century.

- **Vacuum cleaner (1902)** – the inventor, Hubert Booth, used to travel the streets with his invention mounted on a cart. When he found a customer, he would poke his hose through a window, and the dust was sucked out into the machine on the cart. Edward VII was so impressed with it, that he ordered one for Buckingham Palace and one for Windsor Castle.

- **Sliced bread (1928)** – from this came the famous phrase the 'best thing since sliced bread', highlighting the importance of the invention. Within five years of its invention, 80% of bread sales were ready sliced.

- **Suntan lotion (1936)** – this began when Coco Chanel allowed the sun to darken her skin whilst on holiday in France. It caused a sensation at the time, but it took a further 11 years before L'Oréal brought out the first mass-market sun lotion known as Ambre Solaire.

- **Shopping trolley (1937)** – this was invented by a manager of the Oklahoma Humpty Dumpty supermarket. What seems obvious to us now was a stroke of genius in 1937; he realised that having extra large shopping baskets on wheels would boost his trade. In fact, it doubled.

Source: Adapted from *The Week 1999*

How can a business protect a new product from larger competitors?

Patents are used to protect new products from being copied. A business might wish to apply for a **patent** in the following circumstances:

- if it is a small business, which is unable to achieve the economies of scale characteristic of larger companies. A patent will protect the business for a certain period of time, so as to allow the business the opportunity to develop the product further and gain initial consumer acceptance and loyalty

- if the business has spent a significant amount of money on its development. The term 'significant' means different amounts to different companies. Ford, for example, spent £6 billion on the Mondeo – the largest amount of money spent on one product in corporate history

Patent – this is applied for through the Patent Office which is a government agency. The business must then purchase the patent and it will apply for a certain length of time, depending on the market, competition and likely reaction by consumers to the new product. After the patent has elapsed, then there is an open market for the product. In the meantime, competitors will have purchased the product and examined its components and ingredients very carefully, so as to be ready with a competitor product once the patent has expired.

Copyright – this is used for published material so that writers cannot actually copy the text of another writer without specific permission from the publishers. The same applies to photocopying sheet music.

Trademarks – these are used to make a company or a product distinctive from its competitors. They can also be used to demonstrate that a product has been made by a particular manufacturer and therefore hinders competitors attempting to copy the idea.

The product life cycle

One method of analysing the sales and profit of a particular product over time is by examining its **product life cycle**. This is simply a record of sales and how they fluctuate as time passes. The product life cycle model (*see Figure 16.1 below*) allows a company to chart the progress of a product and then make changes to other parts of the marketing mix according to the pattern of sales.

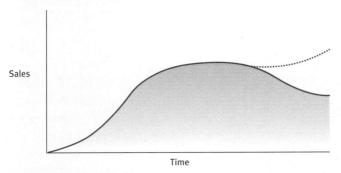

Figure 16.1a   The product life cycle

The product life cycle of any product or brand can be divided into four particular, distinct areas:

■ **Introduction and development** – the product is developed and launched on to the market. Sales usually begin slowly as customers are naturally cautious about anything which is new

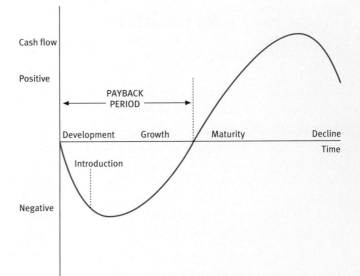

Figure 16.1b   Cash flow and the product life cycle

■ **Growth** – sales begin to pick up as customer interest grows. Sometimes the growth period can be sudden and without warning, resulting in the business losing orders if it has not built up its stock accordingly

■ **Maturity** – sales flatten off as the product becomes well established and more competitors join the market. Frequently the market becomes saturated.

■ **Decline** – the business experiences a gradual fall in sales and must decide whether to extend the product's life, or whether to let it die!

The dotted line represents the effect of an extension strategy.

Question 1

Draw a product life cycle for
a) Concorde
b) Ford Escort
c) Windows 95
d) Direct insurance
e) Beanie Babies
f) Calvin Klein No. 1   [6]

The product life cycle in detail

At different stages of the product life cycle, the consumers and the marketing plan will display different characteristics.

■ Development and introduction

Although these are expressed simultaneously, the development of the product does come before the introduction. **Development** is considered in more detail later in the unit, although it is important to note that a successful development stage does mean the product is far more likely to receive initial praise and acceptance from the customers. The customers that are targeted tend to be summarily known as 'innovators' in that they are seen as the first to purchase.

Introduction is where the product is officially launched on to the market. The scale of the launch may be at a local, regional, or even national level, although businesses that launch at the national level need to be very confident of the prospects of success. The initial launch could be part of a test market where the product is 'trialled' for a period of time and feedback from customers is then used to refine and modify the product accordingly. This then means the launch is more likely to succeed. At this point, the business makes very little profit on sales because of the low volumes which mean the business is unable to achieve the benefit of economies of scale. Due to the limited level of awareness of the product, the business does not need to worry about a wide distribution network. The financial position is likely to be at its most worrying for the business, given that there is unlikely to be a guarantee of the success of the product and a great deal of cash will have been spent on the development process. Advertising is likely to be informative as customers need to find out about new products.

■ Growth

As the product moves into the **growth** phase, the increase in volume means that unit costs can fall due to economies of scale (*see Unit 4 Size of business*), although there is a possibility of other businesses producing copies of the product. This is when patents become significant, because if the product is protected against copying then it will grow more quickly and

earn more profit. Customers are known as 'adopters' at this stage as the trend begins to take off. Due to the growth in demand, the distribution of the product needs to be wider in order to satisfy the demand – this can sometimes catch the business unawares in that it might not have forecast such demand as to outstrip supply. This occurred with the popularity of Teletubbies models as parents queued outside Toys 'R' Us. At this point in the product life cycle, there may be a squeeze on cash flow due to the business producing for sales at a much higher level (*see Figure 16.2*). In the growth stage advertising must be a mixture of information and persuasion as more consumers need to be told about the product, but also because competitors may seek to gain a foothold in the market at this stage.

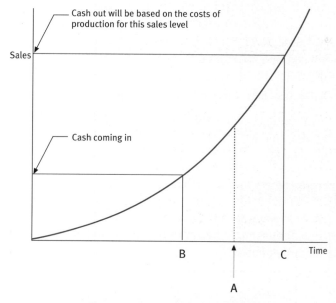

At point A (in time), the business may be receiving cash from sales at B, but producing for sales at C.

Figure 16.2   Growth and the squeeze on cash flow

■ Maturity

Although the product is popular, the increase in popularity falls and the level of sales flattens. At this point, the business is earning most money from the product because it is established. Investment in advertising falls in relation to sales as consumers simply need to be reminded of the product, although as the competition intensifies the advertising needs to become more persuasive. **Maturity** is also a phase where the cash flow for the product is at its greatest, in that the sales level has flattened and the problem highlighted in the previous diagram has disappeared. Expenditure on product development is likely to be low and the business is achieving economies of scale through mass production. However, there is much more intense pressure from competitors at this stage as **Me-Too products** (copies) are launched on to the market. The competitive pressure is usually the cause of a reduction in profit margins as prices are pushed downward.

A second part of maturity is where market **saturation** occurs. This is where the market as a whole ceases to grow in terms of the number of customers, so there remains one of two options in order to increase growth.

a) Encourage customers to purchase (and therefore replace) the product more frequently. This has been done in the car market, with some customers replacing their car every two years, before major problems occur. This way the MOT test is avoided and usually the car will still be under some form of warranty

b) Attract sales from competition, i.e. achieve growth by taking market share from competitors.

Such strategies were considered by Igor Ansoff and have been covered in more detail in Unit 7 Objectives and strategy.

Question 2

In what ways does the advert opposite suggest that the product might be approaching the end of its maturity phase?   [5]

■ Decline

When a product enters the **decline** stage, a business usually considers two choices:
a) to accelerate the decline by having a sell-off, usually at a significantly discounted price in order to ensure the volume is sold
b) to discontinue the product and allow sales to fall at the rate the market decides.

If any advertising takes place, it is likely to be informative, telling customers about the end of season sale or end of line sale. This is typical of Boxing Day Sales for department stores such as Harrods and Selfridges.

■ Extension strategies

Very frequently a business will attempt to prolong the maturity phase of a product. This is usually because the cost of developing and launching a new product is much more expensive. Famous brands such as Mars Bars and Heinz Beans as well as consumer durables such as the Ford Escort have undergone several **extension strategies** at different points during their lives.

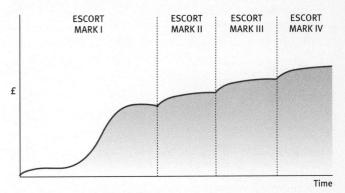

Figure 16.3   The relaunch of the Escort

The Polo mint underwent significant revitalisation during the early 1990s due to a growth in the market share of its rival, Trebor. The Ford Escort, one of the most popular selling cars of all time and launched in the 1960s, has been rejuvenated no fewer than six times! On the other hand, Coca-Cola tried a revamp in an attempt to compete with Pepsi advertising the new cola but loyal consumers did not like the taste and it was quickly dropped in favour of the original flavour and taste. This was an expensive mistake but illustrates the point that even giants in the branded products have to be careful not to change what is established and liked by the consumer. This is one product where a revamp was not the answer.

Question 3

By considering the extension strategies mentioned above of a) Mars Bars and b) Ford Escort, explain what factors might determine the length of time between each extension strategy.   [5]

See Question 2.

Typical examples of extension strategies are:

- Finding a new use for an old product, or a new market – training shoes used to be used entirely for sport, whereas now they are used as a fashion item and the manufacturers have developed the product into a major success, selling far more to the 16–24 age group for fashion than for sport

- Increasing the product range – this practice has been adopted by card shops who have broadened the range from the traditional festive periods and standard message cards to a much wider field

- Change in style – most car companies have adopted this approach, whilst maintaining the name

- Change of name – this may alter the image or establish a global brand e.g. Marathon changed its name to Snickers because it was called that in America. Opal Fruits changed their name to Starburst for the same reason

- Reduction in price – as the market for mortgages has risen and fallen based on economic activity, banks and building societies have fought hard to attract customers away from one bank and into another. A mortgage is usually for 25 years, so customers' attitudes tend to be difficult to change with something as significant as a 25-year commitment. The demand for a change in mortgages has increased following incentives such as £1500 cashback, or very low interest rates for the first few years. Although the number of people borrowing money has not increased beyond the rate of increase in economic activity, the turnover of mortgages has increased by much more

- Offering finance – when products become too expensive to purchase in one go, the business may offer to provide a source of finance, in the shape of a loan to the customer

---

Question 4

What type of extension strategy would you suggest for the following products?
a) Carlsberg Lager
b) A family shampoo
c) Video recorders

Explain your choice.   3 × [3]

Implications of the product life cycle for planning

The product life cycle allows any business to plan ahead. This means it may be able to anticipate possible changes in the shape and position of the product life cycle, with a view to taking action.

- **Distribution** – the channel of distribution will be affected as sales grow because as demand increases, so must the product's availability. Not only will more retailers and wholesalers be needed, but the present middlemen will need more of the product.

- **Advertising** – as competition intensifies, the type of advertising will become more competitive and persuasive.

- **Stock levels** – at the introduction stage, the business will not wish to hold too much stock, in case the product fails. As sales grow, there must be plenty of stock in order to meet the sudden anticipated growth spurts in demand. As sales flatten in maturity, the fact that they are easier to predict means that stocks can fall to a lower level, as long as suppliers are capable of delivering regularly. Obviously in the decline stage, the business will want to hold as little stock as possible to guard against the risk of the demand ceasing, and being left with stock which it therefore cannot sell.

- **Cash flow** – Figure 16.1 demonstrated the problem associated with cash flow. This is the diagrammatic representation of the spreadsheet which the business will take to any providers of finance in order to persuade them to finance the new product. As the product moves through the different stages, the cash flow will alter.

Question 5

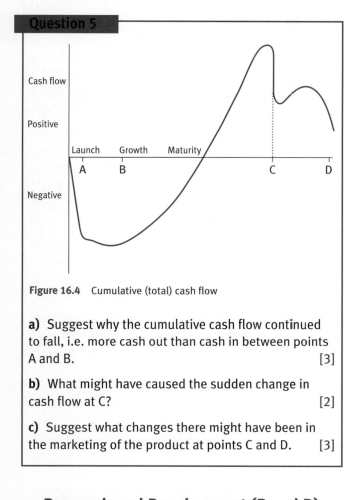

Figure 16.4 Cumulative (total) cash flow

a) Suggest why the cumulative cash flow continued to fall, i.e. more cash out than cash in between points A and B. [3]

b) What might have caused the sudden change in cash flow at C? [2]

c) Suggest what changes there might have been in the marketing of the product at points C and D. [3]

- **Research and Development (R and D)** – although the majority of the R and D expenditure takes place at the start of the project, before it is launched, the business is likely to continue to spend money on it, especially if consumer needs are changing, if only to monitor customers' reaction. Once the product is developed there will be small changes made to the prototype before launching. During the maturity phase, the business will need to anticipate whether or not to carry out an extension strategy. R and D may be needed for an updated version.

- **Pricing strategies** – as the product is launched, the business will need to decide whether it aims to achieve market share, gaining a foothold in the market, or whether it wishes to achieve a high profit margin – rarely do the two happen simultaneously. As the product becomes more competitive, the business will gradually push the price down (which it will be able to afford to do as the cost per unit falls due to economies of scale). Alternatively, it might be in the very fortunate position of being able to charge a higher price because it is sufficiently different from the rest of the market. The Dyson is a good example of a product which commanded a price at the top of the range, despite entering a highly competitive market. This was due to **product differentiation**. Since then competitors have brought out similar products, albeit with slightly different prices.

- **New product development (NPD)** – since product life cycles do not last forever, a business must constantly develop new products, so as to achieve a range of products, preferably with at least one product at each stage of the product life cycle at any one time. This will ensure a broad product portfolio so money from a mature product helps finance the introduction of a new product (*see Figure 16.5*). NPD is considered in more detail on page 188.

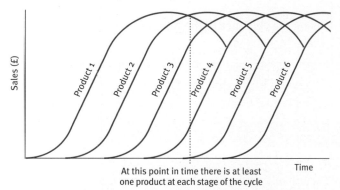
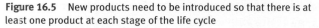

Figure 16.5 New products need to be introduced so that there is at least one product at each stage of the life cycle

Question 6

What problems might a business face if it launches a product at a national level which then fails? [8]

Question 7

Losing keys is a problem for many people. Such a problem was solved by an invention in the 1980s which was a key ring with a built-in sound detector that emitted a 'beep' upon hearing a whistle, or high pitched squeal. Initially, they were priced at £15 and were advertised through specialist mail order companies that sold brand new products. As the market caught on to the idea, the number of copies and imitations proliferated and gradually the price was forced downwards until they could be picked up at a local market stall for £1. The sensitivity of the beeper was so great that it would go off when the TV was on, or a female singer was on the radio, or even when doors creaked. Such was their irritation that many customers ended up taking the batteries out!

Using the above to illustrate your answer, explain how and why the price might have been changed at different stages in the product life cycle.   [5]

Question 8

| | PRODUCT A | | PRODUCT B | | PRODUCT C | |
	Sales	Profit margin (%)	Sales	%	Sales	%
1993	5,000	8%				
1994	7,000	8%			4,000	5%
1995	10,000	9%	1,000	13%	6,000	5%
1996	9,500	10%	6,000	17%	9,000	6%
1997	10,000	10%	13,000	20%	6,000	8%
1998	10,000	10%	15,000	21%	6,500	6%
1999	9,000	10%	14,000	20%	2,000	–1%
2000 forecast	10,500	9%	14,000	19%	500	–5%
2001 forecast	11,000	7%	13,000	20%		
2002 forecast	11,000	5%	11,000	20%		

Using the evidence in the table comment on the three products in terms of the changes in the product life cycle.   [12]

The product portfolio

It is unlikely that you will ever find a successful company that has produced only one product. Even if the business is famous for one product, such as Coca-Cola, there will be different versions of the same product due to the segmentation of the market. Caffeine-free, diet coke and cherry coke are all derivatives of the same product and yet they are sold to different segments of the market for soft drinks.

By widening a product portfolio, a business is not only reducing its risk, but it is also gaining experience in several markets, hence over a period of time it will become more expert at marketing.

Positioning

One method of representing the product a business produces is by using a product mapping diagram. This allows a business to assess not only its own portfolio, but that of its rivals as well. In turn, a business can then 'position' its product into an appropriate segment, especially if the present segment is overcrowded.

The market for washing powder has been heavily segmented by the two major competitors in the market – Lever Bothers and Procter & Gamble. The products vary according to size, tablet, powder or liquid form, biological or non-biological, and so on. When the market began to grow in the 1960s it was simply a case of deciding between a large box and a small box! Due to the increased complexity of the market for washing powder, it becomes necessary to 'map' products according to the following criteria:

a) whether the product is one which does its job efficiently, or whether it is seen to have a 'caring' image

b) whether the product is modern or traditional

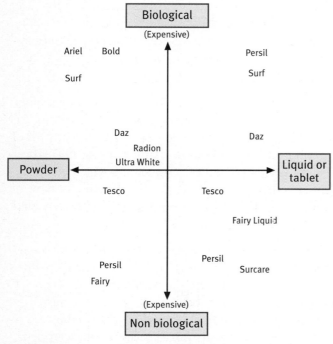

Figure 16.6   Brand positioning of washing powders

Any competitor or indeed any of the businesses competing in this market may then wish to reposition the product in a different market segment in order to create greater product differentiation. This normally occurs if sales are falling and the product needs revitalising.

Boston matrix

Another method of classification for each product within the portfolio was developed by the Boston Consultancy Group, which classified products according to three variables:

■ market share relative to its nearest competitor
■ market growth
■ its position on the grid in relation to other products

Although the gradation was simple (high and low) the **Boston matrix** provided an opportunity for companies to classify their products (*see Figure 16.7*).

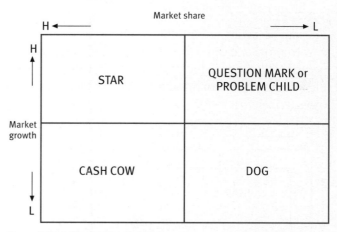

Figure 16.7   The Boston matrix

■ **Dog** – low market share and low market growth; sales have either failed to take off or the product has gone into the decline stage of the product life cycle. If a product is classified as a dog there needs to be significant justification to keep it going. Sometimes it is using up capacity or perhaps it is still selling for a small contribution (*see Unit 43*). No business wants a dog!

■ **Question Mark or Problem Child** – this is a product where the market is growing, but as yet the product itself is unknown to the market. A product in this category might succeed if sufficient money is invested in it; many products begin life like this, although far more drop to the status of a dog than move into the next category. This product is therefore in its introduction stage.

■ **Star** – this occurs when a product has 'taken off' and sales are growing in relation to the market (which is also growing i.e. the product is growing faster than the market). Although this may initially seem attractive to the business, it is unlikely to be earning significant cash flow as the business is investing in more advertising and working hard to establish it into maturity.

- **Cash Cow** – a product in maturity. The phrase cash cow comes from the fact that the product is generating cash and therefore the business is 'milking' the cash cow. Without several products which are cash cows it is difficult for a business to finance new products internally.

The aim of having any product portfolio is for the cash cow to provide cash to fund the question marks or occasionally prop up the dogs. The cash can then help the question marks to turn into stars and then into cash cows (*see Figure 16.8*).

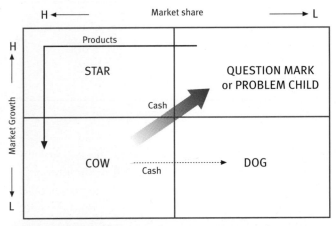

Figure 16.8   The movement of cash and products in the Boston matrix

Question 9

Percentage of products within a company's portfolio

		Cash Cows	Dogs	Stars	Question Marks
Business	1	80%	0%	16%	4%
	2	40%	30%	5%	25%
	3	25%	15%	0%	60%
	4	10%	10%	55%	25%

Comment on the possible consequences for each business of its own product portfolio.   [12]

New product development

A condition of long-term survival for every business is **new product development**. Every product goes through its own life cycle, but very few remain in the maturity phase forever. Consequently, businesses need to look for new products through the process of research.

The process of new product development involves various stages of inventing, testing, building prototypes, retesting, gaining customer reaction, redesigning and so on. The process is therefore as elaborate and as complicated as the business wishes to make it. Some businesses spend very little on R and D, either because they feel the product does not need development i.e. it is simple and straightforward, such as bread, or because they cannot afford the expense.

In fact, those companies which have successfully pioneered new products ensure that despite a drop in sales and profit, the R and D department continues to be well funded and remains an important part of the company.

Psion, famous for its palm-top computers among other products such as a Dacom (which connects laptops to the Internet via mobile telephones), spent nearly 8% of revenue (£10.9 million) on R and D during 1997. The business views R and D as something which is independent of sales revenue. The demand for new products from its customers is the driving force behind Research and Development.

As the process of R and D is carried through for a particular product, the various versions and alternatives are reduced in number as more information is gathered. In addition, there are thousands of new products which do not get any further than the discussion and concept board before being scrapped. A business will aim to allow in its R and D expenditure a proportion which will be used in so-called 'bluesky' products – those which never go beyond the first stages.

Twinkles, tweaks and twists

Recent research on introducing new products has led to some interesting conclusions. The high cost of developing new products compared with changing or upgrading older ones has led to an interesting classification of products:

Twinkles – these are genuine new ideas which are developed into new products. Any new, ground-breaking product, such as microphones replacing keyboards on computers, falls into this category.

Tweaks – these are constant upgrades to existing brands such as a new flavour being added to a range of soft drinks

Twists – these are clever manipulations of products which already exist in order to introduce them to a new segment.

Question 10

Unilever is a business which ranks high on a recently researched R and D scoreboard. In 1998 it spent £546 million, or 1.8% of sales revenue, on Research. At Unilever, R and D ranges from scientific investigation to examining how a brand can be developed further, such as making Persil into tablet form. To quote a senior executive in the company's R and D centre – 'People always wash and eat.' R and D is therefore focused on the long term, meaning that short-term fluctuations in demand tend to be disregarded. With a competitor such as Procter & Gamble investing similar amounts in R and D as well as consumer advertising, there is a school of thought which suggests that if either company cut back on researching new products, the other would gain from continuing its commitment to R and D.

a) Why is R and D expenditure expressed as a proportion of sales revenue?   [3]

b) Explain why Unilever is so committed to R and D.
                                                      [5]

Source: *Management Today 1999*

Question 11

The following quotation was taken from a business magazine: 'During a recession, managers tend to concentrate on the short term. Often the area where cuts come first and deepest in a downturn is in research and development. Not until the mid-1990s did the R and D expenditure of UK companies regain the level it was before the mid-1991 recession.'

Discuss the consequences for a business of reducing R and D expenditure during a recession.

Points for Revision

Key Terms

patents	a method of protecting a product from competition; a patent means that only the company which has innovated and invented the new product can produce it for the period of the patent
product life cycle	the pattern of sales during the 'lifetime' of the product
introduction and development	the product is researched and launched on to the market
growth	when sales increase at a significant rate compared with the introduction
maturity	sales level off and become much easier to predict
saturation	the market stops growing, so to increase market share a business has to become more competitive
decline	sales fall away and the business decides how quickly to kill off the product
Me-Too products	attempted copies introduced once patents (if existing) become extinct
extension strategy	an attempt to prolong the maturity stage of the product life cycle
Boston matrix	a method of classifying a product according to market share and market growth
product differentiation	when a company attempts to make its product significantly different from its competition
new product development	the process of innovating and inventing new ideas and concepts, with a view to developing a successful new product in anticipation of customer needs

Definitions Question:
With reference to a business you know, explain the significance of any three of the above (your teacher may wish to help you choose).   [5] per definition

Summary Points:

1   The sales and cash flow of a product can be depicted diagrammatically by the product life cycle model.

2   A method of establishing the product's position in a market involves either drawing a position map or using the Boston matrix.

3   New product development is one of the most important factors for long-term success in a business although ironically is one of the first areas to experience a fall in its budget when sales drop.

Mini Case Study

Now one of the wealthiest men in the country, James Dyson's name is synonymous with a revolutionary product. He is the pioneer of the Dyson vacuum cleaner which has a unique selling point – it has no bag. The success of the product was a lengthy, painful process for the man who also invented the ballbarrow – a wheel barrow, but with a ball! In all he made 5,127 different prototypes of the vacuum cleaner until he settled on the design which was to make him famous, although he had a real problem persuading other people to invest in it. Having tried the Japanese, famous for their advancement in, and acceptance of, technological products, then the Americans, both of whom provided him with encouraging responses but no real commitment to manufacture, he then decided to set up his own manufacturing process. The main problem was persuading the banks in Britain to lend him the money; each time he was met with the same attitude to innovation – 'You are not a businessman, you are a designer, how can you possibly understand the business principles required to run a successful corporation?' He eventually found a modern-thinking bank manager and set up his own plant in Malmesbury, Wiltshire. Since then, sales have increased rapidly from £3 million in 1994 to £149 million in 1997. He has positioned the product at the premium end of the market and the Dyson is now market leader. In 1998 he spent 7% of revenue on R and D in a 'leading-edge' R and D facility which attracts top designers to the company and includes nearly a quarter of the work-force.

1 Define: unique selling point, market leader. [4]

2 a) Calculate how much the business spent on R and D in 1997. [1]

  b) What might be the problems of a business spending so much on research? [3]

3 Outline the reason why the Dyson is now market leader, despite being one of the most expensive products on the market. [4]

4 Discuss the implications for British industry of the banks' traditional attitude to innovation. [8]

20

Maxi Case Study

The pharmaceutical industry is full of companies with very similar characteristics. The main companies are extremely large, multinational businesses, the chief executives earn six-, sometimes seven-figure pay packages and they all search continually for a new, blockbuster, winning drug.

The latest drug company to hit the headlines was the American business, Pfizer, with its drug, Viagra. The massive media attention which surrounded the launch of the product has meant that analysts have projected a revenue level of $3 billion in five years. Despite the initial success, it still has a long way to go to catch up the best-selling drugs in the world which command sales revenue of nearly £4 billion per annum. However, there has been concern amongst shareholders that a business needs more than one drug to sustain its success and that over-reliance on one drug may cause problems.

All drug companies take out patents on their new products, so relying on one product means that the moment the patent expires, other companies enter the market with their own version. This is made more significant by the fact that the amount of money required to develop a superdrug is high. It can take on average 12 years and £300 million to bring a drug on to the market. In addition, only about one in 10,000 of the products which companies research will be a best seller.

Although the presence of one major drug in a portfolio is attractive, it is not a ticket to success. The company which manufactures the best seller (which is an ulcer treatment known as Losec) is Astrazeneca, not the largest drugs company in the world. Glaxo is particularly sensitive to this issue; in the mid-1990s, Zantac, the world's best-selling drug (a treatment for stomach ulcers), accounted for over 40% of its total sales. In 1996, the patent ran out and the business braced itself to lose about 80% of sales, although most of its sales remained the same. Even so, it continued its drive for new products; Glaxo employs 10,000 people world-wide (about one fifth of its work-force) in R and D and spends £1.15 billion (14.4% of sales revenue) on that area. Such is the investment in research that it is estimated to take 15 years to recoup the investment.

An alternative way of searching for a wider portfolio is through merging. Smithkline Beecham merged with American Home products to create a company worth £75 billion on the stock market. The main objective of such a merger was to pool resources in the R and D laboratories in order to develop the superdrug.

The trick seems to be to plan ahead, so that new products are ready for launch once patents expire. Making progress in technological capability is also important because this means the business can reduce the amount of time it takes to get a product to the market-place, thus giving the product a longer time to pay back.

1 Explain the term 'worth £75 billion on the stock market'.   [3]

2 Either

   a) Analyse how the product life cycle can help companies like Pfizer to manage their product portfolios.

   Or

   b) Using the Boston matrix, suggest how drug companies should manage their products if market share and profit are the main objectives.   [8]

3 What might be the reaction of any two stakeholders to pay packages of seven-figure sums?   [6]

4 Suggest a possible reason for there being very little effect on the sales of Zantac once the patent had expired.   [5]

5 Either

   a) Discuss the factors which would influence the product portfolio for any firm.

   Or

   b) Presentation: Having covered the marketing mix, argue the cases for and against the following statement:

   'It does not matter how competitive the price, how exciting the advertising nor how extensive and efficient the distribution, if the product does not fit the customer's needs, it will not sell – the product is therefore the most important part of the marketing mix.'   [10]

32

Pricing

Learning objectives

Having read this unit, students will be able to

1 understand the different pricing strategies

2 be aware of the different methods of calculating the price of a good or service

3 evaluate the appropriateness of certain pricing methods in different business situations

Context

Next time you visit the supermarket, count the different number of brands of baked beans and look at the prices of each brand. The most expensive is likely to be Heinz (close to 30 pence) and the least expensive may be the supermarket's own brand, or perhaps an unknown brand name. Although the quality may differ slightly, the ingredients and packaging are very similar in terms of cost. So why does Heinz insist on charging the most when Sainsbury Economy Baked Beans cost under 10 pence a can?

The price provides a great deal of information about the quality and image of the individual product. Some companies deliberately charge a price which is lower than the cost, in an attempt to increase market share. Others will deliberately charge more than competitors because it gives the image of quality, respectability and status. For example, Rolls-Royce would probably lose sales volume if it advertised a 25% reduction in price on end of line Bentleys!

Companies will therefore consider many factors when deciding on price, including demand, cost and competition.

What is a price?

Price is defined as the amount a customer pays in return for a good or service.

Although this may seem an obvious statement at first sight, a business will spend a considerable amount of time debating the correct price or prices for its products. The price of the product may change according to the time of year or a change in costs, even though the product itself has not altered.

> **Question 1**
>
> Find out the prices of three newspapers on sale in your newsagents on both a weekday and Saturday/Sunday.
>
> Identify reasons why there is a difference between two newspapers and at different times during the week.   **[5]**

Economic theory revisited

The effect on demand of a price change and vice versa is covered in more detail in Unit 8 Economic theory, but a reminder of the cause and effect is appropriate here.

The relationship between price and demand is straightforward:

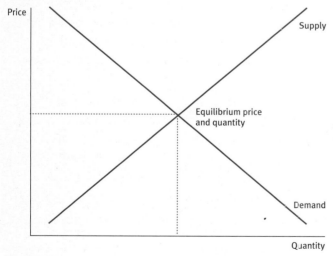

Figure 17.1   Buyers and sellers agree on an equilibrium price

A price increase will result in a demand decrease and vice versa for normal products. There will, however, be exceptions to this. In Ireland during the 19th century, there was a potato glut, meaning that potatoes became cheaper, causing people to buy them less because the amount they saved on potatoes over a period of time meant they could 'trade up' to a higher quality foodstuff. Similarly, fashion houses such as Versace are unlikely to knock money off the prices of their clothes in order to sell more. The exclusivity is a key issue in this case and a reduction in price will mean more people can purchase the item as well as giving the image of a drop in quality, both of which may dissuade loyal customers from purchasing the brand.

On the other hand, change in supply or demand can affect prices.

- A sudden increase in demand due to a change in tastes or purchasing trends will mean the price will increase.
- A fall in demand, due to a recession, will usually result in a price decrease.
- An increase in supply e.g. a glut of strawberries will force the price of strawberries down as farmers need to sell more.
- A reduction in the supply of a product e.g. oil as enacted during the 1970s by OPEC will force the price up, if the product is a necessity.

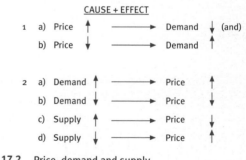

Figure 17.2   Price, demand and supply

Pricing objectives

Before a business chooses its pricing strategy, it must first decide on the objectives that the pricing strategy will fulfil.

■ Profitability

Higher prices do not necessarily mean higher profits. If the business is in a competitive market, then setting the price too high may make it uncompetitive, resulting in a loss of demand. Growth of a business is generated from profit, so the price must allow for the costs of manufacture as well as the costs of dividends, interest and tax. This will help to ensure that there is some profit available for future investment.

Market share

When new products are launched, one of the initial objectives may well be to achieve market share of a certain percentage. If this is achieved, it means that customers are actually trying the product, revenue is flowing into the business and it is using its productive capacity. A business may then change the objective to profitability in the longer term, once brand loyalty has been established.

Competitive advantage

The market for energy is highly competitive, with various sources of energy being used by several companies. Such is the structure of the energy industry following privatisation that gas companies can now supply electricity and vice versa, as well as retailers offering to sell electricity by having a joint agreement with power suppliers. The fuel for heating the home is exactly the same product, so there has been a concerted effort to use price as the main weapon for being more competitive.

Barrier to entry

As companies become larger, it is possible, through the process of achieving economies of scale, to produce more cheaply and therefore charge lower prices.

Many small or new firms suffer when larger firms reduce prices in order to force the smaller firms out of business. When prices fall, the small or new firms are unable to compete as they are unable to gain the benefits of economies of scale. This strategy can be a highly effective way of either eliminating existing competition or preventing new firms from entering the market.

BT has a strong hold over the telecommunications market. Oftel, the regulatory body charged with the duty of monitoring BT's corporate responsibility, has forced BT to charge a minimum amount for calls. BT actually makes more than enough profit from line rental income, and therefore does not need to charge for calls. However, such action would prevent other businesses from setting up in competition to BT, thereby giving BT a monopoly.

Survival

If competition intensifies, then a business may need to reduce its prices, just to encourage customers to purchase. Some revenue is better than no revenue, although this cannot necessarily be sustained in the long run (*see Marginal cost or contribution pricing page 198*).

Pricing strategies

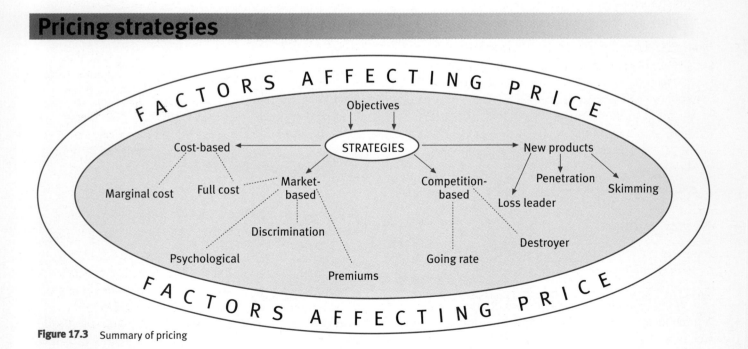

Figure 17.3 Summary of pricing

There are three types of pricing strategy – **cost-based**, **market-based** and **competition-based**.

■ Cost-based

Cost-based pricing is used by calculating the cost of producing a certain number of units of output, and basing the price on that figure. Costs can be divided according to variable costs or total costs. Pricing can therefore be set at a level which either

a) covers the variable or marginal costs, or

b) the full or total costs.

Figure 17.4   Cost-based pricing

The main problem with cost-based pricing is that it takes no account of the price which the customer is willing or able to pay. Companies which use cost-based pricing usually have a primary objective of covering costs, or making a profit i.e. if an order for an individual product does not cover costs, then the business will not consider the order, *ceteris paribus* (all other things being equal).

■ Market-based pricing

This is used by a business that needs to listen to the market (i.e. the customers) in terms of what they are willing to pay. This strategy is more difficult to gauge because it may mean the business charges too high or too low a price initially. With a cost-based strategy, the business usually takes a 'hit and hope' approach to pricing. With market-based, the business will take an approach of 'test and see, then test and see again, until it finds the correct level. This strategy is appropriate where there are several market segments for the same product and so the business may be able to charge different amounts for the same product sold to different people e.g. price reductions for students and OAPs.

Figure 17.5   Market-based pricing

The main problem with this strategy is that it takes no account of the cost of producing a unit of output, so the business may well end up charging a price which customers are willing to pay, but which fails to meet the unit cost.

Companies therefore need to balance the market-based approach with the cost-based approach, by referring back to their objectives to see which objective is the most important.

■ Competition-based pricing

Sometimes a business will price its products with the deliberate objective of beating the competition, even if it is well below the amount that the customer expects to pay and well below the costs. If the business can be more competitive and cause rivals to go out of business, there will be much less pressure to be competitive!

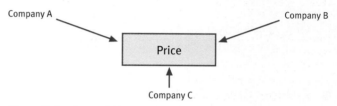

Figure 17.6   Competition-based pricing

This approach takes no account of either the costs or the demand. Consequently a business may end up charging a price which means it makes a loss or undercharging customers, incurring the opportunity cost of the extra revenue and profit which could have been earned.

New products

When a business launches a new product or a new brand it must think carefully about the price. The wrong price may mean that customers are scared off, or that the business fails to capitalise on potential demand. Two possible pricing strategies are employed with new products.

- **Market penetration**
  The price is deliberately set at a low level with a view to gaining customer interest and establishing a foothold in the market. Sometimes the product will be sold at a loss as part of a sales promotion, although the business will hope either that it will be able to increase the price once some brand loyalty has been achieved, or that costs will fall due to economies of scale as demand picks up. Sometimes you will see products with a 'special introductory price' meaning that at the beginning of the product life cycle, the brand is deliberately priced at a low level to gain interest. The emphasis

is therefore on selling a high volume, with the objective of achieving market share, which is more easily achieved if the product is price-elastic i.e. sensitive to changes in price (*see Unit 18*).

■ **Market skimming**

Alternatively, a business might decide to set the price at a high level, with a view to 'creaming' off the profit at the top end of the market. If it is either a new product or a high-quality product, then the business may be concerned with profit from the start. Volumes will obviously be lower and the profit margin will be higher than with **market penetration**. Some companies do this if they wish to recoup some of their research expenditure and there is no obvious competitor. As new competitors gradually enter the market, lured by the attraction of profit, then the price will be forced down. An example of **market skimming** is the recent set of craze products that are going to be sold for only short periods of time which is why prices are higher – manufacturers can 'cream off' the profit when demand is high for a short, intense period of selling.

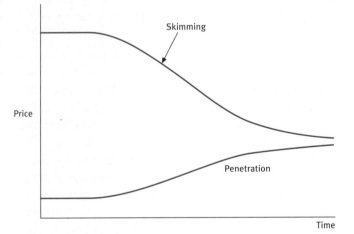

Figure 17.7   The changing price over time for two products

> **Question 2**
>
> Outline and justify an appropriate pricing strategy for the following:
> a) a small corner shop
> b) a company launching a revolutionary pair of designer jeans
> c) a petrol retailer
> d) a carpet manufacturer   [12]

Pricing methods

Cost-based

■ **Marginal cost pricing**

Although cost-based pricing implies all costs must be covered, this assumption means that a business has very little flexibility with its prices e.g. if fixed costs are £4 per unit and variable costs are £2 per unit, the business will aim to charge a price of at least £6. However, as long as the business makes a contribution to the fixed costs (*see Unit 41 Cost classification*) then it will be able to survive, if only in the short run. Hence if it charges exactly £2 per unit, then it will be able to meet its variable costs (materials, labour and variable overheads) and so the material suppliers will still be paid as will the employees. This will mean the business will continue to operate. Charging this level in the long term will mean it cannot pay the fixed costs. Hence it might wish to charge £3 or £4 i.e. less than £6 (total cost per unit) but more than £2 variable cost per unit.

A great deal will depend upon how many products the business is likely to sell when it considers how much more to charge over and above the variable costs. If the company sells 1,000 different product lines, then each product can be priced a little above variable costs, so that the total contribution made by all the products is sufficient to make a profit. If only one product is made, then this approach will mean that profit will not be earned.

This method is therefore based on the variable or marginal cost and is designed to ensure a contribution is earned, hence the name marginal cost or contribution pricing. This method is more appropriate when output levels are changing because if output changes, fixed cost per unit changes, but variable cost per unit stays the same (*see Unit 41*).

> **Question 3**
>
> If a business produces 30,000 units and has a variable cost of £75,000 with fixed costs at £150,000, calculate the lowest price it can charge to survive in the
> i) short term
> ii) long term   [4]

Question 4

Under what circumstances might a theatre company use marginal cost pricing rather than full cost pricing? [4]

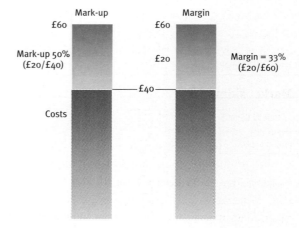

Figure 17.8   Margin versus mark-up

Full cost pricing

This uses the calculation of total cost per unit, and then adds on a mark-up to get the price. **Mark-up** is defined as the percentage of the cost that is added on to the cost to find the price.

e.g. if a 20% mark-up is applied to a unit cost of £30, then the price will be:

$$1.2 \times £30 = £36.$$

Full cost pricing can be used when the fixed costs have been allocated to a particular product, using the technique of full costing (*see Unit 41*) which takes the fixed costs as one lump sum and allocates them to each product according to one criterion.

Mark-up versus margin

A profit **margin**, on the other hand, is used to express the profit as a percentage of the selling price.

Example 1 – A business aims to earn a profit margin of 20% on a product which is sold for £5, so the profit will be:

$$20\% \times £5 = £1.$$

In this example, the costs are the other 80% of the price i.e. £4, so the mark-up on the costs is 25% (of £4) which is added to the profit.

Example 2 – A business has costs of £36 and places a mark-up of 33% (one third) on the costs to arrive at the price.

$$£36 \times 1.33 = £48.$$

The margin is therefore £12/£48 (the percentage of the selling price which is profit) = 25%.

Profit minus pricing

This is a method of pricing which has been pioneered by Toyota and forms a logical link between cost-based

Question 5

a) Brick-It, a building supplier, manufactures bricks for £2 per unit and aims to earn a profit margin of 50%. How much should Brick-It charge? [2]

b) Cement-It supplies Brick-It with bags of cement which cost Cement-It £3 to produce. Cement-It adds a mark-up of 40% to the costs when arriving at the price. If Brick-It aims to make the same margin as in **a)**, calculate the final price charged to the customer for a bag of cement. [3]

and market-based pricing. Toyota first of all works out how much the market (or customer) is willing to pay for a new car (using its own database). It then calculates the profit it needs to earn from each car if it is to meet its target of dividends for shareholders as well as its target for reinvestment. It will then calculate the required cost of production and divide the car into all of its components, calculating the target cost of each individual part. Then it will approach suppliers stating the maximum price Toyota is willing to pay; the suppliers then have to decide whether to accept the order. Occasionally, suppliers may accept the order even though initially they may be making a loss, and hope that they can find gains in efficiency to turn the loss into a profit.

Obviously, not many firms are in such a comfortable position as to be able to dictate terms to suppliers, although there are many suppliers who will queue up at Toyota's door for a contract that will probably last for five or more years.

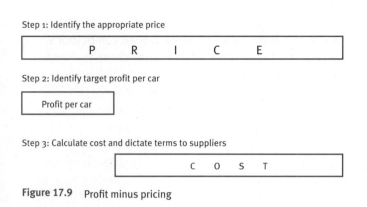

Step 1: Identify the appropriate price

| P | R | I | C | E |

Step 2: Identify target profit per car

| Profit per car |

Step 3: Calculate cost and dictate terms to suppliers

| C | O | S | T |

Figure 17.9   Profit minus pricing

Market-based

■ Price discrimination

This is where the business charges different amounts for exactly the same product. This technique is used by holiday companies according to the time of year. Although the number of hours of sunshine and temperature may make the product (a holiday) slightly different according to the time of year, the product is the same i.e. a set period of time in a particular location. Due to the fact that the customer base is different according to the time of year, the business will decide to charge different amounts. For example, during the school holidays, family holidays are much more expensive than at other times. Most parents do not like their children to miss school, so demand is actually less sensitive to price during the summer holidays. Off-peak pricing applies to many services e.g. rail fares, electricity and gas charges and telephone calls.

Question 6

Virgin charges a wide range of prices for the same product.

The price alters according to the time of departure, the day of departure, the amount of time between the outward and return journeys and the age of the passenger.

Explain why the business does this.   [5]

■ Premium pricing

When a product is considered to be of particularly high value, due to its exceptional level of quality, or the brand image it portrays, then a business may decide to charge a premium for the privilege of purchasing the product. The Ritz Hotel in London charges over £5 for a cup of tea; it is not only that the tea is of high quality, but certain customers are willing to pay for the status and prestige. The same applies to a product from Harrods; carrying it home in a Harrods bag carries a great deal of prestige in some people's eyes, regardless of the product inside.

■ Psychological pricing

A business will play on the susceptibility of a customer by stating a price of £9,995 for a new motor car, or £4.99 for a meal in a restaurant. Many items of clothing are also priced in this way. Although the decision to purchase may well be based on factors other than the price, customers are influenced by the fact that, in the first example, the car costs £9,000 and 'something'. Even though there will be only £5 change from £10,000, the customer will consider the price to be based around the £9,000 mark. This method is sometimes used in conjunction with another pricing method, in that the business will choose a particular price to ascertain the approximate price the market will pay e.g. £10 and then apply psychological pricing to charge £9.99. This method is also used in the Janauary sales.

Competition-based

■ Going-rate pricing

If the product is homogeneous (exactly the same) there is very close rivalry between companies based on the price. Any change in the level of price is likely to mean that customers move to an alternative company.

The petrol retailers such as BP Amoco or Shell make very little profit out of each litre of oil (probably about 2 pence per litre), but they each know that any attempt to increase the price will mean customers will get their fuel elsewhere. At the same time, a reduction will mean the company will gain some sales, but given the very small profit margins, the business will not want to reduce the price for very long. Consequently, such businesses will charge at the going rate and are known as price takers. The business will therefore tend to take its price from the market because of the degree of competition and the homogeneity of the product.

■ Destroyer/predatory pricing

There are times when competition is so intense that a business may embark on a method of pricing which is designed to remove all but the bravest and most efficient companies. Destroyer pricing is therefore employed with a view to pricing the product at such a low level that it forces a company out of the market, although sometimes it forces the rival out of business. In the 1970s, Freddie Laker (owner of Laker Airways) decided to take on British Airways, which at the time was run by the government. Laker began by under-cutting BA, a strategy which was initially successful. But BA was a much larger, financially stable business, so it responded with a series of discounts which ended up forcing Laker Airways out of business.

■ Loss leaders

Sometimes a business will use price as a method of sales promotion. Supermarkets employ this tactic regularly in an attempt to encourage customers through their doors. A product is priced at a level where it will make a loss, although it is hoped that customers will then spend money, while they are in the shop, on the more profitable items. Kwik Save took this to extremes in 1997 when it actually gave away a can of baked beans plus 1 penny i.e. the price was effectively minus 1 pence.

The loss leader is carefully placed within the store to ensure that the customer has to pass many of the other products that are for sale. The retailer will rely on a degree of impulse-buying to compensate for the loss leader item.

Question 7

Supermarkets in Shrewsbury underwent a change in their competitive strategy during 1999 by displaying in each of their stores a trolley of their competitor's goods, next to a trolley of their own, cheaper priced products, in order to prove a point about value for money. Tesco started the battle of the trolleys by comparing its goods to Safeway's then Safeway joined in by visiting Sainsbury's, buying a basket of typical weekly shopping and then comparing its own prices to Sainsbury's. The quotes in the *Shropshire Star* made interesting reading:

Tesco: 'It's a dirty world.'
Safeway: 'It's all healthy competition.'
Sainsbury: 'a cheap gimmick'.

Source: *Shropshire Star* 28/5/99

a) How does the above show that consumers demonstrate little loyalty when prices are suddenly reduced? [5]

b) Explain Sainsbury's reaction to the latest attempt to compete. [3]

Factors affecting price

■ Costs

Despite the need to consider the market and the competition, if a business, in the long run, is unable to charge a price which yields a profit, then it will not survive. Sometimes companies will deliberately invest in new machinery which will reduce their unit costs, because it is less expensive, in the long run, than reducing their prices to a level at which they make a loss.

■ State of the market

This refers not just to the rate of growth of the individual market, but also the number of competitors and the degree of concentration i.e. how much of the market is dominated by a few firms. The state of the grocery market, which is saturated, means that pricing must be competitive. The state of the market for medical cures for illnesses is perpetually in growth, with health services willing to pay large sums of money to acquire wonder-cures, when and if they appear.

■ Competition

The more competitive the market, in terms of the number of firms in the same market, the greater the pressure to use prices as a method of competing. Although a business can emphasise quality and other forms of non-price competition, the price is much easier for consumers to use as an initial comparison. It is only once the quality is compared between products that a balance between price and quality may be made.

Question 8

List four examples of non-price competition.   [4]

■ Customer's perception of value

A business will research the customer's requirement closely. Customers value products in different ways, being willing to pay more for certain products than for others e.g. BMWs were perceived as being expensive, but 'worth the extra' price charged. James Dyson, in selling his range of vacuum cleaners at a price well in excess of the competition, researched his market well, realising that consumers would be willing to pay a much higher price for what was advertised as a far superior product.

■ Marketing mix

For a company to use an effective marketing mix (i.e. one which achieves the desired marketing objectives for the brand or product), the marketing mix must be 'unified'. The price of Calvin Klein perfume must reflect the exclusivity of the retailers, the image of the advertising and the quality of the product. Selling a product which is marketed as having an exclusive image at a price which competes with the budget end of the market will not achieve the company's marketing objectives because it will confuse the customer.

■ Legislation

Every year, the government announces changes in excise duty on alcohol and cigarettes, meaning the businesses that make and sell these products must take a decision. Either they put the tax on to the price of the product and experience a fall in the level of demand or they absorb the increase into their costs, selling the same volume but earning less profit.

■ Weather

At different times of the year certain products become more or less expensive according to the weather. The price to the customer of most staple crops will depend on the quality of the weather during the growing period. A year when the frost is severe may see the price of potatoes rise, due to a shortage. One of the most significant seasonal effects on the Retail Price Index is that of the weather (*see Unit 59*).

■ Product life cycle

Products which are being introduced will be subject to the usual skimming or penetration policies, dealt with in more detail above. As the product enters maturity and competition intensifies, most companies reduce the price to be more competitive. At the decline stage, the price will be lowered with a view to selling off the old product.

■ Distribution channel

As the number of middlemen (wholesalers, retailers, agents) involved in the distribution process increases, the business will need to think carefully about the price which will be charged to the customer. More middlemen means a higher price, because each wholesaler and retailer will add a mark-up to the price in order to earn his own profit. Sometimes a business will cut out the wholesaler and supply direct to the retailer just to avoid the extra mark-up. This is especially relevant in markets that are price-competitive. Being a vertically integrated business allows for more flexibility when deciding on the price (*see Unit 5 Mergers and acquisitions*).

■ Trade cycle

Customers become less sensitive to price changes when the economy is booming than when there is a recession. If incomes are rising (as they do in a period of economic growth), then customers do not take as much care over price differences. When money is less abundant, customers look more carefully for bargains and sometimes 'trade down' (move to a cheaper alternative) (*see Figure 17.10*).

Question 9

Corporate profits suffer worst squeeze for 25 years

In May 1999, the ONS (Office for National Statistics) published some depressing figures about company profits. Not only were staff costs to balance with an annual growth of 6.6% but the cost of preparing for the Euro and the millennium bug was also identified as causing a dent in profits. In addition, some companies reported that price competition had brought the toughest trading conditions for 25 years. This meant that investors were warned to be particularly suspicious if any company claimed encouraging profit growth forecasts.

Source: *Financial Times*, 25/5/1999.

Explain the problem for a) companies b) the economy as a whole, if costs are rising, but prices must be kept low due to competition.   [10]

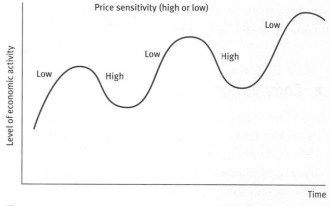

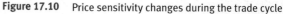

Figure 17.10   Price sensitivity changes during the trade cycle

■ Exchange rates

Regardless of whether a business exports or imports, it is still likely to face competition from abroad, which will be either helped or hindered by exchange rates. A stronger domestic currency will mean that a business selling abroad will earn less revenue when the foreign currency is translated back into pounds. This has been one of the main reasons why multinational companies based in Britain have experienced problems when trading abroad in recent years. A stronger currency also means that companies will face greater competition, because the foreign companies do not have to charge as much to earn the same revenue. The only advantage of a stronger currency in this case is if the business imports some of its raw materials (*see Unit 61*).

Points for Revision

Key Terms

cost-based pricing strategy	pricing based on the cost of production
market-based pricing strategy	pricing based on potential and effective demand
competition-based pricing strategy	pricing based on competition
market penetration	a new product is given a low price with a view to gaining a foothold
market skimming	the price is deliberately set higher in order to cream off the profits
marginal cost/ contribution pricing	price is set based on the level of marginal cost (or just above) in order to make a contribution
full/absorption cost pricing	the unit cost is calculated (i.e. total cost per unit of output) and then a mark-up is added
mark-up	a percentage of the cost added to find the selling price
margin	the percentage of the selling price which is profit
price discrimination	different prices charged for exactly the same product in different markets
psychological pricing	prices set at a level designed to coax the customer into a purchase (e.g. £5.99)
going rate	competitors charge about the same amount as each other for exactly the same product
destroyer/ predatory pricing	the price is set low with a view to competitors either going out of business or at least leaving the market

Definitions Question:
With reference to a business you know, explain the significance of any three of the above (your teacher may wish to help you choose).   [5] per definition

Summary Points:

1   Price is one of the most significant elements of the marketing mix and is used to gain a competitive advantage.

2   Several pricing strategies might be employed – cost-based, market-based and competition-based. Different strategies and pricing methods are appropriate in different circumstances.

3   When a new product is launched into the introduction stage of the product life cycle, a business may wish to choose either a penetration or a skimming strategy in order to achieve its marketing objectives.

Mini Case Study

Drive-It is a car and van rental business. It owns 35 vehicles of varying sizes in its fleet and hires out the vehicles for periods of time from one day to a month. On one of its vehicles, the Vauxhall Vectra, it has allocated the following costs per hire:

Admin. and marketing   £2,000 per annum
Depreciation   £12.50 per day, whether or not it is hired
Service costs   £3.25 per day if hired
Insurance costs   £8 per day if hired

The business operates on a six-day week, 50 weeks a year, and the car is hired out on 200 days. The business uses a full cost pricing method, adding a mark-up of 25%.

A local competitor has just announced that it is cutting its prices and will be charging a rate of just £24 per day as part of an introductory offer which will hopefully encourage customers to hire its cars. Drive-It knows that the competitor will not be able to sustain the introductory offer, but is conscious that its business may suffer from a fall in revenue as a result.

1 What is the name of the strategy being adopted by the competitor?   [1]

2 Calculate the cost per day of hiring out the Vectra and hence the price charged to customers.   [6]

3 Calculate the lowest price that Drive-It might charge in response to the competitor, stating your assumptions.   [3]

4 Using your answers to 2 and 3 and stating your assumptions, discuss the possible pricing strategies open to Drive-It.   [10]

20

Maxi Case Study

In May 1999, BA announced a reduction in profits of 61%, mainly due to the fierce competition on some of the major north Atlantic routes. The main cause of this was the Asian crisis which had reduced demand for flights to the Far East; in response to this, the Asian airlines moved the spare capacity to the north Atlantic routes. The other reason was the intense competition at the budget end of the market from companies such as easyJet and Ryanair. This had placed significant pressure on all companies to reduce their prices.

EasyJet, founded in 1995 by Stelios Hajiloannou, was originally set up to take advantage of the growing segmentation in the market; not only were airlines charging various amounts for the same journey, albeit in different seats, they were also beginning to offer cut-price, no frills journeys. EasyJet targeted the latter, recognising the growth in the market segment and therefore the potential profits.

By 1999 easyJet owned a mere 12 Boeing 737s although it has since taken delivery of a further 12. Its revenue was just over one third of BA's profit, and yet it was able to earn a profit margin of 3%, resulting in pre-tax profits of £2.3 million. Part of its success is due to the fact that easyJet reduces its costs by offering no free food or drink on board, although it must invest heavily in advertising to ensure people know about the low prices. It uses the Internet to allow customers to purchase tickets, cutting out the middlemen for further cost savings. In this case, because the cost of an extra journey on an aeroplane is so low, it means that most of the price is profit. BA's low-cost subsidiary, known as Go, was predicted to make a loss for the first three years of its operation even though it is part of a much larger company. Go began in 1998, following the success of easyJet. This demonstrates the insignificance of economies of scale at the budget end of the market.

Robert Ayling, BA Chief Executive, responded to the drop in profit by announcing a plan to improve the performance of BA by reducing the number of cut-price economy class seats. Instead, it planned to market its business class travel more aggressively, having developed a new style of seat which turns into a bed, aimed at the long-haul market. This would allow the business to charge much higher premium prices for these air journeys. Arguably, BA was being a little too impatient, given that easyJet did not have things easy at the start, with a loss in the first year of £50 million and £3.3 million in the second year, although this has since turned into a healthy profit. This could be due to the fact that easyJet is a private limited company, so it does not have to wait for reaction from the city or the institutional investors in order to take decisions.

There was more action at the budget end with competition from Ryanair, another no frills airline, which offered free seats at the start of 1999. If a passenger travelled from London to Glasgow or Dublin, the seat cost an incredible £29.99, but the extra seat was free! At the same time, Go responded with return flights to Rome and Bologna for £70.

The extra capacity due to the increase in the number of aeroplanes being assigned to cater for the no frills market has actually pushed prices further down, although with a free journey, Ryanair was charging less than the marginal cost which is not a strategy it would want to adopt for long.

So confident was easyJet's owner of the success of his company, that he actually set up a competition to predict the amount of losses Go had cost BA during 1999. Well over 2,000 people entered the competition, although BA did not include the loss in its profit announcement.

Source: *Financial Times* 26/5/99; *Sunday Business*, January 1999; easyJet website

1 Define: subsidiary, budget end of the market, profit margin. [6]

2 Outline the evidence which suggests that size is not necessarily the key to low prices. Why might this evidence be surprising? [6]

3 Calculate the revenue of easyJet, to the nearest million pounds. [2]

4 Using supply and demand diagrams, explain the effect of the Asian crisis on north Atlantic air travel prices. [6]

5 a) Which costs will make up the marginal cost of an air journey? [2]

b) Why would Ryanair charge less than marginal cost? [2]

6 a) In such a low-margin business, why is volume so significant? [3]

b) Explain why the change in BA's strategy might be beneficial to the company's profit margin. [3]

7 Either

a) Outline the possible pricing strategies mentioned. Discuss the appropriateness of the strategies given the segmentation of the market.

Or

b) Prepare a presentation which states which type of pricing strategy the business has used, justifying and explaining your choice. [10]

40

Elasticity

Learning objectives

Having read this unit, students will be able to

1 define price and income elasticity

2 calculate and interpret elasticities

3 understand the factors that influence elasticity for a range of products

4 understand the significance of elasticity for a business

Context

Most businesses will regularly try to increase demand for their products by lowering prices. The attraction of buying the same product at a lower price causes consumers to feel that they are getting a 'bargain' which prompts extra demand. Sometimes businesses are forced to put their prices up when the Chancellor of the Exchequer places extra taxation on certain products e.g. petrol; he targets petrol because he knows that demand is not likely to fall significantly due to the rise in tax. A business that makes luxury products will benefit from a growth in consumers' income because consumers have more money to spend, although a bread maker is not likely to feel much benefit from the increase in income. The extent to which demand changes following a change in another variable is measured by elasticity of demand.

The concept of elasticity

Elasticity is a measure of responsiveness. A business likes to be able to predict the likely response to a change in any of the factors that affect demand. If such a response can be predicted with some degree of accuracy, then a business will be better placed to anticipate changes in the market.

Factors of demand revisited

Unit 8 Economic theory covered the four factors that affect demand. These are:

- Price of own product
- Price of competitor's product, whether it is a substitute or a complement
- Income
- Consumer tastes and trends

Price elasticity

If a business increases its price, demand will fall and vice versa. This is demonstrated in the demand schedule for a particular product (*see Figure 18.1*).

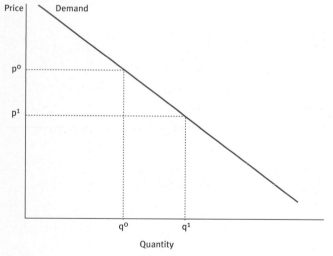

Figure 18.1 Demand schedule

If the price is reduced from p^0 to p^1, demand will increase from q^0 to q^1. The extent to which demand

increases when the price falls will be significant when making the decision whether to increase the price. This relative change in demand following a change in price is measured by the price elasticity of demand.

e.g. supposing a business reduces the price of a product from £20 to £18. As a result, demand increases from £10,000 units to 12,000 units.

In percentage terms, the price has decreased by $\frac{£2}{£20}$ = 10%, and in response to the price change, demand has increased by $\frac{2,000}{10,000}$ = 20%. These two changes are related by a formula:

price elasticity of demand
$$= \frac{\text{percentage change in quantity demanded}}{\text{percentage change in price}}$$

Substituting the numbers: $\frac{20\%}{10\%}$, the product under investigation has price elasticity of 2.

Question 1

If the price of a product falls from £15 to £12 and demand increases from 4,000 units per month to 5,000 units per month, calculate the price elasticity of demand for the product. [3]

Question 2

If the price elasticity of demand for high quality apple pies is estimated to be 0.8 and a business increases the price by 20%, what will be the likely change in demand? [3]

Question 3

Manacle Ltd has decided to reduce the price of its safety chains which it sells to security firms. The price is presently £3 per metre, although a price reduction of 5% is likely to increase demand by 12%. Present demand is 5,000 metres per week.

a) Calculate price elasticity of demand. [1]

b) Calculate the new level of demand, following a 5% reduction in price. [2]

c) Calculate the revenue before and after the price change. [4]

One of the principal factors that determine whether the business decides to increase or reduce its price will be the level of elasticity. If, for example, the price of petrol is increased, then the demand will fall but by a smaller percentage than the change in the price e.g. price increase = 10%, demand decrease = less than 10%. In these cases calculating the price elasticity of demand will give an answer that will be less than one. In this instance, the demand for the product is referred to as being price **inelastic**.

Alternatively, if, following a price reduction of 10%, demand rises by more than 10%, the answer to calculating the price elasticity of demand for the product will be more than one. In this instance, the product is referred to as being price **elastic**.

Table 1

Demand change greater than price change	Price elastic
Demand change less than price change	Price inelastic
Demand change equal to price change	Unitary elasticity

Effect on revenue

A company will consider the effect on revenue as one of the main factors that determine whether or not the price should be changed. The effect on revenue will therefore depend on the elasticity e.g. if the price of a product is increased from £3 to £3.36 (12%) and demand falls from 1,000 units per day to 950 units per day (5%), the effect on revenue will be:

Before   £3   ×   1,000   =   £3,000

After   £3.36 ×   950   =   £3,192

i.e. an increase in revenue of £192.

In the above case, the price elasticity = $\frac{5\%}{12\%}$ = 0.42

which is inelastic.

Therefore if the demand is price inelastic and the business has an objective to increase revenue, the price must be increased. Alternatively, if the demand is price elastic with the same objective the price must be decreased.

Question 4

The price of a product is decreased by 4% from £5. The result is an increase in quantity purchased by 6,000 units from 100,000 units.

a) Calculate the price elasticity of demand.   [2]

b) Is demand for the product price elastic or price inelastic?   [1]

c) Based on your answer to b) suggest whether the business was justified in its decision to reduce the price, if the objective was to increase revenue. No calculations are necessary.   [3]

d) Justify your answer to c) with appropriate calculations.   [4]

Question 5

A manufacturer of saucepans is considering a price increase of 6%, with a view to developing a more up-market image.

	Now	Proposed
Price	£70	£74.20
Unit cost	£40	£44
Monthly demand	12000	11640

a) Explain the change in unit cost following the proposed price increase.   [3]

b) Calculate the change in i) revenue ii) profit, following the price increase.   [5]

c) Is the demand for saucepans price elastic or price inelastic?   [3]

d) Comment on whether the business should increase its price by 6%.   [4]

Cross price elasticity

All businesses will operate in a market where the price of a substitute could increase or decrease, as could the price of a complement. Examples of substitute products are tea and coffee. If the price of tea is increased, the demand for coffee will increase, because it has become relatively less expensive.

Alternatively, the price of CDs may increase, which may reduce the demand for CD players. Because the demand for CD players is derived from the demand for CDs, the two products are known as complements. The effect on the demand for one product can depend on the price of a competitor. This can be measured by

cross price elasticity of demand

$$= \frac{\text{percentage change in demand for product A}}{\text{percentage change in price of product B}}$$

Question 6

A competitor of Tiger's Maid reduced its prices by 4p to 36p in an attempt to gain market share. Tiger's ice-cream sales consequently fell by 1%.

a) Calculate the cross price elasticity of demand.   [2]

b) Indicate whether the competitor would be pleased with the outcome.   [6]

Whether the answer to cross price elasticity is positive or negative will depend on whether the products are complements or substitutes e.g. Products A and B are complements. If the price of A increases, demand for product B will decrease because the total package of A and B together has become more expensive. The answer to the cross price elasticity is therefore negative if the products are complements.

If, on the other hand, products A and B are substitutes, then an increase in the price of A will make product B appear relatively less expensive, therefore the demand for B will rise. The answer to the cross price elasticity is therefore positive if the products are substitutes.

Question 7

Wash-It has developed a range of hygiene products, sold under the company's brand name. Two products within the range – shampoo and conditioner – are sold together. Wash-It is intending to reduce the price of shampoo by 30 pence, to £3.30. As a result, demand for conditioner is expected to rise from 40,000 units to 42,000 units.

a) Calculate the cross price elasticity of demand for conditioner.   [3]

b) What additional information might you need before advising the business whether or not to change the price of shampoo?   [3]

Income elasticity

There are certain products whose demand will depend on the level of income within an economy. The demand for all products is, to a greater or lesser extent, sensitive to levels of income e.g. if there is a recession, and the level of disposable income falls, then there is likely to be a reduction in demand for all products. Some products will be more affected than others and the effect of a change in income on the level of demand for one product is measured by:

income elasticity of demand

$$= \frac{\text{percentage change in demand}}{\text{percentage change in income}}$$

e.g. demand for hi-fis is 10,000 per month at Weaker Sounds plc. Income is predicted to rise by 2% over the next 12 months and the products have an income elasticity of 1.7. The effect on demand can be calculated substituting into the above formula:

$$1.7 = \frac{\% \text{ change in demand}}{2\%}$$

therefore % change in demand = 3.4%

The new demand is therefore 10,000 × 1.034 = 10,340 units per month.

Question 8

Rank the following products in terms of how much demand will change if incomes change. Justify your ranking.

Wallpaper
Mobile phones
Bread
Baked beans
Washing powder
Mortgage interest payments   [6]

The level of income can be measured in several ways:

a) Growth in Gross Domestic Product (per capita of population)

b) Increase in real wages

c) Increase in disposable income

If the increase in income results in an increase in demand which is relatively larger than the increase in income, the product is said to be income elastic. Products that fall into this category tend to be luxuries or non-necessities, such as cars, or household products. These can be referred to as big-ticket items because of the significant amount of expenditure and the nature of the product, meaning the purchase of such items tends to be one-off.

Alternatively, products such as bread, milk and other basic foodstuffs tend to be income inelastic in that a change in income will have little effect on demand. Some products are actually demanded less due to an increase in income. These tend to be tertiary brands i.e. those at the bottom end of the price range. When incomes rise, consumers 'trade up' i.e. buy the more expensive substitute.

Question 9

The staff at Hodson & Sons garage all received a substantial wage increase as a reward for an extremely good year. The average pay increase was 10%. As a result, the local bakery noticed an upsurge in demand for its fresh cream cakes that previously had not been bought by the garage staff as they claimed the cakes were 'just that bit too expensive'. The increase in the sales volume of the cream cakes was 15% and yet the sales of bread rolls had shown only a 3% increase.

a) Calculate the income elasticity for both the cream cakes and the bread rolls. [4]

b) Suggest one reason why the answers in a) are different. [2]

c) Why is the government able to continually increase the tax on products such as cigarettes and petrol? Ignore any social issues. [4]

Advertising elasticity

If a business launches a new advertising campaign, it will have studied the likely effect on demand. Although this is difficult to gauge, a business will be keen to assess the effectiveness of its advertising in order to achieve the lowest possible ratio of advertising to sales revenue. The impact that a particular advertising campaign has upon the demand for a product is measured by

advertising elasticity of demand

$$= \frac{\text{percentage change in quantity demanded}}{\text{percentage change in advertising}}$$

e.g. if advertising expenditure is increased from £10 million to £12 million per annum (20%) and demand increased from 40 million units to 46 million units per annum (15%), then

$$\text{advertising elasticity of demand} = \frac{15\%}{12\%} = 0.75.$$

Another method of assessing whether advertising should be carried out uses the formula

$$\text{advertising : sales ratio} = \frac{\text{advertising expenditure}}{\text{sales revenue}}$$

e.g.

	Advertising expenditure	Sales revenue	Advertising sales
before	£50 m	£800 m	6.7%
after	£70 m	£880 m	12.6%
% increase	40%	10%	

In the above example advertising elasticity $= \frac{10\%}{40\%}$, so demand is advertising inelastic, which is backed up by an increase in the advertising to sales ratio. Although the extra cost of advertising is £20 million, compared with the extra £80 million revenue, it is the percentage change which is more important.

Question 10

Advertising expenditure for a brand of coffee was raised from £100,000 to £120,000 per annum. As a result sales volume rose by 30%.

a) What is the advertising elasticity of demand? [2]

b) What other information is needed to assess whether the additional expenditure was cost-effective? [4]

Question 11

	Advertising elasticity	Income elasticity	Price elasticity
Product			
X	1.8	0.7	1.3
Y	0.7	1.8	0.5
Z	1.4	−0.1	2.1

The above figures relate to three products – contact lenses, own brand cereal and mobile phones. Suggest which product corresponds to X, Y and Z above, giving your reasons. [10]

Factors determining the level of elasticity

■ The nature of the product

If the product is a necessity such as milk or bread, any change in price will have little or no effect on the level of sales. These products are classed as being price inelastic. However, if the product is a luxury good such as perfume or after-shave, a change in price will have a significant effect on the amount demanded. These products would be classed as being price elastic.

■ The number of substitutes

Where there are several substitutes, a change in the price of one product will lead to a greater change in the quantity demanded. If, for instance, the price of one brand of washing powder increased, it is more likely that the subsequent fall in demand would be proportionately greater as consumers switched to cheaper alternatives. In this instance, the washing powder would be price elastic. Alternatively, where there are no real substitutes, any change in price will have little effect on the level of demand.

■ Complementary products

Goods that are frequently purchased and used in conjunction with each other will normally be price inelastic; it depends upon the degree of complementarity. An increase in the price of one product may lead to a significant change in the level of demand. For example, in the mid-1970s when there was a quadrupling of the price of petrol there was a significant increase in the demand for small cars. However, paper and books are not so complementary and therefore a change in the price of paper will not have a significant effect on demand for books.

■ Size of price change

A large change in price is more likely to have a proportionately greater effect than a small one. Changing the price by 1% here or there will not have the same effect as a wholesale price increase or reduction which will receive more attention.

■ Level of price

A change in price of cheaper goods will not have such an effect on demand because the nominal (actual) change will be smaller than for more expensive goods. If a car manufacturer reduces prices by 10%, this could represent a saving of thousands of pounds.

■ Previous change

A business which has continually reduced its prices or continually claims that the 'bonanza sale' of its products 'must end soon' will face less of a reaction from customers than a business that is promoting itself in this manner for the first time.

Difficulties in using elasticity

■ Assumption of *ceteris paribus* (all other things remain equal) – the different measurements of elasticity make a clear assumption that only one factor can change demand at any one time e.g. if the price decreases, then demand will increase and only the change in price can be measured in terms of its effect on demand. In reality, demand may be affected by income, price of competitors and advertising at the same time. Elasticity can therefore only be used with uni-variate analysis (change in only one variable at once)

■ Difficulty in measurement – unless the business has already changed its prices and all other factors have stayed the same (*ceteris paribus*), the predicted change in demand is difficult to estimate. Even if the above is applicable, creating the same circumstances for a price reduction is impossible. Therefore elasticity is very difficult to measure accurately.

Points for Revision

Key Terms

elasticity	the responsiveness of demand to a change in another variable
price elasticity of demand	the response of demand to a change in price
elastic	demand changes by a greater proportion than the change in the other variable. The answer to elasticity is greater than one
inelastic	demand changes by proportionately less than the change in the other variable. The answer to elasticity is less than one
cross price elasticity of demand	the effect on demand for one product of a change in price of either a substitute or a complement
income elasticity of demand	the effect on demand for one product of a change in the level of income
advertising elasticity of demand	the effect on demand for one product of a change in the level of advertising

Definitions Question:
With reference to a business you know, explain the meaning of any three of the above (your teacher may wish to help you choose).   [5] per definition

Summary Points:

1   Elasticity measures the responsiveness of the demand for a product to a change in one of the factors that affects demand.

2   Elasticity is difficult to measure and therefore several assumptions need to be made when using the concept in business decision making.

Mini Case Study

Having monitored the sales of leading brands in its own stores, a well known supermarket chain is considering the launch of a luxury ice-cream. The choice is between launching its own label or using a distinctive name to build brand recognition. Haagen-Dazs has been stocked for some considerable time and, according to a survey of sales conducted by the supermarket, is especially popular with socio-economic groups A, B and C1.

The supermarket was aware of the nature of the advertising campaigns that had been used by Haagen-Dazs ice-cream and was confident that consumers viewed such a product as an indulgence. When questioning consumers at the supermarket, it was quite clear that Haagen-Dazs was seen as a justifiable treat that was purchased often at the end of the week.

This matched the data that the supermarket had been collecting from the recently introduced storecard which is a promotional scheme to enhance consumer loyalty run on similar lines to that of the Tesco storecard. The storecard provided details of individual consumer purchases and clearly indicated that sales of Haagen-Dazs and other leading brands of luxury ice-cream were buoyant.

Further research suggested that rival supermarkets were selling luxury ice-creams under their own-brand labels, making the market for such products more price-sensitive. The supermarket chain decided to test how sensitive this product was by increasing the mark-up on the established brand name, Haagen-Dazs, at a couple of its stores. At the same time it investigated the significance of income in relation to demand for this particular brand.

The research was conducted over a four-week period and the results were as follows:

	Price	Average sales per week
Haagen-Dazs	£3.00	120
	£3.25	115

The supermarket had an agreement with the distributors of Haagen-Dazs that, provided sufficient boxes of ice-cream cartons were purchased, the equivalent of a minimum of 120 cartons per week for each store in the supermarket chain, the buying cost would be reduced from £2.00 to £1.80 per carton.

---

1 a) Calculate the price elasticity of demand for Haagen-Dazs when the price is increased from £3.00 to £3.25. [3]

   b) Comment on your answer given the nature of the product and the market conditions. [5]

2 Calculate

   a) revenue **b)** profit for before and after the price change. [5]

3 a) Using your answer to question 2, advise the supermarket which price to charge. [3]

   b) Would your answer to **a)** change if the supermarket decided to proceed with the launch of its own brand? [4]

20

Maxi Case Study

Getting across the Channel has never been easier; the wide range of different modes of transport – Eurotunnel, ferry, Hovercraft or catamaran – means the consumer has a great deal of choice compared to the days when the only form of transport was a ferry.

There are the occasional problems with all modes of transport across the Channel; either the weather is too rough, which leads to the cancellation of ferry crossings, or a dispute may mean the Eurostar service is delayed.

Since the building of the Channel Tunnel the degree of competition has intensified with the consumer being the main beneficiary.

Life for the cross-Channel companies has not been easy. The growth of traffic preferring Eurostar, the 'dry land' option, and the EU's decision to end duty free shopping have tested the ingenuity of their marketing executives to the full.

One strategy that was quickly adopted was the merger between P&O and Stena Lines, which has enabled the combined company to compete more effectively.

However, the loss of duty free revenue in 1999 led to the ferry companies and Eurotunnel announcing that large price increases would be needed for the summer of 2000 if the companies were to maintain their level of revenue and profitability. Actual figures were not given by some of the cross-Channel companies, though the holiday tour operators were told to expect increases of about 30%.

Hoverspeed was more specific, stating that a family of five travelling by car would have to pay an additional £15, making the fare £60 from Dover to Calais. The large increase in fares was attributed entirely to the loss of duty free sales.

This worrying news for the cross-Channel companies came at a time when the number of customers wishing to travel to Europe was continuing to increase. The number of visits abroad had increased by over 120% between 1981 and the mid-1990s. This was due partly to the increased prosperity of UK residents although low inflation by the end of the 1990s had increased consumers' incomes still further and as a consequence the demand to travel abroad was still rising.

The reaction to the proposed price increases announced by the cross-Channel companies was greeted calmly by the holiday tour operators. They indicated that they would not necessarily pass on the fare increases to consumers and, if they did, the increases would not be as high.

The plight of the ferry companies was serious; some analysts suggested that duty free sales could account for as much as 50% of their revenue, whilst Eurotunnel collected up to one third of its revenue from duty free sales.

Both groups of companies expected to see an increase in the amount of advertising in an attempt to entice consumers into travelling by their particular mode of transport.

The ferry companies were most concerned at the comments of a shipping analyst from GP Wild International, who stated there was plenty of evidence to suggest that the price elasticity for ferry services was elastic. The consequences for the ferry companies hardly bear thinking about. More news concerning disputes with the French train drivers that led to the postponement of Eurostar trains would be regarded by them as good news indeed.

1 Explain the following terms: marketing executives, low inflation.   [4]

2 Discuss how knowledge of price elasticity of demand might affect the holiday tour operators who buy spaces on the cross-Channel ferries to sell in their package deals.   [8]

3 Explain why demand for ferry journeys might be price elastic.   [4]

4 What might be the effect of the merger of Stena Sealink and P&O Ferries on the industry as a whole?   [6]

5 Discuss why ferry companies might be interested in:

a) income elasticity of demand

b) advertising elasticity of demand   [8]

30

Distribution

Learning objectives

Having read this unit, students will be able to

1   identify the various distribution channels used for getting products to customers

2   understand the differences between franchising and direct selling

3   appreciate the factors involved in selecting and using the most appropriate distribution channel

Context

If you were to enter any local supermarket and see the vast array of products, you might wonder what route these products had taken to arrive on the shelves. Some will have been made on the premises such as bread and cakes, whilst other products will have travelled half-way round the world and will have been handled by several people and machines before eventually being placed on the shelf.

However, it may be the case that you do not purchase all your food from the supermarket. Items such as milk or eggs can be bought direct from the farm, others can be delivered to your door, either from the supermarket or from a mail order company. Some of you may already have purchased items through the Internet. Whatever the source of your purchases, the products will have come through a variety of distribution channels.

Channels of distribution

There is little point in a business spending large sums of money encouraging consumers to buy a particular brand of hair shampoo and providing a sales promotion incentive, if the shampoo has not been placed in the 'correct' retail outlet. If an image has been created for a product, the outlet from which it is to be sold is of paramount importance if the image is to be maintained. Selling reject clothes in the local charity shop or on a market stall is acceptable but it would not be appropriate to sell them in Harrods. A business has to consider carefully where its product is sold in relation to where its potential customers are located. Market research ought to have revealed the most likely geographical areas and the socio-economic groups to which those potential customers belong. This information should then be borne in mind when choosing which outlets should sell the products.

However, there are occasions when the outlets that want to sell the products of a business are not the ones that the business would select. Much media attention has focused on disputes between the major supermarket chains and sportswear manufacturers such as Adidas and Nike. The supermarkets wanted to sell the sportswear at prices that would affect the image of the products and, more importantly perhaps, the other retail outlets that sold the sportswear.

The **channel of distribution** refers not only to the final outlet where consumers can purchase the products of their choice, but the route that is taken from the manufacturer to the consumer.

The channels

The main channels of distribution are shown in Figure 19.1.

The different channels of distribution are of various 'lengths' depending upon the type of product and other factors that are discussed below.

An understanding of the functions of the components, or intermediaries, of each channel is important before addressing the factors that a business takes into consideration when selecting the most appropriate channel to use.

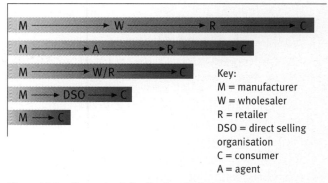

Figure 19.1 Channels of distribution: from the manufacturer to the consumer

Wholesaler

The role of the **wholesaler** is to act as a communicational link between the manufacturer and the retailer. The traditional role of a wholesaler has also been to buy large quantities from the manufacturer and sell smaller quantities to the retailer. This process of 'breaking bulk' is essential if the many small retailers are to be able to supply their consumers in the quantities that are demanded. No manufacturer wants to or is able to deliver just a few items to the thousands of retailers scattered all over the country.

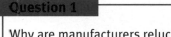

Question 1

Why are manufacturers reluctant to deal directly with consumers or small retailers? [6]

Advantages of using a wholesaler

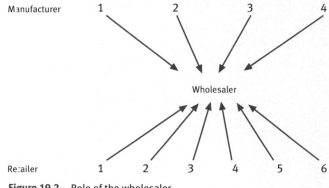

Figure 19.2 Role of the wholesaler

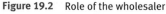

- The existence of the wholesaler enables the manufacturer to deliver to only a few locations instead of to every retailer, saving time and therefore money.

- The role of being a link between the manufacturer, the retailer and the consumer is one of the major strengths of the wholesaler. Undertaking this role as a link is cost-effective for the manufacturer. Instead of having to communicate separately with individual retail outlets, communicating with just a few wholesalers saves time and consequently money. Imagine the cost of writing to and analysing all the replies from individual retailers.

- The wholesaler helps the manufacturer by providing valuable information about the trends in the market which are provided by the retailer. Such information can help the manufacturer plan its production schedules.

- If any complaints are received about a product by the retailer they can be passed back to the manufacturer via the wholesaler, providing the manufacturer with information that may lead to improvements in the product concerned.

- The wholesaler allows the retailer to purchase many of the products it needs from one location, saving the time and the inconvenience of dealing with a range of manufacturers.

- Being local, unlike many manufacturers, the wholesaler is convenient for all the retailers in the catchment area, again saving the retailer valuable time and money in travel.

- There will be more choice at a wholesaler than that available from one particular manufacturer because the wholesaler will stock products from a range of manufacturers.

- The retailer will probably enjoy the benefit of credit facilities provided by the wholesaler which will enhance its cash flow. Such a service would not be provided by the manufacturer unless the retailer was purchasing extremely large quantities, something most retailers do not do.

Disadvantages of using a wholesaler

- In return for providing services to the manufacturer as outlined above, the wholesaler will add on its profit margin to the price which will mean the customer will have to pay more for the product.

- The service the retailer receives from the wholesaler may reflect badly on the companies whose brands of goods have been bought.

- The manufacturer has less control over where the product is sold or for what price it is sold.

- There are fewer opportunities for the manufacturer to market the product at the wholesalers, where it will be competing with other manufacturers' brands.

Cash & carry

The majority of cash & carry stores such as Booker, Makro and Today's operate on similar lines as a wholesaler in terms of breaking bulk and being located for the convenience of retailers. But they differ with regard to payment for the goods purchased.

At cash & carry stores, there is greater emphasis on paying immediately for the goods, although certain retailers with a well established reputation are eligible for credit facilities. They also sell to a wider range of retail outlets, some of which may be only occasional buyers such as sports clubs wanting to buy a supply of crisps to sell in the bar.

Regional distribution centre

Supermarkets have increased their share of the retail market considerably over the last 20 years. The number of small independent retailers has continued to fall. Not only have the small grocers diminished in number, but the majority of our purchases of meat and bread are now made through supermarkets. As a consequence, the supermarkets have bought much larger quantities from the manufacturers. In an attempt to streamline the delivery of products to supermarkets located all over the country, **regional distribution centres** were built to take delivery of a large proportion of the supermarkets' needs (*see Figure 19.3*). The products are distributed to suit the needs of the various stores throughout the country. Each supermarket feeds its requirements to the distribution centre via a computer and takes delivery on a 'just-in-time' basis. This process reduces the need for the individual supermarkets to have large storage facilities and they can therefore use the majority of their space for selling. The other reason (and probably the main reason they started doing this in the first place) was to cut out the middleman and therefore be more competitive with their prices.

Other national retail chains operate in a similar manner. Argos has several distribution centres; one of the latest was opened in 1998 just outside Stafford, strategically placed just a few hundred metres from Junction 13 of the M6, for ease of access to its stores.

Figure 19.3 Regional distribution centres

Agents

An **agent** is an intermediary between the producer or the seller and the consumer. Agents can simply perform the task of selling the product or service on behalf of the seller. For performing this task, the agent will receive either a fee from the consumer or, as is more likely, will charge commission on the sales which is payable by either the buyer or the seller. Until recently the use of agents was almost the only way to buy a foreign holiday. Travel agents are still the most popular way for consumers to select and purchase their holidays, although more consumers are now buying their holidays and flights on the Internet.

Buying tickets for pop concerts is still done through an agency in the majority of cases, though telesales and buying on the Internet are quickly eroding the agent's dominance. Until recently agents were the main channel used to purchase financial services such as

insurance and investments, but as with the previous examples, alternative channels of a more direct nature are available through the Internet.

Agents play a vital role for businesses trying to sell products abroad. The agent is not the owner of the goods at any time of the procedure involved in their sale. The agent will, however, attempt to gain the best possible price for its client because, in many instances, the value of the sales will determine the amount of commission earned. Selling in a foreign country can be fraught with difficulties, in terms of finding appropriate customers, understanding regulations and gaining payment. Hiring the services of an agent who knows the country and the best way of trading in that particular country can be worth the additional expense.

Question 2

What savings would be made by hiring an agent to sell a company's products to a foreign country? [5]

Retailing trends

There is a large range of retail outlets used by the consumer. The traditional retail outlets are listed below (*see Figure 19.4*).

Independent sole traders	P. Eldershaw (Butchers)
Voluntary chain stores	Spar
Multiple chain stores	Virgin Stores
Variety chain stores	W.H. Smith, Boots
Department stores	Rackhams, Debenhams, Harrods
The Co-operative	
Franchise stores (multiple chains)	McDonald's, Tie Rack
Mail order	Janet Fraser

Figure 19.4 Traditional retail outlets

The trend is for more consumers to want to shop out of town where there are facilities to park and a wide range of stores. The Metro centre near Gateshead and the Merryhill centre near Dudley in the West Midlands are good examples of these shopping malls. All the major national chain stores are accessible in pleasant shopping conditions, mainly under cover.

The result of such shopping centres with larger retail outlets is the demise of the small retailer. This trend has had repercussions on the manner in which products are distributed and the channel of distribution that is used. More products are being distributed through shorter or more direct channels because of the quantities involved.

A further problem for the independent retailer operating a 'corner' shop is the emergence of petrol stations expanding their traditional sales of petrol and a few car accessories into being a 'stop and shop' enterprise that caters for the complete range of possible impulse purchases. Several independent newsagents have suffered from garages selling newspapers and confectionery, once the domain of the former. This, too, has affected the manner in which products are distributed. Petrol companies have the advantage of negotiating large discounts for bulk buying which make it difficult for independent retailers to compete. The garage shops are situated in prime sites and do not have the problem of providing parking facilities. There are now approximately 900 Shell Select shops in the UK, Texaco's Star Shops have around 400 outlets, but both are insignificant when compared with BP and Esso each with approximately 1,500 outlets. Some of the independents have tried to retaliate by joining voluntary chain store groups such as Spar, Londis and Mace, that buy together and have their own-label foods as a method of competing.

Franchises

A **franchise** is an arrangement between a person who wishes to operate a business under the name of the franchise and the company itself. A good example of a franchise is Benetton.

Franchising is a compromise between owning one's own business but having the financial and marketing expertise and brand recognition of a large company. For the privilege of 'owning' a franchise and not having to worry about the initial set-up costs in quite the same way as starting a business on one's own, the franchisor (the owner of the franchise) will charge royalties to the franchisee (the person buying the franchise).

The number of franchise retailers has increased over recent years. The most famous franchise business is undoubtedly McDonald's, though the likes of Burger King, Body Shop, Dunkin' Donuts and Tie Rack are equally well known, certainly in the UK. However, if you were to visit almost any country in the world, the name McDonald's would be instantly recognised by all. This is not just because of its franchise but its marketing strategy as a whole.

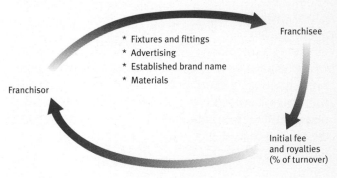

* Fixtures and fittings
* Advertising
* Established brand name
* Materials

Franchisor

Franchisee

Initial fee and royalties (% of turnover)

Figure 19.5   Franchisor and franchisee

The level of royalties paid to the franchisor, calculated as a percentage of the sales revenue, varies considerably between franchises. McDonald's charges the franchisee between 5.75% and 18.5%, whereas Burger King charges approximately 3.4%. In addition, in exchange for the use of an established brand name, the franchisee will have to purchase the required products from the franchisor. This is necessary if the product is to remain the same throughout the countries around the world and within individual countries. The fixtures and fittings for the outlet are provided by the franchisor for an initial payment by the franchisee.

Question 3

Suggest reasons why McDonald's chooses to charge its franchisees such a wide range of percentages.   [4]

The trend for franchise businesses is similar to that of all retailers, in that there are now fewer but larger businesses holding franchises, rather than smaller, more numerous holders previously. There are just under 500 franchised outlets of Burger King, the majority of which are owned by large business chains such as Granada, which owns nearly 100.

Direct selling

This is where goods are sold directly from the producer to the consumer without the need for any middlemen or intermediaries.

Direct selling can be conducted in a variety of ways, e.g. 'home parties' as done by Tupperware, where the products will be displayed to consumers in the comfort of their own home and orders are made directly to the producer. There are several examples of other companies joining in on this approach; the Body Shop, in an attempt to boost sales, decided to expand its home shopping facility referred to as Body Shop Direct. By the middle of 1999 it had over 1,600 consultants around the UK. Body Shop expanded its website in order to give information about its location of consultants and its range of products.

Virgin Vie, the Virgin cosmetics company, also decided to concentrate on direct selling in an attempt to boost levels of sales that were considered disappointing.

Mail order

The goods are selected in the customer's home and are ordered from the mail order company, either by phone or by post.

This method of selling directly to the consumer has been in existence for decades. However, it is no longer purely for those who want to spread the cost of buying items over several months or years to ease the burden of the expense. It is also for those who prefer to choose goods without having to visit the shops and thus avoid travelling expenses. There are still consumers who prefer to purchase from the comfort of their own home and who have no access to the modern version of direct selling or mail order, which is buying online; using the Internet to purchase products. Being able to flick through the pages of a catalogue is still a major selling point for the mail order companies such as Argos, Littlewood and Great Universal.

A modern version of the catalogue was introduced by Next who produced a sophisticated 'Directory' which captured the imagination of its consumers. Even the traditional method of buying food has been encroached upon by the mail order approach. Previously, the only food that was ordered from home and delivered directly was the take-away. Somerfield acquired a catalogue grocery mail order company called Flanagans and renamed it 'Supermarket Direct'. This is based in South London and will complement its other home shopping businesses based in Bristol. A Somerfield spokesperson, speaking in 1999, intimated that this acquisition was a strategy to compete with rival retailer Iceland's home shopping facilities.

The increase in home shopping will have repercussions on the channel of distribution for food as more warehouse facilities will be required to service the mail order firms.

Telesales

Telephone sales are usually associated with the 'courtesy' call offering double glazing, finance, new kitchens etc. A less aggressive version of telesales is the customer call centre considered in the maxi case study in *Unit 11*.

Television sales are growing as a result of digitisation. Shopping channels are already available, though not to the same extent as in America. Telesales is a convenient method of purchasing a wide range of products from the comfort of the customer's home. Goods are ordered directly from the company that advertises on the sales channel.

Question 4

Suggest how finding information on top brands on the Internet would be useful to a marketing executive. [8]

Online shopping

This is shopping, again from the comfort of home, using the Internet, both to view the products and to order them.

Somerfield is not the only supermarket chain that is keen to diversify into the home shopping market. Tesco, the leading supermarket chain, launched Tesco Direct which enables customers to order via the web and have their shopping delivered the following day. Such is the demand for this facility that Tesco hoped to have over 100 of its stores operating the service by the end of 1999. Tesco has used direct mail to advertise its service and has had its new logo for Tesco Direct painted on special delivery vans. Many of the traditional high street retailers are also using the Internet which drastically alters the channel of distribution. Instead of products being sent from the manufacturer to regional distribution centres to retail outlets in the high street and finally on to customers, the use of the Internet misses out the need to send products to the retail stores and in some cases the products will be sent direct from the manufacturer.

Manufacturer   Online via the Internet

→ Consumer

Figure 19.6   The latest trends: online shopping

The idea of avoiding the queues for city centre car parks and the jostle within the shops, when the time could be better spent at home, has been used to good effect by eToys. Avoiding Toys 'R' Us on a busy Saturday is an obvious selling point that has led to eToys serving over 350,000 customers within 18 months of starting.

This example of e-commerce is without doubt just the tip of the iceberg. Customers simply click on to the website and make their order with another click of the mouse.

It is possible to buy a wide range of products online. The use of travel agents has been challenged by online bookings for flights and holidays. EasyJet's website offers discounted flights compared with the cost of its flights booked over the telephone. A phone call to easyJet will inform you of its website and the additional savings that can be made without having to wait patiently in a call queue. For those customers who prefer to speak to a human being, easyJet has incorporated into the website the facility to be rung by a representative which is achieved by clicking on the relevant icon.

Websites with their accompanying banner adverts make **online shopping** a viable alternative to traditional methods.

The massive growth in online shopping may require some of the businesses involved to establish distribution centres to meet the increase in orders.

Question 5

Suggest why there may still be a need for normal retail outlets in spite of the growth of shopping online.   [5]

Internet facts

- According to Datamonitor, a market analyst, there will be over 250 million customers online within the next four years and over 300 million by 2005.

- According to Verdict Research, nearly 50% of the UK's top 100 retailers have websites but to date only about 15% are able to trade online.

- A MORI poll conducted on behalf of Hewlett-Packard found that just over 25% of respondents who were already online had purchased goods via the web.

- The purchases were for books, CDs, theatre tickets, flights, holidays and computer equipment.

- MORI also suggested that a quarter of the high income earners who were not already connected expected to be online by the end of 1999.

Question 6

Anderson Consulting stated in 1998 that e-commerce business had helped to increase revenue by between 10 and 20% whilst cutting costs by between 20 and 45%.
Explain how these figures may have been achieved.   [5]

Physical distribution

This is concerned with the actual movement of the products and has recently become more important as the cost of moving goods from the manufacturer to their final destination has escalated dramatically. Consequently, more thought has been given to how this **physical distribution** can be achieved at the lowest possible cost. Competition within markets has become so intense, ensuring that the minimisation of distribution costs may provide a competitive edge for a business.

The major costs involved with the movement of goods are:

- Wages — Drivers' and handlers' wages have increased in recent years
- Machinery — The lorries, ships, rail wagons, containers, lifting gear (from dock cranes to fork lift trucks)
- Warehousing — The costs of building, the land, maintenance costs including security
- Packaging — Boxes and other protective layers

All the above are costs that have to be 'added' to the cost of the product. Consequently distributors have taken a variety of measures in an attempt to minimise these costs.

Physical distribution changes

The size of lorries has over the last decade increased significantly – 30 and 40 tonne lorries are now commonplace on our motorways. Using larger lorries allows the transporting business to benefit from economies of scale by carrying much larger payloads.

The methods of loading and unloading have been modernised, not just for bulk orders but even for smaller loads. Much of the builders' materials that individual consumers may order from their local builders' merchants is delivered with the benefit of integral cranes attached to the lorry which can be used to unload large bags of sand or just 100 bricks.

Lorry with integrated crane

Distribution of products and materials has had to alter as more and more businesses operate JIT ('just-in-time') methods (*see Unit 28 Stock control*) and therefore require more deliveries.

Selecting the appropriate channel of distribution

Several factors have to be considered before selecting the channel of distribution that is most appropriate for the product in question.

■ Type of product

Consideration needs to be given to the characteristics of the product. Its size, shape, weight, value and fragility are all of concern. The ideal route for an expensive and fragile piece of jewellery, pottery or glassware would be the shortest, direct from the manufacturer to the consumer. However this would not be practical, in terms of the cost to the manufacturer. In this instance, concerns over security and manhandling are outweighed by the practical and cost issues.

Similarly, if the product to be distributed is a 'low-value good', this might also suggest a short route in an attempt to minimise costs. Unfortunately, many low-value goods such as crisps are sold in so many types of retail outlets and in varying quantities, that a short, more direct channel is out of the question.

If the product is unique, having been made to order, then the shortest channel linking the manufacturer to the consumer is appropriate. This channel will allow for consultation between the two parties and ensure that the specific customer requirements have been met. Consultations could also take place to arrange for the delivery as and when required. For the producers of, for example, submarines and specialist machinery, a direct channel is the most appropriate.

Consumers

The consumer segment that is being targeted will influence the outlet in which the product will be sold and therefore which channel of distribution will be required.

Quantity to be delivered

The number of items to be delivered is important; if only a few are required it would not be cost-effective to use a short channel as the manufacturer would be involved in transporting just a few items many times over. Under these circumstances it is preferable to use a longer channel involving a wholesaler.

Frequency of delivery

Delivering on a regular basis may make it worthwhile establishing a particular channel for the items involved; however, for the same reason, frequent deliveries would probably necessitate a longer channel.

Location

Distribution to an isolated village would not be economical for a manufacturer so a longer channel would need to be used. Goods being exported may require the expertise of an agent. Goods that are sold all over the country or the world would require a longer channel.

Budget

This will be of significance, especially when the physical distribution factors are considered. If the right equipment is not available the choice of channel may be out of the hands of the manufacturer.

Question 7

Select the most appropriate channel of distribution for the following products (justify your choice):
i)   Cans of a branded soft drink
ii) Holiday canal barges
iii) A daily newspaper   [12]

Points for Revision

Key Terms

channel of distribution	the route that a product takes from manufacturer to consumer
agent	acts as an intermediary between the seller and the customer
wholesaler	provides a link between the manufacturer and the retailer
regional distribution centre	a large-scale depot used by a national retail chain to distribute goods to its own stores as and when required
franchise	the right to trade using the name and products of a business (the franchisor)
direct selling	the shortest channel of distribution, where the manufacturer will sell to the consumer without the use of an intermediary
online shopping	using the Internet to purchase goods and services
physical distribution	the equipment that is actually required to move goods from the manufacturer to the consumer

Definitions Question:
By referring to a business you know, explain the significance of three of the above terms (your teacher may wish to help you with the choice).   [5] per definition

Summary Points:

1 There are various channels of distribution available to ensure that goods and services reach the consumer.

2 The methods of shopping used by consumers are changing rapidly and consequently affecting the channels of distribution.

3 The physical distribution of goods has become more sophisticated due to technological progress.

Mini Case Study

The Arcadia retail group, which consists of Dorothy Perkins, Top Shop, Principles and others, has invested heavily in the Internet.

Christmas 1998 was a poor one for the likes of Dorothy Perkins and others within the group. As a consequence there was a need to find a method of competing, hence the move into selling via the Internet.

The initial plan was to become a service provider, allowing access to the World Wide Web. Arcadia has captured, it claims, a significant share of the Internet clothing market within the UK. Sales figures indicate that the 'Net shop' is the 92nd most successful store in the whole of the group and there are over 1.5 million visitors to its website each week. As a result, an additional 50,000 names have been added to the home shopping mailing list, many of whom have visited the site from overseas, which may present problems if purchases are required.

Being a service provider means for Arcadia that it is able to influence which websites are the easiest to access. Although surfers are free to gain access to anything on the net, some element of control by acting as a service provider gives the business a head start if someone is interested in looking for clothes to buy.

Expanding its operations on the net, Arcadia hopes that its share price will improve. Recent redundancies and cost-saving measures achieved a small recovery in its share price but much will depend upon the success of its investment in the shopping of the future.

Adapted from 'Top Shop chain fashions Internet expansion drive' by Kirstie Hamilton (*The Sunday Times* 28/3/1999).

1 Suggest how the channel of distribution might change if more Dorothy Perkins customers purchased goods using the Internet as opposed to visiting one of the stores.   [6]

2 What are the limitations of shopping online compared to visiting an actual store?   [5]

3 To what extent should Arcadia be pleased with the level of sales achieved via the net?   [4]

4 Why might visitors to the website from abroad create problems if they wished to purchase goods?   [5]

20

Maxi Case Study

Malcolm Walker, the chairman of Iceland and entrepreneur, is cast in the mould of a Richard Branson, who started his business with £60 and has seen his business grow to a value of £477 million. Walker will probably be remembered more for his comments on GM ingredients ('Frankenstein food') than for his innovative style.

Iceland had well over 750 retail outlets throughout the UK selling freezer foods to customers mainly from socio-economic groups C2 and D rather than the higher groups, who only frequent the stores when food is required for special occasions, such as parties and barbecues.

Walker had never been afraid to adapt as the market changed and, as a consequence, he was quick to see how to provide a more convenient service to his customers.

He started his home delivery service in an attempt to remain competitve with his main rivals and to cater for his customers who did not have a car. Walker had originally been opposed to Sunday trading, but research told him that over half of his customers did not have access to a car during the week. When Sunday trading started in earnest, the housewife had a car at her disposal and therefore was tempted to shop out of town, where most of Iceland's rivals were located.

This could have been a major problem for Iceland, as nearly all its stores were in town and city centres. Consequently, Iceland offered a free home delivery service for customers who lived within a 10-mile radius of its stores. The only proviso was that the customer spent at least £25. The scheme was an instant success, with customers using the service spending on average £40 and the majority of deliveries falling within two miles of stores.

Iceland is still the only supermarket chain to offer a delivery service from all its outlets. Although the service has meant increased expenditure on physical distribution, staying in the town centres appears to have been successful for Iceland and its customers. Revenue from home delivery sales accounted for 11% of total sales by the early part of 1999.

Adapted from an article by Dominic Rushe (*The Sunday Times* 23/5/1999).

1 Define: entrepreneur, socio-economic groups.   [4]
2 What would be the increased costs for Iceland's physical distribution, having introduced the free delivery service?   [6]
3 Discuss the factors which Iceland might consider when assessing the best channel of distribution to use.   [10]
4 Discuss the appropriateness of an online shopping facility for Iceland.   [12]

32

Promotion

Learning objectives

Having read this unit, students will be able to

1 demonstrate an understanding of above and below the line promotion

2 recognise the differences between advertising and sales promotion

3 identify an appropriate promotional mix for a given situation

Context

It is difficult to escape the constant bombardment of promotion in our everyday lives. Whether we are watching television, listening to the radio, reading a newspaper or magazine, surfing the net, or even just walking around the shops, there is little respite from some sort of promotional activity. You can no doubt recall a variety of advertising slogans or recognise a can of Coca-Cola regardless of the language on the can.

Promotion has instilled brand names into our subconscious. Kit-Kat is so well known that a recent television advertisement for the snack bar featured only a picture of Loch Ness, the words 'Have a break' and a glimpse of the logo; such is the power of promotion that just three words were sufficient to associate them with a product.

Promotion can involve large amounts of expenditure; Ford spends $1 billion a year. Today there are many ways to promote a product or service. Advertisers have to be aware of the technologically sophisticated consumer and spread the promotional budget far wider to capture the customer. More and more television channels are available to the viewing public, the choice of radio stations has increased, the number of magazines that are read on a regular basis has grown rapidly and with the expansion of PC ownership providing more potential customers with access to the Internet, advertisers are having to adapt their strategies to ensure that the appropriate customer is reached.

The role of promotion

Promotion is used as part of the marketing mix in an attempt to persuade the customer to purchase the products or services of the business. It is up to the business to establish what the needs of the customer are as well as establishing which customers are likely to consider purchasing its products.

The principal objective of promotion is to increase the desire of the customer to buy the products or services on offer. In addition, promotion is used to inform the customer of the product and explain its benefits and uses.

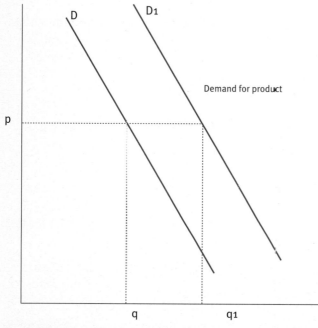

Figure 20.1   Promotion attempts to increase the desire to purchase

Promotion, if successful, can alter the elasticity of a product, making it less elastic and thereby less likely to lose sales if either the price increases or alternatives are available at a cheaper price. This is particularly helpful for e.g. manufacturers of breakfast cereals to add value to their product.

DAGMAR

It is important for promotion to help the customer to become aware of the product and to understand its selling features and distinctiveness. Using DAGMAR (Defining Advertising Goals Measuring Advertising

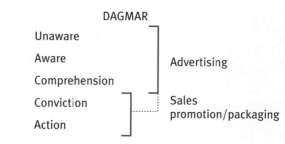

Figure 20.2   DAGMAR promotion guideline

Results), promotion has an important role to fulfil. Promotion can then be used to 'sell' the product or service by explaining exactly what it does and creating an image for the product that makes it more attractive to the customer.

The promotional mix

The **promotional mix** consists of a variety of methods in order to gain sales. The mix consists of above and below the line activities, all used in an attempt to inform and persuade the customer to purchase a particular product.

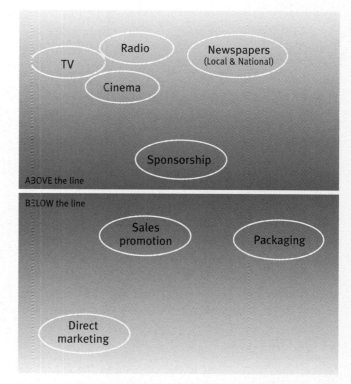

A variety of different promotions to entice the consumer into buying the product

Above the line promotion

Above the line involves the use of media over which a business has little control. Advertisements and promotional offers are broadcast and may or may not be received by the targeted customer.

Above the line promotion relies on the use of **media** such as television, radio and cinema, where there is no personal contact with the customer. Although there is some attempt to target the customer by careful consideration of the timing of the advertisement, there is no attempt to contact individual customers.

Advertising

Advertising is a method of communicating with the mass market which has to be paid for.

Purpose of advertising

One of the main purposes of advertising is to create a distinctive image for the product to enable the business to add value to the product or service. Value is added to a product if the customer is prepared to pay more because a perceived additional benefit can be derived from that product. There are two types of advertising that can be used in an attempt to persuade a customer to purchase a particular product.

■ Informative

As the name suggests, **informative advertising** informs customers that the product exists. Either the product is new to the market, or it is an established brand but has been improved or a new product has been added to the product range. For example, many toothpaste advertisements concentrate on how they combat plaque or gum disease, whilst an advert for a new snack food will probably concentrate on its ingredients.

■ Persuasive

Persuasive adverts appeal to the customer by suggesting how life will be better if the product is purchased. There are occasions when the same message can be

imparted by suggesting the difficulties or problems that may be encountered if the product is not purchased. Many of the adverts will compare one product with another to highlight how theirs is better because it is faster, cheaper to buy or operate, smaller, quieter, easier to use, etc.

> **Task 1**
>
> Collect four advertisements of your choice from a newspaper or magazine and state with reasons which type of advertising is used.   [8]

AIDA

It is important for all advertisements to satisfy the 'AIDA test'. This is similar to the guideline DAGMAR and is a useful guide in judging whether an advertisement is more likely to succeed.

AIDA represents:

- **Attention** – without gaining the attention of the customer, the message cannot be successfully delivered

- **Interest** – once the attention of the customer has been gained, the advertisement must maintain the interest of the customer throughout, in order for the message to be delivered and understood

- **Desire** – it is important for the advertisement to create a level of desire for the product that leads to positive action on behalf of the customer

- **Action** – if the advertisement has been successful, the customer will actually purchase the product or service and will not be diverted into buying an alternative at the point of sale

Method of attraction

Gaining the attention of the customer relies upon the advertiser ensuring that an appropriate method of attraction is used. The method will normally depend upon who is the target of the advert in that the customer should be able to empathise with the character, humour, or situation portrayed.

The most popular methods of attracting the attention of customers are:

■ Famous people

Procter & Gamble's Max Factor cosmetics signed up Madonna to help promote its Gold Range of cosmetics. Seeing a famous face on the television or in a magazine gains the attention of the customer, allowing the message to be imparted to a captive audience.

Walkers Crisps has regularly used a famous person to gain the attention of its target audience e.g. Gary Lineker and Michael Owen. In this case, Walkers actually corrupted the name of the flavour of crisps to generate added interest in the product i.e. Salt and Lineker, Cheese and Owen.

'Salt and Lineker' with 'Cheese and Owen': a top match for Walkers

The famous person who is selected depends upon the product and the customer segment to be targeted.

Choosing a famous person to gain the attention of the customer does not always guarantee success; Yardley, another cosmetics brand, chose Linda Evangelista, a Canadian model, to front what is decidedly a very English product and managed only to confuse the customer as a result (Yardley has subsequently gone into receivership).

Task 2

Choose three advertisements from newspapers, magazines or television that feature a famous person. Based on the character and image of the person, suggest which customer segment is the target of the advert.   [3]

■ Comedy

Several adverts use comedy to gain the attention of the customer; some use a famous person to convey the comedy. Rowan Atkinson appeared in a series of Barclaycard adverts as a hapless MI5 agent.

■ Cartoons

Kellogg's Rice Krispies, Frosties and Coco Pops all use cartoons.

■ Sex

Adverts for men's magazines such as *FHM*, *Maxim*, *GQ* and *Esquire* often feature women in some sort of seductive pose to gain the attention of the reader. Another example is the controversial advert for Wonderbra. The magazine advert features a young woman wearing one of the company's garments and has the phrase 'I can't cook; who cares?' strategically placed upon the page.

■ Financial incentives

D.F.S., the furniture retailer, is constantly bombarding the customer with financial incentives to attract his/her attention which is also a method of sales promotion.

Question 1

Suggest four factors that would influence the method of attraction used by a business for its product or service.   [4]

Media

■ Television

Advertisements on the television are becoming more sophisticated in an attempt to gain the attention of the consumer. In 1999, Guinness spent over £1 million on an advertisement which showed an unusual surfing scene with horses joining the surfers 'riding' the waves.

One of the difficulties for companies wishing to advertise on television is the growing number of channels that are available thanks to digital technology. The number of potential customers watching any one programme is actually falling because of the vast choice. However, the benefit is that it may be possible to take advantage of the specialist programmes to target a more specific audience.

Task 3

By using your own market research, find out which television advertisements members of either your family or your peer group can remember seeing in the last few days. What is it about the adverts that they remember?

■ Radio

The use of commercial radio as an advertising medium has expanded rapidly over the last 20 years.

Commercial radio is listened to by over 60% of listeners under the age of 55. With the growth of radio stations to as many as 265 in 2000, there are plenty of potential customers to target. Once Virgin had started its commercial station in 1993, its progress as a medium for promotion took off in a dramatic fashion. BRMB ran a famous advertising campaign by staging a blind date wedding competition: individuals were encouraged to enter a competiton to marry someone they would not see, apart from in photographs, before the wedding ceremony. The prize included a rent-free apartment in Birmingham, a new car and a luxury foreign holiday for the honeymoon.

The promotional publicity was beyond the expectations of the radio station as the wedding was featured in all the national newspapers and on the television news and prompted several debates as to the ethics of such a promotion. Ironically, the marriage ended in divorce soon after.

■ Cinema

With the large growth in cinema audiences since the early 1990s, there has been a corresponding increase in the amount of cinema advertising.

■ Newspapers

A wide range of national newspapers can be used to place advertisements. Although these adverts cannot target individual customers, there is a good chance of targeting the right segment of the market.

This is because there are differences in the readership of these papers. Socio-economic groups A, B and possibly C1 are more likely to read *The Times* and the *Daily Telegraph* as opposed to the tabloid papers, such as *The Sun* and *The Mirror*. More than half the population over the age of 18 read a national newspaper on a regular basis so this provides a cost-effective method of 'contacting' many potential customers.

Local newspapers are also well read by adults, the vast majority are evening papers and offer news pertaining to the local area. Consequently they provide an ideal medium for local businesses which can use the classified advertisements section or may decide to take a display advertisement. Both types are relatively inexpensive and yet have a large circulation.

■ Magazines

The number of titles on the market grew during the late 1990s. The number of magazines aimed at teenagers of both sexes was a real growth area, especially for men's magazines. As the number of such magazines increases, there are more opportunities to target specific segments of the market, making this an excellent medium to use for products that are used by the readership.

Specialist magazines, especially for computers, make the task of reaching the target market that much easier; however this virtue must be balanced by the fact that many readers may be saturated by the amount of adverts in these magazines, reducing their effectiveness.

National Newspaper Circulations

Dailies	March 1999	Feb1999	Month-on-month % change	Oct 1998 March 1999	Oct 1997 March 1998	Year-on-year % change
The Sun	3,813,381	3,698,805	3.10	3,698,646	3,723,163	-0.66
The Mirror	2,303,510	2,301,499	0.09	2,298,214	2,290,380	0.34
Daily Record	691,811	700,497	-1.24	680,442	677,565	0.42
Daily Star	514,680	534,704	-3.74	536,242	591,255	-9.30
Daily Mail	2,362,184	2,346,502	0.67	2,347,022	2,253,898	4.13
The Express	1,085,550	1,091,790	-0.57	1,095,484	1,183,321	-7.42
Daily Telegraph	1,045,336	1,043,653	0.16	1,043,330	1,084,446	-3.79
The Times	746,403	755,359	-1.19	748,761	806,240	-7.13
The Guardian	401,494	400.600	0.47	396,984	403,192	-1.54
FT	385,803	380,581	1.37	382,082	342,570	11.53
The Independent	224,306	220,203	1.86	221,310	234,043	-5.44
The Scotsman	79,775	80,332	-0.69	79,760	n/a	=

Sundays						
News of the World	4,313,582	4,296,652	0.39	4,252,692	4,409,772	-3.56
Sunday Mirror	1,933,074	1,985,075	-2.62	1,986,913	2,138,296	-7.08
Sunday People	1,620,105	1,662,080	-2.53	1,676,721	1,797,608	-6.72
Mail on Sunday	2,319,272	2,326,195	-0.30	2,325,750	2,209,387	5.27
Express on Sunday	1,005,926	1,010,122	-0.42	1,005,987	1,102,595	-8.76
Sunday Times	1,366,464	1,377,297	-0.79	1,367,776	1,351,847	1.18
Sunday Telegraph	808,826	816,978	-1.00	814,986	863,180	-5.58
The Observer	401,403	406,937	-1.36	404,672	420,182	-3.69
Independent on Sun.	255,982	252,105	1.54	253,240	272,101	-6.93
Scotland on Sunday	118,492	124,437	-4.73	125,199	n/a	=
Sunday Business	55,123	56,065	-1.63	52,084	n/a	=

Source: *Marketing* 22/4/99

Figure 20.3   Newspaper circulation figures

Question 2

a) Suggest how a business would use the information in Figure 20.3 when planning an advertising campaign.   [8]

b) With reference to Figure 20.3, how would you calculate the most cost-effective newspaper, given the cost of a full-page advertisement in *The Sun* and the *Daily Express* is approximately £35,000 and £20,000 respectively?   [4]

Question 3

Using Table 1, suggest how it could help in the process of selecting the most appropriate media for an advertising campaign for:
  i) a children's toy
  ii) a new chocolate bar
  iii) a mobile phone

Justify your suggestions.   [12]

Table 1

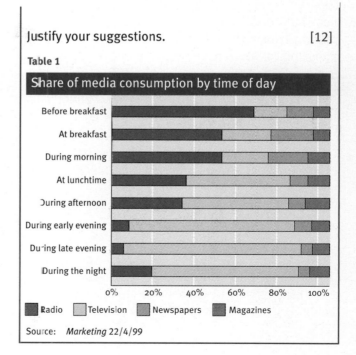

Share of media consumption by time of day

Before breakfast
At breakfast
During morning
At lunchtime
During afternoon
During early evening
During late evening
During the night

0%   20%   40%   60%   80%   100%

■ Radio   ☐ Television   ■ Newspapers   ■ Magazines

Source: *Marketing* 22/4/99

■ Posters

Although the majority are static and limited in the amount of detail that can be effectively imparted to the customer, posters are regularly used to support an advertising campaign, acting as reinforcement to other adverts by reminding the customer of the advert and the product.

There is a role for poster adverts, especially for regional events or products and services. It is impossible to use the London Underground and fail to notice the many poster adverts for local theatres and concerts. As a very cheap medium, posters are useful for all sorts of local events including the village summer fayre.

There has been a dramatic increase in the usage of posters as marketing experts have become more adventurous and imaginative as to where a poster can be placed and what can be put on them. The growth of posters outdoors has been nearly 60% since 1995, with revenue of well over £500 million.

Innovations have led to e.g. posters at bus shelters reacting to movement and emitting sound messages.

Others use fragrance diffusers to produce the aroma of various products such as coffee and perfume. There have been some instances of whole tube stations being branded for Capital Radio and even a branded escalator at the Bank tube station for American Airlines. Clever poster advertising has been placed on No Smoking signs by Nicotinell. Another poster campaign which many may relate to, travelling home on a crowded tube after work on a balmy summer's evening, is on the grab handles, which have been branded by Elida Fabergé deodorant!

Buses have for many years carried posters, but of late have become mobile advertisements on a grand scale with, in some cases, the whole bus being converted into one giant advertisement. With advanced research techniques it has become possible to map demographic areas where advertisements are more likely to be seen and heard by the targeted customers.

■ On the Internet

The use of the Internet as an advertising medium is one of the main growth areas. Websites are being put online at an incredible rate. The major advantages of the Internet are the ease with which an advert can be updated, and the ability to target segments of customers.

E-commerce and the sale of products over the net are still in their infancy and yet, for many, they are a natural way to ascertain information about a wide range of products (*see Unit 19 Distribution*).

Compaq, now the owner of the search engine AltaVista, has used this to reach subscribers with a wide range of advertisements on websites. These advertisements, known as 'banner ads', started in 1994 and were reputed to be worth $1.3 billion by 1998, according to Internet Advertising Bureau.

UK advertising revenue, according to Fletcher Research, for 1998 was approximately £15 million but was expected to be around £268 million by the year 2001.

Virgin launched its website in the summer of 1999. Sir Richard Branson, the owner of the Virgin label, spent £50 million investing in the Internet, of which nearly £500,000 was spent by Virgin Atlantic. The Internet will then be used to target specific customers (*see Direct marketing later in this unit*). Microsoft has gained by far the most advertising revenue from online advertising, signing a contract estimated to be in the region of £54 million with Bank One to advertise its credit card services. This American bank has probably opened the door for other marketeers to encourage their clients to use the Internet as a medium for advertising their products. A spokesman for Bank One suggested that the Internet was a marketing channel that would complement the more traditional advertising channels (*details are available on* www.bankone.com).

In addition, Channel 5 launched its net site (www.channel5.co.uk) with Melinda Messenger marketing the site in a series of advertisements that featured in *The Sun* newspaper. The site's e-mail section sells Melinda Messenger merchandise.

Task 4

For the above media make a presentation of the advantages and disadvantages and recommend which would be most suitable for a product or service of your choice. [20]

Successful adverts

Adwatch in *Marketing* magazine measures the response of any particular advert. Pringles has been a huge success according to Adwatch.

The marketing of the Renault Clio is a good example of how the marketing mix has been carefully chosen to ensure that the targeted customer is reached. Apart from the advertising on television, a series of adverts appeared in selected magazines appropriate for the segment of both male and female customers along with a poster campaign, used to remind customers of the brand name. All the adverts were constructed to ensure the customer was provided with all the information with regard to the improvements that Renault had incorporated into the latest model of the Clio. The safety features introduced played a prominent part within the advertisement.

Constraints on advertising

To ensure that advertisements are of an acceptable standard several laws exist to protect the customer from adverts that may be misleading or may attempt to exploit the customer (*see Unit 58 Legal environment*).

The Advertising Standards Authority (ASA)

The role of this independent body is to ensure that all adverts are 'legal, decent, honest and truthful'. The ASA also attempts to ensure that adverts do not cause offence to anyone.

If a member of the public takes offence at any advertisement, reporting this to the ASA will lead to the body investigating the claim. If the ASA receives several complaints about the same advert it is more likely to make a recommendation that the advert is altered or stopped from being shown or announced. The ASA now has the power to check poster adverts before being displayed if the company in question has previously had a complaint against one of its adverts upheld.

The ASA did receive a lot of complaints about an advert on Channel 4 which showed scenes of gunfights as part of an advert for Film Four. A picture of a man pointing a gun at the reader of newspaper adverts placed in *The Times* and *The Sunday Times* alongside a man lying in a pool of blood was found to be offensive by the ASA. It was considered that scenes appearing in newspapers would probably be seen by children. The organisation also prevents the continual appearance of certain brands placed in strategic positions in film scenes, in order to gain exposure to the audience.

The Committee of Advertising Practice (CAP)

This body has suggested the formation of a trustmark scheme for adverts and promotions on the Internet. Such a scheme is an attempt to ensure that adverts on the Internet are policed properly.

Ethics

How provocative an advert can be, without fear of offence or accusation or exploitation, is a very difficult judgement to make. No one has objected to the trend for a more hard-hitting approach in the 'Don't drink and drive' campaigns that feature each Christmas. Many of the scenes that are shown for this are brutal, but necessary, if the campaign is to work.

The approach to advertising to children is another matter; Sweden has banned television adverts aimed at children altogether.

The Incorporated Society of British Advertisers was quick to attack a demand by Friends of the Earth, who wanted a ban on children's adverts after 9 p.m.

Publicity

This term can have a variety of meanings; publicity is communication to the market which is unpaid. It can therefore be positive or negative; by not paying for it, the business may prosper or suffer due to media attention.

Question 4

Think of a piece of **a)** positive publicity and **b)** negative publicity. What do you think will have been the effect on the business? [6]

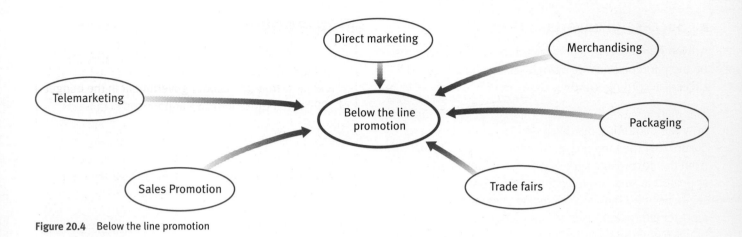

Figure 20.4   Below the line promotion

Below the line promotion

Below the line promotion is much more specific and uses media over which the business has control such as **direct marketing** and **sales promotion** offers on its packaging.

Below the line promotion includes the use of sales promotion, mailshots (direct marketing), packaging, **merchandising**, telemarketing (personal selling), public relations and trade fairs.

This type of promotion relies on media that are operated by the business itself.

The main attribute of this type of promotion is that a business can target specific customers more easily than is the case for above the line. The use of database material is vital to the success of these methods of promotion. Nevertheless, there are some difficulties with this approach in that the targeted customers may become resistant to constant direct mailing and telephone calls.

They are frequently used as an incentive for new products trying to establish themselves in the market; alternatively sales promotions are used as a method of extending the life of a product (*see Unit 16 Product*).

Sales promotion

Sales promotion is divided into two parts:

- Into the pipeline, which refers to attempts by

manufacturers to encourage retailers and wholesalers to stock the product

- Out of the pipeline, which refers to attempts by manufacturers to encourage customers to purchase

It is important to understand that sales promotion includes more than just a money-off voucher on the packet of a fast moving consumer good (FMCG). In order for the customer to purchase the product from the retailer, the latter has had to be persuaded to stock the product in the first place. For this to be achieved, the company selling the product will have had to educate its sales-force on the distinctive selling features of the product in order to help it persuade the retailer to stock it.

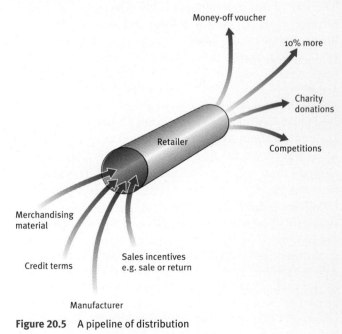

Figure 20.5   A pipeline of distribution

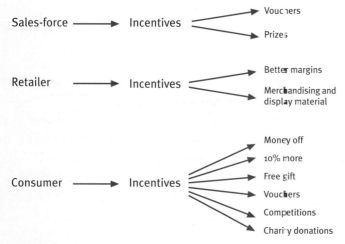

Figure 20.6

The chart shows that sales promotion has three distinct elements:

■ Sales-force

If the business is to ensure that its products end up on the shelves of the required retail outlets, the sales-force must have done its job well.

In order for it to do this, the sales team needs to know all about the product and be motivated to sell it properly to the retailers.

There is a variety of incentives that are available to sales-forces e.g. competitions for the best salesperson of the month or year may motivate only those who feel they have a realistic chance of winning. Ann Summers, the underwear company, has a policy of recognising the achievement of each of its employees during the year at the annual sales conference, where the best employees are awarded prizes. An alternative that has proved very popular with companies is the use of vouchers that are given out to the sales-force. The vouchers are redeemable in well known chain stores such as BHS and Marks and Spencer. It is estimated that the incentive industry issues approximately £500 million of vouchers and prizes every year.

Kingfisher, the holding company, is one of the largest suppliers of vouchers and appeared unconcerned about the recently announced tax change (*see Question 5*). A spokesperson for the company thought that businesses would be prepared to pay more to gain more vouchers to compensate sales staff.

Other incentives such as travel vouchers or tickets are not yet included in the changes.

Question 5

Businesses that regularly rewarded their sales-forces with the incentive of winning a competition received a severe blow from the Labour government in the budget of 1999 when Gordon Brown announced significant changes in the tax laws by classifying vouchers as a benefit to be taxed. These non-cash vouchers are eligible for NICs (National Insurance contributions). To what extent would you agree with the statement that Gordon Brown's actions have reduced the value of the vouchers in the eyes of the sales-force?   [7]

Trade fairs

This type of sales promotion enables the producer to meet the potential customer personally. The stands are manned by trained sales staff who are ready to meet the needs of the customers.

The Motor Show, held either in London or at the NEC Birmingham, is one of the largest and busiest fairs of the year. Other fairs such as the Ideal Home Exhibition provide an opportunity for the products to be seen by the customer rather than having to rely on glossy brochures and advertising pictures. The sales staff at the fairs are able to conduct formal or informal research into the views of the customers.

■ Retailers and wholesalers

Retailers require incentives to stock goods that may need to replace existing brands because of limited space on the shelves. The retailer will want to know whether it will be worthwhile stocking a new product that may not sell. It is up to the sales-force to convince the retailer that the new product will sell by informing the retailer of the imminent advertising campaign and the display material that will be made available to give the new product prominence within the shop. In addition the profit margin will be a high priority to the retailer; the sales-force will need to ensure the margin is favourable and that there are sufficient incentives to stock a large quantity. The latter is usually achieved by offering a further discount on the amount bought. A bulk-buying discount is standard practice.

There may be other incentives offered depending upon the type of product and the type of retailer that is buying the product.

Question 6

Why might it be worthwhile for a producer of an FMCG product to offer more and better incentives to a supermarket chain than to a range of independent retailers?   [5]

■ Customers – out of the pipeline

The final part of the sales promotion is the incentives at the point of sale that are offered to the customer. If the advertising has been successful, the potential customer has been informed of the new product, should understand what it is and why it ought to be bought. The 'action' part of the process is where the most danger lies for the producer of the product.

Upon entering a retail outlet with the advert still fresh in the mind of the customer, he or she is faced with an array of products of a similar type. It is at this point the customer may waver and either return to a regular brand or get distracted by another brand as a result of the packaging or an incentive that appears too good to miss.

Providing a final incentive is an attempt to ensure the product that has been advertised is selected over all the alternatives available.

There are many different types of sales promotions that are used for customers. Which is used will usually be determined by the product and the type of customer.

■ **Free offers**
   Such gifts range from small toys that are often given out with cereals to a free radio or travel case if a particular insurance or credit card is applied for. Magazines are constantly giving away free CDs, cosmetics and photographs of the latest pop idol to the appropriate customers.

■ **Money off**
   Special price-off stickers or flashes are added to the packaging of the product to draw to the attention of the customer the reduced price.

■ **Credit facilities**
   D.F.S., the furniture store, has always offered incentives for customers to purchase a new three-piece suite by extending the period over which payment can be made. 'Buy now, pay later' is a further inducement, as is free credit for a certain number of years.

■ **X% more**
   More for your money is also popular especially for FMCG items that are sold in a highly competitive market e.g. chocolate bars and cans of beer. 'Buy one get one free' or 'two for the price of one' are typical offers. Many products are available with this type of sales promotion. Pepsi Cola used this but on a grand scale; buy 12 and get an extra 6 free. Supermarkets use this technique in conjunction with certain manufacturers to increase the turnover of some items.

■ **Coupons or vouchers**
   These can be used to give money off or to encourage customers to collect a certain number which can then be redeemed for another gift or free next purchase. The idea of such incentives is to try and establish the habit of buying this particular brand and to establish brand loyalty.

■ **Competitions**
   The opportunity to win a holiday of a lifetime is still a very popular sales promotion and can be found on an enormous range of products.

■ **Charity donations**
   Various companies have chosen this type of promotion for their products. The manufacturer promises to donate a certain amount of money to charity if you buy the product. Positive publicity is also gained by the company for such a promotion.

Sales promotion and the mix

Sales promotion still has an important role to play within the marketing mix being used by companies in an attempt to inform and entice customers to purchase their products.

Pepsi has used several sales promotions on its packs of drinks for Spice Girl CDs to build up a useful database which was then targeted for the launch of its pager featuring the Pepsi brand name. The pager can be used in the normal way but automatically informs the owner of Pepsi news and musical updates, normally of Pepsi-endorsed pop artists such as The Spice Girls, Boyzone and Eternal. Pepsi also launched a website from which tickets for pop concerts can be purchased.

Pepsi promotion: What message is being sent to the buyer?

Merchandising

Merchandising is another form of incentive at the point of sale that is used to entice the customer into buying. It concentrates on how the products are presented to the customer. The display stands, the actual display of the goods and the general ambience of the outlet itself can influence the purchasing behaviour of customers. Companies are quick to provide display bins for new lines of chocolate bars or for existing ones on special offer. Not only do such displays draw attention to the goods but they actually encourage impulse buying. Supermarket displays that are adjacent to the check-out tills are a case in point where sweets are available, possible to encourage parents to pacify bored children waiting patiently or otherwise in the queues.

Themed displays are used to coincide with special events that increase the consumption of certain items e.g. back to school displays.

Packaging

Packaging can also be used to highlight the brand name of a product. In order to achieve this at the end of 1998, Virgin redesigned its cans of cola to incorporate a new logo which was larger and written horizontally instead of the previous vertical logo. Packaging can be used to extend the product range or the number of variants that are available for a given product.

Pringles, the savoury snack crisps, was faced with the problem of attracting the smaller retail outlets to stock a product which took up too much room on limited shelf space. This problem meant that many potential customers who might have purchased Pringles on impulse were unable to do so unless they made their purchases from a supermarket. As a result, Procter and Gamble introduced the smaller 56g tube to enable retailers to stock Pringles and thereby boost sales along with the larger tubes by 44% in less than a year. Alongside the Pop Box (25g size), packaging has enabled Pringles to satisfy a wider range of customers.

United Biscuits launched a unique packaging for its Jaffa Cakes, making Jaffa the first biscuit to be sold in a resealable tube along similar lines to that used by Pringles. This idea had been tested in several Tesco

Six free cans in Pepsi multipack

stores in 1998 and had been a success; as a result the national launch took place in 1999. McVitie's saw this new packaging as an additional method of packaging Jaffa Cakes, but would continue to use the traditional carton as well. Pringles used packaging to establish an additional segment of customers by launching the 'lunchbox' pack called the 'Pop Box'. The idea was that the normal tube of Pringles could be made to last all week by placing a small quantity in the Pop Box as part of a lunchtime snack for children.

The Pop Box was shaped to take the Pringles crisps and be a feature in itself.

Pringles – packaged for a segmented market

Nestlé's Shreddies combined a promotional offer of a Sampler CD with a variant on the normal packaging for the cereal. The front of the packaging was designed to feature the CD which was incorporated into the shape of Disney's Mickey Mouse.

The selection of such a promotional offer and the redesigned packaging to complement the offer clearly illustrates the importance of establishing a mix that is compatible with the targeted customer.

There are many functions that packaging performs:

- It protects and preserves, thereby extending the shelf life of the product

- It allows the retailer to display and stack more easily

- It is a form of advertising and allows the customer to recognise the brand

- It provides a mass of information, thereby complying with the legal requirements to display the weight, place of manufacture, sell by date if applicable and ingredients. In addition, instructions for use can be given, along with the bar code and sales promotional offers.

- It adds value by turning a product into a gift. Presentation packaging can help create an image for the product that allows more to be charged.

- It provides the means to carry; this is important when many items are sold in larger quantities today. The multipack is sought out by the customer and therefore carrying becomes a factor in the decision making process.

- It provides the flexibility to sell the same product to a variety of customers. Cereals are sold in giant packs, variety packs etc. as are Liquorice Allsorts and Coca-Cola.

Question 7

What factors would you take into consideration when designing the packaging for toothpaste, perfume or after-shave?   [8]

Sponsorship

Sponsorship flourished, especially after the advertising of cigarettes was banned on television. Sponsoring a motor racing team or a world snooker competition was a method of advertising on the television without falling foul of the law. Today sponsorship is common-place throughout sport. Companies are all keen to get their particular name or brand name associated with particular sporting events that will receive high-profile publicity both on television and in the press. Cadbury was one of the first major companies to sponsor a particular television programme in an attempt to raise the profile of some of its products at peak viewing time. Its sponsorship of *Coronation Street* was seen as a coup in the marketing world.

Direct marketing

Of all the forms of promotion this has probably been the biggest growth area in recent years. Such is the pace and importance of **direct marketing** that there are now annual awards presented by the Direct Marketing Association in conjunction with the Royal Mail.

The ability to target directly a specific customer is seen to be much more productive than the general sweep approach of above the line marketing on the television. With advances in technology, IT especially has provided the means by which selling directly to an individual customer has become commonplace.

Direct mail/Mailshots

These can be achieved using a variety of methods of delivery from door to door:

- By post with the Royal Mail – it is reliable and all households are accessible; but it is expensive
- Solus deliveries – leaflets are delivered by hand thereby giving total control over the process. Often used for the delivery of catalogues, this type of delivery can be expensive
- inside local newspapers – the most popular method of delivering leaflets door to door and comparatively cheap. But there is a danger of overload, with the customer becoming immune to so many inserts. Furthermore, there is less control over delivery as the doors selected are those the paper is delivered to anyway
- Shareplan deliveries – similar to Solus, but involves sharing the cost of delivery as companies combine the delivery of leaflets with several others always providing they are not in competition with each other

Since the start of the 1990s, the sophistication of direct marketing has been developing at a rapid pace; a lot more attention has been given to the standard and the format of what is put through the letterbox. The problem facing all companies that use direct mail is how to catch the attention of an otherwise bored customer who is continually faced with unwanted junk mail.

Avco Trust, a business many had never heard of which provides loans for home improvements, was reluctant to highlight the usual methods of 'selling' loans by emphasing the low interest rates. Instead its mailshot featured a message printed on what was a carefully designed packet to imitate a well-known brand of wallpaper paste. As a result, the company achieved a 7.6% response rate (companies will normally be delighted with a 5% return) and issued loans to the value of £3.6 million. The normal mailshots had brought in loan business to the value of £2.3 million.

Telemarketing

This is another form of direct marketing that has expanded rapidly in recent years. Cold calls from double glazing companies may have tarnished the image of this approach, but the financial services sector has used this method with a high degree of success, especially when customers are used to telephone banking. Although the success rate is less than if a salesperson calls, it is considerably cheaper per call (*see page 223*).

Which media to use?

Whether above or below the line promotion is under consideration, there are several factors that will affect the media or combination of media to be used.

Budget

The amount of finance available and the cost of a particular medium are of paramount importance to any business. In simple terms, a sole trader cannot afford to advertise on national television, nor would it be necessary.

Number and location of customers

If the potential customers are located within a small region of the country as opposed to a product that is sold nation-wide, then media that serve the local area are likely to be far more successful and affordable. The type of customer is also important to consider. If, for example, a business was targeting socio-economic groups A and B, this would influence which newspapers to advertise in.

The type of product

Much will depend upon the features of the product that need to be emphasised to the customers. Advertising a new washing powder which washes even whiter would not be best served by commercial radio. Obtaining the right mix of promotion (in relation to the marketing objectives) is one of the most important parts of the decision making process.

Appropriateness of media

Products which aim to develop an exclusive image do not tend to be advertised on television. Products such as crafted shooting sticks may be advertised in magazines such as *Country Life* because of the target market.

Points for Revision

Key Terms

promotion	the collective manner in which the customer is informed and persuaded to purchase products
promotional mix	the combination of advertising, publicity, sales promotion, and direct selling
above the line promotion	general promotion which is not able to target specific customers
informative advertising	usually used for new products, highlighting the key features of the product
persuasive advertising	the emphasis is on how a product is better that the competition and why it is essential to consume
media	the vehicles by which advertising and promotion are carried out e.g. television, radio, magazines
below the line promotion	promotion that targets specific customers by direct contact
sales promotion	an incentive at the point of sale
merchandising	a further incentive to buy, concentrating on the display of products
direct marketing	when a business deals directly with a customer either by post or phone

Definitions Question:
By referring to a business you know, explain the significance of three of the above terms (your teacher may wish to help with your choice).   [5] per definition

Summary Points:

1   There are two types of promotion, above and below the line.

2   Promotion includes advertising and sales promotion and direct selling combined with publicity.

3   The type of promotion used depends primarily on the nature of the market and the customer.

Mini Case Study

Jigsaw, the name given to the consortium of Cadbury Schweppes, Kimberly-Clark and Unilever, was conceived in an attempt to reduce the costs of direct marketing by sharing information and some of the overheads. The consortium was set up to enable its members to compete with some of the large retailers in the market. The three companies have since worked together to publish three magazines that are to be aimed at socio-economic group C1, C2, D and E females between the ages of 25 and 45. The majority of the targeted females have children.

The three magazines are no ordinary publications; they are customer magazines.

Following a test market of approximately 150,000 households, it was the intention of the consortium to send out a magazine to about a million households throughout the country.

The magazines, known as Best Brands, Customers' Choice and Voilà are different in their design, yet have the same content, each containing information on the brands of the three companies as well as items of interest such as recipes and beauty hints. There are advertisements for other businesses, including holidays with Eurocamp.

To appeal to the targeted customers, the magazines contained vouchers and coupons that could be redeemed. In addition, there were questionnaires that were intended to give the consortium an indication as to the likely customer profile of the readers, which is so important if direct marketing is to be successful.

It was the intention of the consortium to select the most popular magazine from the three to enable the national launch to be completed by the end of 1999.

1 Which type of promotion was being used by the consortium?	[1]
2 What is the name for the type of sample mentioned in the case study?	[1]
3 Why is an accurate customer profile important if direct marketing is to be a success?	[4]
4 Why did the magazines include vouchers and coupons?	[3]
5 Suggest how the consortium would save money on the costs of collecting information and overheads.	[5]
6 Discuss whether the use of above the line promotion would be appropriate for these magazines.	[6]

20

Maxi Case Study

Young television viewers, especially those aged between 10 and 15, have deserted the screen in their thousands, preferring to occupy themselves with their play-stations or PCs, and adults spend more time surfing the net in an attempt to find a last-minute bargain for their summer holiday. For those left still watching the television, there are many more channels to choose from which has meant that the actual number watching any one channel has fallen dramatically. Unfortunately for the producers of television channels, the combination of more alternative media for advertising, coupled with the increase in advertising rates, has meant that many businesses are questioning the cost-effectiveness of television.

The cost of advertising in America has risen dramatically over the past few years. A prime-time slot in the middle of *ER*, the hospital soap series, has increased from $180,000 in 1995 to $478,000 in 1999.

The increase in the cost of advertising on television has, in part, been caused by a surge in demand that has forced up the rates that businesses have to pay. This has occurred as some businesses have decided that more slots are needed to gain the same amount of coverage or to ensure that the same number of potential customers see their product or service. Some businesses have found ways of circumventing these increases in costs, by attempting to get their products placed on to the screen as part of the programmes or actually sponsoring the programme, something that Cadbury has done with great success by sponsoring *Coronation Street*. Other businesses have looked elsewhere to gain cost-effective exposure.

The main drift away from television, however, has been as a result of the surge in direct marketing, which appears to be more suited to accurate targeting of customers, either by telephone or by mail. Making personal contact provides a better opportunity to make a sale than a television advert that might not even be seen by the people at whom it is aimed.

The use of one type of direct marketing, mailshots, has grown at 15% per annum since the early 1990s. Targeting door to door, based on geodemographics, enables a business to contact potential customers whose profiles appear to mean they are more likely to be interested in the products being sold.

Allied Domecq had found advertising its chain of public houses almost impossible given that they all have different names. However, the direct marketing approach of door-to-door leaflet drops has proved successful because marketing literature can be tailored to suit individual areas and therefore individual public houses in that particular area.

Of greater significance is the inability of television to provide samples that instantly put the customer into contact with the product being marketed. But it is not all doom and gloom for television, as many businesses see a place for both direct marketing and television. PG Tips used a combination of both when it launched its pyramid tea bags. The television was used to inform the customer and establish some sort of brand recognition, whilst samples were distributed door to door; below the line was feeding off above the line promotion.

1 Define: cost-effectiveness, geodemographics, above the line promotion. [6]

2 With evidence from the case study, suggest why direct marketing has increased in popularity. [5]

3 Under what circumstances would it be more likely for a business to use telemarketing instead of mailshots? [6]

4 Draw a demand and supply diagram to explain the reason for the increase in the cost of television advertisement rates during a popular soap programme. [4]

5 Suggest why television, despite the fall in popularity, will always survive as the main medium for advertising. [6]

6 Discuss why PG Tips used a combination of media for its promotional campaign. [8]

35

Marketing strategy

Learning objectives

Having read this unit, students will be able to

1   identify the link between strategy and objectives

2   understand various marketing strategies which firms employ in order to meet their marketing objectives

3   appreciate the significance of different strategies in different business situations

Context

Fifteen years ago, very few firms made any claim about being 'environmentally friendly'. This was because, at the time, the issues of harmful gases or testing on animals were not at the forefront of consumers' minds. It was only when scientists discovered the hole in the ozone layer and global warming that companies began to realise a change of strategy was required. Since then, not only have companies placed enormous weight on how environmentally friendly their products are, but they have actually begun to make products specifically aimed at the typical 'eco-warrior'. The shopping basket of the 'warrior' contains only products which are not tested on animals, those made from recycled paper, or those made with no extra chemicals. Concerned consumers will also purchase from those companies that have a sound environmental health record. This change in strategy has come about following research into customer attitudes and new marketing objectives.

What is marketing strategy?

A **marketing strategy** is a long-term plan which is designed to meet the company's **marketing objectives**. In Unit 7 Objectives and strategy, a clear link was made between the two. The importance of strategy is that it relies primarily on clearly stated marketing objectives, and once the strategy is defined and made clear to the marketing team, it must be carefully researched. The implementation of the strategy is carried out using the four Ps of the marketing mix, otherwise known as product, price, place and promotion. There are always constraints on achieving the strategy which the business must take into account when setting the marketing objectives.

- Customers
- Competition
- Exchange rates
- Interest rates
- Marketing budget
- Distinctive competence of company

Question 1

Explain how each of the above might affect the marketing strategy of a business of your choice.　[12]

Figure 21.1　Marketing strategy within the marketing function

Marketing objectives

Marketing objectives have been covered in greater detail in Unit 11 Introduction to marketing. All objectives within a business will stem from the mission statement (*see Unit 7 Objectives and strategy*). Once the mission statement has been agreed, objectives can be set with a view to achieving the mission statement. By way of reminder here are some examples of marketing objectives:

- to increase market share
- to increase market share in relation to competitors
- to gain a foothold in the market
- to establish a product as a market leader

These examples fulfil the requirement that an objective must be easy to assess i.e. the business must be able to state categorically whether or not the objective has been achieved. However, in order to provide even more guidance on the nature of the objective and whether the business is on course to achieve the objective, it is possible to develop the objective in greater detail, using time scales and levels of performance e.g.

- to increase market share by an annual average of 2% over the next five years, or

- to gain a foothold in the market by establishing a market share of 3% in the first year, or

- to sell 300,000 units, at a margin of 5%.

Sometimes the business may also link the marketing objectives to objectives that are set in other parts of the business e.g. to achieve financial payback of the marketing budget within two years.

Scientific data versus a hunch

Sometimes the data collected in market research does not justify the cost of collection. Despite a thorough, carefully planned and scientific approach to collecting data, there is always a chance of error. The alternative to spending large amounts of money on research is to go on instinct. There are many examples of entrepreneurs who do this, either because they trust their own feelings more than market research data, or because research would be entirely inappropriate.

When Alan Sugar launched the Amstrad home computer, he refused to carry out research because he knew that very few people could conceive of the idea of a home computer, because it was such a revolutionary product. Sir Richard Branson chooses his product portfolio more on his gut feeling for the growth of the product than on any substantial evidence.

Examples of marketing strategy

Global marketing

Whether consumers wish to buy a can of Coca-Cola or a Big Mac in Prague, Tokyo or Los Angeles, the product will be identical.

With the growth in multinational businesses, there are now more opportunities to sell products throughout the world. Mass markets are in many instances now global markets, providing the opportunity for businesses to increase the sales of their products in an attempt to reap the benefits of economies of scale.

Where products are standardised i.e. when the same parts are used with only small variations, selling throughout the world is an essential strategy in order to reduce the unit cost of the product and therefore remain competitive. Selling products in such large numbers not only helps to reduce the unit cost of the product but increases the amount of revenue for the business. This revenue can be used to finance research into new products in an attempt to maintain market share by identifying local tastes and cultures and adapting the product to meet individual needs.

Despite the obvious advantages of **globalisation**, obtaining them is not necessarily straightforward. Marks and Spencer ventured into Europe, opening shops in France and other European countries, but was unable to sustain the level of sales to make the outlets profitable, culminating in an announcement in mid-1999 that it was to close some of its European stores, including the one in Paris. It was reported that the French were unable to

grasp the image of Marks and Spencer which appeared dated when compared with other similar outlets.

A more successful business that has achieved globalisation is Unilever. Such is the success of Unilever that its organisational structure is based upon regions of the world: Europe, North America, Africa and the Middle East, Asia and the Pacific, and Latin America. Many of its products are sold throughout the world; washing powders, Lipton tea and deodorants are good examples of this.

Globalisation has allowed Unilever to spread the cost of research; it has a network of research laboratories and innovation centres throughout the world. Another major advantage of globalisation is that the business is able to cope with the slowdown in economies in a particular area of the world. This way, if the economies of Latin America and the Pacific rim are in recession, buoyant sales in other regions of the world can compensate and 'subsidise' a lack of sales in these areas.

Globalisation can mean there is a need to alter the strategy for a particular region of the world. Unilever, hit by the economic crisis in south-east Asia, had to alter its strategy from achieving high growth to one of maintaining and protecting its market share in the region. Niall Fitzgerald, the Chairman of Unilever, refers to the process of glocalisation – **global marketing** applied to a local market.

Question 2

What are the difficulties of having a standardised product throughout the world?   [6]

Niche marketing

A business may wish to concentrate on a particular specialised segment of the market rather than attempting to appeal to the mass market. This is referred to as **niche marketing**.

Such a strategy is often used by smaller businesses that are unable to compete with the dominant businesses within the market, due to lack of resources and inability to exploit economies of scale. Despite the obvious attraction to small companies, niche marketing is also undertaken by large, dominant businesses when attempting to widen their product portfolio. If a small business can exploit a niche market it may well be highly profitable because larger firms are unlikely to be willing to deal in the small volumes that are likely to be sold; consequently, the small business will have little or no competition.

Many of the businesses that operate within a niche market are specialist firms which have a unique skill or a unique product to be sold. The trend in the publication of magazines has become more niche orientated; the number of specialist magazines increased significantly during the latter part of the 1990s. The number of titles that cater for specific segments of the market now includes magazines for men in specific socio-economic groups and specialist magazines for consumers who may wish to purchase products from the comfort of their own home e.g. Best Brands and Voilà published by Jigsaw, the marketing consortium.

If a successful strategy is operated to establish a niche market, the unique element of the product or service may mean that the price that is charged to the consumer will be high. This is because products in such markets are less price-sensitive. The price elasticity of the product or service will be more inelastic (i.e. less than one).

Simon Drew, an artist with two shops in Dartmouth, has managed successfully to establish a niche market for pictures and mugs. His unique ideas, which he draws, have led to the production of pictures, postcards, mugs and sweatshirts bearing his own artwork. Although the volume of products is relatively low when compared with the mass manufacturers, the margins he can earn on his individual style of artwork is sufficient to keep his business operating successfully.

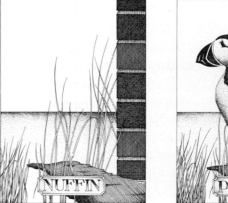

Examples of Simon Drew's successful works

Question 3

What are the advantages and disadvantages of trying to achieve a niche market?   [6]

Market-led versus asset-led strategy

The reason why marketing has become such a huge industry is the requirement of companies to find out customer needs and satisfy them at a profit. Failure to achieve this objective means losing market share to the competition. This approach is known as market-led marketing, whereas some companies concentrate on their distinctive competence and expertise when it comes to new products. In a sense this moves towards a product-orientated approach, by using the assets of the business to launch a new product. James Dyson's latest product, a washing machine, was launched on the back of his success with the vacuum cleaner. The main assets of Dyson Appliances are the innovative approach to new products and the varied colour schemes – these were used in the marketing of the new washing machine.

Segmentation

This has been considered in detail in Unit 11 Introduction to marketing. Segmentation frequently occurs when there is an obvious subdivision of the type of customer who buys the product. The railway companies are good examples of businesses which have responded to this by selling the same product to different customers at different times of the day for different prices. The East Anglian Water Company announced in July 1999 that it was intending to introduce a different price tariff for different times of the day. A higher price would be charged for using water between 7am and 9 am and between 5pm and 7pm in the evening. This was announced as an attempt to regulate the demand for water.

Task

List three other industries that operate price discrimination.

Marketing plan

To ensure that the objectives of the business are implemented in an appropriate manner, a plan is drawn up which can then be used to communicate the marketing strategy to employees and assess progress. Assuming the strategy has been agreed, the plan is based on research and the various elements of the marketing mix.

In the same way that a business plan is put together, the **marketing plan** will contain details of objectives, costs, forecast revenues and constraints.

Many businesses will conduct a SWOT (*see Unit 9*) and PEST (Political, Economic, Social and Technological) analysis prior to the drawing up of the plan. A particular segment may have been targeted following assessment of the likelihood of success and consideration of the product positioning. Depending upon the size of the budget for the particular product or range of products, the plan will be drawn up to fit the budget and objectives and strategy that have already been decided upon.

Once the plan is in place it can be used to review progress and monitor any difficulties using a variety of techniques such as variance analysis (*see Unit 45 Budgeting*). A **marketing audit** can then be put into operation to assess the effectiveness of the marketing mix that has been decided upon.

All good marketing plans have a degree of flexibility to allow for a change in circumstances caused by the economic climate, competitors' actions and new legislation.

Orange had formulated a strategy to achieve market growth and to expand across Europe. Its marketing plan involved a greater emphasis on its 'pay as you go' phones, attracting customers who may not otherwise have contemplated becoming a mobile phone owner and user. In addition, Orange was keen to ensure that its customers remained loyal despite the intensity of the competition. Research had shown that the longer customers were with Orange, the more they used their phones. From its marketing audit, Orange found that over 20% of its Talk 15 customers who joined in 1996 had subsequently move to higher Talk plans with the company.

Question 4

Produce a market plan for a business that produces fruit juice and is faced with new competition from a company selling exotic flavours.   [5]

Brands

Very frequently, a business will rely on brands in order to help it achieve its marketing objectives. For example, if a firm is aiming a product at a specific segment, the customer needs to identify the product as filling that particular segment. Hence the product must have a distinct image which is different to the competition. A brand is therefore a product that displays the following characteristics:

- It is different to all other products. This differentiation may be achieved in a multiplicity of ways – price, quality, packaging, advertising, after-sales service are some examples

- It must have a distinctive image, which is normally built through investment in advertising

- It must be consistent – when Coca-Cola changed the flavour in the early 1990s, it lost sales to Pepsi, because it was breaking with a tradition that consumers wanted to continue

Branding can therefore be classified in a number of ways:

- Company brand – The Halifax advertises itself as a bank from which customers can get 'extra' help.

- Individual product brands, such as Windows 98 and Office 2000, where there is no apparent link with a manufacturer and the product stands on its own.

- Line brands – e.g. Tetley tea bags (made by Lyons) are a good example of this in that they are not only produced in a variety of packaging formats, but there are round tea bags, pyramid tea bags and even tea bags with drawstrings, all under the Tetley name.

- Family brands – such as Kellogg's breakfast cereals. Anything with the name Kellogg's on it conforms to a particular high standard of product.

- Own-label brands – sold under the flagship name of the supermarket e.g. Tesco baked beans.

- Tertiary brands – those that are sold under a particular family name, such as Tesco Value. They are sold with distinctive (simple) packaging, in Tesco's case blue stripes on a white background, and are designed to compete at the bottom end of the market.

Due to the fact that branding is about building a set of values around which a product can be made to appear more attractive and therefore inspire sales, branding does not always have to be for a consumer product.

Supermarket own-label brands

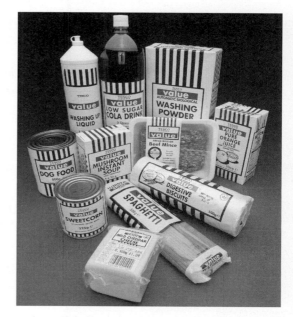

Supermarket tertiary brands

Two such examples of a brand are *Coronation Street* and Melinda Messenger; both have an image and adoring audience and the names can be used to promote products. For example, Channel 5 signed up Melinda Messenger in 1999 to help promote its website, hoping that the name of the former model would attract more people to the website, especially as she was allowed to have her own dedicated section on the website. Cadbury's is associated with *Coronation Street* through sponsorship.

Points for Revision

Key Terms

marketing strategy	a long-term plan which is formulated to achieve the marketing objectives
marketing objective	specific target that is set to provide focus for the marketing teams e.g. increase sales revenue by 400,000
global marketing	finding markets in any part of the world in order to achieve economies of scale
globalisation	similar to global marketing, but pays closer attention to local markets
niche marketing	focusing on a specialised, well defined part of the market
market-led marketing	a strategy which responds to customer needs
asset-led marketing	a strategy which generates ideas and products which are based on the company's assets e.g. one of its brands
marketing plan	the programme of how a business plans to achieve its objectives through the strategy, focusing primarily on the marketing mix
marketing audit	a review of the effectiveness of the marketing plan

Definitions Question:
By referring to a business you know, explain the significance of any three of the above
(your teacher may wish to help you choose).   [5] per definition

Summary Points:

1   Marketing strategy is a long-term plan which is necessary for the achievement of marketing objectives.

2   The marketing plan is used to achieve the marketing strategy, through implementation of the four Ps.

Mini Case Study

The gradual reduction in the price charged by food retailers has led the main players in the industry (Sainsbury, Tesco, Safeway) to think again about their portfolio of brands. Apart from competition between the large companies, there has been a gradual influx in the past 10 years of foreign-based retailers who are able to offer products at dramatically lower prices. Stores such as Aldi, Netto, and Lidl have slowly gained a foothold in the market by undercutting the established retailers, so that shopping can be purchased at between 50% and 60% of the prices a customer would have to pay in a main retailing store. The foreign companies have deliberately targeted a lower income segment – socio-economic groups C2, D and E. They achieve this in a variety of ways, apart from attracting them through lower prices. In addition to selling unknown brands, profitability is achieved in three other ways:

1 By locating on cheap land, close to the large retailers

2 By having the most basic merchandising – sometimes customers have physically to get into the cardboard boxes housing the products

3 There are no bar codes on the products; check-out staff must remember the prices for the 800 or so lines

In response to falling sales, Safeway responded with its own tertiary brand, the 'Safeway Saver'. This is packaged in red and green and the company actually states on the packaging that it is confident the product represents value for money. There are about 200 lines in this tertiary brand and they are aimed at the same type of customer that initially deserted Safeway in search of the foreign retailers' cheaper prices.

1 Define the following terms: merchandising, profitability.   [4]

2 What characteristics will the products that are included in the tertiary brand line display?   [4]

3 Explain how each of the three methods employed to improve profitability will help achieve this objective.   [6]

4 Explain Safeway's marketing strategy and comment on the problems it might have faced when introducing the saver line.   [6]

                                                                                                                            20

Maxi Case Study

The Prudential Insurance Company has recently been through a period of change which has transformed its image. Traditionally it had been a company famous for the phrase 'The man from the Pru', based on the large number of direct salesmen employed to collect premiums from customers on a regular basis.

Following the problems at the end of the 1990s when the company was accused of selling pensions incorrectly, it has undergone radical change. Sir Peter Davis, the chief executive of the Prudential, has stated that its aim is to be the largest long-term savings company in the industry. Such an objective may be achieved only at the expense of profit, following the government's ruling that financial companies must reduce their annual management charge for the new stakeholder pensions from 4% to 1%. Shortly after the announcement by the government, Lloyds TSB announced its plans to buy Scottish Widows in an attempt to achieve greater economies of scale, reflecting the need for volume sales.

At the time, the customer base of the Prudential was seen to be moving away from traditional pensions to lower cost products, which meant a further reduction in profit. To improve its profit margin, the Prudential took several steps:

1 4,000 job cuts were announced in June 1999, mainly from the direct sales-force, aimed at saving £200 million per annum

2 The company bought Scottish Amicable for £2.7 billion in an attempt to boost sales revenue

3 It made a conscious effort to reach a greater number of up-market customers, without sacrificing the traditional low to middle income customer base. This was done because economies of scale were easier to achieve through higher premiums. This part of the marketing strategy was achieved by reducing the number of direct sales-force. There was much greater potential for an increase in sales volume by using Independent Financial Advisers, postal accounts and phone accounts. The Internet is also becoming a more important part of the promotion of the product.

Such changes were designed to widen the product range as well as increase the number of distribution channels available to the business. The drive for new products meant that by 1999, 45% of its income came from products that did not exist in 1995. As part of its marketing strategy, the business launched the Egg account in 1998, which actually achieved its five-year target in just seven months, attracting £5 billion in savings and 500,000 customers. As a result, a new objective has been set, which is to attract two million Internet customers in the five years from 1999. This ambitious target is based on a potential market that is growing, although there are still 30 million customers who are not online and therefore the Egg account is inaccessible to these people. It offers a rate of 0.5% above the base rate, which its competitors do not believe is sustainable; the Prudential also aims to break even on this account by cutting costs. The Internet offers an easy method of banking, with the added advantage that costs are approximately four times lower than using a telephone call centre to manage the accounts.

Source: *The Times 28/4/99, Financial Times 29/6/99*

1 Define: chief executive, break even. [2]

2 Explain why the Prudential had to aim towards increasing the volume of sales. [5]

3 Given the cost of employing someone to collect money and the ease with which a customer could have paid money through a bank account, explain the original reasons for collecting money through the sales-force. [5]

4 Suggest the problems that might occur when formulating a new marketing strategy for Lloyds TSB and Scottish Widows following the merger. [4]

5 Analyse how the changes made to the marketing mix might have helped the Prudential achieve its objectives. [6]

6 Explain two implications of developing the new products that quickly accounted for 45% of 1999's income. [4]

7 Based on the evidence in the article, describe, in no more than 100 words, the marketing strategy of the Prudential. [4]

8 Discuss the appropriateness of the marketing objectives for the Egg account, in the context of the recent changes the company has made. Consider both short- and long-term objectives. [10]

40

'Friday afternoon'

End of section test

1 Define marketing. [2]
2 Explain the meaning of market segmentation. [2]
3 How is market share calculated? [1]
4 Explain the difference between product orientation and market orientation. [3]
5 Define unique selling point. [1]
6 Suggest two marketing objectives. [2]
7 Give an example of a product which has a competitive advantage. [2]
8 Suggest two reasons why marketing has become more significant in recent years. [2]
9 What is secondary data? [1]
10 What is a quota sample? [2]
11 When might a firm use quota sampling? [1]
12 What is the difference between a bar chart and a histogram? [2]
13 Give two advantages of presenting data in index number form. [2]
14 When might a business use a pie chart to represent data? [2]
15 Define median. [2]
16 Explain three characteristics of the normal distribution. [5]
17 What does the inter-quartile range demonstrate? [2]
18 Describe the Delphi technique of forecasting. [2]
19 Name two elements of any time series. [2]
20 Why is it necessary to centre a four-point moving average? [3]

21 What is the difference between an actual value and an expected value in decision trees? [3]
22 In a decision tree, what does a) a square b) a circle represent? [2]
23 What ratio is used to show the importance of research and development in a particular company? [1]
24 What are the four stages of a product life cycle? [2]
25 Give an example of an extension strategy, with reference to a specific product. [3]
26 What characteristics of market share and market growth might be displayed by a) a cash cow b) a question mark or problem child? [2]
27 What is a product portfolio? [1]
28 Define product positioning and give an example of an industry which might carry out this assessment of its product portfolio. [3]
29 Explain two pricing strategies. [4]
30 Explain marginal cost pricing. [2]
31 When might a firm adopt price discrimination? Give an example of a firm which uses this method. [3]
32 Explain the usefulness of cross price elasticity to a multi-product firm. [3]
33 What is the formula for price elasticity of demand? [1]

34 How might an understanding of price elasticity of demand help a business to make decisions on its price? [4]

35 State two problems of using elasticity. [2]

36 What is the difference between above the line and below the line promotion? [2]

37 What is the difference between into and out of the pipeline promotion? [2]

38 Give three examples of below the line promotion. [3]

39 What factors determine the success of promotion? [4]

40 Explain why direct marketing is becoming more popular amongst certain industries. [3]

41 Distinguish between asset-led and market-led marketing. [3]

42 List two possible distribution channels. [2]

43 Explain why the Internet is becoming a more popular channel of distribution. [4]

100

'Friday afternoon' 1

The Soup Makers manufactures a range of soups which it sells to a variety of customers. Details of the products are provided in Figures 22.1 and 22.2:

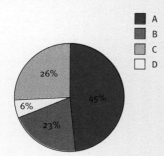

Figure 22.1 Product performance by sales revenue

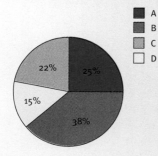

Figure 22.2 Product performance by profit

Product A: sold to a major supermarket chain as an own brand.

Product B: sold under the brand name of The Warming Range, this is the oldest and best known brand of the business. The managing director makes sure all his sales-force understand the significance of The Warming Range because it generates most of the profit.

Product C: a recently introduced brand, positioned at the top end of the market, known as The Luxury Range; targeted at high-class catering establishments. A recent order was won from the Dutch embassy which provides evidence of the exclusiveness of the product.

Product D: an international brand, sold to a large American restaurant chain, as the quintessential English starter to a three- or four-course meal.

The managing director is thinking about introducing a fifth product to the range in order to use up the last 10% of capacity at its factory, although he is anxious not to launch a new product which might reduce the sales of one of the present brands. The company has developed a name for itself in the soup market and prides itself on its strength as a company to strive for product excellence. The managing director is sure that this is the reason why customers continue to purchase its products in abundance.

1 Using all the information available, analyse the product portfolio for The Soup Makers. [6]

2 a) Why might a bar chart be more helpful in presenting the data in Figure 22.2? [2]

b) Calculate the angle for the sales revenue for Product B. [1]

3 How might a knowledge of the Boston matrix help the managing director to launch another product? [5]

4 If a fifth product is launched, briefly explain whether this would be an example of asset-led marketing or market-led marketing. [3]

5 Explain why Product C is an example of niche marketing. [3]

20

'Friday afternoon' 2

Michael Case listened carefully to his marketing director, James Aston, who was coming to the end of his monthly report. Michael was rather concerned with the prediction that the market for neon strip lights was changing towards the more efficient, longer lasting, but expensive alternatives. The company's main customers were small businesses that operated in industrial units of about 10,000 square feet. It supplied the customers with a variety of strip lighting for offices and small factories, offering to deliver anything from 5 to 500 units. This meant that delivery costs were high, but the volume of sales meant that profit could be made. James was suggesting that the company might be able to increase its volume further with a price cut of 12% per unit which would lead to extra volume, given that the estimated level of price elasticity is 1.8. The present average unit price is £14, with a variable cost of £9. Monthly volume is 10,000 strip lights.

The company had a distinctive competence in strip lighting and wanted to launch a new product in anticipation of the change in market tastes. The idea for a new strip light which conserved energy was discussed at the meeting between Michael and James, although James agreed that he should carry out some research before putting a prototype to the test.

1 Calculate the change in
   a) sales volume   [3]
   b) sales revenue   [3]
   c) total contribution   [4]

2 What other factors would the business consider before changing its price?   [3]

3 Suggest how the business might forecast the sales of the new product.   [2]

4 Explain two possible marketing objectives for the new product.   [5]

─────
20

Maxi Case Study

James Tibbetts hit on the idea of a new design of shoe-cleaning brush when carrying out research for his degree in Design and Technology. He was experimenting with a variety of designs with the objective of finding the most efficient way to allow a consumer to carry the brush in a top pocket. The brush had two ends – one was impregnated with a small amount of polish, the other was to make the shoe shine. Initially the idea was test marketed with a sample of consumers who were very enthusiastic about the product because of its unique functional properties. However, when he approached supermarkets and shoe shops in Britain, he was disappointed with their response. Not only were they looking for a product which was unique, they were expecting James to provide marketing support for them. This was beyond his means because he had formed a small limited company in order to be awarded a patent, and this had taken up most of his seed capital and he could not afford to conform to their demands. Instead, he found an agent specialising in marketing products abroad who put him in touch with several retail chains based in northern Italy.

Far from the attitude demonstrated by the British retailers, the Italians welcomed his invention with open arms. He arranged to have the product manufactured in Britain and went into a joint venture with a large brush manufacturer which agreed to share its profits. Although his initial objective was to penetrate the market with a 2% market share (150,000 shoe brushes), within the first six months he had sold 400,000. Initially he was aiming at the business market, although in the end, the fashion-conscious Italian men were the main purchasers of the brush. The brand, known as Top-Shoe, was priced aggressively at £1.95 and it was estimated to have a life of 20 thorough shines. As the product reached maturity, James decided to extend the range of products under the Top-Shoe brand with a variety of other pocket-sized gadgets. The Top-Comb, Top-Teeth and Top-Shave were all products which were aimed at the fashion-conscious male who needed quite literally a quick wash and brush up before going out after work, but who had not time to go home.

Such was the success of the product range that it was eventually adopted in three other European countries and targeted at the same type of consumer. James then used the profits from the initial success to develop a travel pack which was to be marketed under the Top-Shoe brand name and aimed at business travellers; although such products were handed out on business class air journeys. James felt that there was enough backing from the brand name for him to launch into the European market. He therefore began the process of sending mailshots to the boards of directors of all companies which he felt were appropriate to be targeted for his new product.

1 Define: seed capital, maturity.   [4]

2 Suggest how James might have carried out the research amongst customers, when test marketing the Top-Shoe.   [5]

3 Identify the evidence that the strategy for the Top brand was an example of niche marketing. What advantages might this approach have had for the company?   [8]

4 What sort of marketing support might the British retailers have expected from James?   [4]

5 Explain the usefulness of developing the brand name in this case.   [6]

6 What factors should James consider when deciding the most appropriate method of distribution for the Top brand products?   [5]

7 Develop and justify a marketing strategy for the new product.   [8]

40

Operations management

Introduction to production

Learning objectives

Having read this unit, students will be able to

1. explain the significance of production in the creation of wealth

2. identify some of the important issues that relate to production

3. identify the measures of performance used in assessing productive efficiency

Context

One of the many objectives of production is to make a product that is worth more than the value of the parts involved in its manufacture. The desk you are working on began its life as a variety of raw materials – wood, steel and possibly some chemicals. The process of production will have converted the materials using labour and machinery into a finished product. Depending on the market for desks, the business will hopefully have sold the desk for more than the cost of all the materials, labour and overheads used to run the machinery and assemble the desk. This will have led to some profit being made by the manufacturer. In addition, the raw materials suppliers and their work-force, the business that transported the product, the work-force of the desk manufacturer as well as the shareholders will have increased their income as a result of producing the desk. Clearly, if the product had been made poorly or had taken a long time to build, the business might have made a loss. Only by being efficient and well organised at the work-place will a business be able to manufacture a product according to customer needs, at a profit.

The objective of production

The process of **production** is about converting inputs, such as raw materials and/or components, labour and capital machinery, into finished products ready for sale to the customer. This will involve **adding value** (*see Unit 1 Business activity*) so that the revenue earned from selling the product is greater than the cost of all the processes involved in putting the product together and selling it to the customer. The customer may be a consumer who is buying the product to eat, or it may be another manufacturer which is using a partly-assembled product in its production process. The conversion process may produce waste products, which can sometimes be recycled and used elsewhere in the production process of another firm e.g. Marmite uses the waste products of brewers (yeast extract).

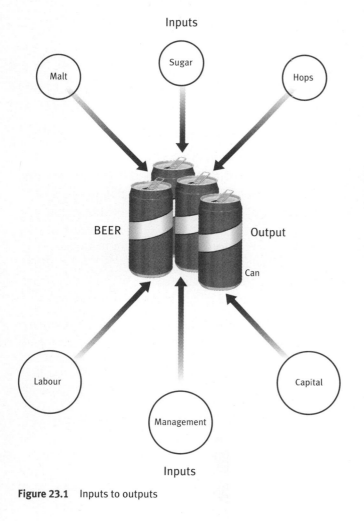

RAW MATERIALS

Inputs

Malt

Sugar

Hops

BEER

Output

Can

Labour

Capital

Management

Inputs

Figure 23.1   Inputs to outputs

Question 1

Select your favourite main course that you would purchase at a restaurant. How much do you think the materials cost? How much is the added value (price – cost of bought-in materials)? Explain briefly how the restaurant adds value.   [4]

Frequently production is seen as a dirty word, conjuring up pictures of workers covered in grime, struggling with large items of machinery. In fact, the process of production is now carried out in almost sterile conditions, with a high level of technology facilitating the process which is aimed to design and produce products according to customer demands, at a profit.

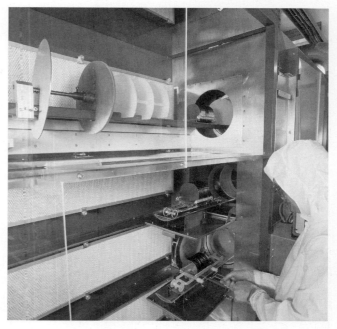

Dirty factories are a thing of the past

How does production fit in?

Production therefore links in with all the other parts of a business:

■ **Marketing** – to ensure that the correct specification is achieved, within the desired delivery time at the right price

■ **Finance** – to ensure that the business makes a profit, but that it can afford the machinery required for efficient production

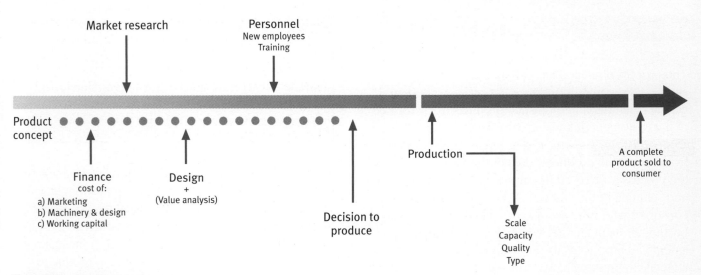

Figure 23.2   From concept to consumer

- **Design** – so that when a new product is designed, the production department can be sure that it is possible to manufacture it within a target cost which means it can be sold at a profit

- **Personnel** – to ensure that employees are given jobs which help them to be enthusiastic about their work. This will lead to greater motivation and higher levels of output and quality

- **Management** – to co-ordinate the flow of resources within the factory so as to maximise output and quality

---

Question 2

Choose a product with which you are familiar. Consider how other parts of the business need to be linked with production.   [6]

How can production be measured?

A business will always aim to make as much saleable output with as few inputs as possible. The higher the output in relation to the input, the greater productive efficiency or **productivity**. There are various methods of measuring this:

- **added value per product** – this is particularly relevant when the business has made a unique product or version of a product, meaning it can be sold for a larger profit margin e.g. Dyson sells its vacuum cleaners at a vast profit margin because of the added value it creates on the production line and in the marketing of the product. This measurement can be extended to calculate added value per employee (*see Unit 1 Business activity*)

- **output per employee** – measured by number of units made / employees

- **sales per employee** – measured by number of units sold / employees; alternatively this could be measured by revenue per employee; notice the difference between this and the above is the assumption that products which are made are necessarily going to be sold. Retailers refer to sales per square foot of selling space, because this is more appropriate given the nature of retailing

- **output per machine** – this can be used when a business is capital-intensive or when a business is considering buying a new, more technologically advanced machine. Another version of this is sales / capital (net assets) (*see Unit 38 Ratio analysis*)

- **profit per employee** – this can be used to determine how much each employee is contributing to operating profit. This is sometimes used as evidence for the work-force to be increased or decreased, especially if profit per employee (before wages) is less than the average wage.

■ **items sold per hour** – another measure used by retailers, when assessing the number of employees it needs at different times during the day, week or year according to the expected amount sold i.e. more checkouts need to be open and more shelves need to be stocked

Don't use...

Question 3

Find five sets of company reports and calculate operating profit per employee and sales per employee. Discuss the differences across the companies you have chosen and try to identify reasons for the differences.   [15]

Broadly speaking, as productivity increases, a business can make products at a lower cost per unit. Some businesses have traditionally taken the view that quantity is the main objective, with no regard whatsoever for quality. The Communist government of the USSR simply ordered manufacturers to produce a certain number of cars within a production period. The emphasis was very much on producing the required amount, which meant that quality was ignored! Such an approach in today's business world would not last very long.

Question 4

The following information was collected from the internal accounts of a business.

	Year 1	Year 2
Sales per employee	£80,000	£110,000
Output per employee	£110,000	£120,000
Profit per employee	£8,000	£11,000

Using the information in the table, suggest which changes might have taken place in the business to have caused the changes in these levels of productivity.   [4]

The pressure on businesses to be highly productive can make a business focus entirely on productivity, with the aim of driving down its costs. This means it can therefore reduce its price, which, in turn, will lead to an increase in demand by making its products more

competitive. The business can then decide if it prefers to charge the same price for the product and earn a larger profit margin (*see Unit 18 Elasticity*).

What is production all about?

The following provides a brief summary of every part of production which can contribute to greater efficiency. It also summarises the individual topics covered in much greater detail in the units in this section.

Location – a business will need to look carefully at its chosen **location** with respect to many factors. It may want to be close to its suppliers, so as to be sure of reliable delivery, or near to its main customers, so they can save costs when visiting the business.

Stock control – as a business produces more units of output, it will need to order more units of raw materials and components. This has a consequence for the costs of holding stock as well as the costs of borrowing money in order to buy the stock. When stock is lying around in a warehouse it is adding costs, not adding value. In recent years, therefore, businesses have tried to move towards a 'just-in-time' approach to **stock control** and production, in an attempt to reduce such costs.

Quality – as customers have demanded higher specifications of products, businesses have needed to invest heavily in a more efficient process of checking quality. Quality can mean producing products which rich people purchase, but this is an outdated definition. **Quality control** concerns the process of meeting the needs of customers now and in the future, by making sure products are manufactured 'right first time'. There has been significant investment in this respect over recent years.

Technology – as knowledge and awareness of technological development have progressed, businesses have been able to purchase machinery which not only replaces human beings on the production line, but also produces products more quickly and with more accuracy. Technology is also prevalent in the process of designing a product. If a business discovers a new market, it will need to design its product quickly to steal a march on competition. Computers in the design process mean that several stages of prototype production can be omitted, thereby reducing costs. The process of replacing humans with machines in the process of production is known as moving from a labour-intensive to a capital-intensive business.

Technology means a more capital-intensive business

Type of production – some products are unique and are therefore produced as a one-off e.g. a wedding cake. The added value is represented by the higher price. With other products, mass production is used – the process of making products using a repetitive manufacturing process, either a batch of products in one go e.g. loaves of bread, or a flow production line, such as the one used for the Model T Ford. These cars flowed off the line at a rate of one per minute in 1924.

Scale of production – as a business expands, the scale of production will need to increase to cope with the extra output. One advantage of this is that a business can achieve economies of scale (*see Unit 4 Size of business*), which can further allow it to charge a lower price. The use of capacity is particularly important when a business has invested heavily in machinery. Alternatively a business may decide to operate on a smaller scale and subcontract some of its production to other companies which may have greater expertise.

Layout – the way that a business organises its machines so that one process leads efficiently into another can determine the length of time it takes to produce and therefore its productivity. Morgan Motor Company has to put the wheels on the chassis of its car first so that it can be wheeled from workshop to workshop! A more efficient **layout** would mean less time pushing and more time building.

Planning – the **planning** of materials, labour and capital machinery must be done before the production takes place – a business needs to make sure that inputs are at the production line in time for production, but too much time in advance of production can mean wasted resources. This is solved by a technique called critical path analysis (*see Unit 31*).

Design – this refers to the product fitting the needs of the customer in terms of the function it performs. A business will need to innovate continually to produce new, exciting, interesting designs for its products. Consider, for example, how the **design** of a computer keyboard has changed in recent years.

Points for Revision

Key Terms

production	the process of converting inputs into outputs
added value	price – cost of bought-in parts
location	the geographical siting of a business
type of production	the way a product is manufactured
stock control	how businesses ensure the correct level of stock is held
quality control	the process of managing the minimisation of waste
planning	a management function which organises the production
design	creating the correct specification for the customer
layout	the organisation of the order in which machines are sited and products are made
productivity (productive efficiency)	the ability of the business to convert inputs into outputs

Definitions Question:
By referring to a business you know, explain the importance of any four of the above terms (your teacher may wish to select the terms).   [5] per definition

Summary Points:

1   Production is one of the major functions of business and is otherwise known as operations.

2   It is important to consider other parts of the business, such as marketing, or finance, when making decisions within the production department.

3   The primary objective of the production department is to add value in the most efficient manner.

4   There are several measures of productivity, the most appropriate of which depends on the nature and activity of the business.

Mini Case Study

Rain-Hold Ltd manufactures uPVC frames for windows and doors which it sells to the building trade and a variety of cut-price double glazing companies. It uses a very simple heating and moulding procedure in making a range of products employing a combination of labour and capital. This process adds sufficient value to earn the company large profits. Details of costs are as follows:

Raw materials = Plastic pellets	£10
Additional plastic coating	£ 3
Labour	£15
Other overheads	£15

Production has been stretched to full capacity by an increase in sales revenue; the workshop, originally built for 20 employees and three machines, now houses 30 employees with the same amount of machinery. The result has been falling productivity and the business is considering moving towards a more capital-intensive process of production by purchasing two brand new, state-of-the-art moulding machines. James Swift, the marketing director, was delighted with this proposal because it would allow the business to be more competitive. However, Kate Lock, the accountant, was expressing caution over the finance required. She has prepared the following information, based on observation of past output figures:

Figures of output are weekly

Units of labour	Output with 3 machines	Output per unit of labour (3 machines)	Output with 5 machines
20	50	2.5 frames	75
30	70	2.33 frames	120

1 Define: full capacity, productivity. [4]

2 Calculate the added value, assuming the average selling price of each unit is £75.00. [2]

3 Calculate the weekly output per unit of labour for 20 units and 30 units of labour, using five machines, and advise the business of the most productive combination of labour and capital. [4]

4 Evaluate the problems which the business might encounter when moving to a more capital-intensive process. [10]

20

Maxi Case Study

Designs on Crystal Ltd is a Scottish business which buys in a variety of pre-made glass – mainly tankards, tumblers, rose bowls and decanters, and creates a unique design, according to specific customer requirements, which is etched into the glass using a variety of technical processes. A recent order which it won was for the Carlsberg/Liverpool F.C. 'player of the month'. Ten years ago when sales were growing, the business moved to its present premises; instead of renting property, it decided that purchasing a building would be better because the rent being paid on the old building would be more than the interest on the loan needed to purchase the new property. James McDrew, the managing director, found an old army building which was ideal for the business. The design of the building lent itself to the four-stage process of production, in that each employee could work in a separate area and pass work on at his/her own speed. The four stages are

1 artwork, using Corel draw software to create the required design and lettering

2 printing, to turn the artwork into a stencil that will etch on to the glass

3 application, where the design is actually etched on

4 firing, finishing and packing, after which the product is sent to the customer

Examples of products from Designs on Crystal Ltd

The business is not in a particularly competitive industry; in this case this means that demand is not particularly sensitive to prices. Any reduction in costs can therefore immediately result in greater profit, because the business does not need to put the prices down in order to compete. The scale of production can help to determine the profit, assuming break-even point is reached – one example is the cost per glass: if the business buys 12 glasses of a particular type, it will pay £4.70 per glass; once the business orders £500 of this type, it is charged only £3.70 per glass.

It prides itself on high quality and each employee is expected to inspect the product and 'sell' it on to the next process. If there is any doubt over the product's quality, it does not go through to the next stage. Reworking is impossible, so individual products are scrapped if there is a fault at any stage. Precision of the design on the glassware is the main selling point and the cost to Designs on Crystal of a customer taking the product out of its packaging, only to find a blemish in the glass, is far too great for the company even to consider; so the philosophy on quality must be to get it right first time.

Table 1

Year end Oct	1998	1997	1996	1995	1994	1993	1992	1991	1990
Sales	207091	170864	165388	151355	174023	134367	117220	156901	136303
Gross profit	91736	68942	59645	55501	64312	37178	79722	108568	88683
Overheads	67144	56369	61943	58552	43361	53055	82670	78130	67810
Operating profit	24140	12573	−2298	−3051	20951	−15877	−2948	30438	20873
Staff	7	7	7	8	7	7	6	10	10

James is delighted with the recent performance of his business. He says: 'The upturn in turnover and profitability over the last few years has been due to the focused effort to drive forward and become more efficient and target our strengths.'

The business has also made investment in new equipment. One recent example of this is the purchase of a computer, laser printer and scanner used in the design process. This means it can cut out the process of filming, the use of the chemicals and the time involved, all of which is estimated to save the business £12.50 per order. The actual cost of the new equipment was £1500.

The business holds buffer (or safety) stock of about two months' sales; the cost of the glass is about one-third of the final sales value. In 1998 the business turned over £200,000, made up of about 1,000 orders at an average value of £200 each, although sales per month fluctuated between £10,000 and £28,000 per month.

1 Define: scale of production, break-even point, quality. [6]

2 a) How many glasses must the business purchase to achieve the discount? [1]

   b) What is the value of the buffer stock (i.e. cost value)? [4]

   c) State two reasons why the business needs to hold such a high level of stock (two months of sales/production). [2]

3 a) How many orders did it take (at an average saving of £12.50) to pay for the investment in the scanner? [2]

   b) What other factors might the business have considered when taking the decision to purchase the new scanner? [4]

4 Copy the information in Table 1 into a spreadsheet. Calculate the changes in productivity over the time period and suggest reasons why the productivity has altered. (Choose your own measures of productivity based on the information provided.) [8]

5 What factors might the owner have taken into account when moving to the new location? [5]

6 Evaluate the various methods employed by the business which add value. [8]

40

Location of industry

Learning objectives

Having read this unit, students will be able to

1 identify the factors that affect a business's decision to locate

2 evaluate the significance of such factors in different business situations

3 identify recent trends in location

Context

Anyone involved in the surveying/property business will tell you that the three most important factors affecting the success of a business are location, location and location! Consider the issues facing Shell, the oil company, when deciding where to locate its oil refineries. It must consider a multiplicity of factors e.g. how easily the crude oil can be transported to the refinery, which obviously depends on where the oil has been found; then it must consider the availability of suitably qualified labour within a particular area, along with the cost of building the plant and hiring the labour. It must also consider the location of its customers, in that the petrol retailers (also, incidentally, owned by Shell – *see Unit 5 Mergers and acquisitions*) will need to gain access to the fuel at short notice. Shell might even consider that the government may provide finance for the refinery, but with the condition that it locates in a particular area of high unemployment. Shell will arrive at the decision only by balancing the various benefits and costs of available sites and evaluating each factor in terms of its importance within the overall decision. For example, access to the North Sea oilfields may well be more important than being close to its retailers, because the cost of transporting from the oilfield to the refinery may be much cheaper per mile travelled than the cost of moving the petrol in road tankers to the petrol stations. Alternatively, if the government is providing grants for creating jobs, but the unemployed do not possess the technical skills, and the training costs outweigh the government grant, this will also affect the decision.

Types of location

There are four main types of industrial location (costs are included below):

- **Office space** – used primarily by service companies, but also major manufacturers who have a separate headquarters away from their manufacturing facilities e.g. Unilever, which has many production facilities around the world, has its headquarters in London. Normally this type of location is the most expensive due to its scarcity.

- **Retail warehousing** – this may be located on out-of-town retail parks such as Fosse Park in Leicestershire which is full of enormous warehousing facilities for major businesses to use for distributing their products.

- **Retail** – refers to high street locations; such property has become less expensive in areas where out-of-town retail parks have become more widespread and the demand for a high street presence has fallen. However, costs remain high in cities and large market towns.

- **Industrial** – usually the cheapest, given the amount of locations available and the level of demand and the fact that it is located furthest away from centres of population.

Rental costs

Costs of particular types of space in 1999....

Office: London is normally the most expensive, costing up to £55 per square foot per annum. One square foot is about the same area as that of a waste-paper bin (which probably costs about £5 to buy) i.e. a business will have to pay 11 times the value of the bin, just to be able to pay for a space to put it.

High street: this is calculated in zones of 20 feet from the front window to the back of the shop. In a market town such as Norwich, Norfolk, the most expensive space is £180 per square foot for the first 20 feet. Thereafter, the cost per square foot is reduced by

50% every extra 20 feet away from the window. For example, if the shop is 100 feet long and the starting zone is £100 per square foot, the last zone will cost £6.25 per square foot.

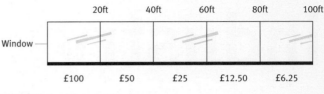

Figure 24.1   Price of shop space

Retail warehousing/out-of-town retail:

typically £10–£20 per square foot. The rates will vary according to the popularity of particular areas which normally depends on the density of population. However, strong demand for space can push up rental values. In 1999 Fosse Park saw rents reach £60 to £75 per square foot due to competition for space.

Industrial: £1.50–£7.00 per square foot per annum; there is an enormous variety of properties available because the factors determining most industrial locations are less stringent than those for high street shops, for example.

Question 1

What type of property are the following businesses likely to seek? State your reasons.
Hint: there may be more than one type.
a) Marks and Spencer plc
b) Harry Ramsdens plc
c) The Body Shop
d) Tarmac (construction business)
e) Blue Circle Cement
f) Barclays Bank
g) Sony   7 × [2]

Factors affecting location

- Availability of property – if a particular type of location is in plentiful supply, then a business may adapt itself to move to such a place, given that the price may be cheaper; on the other hand, a business may be forced to wait for some time for the property which fits its needs, especially if location is significant for sales (e.g. high street stores)

■ Cost of property – if there is a high level of demand for such property from a variety of businesses, then the forces of supply and demand will dictate that the price will increase. In Figure 24.2, with a sudden increase in demand for a particular type of property, the price will increase from p_0 to p_1, because there will be no immediate increase in the supply of property.

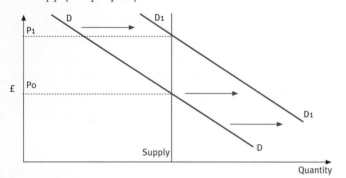

Figure 24.2 Demand and supply diagram

■ Popularity – if a particular location becomes suddenly more desirable, it will normally take about 36 months for more space to be provided, following the sudden increase in demand; this lead time will include obtaining the necessary planning permission as well as constructing the actual building.

■ Cost of local labour (within the **local labour market**) – this is frequently the rationale behind businesses locating manufacturing plants in south-east Asia. The jobs do not require a great deal of skill and the cost per day is so much cheaper. Even if the level of productivity is much lower in Third World countries, a wage rate of £3 per day for workers in the Levi factory in Manila is a far cry from the £14 per hour paid at its Northampton plant

■ Infrastructure – a business will want to be able to deliver products to customers quickly and be on an accessible route for receiving goods from suppliers; if neither of these is the case, then the costs of the business will rise. This is an advantage of moving into a purpose-built industrial estate or into a region which is well served by efficient transport networks and the other elements of the **infrastructure**.

■ Availability of government assistance – when Nissan made the historic and pioneering decision to move to Tyne-Tees, it was made clear that the government had offered some very favourable incentives. During the 1980s as part of the government's attempt to help the economy to grow, it set up various **Enterprise Zones** which carried with them some attractive financial advantages e.g. free rates for 10 years and a 100% depreciation allowance on any long-term investment in the first year i.e. if a business bought plant and machinery worth £5 million, it could write off the investment in the first year for tax purposes. This meant profits would take a drop and might even mean the company made a loss, so it also meant the company did not need to pay tax that year (*see Unit 35 Profit and loss account*).

■ Type of company – the requirement of a manufacturing business as opposed to a service business will vary according to the factors above. Some industries, known as **footloose industries**, have no defined requirement as to where they must locate i.e. the geographical location is not significant. Examples of these are government departments such as the National Savings Bank, with a headquarters in Durham. Companies which use a telephone sales approach to all their marketing are another example of a footloose industry. As long as the location meets the business's other requirements, it has relative freedom to locate anywhere it wishes.

■ Location of customers – if a business relies on one customer for the majority of its income it may well decide to locate within easy reach of this customer. This will allow it a much faster response time if the customer changes its requirements as well as allowing the customer to operate a just-in-time stock holding policy. It will also mean that a fast response time can lead to the supplier holding a low level of stock. There is a famous example of a carpet manufacturer (*also referred to in Unit 30 Lean production*) that is located within two minutes' drive of the Nissan factory so it does not need to hold large amounts of stock and begins to cut the carpet only when the car hits the final assembly line. Some businesses will aim to deliver within 24 hours and must therefore choose a location which will allow this to be achieved at a minimum cost (*see case study on Enta at the end of this unit*). Some supermarkets will need to locate in an area where there is a sufficient density of population to justify the investment or perhaps in a town centre, where the footfall is particularly high e.g. Tesco plc has begun to differentiate its stores, according to location. The recently opened Metro stores are located in city centres, normally close to areas where many professional people work – lawyers, financiers etc. The range of goods is smaller than the usual retail outlet and targets these buyers.

Tesco Metro Store

The 'top-up' shop, as it is known, offers goods at a slightly higher price, given the socio-economic grouping of the customers.

■ Location of suppliers – when raw materials are in plentiful supply, but difficult to transport, there is likely to be a cluster of businesses located close to each other all in the same industry. A traditional area for the brewing industry, where such companies as Bass, Carlsberg, Tetley and Marstons all have manufacturing facilities, is Burton-on-Trent. The reason is the quality of the spring water used in the brewing process. As a result of these manufacturers locating in Burton, Marmite followed suit; the main product used by Marmite is yeast extract, which is a by-product of the brewing industry.

■ Proximity to competitors – if a business observes a competitor making profit from a particular location,

Marmite factory

it may well choose to locate in the same area. Morrison's supermarket chain actually waits until other main supermarkets have had a store in a particular town for some years and then builds its own store – an interesting way of carrying out market research! At the other end of the scale, Silicon Valley in California is a famous location for the computer industry, external economies of sale being the main reason.

■ Proximity to industry e.g. most financial companies need to have a presence in the City of London because of the benefits of computer networking following the Big Bang (which happened in 1986, meaning stockbrokers were connected via computer cables).

■ Rent or buy – some businesses will not be able to purchase a location because of the financial outlay, so will elect to rent the property. Sometimes it is impossible to purchase certain property e.g. in the City of London, most of which is owned by the Duke of Westminster, so businesses must rent.

■ Language requirements – if a French company's employees all speak French and German, it makes sense to look carefully at German locations if the opportunity for expansion arises. Choosing other countries might necessitate training in the local language.

- Climatic conditions – the Canary Islands have prospered as a holiday resort due to their geographical location making them an attractive destination for sun worshippers.

- Opportunity for **sub-letting** – when a business signs a contract to use a particular location, it may wish to sub-let some or even all of its location if it cannot use the space efficiently e.g. if demand drops and a business needs to cut costs, but does not want to lose the chance of using the same location in the future if and when demand picks up again. Permission to sub-let will be written into the contract at the beginning.

- Features of property (retailers) – the size, position, infrastructure and appropriateness for certain displays of goods will all determine whether retailers will choose a particular location.

- Planning permission – if a business wishes to extend a building to allow for extra capacity or perhaps storage space, it will need to obtain planning permission. Certain properties, such as listed buildings, will not be granted such permission, which can, in turn, affect the future value of the property.

- Expected return due to new location – a business must be able to make a return well in excess of the cost of location. This can be a significant factor especially if short-term returns are necessary e.g. for hi-tech firms who have raised the majority of their finance using venture capital (*see Unit 40 Sources of finance*).

- Obsolescence of building – as the requirements for modern-day business have relied more on technology, some buildings have needed to be adapted. Raised floors have been needed to allow for wiring for computers, air conditioned offices have become a necessity in some cities in the summer so piping and conduits have been needed. Some buildings have simply not been constructed to allow for this which has necessitated their demolition and rebuilding. Others, however, have been built with future requirements in mind which makes adapting to new technology much cheaper.

- Owner's preference – it has been said that location can depend ultimately on the owner's preference; perhaps the managing director wishes to be close to her parents, or within easy reach of the best school in the area. Or, perhaps, the managing director's husband may want to be near the local golf club! Although not based on any financial or commercial logic, this factor can exert considerable influence on the final decision.

A 1950s building

- Globalisation – as markets have become ever more widespread, it has become possible to choose a location anywhere across five continents; with transport and telecommunications becoming much more efficient, companies have been able to search for the lowest cost route.

- Tradition – for whatever reasons, a business may traditionally have been located in a certain region and moving away for commercial reasons will be resisted e.g. Norwich Union maintaining its HQ in Norwich, despite cheaper and possibly more suitable alternatives. **Industrial inertia** occurs when the traditional reason for a particular location is no longer applicable e.g. suppliers of shipyards in the north east located close to the shipyards, but once these closed down, there was no longer a need to stay there.

■ Size – although a business may move to increase its capacity, it will not want to fill such capacity immediately if it expects further demand increases. Otherwise it will be in the same position as it was before the move; in other words it must allow room for expansion.

Question 2

In each of the following examples, consider the above factors affecting location and choose the three most significant factors affecting the location of each business. You might not choose the same five each time, nor will you agree with other members of your class each time. Be prepared to argue the case for your own selection. State three other pieces of information about the business you would like to know before making the final decision.

Business 1: a small retailer which sells high quality delicatessen food such as spices, herbs and pulses

Business 2: a national distribution company with three main customers, each 100 miles from each other, contributing 30% of the revenue. The business prides itself on 'next day delivery'.

Business 3: a steel manufacturer, reliant on coal, distributing and receiving its product by rail. It has a virtual monopoly on the supply of steel within the economy.

Business 4: a double glazing business that receives glass from the manufacturer and fits it into frames. It markets itself using a telephone sales team and travelling sales representatives.

$4 \times [15]$

Question 3

A petrol retailer has identified three different locations for its third petrol station. It has to compete with the multinational businesses such as BP and Esso, as well as the local hypermarket which has just begun to sell petrol. It has identified six main factors which will affect its decision and has given each site a mark out of 10 as to how appropriate that particular site is in achieving its objective e.g. Site 1 is the most expensive, so it has a mark of 4, compared with the other two.

Factors affecting the choice of site

	Site 1	Site 2	Site 3
Cost of site	4	6	9
Access to supplier	6	7	8
Proximity to competitors (higher number denotes being further away)	9	6	4
Possibility for future expansion	2	5	6
Proximity to customers	7	7	5
Personal preference	8	6	4

a) Rank the above factors in order of priority, weighting the most important with the number 6 and the least important with the number 1. Justify your choice. [5]

b) Multiply the rank by each of the scores e.g. if you think Access to supplier is the most important, rank it with 6, then multiply 6×6 for site 1, 6×7 for site 2 etc. and add up the totals for each site. Which is the best site? [4]

c) What might persuade the owner to choose one of the other sites as an alternative to your suggestion? [4]

Question 4

A business has decided to locate much closer to its two customers and is considering two sites – A and B. It delivers products to customer 1 by rail and to customer 2 by road. Collection of its materials is done from one location – Port Sea. Apart from the labour cost, the cost of manufacturing is the same at both.

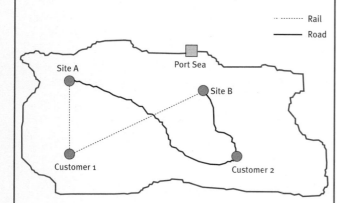

Table 1

	Site A	Site B
Labour costs (per month)	£10,000	£12,000
Rent costs (per month)	£40,000	£35,000
Rail (50,000 units per month)	£0.60 per unit	£0.75 per unit
Road (50,000 units per month)	£0.30 per unit	£0.20 per unit
Collecting supplies	£5,000 per month	£2,000 per month

a) Using the information contained in Table 1, calculate the difference in monthly costs of operating at site A and site B. [6]

b) If the delivery to customer 1 dropped by 10,000 per month and delivery to customer 2 increased by 10,000 per month, how would your answer to **a)** alter? [4]

c) What other information would you need before taking the decision whether the business should choose site A or site B? [5]

Recent trends

- During the **property boom** of the 1980s, businesses looked to move away from London as the cost of property soared. If such a move fitted in with the business's requirements, it could achieve a significant saving.

- Such savings have been less significant following the reduction in rental costs of office space in recent years due to a) over-supply – Canary Wharf still remains under-utilised, and b) a drop in demand due to the recession. This has led some companies to move back to London.

- The building of Terminal 4 at Heathrow has made location close to this airport much more attractive; as a result, the cost of renting has increased.

Heathrow

- Leases have reduced in length due to excess supply of property and demand of tenants not to be tied to a long-term commitment e.g. average shop lease from 25 to 15 years; central London offices from 25 to 10 years. An option to terminate a lease after 10 or 15 years can be built into a contract, but this can sometimes result in a financial penalty.

- Demand for office space is now highly influenced by level of technology. Hot-desking – the process of having a flexible office, the use of personal computers and telecommunications systems have meant less need for so many places to work and file records. It is quite likely that over-supply of office space will continue.

Points for Revision

Key Terms

local labour market	the supply and demand for labour within reach of the business
infrastructure	the transport networks surrounding the location
enterprise zones	areas where the government offered financial incentives for location
footloose industries	industries which are not required to locate in a particular area
sub-letting	business 1 rents from the owner, but also lets a part of the building to business 2
industrial inertia	when the traditional reason for a business locating in a particular area is no longer important
property boom	refers to the period in the mid to late 1980s when the cost of property rose quickly (*see Unit 60*)

Definitions Question:
By reference to a business or businesses of which you have direct knowledge or experience, explain the significance of any three of the above (your teacher may wish to choose the definitions for you).   [5] per definition

Summary Points:

1. The location of a business can have a significant effect on its profitability and efficiency.

2. There are four types of location which a business can choose – office, high street, retail warehousing and industrial.

3. The cost of the location, in terms of rental costs, will depend on the type of location.

4. There are many factors which affect the location of a business, although a great deal will depend on the nature of the business and its industry.

5. The lowest cost option has become less important in recent years.

Mini Case Study

Paradise Pictures, a picture frame business, specialises in renovating and selling frames for old paintings. Presently it is based in cramped conditions in the centre of a major city, having started the business there 120 years ago. The family lives on the edge of the city and all six members of the family work in the business. Recently local customers have complained when picking up their frames of the difficulty of carrying these to the car park 500 yards away.

Patrick Paradise, the chairman, has also developed the export market and organising collection and delivery has been difficult because the city is poorly served by motorways. Peter Paradise, the distribution manager, is very keen to locate closer to the ferries, given that the export market is growing compared with the static local market, and he has found a site in Kent. Paula Paradise, the sales manager, is worried about losing local customers who have been loyal for many years and is therefore reluctant to move.

The Kent site will cost £200,000 and will probably generate additional net cash flow of £60,000 per year to begin with.

A compromise solution is to find a wholesaler in Kent to act as a distributor.

Perry Paradise, the accountant, requires a decision as to whether the business should:
 i remain at its present site
 ii move to the Kent site
 iii remain and use a wholesaler

---

1 Define: export market, wholesaler, cash flow. [6]

2 Calculate the payback period of the Kent site, stating your assumptions. [2]

3 Evaluate the factors affecting Paradise Pictures regarding the three options. [12]

20

Maxi Case Study

Enta Technologies is a business based at Stafford Park, Telford, Shropshire and is one of a large number of successful businesses that the Telford Development Corporation has attracted in recent years. This was done by offering incentives such as free rates for 10 years and depreciation allowances. The enticement of high unemployment in the region meant there was a plentiful supply of labour. A motorway facilitated short delivery times.

The business manufactures for the computer industry according to customer requirements – sometimes the business will provide hard drives, keyboards or mice as well as fully assembled computers (total output = 20,000 'kits' per month) and has grown from a turnover of £60,000 to £80 million in just eight years!

In 1995 it moved into one of the most singularly designed buildings you could expect to see for a business that makes computers. It is shaped in the style of a Taiwanese Pagoda (*see photograph*) with a specific objective in mind; customers who regularly visit the site to discuss their individual requirements will remember it!

Computer companies are normally housed in rather bland, functional buildings, whereas Enta Technologies allows instant recognition and an image which works to differentiate the business from its competitors. This is particularly important in an industry which is highly competitive and dynamic.

Jason Tsai, the founder of the business, states that a significant factor affecting the decision to locate its business in Telford was the geographical position. Telford is central to England and is within three hours' travelling time of 80% of Enta's customers; it promises to deliver its computer kits (part-assembled computers) and fully assembled computers by 11 o'clock the next day. Such a fast delivery time is demanded by the 5000 or so customers who are retailers such as Dixons and businesses that sell customised computer packages using direct marketing to gain business. Only 20% of business is generated abroad, so the products are flown from Birmingham.

The second main reason was the language – English is the second language in Taiwan and the owner was relatively fluent in English. Another reason was the quality of the British work-force. Jason Tsai took a pragmatic view to paying wages – 'The amount I pay employees is reflected in the quality of work they provide – low wages = low quality! And our customers would simply go elsewhere if this was the case.'

The only financial aid the business has received was given by the Department of Trade and Industry which offered a grant for each person employed. In 1995, it offered £4,400 as a lump sum for each extra person employed at the time of moving in to the new premises; since then the business has increased its employees from 30 to 100 people, although only six are actually employed on the production line. The only condition of the grant was that if the business had to make any redundancies, the money would have to be repaid.

1 Define: highly competitive, direct marketing.   [4]

2 a) Calculate the average annual percentage increase in turnover during the eight years of the business's existence. How useful is this figure to potential investors?   [4]

   b) How much money did Enta receive from the DTI in the form of grants for new employees?   [2]

3 Given that only six out of 100 employees work on the production line, describe the functions which might be performed by the other 94 employees. Think about the nature of the business.   [5]

4 a) State the main reasons why Enta chose Telford for its factory.   [2]

   b) Explain why high unemployment in a region is particularly attractive to a business like Enta. You may wish to use a supply and demand diagram in your answer.   [6]

5 What characteristics does the computer industry display to warrant such a peculiar design of building in Telford?   [4]

6 Apart from the factors highlighted in the text, discuss the other factors which Enta may have considered when deciding to locate at Telford.   [8]

Technology

Learning objectives

Having read this unit, students will be able to

1   identify the various applications of technology within a business

2   understand and appreciate the significance of technology to industry

3   appreciate the problems of technological advancement and how a business needs to address such problems

Context

Look at any food product displayed on a shelf in the local supermarket and ask yourself what technology has been used to put it there for you to consume.

If a crop is involved, technology would have been used to enhance the growing of the crop, to develop the pesticide to protect the crop or even to develop a new species of the crop.

The 'manufacturing' will have used sophisticated technology to freeze-dry the crop and regulate its temperature until required, cook it, pack it and palletise it automatically ready for distribution to a regional distribution centre.

The retailer will have used technology to order the product, having installed a scanning machine that you probably thought was just to enable the check-out assistant to price your chosen products and total your bill.

Or were you able to look at the product on the virtual shelf displayed on your PC because you are one of a growing number who shop on the Internet, to date, the ultimate in technology for your convenience?

Technology is all around us and plays a significant part in the continual desire of businesses to gain a competitive advantage. It is the vehicle to providing new products, improved products or the same products at a lower cost.

Why is technology important?

If you read the annual report of any company you will usually see some reference to technology regardless of the type of business.

BT – 'Now it is possible for a strand of glass as thin as a human hair to carry 40,000 telephone calls simultaneously.'

Marks and Spencer – 'Our sophisticated use of technology is central to delivering the services that customers want' … 'We are substantially increasing investment in information technology to drive sales, enhance customer service and improve efficiency.'

Boots – When referring to understanding their customers, 'Today we are using increasingly sophisticated technology to achieve this.'

The General Electric Company (Marconi) – 'A continuing stream of innovations has underpinned breakthroughs into new markets.'

If you look at the advertisements in newspapers and magazines, you will find that many feature products which are smaller, faster or more advanced; all highlight the technology involved.

Businesses are constantly attempting to improve the products they sell. This may mean applying technology to improve how the product is designed or how the factory is organised. Both may bring about valuable savings in costs that can either be passed on to the customer or increase profits. But it is not just for consumer products that technology plays such an important role in the struggle for advancement. In the medical field, it has been used to develop equipment and drugs to combat disease which were until very recently viewed as fiction or fantasy. Picker International, part of the multinational company GEC, has pioneered image-guided surgery equipment which allows a surgeon to work with total accuracy when making incisions for neuro and spinal surgery. It is also possible to send images via the Internet for viewing by doctors anywhere in the world. We the customers benefit from the technological progress, but for the businesses it may be their passport to survival and profitability.

Technology provides the vehicle to increased productivity; the utilisation of technology usually means that a business will become more capital-intensive, the benefits of which further enhance the competitiveness of the business.

The application of technology

It was mentioned in the context section that technology can be used in any or all stages of production. The technology used today to produce the food we eat and to extract the raw materials (primary sector) that are required by any industrial economy is highly evident.

Technology at work

Manufacturing businesses (secondary) have altered their methods of production dramatically as a result of technology (*see photograph overleaf*).

For the service sector of the economy (tertiary) consumers can now book their holiday on the Internet having first visited one of the many sites that have actual pictures from camera links. Watch an old James Bond film and compare the special effects with a film of today. *Titanic* was filmed using many special technological techniques that created the illusion necessary for the sinking of the ship.

Technology is being used to help address some of the problems with congestion on our roads. Several schemes already in existence in an attempt to reduce congestion rely on modern technology such as the scheme in Leicester which is an attempt to reduce the flow of traffic on certain main roads at particular times of the day. Smart cards which can be scanned are used to enable the motorist to be charged for using a particular route at a given time. Other towns and cities are considering a form of road pricing to alleviate the difficulties of ensuring that the appropriate 'fee' is paid for the road used.

The robot's role in manufacturing

Production

Technology is utilised throughout the process of production.

At the design stage **computer aided design** (CAD) has had a dramatic effect upon the number of ideas that can be generated and tested in a small amount of time which in turn helps keep costs to a minimum. Coupled with the application of virtual simulation, designers are now able to view their ideas from many angles without the need to even produce a prototype, again saving cost. Given the level of competition in many of the world's markets it is essential that companies are able to update their products with a shorter lead time; CAD is the vehicle that enables this to be achieved. Architects are now able to 'draw' their buildings on computer and walk through the rooms they have created. Furthermore they can calculate the engineering requirements as the design of the building is altered, without building anything! Therefore the designer's time can now be spent actually creating rather than having to keep checking whether an idea is feasible, via the production of models. The computer aided design facility enables the car designer to calculate the efficiency of the design by utilising a simulated wind tunnel; this provides data on the drag factor of the car which is of significance for fuel consumption figures. Technology has allowed the development of many new materials to be used in producing industrial and consumer goods. *Tomorrow's World* need be viewed for only one week to learn about a new material that is to be used for a new or existing product.

Technology has brought many new products to the market by providing the means for cost-effective research. The growth of the so-called 'neutraceuticals' (food which improves your health as you eat it!) has been the result of intense competition between Johnson & Johnson and Unilever. Technological research has led to the launch of a margarine that actually reduces the cholesterol level of the consumer.

Manufacturing

Computer aided manufacturing (CAM) is now commonplace within any modern factory. To enable JIT (*see Unit 28 Stock control*) to operate, this technology is required to ensure all the right parts are ordered at the right time and are delivered on time for them to be used on the production line. Processes that involve measuring temperatures constantly, such as the brewing industry, rely on computer technology to undertake these laborious but essential checks and to do so more accurately, more frequently and much more cost-effectively than an operative could. Technology allows many of the quality controls to be undertaken automatically and more reliably.

Marketing

Much of the technology that a business uses is **information technology**.

Recently a marketing expert with IBM made predictions of IT applications for the 21st century, many of which are already well beyond the concept stage.

The use of intelligent packaging has been well reported in the press and in company literature. Much of our food will be packaged to include sensors which will clearly show when the item is no longer fit to eat. Another application of smart packaging will be to contain a sensor that can be 'read' when it has been used and as a consequence will automatically be reordered by the consumer's computer which will be linked to the supermarket's website. IT is very much at the forefront of retail advances for the benefit of consumers. Shopping on the Internet has already been referred to, but the uses of the technology continue to grow. Sainsbury's announced at the end of 1998 that it was hoping to use the Internet to build a **database** of customer's e-mail addresses. This data will then be tied into the reward card (or loyalty card) system which will in turn allow the supermarket to promote the right kind of offers to the appropriate segment of consumers. Given the consumer's thirst for 'information', a website will be available for the customer to check the number of points accumulated on the reward card and how to redeem the points on line. Details of the scheme can be found on Sainsbury's site at www.sainsbury.co.uk. Not surprisingly, Tesco announced that it was to provide a very similar scheme on the Internet.

> ### Question 1
> How might IT be of help to a company wanting to prepare a cash flow forecast as part of its business plan? [3]

> ### Question 2
> How would a business utilise a database? [2]

> ### Question 3
> Suggest how a business could benefit from using any two from the following list:
> Video/tele-conferencing
> Internet
> Electronic (e-) mail
> Fax
> ISDN
> e-commerce [4]

Technology in the working environment

Ten years ago, many were predicting that home working and the virtual office would be commonplace. Businesses would all be using ISDN (Integrated services digital network) to enable them to send vast amounts of information down the telephone line at great speed. All businesses would be operating their sales conferences utilising video conferencing and the Internet would be the vehicle used to sell their products to the customers who would be sitting at their computers choosing products they wanted from virtual shelves. Yet today, at the turn of the century, the reality is not as predicted. A survey conducted by Richard Ellis at the University of Cambridge stated that many companies consider there is a need for their employees to interact and socialise, something the technology does not cater for. The concept of hot-desking (*see below, The place of work*) was operated by only 10% of employees at companies which made this facility available. The number of companies involved was only 15% of those surveyed.

Although the majority of offices today are awash with technology, the survey highlighted that to many of the companies asked, much of this technology was not considered to be of vital importance. Of all the technology available in the modern office, the item that was considered to be vital was e-mail, whilst video conferencing, although used by 55% of the companies surveyed, was considered to be vital by only 6%!

The survey indicated that technology provided the opportunity for large increases in productivity. Much time is spent by employees commuting to work, which could be used for more productive purposes. Neil McLocklin, who is a member of the workstyle consultancy group at BT, suggested that commuting took, on average, eight working weeks annually. Consequently many companies are looking at ways to increase the output of their employees. Technology is, however, only a part of the answer. For all its obvious advantages there has to be a change in attitude by the work-force and this will take time.

The problems of technology

To many, the prospect of technological progress can be seen only as an advantage. The customer is provided with a greater choice of products with a higher level of quality, often at a cheaper price. Business is able to provide its customers with the above at a cheaper cost and consequently with a higher profit. However, the fact that technology is continually changing can be a problem in itself. The pace of change has meant that business has to be able to cope with this, normally in the form of extra cost for both training and investment.

Cost

More money has to be allocated for research and the provision of the new technologies. The significant level of capital investment required for the purchase of the hardware if CAD, CAM or any application of information technology is to be used, may be prohibitive to a lot of the smaller businesses. In addition there are the set-up costs of installing new technology; not only might the training of operatives take time, assuming there has been no resistance to their introduction, but it will also be quite expensive.

Human

Utilising technology, in many instances, has consequences for the existing work-force. If a drinks business has invested in a new machine that is capable of packaging cans of cola into trays which in turn are automatically put on to pallets ready for distribution, there will be a fall in the demand for labour. The technological advance has led to capital substitution, creating unemployment for those workers who used to undertake the packaging procedure. The business may have to pay redundancy money to those affected. The remaining workers still required in the packaging department may face a change in the nature of their work. Prior to the installation of the new technology, their work might have involved several different tasks and consequently different skills; subsequently, their task might be only to 'mind' the machine, drastically reducing the skill required and the variety of tasks to be performed. This in turn may have consequences for the level of motivation that the new job provides (*see Units 49 and 50*). Such consequences are areas for thought for management as it continues to introduce more and more technology that reduces the input of the worker. Joan Woodward, in *Industrial Organisation: Theory and Practice* (Oxford University Press, 1965), highlighted the difficulties of introducing new technology into the business organisation.

Technology has led to other problems which affect us all. As improvements have been developed in the field of medicine, the life expectancy of the population increases creating an additional burden upon the employed population. Governments are now faced with the economic problem of choice with regard to priorities for expenditure. Provision for the elderly is expensive, but the government has to ensure that companies do not face too high a burden of taxation if sufficient profits are to be available to plough back into the business in order to remain competitive.

But technology has also provided new jobs within the economy. Anyone with computer skills is more likely to gain employment.

The place of work

Technology has already started to have a dramatic effect on how and, most interestingly, where workers perform their job. Today's office hardware enables a business to operate a 'hot-desking' system. No longer, as has been the tradition, is there one desk for every employee; now one desk may be used by many as their needs dictate. With more people working from home there is less need to provide such a large amount of office space and equipment, thus reducing costs for the business.

The working environment has become much more reliant on the machine, the robot and the computer and, as a consequence, the ability to control one's own working environment is very limited. Similarly, there have already been instances when the technology has 'reacted' automatically to a given situation, which has compounded the problem rather than alleviated it. The infamous Black Monday Stock Exchange share price crash of 1987 was allegedly caused by the 'over-reaction of the equipment that went into "sell" mode'. More recently (November 1998), the reliability of electronic trading was called into question again when on the London International Financial Futures Exchange, £11.5 billion of German bonds were put up for sale by mistake! A young trainee who thought he was working on a simulated version of the market inadvertently ended up 'playing' on the real thing as a result of a failed security system on the computers.

Question 4

Suggest some of the human consequences of the growth in the number of employees working from home. [5]

Points for Revision

Key Terms

technology	a process of creating solutions to problems within the business environment, utilising the resources available. The result of technological advancement is improved efficiency and better or new products
CAD	computer aided design is a way of utilising computer programs to generate, amend and solve design ideas. Such a system provides large savings to the business, especially by reducing the length of the lead time
CAM	computer aided manufacture utilises computers to help organise and operate the smooth running of the productive process. CAM is vital if lean production is to operate successfully
information technology	electronic means are used to store and use information more quickly and at a lower cost to the business
database	a collection of information which can be stored, used and manipulated
hot-desking	using one desk for the benefit of many as and when required

Definitions Question:
By referring to a business you know, explain the significance of three of the above terms (your teacher may wish to help you with the choice).   [5] per definition

Summary Points:

1 Technology provides a vehicle for businesses to remain competitive via the introduction of new or improved products, often at a cheaper cost.

2 Technology has meant that businesses have to learn how to cope with constant change as a result of the pace of technological development.

Mini Case Study

Went's Clothing plc is a large multinational business that makes clothes products, with factories in Europe and Asia, selling to over 2,000 different retailers. Its growth in size has made communication between countries and employees difficult to manage because of the vast number of messages which need to be conveyed both within the business and to customers and suppliers. The problem has resulted in two potential orders being lost to competitors because the faxed orders have been misplaced. In addition, the company has incurred extra costs as a result of delayed messages.

In an attempt to solve these problems, Went's Clothing is thinking of implementing an electronic mail software package system (e-mail) using some of its existing hardware. This will require investment in new computer equipment because some of the present terminals lack the memory and processing speed. The extra fixed cost arising due to the new assets would be £250,000 but since the lost orders were worth £150,000 the board was keen for this to go ahead. The financial director, Alex Went, provided further proof of the worthiness of this idea by claiming that e-mail would save an average of 80 pence per call. The present number of calls is 350,000 per annum.

1 Define the following: investment, hardware. [4]

2 a) How many calls would the business need to make to break even on the new system? [2]

   b) Based on your answer, should the business go ahead with this? State your assumptions. [4]

3 Evaluate all the issues which the business will consider when making the decision whether to implement the e-mail system. [10]

$\overline{20}$

Maxi Case Study

Sainsbury plc has gradually adopted more technologically advanced procedures in its outlets in recent years. Despite earning a turnover of nearly £12 billion from its supermarkets alone, it has faced continuing and intensive competition from close rivals such as Tesco and Safeway. It therefore seizes upon every opportunity to reduce costs and satisfy customers in an attempt to gain a competitive edge over its rivals.

Although the technological developments are now commonplace throughout this industry, it is difficult to imagine how Sainsbury's would manage without them. The most significant form of technology used by the business is its EPOS or electronic point of sale system. This is the process whereby a product is passed over a laser that reads the bar code on the side of each and every product. It is tempting to think that the sole purpose of this is to calculate the bill more quickly, given the multiplicity of special offers and multibuy deals which Sainsbury's offers, or that EPOS is just a device to enhance customer convenience by ensuring that the wait at the check-out is kept to an absolute minimum.

In fact, the device provides Sainsbury's with three very important pieces of data:

1 The purchasing patterns of customers as a whole, so that the buying department can quickly identify changes in purchasing trends and is therefore able to contact the supplier quickly

2 The ability to order stock, given that the computer tells the store how many items of stock have been sold by a particular time during the day

3 When used in conjunction with the customer's reward card, it is possible to ascertain what individual customers are purchasing, in what quantities and when. This provides Sainsbury's with the opportunity to market special offers directly to 'selected' customers

The data is actually collected by the store's computer and transferred overnight to the headquarters in Blackfriars. The purchasing department then analyses the data with a view to contacting suppliers to change their orders according to consumer purchases. It will also tell the business how much each store has in stock at a particular time and how much it will have available to sell that day, since the orders sent in the previous day are in transit.

However, the computer is unable to build in what the company might call 'external shocks'. For example, supposing Heinz suddenly launched a promotional offer of Buy-one Get-one-free for their cans of beans. Suddenly, Heinz beans will become more attractive in comparison to Sainsbury's own brand. Left to its own devices, the computer will simply tell the buyers there has been a fall in sales, but the manager at the store has the flexibility to identify exactly when the offer will finish or decide that he wants to run an offer of his own and can change the orders accordingly. Technology has thus allowed for the decentralising of the ordering process.

In addition, the manager is able to review the process as he walks about the shop and can change orders with a handset. Simply by scanning the bar code on the shelf and entering a new volume, the manager can alter an order which has already been sent to the head office. The technology thus allows the business to be managed with greater flexibility (the manager can override the system), which allows for a better control of stock.

Just-in-time can therefore be operated, given the very close liaison this technology allows with the suppliers e.g. if McVities is told that Sainsbury's in Hemel Hempstead needs 10 cases of biscuits, when the cases arrive at the Sainsbury's depot, instead of going into storage, the computer sends a message to take them off one lorry (from McVities) and put them immediately on to the lorry for Hemel Hempstead, allowing for a much quicker turnover of stock.

A final application of technology is the growth in the number of personal computers in each store; depending on the level of seniority, managerial staff can key in to various databases. For instance, ordering by e-mail (internal and external) can be done. In addition, there are programmes to calculate the productivity of labour for the manager. All this means he/she can spend a greater amount of time with customers and staff and not filling in endless amounts of documentation. Obviously, installing personal computers into every store at once would be prone to error, so the business operated a pilot scheme to get through the teething errors, before trialling it in a particular area.

Close links with the supplier become very important when using this JIT approach – a recent promotion of two for the price of one on Carlsberg lager resulted in more lager being sold in two weeks than in the previous nine years. Prompt delivery, facilitated through technology, meant there were some very happy customers.

With 21,000 lines and 1 million items over 42,500 square feet, it is difficult to imagine how ordering was ever done by phone!

1 Explain the terms: competitive edge, just-in-time.   [4]

2 a) How would a supplier benefit as a result of Sainsbury's usage of EPOS?   [5]

  b) What problems might a supplier encounter because of Sainsbury's EPOS?   [5]

3 How has technology used by Sainsbury's helped it gain customer loyalty?   [4]

4 Imagine you are responsible for the direct marketing undertaken by Sainsbury's; explain how you would utilise the data from EPOS to increase the sales of particular products of your choice. What other data would you require?   [10]

5 a) What evidence is there to suggest that technology would reduce costs?   [6]

  b) What evidence is there to suggest that technology would increase costs?   [6]

40

Value analysis

Learning objectives

Having read this unit, students will be able to

1 understand the model of value analysis and how it can be applied in business

2 apply various products to the model and assess its usefulness to the business

Context

Look at almost any car, either in a picture or preferably at first hand, and ask yourself what you notice first. Is it the shape, the colour, the make or a combination of these and other factors? Now simply remove one or all of the hubcap covers from the wheels, with the owner's consent! The difference is very noticeable. The whole image of the car has been transformed. Few customers would be satisfied with the product without the hubcaps. The 'changed' appearance of the car reduces the value of the car in the eyes of the customer. Gaining value for money is an important aspect for customers, in their decision whether to buy a product.

Customers may feel that a product is expensive, but given the 'additional' features that are included, this makes the product 'worth' the extra money. The Dyson vacuum cleaner is a case in point. It is much more expensive than many of its rivals but is seen as superior in performing the task of cleaning and as a consequence is good value for money.

Customers look for a product that is going to perform its function well, look good and not cost the earth! Consequently, businesses spend a lot of effort ensuring they have the balance of these attributes right. This requires the process of value analysis.

Task

Either:
Select three products that you buy and suggest which are the most important features for each one,
or:
The next time you visit a restaurant or fast food outlet list the main features of the 'product' that were important to you.

Value analysis defined

Value analysis is concerned with giving the customer what is required at the lowest possible cost. However, that does not mean a reduction in the value of the product or the ability to meet the customers' requirements.

In other words, businesses try to satisfy their customers in the most economical way possible.

All designers of products have to take into consideration three main areas of concern:

■ **function** – a vacuum cleaner must be capable of collecting dirt, whilst being easy to use and manoeuvre, preferably without causing damage to the carpet.

■ **cost** – it must be affordable, or be perceived as being good value for money – a disposable cup, given its function, cannot be too expensive.

■ **aesthetics** – its looks may be very important. A fashion item must look good regardless of the cost and its ability to function as clothing.

The aim is to achieve all these simultaneously without unjustified extra cost.

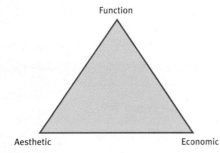

Function

Aesthetic   Economic

Figure 26.1   Design triangle

The priority of the features depends upon the actual product and the needs of the customer.

All products to a greater or lesser extent will need to incorporate all three elements. Under the bonnet of a car there are many parts for which the functional element is fundamental to the car's progress. Yet the actual looks of that particular part are of little or no consequence to the customer.

It is important however to keep the cost of the parts as low as possible because the final cost of the car is crucial in such a competitive market. Cutting the cost by using a cheaper alternative for the battery may be counter-productive if this leads to the car failing to start.

Deciding priorities between the three elements for a product is therefore very much a balancing act which requires careful consideration.

Question 1

Which components of a box of chocolates could be considered a high priority in terms of **a)** function **b)** aesthetics **c)** costs?   [6]

Question 2

Which components of the box of chocolates could be given a high priority in terms of cutting costs without affecting the value to the customer?   [2]

Question 3

For the products illustrated below suggest the order of priority for the main aspects of value (function, cost and aesthetics).   5 × [2]

Value analysis in operation

Imagine a design team which was given a free hand to produce a new perfume and its packaging, but was told that it did not have to consider the cost at all! It is quite likely that the end product would be of a very high quality but it is also quite likely that very little would be sold because of the price. High-quality goods are usually expensive to manufacture and are seen by customers as such. But there is a maximum that customers are prepared to pay for any good, regardless of the additional quality.

Reducing the cost of the product without affecting the quality will increase the profitability.

To be able to produce the right product or provide the right service at the right price requires careful thought and planning. It is essential to utilise the skill of several experts. The value analysis team usually consists of people from different departments within the business to ensure the different aspects of the product or service are given the necessary attention. The representatives may include design, technical, financial and marketing experts, all with something to contribute. At each stage of the value analysis they will be looking for ways to reduce the cost of production without reducing the quality and therefore its value to the customer. This may mean simply finding an alternative material that can be used.

All aspects of the production process will be reviewed, as they all contribute to the cost of the product or service in question.

How many people are involved in the value analysis process usually depends upon the size of the business and the type of product involved. There is a danger that if the team is too large it may become cumbersome and expensive which is counter-productive (*see Unit 4 Size of business*).

If on the other hand they do their job well, the value analysis will ensure that the optimum value is gained for the product at the lowest possible cost.

The value analysis process

- The first step is to decide which aspect ought to be investigated; this may well be a consideration of any problems that are apparent in the design of the product.

- Once areas for investigation have been drawn up there will need to be a plan for the collection of all the relevant data.

- The data that has been gathered will then be carefully evaluated and an agreed solution established.

The process in detail:

- Which problems are considered will probably depend upon whether the product is already on the market or is still at the concept or **prototype** stage. For the latter, the investigation will centre on finding the most efficient method of production, the most cost-effective materials to use and the actual design for the finished product. Using prototypes as part of the value analysis process is appropriate for many goods, not just cars and planes. Although these are obvious examples, prototypes are used for toys, to ensure there are no parts that have sharp edges, or parts that will fall off too easily. For existing products, the problem areas may be self-evident due to customer reaction, feedback from the shop floor highlighting difficulties with the assembly or from the suppliers.

- Any of the above areas for concern will require more information in an attempt to assess accurately the 'value' of the product, if reductions in cost can be made without adding to the costs, or if improvements can be made which will add value without increasing the costs. This information may be collected at the embryonic or development stage in the 'life' of the product. Many alternative uses for a product which will widen its appeal to a larger range of customers (providing a larger consumer base) can be generated very cheaply using **morphological studies**. This is a method of generating many ideas very quickly and consequently more cheaply (*see Figures 26.2 and 26.3*).

Utilising a matrix with just two axes will enable a lot of ideas to be generated:

Occasions / places

	Donald Duck	Mickey Mouse	Teletubbies	
Tennis matches				
Rugby				
Cricket				
Proms concert				
Motor show				
Alton Towers				

Characters

Figure 26.2   Novelty caps for all occasions

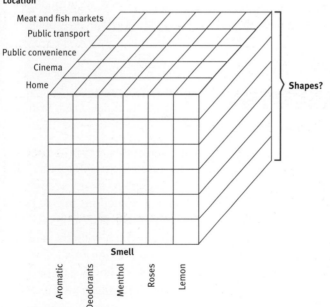

Figure 26.3   Developing concepts for air fresheners

Question 4

a) Using the matrix approach with either 2, 3 or 4 categories, how many ideas can you generate?   [5]

b) How many of these ideas are worth pursuing – how would you decide?   [5]

Thinking of different areas where an air freshener (*Figure 26.3*) might be used, in conjunction with the type of smell that is to be used and the type of dispenser for the contents, quickly provides the business with a large range of ideas in a very short period of time. In this case 125 alternatives are possible. Careful research can be made into the suppliers that could be used in an attempt to gain the best deal for the provision of the materials needed. An assessment will then need to be made to check whether a cheaper material will still enable the product to function properly or, possibly equally importantly, will the material reduce the aesthetic aspect of the product?

The data for products that are already on the market will often come from market research. Questionnaires are frequently used by businesses to ascertain the views of customers. You may well have been asked to fill in a short questionnaire to gauge your opinion at a restaurant or the local franchise of Dunkin' Donuts. This is a cheap and effective method as it provides up-to-date information about customer reactions to a given product or service. Asking for information at the point of sale ensures the replies are more likely to be accurate as views are given whilst reactions are fresh in the mind of the customer (*see Unit 12 Market research*). This information may provide useful data about the priority the customer places upon function and price. Questions can be carefully worded to ascertain how useful the customer finds the product or the amount of esteem that is attached to owning the product.

One of the problems of carrying out value analysis is that it should involve people with differing responsibilities and who operate in different departments. Consequently there is a need to organise the collection and analysis of data. There may also be a conflict of interest as the different departments may wish to give different priorities to the function, aesthetics and cost of the product.

- The final evaluation of the data and the subsequent recommendation ought to be chosen on the basis of which provides the greatest level of value overall. This can be done by using either a simple checklist (*see Figure 26.4*) or a matrix (*see Figure 26.5*) which highlights the alternatives and the contributions to value of each.

Criterion	The possible materials to be used			Total
	A	B	C	
COST	4×3 (12)	4×1 (4)	4×5 (20)	36
LOOKS	1×1 (1)	1×3 (3)	1×2 (2)	6
ROBUST	5×2 (10)	5×5 (25)	5×4 (20)	55

Each criterion is weighted in terms of importance for this product.

The looks are the least important aspect of its value and therefore have a weighting of (1), whereas the robust nature is absolutely vital for the product and therefore has a high weighting (5).

The mark for each material is then awarded out of 5, where 5 is very good and 1 is poor. Therefore in this example material C is the cheapest to use, B looks the best and B is the most robust for the function it has to perform.

The advantage of this type of assessment or evaluation is that it can be adapted to cater for any changes in circumstances. If for some reason, perhaps a change in fashion, the product's looks are now considered to be important, the weighting can simply be altered to take account of the change.

Figure 26.5 Matrix for assessing alternatives

Checklist for value analysis

Function of each component of the product
  i)   What does the component do?
  ii) Is it vital?
  iii) Could it perform another function as well?
  iv) Could this component be used for other products as well?
       (standardisation)

Materials to be used
  i)   What can be used?
  ii) Is there an alternative
  iii) Is the alternative cheaper
  iv) Does the material last?
  v)   How much waste is created?
  vi) Can this waste be reduced?

Manufacturing
  i)   Can any time be saved in the manufacturing process?
  ii) Could it be produced elsewhere more cheaply?
  iii) Could a machine be used instead of labour?

Figure 26.4 Example of a checklist

Question 6

Look at Figure 26.5 then

a) suggest what type of product this matrix has been used for [1]

b) justify your suggestion [5]

Points for Revision

Key Terms

function	the ability to perform the task for which the product was intended
cost	does the price fit the value the product brings to the customer? will the customer for whom the product is intended have the ability to purchase the product given his or her level of income?
aesthetics	the look of the product and the image it portrays to the customer. This may refer to the style, shape, colour and whether it portrays quality
prototype	a mock-up model of the product or a first attempt of the finished product. This is often used for testing purposes before going into full production
morphological studies	the generation of many ideas in a short period of time and consequently in a cost-effective manner

Definitions Question:
By referring to a business you know, explain the importance of any two of the above terms (your teacher may wish to select the terms).   [5] per definition

Summary Points:

1   Value analysis should involve a range of people who are attempting to consider all aspects of a product, from the materials used, how it is produced, the uses to which it is put, whilst taking careful note of the product's function, its looks (the aesthetics) and the cost.

2   The objective is to maintain or increase the value of the product in the eyes of the customer without increasing, and preferably even decreasing the cost of production.

Mini Case Study

Carman Prints Ltd produces a range of tea towels and beer towels. Its major customer is a well known high street chain of retailers which buys over 60% of the tea towels that are produced at its factory in Leicester.

The owner of Carmar Prints, Mr Patel, is concerned, as he always is prior to the annual renegotiation of contracts with his major customer. This year he is even more worried, having read the high street retailer's half-year results report. The report clearly stated that 'values are being re-examined to ensure that our customers continue to be offered attractive prices without any loss of quality.' In addition reference was made to the present economic climate which meant the retail sector was likely to remain highly competitive into the future. As a result, measures would be taken with suppliers to ensure improved values.

Mr Patel realised he would have to react quickly, knowing that his biggest buyer would be pressurising him to offer a lower price whilst maintaining the quality of the product. He immediately contacted his suppliers abroad to see if he could negotiate a lower price for the cloth that he used. He managed to reduce the price of the cloth by only 4p a metre; any further reduction would require his company to accept a thinner cloth. When he asked his printers if they would consider reducing their prices for the work they did on the tea towels he was offered a choice. He could pay less for the printing but it would mean using a different process which would affect the life of the print on the tea towel.

1 Define: high street chain, economic climate. [4]

2 Suggest what would be the most important aspect of value for the tea towel. Justify your choice. [4]

3 By using the process of value analysis, make a recommendation for Mr Patel as to how he might be able to satisfy the high street chain. [4]

4 Discuss the problems for Mr Patel when applying value analysis. [8]

20

Maxi Case Study

The name Skoda used to be synonymous with unreliability. Since being taken over by Volkswagen, a transformation has been evident at the assembly plant near Prague in the Czech Republic. The amount of care which now goes into the car has vastly improved its image and its competitiveness in the European market.

Firstly, Skoda spend a considerable amount of time analysing market potential and customer expectations and desires. As a result of this research, the specifications for the car's dimensions, acceleration and driving characteristics are recorded.

Using ergonomic principles, legal requirements and performance parameters, the design is considered to meet the following objectives:

a) Satisfying future market requirements

b) Setting the trend in further development

c) Presenting its own identity

An acknowledgement of environmental issues has made Skoda (as with all car manufacturers) conscious of the need to find alternative materials in order to increase the ability to recycle materials, to lighten the cars produced and consequently decrease their fuel consumption. In addition, greater consideration is given to the aerodynamics of the car, again in an attempt to reduce fuel consumption. While considering all these points, there is still a need to ensure the functional qualities are not lost or reduced.

Once the outer shape of the car has been designed, the interior will follow, as it is derived from the external shape. A great deal of time is taken to ensure a balance is achieved between the shape (and therefore the look of the car) and the aerodynamics. This is done by constructing a clay model after the CAD process has been undertaken. The clay is built up on top of a wooden frame (see *photograph 1*). The use of clay or a Plasticine type material allows the designers the opportunity to 'shave' bits off or add bits without costing large amounts of money (see *photograph 2*). It is only when the designers are happy with the shape that a metal mock-up will be produced, which is held together using a wooden and metal frame (see *photograph 3*).

There are stringent safety rules and features to build into the design. Building a car that is strong enough to withstand a front-on collision or a side impact is easy enough, but to achieve this without reducing the aesthetics and without adding substantially to the weight of the car is quite an achievement (see *photographs 4 and 5*).

The interior of the car must ensure that all the controls are ergonomically sound whilst providing sufficient comfort for driver and passengers. Much of the design for the interior is done by computer, using a digital mock-up. Further crash tests are simulated to comply with legal requirements. Once these tests are complete, the interior design can be completed, concentrating on the overall appearance in order to achieve an individual identity and fulfil customer requirements at a price that is right for the market (see *photograph 6*).

1

Clay is built up on
a wooden frame

2

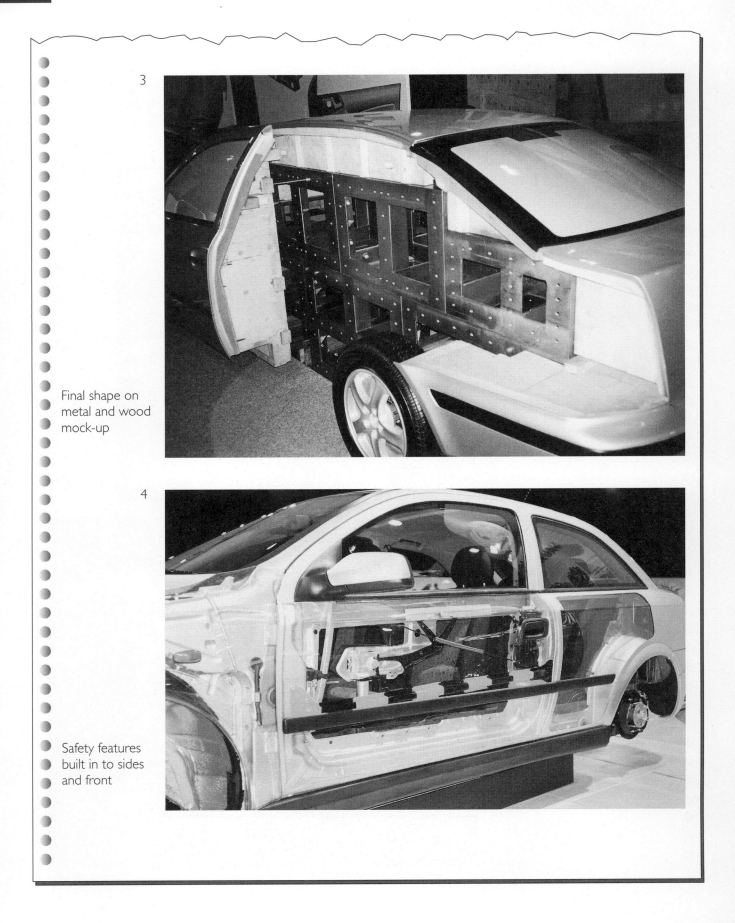

3

Final shape on metal and wood mock-up

4

Safety features built in to sides and front

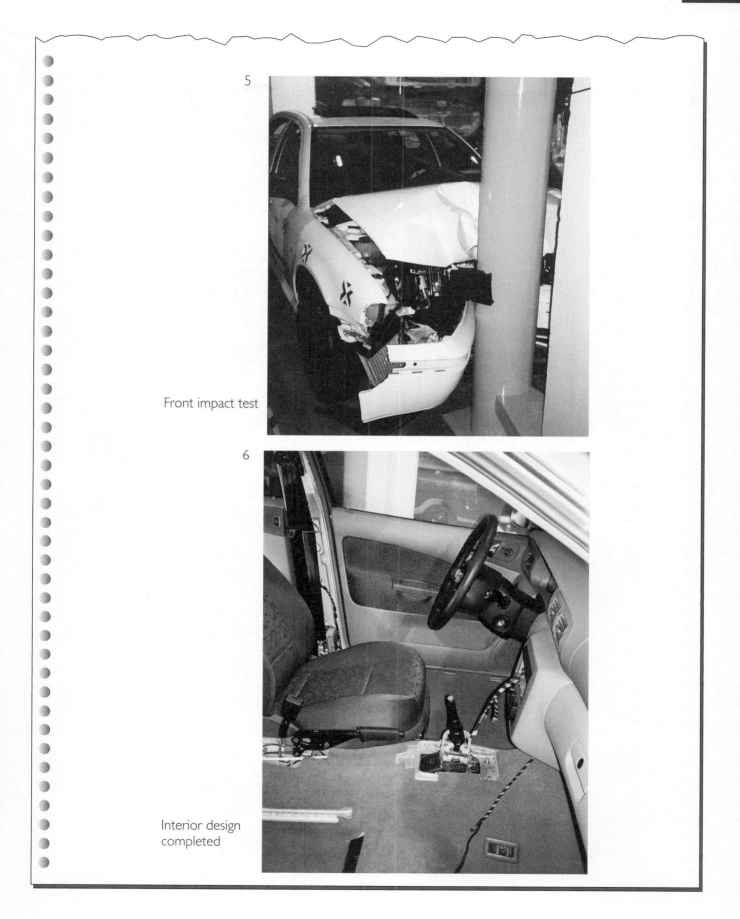

5

Front impact test

6

Interior design
completed

1 Define: prototype production, legal requirements, ergonomically sound.   [6]

2 Using the evidence in photographs 1 and 2, suggest how this method of design contributes to the achievement of aesthetics, function and economic cost.   [6]

3 Why would Skoda benefit from using CAD in the design stage of production?   [3]

4 Suggest the order of priority for the interior of a car in terms of functional qualities, aesthetics and economic costs. Justify your choice.   [7]

5 Either

   a) You have been asked to prepare a numerical matrix to assess the alternatives for the material to be used in the production of the dashboard fascias. There are three materials that could be used: leather, reinforced plastic and walnut. Explain your choice of criteria to assess the different materials.

   Or

   b) Using the value analysis triangle provided in Figure 26.6 plot the three materials within the triangle and justify your choice.   [8]

   —
   30

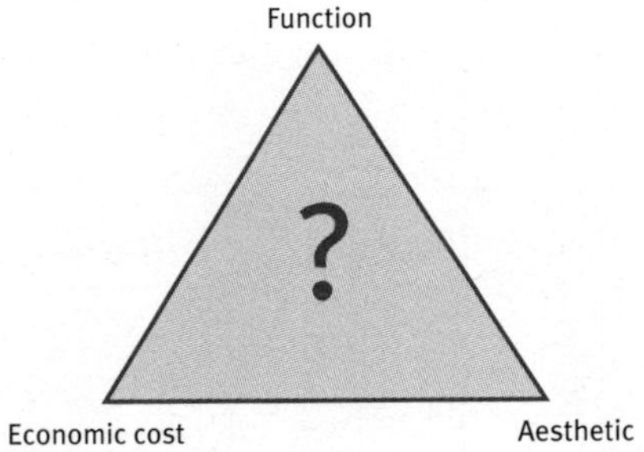

Figure 26.6   Value analysis triangle

Types of production

Learning objectives

Having read this unit, students will be able to

1 distinguish between the different types of production employed in business

2 understand the factors that determine the type of production

3 make judgements as to the most appropriate type of production for a given business situation

Context

If you were to compare the way a Morgan car and a Toyota Corolla are produced, you would notice some stark differences. Morgans are manufactured using a traditional method of production with little regard for productive efficiency. The business has always sold the car on the basis of it being predominantly hand-made, including even hand-cutting the sheet metal into shape. The layout, level of stock and machinery would strike you as being nothing but old-fashioned. On the other hand, Toyota, pioneer of the modern production system, employs not only modern machinery, but also a modern way of thinking about how production should be organised.

Many factors, such as finance, customers, space, skill levels, management and competitors, determine how a business creates its products.

Job production

Job production is the manufacture of individual products, often referred to as 'one-off' or unique products. These products are manufactured to meet the individual needs of the consumer. The quantity produced is often just one unit, though it is possible to produce in a larger quantity and there may well be variations that make each unit an individual product. Each stage of the process is organised and completed, until the unique product is finished. Only then would production on another product be started e.g. a surgeon conducts an operation on a patient from start to finish, he does not 'open up' several patients, then return to each to make repairs and then finally stitch them all up!

A large proportion of job production is undertaken by small companies who specialise in meeting the needs of consumers with highly specific individual requirements, this being one way in which a small company can compete with larger companies. However there are examples of job production, known as **project production**, that are undertaken by large companies, usually when the one-off item is highly expensive such as the new Severn Bridge linking the English and Welsh sections of the M4. In this case there was only one customer – the government. The scale of operation will depend upon the product involved; compare the production of hand-made clothes, manufactured to fit an individual consumer, with producing an aircraft to meet the requirements of an airline company such as Virgin. The latter will obviously be on a much larger scale. However, the volume of product in question will always remain small.

Main characteristics

- **Number of goods produced** – individual or a small quantity; job production can be repeated at a later date, whereas project production is literally one-off

- **Variation of goods produced** – as production is geared to meet the individual requirements of the consumer, the variation will be enormous

- **Capital equipment required** – more likely to be **labour-intensive** than **capital-intensive**. Due to the individuality of the product, there is less need for automation. In addition, because of the low-volume production, the unit cost will be higher and therefore the price will be higher because of the lack of opportunity to benefit from economies of scale (*see Unit 4 Size of business*)

- **Labour requirements** – given the need to satisfy the individual requirements of the customer, the work-force needs to be flexible, capable of producing 'one-offs'. This flexibility requires a much higher level of skill. As a consequence of the skills required, the cost of labour is high. Even specialists such as architects, engineers and JCB drivers need to be able to perform a variety of tasks within their area of expertise

- **Finance** – although the cost of producing individual products is high due to the level of wages and the inability to benefit from economies of scale, there are 'savings' when compared to other methods of production. The comparatively low level of **work-in-progress** is possible because material needs to be purchased only when required. The material is worked on immediately, providing 'added value' (*see Unit 26 Value analysis*). There is no need to hold high levels of stock which tie up valuable cash that could be better utilised in other areas. There is also no need to operate expensive stock control systems to manage large quantities of stock effectively

- **Production process** – because this method of production requires the completion of one product before work can start on another and because each product or job is unique, there can be little or no systemised layout within the factory. The utilisation of the factory space will be determined by what is being produced. This highlights the obvious flexibility of job production. This process is also considerably easier to monitor and rectify if any problems occur. It will also be possible to alter the requirements during the production process to cater for any changes the customer may ask for. Planning becomes significant in these cases; frequently one-off construction projects e.g. the M25 will necessitate the use of a network diagram (*see Unit 31 Critical path analysis*) to help with planning and control

- **Demand** – job production depends upon orders being taken to produce specific items; unfortunately demand for such products is very hard to predict with any degree of certainty which makes planning and costing difficult. Working out how long a new product will take to complete is not easy! How many hours will a particular worker need to complete the order? The order may require the workers to experiment in order to find an appropriate way to meet the customers' requests

Question 1

Give five reasons why a designer outfit shown in Milan might be very expensive to buy.   [5]

Project production: construction of the Severn bridge

Question 2

Highlight the characteristics of constructing the Severn Bridge that make it a prime example of project production.   [5]

Batch production

Batch production involves the manufacture of a quantity of products or parts of a product. These are produced in a batch, all at once, before the next quantity or batch is manufactured. This involves breaking down production into various processes. It is essential that all items within a batch must pass through a particular process before the batch can move on to the next process e.g. when plates are made, they go through several stages – biscuit firing, glazing, polishing etc. – and the glazing cannot begin until all plates have been removed from the kiln. Dividing the process into a number of stages enables some **standardisation** to take place whilst allowing variations between batches.

Bread is another obvious example where the processes involved are the mixing of the ingredients, the shaping of the dough mixture and finally the baking. Although the process remains the same, each batch may differ in terms of the ingredients, the size and shape and the baking time, thus allowing the producer to supply a range of products to a variety of customers.

Batch production: pottery being made

Main characteristics

- **Number of goods produced** – this will be greater than job production. The size of each batch will be determined by the demand

- **Variation of goods produced** – there can still be a wide variety but the differences must be within the capabilities of the processes that are necessary to produce the products. Using the same production processes a manufacturer of umbrellas can meet the customers' needs for ladies and men simply by offering two sizes. Both groups of consumers may have a range of colours and all customers may have any logo printed on the umbrella

- **Capital equipment required** – because the quantity of production is larger it is necessary to operate more machines. The utilisation of machines that are undertaking repetitive processes means that there will be a need to employ maintenance staff to keep the machines in good working order. With only one machine there may also be the need to retool the machine to cope with changes within each process; much emphasis will lie with the work-force – the speed of changing the setting can dictate the overall level of **productivity** within a factory

- **Labour requirements** – due to the fact that the same process may be repeated for each batch, the level of skill required of the labour force is not as high as that required for job production. The repetition often means that the workers are able to give their attention to just one of the processes, speeding up as they become experts. The lower level of skill may mean that training of new workers is cheaper and that lost staff are easier to replace. Many workers will not see the final product, adding further to the lack of motivation (*see Unit 50 Non-financial motivation*)

- **Finance** – using more machines requires additional capital, although the level of production will help reduce the unit cost (*see Unit 4 Size of business*). There will be more work-in-progress and this will require storage space as batches wait to be processed, adding further to costs

- **Production process** – the layout of the factory will now need to be considered and will be determined by the type and number of processes involved. It may simply be a question of ensuring that the raw materials come into the factory at one end and the completed products leave the factory at the other. Thwaites Brewery in Blackburn has organised its batch processes by starting with all the required ingredients at the top of the factory which is several storeys high. The finished product, either in cans or barrels, leaves via the ground floor

- **Demand** – batch production satisfies the majority of demand for products within an economy. Products manufactured via this method are aimed at a much larger and wider market than goods made via job production. Owing to the variation within the production process, consumers are able to purchase products that have a degree of individuality at a cheaper price than the goods produced via job production

Question 3

Why might a printing company be a good example of batch production?   [5]

Question 4

Discuss the main difficulties of operating a batch production system for a small baker.   [8]

Flow production

This originated in the writing of Adam Smith when he described the significance of **specialisation**, whereby one person doing the same job over and over again would become an expert at that particular function. Consequently, the job would be done more quickly and so productivity would rise; this was made possible only by the invention of machinery that allowed such work to be carried out. The work of Adam Smith was adopted by Henry Ford, through the famous Model T. The factory at Detroit employing a **flow production** system broke all records of productivity and created a benchmark for other companies to emulate. Flow production is the process of organising production on an assembly line so that the speed of inputs is exactly the same as the speed of output i.e. production is continuous with one unit of output at each point in the assembly line (**workstation**); each unit passes on to the next workstation immediately after it has been worked on. Companies will use this process when making products which are standardised. The entire process of e.g. assembling a car is divided into several hundred highly specialised tasks. The process tends to be capital-intensive and many of the work-force operate machines or perform one specific task e.g. fitting the casing on to a remote control 1,000 times a day.

Main characteristics

- **Number of goods produced** – a large volume of products can be produced leading to economies of scale: as production runs become longer, the business will benefit from a lower cost per unit (*see Unit 4 Size of business*). This will allow the business either to earn a higher profit margin or to maintain the present margin but reduce the price, thereby becoming more competitive.

- **Variation of goods produced** – although standardised, variety is possible within the limitations of the machinery e.g. cars are assembled using flow production, but there can be variations of colour, size of engine, gearbox, electrics, models – all produced on the same assembly line

Flow production: cars on an assembly line

- **Capital equipment** – unlike batch production, this process requires enough workstations for there to be one unit of output per workstation (*see Figure 27.1*) e.g. if a motor car needs 350 different tasks carried out during its final assembly there must be sufficient machinery and space to allow these 350 functions to be carried out simultaneously. This requires heavy investment in machinery, so flow production is likely to be capital-intensive as opposed to labour-intensive

- **Capacity utilisation** – due to the high level of capital-intensity, firms will need to be sure of operating the process at full, or near to full capacity. Most firms aim to use between 50% and 90% of capacity. Flow production will allow the business to produce greater output, but this benefit will be partially offset by the costs of the extra machinery. To make any cost savings, it is likely that a flow system will need to be operated close to **full capacity**, otherwise the increase in unit cost will be too high to justify the capital expenditure

- **Labour requirements** – the system and not the individual operator sets the pace of work – this is one of the main problems with flow production. Such problems can cause industrial disputes and unrest in the work-place. Negotiations between unions and management are often required to balance motivation with the need to achieve productivity targets. The level of skill required fell due to specialisation, as developed by Henry Ford. The problem of having one person doing the same job is how to motivate an operator who does the same job (which takes one or two minutes) for eight hours a day, five days a week, 48 weeks of the year! Efforts have been made to develop a range of skills within a production area (*see Unit 50 Non-financial motivation*) to counteract this problem

- **Production process** – back-up systems: consider what would happen if the entire line was stopped due to faulty machinery. Operators would be paid to do nothing as the problem was fixed, stock would be left standing still adding to costs and customers would suffer from late deliveries. Hence the business needs to spend a significant amount of time maintaining the machines to the

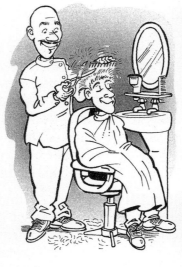

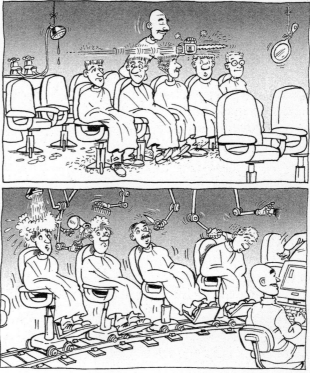

Figure 27.1   The difference between job, batch and flow

highest standard. A defect, even when spotted immediately, can be expensive to correct given the need to shut down the entire process

- **Reliance upon suppliers** – if the process is designed to operate on the least level of stock, the business will require suppliers to be on time. Toyota places such emphasis on prompt delivery that suppliers travel with an entire set of spare tyres, in case of a multiple blow-out

- **High levels of work-in-progress** – if a computer needs 100 different parts to be installed, there will be 100 units of output in work-in-progress. In addition to this, there will be stock waiting to be added on to the product e.g. circuit boards (*see Unit 28 Stock control*)

- **Efficient material handling systems** – as the product moves along the production line, the materials which are needed to process the product must be ready when it arrives at a particular work-station. Consider the problem a TV manufacturer might face if the screens were not there at the right time ready to install. The production line would need to be stopped, with serious effects on costs

- **Scientific design of each operation** – setting up the process in the first place needs a high level of technical skill, because the length of time of each job needs to be designed so that all jobs run smoothly into each other.

- **Quality control** – with batch and job production, products can be tested easily at different stages of production. With flow production, quality control traditionally occurs at the end of the process. Consider the cost involved in identifying and correcting a defective product when the fault is spotted two hours after it has occurred. Not only must all the finished goods that have been produced in the meantime be rectified, but also the work-in-progress that has gone through the faulty workstation needs to be corrected

- **Demand** – a firm would make the decision to use this type of production only if there was a high and continuous level of demand. This has clear implications for marketing and the market research function

Question 5

A business produces 1200 units per month with a capacity of 1500 units. Due to evidence of increased demand, the company intends to increase its capacity. The only machine available will increase capacity by a minimum of 800 units per month. Demand is estimated to increase to 2000 units per month over the next two years.

a) Calculate the capacity utilisation before the expansion. [1]

b) What will be the new capacity utilisation in two years' time? [2]

c) Why might the company be concerned about the use of capacity within its plant? [5]

Question 6

Consider the following products and suggest the most appropriate type of production units, giving reasons for your choice:
a) wedding cake
b) biros
c) the Millennium Dome
d) sticks of rock
e) designer jeans
f) a housing estate
g) televisions   7 × [2]

Question 7

Why might the canning process at a brewery be appropriate for a flow production system? [5]

Factors affecting the decision to move to a more modern production system

There are several reasons why a business might modernise its production; it might be to fulfil extra demand or to produce products more quickly or to reduce the level of wastage. Whatever the reason, the ultimate objective is likely to be greater productivity.

In more detail the reasons are:

- **Demand** – the business may well be moving into the mass market or its present customers may have increased their orders. The business must consider the degree of certainty with which it forecasts extra demand into the long run. However, the business would need to consider the problems it would face if a major customer suddenly pulled out just after the business had invested in a new production system

- **Work-force reaction** – jobs will become more specialised and it is likely that the variety of tasks and skill required will decrease. It may also mean that the work-force loses the team approach that is sometimes adopted in batch production. Flow production may require individuals to work on their own. The management will need to be aware that there may some resistance to change (*see Unit 55 Managing change*). This issue may be resolved through extra training (*see Unit 54 Recruitment and contracts*); as new machines are required, the business will need to equip the work-force with the necessary skills to operate them; this will automatically incur extra costs as it will no doubt take time for the work-force to gain experience operating the new machinery which may also mean lost output

- **Finance** – not only will extra fixed assets (*see Unit 36 Balance sheet*) be required, but the business will also need to invest in the extra working capital (*see Unit 34 Cash flow and working capital*) needed to operate at a higher level of output

- **Redundancy** (*see Unit 54 Recruitment and contracts*) – new, more automated machinery could well result in redundancies. This not only breeds discontent due to insecurity, but also means further costs for the business in redundancy payments

- **Suppliers** – it is sometimes automatically assumed that an increase in output can easily be managed. If the suppliers are at full capacity, a new supplier will need to be found, contracts drawn up and negotiations will need to take place continuously to ensure a close working relationship

- **Space** – not only must space for the new machines be found, but space for stock, from raw materials to finished goods, is required

- **Effect on other parts of the business** – extra output may mean more pressure on the promotion budget to achieve the extra sales; in turn, the business will need to find more distribution outlets and arrange for the transportation of the extra output

Points for Revision

Key Terms

job production	making a one-off product, which may be repeated later
project production	a one-off, unrepeatable product
batch production	producing goods in batches with a range of processes
flow production	continuous production with the speed of inputs the same as the speed of output
labour-intensive	when the majority of the production process is undertaken by the work-force. Labour costs will represent a high proportion of total costs
capital-intensive	when the majority of the production process is undertaken by machinery. Capital costs will represent a high proportion of total costs
productivity	the ability of the business to turn inputs (e.g. materials and labour) into finished goods. Also known as productive efficiency
capacity utilisation	the extent to which a business uses its capacity level of output (measured by current output as a percentage of available capacity)
work-in-progress	partly manufactured products
specialisation	the process whereby labour concentrates on one particular skill
standardisation	utilisation of one part in a variety of products e.g. windscreen washer bottles in different models of cars
workstation	an area within the assembly line where a particular process takes place

Definitions Question:

By referring to a business you know, explain the meaning of three of the above terms (your teacher may wish to help you in your choice). [5] per definition

Summary Points:

1   There are three main types of production – job, batch and flow.

2   The decision as to the most appropriate will depend on a variety of different factors; namely the number of goods required (demand), the variety required (by the customer), the amount of capital equipment needed, the skill of the work-force, finance available, the practical considerations of implementation.

3   The business must evaluate the likely costs and benefits associated with changing to a different process; it is unlikely that a business will be able to change to a different process without facing considerable problems.

Mini Case Study

By 1998, Cobblers Ltd, a small manufacturer of hand-made shoes, had been selling its shoes to selective department stores and independent tailors for 30 years. The owner, James Cobbler, was worried about the growing number of competitors from abroad. Such competitors were manufacturing similar quality shoes at a cheaper price. Cobblers employed job production, with each of the 10 employees making a pair of shoes from start to finish. James realised that he needed to improve the productivity of his work-force if the business was to compete successfully. He decided to buy some machinery to increase the speed of production which unfortunately meant he had to make two employees redundant.

Fred, probably the most experienced craftsman, became responsible for the machine which cut and shaped the leather into both soles and uppers. The next machine was used for stitching the shoes together. As a result of this change, James noted an increase in the productivity of his work-force (see Table 1), despite the frequent mumbling behind his back about the new working processes.

The other problem was that when he made shoes to order, there was no problem with stocks of materials because he ordered them only when required; with the new machinery, there were piles of partly finished shoes all over the place. At the time, he was sure he had taken the right decision, although now he is not certain that the benefits outweigh the costs.

Table 1
Before introduction of machines: output = 50 pairs per week
After introduction of machines: output = 80 pairs per week

1 Define the following terms: job production, productivity.   [4]

2 a) Using Table 1, calculate output per employee before and after the introduction of the new machinery over the years in question.   [3]

   b) Explain why the productivity changed having installed new machinery.   [5]

3 Discuss the likely problems faced by James Cobbler having introduced machinery into the production process.   [8]

20

Maxi Case Study

Zeneca was formed due to the demerger of ICI in 1992 and has since achieved excellent levels of growth. It manufactures agrochemicals (pesticides and herbicides) which are sold to farmers. The science director of the specialities business was struggling over the latest decision facing him. It concerned the manufacture of a chemical known as FLP which is used in the production process. Zeneca presently manufactures FLP using batch production, and has significant experience in this area although several issues have forced the company to consider changing to a more continuous flow production process. The present system produces FLP in large batches capable of a capacity of 2000 tonnes a year, whereas the new system, which would be much more technologically advanced, would be used to produce between 2200 and 2500 tonnes a year on a continuous basis, depending on demand. (*See diagram below for more details.*)

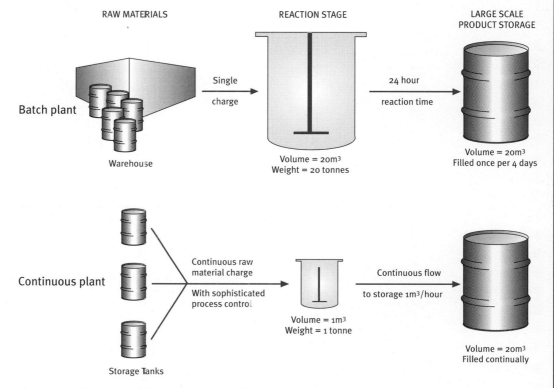

Figure 27.2   Comparison between batch and continuous production

The main justification for the change was the increase in demand for FLP. If the company did make the change it had to be sure of extra demand because there would be an increase in capacity and if output fell too far below the new capacity, the unit cost would rise significantly. During the past five years, the market for FLP has grown by 25% and there would certainly be some demand within other parts of Zeneca for FLP; previously those other parts of Zeneca had purchased FLP from other suppliers.

One of the ingredients required for the manufacture of FLP is a highly corrosive substance. All the ingredients are presently produced by Zeneca.

The finance department has produced the following information:

Table 2

	Batch	Continuous
Fixed costs	£2 million per annum	£2.6 million per annum
Variable costs	£2,500 per tonne	£2,200 per tonne
Capacity	2000 tonnes	2500 tonnes

Given the nature of the competition, this would give the company a significant competitive advantage even though it would take 18 months to build the plant.

Rager, a German company, had experienced recent problems with batch technology based on the environmental hazards caused by the corrosive material. In addition, there were some firms waiting to enter this new market. One of these, Maltus Inc, had already invested in a new plant although it had problems finding a material supplier. Dupus, another potential competitor, was facing environmental pressure to spend money on cleaning up its plants although it had a large internal demand for FLP; if Zeneca invested before Dupus, then Dupus would buy from Zeneca with a long-term contract of about 1000 tonnes per annum. Presently output at Zeneca is 1200 tonnes a year.

The personnel director commented on the excitement among employees at this proposal, and in addition, several members of the senior management team were highly enthusiastic about the investment. Three such supporters were based at the Riverland facility, which had been proposed as the site for changing the process involved in the manufacture of FLP. There had been a decline in the output at Riverland in recent years and the site certainly had the space to expand, although the employees would have to receive some training to equip them with the appropriate skills for the continuous technology.

The union had expressed disquiet about the possible increase in capital-intensity and the effect this might have on redundancies. Zeneca had a clearly stated policy that asserted their commitment to keeping trained staff even if demand fell.

1 Define: unit cost, competitive advantage, capital-intensity. **[6]**

2 Work out the unit cost of producing under batch production and continuous production at the following levels of output: 40%, 60%, 80% and 100% of capacity. Plot both lines on a graph and estimate the level of output after which continuous production becomes more efficient. (You may wish to answer this question using a spreadsheet.) **[14]**

3 What are the pros and cons of a policy that keeps staff employed irrespective of the level of demand? **[5]**

4 Discuss the factors that Zeneca will need to consider before changing from batch to continuous production. **[15]**

40

Stock control

Learning objectives

Having read this unit, students will be able to

1 understand the factors that affect the level of stock held by a business at any one time

2 draw and interpret a stock level diagram

3 understand the significance of just-in-time stock control for a business

Context

Consider a business like Bassett's, the manufacturer of liquorice allsorts, and its need for stock. Not only will it require the storage of ingredients ready to be put into enormous mixing containers, but it will also need stocks of finished goods to be ready for dispatch to retailers. This is in addition to the materials that are already in the process of being turned into sweets. While the stock, in whatever form, is in the business, it is not making any money for Bassett's, hence the need to move it as quickly as possible through the manufacturing process. Many factors will determine the level of stock being held and a business will need to consider the costs of too much stock against those of too little stock e.g. how many types and quantities of sweets should a shop stock?

Over the past two or three decades, following the lead of the Japanese, control of stock has become a significant issue in the drive to reduce costs, make production more flexible and suppliers more reliable.

Types of stock

Stock can take three basic forms:

- **Raw materials and components** – these represent the materials before they are processed either on an assembly line or as part of the manufacturing process. Not all businesses will hold raw materials; this largely depends on the principal activities of a business e.g. a house builder will buy the bricks as opposed to the crushed stone which goes into the brick-making process

- **Work-in-progress** – all the stock which is at some point on the production process, whether it is stock which is being worked on or stock that is partly finished and waiting for the next batch process (*see Unit 27 Types of production*). Car companies devote areas of the workshop to sub-assembly i.e. they manufacture some of the body parts separately and hold them in stock to be used as and when required. This can also involve finished goods which are being tested within quality control

- **Finished goods** – all the stock that is waiting to be delivered to the customer

Figure 28.1   The artist's studio

Activity

In Figure 28.1, try to identify the stock that is raw materials, work-in-progress and finished goods; think about the consequence for cash flow (negative or positive) in terms of when money will flow in and out of the business for each of these types of stock.

The theory

When a business considers the amount of stock it needs to hold at any point, it must balance the costs of holding stock against the costs of not holding stock. These costs are not easy to calculate, which, ironically, in the past has made the decision more straightforward i.e. hold enough stock 'just-in-case' there is likely to be a problem.

Costs of holding stock

- **Administration** – with more stock to administer and keep secure, these costs will rise

- **Insurance** – if the level of stock rises, then the value of the business (on the balance sheet, *see Unit 36*) will rise; this may well prompt insurance companies to increase the premiums payable

- **Possibility of theft and damage** – consider the extreme of having only one unit of stock – this will be carefully guarded, particularly so if it is expensive. The other extreme is to have a warehouse full of the same stock; less care is spent on each item because a mentality can set in of 'we have plenty of spares in the back, so don't worry about the odd breakage/spillage etc.' Damage can be caused through a variety of reasons, although deterioration is a concern for food retailers and producers alike. Supermarkets refer to this as shrinkage

- **Obsolescence** – large amounts of stock can also lead to a greater chance of obsolescence (becoming out of date or unfashionable) when the business is caught out by a sudden change in market demand or a change in technology – this is a constant area of concern for computer manufacturers and retailers. Frequently obsolescence will prompt the business into a stock sell-off at greatly reduced prices

- **Cost of storage** – warehouse space is an expense that must be paid to have the facility to store goods so that they can be found as and when customers need them. This gives some flexibility to the business so that it can supply customers quickly

- **Costs of finance** – this is certainly the most significant issue when interest rates are high. Stock is normally purchased from suppliers on credit i.e. with payment being made some time after delivery. (There are a few fortunate companies, which, by the nature of their business e.g. supermarkets, or the control they have over their supplier, will be in the enviable position of being paid *before* the stock needs paying for.) The business will need to pay for materials before the money comes in from selling the finished goods. When the outflow of cash occurs, the business will need to use a source of finance (normally an overdraft – *see Unit 40*) to pay the suppliers. This will incur an interest cost for the business. (*This problem is dealt with in more detail in Unit 60 Interest rates.*)

- **Opportunity costs** – by tying money up in stock, the business is unable to use that money elsewhere to earn an alternative return

Costs of not holding stock

- **Inability to satisfy sudden large orders** – this will mean the business loses revenue and will incur an opportunity cost. The benefit foregone in this case is the lost revenue. Alternatively, the business may choose to meet the sudden large order, but be unable to meet its usual orders, letting regular customers down. In these circumstances the business will need to balance the benefits of the new customer against the potential costs of losing those who are regular buyers

- **Loss of goodwill** – this is almost impossible to quantify with any degree of accuracy as it represents future sales that will not now be earned by the business because it proved unreliable to a customer, due to lack of stock

- **Longer delivery lead times** – this is particularly important in highly competitive industries where non-price competition is used heavily. One way of competing is on fast delivery times. Viking Direct (a stationery supplier) always promises 'next day delivery' which means it must hold several of the same unit in stock at any one time. Clearly the benefits of meeting orders quickly, and the consequent level of revenue it earns, outweigh the extra costs of holding

Traditional approach to stock holding

In the past a business would naturally make a comparison between the costs of holding and the costs of not holding, although there were other complications. Businesses tended to adopt a 'just-in-case' policy; this is exactly what it suggests, that there was such a degree of uncertainty in ordering materials and components that they ordered stocks just in case they were needed. The costs of holding stocks were not too significant but suppliers were notoriously unreliable, as were delivery companies. There were cases when a business would order the same volume from two separate suppliers, just in case one was late or simply failed to appear. Quality was unreliable, so the solution was to order enough so that a back-up was available.

The theoretical optimum volume to order is represented in the diagram overleaf (*Figure 28.2*).

As the amount ordered increases, the cost of running out of stock (**stock-out**) will decrease. But as the amount of stock rises, so does the cost of holding. The business will therefore arrive at a theoretical optimum amount of stock to order that balances the two costs. This amount is known as the **economic order quantity**.

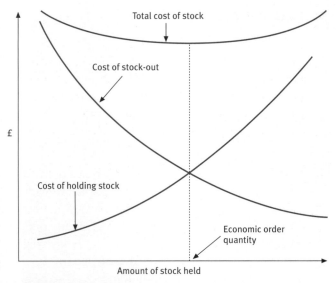

Figure 28.2 Economic order quantity

The final issue that the business will consider will be the likelihood of achieving economies of scale from purchasing (*see Unit 4 Size of business*). Some suppliers will insist on allowing bulk purchase discounts only if the business buys in bulk and receives in bulk. Again, the balance of the costs is the same; whether the savings made by purchasing in bulk will offset the extra holding costs.

Buffer stock

This represents the safety stock, below which the business is unwilling to allow stock levels to fall. The level of **buffer stock** will therefore depend on a multiplicity of factors:

- Amount of space available for storage
- Pattern of demand and likelihood of a big order
- Insurance costs
- Chance of deterioration and/or obsolescence (going out of date or out of fashion)
- Cost of finance (interest rates on the overdraft)
- Opportunity costs
- Cost of delivery and administration
- Speed of production and type of production
- Reliability of suppliers
- Length of product life cycle (*see Unit 17 Pricing*)
- Peace of mind of owner

Question 1

What are the two most significant factors which determine the buffer stock for

a) a yogurt manufacturer?
b) a building company?
c) a fireworks manufacturer? [6]

Question 2

A business has approached a supplier for delivery of 60,000 units, in two equal instalments of 30,000 units, at a cost of £4 per unit. With this pattern of delivery, the cost of storing the units will be £18,000. However, if the business receives delivery of all 60,000 at once, the supplier will charge only £3.80 per unit but the cost of holding will rise to £32,000.

a) Explain the reason why the cost of holding does not double when the number of units in storage does. [2]

b) (i) Calculate the saving to the company of purchasing the 60,000 units in one delivery and compare this with the extra costs of holding. How much extra will the company end up spending with the larger delivery? [3]

(ii) Despite the extra cost, give other reasons why the business might order a larger amount. [3]

Diagrammatic representation

It is possible to represent stock movement on a diagram which shows the minimum and maximum stock levels, the level of buffer stock, the **reorder level** and the time taken between ordering and receiving goods (lead time).

Figure 28.3 represents a business that receives 60,000 units every three months. The **lead time** for delivery, for whatever reason, is one month, with a reorder level of 30,000 units. One month after the stock has been ordered, delivery arrives when the buffer stock is reached (10,000 units).

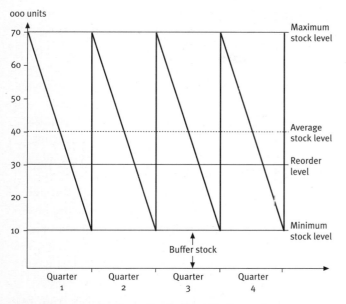

Figure 28.3   Diagram illustrating the role of buffer stock

Several points are worth noting from the above diagram. The diagonal lines indicate that stock is used constantly at a rate of 20,000 per month. Suppliers are also assumed to deliver on time and it is also assumed that all the stock is of the right standard for use. This means the buffer stock is not used and therefore performs its intended role i.e. as a safety back-up. The dotted line represents the average level of stock. For half of each time period the stock level is above this line and for the other half it is below this line; therefore the line represents the average amount held at any one month in the year.

e.g. in the above example the maximum stock held after each delivery is 70,000 units and the minimum held (i.e. the buffer) is 10,000 units. The average level will therefore be 40,000 units (half-way between 70,000 and 10,000).

Alternatively: $\dfrac{(\text{Maximum stock} + \text{minimum stock})}{2}$

$$\dfrac{(70,000 + 10,000)}{2} = 40,000 \text{ units}$$

This diagram also helps us to identify one of the main measures which is used to assess the necessary level of stock as well as the speed of usage. Such a measure is called **stock turnover** and is calculated by cost of sales/stock. (*This is treated in more detail in Unit 38 Ratio analysis*). In the above example stock turnover is 4 i.e. stock has been received into the business and used again four times a year; clearly as the speed at which stock is used up over a year increases, with the same delivery amount, the turnover of stock will increase.

Worked example

Consider what might happen to Figure 28.3 with a usage rate of 60,000 per month. Figure 28.4 shows how the changes will be represented. The new usage will mean that the business will use up the delivery and therefore reach the buffer stock within one month. Let us say that the supplier is physically unable to deliver a greater quantity (perhaps because of the size of the lorries), so it delivers the same amount more frequently – in fact it will deliver once a month. With a delivery once a month, the stock turnover will be 12 times a year, but because the supplier is delivering the same quantity, the average stock level held will be the same.

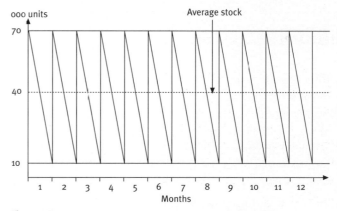

Figure 28.4   Higher stock turnover means more efficiency

Companies with a higher stock turnover tend to be more efficient because for a given level of demand, they are holding less stock. In the above example, although the average level of stock is the same, the demand for the stock is much higher, so the business will incur similar holding costs, but with higher revenue, the percentage of the revenue that is taken up by holding costs will be less.

Question 3

A business uses stock at a rate of 500 per week and holds a buffer stock of 100 units, receiving stock from the supplier once a week.

a) Represent this on a stock level diagram for an eight-week period.   [4]

b) What is the maximum level of stock?   [1]

c) Suppliers take two days to deliver and the business operates a five-day week from Monday to Friday. At what level of stock will the company need to reorder the stock? What is the average level of stock? Show both of your answers on the diagram.   [4]

d) The business decides to receive its deliveries once every four weeks. *Ceteris paribus*, how will this change the maximum stock level, minimum stock level, reorder level and average stock level? You may need to redraw the stock level diagram to assess the changes.   [4]

Modern approach to stock holding

If the business decides that the cost of holding all the stock is too much, how does it go about **destocking** (reducing the level of stock held)? Firstly, it must arrange with the suppliers to deliver a smaller amount, but more frequently. Then it must arrange for more frequent delivery to be received, which will presumably increase the administration costs. Materials are likely to be stored in the same place, but initially more of the space will be unused, which is inefficient. The company may also lose any bulk purchase discounts, although it will be ordering the same amount and close negotiation with the supplier will probably mean it maintains the discount. Overall, there does not seem to be any short-term advantage in holding less stock although in the longer term the business ought to save money.

Two methods can be employed to reduce the amount of stock held:

– **Consignment stock**; this is where the stock is actually held by the customer and therefore the customer provides the warehouse facility. Initially this would seem entirely disadvantageous for the customer, but the stocks are paid for only when used which means the customers controls its own costs and the supplier reduces its level of stock.

– **Just-in-time management**; this is dealt with in more detail in Unit 30 Lean production. Essentially it involves the business holding the lowest level of stock by receiving materials and components only when they are needed. There is a famous case of

Nissan ordering a carpet for one of its cars and the lead time being a matter of 42 minutes (which means the supplier finds out stock is required only when the car hits the final assembly line!) Just-in-time was pioneered in Japan in the 1950s at Toyota, but it was not until the 1970s that the western world began to consider its benefits. At the time, interest rates, and therefore the cost of financing stock, were over 20% in the UK and manufacturers were looking hard for ways of cutting costs. It works using the kanban system that calls through for the stock when it gets close to the lowest level possible. JIT therefore became a method not only of saving costs of holding and financing stock, but also of releasing working capital to be used elsewhere in the business (*see Unit 34 Cash flow and working capital*). There are obvious advantages to be achieved from JIT stock control, which are all associated with holding very little stock:

■ Low stock holding costs

■ Low finance costs

■ There is pressure on the business to produce products with 0% defects, because once the goods have been made, they are shipped off to the customer at once. This forces the business to consider quality in much more detail (*see Unit 29 Quality*)

■ Production becomes generally more efficient because there is no excess stock to allow it to make mistakes e.g. if a business makes pottery and it has lots of stock in its warehouse, it can replace faulty goods easily by using some of the excess stock – with no excess stock, there is no chance to replace it, hence the need to get the product right first time

■ Less space is used for storage and more can be used for manufacturing or perhaps retail space

Yet the problems are many:

■ Very close liaison is required with suppliers; if the suppliers are late, this can cause many problems for the business as the production process grinds to a halt. JIT can also be extended to retailers: Sainsbury's operates JIT stock control; if one of its suppliers is late the lorry is sent to the back of the queue!

■ Someone in the **supply chain** will need to hold stock; for this system to work, it is unlikely that all the businesses involved in getting products from the manufacturer to the customer will be able to use JIT. Hence the continuing need for warehouses.

■ Traffic systems – in Japan, JIT is sometimes referred to as 'just-in-trucks' as the stock is held up in the traffic systems. In 1996, when the earthquake in Kobe struck, business was immediately paralysed, not because the work-force could not get to work, but because the stock could not be delivered when the central highway collapsed. With Toyota holding only four hours of stock, it is easy to imagine how sensitive the business might be to traffic jams. However, such businesses are so convinced of the benefits of JIT that they have persuaded suppliers to locate very close by in order to ensure prompt, reliable delivery.

Points for Revision

Key Terms

buffer stock	safety stock kept for emergency use
reorder level	the level of stock at which the business must order another delivery; this level depends mainly on the speed and reliability of suppliers
stock turnover	cost of sales divided by average stock level; the number of times stock is used and replaced within a time period
lead time	time taken between order being placed and delivery being received
consignment stock	arrangement between customer and supplier for customer to hold stock, but to pay for it only when the stock is used
just-in-time stock control	receiving delivery just before the materials are needed
economic order quantity	traditional method of calculating amount to order, balancing costs of storage with economies of scale
destocking	running stock down to a lower level
opportunity cost	benefit foregone of next best alternative use for money
stock-out	running out of stock
supply chain	the line of supplies at different stages of production involved in creating the finished product

Definitions Question:
By referring to a business you know, explain the significance of any three of the above terms (your teacher may wish to help you choose the terms).   [5] per definition

Summary Points:

1. A business will need to hold stocks of raw materials, work-in-progress and finished goods.

2. Holding too much stock or too little stock incurs costs and a firm must maintain a balance between too much stock and too little stock.

3. JIT reveals inefficiencies in the production process that can then be solved; large levels of stock tend to hide these problems.

4. By reducing the average amount of stock held, the company reduces the costs of financing the stock, which becomes particularly significant when interest rates rise.

Mini Case Study

Hold and Deliver (H and D) Ltd is a wholesaler based on an industrial estate near the M6 in the Midlands. It receives products from various manufacturers located in the Far East and supplies various toy stores in the area, priding itself on prompt delivery.

One of its new products is the Pro-Yo, a designer yo-yo, although this is only one of several products stored in its warehouse. Given the nature of these products, the product life cycle tends to be both short and difficult to predict. Based on the last craze for these types of product (which was the tamagotchi), the business made and sold 100,000 in one year, although sales rapidly declined in the second six months.

Over recent years the M6 near the warehouse has become increasingly congested as more businesses have located on the industrial estate. This has caused several problems for H and D, given its reputation with customers.

The business has recently decided to work on a maximum stock level of 10,000 Pro-Yos with a buffer of 2,000 in order to meet orders promptly. It is also aiming for a stock turnover of 12 times per year.

1 a) Calculate the total usage of stock during the year.   [2]

   b) Draw the usage of stock during a year.   [3]

   c) The average level of stock is 6,000 (make sure you can explain this to your teacher.) The cost of holding the stock is £0.50 (not including finance costs) per unit and the interest rate is 10% per annum. Each unit of stock is valued at £3 each. Calculate the total cost of holding the average level of stock for a year.   [5]

2 What are the implications for stock levels with a product such as this?   [4]

3 a) How might the problems caused by the motorway affect this company?   [2]

   b) Recommend possible solutions to this problem.   [4]

$$\overline{20}$$

Maxi Case Study

Saxton Ltd is a business that supplies a variety of business equipment world-wide. It has 13,000 different product lines, which range from computer supplies and office furniture, to stationery and filing equipment. The business has grown quickly over recent years, with turnover from all its operations topping £4.5 billion using a catalogue as its main promotional material. Despite the business making every attempt to keep costs low, its prices are not the cheapest in the industry because part of its unique selling point is a lead time of just one day. This means it must hold enough stock to fulfil its promise, which obviously adds to its costs. A telesales team arranges orders when a customer calls and once an order has been placed it is then passed via a computer to the main warehouse. In the UK, this is situated in Berkshire, close to the M1 motorway, occupying an area of 160,000 square feet, dealing with 10,000 orders per day. In order to move the stock quickly, the business employs a semi-automatic conveyor system that loads the products on to lorries. Due to the large amount of product lines being held at any time, there is an average of £7.5 million worth of stock in the warehouse. The appropriate level of stock for each product line is determined, amongst other things, by past demand patterns. The main objective within the warehouse is a fast turn-around of stock, without compromising the level of service and the ability to meet customer demands within a day. In 1999, the stock turnover had actually increased to about 10 times per year. Information about previous years is contained in Table 1:

Table 1

(£ million)	1997	1998
Cost of sales	50	70
Average stock	8	9

The business also has a 'free returns' service. This means that wherever the products have been delivered in the country, it will pick them up from the customer's door and return them to its warehouse. This occurs on approximately 5% of all deliveries. Peter Hankin, the distribution manager, describes several cases of how this service has been taken for granted. One in particular that he reported referred to a church steward who once ordered 200 garden chairs on a Thursday and returned them on the Monday describing them as inappropriate – something about the colour being 'not quite appropriate to the décor of his garden'. In addition, the business offers free delivery for orders over £25 and guarantees the products for a year. These mean that the profit margin is squeezed if the price is to stay close to that of its competitors.

1 Define the following terms: unique selling point, lead time, profit margin.   [6]

2 a) Calculate stock turnover for 1997 and 1998.   [4]

  b) (i) If the interest rate in 1999 was an average of 4.5%, calculate the cost of financing the average stock level for 1999.   [1]

    (ii) What reservations do you have about this calculation?   [4]

3 a) Suggest why Saxton Ltd might have aimed to achieve an increase in stock turnover.   [4]

  b) What problems might the business have faced when attempting to increase its stock turnover?   [4]

4 Apart from extra stock holding costs, identify and explain the evidence within the case to suggest why Saxton's prices were not 'the cheapest in the industry'.   [4]

5 Evaluate the usefulness of just-in-time stock management to Saxton Ltd.   [8]

35

Quality

Learning objectives

Having read this unit, students will be able to

1   define the meaning of quality in various contexts

2   identify the significance of quality for various stakeholders

3   appreciate the various methods of quality control that can be employed by a business

Context

No company wants to feature on the BBC's *Watchdog* programme as an example of how not to provide a quality product or service to the customer. The Ford motor company was featured heavily because of an alleged fault on the steering of the then comparatively new model of the Mondeo.

A family reading the Travel supplement of *The Sunday Times* would not be impressed with a low-cost airline given a score of 0 out of 10 following a customer survey! Many of the poor-quality features were not on the flight itself, but in the booking arrangements, the quoted price and the check-in procedure. So the concept of quality covers a wide range of attributes related to the product or service.

Consumers are now able to 'shop around' for the best deal, no matter which product or service they are interested in, as the competition to win the order intensifies. Britain's industrial scene has succumbed to many pressures from foreign competition, one of which has been a better quality of product or service. Giving quality a high priority is therefore not only desirable but essential to maintain sales and as a consequence profit.

What is quality?

Many businesses today refer to 'quality' in their promotional material:

Quality starts when a potential customer first makes contact with a company, whether to make an enquiry or to place an order. And finishes..? Many businesses agree that it ought not to finish, as quality should continue to be of concern to a company long after a good or service has been purchased. A woman purchasing an item of clothing not only expects good service whilst in the shop, but expects that item to wear and wash well. Furthermore, if there is a subsequent problem, the customer quite rightly expects a satisfactory remedy if the clothing is faulty.

Quality should therefore be seen as a package which covers the whole process of buying and using a product or service. As a consequence, quality is given a high profile within the production process of a manufactured good. If a high standard of quality can be achieved by producing to a high specification, it is more likely that the customer will come back for more.

Question 1

Select two products that you use most days; make a list of what you consider to be important when buying your chosen products.   [4]

Question 2

Either watch a series of TV commercials or browse through a couple of magazines and note the number of times quality is mentioned or implied and how it is referred to.   [5]

Why is quality important?

- Quality is an essential requirement in the process of satisfying a consumer.

- It is essential for businesses to be able to satisfy their customers if further sales are to be made, either by the same customers or new ones who have been recommended to try a given product by those who are satisfied.

- It may provide the **competitive advantage** that the business is hoping to gain. It can be an important part of the perception of the product; part of the image of the product that makes it distinctive.

- Good quality helps reduce the number of complaints about the product and therefore reduces the likelihood of its reputation being damaged and loss of any subsequent sales. It also avoids any reduction in the **goodwill** of the business, which can be a valuable asset. The fewer products that are returned, the lower the cost of providing replacements or the cost of correcting any faults.

- Competition and the growing willingness of customers to complain if they are not satisfied have meant that businesses must give quality a much higher priority than in the past. The level of expectation with regard to quality is now very high.

This can in part be attributed to the fact that customers are more informed, probably as a consequence of the number of consumer programmes on the television and the improved availability of information about consumer rights thanks to the work of bodies such as the **Consumers' Association**.

Question 3

Why are faulty goods that are returned by the customer costly to the business?   [4]

How is quality achieved?

Traditionally quality was tested at the end of the production process to ensure the job had been done properly. This would require a team of inspectors who would check for faults in the finished product. It was costly to rectify faults at such a late stage and meant that workers were not encouraged to build in quality; this was someone else's responsibility. In the diagram above right two variables are demonstrated. Firstly, the cost of inspection falls as the required level of quality falls – if a business does not take the issue of quality seriously, then it will not spend very much on inspection. Alternatively, the costs of failure will increase, because as fewer products go through the testing process, a greater amount will end up with the customer, who will return them to the manufacturer demanding either a refund or a replacement.

Traditional quality control policies centred on a firm's attempt to balance these two costs by choosing the level of quality which minimised the cost of both inspection and failure. The total costs on the diagram are represented by the sum of the vertical distances of each bar – 95% produces the lowest total cost. This suggests that the business would be happy with a 5% level of defects.

This traditional approach uses sampling techniques for the 'selection' of products to be tested to ensure they are acceptable. Many businesses used, or in some cases still use, control charts to ensure products are produced within acceptable limits.

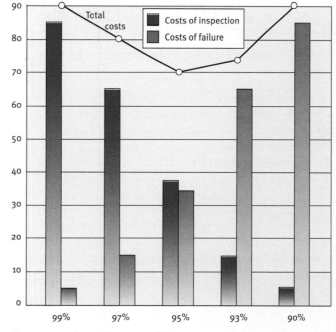

Figure 29.1   Inspection versus failure

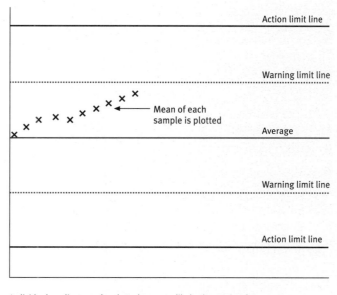

Individual readings can be plotted, or more likely, the mean value of a sample from a batch is plotted.

If X lies between the two warning limit lines, production can continue until the results of the next sample are known

Figure 29.2   Control chart

Samples are taken and plotted on the control chart. The chart shows the tolerance levels within which the product's specifications must fall. This may be weight, length, or width. The results can then be used to determine whether any action is necessary to rectify a potential or actual fault.

The tolerance levels are determined by the product and customer requirements.

The manufacturer has to decide between:

- possibly excessive inspection, followed by rejection of products, which occurs because the sample tested had sufficient faults to suggest that the batch overall would have too many faults (producer's risk)

- allowing products to be sold to the customer who accepts the goods but subsequently discovers they are faulty and therefore should have been rejected (consumer's risk)

Obviously, the latter (consumer's risk) is much more serious because of the damage to the reputation of the business and the cost involved in replacing the product.

Today, the emphasis is very much on building quality into the product and the work-force is responsible for the quality of what it produces.

The whole process of providing the customer with what is required involves quality. Philip Crosby, an American writer on business, refers to four 'absolutes' of quality management in his work *Quality is free* (1979, McGraw-Hill):

  i) quality means conforming to requirements
 ii) quality comes from prevention
iii) quality performance standard is zero defects
 iv) quality measurement is the price of non-conformance

BMW defines quality as:

  i) being able to adhere to specification
 ii) being able to meet customer expectations
iii) being attractive in the market

Quality is achieved by understanding that customers expect good quality and that goes beyond the simple 'does it work?' and 'will it last?' approach. The Japanese believe in offering the customer high quality, with reliability, low running costs, good specifications at affordable prices! And how is all this achieved?

- It ought to start with listening to what the consumer wants, via market research and feedback from existing customers. Knowing what the customer wants can then be used to set the standard to which the product must conform.

- The next area of concern is related to the design of the product. To ensure that quality features in the design stage, planning and testing prototypes is important to ensure that consumer specifications can be met. Consideration of the materials to be used is very important; there may be a tendency to select the cheapest materials in an attempt to reduce costs. This will, in many cases, be a false economy.

- When actually producing the product, care should be taken throughout the process of production so that there is sufficient quality control built into the system to ensure that tasks are performed to the specified standard. To ensure this is done carefully there is a need to 'educate' the work-force.

- The people involved in the business are vital to the success of delivering quality. They need to have and take responsibility for the quality of the products produced. They must be able to work as a team to ensure the success of the process from inception to sales.

- Dr W. E. Deming*, an expert on **statistical quality control**, put forward 14 points to ensure that businesses would be able to achieve an all-round improvement in their performance. The points were:

1 Create a sense of purpose for improving the product or service
2 Adopt the philosophy necessary for quality
3 Cease dependence on inspection to achieve quality
4 Stop awarding business on the basis of price alone
5 Improve constantly in every activity within the business and therefore reduce costs
6 Introduce training on the job for everyone
7 Institute supervision to help everyone to do a better job
8 Eliminate fear and everyone will work more efficiently
9 Break down departmental barriers
10 Eliminate slogans and targets for the workers
11 Eliminate work standards which aim at quotas; offer help instead
12 Remove barriers to pride of workmanship
13 Introduce a programme of education and retraining
14 Ensure that everyone works in teams to achieve the transformation

* in *Out of the Crisis* (1986, MIT Center for Advanced Engineering Study)

It is of interest that it was the Japanese who were the first to adopt the Deming approach to quality because during the 1960s western businesses refused to accept that quality was a major issue.

Quality in practice

The total quality approach, often referred to as **Total Quality Management** (*see Unit 30 Lean production*), was seen as the way forward. Kemble Instruments, a business manufacturing laboratory equipment such as an automated blood checking machine for the testing of AIDS, had operated during profitable times on the basis of producing the goods to meet demand and giving quality a low priority. However, when the recession struck and several businesses were chasing very few orders, quality suddenly became an issue.

Kemble adopted TQM in an attempt to ensure that its products were of the highest quality and to provide the business with a competitive advantage. The business changed emphasis to producing only what was required and took great steps to ensure that quality was achieved first time. Workers were quick to respond to the challenge of being given the responsibility for what they produced. Many were able to make suggestions as to how best to improve the production of a given part or how time could be saved in collecting the components for their particular workstation; after all they were the experts. It was they who were producing the goods daily.

By adopting this total approach to quality the business managed to reduce the level of faults from 6% to 0.6%, and reduced the amount of stock held by half. This was achieved by operating a package of measures: JIT, a form of **quality circles** (*see Unit 30 Lean production*) and job rotation.

The Japanese approach has been to ensure that there is a commitment to a zero defect product. Much depends upon ensuring that the components are of a high standard and this in turn requires an agreement with the suppliers to operate a similar approach to quality. This is often gained by guaranteeing the supplier business for a given period of time.

Ford has taken a slightly different approach with its suppliers, by offering a marketing incentive. It offers an award, the 'Ford Q1', if the supplier can comply with a stringent quality process. Each supplier to qualify must:

- ensure there is a consistent quality of components

- be committed to improving the quality of components

There has to be documented evidence of these procedures. In return the supplier is guaranteed contracts for a certain length of time.

Texaco set up QATs (Quality Action Teams) to encourage teamwork and to get as many of the workers involved, just as quality circles (*see Unit 30 Lean production*) attempt to do. Texaco accepted that as the customer was insisting on a better service and product, the business had to provide it. The total quality approach helped achieve this but also increased productivity, which increased profits as costs fell.

IBM puts a premium on quality when purchasing from suppliers. According to business strategist Tom Peters, the percentage of defects within an order determines the amount paid by IBM. As the percentage of defects increases, the price paid for the products is cut. This financial incentive may work for suppliers to IBM and encourage other businesses in the chain of suppliers to do likewise.

Jaguar has relied on the use of technology to achieve quality. Its brochure distributed at the 1998 Motor Show for the launch of the S-Type stated:

'Precision engineering delivers the highest levels of quality. The all-new production facility uses sophisticated plasma welding techniques; laser cameras check critical dimensions throughout the assembly process, for the utmost precision and quality.'

It is of interest to note how attention to quality has been highlighted as a marketing point.

The Group Chief Executive of Diageo states in the 1998 report:

'My job is simple. It's to make sure that everyone in this company is obsessed with delighting our consumers.'

Quality bodies

The British Standards Institute 'offers' certificates to show that certain quality procedures are undertaken. Many businesses have applied for these as a method of showing potential customers that they take quality seriously. The certificates show that quality standards have been achieved. The **BS5750** was the most common 'award'. It is a procedure standard. Companies must be able to show that they operate a set procedure for ensuring that quality can be achieved. Many thousands of businesses throughout the country have gained BS5750, from small health centres to multinational manufacturers.

Many businesses now insist that their suppliers are registered BS5750.

All who deal with a business with BS5750 know the validity of its quality system (the international version of this is ISO 9000 – 9002).

BS5750 is divided into three parts and a business can select which part is the most appropriate for its needs and customers.

i)   Specification for design, manufacture and installation
ii) Specification for manufacture and installation
iii) Specification for final inspection and test

The BSI also offers a system of product certification:
i)   The BSI Kitemark which carries BSI's assurance that products comply with national or international standards
ii) The BSI Safety Mark which can be applied when the standards cover specific safety requirements

BSI symbol (Kitemark)

Seeing such a symbol instils confidence in the potential customer.

Points for Revision

Key Terms

competitive advantage	a particular feature that a business is able to claim makes its product stand out from the others in the market, thus enabling that business to sell more or charge a higher price
goodwill	an intangible asset usually related to the reputation of the company; the value of goodwill is difficult to calculate, but can be significant (*see Unit 36*)
Consumers' Association	an independent body which campaigns for improved standards of consumer protection; it publishes *Which?* magazine.
statistical quality control	a technique to measure the degree of accuracy of production; it makes use of tolerance levels, normal distribution curves and standard deviation
Total Quality Management	a method designed to reduce or even prevent defects from occurring during the production process (*see Unit 30*)
quality circles	a method of solving particular problems within a given workstation; a group of usually four to 10 workers will meet at regular intervals on a voluntary basis
BS5750	the number given to the standard for quality control procedures by the British Standards Institute

Definitions Question:

With reference to a firm or firms of which you have direct knowledge or experience, explain the importance of any three of the above terms (your teacher may wish to select the terms).

[5] per definition

Summary Points:

1 Quality is now essential in this competitive age. It no longer refers just to the standard of the product. Quality now includes all aspects of the business and their relationship with its customers.

2 The Japanese have taken the lead in the adoption of various techniques designed to improve quality.

3 Quality control is now built into the production process and ought not to be undertaken at the end of the process.

4 Quality is the responsibility of all the workers and not an inspector.

Mini Case Study

The Kings Rock Company is based in Southport, Lancashire. It manufactures confectionery rock using a small amount of machinery and staff with many years' experience. Presently, the question of quality is dealt with by the supervisor who inspects a sample of each batch of sticks of rock for length and width, but more importantly for the clarity of the lettering. This process is checked at the end of production, using a sample of 100 sticks per day.

Depending on the day of the week, he rejects on average 6% of the 4,000 sticks produced every day. These are sold in the corner of the factory shop for 50p per stick (the normal selling price for each stick is £1).

To produce the rock, a sugary mixture is passed through a machine which is old and rather unreliable. The rock is then cut by one of the employees by hand. The owner is concerned not only with the loss in the shop, but some poorly made rock is getting through the system to be sold at the local souvenir shops. With such a competitive market, in a low-margin business, this is an expensive mistake to make.

There is a also high labour turnover mainly due to the tedious nature of the job. This can have serious consequences for quality.

---

1 Define: low-margin business, labour turnover.   [4]

2 a) If the unit cost of a stick of rock is 60p, calculate the loss per week of the reject rock.   [2]

   b) Why might the business continue to sell at a loss?   [2]

   c) With a 0% reject rate, how much extra profit will the business earn?   [2]

3 Suggest the main reason why the owner would be concerned about reject rock being sold in the souvenir shops.   [2]

4 Develop a quality control programme which would solve the present problems facing Kings Rock.   [8]

                                                                                              20

Maxi Case Study

Ishida Europe Manufacturing Limited assembles packaging and multi-weighing machines for the food industry. The factory and headquarters of the company are located in Birmingham.

The plant assembles about 30 multi-weighing machines a month for companies such as Walkers, Golden Wonder and K.P.

It also assembles:

- Weighing conveyor systems which can reject items of an incorrect weight
- Automatic case packing equipment
- Bag-making machines which convert rolls of plastic film into bags for a variety of food products

Ishida's mission statement includes reference to quality, stating that it:

....'aims to be a world-class manufacturer of innovative, high-quality industrial weighing, packing and associated equipment which exceeds customer expectations for quality, delivery and performance.'

How do we achieve our mission?

Innovation solutions	• Understand customer requirements • Involvement in specification process • Utilisation of Engineering knowledge base
Manufacturing best practice	• Employee involvement • Investment in plant equipment • Continuous improvement of methodology
Quality products	• Operation of ISO Quality System • High quality supplier base • Investment and utilisation of technology
Customer satisfaction	• Commitment to lead times • Feedback from customers • After sales service and support
Employee development	• Recruitment of high calibre individuals • Investment in training and development • Empowerment

Ishida's mission statement: how it achieves its mission

The problem facing Ishida is how to implement such a policy for quality. The business is constantly faced with the dilemma of meeting its customer delivery date and ensuring its products meet the customer's requirements in terms of quality. Rushing the assembly of a machine to ensure the delivery date is met may lead to a reduction in quality and consequently a dissatisfied customer; spending more time ensuring the machine is of the highest quality may mean a delay in delivery. This could be serious as the customer may well be contemplating closing the factory whilst the new machinery is put in place. Any delay in delivery would be very costly.

The battle to ensure the finished product is of the highest quality, but completed within the allotted time, starts immediately after the order has been placed. Ishida has an approval procedure that involves the design office. Ishida has invested heavily in CAD (computer aided design), which allows the design office to produce a list of jobs which means the production team can check whether it can meet the lead time. During the approval stage, a list of all the parts required to produce the finished machine is drawn up. It is only after this procedure is complete that an order is accepted. One of the major problems facing Ishida is that each product assembled is unique and despite employing highly skilled operators, mistakes can still be made. In an attempt to eradicate mistakes, a 'Critical Inspection List' is written as a warning to the assemblers as to likely difficult assembly procedures.

On the shop floor, assembly takes place within individual bays, where an individual worker is responsible for the whole of the assembly of a packaging machine. Each bay has a trolley ready and waiting with all the required parts to assemble the equipment, prepared at the approval stage. Unfortunately, the assembler can waste valuable time hunting for the appropriate part amongst the many haphazardly placed on the trolley. The assembler assumes the parts have been checked by the stores team whose responsibility it is ensure that all parts that arrive at Ishida are perfect to use.

One of the dilemmas facing Ishida is whether it is better to rely on one or two suppliers who can guarantee delivery of parts on time and of the right quality, or use more suppliers in an attempt to foster greater competition and cheaper prices. Ishida has gone for the former, building up partnerships with single suppliers which can provide the goods to its exacting requirements. However this has its limitations; expecting a single supplier to provide additional parts quickly may not be physically possible or otherwise compromise the quality of such parts.

By building such partnerships, Ishida has even brought employees of the supplying businesses to see how the supplier's parts are used in the finished product and assembled into the packing machines. This is an attempt to improve the standard of the parts produced and reduce the number of parts that are of an inadequate standard.

The assembly workers, whilst assembling a machine, write out a list of any problems that they encountered in the building of the machine and note any parts that were issued unnecessarily. In addition they fill in a time sheet that gives an indication of how long it has taken to assemble particular sections of the machine in order to be able to have some idea if similar machines have to be built in the future. They also record time taken to rectify any errors or where the route card was not clear or inaccurate (the route card is the suggested order of assembly). The assembler will also include the amount of time when it was not possible to carry on working on the machine because of problems (down time). Contact with the engineering office is possible if there is a question over drawings or a part does not fit.

All workers, especially the less experienced, are encouraged to keep their own notes for the assembly of the machines, which can be used as helpful reminders and as an additional aid to the route cards.

Certain quality checks are built into the assembly process to avoid wasting valuable time having to dismantle the machine if a fault arises that could have been easily rectified before the next stage of the assembly had taken place. Once the sub-assembly has been completed, the team leader will inspect the work. Once the machine is completed, the final inspection is undertaken and an interesting additional form of inspection takes place. Personnel from Ishida's different departments will meet and study the assembled machine to ensure it meets the requirements as specified by the customer. The engineer drawer, quality assurance, sales and the assembly team leader will view the machine from differing perspectives.

1 Define the following terms: mission statement, CAD, lead time, down time. [8]

2 What will be the difference in perspective for the personnel from quality assurance, sales and the assembly team leader when looking at a completed machine? [6]

3 How would the implementation of quality circles be of benefit to Ishida?
(*You may wish to refer to Unit 30 to help you with this question*) [4]

4 What are the major problems for Ishida of relying upon a single supplier? [4]

5 To what extent does the quality programme described above resemble a Total Quality Management programme? [6]

6 What are the problems of having fixed lead times when quality is so important? [4]

7 Discuss whether you think that the quality programme in place is sufficient to ensure customer satisfaction. [8]

40

Lean production

Learning objectives

Having read this unit, students will be able to

1 understand the main terms associated with lean production

2 evaluate the consequences of, and benefits for, a firm introducing lean production

3 appreciate the difficulties of using lean production

Context

Toyota Motor Manufacturing (UK) recently spent over £150 million on its new factory in North Wales (Deeside), where engines will be produced for the Toyota Avensis and the Toyota Corolla. The emphasis within the factory is very much on lean production, producing car engines more quickly and building in quality at every stage of the production process. Toyota refers to the 'TPS' – Toyota Production System, which relies on the usage of JIT (just-in-time) and jidoka (the automatic system of stopping the production line as soon as faults are detected). As a result of operating a lean production system, Toyota feels confident it will be able to be highly competitive with the other major car manufacturers.

In the highly acclaimed book, *The Machine That Changed the World* (James Womack, Daniel Jones and Daniel Roos, Rawson Associates, NY, 1990) evidence was quoted to show how much leaner Toyota was compared with General Motors in the production of cars. Not only were the Japanese more productive in terms of the number of cars produced, but these cars were produced in a smaller space, with fewer workers who took less than half the time to produce a car. If this were not enough in terms of giving Toyota a competitive advantage, the Japanese cars were produced with less than a third of the faults found on General Motors cars. By taking this approach to manufacturing , the Japanese had set the benchmark for the world's car manufacturers to follow and attempt to emulate.

Lean production explained

Possibly as a result of the emergence of global markets as opposed to national markets, the degree of competition between businesses has risen dramatically. More businesses are competing in a much wider/larger market and as a consequence are faced with the problem of how to generate a competitive advantage.

Lean production, with its origins in Japan, is a collection of working practices which, if implemented successfully, is designed to enhance the quality of products whilst attempting to reduce the cost of producing them. Both aspects are important ways in which to compete. Consumers are looking for reliability, punctuality, quality at a competitive price. The utilisation of 'lean production' goes a long way to addressing all these concerns.

'Lean' represents an attempt to minimise costs and enhance quality in the widest possible sense. Lean production should therefore mean higher levels of productivity, for both its labour force and capital equipment, which in turn may mean a reduction in the size of the labour force required and consequently a reduction in costs. Such a reduction in work-force will be seen only if the overall quality and level of output are not reduced as a result of the smaller number of employees. Less stock should be required at any one time and less space is needed to produce the goods. Lean production should result in fewer defects, thus improving the quality of the product and ensuring customer satisfaction. The quality of the product can be improved only if the work-force is content and plays a full part in the decision making process.

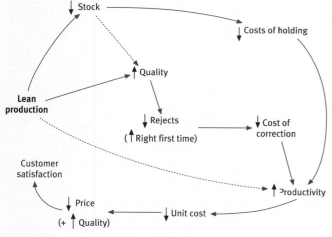

Figure 30.1 Lean production explained

The key elements to lean production are:

- time-based competition – reducing the time taken from the inception of the product or the product concept to starting the actual production (lead time)

- cell production – the organisation of the production process into small teams

- just-in-time management – cutting the amount of stock in the business

- jidoka and quality circles – the contribution of the work-force with regard to suggestions for the solving of problems on the shop floor

- total quality management – ensuring the efficient utilisation of production methods, machines and labour

All the above are employed to make the business's production process more efficient and, therefore, the business more competitive. This represents a complete approach to production and requires a different outlook or philosophy as to how goods are produced.

Time-based competition

Assuming it is understood that time is money in business, attempting to find ways of saving time will save the business money by cutting costs. The Japanese found that if they could develop their products more quickly, not only would there be a reduction in development costs but this time-saving might mean that their product would be available to the consumer sooner than a competitor's. This could be achieved by a greater usage of CAD (computer aided design). Akio Morita, the founder of Sony, always worked on the objective of getting Sony's products into the mature phase of the product life cycle before competitors had entered the market (*see Unit 16 Product*).

Time-based competition is also concerned with reducing the amount of time it takes to produce the product and therefore make it available to the consumer.

Down time (or idle time)

The time taken to set up the machines to produce particular parts of a car; for example, the presses which stamp out the different panels, doors, roof, bonnet and boot can take several hours to change. Whilst they are being changed no production is actually taking place in that section of the factory and this is known as down time. If a way could be found to reduce the time it takes to change the machines, vast savings would be made. Time-based competition has led businesses to consider any part of the productive process where time can be saved. This has led to a careful consideration of where components are placed prior to being used on the production line.

Cell production

Cell production is where the work-force is divided into teams. Each team is responsible for a particular part of the production process. Responsibility includes quality control, health and safety at work, job rotation (allowing the work-force to change tasks within teams). The cell is made up of several teams; the idea is that each cell 'sells' the part-finished product on to the next cell which receives it as an internal customer.

Just-in-time

The traditional approach to stock control was one whereby businesses held stock 'just-in-case' it was needed. This meant that problems at the work-place were, in effect, 'covered' by excess stock. Consider the causes of the work-place grinding to a halt – these might be machines being unreliable, suppliers delivering late, quality being low and even industrial action (strikes) meaning part of the process was shut down, while the other part was still operational. With plenty of stock, the business could still keep on working, so a business would not normally look at these problems when they occurred. By reducing the stock to a minimum, the business is placed in a riskier position; if the supplier is late or delivers low-quality goods, or machines break down, with a much lower stock level, the business could suffer very quickly from lost output or could be employing work-force with nothing to do. This would force the business to look into solving the problem, whereas before it didn't need to because it had the stock to fall back on (*see Figure 30.2*).

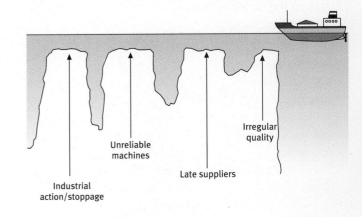

Explanation: If stocks are high enough, this can 'cover' the problems. By reducing the stock levels, the problems are 'uncovered' and are more likely to be solved

Figure 30.2

The overall aim of **JIT** is to produce goods that meet exactly the requirements of the customer at the lowest cost when they are required. Toyota has invested heavily in the method of 'just-in-time' because of the huge savings that could be made by ensuring that the stock of components needed to build its cars arrived on the production line just in time to be used. This method allows savings to be made by reducing the amount of stock that has to be stored at any one time. This in turn meant that less space would be necessary for storing parts.

Stored stock is not adding value to the business, it is only adding costs because the stock is not actually doing anything. Added value is achieved only when stock is being used to help complete the car, and stock held in storage is in fact costing the business money.

Just-in-time involves the delivery of stock to the work-place – be it a production line or a retailer's shelf, with a view to minimising the time it spends waiting to be used or bought. Given the complexity of manufacturing a motor car or stocking 20,000 different lines at Sainsbury's, this process requires careful planning.

Toyota solved this problem by introducing a card system known as **kanban**. This is a system that uses a card which is attached to all items in the production process.

Each item or part has a number which is printed on the card using a bar code. Every time an item is used, the kanban is removed and delivered to a computer terminal where the computer reads the code on it and automatically reorders the parts, or ensures more are collected from the small stock held within the business. Therefore the entire production line is governed by the kanban, which ensures there are enough parts in the right place at the right time.

This system means that the assembly line does not have to be cluttered with parts waiting to be used, thus saving space. In stock control terminology, the system operates on a minimal buffer stock. Less stock causes fewer costs to be incurred, as there is less cash tied up in stock (*see Unit 28 Stock control*). In the early 1990s, Nissan had managed to reduce the process of ordering and receiving stock from one of its suppliers to 42 minutes (synchronous supply).

This illustration highlights the need to ensure the assembly plant has a very good working relationship with its suppliers. Many manufacturers who use JIT use fewer, more reliable suppliers which not only deliver on time but several times a day. In the article opposite the supplier was the French business Sommer Allibert which had decided to relocate its factory within just two miles of the Nissan plant, enabling it to deliver the carpets on time! Over 100 deliveries a day were made from the carpet supplier to Nissan.

Apart from ensuring that the components arrive on time, there are other considerations if JIT is to operate successfully:

- Regular demand will help JIT production to be used effectively. If there is a fluctuating pattern of demand, then JIT may be difficult to achieve, because of the flexibility needed in the amounts delivered by suppliers

- A large capital outlay on a computerised stock control system using kanban

- The quality of the parts has to be perfect because at any point very little stock is held for as short a time as possible. Therefore every unit of stock received must be perfect. This means that the supplier has to ensure that its suppliers in turn are quality-conscious. As a consequence suppliers are involved at the planning and design stage in an attempt to iron out any difficulties before production commences. However, one criticism of JIT is that large businesses pressurise smaller suppliers into holding stock. If the supplier has to deliver several times a day, but does not have the technology or finance to operate JIT, it will be forced to act as a warehouse for the larger manufacturer

- This in turn requires the labour force to be capable of checking for and correcting problems as and when they arise. The work-force needs to be much more flexible in its approach to the job to ensure that the production line runs smoothly. This provides the workers with some responsibility, which in itself is a form of job enrichment (*see Unit 50 Non-financial motivation*)

- JIT requires good labour relations to be in place. Not only is more expected from the work-force, but there is no place for disruption to the production process with so little stock

Making it just in time

By Andrew Griffiths

NISSAN is setting new standards in manufacturing, with supplier relationships that have slashed delivery times to just 42 minutes in one case.

In the latest development of "just-in-time" methods, whereby parts are delivered as they are needed, the Tyneside car-maker has introduced the concept of "synchronous supply".

The system under which specified parts are manufactured and sent in sequence to the correct vehicle is so accurate that there are no checks before fitting, even though there can be scores of variations in parts.

The advance is another indication of the struggle facing Ford, Rover and Vauxhall, which are already finding it difficult to keep up with Nissan in terms of productivity and efficiency.

Synchronous supply works in its most impressive form in the link between Nissan and Sommer Allibert, a French-owned carpet and trim manufacturer that recently set up a satellite plant just two miles away from the car factory.

Sommer lorries make the trip along Nissan Way an astonishing 120 times a day, supplying 5,000 pieces of carpet, parcel shelves and boot linings, which match precise orders that are sent along a computer link just minutes earlier.

As each painted Micra shell starts its journey in Nissan's massive complex, a special coding tag triggers a message to Sommer that specifies one of 120 variations for these components, depending on colour, engine size, extras and whether the model is left- or right-hand drive.

At Sommer the correct piece is selected, trimmed, and has its plastic extras fitted, before being stacked in sequence and loaded in small batches. On arrival, the Sommer driver takes the stock straight to the assembly line.

Eric de la Villegeorges, Sommer's managing director, says that back-up systems in the case of computer failure or vehicle breakdown mean the system is virtually failsafe.

"If we don't supply a part immediately it would shut down the plant," he says.

Terry Hogg, Nissan's production control director, says that the system brings 100pc savings on inventory, 100pc savings on internal handling, and 90pc to 95pc savings on space, as well as productivity advantages.

Mr Hogg says that although the process can increase the cost of components, with bigger fuel bills and the additional wear and tear on vehicles, the higher costs are outweighed by savings. Sommer benefits by keeping its own stock levels low.

Six companies who have set up plants within a few miles operate the system for exhausts, seats, door panels, consoles and headlinings. There are 460 deliveries a day, taking 20,000 parts to Nissan.

This and other methods has enabled Nissan to reduce its average inventory for European-originated parts to 1·6 days—five times better than the next best in Europe. The industry average is 20 days.

In 1993, the target is to get it down to one day—another indication of how the Japanese manufacturer is pulling away from the competition.

Other parts are delivered up to four times a day. For the new Micra, which goes on sale in Britain next year, Nissan has extended its "milk round" collection system, which started in the Midlands, to cover Hertfordshire.

This involves using a single parts supplier to make a regular tour of suppliers in an area and collecting from each before going on to the plant, reducing mileage by 2·3m miles a year.

Previously, each supplier made individual haulage arrangements, wasting resources and adding to traffic congestion.

Another feature of the supply chain is the minimal use of disposable packaging. The majority of components are delivered in specially designed units that can be used by assembly workers as dispensers and that can be refilled back at the supplier.

Question 5

Suggest why a business which supplies a computer assembly plant might relocate much nearer to its customer (you may wish to refer to Unit 24 Location).   [3]

Question 6

Explain how JIT reduces costs. Ensure you refer to
 i) stock
 ii) work-in-progress
 iii) finished goods   [6]

Question 7

Imagine you are responsible for the wage negotiations on behalf of the work-force at a business that is about to introduce JIT. List the reasons why you would argue for a higher wage rate for the work-force.   [5]

Question 8

What are the main problems facing a business operating JIT?   [5]

Jidoka

With so little stock waiting to be used on the production line and with very little buffer stock, the importance of keeping the line operating to ensure parts required at the next stage of the assembly process are available is paramount. Therefore all workers must be able to detect and identify faults quickly. Spotting faults early means that they will be less likely to create difficulties further down the production process.

In addition, such faults will be cheaper to put right if other stages of the production process have not yet been involved. If there were a fault with a car windscreen seal and it were not discovered until after the windscreen wipers and the electric circuits for the heated screen had been connected, the costs of correcting the fault would include dismantling the features that had been added to the windscreen. Identifying the fault before assembly is preferable. **Jidoka** requires money to be spent on electronic sensors that can detect a fault and stop the production line and so prevent the fault being repeated or being made worse due to late detection.

The work-force is also encouraged to look for faults and individuals are expected to attempt to solve the problem themselves. If this is not possible the production line is halted until a remedy is found.

Quality circles

This is a process that involves a group of workers, normally between four and 10, meeting at regular intervals, usually on a voluntary basis, to discuss problems of their choosing and attempting to find remedies to these problems. The workers tend to concentrate upon problems that affect their own workstation. Many of the problems are related to manufacturing quality and ways to improve productivity. The philosophy behind **quality circles** is that it is the workers who are actually on the production line who are in the best position to make suggestions as to how to remedy difficulties or make recommendations for improvements. In addition, encouraging the employees to be involved in the decision making process offers a sense of responsibility and involvement, both considered important in terms of motivation (*see Unit 50 Non-financial motivation*).

If suggestions are acted upon by management there is a sense of achievement which again may be seen as a source of motivation for the work-force. However there may be some reluctance by the workers to make suggestions which lead to a reduction in the amount of labour required. Therefore, operating quality circles requires an understanding between employer and employee, effective communication between the two groups and ability of management to delegate responsibility to the workers. Many businesses operate quality circles and not just those involved with the production of cars. Lucas Aerospace, Wedgwood and British Airways all operate such a scheme. British Airways has found significant levels of success with this approach by encouraging all employees to concentrate on the customer i.e. the end-user of the product.

Some businesses operate a form of quality circles but do not provide the time for the employees to meet during the working day. Instead, they operate a 'suggestion scheme' and offer rewards for suggestions that are implemented and save the business money. Rewards range from just a few pounds to several hundred pounds. The danger of this approach, however, is that an expectation grows that the workers *should* make suggestions, as was the case at Leyland trucks where it was assumed each worker would make at least 20 suggestions every year. However, there has been evidence in America that quality circles have been used as a way of reducing the power of trade unions (*see Unit 53 People in groups*) given that it gives more responsibility to workers and helps them enjoy their jobs.

Toyota considers suggestion schemes as an integral part of the business's philosophy of looking for improvements on a continuous basis. The Japanese refer to this striving for continual improvement as '**kaizen**'.

Kaizen

Kaizen is seen as a vital, yet simplistic way in which to reduce 'muda'. This is a Japanese word for waste of any kind. For example, reducing the amount of time needed to move stock to be used on the production line, thus reducing costs.

Kaizen is the key to all that is considered important if a business is to survive in the modern competitive world.

Striving for continuous improvement, by involving the workers for their ideas, their flexibility of approach and their ability to operate in 'teams' or 'cells' is the key to enhancing performance. Each cell is responsible for its own work, the quality of that work, its level of stock by implementing the kanban system and making improvements at its own workstation.

The theory behind kaizen is that:

- All the activities of the business should be geared to its customers. In many instances the customer is the next stage in the production process (an internal customer, as opposed to the external customer, the end-user of the product). Anything that can be done to help the customer is considered important.

- It is essential to communicate clearly so that all concerned are aware of the potential problems and can therefore be in a position to make suggestions for improvements.

- It is vital to the success of the business in its use of kaizen that there is a reliance upon its work-force to be actively involved in the adoption of this continuous improvement and elimination of waste.

- There is an emphasis upon the improvement of the production process, rather than just being concerned with the end result, namely the finished product.

Question 9

Suggest why some businesses may be reluctant to introduce quality circles.   [4]

Question 10

What is continuous improvement?   [2]

Question 11

Devise a training programme for new workers in an attempt to make them aware of the need for kaizen.   [5]

Question 12

State how the customer will benefit from a kaizen approach.   [5]

Total Quality Management

As Tom Peters states in his book *The Pursuit of WOW!* (Vintage, 1994):

'No doubt about it, superior quality is a must for competitive success these days.' But he sounds a note of caution, suggesting that it is not just a case of management adopting a Total Quality approach and assuming all will be well;

'... it's about products that work unerringly.'

As Bosch stated in its advertising campaign at the end of 1998: 'Excellence comes as standard.'

Businesses now have to ensure that quality exists as a matter of course rather than as an additional feature that customers will have to pay for.

TQM involves management implementing a programme of improvements in the organisational processes that operate within a business. Careful control of the processes ought to ensure a better quality product will be produced, which in turn will satisfy the customer's expectations.

It ought to be made clear that TQM is not the same as TQC (Total Quality Control). The latter involves the utilisation of kaizen by *all* the employees of the business, regardless of their status within the business, whereas TQM is the responsibility of management.

TQM helps businesses to:

- focus on the needs of the customer

- gain quality in all aspects of the business's operations, not just the quality of the actual product or service

- analyse all the processes involved in an attempt to remove wastage

- encourage a team approach to reducing problems and finding methods for continual improvement

There are however some problems to consider with the adoption of TQM. Training needs to be thorough and involves additional costs for the business. It requires everyone within the business to be committed to the process. Communication between everyone has to be excellent, to ensure all are aware of what is trying to be achieved.

Points for Revision

Key Terms

JIT	just-in-time refers to the manner in which parts are ordered and made available prior to being used. The idea is to ensure that the parts are delivered just before they are to be used, thus reducing costs
kanban	a bar coded card that triggers the reordering of parts; essential if JIT is to operate successfully
jidoka	an automatic fault detection process which can stop the production line to prevent further goods being produced that are faulty
kaizen	a system of continuous improvement
Total Quality Management	a management process for improving the quality of products
quality circles	workers meet on a voluntary basis in an attempt to find solutions to problems, usually within their workstation
cell production	a method of organising workers into groups which are then responsible for the production and quality of the goods produced

Definitions Question:
By referring to a business you know, explain the significance of three of the above terms (your teacher may wish to help you with the choice).   [5] per definition

Summary Points:

1. Lean production is a corporate way of life, a total approach which encompasses everyone within a business in an attempt to maximise the quality of the product.

2. It requires low levels of stock, with quality accepted as standard, with management who operate by consensus, and see effective communication as essential; suppliers are few in number but are viewed as partners who are prepared to make many deliveries on demand.

Mini Case Study

A. Busi Ltd operates a medium-sized factory on the outskirts of Birmingham.

The founder of the business arrived in this country from Italy in the early 1950s.

The business manufactures make-up containers such as eyeliner and eye shadow boxes, mascara and lipstick tubes. This is a competitive market and consequently the managing director is very cost-conscious in an attempt to maintain profit margins.

Recent concerns have been over the value of stock that is stored in the factory. Cartons of the plastic strips that form the basis of the boxes are piled up to the ceiling. The production manager justifies this high level of stock by suggesting that it enables the business to meet any unexpected orders without delay, as the materials required are ready to hand.

On further investigation, it was discovered that there was sufficient stock for two months' production. Concern was expressed that too much money was being wasted paying for all this stock to be stored for such a length of time. To add to the business's problems, the paint used to spray the boxes for the various make-up containers was also stored in large quantities. There were even colours that were no longer used as fashions had changed and certain colours were no longer 'in'.

Being a traditional business, many of the processes involved in the production of the containers had not changed for many years. However problems were starting to emerge as a result of the higher levels of production that were being undertaken as a consequence of gaining an order from a high street chemist chain to supply containers for its 'own-brand' make-up.

Many of the workers were highly experienced but had not been allowed a say in the running of the business, probably because the owners had taken the view that they and not the workers knew best. It was clear however that something had to be done about the way in which the stock was stored, if the business was to remain competitive.

1 Explain how the business is wasting money having such a large amount of stock.   [5]

2 a) How might the introduction of just-in-time help the business?   [5]

    b) What would be the problems facing Busi Ltd if it were to introduce just-in-time?   [4]

3 Prepare a case for the introduction of quality circles at Busi Ltd.   [6]

<u>20</u>

Maxi Case Study

There have been several references to Toyota in this unit, only because the business provides a benchmark for most manufacturers world-wide in terms of its productive efficiency used in what is known as the Toyota Production System (TPS).

The system of production it employs has a basic aim – to reduce waste; managers and employees have been educated to question the need for every process, sequence and work-in-progress stock. By removing unnecessary parts from the system, the objectives of reducing costs and increasing quality are achieved. Quality rises as productivity rises because a big part of eliminating waste is removing defects.

Although this is a radical system, it does have its roots in the production system set up by Henry Ford in that it is still a conveyor belt system with division of labour; each worker handles one step in the process and the suppliers are relied upon to keep the system running. However, the TPS has one or two 'twists' to it which make it different.

The origin of the TPS lies in the fact that the volume of output in post-war Japan was much smaller than that in America. Toyota could not employ specialised equipment, and machinery not only had to perform different tasks but had to adapt to different models. It did not have the space to store vast amounts of stock, so had to ensure reliable suppliers delivered on time. This was coupled with the need for mutual trust between employees and management following some drastic restructuring in Japanese industry in the 1950s. The work-force agreed to job cuts only as long as those who remained were promised lifetime employment.

The managers are therefore willing to delegate as much responsibility as the workers feel they can accept; to this extent, workers are in a position to stop the work flow if necessary; this is built in to the production targets which allow for a down time of 5% due to the various problems which can occur on any production line. Employees can put in their own ideas to improve the flow of products and are continually encouraged to do so; the rigid job specifications of the past have disappeared and they are provided with multiple skills. The management claims that the more responsibility, the greater the motivation; if employees are permitted to spend time in a productive, challenging environment, experience has shown this will produce a form of creative tension which clearly motivates the workers at Toyota. After all, there is nothing more dull than working for hours in an unproductive manner.

Toyota attributes the success of the TPS system to three basic conditions:

1 Top management must give strong, visible commitment to the system

2 All employees must participate

3 The business must provide employees with necessary skills, through training

The system also encompasses the suppliers of raw materials and components, ensuring the smoothest flow of products. Independent suppliers are seen and expected to participate on an equal footing. The just-in-time approach can help suppliers reduce stock in the same way that it reduces the manufacturer's stock. Interestingly, suppliers also benefit from improved management–employee relations because of the scope for expanded work.

The conveyor belt system therefore starts with the customer order and culminates in the delivery of products. The main focus is always on the customer, not on the manufacturing process – this is the origin of just-in-time, which Toyota describes as 'making only what is needed, only when it is needed and only in the amount that is needed.' This uses the concept of levelled production – using resources evenly throughout the day and week, producing items using a continuous flow system and establishing a pace of work in every process which is the same as the pace of demand in the market-place (known in the TPS as takt time).

Instead of producing and hoping to sell, the entire process is governed by customer demands. The kanban (Japanese for signboard) system pulls through components and parts for production. The flow system then ensures not only that the product moves through the process without stopping, but, by definition, it must lead to the lowest possible level of stock. Once stock begins to build up, the inefficiency of production builds with it.

Building quality into the process is of paramount importance; it originates from Toyota's founder whose first invention was a loom. The machine was designed to stop immediately a thread snapped. Stopping work means problems are solved as they occur, thereby eliminating the waste that could result if it were not stopped immediately. This is where the jidoka process is used, preventing defects from occurring again by stopping the line. In turn, this means that workers do not have to inspect machinery continually – it stops itself when a fault is detected. This therefore frees up their time to concentrate on tasks that require skill and judgement.

The final element of the Toyota approach is kaizen, whereby teams of workers are expected to aim for continuous improvement. This means not just 100% quality, but achieving 100% quality all the time, then aiming to do this more quickly, so that perfect products can be manufactured at a lower cost. The process is therefore never-ending. Toyota divides this into work kaizen, which aims to solve the problem by altering the actual job carried out, and equipment kaizen, which aims to modify the sequence and process of work, through better capital equipment and a more efficient layout.

The system is also adapting and changing to new surroundings and market conditions – globalisation, technological advances and the drive for improvement make sure the company never rests on its laurels. Toyota likes to quote several examples of how it adapts and continues to improve productivity. In one plant in North America, it reduced the time required to change one of the stamping machines (used to shape metal) by a staggering 94%, meaning it could increase the number of change-overs by 300%. This led to a tremendous improvement in the flexibility of the business to respond to changing market circumstances. Stock was reduced by 83% and output increased by 140%.

Customer demand is the dynamic that drives the Toyota Production System. All activity in the system occurs in response to real demand, as expressed by customer orders. The system thus contrasts with conventional, "push" systems, where processes make items regardless of actual end demand.

Jidoka

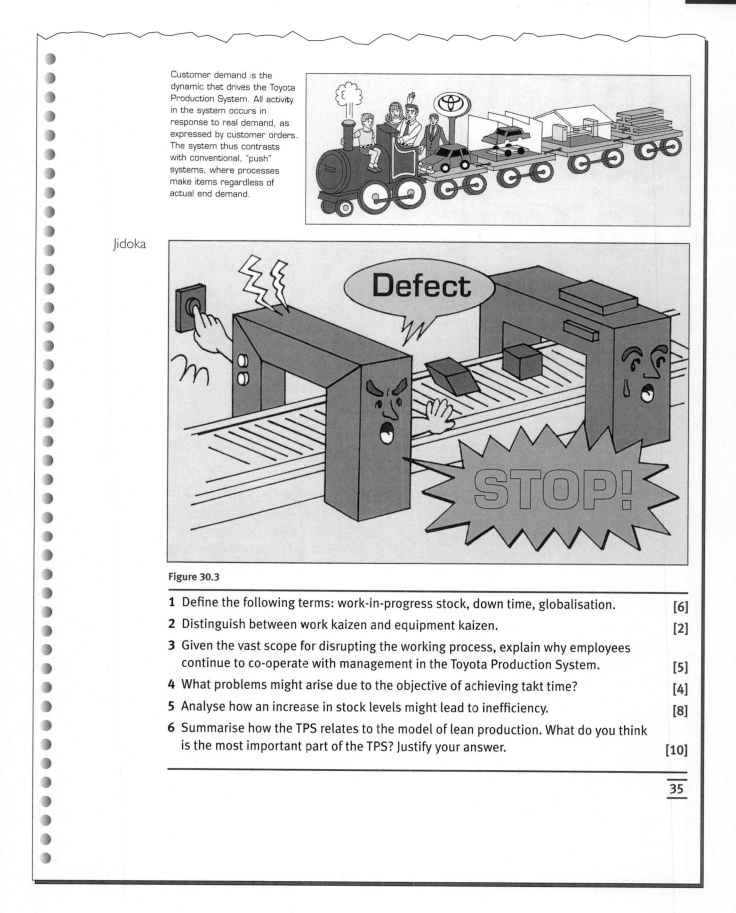

Figure 30.3

1 Define the following terms: work-in-progress stock, down time, globalisation. [6]

2 Distinguish between work kaizen and equipment kaizen. [2]

3 Given the vast scope for disrupting the working process, explain why employees continue to co-operate with management in the Toyota Production System. [5]

4 What problems might arise due to the objective of achieving takt time? [4]

5 Analyse how an increase in stock levels might lead to inefficiency. [8]

6 Summarise how the TPS relates to the model of lean production. What do you think is the most important part of the TPS? Justify your answer. [10]

Critical path analysis

Learning objectives

Having read this unit, students will be able to

1 identify the nature of problems which can be solved by using critical path analysis

2 draw and interpret networks

3 identify the application of Gantt charts within the use of network diagrams

Context

One of the largest construction projects ever to take place was the Channel Tunnel. The actual construction probably took the best part of five years, in addition to the planning process involved before the first excavator began digging. Such a project required thousands of different tasks to be planned and co-ordinated, involving labour materials and various pieces of machinery. Each task will also have taken a different amount of time, which further complicates the planning process. Some of the tasks took place simultaneously, whilst some had to be scheduled before others e.g. the tunnel had to be dug before the rail line could be laid. Each activity will have been planned to take place for a certain number of days, weeks, months, or even years. It would have been pointless and very inefficient if the physical resources required for laying the track had been brought together at the beginning of the project when they would not have been needed for about two years! This would have resulted in a huge cost for Eurotunnel's shareholders given that they would have been paying for the resources simply to wait their turn. In order to plan for efficient scheduling of resources, create deadlines which act as a target for completion and control costs of major projects like the Channel Tunnel, Eurotunnel will have used critical path analysis. This allows all activities to be displayed in diagrammatic form, so as to calculate exactly when the resources are required and for how long. This process can then be used to organise and plan resources so that the business maximises their use and at the same time attempts to minimise costs.

The nature of problems

Critical path analysis (CPA) may be used where the business faces problems that display the following characteristics:

■ dependent activities – although certain activities can take place simultaneously, some activities can take place only once others have finished e.g. the roof of a house cannot be constructed until the walls have been built, hence there is no need to order the roof slates when the foundations are being laid

■ deadlines – if you have ever driven past a civil engineering project e.g. a new by-pass or bridge, you may well have read the claim 'completed six months before deadline'. Such projects will have involved a CPA approach and may also have included a financial incentive for early completion

■ restricted resources – sometimes a particular raw material or skilled labour may be in short supply. The business will therefore have to prioritise those activities according to their place in the network or their need for the specially skilled labour.

Activity

Think of various 'projects' that display the characteristics for critical path analysis. These might be school-based, home-based or even business-based! Write down the separate activities involved and try to establish a logical order in which the activities ought to be carried out.

Diagrammatic representation (network diagrams)

Node ——→ Activity

Figure 31.1

A node denotes the start and finish of each activity and an arrow denotes an **activity** which has a duration.

To demonstrate how activities are drawn to represent a project, here is a project with four activities.

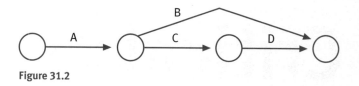

Figure 31.2

The above means A begins on its own, then B and C may begin once A has finished. D may start once C has finished.

Figure 31.3 below displays a network in which A and B begin together, C follows B, D follows A and E follows C and D.

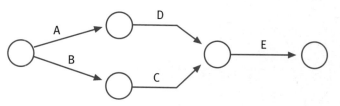

Figure 31.3

Question 1

Draw a network using the following information:
A, B and C begin together. D follows A, E follows B, F follows C and E.   [4]

Use of the dummy activity

Consider the following set of activities: A and B begin together, C follows A and B, but D follows only B. E follows D and C. If Figure 31.3 is examined D follows A and C follows B, and C is independent of A. However, in this example, C is dependent upon *both* A and B while D is dependent only on B. To make the required link between A, B and C needs the use of a **dummy** activity, otherwise there would be no obvious dependent link between C and B.

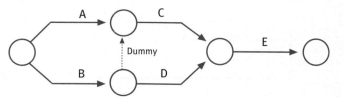

Figure 31.4

The dotted line represents a dummy activity. This is used to ensure the logical dependence of each activity is represented. Now we can see that C can begin only once A and B have been completed, but due to the direction of the arrow on the dummy activity, activity D is waiting only for A.

Activity

If the arrowhead on the dummy activity were pointing the other way, describe to your teacher the order and dependencies of the network.

Each node is divided according to the following:

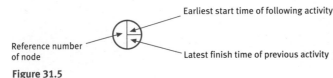

Reference number of node

Earliest start time of following activity

Latest finish time of previous activity

Figure 31.5

Once the **network diagram** has been drawn, the times of each activity must be inserted on each arrow with a view to calculating the following:

- **Earliest Start Time** of each activity = the earliest time an activity may begin, which will depend on the duration and order of previous activities.

- **Latest Finish Time** of each activity = the latest time an activity must finish, so that the entire project can finish within the minimum duration time.

- **Minimum duration** of the project = the earliest time the project may finish, given the order and duration of all the activities.

In order to demonstrate this next step, the following example of a manufacturing process will be used, with information in Table 1.

Table 1

Activity	Description	Preceded by	Duration
A	Order and deliver component A	–	8
B	Order and deliver component B	–	5
C	Record sales/purchases on spreadsheet	–	1
D	Receive and check all components	A,B	2
E	Manufacture stage 1	D	6
F	Sub-assembly 1	D	8
G	Manufacture stage 2	E	3
H	Dispatch to customer	F,G	1

This will result in the network diagram in Figure 31.6.

The node which follows activity C must be the last node of the entire project, otherwise the activity would be left 'dangling' without any calculation to be performed on it i.e. the project must begin from only one node and must end on one node.

Earliest Start Time (EST) of the following activity

- Node 1: the EST of the first three activities is 0.

- Node 2: B takes 5 days, but the table states that D may begin only when both A and B have finished, so the EST of D is 8 (it cannot start until A, the longest of the two activities, has finished).

- Node 3: the EST of D is 8, so 8 + duration of D, which is 2, gives the EST of E and F as 10 days.

- Node 4: EST of E is 10 days, + duration of E means EST of G is 16 days.

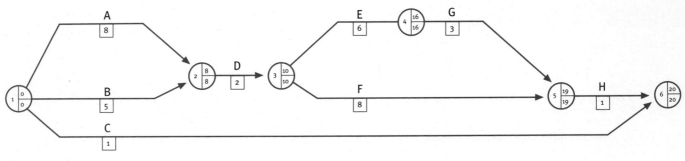

Figure 31.6

- Node 5: EST of F is 10 days, + duration of F is 18, but the EST of G is 16 days + duration of G (3) which means H cannot take place until 19 i.e. until the latest of both G and F.

- Node 6: H and C take 1 day which means that the earliest time the project can finish is 20 days.

This gives an indication of the minimum duration time of the project.

Latest Finish Time of the previous activity

If the project is to finish within 20 days, activity H must finish within 20 days, so activities F and G must finish by day 19.

The LFT on Node 5 = 19.

Node 4: 19 – duration of G (3) = 16.

Node 3: careful! LFT of E is 16 (see Node 4) – 6 is 10 days. 19 – duration of F (8) = 11 days, so the lower of the two numbers must be the LFT of activity D. Try completing the project in 20 days, if the LFT of Activity D was 11 – it is impossible without shortening other activities!

Node 2: 10 – 2 = 8.

Node 1: this must be zero i.e. the lower of 8 – 8 = 0 (activity A) and 8 – 5 = 3 (activity B) and 20 – 1 = 19 (activity C).

N.B.: When calculating EST, and two activities run into one node (see Figure 31.7), the earliest start time is either 14 or 17. 17 is used, because Z cannot start until both X and Y have been completed and Y takes 7 days.

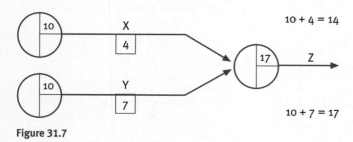

Figure 31.7

When calculating LFT, and two activities come from one node (see Figure 31.8 below), the latest finish time of R is either 6 or 3. 3 is used, because if R is completed any later than 3, then the latest finish time of S will increase, thereby increasing the duration of the project.

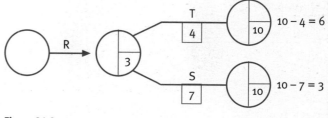

Figure 31.8

Float

One of the main purposes of the network diagram is to identify which activities can be delayed, or, put another way, if an activity is delayed, will the delay affect the minimum duration time? This can be done in two ways:

- **total float**
- **free float**

Total float represents the amount of delay available on any single activity which does not delay the project duration i.e. how long an activity can be extended/postponed so that the project is still finished within the minimum duration time.

It is calculated by:

Latest Finish Time (LFT) – Earliest Finish Time (EFT) of an individual activity

A common error made by students in exams is to confuse which activity is being considered. LFT is already displayed in the network, although EFT is not.

EFT can be calculated as:

EFT = EST + Duration or Duration + EST

So Total Float = LFT – (Duration + EST)

Removing the brackets,

Total Float = LFT (at end of activity) – Duration – EST (at beginning of activity).

Question 2

Copy the following two networks and the duration of each activity, then calculate the Earliest Start Time and Latest Finish Time of each activity, filling in each node accordingly. How long will each project take?

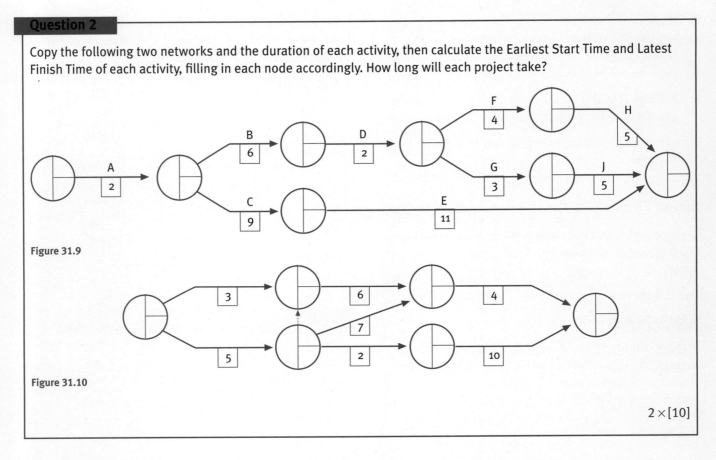

Figure 31.9

Figure 31.10

2 × [10]

Using the diagrammatic version:

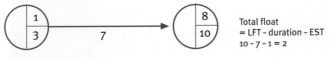

Figure 31.11

Total float
= LFT - duration - EST
10 - 7 - 1 = 2

For the project drawn in Figure 31.6, the total floats are in Table 2:

Table 2

Activity	LFT	–	Duration	–	EST	=	Total Float
A	8	–	8	–	0	=	0
B	8	–	5	–	0	=	3
C	20	–	1	–	0	=	19
D	10	–	2	–	8	=	0
E	16	–	6	–	10	=	0
F	19	–	8	–	10	=	1
G	19	–	3	–	16	=	0
H	20	–	1	–	19	=	0

Activities with total float of zero represent those activities which cannot be delayed without delaying the entire project. Such activities (in our example A,D,E,G,H) represent the **critical path**.

Activity

Consider what would happen to the minimum duration time if
a) Activity E increased by one day, or
b) Activity F increased by one day

In each case, follow the calculation of EST through to the last node and then work backwards to the node before each activity in the question above.

Free float represents the amount of delay available on each activity which does not delay the EST of the next activity. It is calculated by:

EST at end – duration – EST at beginning

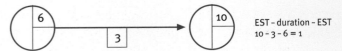

EST - duration - EST
10 - 3 - 6 = 1

Figure 31.12

For the network in Figure 31.6 above, this would be:

Activity	EST (at end)	–	Duration	–	EST (at beginning)	=	Free Float
A	8	–	8	–	0		0
B	5	–	5	–	0		0
C	20	–	1	–	0		19
D	10	–	2	–	8		0
E	16	–	6	–	10		0
F	19	–	8	–	10		1
G	19	–	3	–	16		0
H	20	–	1	–	19		0

Free float tends to be more appropriate when the delivery of materials must be on time or when labour is involved in other activities and cannot be moved on to another job; in the above case, for example, F can be delayed by 1 day and H will still be able to commence on time.

Question 3

Using the following network, calculate total float, free float and minimum duration time. State the critical path.

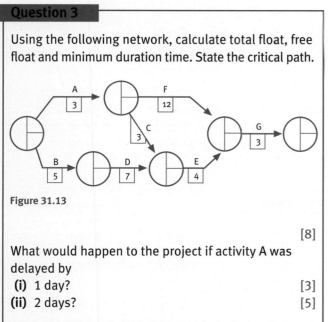

Figure 31.13

[8]

What would happen to the project if activity A was delayed by
 (i) 1 day? [3]
 (ii) 2 days? [5]

Hint: It may be helpful in (ii) to redraw the project and recalculate EST and LFT, finding the new total float figures and if there is any change in the minimum duration time.

Gantt charts

One of the uses of CPA occurs when there is a particular shortage of a resource which is needed to accomplish the project e.g. labour. It is possible to construct a **Gantt chart** in order to represent the usage of labour and to identify when activities may need to be delayed due to such shortages.

Consider the following network:

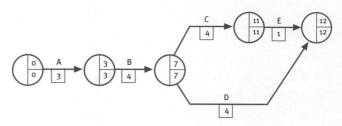

Figure 31.14

Each activity requires the following number of employees:

A   5   The business has a total of 11 employees available at any one time. Initially it would
B   6   appear that each activity can be performed, but closer examination of the network
C   9   reveals that C and D will be taking place at the same time.

D   4

E   5

We begin by plotting a chart which shows each activity over time:

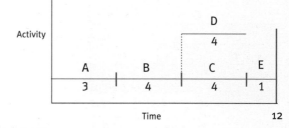

Figure 31.15

We can then multiply each activity's time by the number of employees required e.g. activity A requires 5 employees for 3 days, so we can draw a block histogram (which shows the resources taken up by each activity and its labour requirement) with a dimension of 5 × 3 to represent activity A's requirement of labour. Doing the same for each activity, assuming each starts at the Earliest Start Time, produces the following:

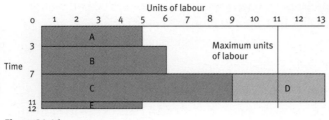

Figure 31.16

You will observe that by performing C and D simultaneously, the number of employees required exceeds that which is available because a second assumption is that employees cannot start another activity until the one on which they are working has been completed. It is therefore necessary to prioritise whether C or D should happen first.

This is where total float can be used to aid the decision making process:

	LFT	–	DURATION	–	EST		Total float
A	3	–	3	–	0	=	0
B	7	–	4	–	3	=	0
C	11	–	4	–	7	=	0
D	12	–	4	–	7	=	1
E	12	–	1	–	11	=	0

D has greater float, so C has less delay time, therefore C must be done first. Rearranging the diagram produces this result.

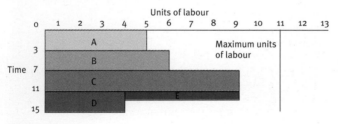

Figure 31.17

Even though the project has gone over the original minimum duration time by three days this is still the shortest time in which the project can be finished given the constraint of labour.

Using the network below in Figure 31.18, draw a Gantt chart given the labour requirements set out below the diagram.

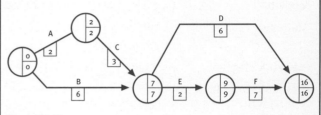

Figure 31.18

Activity	Labour requirement	Float
A	3	0
B	4	1
C	7	0
D	5	3
E	5	0
F	3	0

Labour restriction: There is a maximum of 10 units of labour available per day. An activity can begin only when the required units are available for that activity. Assume each activity can begin on the earliest start time.

a) By drawing a Gantt chart, show that the project can be completed within the minimum duration time and show how much unused labour there is to spare.   [8]

b) Why might unused labour be a problem for a business?   [4]

Points for Revision

Key Terms

activity	part of a project requiring a set period of time
dummy	an activity which takes zero time and is intended to display the logical dependency with other activities
network diagram	pictorial representation of the project
Earliest Start Time	the earliest time that an activity may commence, given the constraints of the preceding activities
Latest Finish Time	the latest time an activity must be completed, so as to be able to complete the project within the minimum duration time
minimum duration time	the earliest time the project may finish given the order and duration of all the activities
total float	the amount of delay on each activity such that the project is not lengthened
free float	the amount of delay on each activity such that the EST of the following activity is not delayed
critical path	the sequence of activities, which, if delayed, will result in a lengthening of the minimum duration
Gantt chart	a method of charting the sequence of events which can be combined with resource requirements

Definitions Question:

By referring to a business you know, explain the importance of any two of the above (your teacher may wish to help you choose).   [5] per definition

Summary Points:

1 Critical path analysis is used in the planning and execution of projects.

2 Such projects display certain key characteristics of logical dependency, deadlines and the need for resource allocation.

3 A network diagram is used to represent the order and timing of activities.

4 Float (both free and total) can be used to identify those activities which cannot be delayed without delaying ensuing activities.

Mini Case Study

Sell-It plc is trying to capture a larger share of the market by planning an aggressive advertising campaign. There are several tasks which need to be completed before the advertising campaign can be shown on television. These activities have been given letters (*see below*).

Activity	Description	Preceded by	Duration (weeks)
A	market research	–	3
B	collation and presentation of data	A	1
C	planning format of advert with advertising agency	B	2
D	filming advert	C	3
E	buying TV slots with ITV	C	1
F	control and review using panels	D and E	1

1 Define: advertising campaign, presentation of data.   [4]

2 Explain why critical path analysis can be applied to this particular project.   [4]

3 a) Draw the network and for each activity calculate

   (i) total float

   (ii) free float

   b) What is the minimum duration for the project?

   c) Identify the critical path.   [7]

4 How can the calculations in question 3 help the business?   [5]

20

Maxi Case Study

Tettenhall College is an independent school located on the edge of Wolverhampton. It is a coeducational school with day pupils and boarders, the latter representing about a quarter of the school roll. It was founded in 1863 by some local businessmen and has subsequently prospered by keeping abreast of the needs of its customers.

Several years ago it built a girls' boarding house in response to a researched need for boarding places for a growing number of parents who were keen to place their daughters in a caring environment with modern facilities.

Once the tenders to build the boarding house had been assessed and the contract awarded, the local builder, Harold Fidler Ltd, prepared a list of activities and durations which had to be completed (see below).

However, the builder wanted to find out if any of the activities needed careful scrutiny to ensure that the completion of the project was not put in jeopardy. The table was unable to show this in sufficient detail. Consequently a network diagram was necessary to highlight which activities were critical to the project.

Activities	Description	Preceded by	Duration (days)
A	Lay foundations and build structure	–	80
B	Build stairs	A	30
C	Build roof	A	40
D	Windows	A	8
E	Plasterer	A	70
F	Carpenter	BCDE	70
G	Electrician	BCDE	84
H	Heating	BCDE	70
J	Plumbing	BCDE	63
K	Floor covering	FGHJ	28
L	Decorator	FGHJ	35

Which activities were able to take place concurrently and which had to be completed prior to others starting is shown in Figure 31.19:

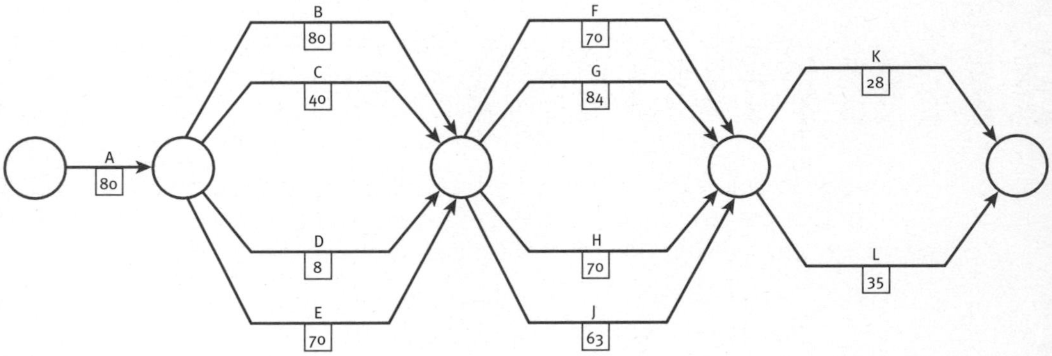

Figure 31.19

A similar process was contemplated for a new nursery and prep school to be built within the existing grounds of Tettenhall College. The idea was to sell the site of the prep school, which was located about half a mile away.

The architects, Alan Cotterell Practice Limited, drew up a Gantt chart of all the activities prior to the actual construction. The time taken between the design brief being issued and the start of the construction of the building was approximately seven months. The building was completed on time, less than a year later.

1 Define: design brief. [2]

2 a) Copy the network diagram in Figure 31.19 and calculate the earliest start times and latest finish times. [6]

b) State the minimum duration for the project. [1]

c) What is the critical path of the project? [1]

3 a) What other activities, apart from the actual construction, need to be undertaken before the school begins to receive payback for the investment? [3]

b) The actual construction time took up nearly 75% of the entire project. What other activities would have occurred prior to building commencing? [3]

4 Activities F, G and J require a particular skill for their completion. The skill level is required in the first five days of these activities but only one member of the subcontractor's team is qualified to carry out the task. Draw a Gantt chart to demonstrate the use of this skill level in which F, G and J must be carried out, so that the entire project is still finished within the required time. [6]

5 Discuss the likely constraints that would face the architects and the builders before and during the construction of the nursery and prep school (think about the possible stakeholders involved). [8]

30

'Friday afternoon'

End of section test

1 What is the definition of production? [2]
2 Explain the importance of added value for a business making coffee cups. [3]
3 Why is it important for the production department to communicate closely with the marketing department? [2]
4 Why might a business not always locate at the cheapest location? [3]
5 State four factors (other than cost) affecting the location of a business. [4]
6 State two advantages and two disadvantages for a business intending to use computer aided design. [4]
7 How might the work-force be affected when a business uses computer aided manufacture? [2]
8 State the three factors of value analysis. [3]
9 Outline the role of value analysis within a business. [3]
10 Explain, by using an example for each, the difference between job, batch and flow production. [6]
11 State four factors a business might consider when moving from batch to flow production. [4]
12 State the three types of stock held in a manufacturing business. [3]
13 Briefly explain three factors which affect the level of buffer stock held by a business. [3]
14 Explain just-in-time production. [2]

15 Why are suppliers important if a business wishes to adopt just-in-time production? [3]
16 Define quality. [2]
17 Explain why an increase in quality leads to cost savings. [4]
18 What is meant by kaizen? [2]
19 What problems might a business face when introducing lean production? [3]
20 Outline three differences between lean production and the more traditional approach to production. [3]
21 Define total float. [2]
22 Outline three characteristics which make a problem suitable for critical path analysis. [4]
23 What is a Gantt chart? [2]
24 What are the main characteristics of cell production? [4]
25 What is the purpose of the kanban? [2]

75

'Friday afternoon' 1

Mousecroft Ltd manufactures fireworks and orders products to be delivered every two months. Each delivery is for 1000 units and the buffer stock is 100 units.

1 a) How much stock is used per month? [2]
  b) What is the average level of stock? [2]

2 What would be the answers to the above two
questions if, *ceteris paribus*,
  a) delivery was made every month?   [2]
  b) delivery increased to 1600 units per two
     months?   [3]

3 Using the figures for question 1, each unit of
stock has an average value of £5 per unit,
and is sold for an average price of £9.90.
Calculate the profit for a year.   [3]

4 What problems might Mousecroft face when
controlling its stock?   [8]

                                                    ——
                                                    20

'Friday afternoon' 2

Bilder Ltd has been offered a contract for an extension
to an existing plant presently run by Mott-Tech, a
computer manufacturing firm. The project officer for
Bilder has put together a list of activities in the table
below which will allow Bilder to use a network
diagram in the planning of this project.

Table 1

Activity		Time taken	Preceded by
A	Obtaining planning permission	42 days	–
B	Arranging for land to be levelled and foundations laid	5 days	A
C	Foundations built	5 days	B
D	External walls and roof constructed	21 days	C
E	Road connection between extension and old plant built	10 days	A
F	Air conditioning and wiring built in	6 days	D
G	Machinery installed for extension	3 days	E, F
H	Extra stocks ordered and delivered for machinery	4 days	G
J	Labour hired and trained	14 days	A
K	Plant performs first production run	1 day	J, H

The nature of the computer industry is such that any
delay could cost Mott-Tech dear, so Mott-Tech has
offered a bonus of £5,000 for the project to be
completed within 90 days.

1 Outline why the above project is suitable
for critical path analysis.   [3]

2 a) Draw the network and demonstrate
     whether Bilder will be able to earn the
     bonus.   [5]
  b) Calculate total float for all the activities
     within the project.   [5]

3 What happens to the project if
  a) activity F is delayed by 5 days?
  b) activity J is delayed by 10 days?   [4]

4 Would you rather experience a delay in C
or H? Explain your answer.   [3]

5 Discuss how an increase in the pace of
technological change might affect Mott-Tech's
sales and costs.   [10]

                                                    ——
                                                    30

Maxi Case Study

Sachsis is a medium-sized company, located in Northampton, which supplies car manufacturers in Europe with metal parts used in the sub-assembly of chassis. The company produces four different products, one of which is sold to a Swedish company which makes lorries, though Sachsis finds it difficult to achieve economies of scale with this product due to the long change-around time on the press. This is because of the size difference of this product compared with the others. Despite such large contracts for the other three products from the likes of Nissan and Vauxhall, the company's owners attribute this problem to the fierce competition in the early 1990s for contracts which forced prices down and squeezed margins. Although initially they earned a profit margin of only 4%, the company was gradually managing to increase this, aiming for 9% (the industry average) by careful cost control and increased volume.

Over the past five years, the chairman, Mr Andrew, has made continual pleas to the work-force to improve the level of output (with promises of increases in pay) and output has increased from 1 million units to 2 million units; unfortunately, pay increases were not forthcoming because the number of reworks and waste products increased by 35%. The work-force was becoming increasingly uneasy about the owner's growing demands for improvements in output; its argument was that the quality control department (which was housed in a separate building to the main production plant) should be checking the goods and dealing with any problems. According to the union representative, the work-force seemed to be getting the blame for everything, despite achieving what the management wanted. Mr Maurice, the accountant, explained that whilst output, sales and profit had increased, productivity had gone down (see Appendix 1). This meant that margins had to be kept very tight and pay increases had to be avoided at all costs.

At present the company uses batch production which allows large quantities of the same design to be produced: this means the company must store goods until they are required by the car assembly plants. Mr Cordant, the production manager, claims this is a necessity because Nissan and Vauxhall operate a method of just-in-time production and so Sachsis must be able to supply goods at short notice. During last year, the delivery rate to customers of product W was 2,000 per month at £250 per unit and it received materials every two months which were designed to supply two months' production and maintain a buffer stock of 1,000 units. Unfortunately, after six months, demand dropped to 1,000 units per month for the rest of the year. Sachsis was notified well in advance of this change, and reduced its order of materials to 1,000 per month (with the same delivery pattern from its suppliers).

With the growth of Nissan in Europe, the company is considering locating a new production facility somewhere in Europe which will also allow it to bid for a contract to supply European car producers. Mr Andrew has found a location in Turin – an old, run-down warehouse close to the Fiat factory which would require an investment of £5 million in new machinery and repairs to the building. Mrs Andrew, the marketing director, is more concerned that if the business is to create more manufacturing capacity, it should look to expand its own factory to use a flow system which would also cost £5 million. Mr Cordant, however, has just returned from a management seminar on Total Quality Management (TQM) and claims that a new philosophy is required across the entire business to manage quality and output more effectively which will involve the implementation of quality circles. Mr Andrew, on the other hand, simply sees TQM as a management fad rather than something that will benefit the company.

Appendix 1

(£000)	1995	1996	1997	1998	1999
Turnover	8,000	10,000	3,000	14,000	16,000
Operating profit	320	420	600	660	680
Number of employees	30	40	54	60	70

1 Define:

   a) economies of scale

   b) profit margin of only 4%

   c) batch production

   d) just-in-time

   e) buffer stock

   f) quality circles   [12]

2 Using the figures in Appendix 1, provide evidence which demonstrates the change in productivity over the time period.   [8]

3 Discuss the factors of location that Mr Andrew might have considered when examining a site in Turin for a new production facility.   [10]

4 Discuss the factors that the business might consider when deciding to move from batch to flow production.   [12]

5 a) Discuss how the introduction of a Total Quality Management programme might help to solve the company's problems of industrial unrest and decreasing productivity.   [12]

   b) What problems do you foresee in Sachsis's attempt to implement such a system?   [6]

6 a) Using graph paper, draw a stock control chart for the past year of product W. Assume opening stock is 5,000 units.   [6]

   b) From the diagram, establish the average value of stock held for the first six months and the second six months.   [4]

   c) Calculate the cost of financing the average level of stock for the year if the interest rate was 10% per annum for the first quarter of the year and 12% per annum for the remaining three quarters.   [8]

7 Using the case study, demonstrate the importance of other parts of the business to operations management.   [12]

90

Accounting and finance

Introduction to finance

Learning objectives

Having read this unit, students will be able to

1   appreciate the role of finance in business

2   identify the various financial statements used in business

3   understand that the financial sector of a business complements the other parts e.g. marketing, personnel

4   identify the various conventions and principles used in compiling financial statements

Context

One of the most frequently asked questions about a particular business is 'How well is it doing?' Although stakeholders of a business will have different interests in the performance of a business, they will still want a broad picture of the company. Ironically, such a broad picture can never be given because there is no possible way of making a financial statement without further qualification. By being more specific about the nature of the financial information required, a stakeholder can glean information that is far more meaningful. Pizza Express, the resturant business, like every public limited company, publishes an annual report which is for its shareholders and other stakeholders of the business; this provides important financial information for them e.g. the level of profit it has earned, the amount of dividends it has paid out, the amount of revenue it has earned, the value of its assets, the amount of cash flowing through the business or the amount of borrowing undertaken. This represents part of the financial situation of the company. Alternatively, the chairman may want to know the break-even level of one of its new software products, or how the company's overheads are being accounted for, or the monthly cash flow forecast or to assess the budget plans. All to this information is considered under the headings Finance and Accounting.

Definition of finance

Finance is defined as anything that allows the business to operate. This is meant in the broadest sense; running machinery, purchasing materials, investing in a patent, paying the work-force, running an advertising campaign, all need some form of finance in order to happen. Finance can come in various forms depending on what the business needs it for e.g. buying a new piece of machinery is unlikely to require the same type of finance as that which is required to pay wages on a weekly basis. Sometimes the business can generate the finance itself (internally) although on many occasions it will need to rely on external sources. The phrase 'to be financed by' means 'the business will raise the money from' – a frequently used expression in business decisions. Of equal importance is the assessment of how the finance will be used and the return it will make for the business.

Question 1

Divide the following into sources (whether the business is finding/creating finance) or uses (whether the business is using finance).
a) Running down stock i.e. selling it and not replacing it
b) Paying suppliers
c) Being given credit by suppliers (goods are received but are not paid for)
d) Shareholders investing money into a firm
e) Shareholders being paid dividends
f) Selling goods on credit to customers
g) Increasing the amount of money on the overdraft

[7]

Definition of accounting

Accounting terms need to be understood as the majority of company statements use them as if they were everyday language.

In his book *Finance for the non-financial manager* (Thorsons, 1989), John Harrison quotes a famous section from Charles Dickens's *David Copperfield* in which Mr Micawber states:

'Annual income: twenty pounds; annual expenditure: nineteen pounds nineteen and six; result: happiness. Annual income: twenty pounds; annual expenditure: twenty pounds nought and sixpence; result: misery.'

Accounting is the process which allows the business to control its expenditure and focus on profit and cash flow. It is divided into two distinct areas:

■ Financial accounting

This involves reporting to the shareholders of the business in terms of the assets, liabilities, profit and cash for the entire financial year. **Financial accounting** is mainly for external users such as shareholders, suppliers and banks who utilise the annual report. There are several accounting rules which determine the accuracy of **accounts** (*see below*).

■ Management accounting

This focuses on more detailed internal accounts than the above so that a business can analyse its performance internally. This allows the business to:
1   calculate the break-even level of output
2   evaluate the performance of particular departments
3   set clear, definable financial targets
4   monitor cash flow on a monthly basis

Any assessment of longer-term investments can be carried out using cost benefit analysis which is also an internal issue.

Financial accounting, therefore, is about reporting past information about the business, whereas **management accounting** is about running the business in the present and making decisions for the future.

Annual Report

A large amount of financial information can be found within an **annual report**. Every business that is fully quoted on any stock exchange must publish an annual report. Most reports take the same format:

Summary of results – this section provides an overview of the company's results, normally referring to the main numerical areas of interest for the shareholder e.g. dividends and profit

Aims of the company – this is intended to give
readers a feel for the activities and objectives. Recently
businesses have referred to these general statements as
mission statements (*see Unit 7 Objectives and strategy*)

Chairman's statement and report – this
provides an overall synopsis on the company and the
state of the markets it operates in in terms of whether
conditions have worsened or not

Directors' report – this includes a summary of
each part of the business, whether by product, location
or both. It provides a detailed account of investment
plans and reports on the previous year. It also provides
the reader with a summary of accounting policies

Auditor's report – directors are faced with the
problem of producing an analytical opinion on their
own performance, so the law states that an **auditor** must
first check that the accounts represent a 'true and fair
view' of the business at the time they are put together
(which is not necessarily the same as when they are
published). The idea behind this is to protect the
interest of shareholders and potential shareholders

Financial statements and notes to the
accounts – including three statements, all required
by law to appear in the report, which relate to the time
reference of the report itself: profit and loss account,
balance sheet and cash flow statement. The notes
provide more detail of the directors' pay and share
options as well as how each individual figure was
calculated

> ### Task
>
> Look through the annual reports of three companies
> (preferably in different markets) and attempt to find
> the following information:
> - what the business does
> - the stated objectives of the business
> - earnings per share
> - revenue or turnover
> - number of employees in the business
> - the name and salary of the highest paid director

> ### Question 2
>
> a) Which company has the highest paid director ?
>   Is this reflected in the amount of profit or turnover
>   earned for the business? Is it related to the
>   number of employees?   [5]
> b) Should directors' salaries be linked to performance?
>   If so, what criteria would you suggest would be
>   appropriate for determining executives' pay?
>   [5]

Stakeholders

All stakeholders will have an interest in a particular
aspect of the annual report:

Shareholders: the business will be paying
dividends, which normally increase from year to year,
not only to protect the investor against inflation but
also to ensure the dividend increase compares with
competitors'. Shareholders will also wish to see the
profit increasing over a period of time and the business
investing in new assets with a clear, well defined
strategy for growth.

Managers: if the business is profitable, with a strong
cash flow, then they are likely to keep their job.

Customers: if the customer is a sugar buyer for a
supermarket and approaches Tate and Lyle, it will want
to find a statement (possibly in the objectives section)
that it is committed to identification and satisfaction of
customer needs. Similarly end-user customers will wish
to see a clear statement about customers' needs being
satisfied.

Pressure groups: if consumer groups, such as
Which?, identify a business that seems to be making
excessive profit, possibly at the expense of customers,
they will use the report to gather evidence which
supports their case.

Directors: the main way that directors are judged is by increasing the wealth of shareholders. A convincing annual report will obviously be in their interest because it will hopefully encourage present shareholders to maintain their investment in the business, as well as encouraging new shareholders to invest.

Government: the government will want to use an annual report with a view to encouraging foreign companies to locate in the UK. It will also want to see directors being responsible about pay awards; the Cadbury Report on corporate governance made clear rules on communicating correct, relevant financial information in the annual report. The Accounting Standards Board (ASB) also exists to ensure accurate, meaningful accounts are drawn up.

Suppliers: they will wish to see a positive cash flow, and possibly the company making a statement of intent in their objectives with regard to prompt payment of suppliers.

Employees: they will be concerned with their job security and will therefore consider the amount of capital investment and potential cost savings which the company may be aiming to make in the future (because cost savings normally mean redundancies). Unions (*see Pressure groups*) will also want to assess the level of increase in executive salaries to ensure the employees receive the same increase.

Figure 33.1   Stakeholders and their stake

Question 3

Protex manufactures tarpaulin, a canvas made from a special material which is totally wind- and rainproof.

The business has just been hit by a recession in the country it exports to as well as receiving news that its supplier of the material has just been taken over. The resulting drop in sales and profit has led the business to announce redundancies, but not for the senior managers. If you were a newspaper reporter writing an article on this company, identify the principal stakeholders who would be affected by the reduction in sales. What financial information would you wish to extract from the business to place in your article?

[10]

Financial statements

Balance sheet, profit and loss, cash flow statement

Although these financial statements will be considered in more detail later in this section, a firm understanding at this stage will help you later on, when the accounts are analysed.

Balance sheet – shows the 'stock' of assets which the business owns and which is balanced against the amounts of money which the business owes. It applies to a precise point in time (in the title it will state 'as at 31/12/00').

Profit and loss – calculates the surplus (or deficit) of income over all of a company's costs. Income is earned by selling products and costs are deducted which apply to the products sold (such as material costs) or to the accounting period e.g. rent for the year.

The balance sheet is therefore the 'stock' of wealth at a point in time and the profit and loss is the flow of income and expenses during the year which results in the company being either

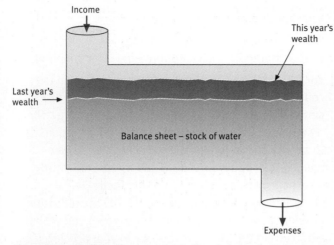

Figure 33.2   Profit and loss represents flow: balance sheet represents stock

a) wealthier (income greater than expenses, in which the case the balance sheet wealth increases, due to profit)

b) poorer (income less than expenses, in which case the balance sheet wealth decreases, due to a loss)

The above analogy represents the balance sheet and profit and loss account. The balance sheet is represented by the stock of water in the tank at one time. This stock is constantly changing, given the fact that income is always flowing into the business (we hope) and expenditure is (unfortunately) always flowing out of the business.

Cash flow – the third and final statement concerns the flow of cash through the business. This is not the same as a cash flow forecast, which represents the predicted cash flow on a short-term basis over a period of time into the future. Rather it is a record of how cash has moved into and out of the business, in broad totals, over the past year.

Accounting principles or concepts

When a business draws up its accounts, there are several rules and regulations which it must follow. This is to ensure some degree of accuracy is maintained as well as common rules between each company. These rules are known as **accounting concepts or principles**.

Matching (or accruals) principle: states that a business must match revenues with costs of goods sold or costs which relate to an accounting period e.g. if a trader purchases 100 paintings at £30 each and sells 40 of them for £60 each, how much profit has been made? There are two versions:

Income = 40 × £60 = £2,400;
expenses = 100 × £30 = £3,000
so loss = £2,400 – £3,000 = £600. This fails to recognise the fact that there will be goods in stock which can be sold in the future and is therefore INCORRECT

The CORRECT version is:
income = 40 × £60 = £2,400;
expenses = 40 × £30 = £1,200
so profit = £2,400 – £1,200 = £1,200.

The business must 'match' against the revenue earned, the cost of the goods which are sold. Those that remain unsold can presumably be sold during the next accounting period. A similar reference to the matching principle is made with depreciation (*see Unit 37 Asset valuation*).

Materiality: when accounts are drawn up, the figures should focus on items which are significant financial matters, rather than those of little or no importance e.g. British Steel will be much more concerned about the value of its plant and equipment than about the stock of paper in the photocopying office. On the other hand, a market trader selling writing paper will be much more concerned about the stock of paper than about the value of the petrol in his van.

Objectivity: when accounts are drawn up, there should be no personal, subjective calculation of values i.e. the asset value of a business must not be calculated based on opinions of directors. The aim is to avoid overvaluing the business, possibly due to the fact that the business is about to be bought by a third party e.g. via a takeover.

This diagram provides an overview of the movement of finance within business. You will find it useful throughout this section.

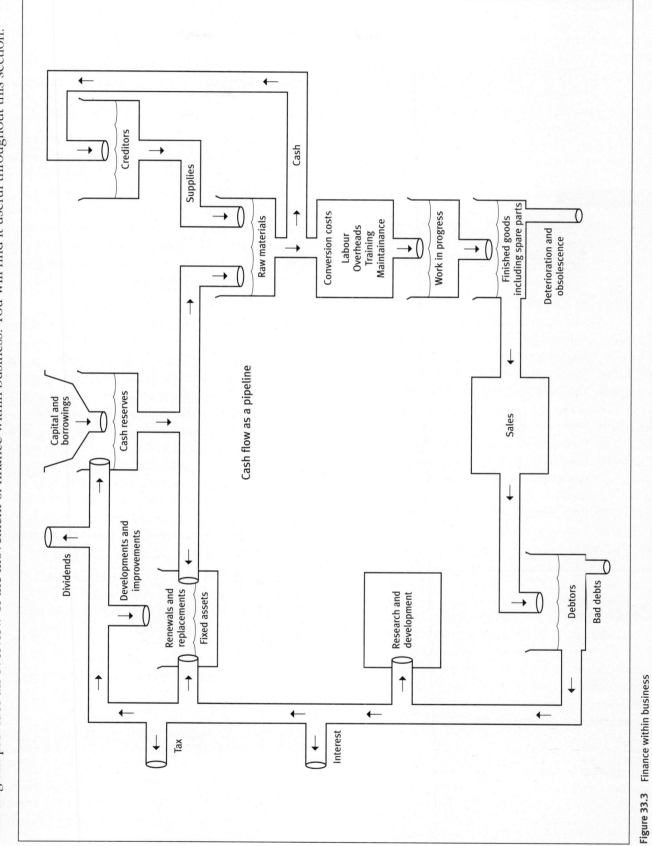

Figure 33.3   Finance within business

Realisation: this states that a sale is recognised when the goods change hands and not when cash is received. Occasionally, e.g. in grocers, newsagents etc. there is a significant amount of cash sales (sales where cash changes hands at the same time as goods). A majority of businesses deal on credit, so the sale is recognised when the ownership of the product passes to the customer. The same principle arises with a business purchasing products from its suppliers.

Question 4

Consider the following set of events and advise when Mr Field should recognise **a)** the purchase of the parts, and **b)** the sale of £2,000. Explain your answer.

1/5/00	Mr Ram sends an order to Mr Field for 200 hole punches at £10 each
3/5/00	Field sends confirmation of receipt of order
4/5/00	Field orders parts from supplier
7/5/00	Supplier despatches them to Field
8/5/00	Field receives parts from supplier and starts work
12/5/00	Ram sends deposit of 10% for hole punches
15/5/00	Field despatches hole punches to Ram
16/5/00	Field sends invoice (a document which requests payment) to Ram, with 30 days' credit
17/5/00	Hole punches arrive at Ram
26/6/00	Ram eventually pays Field

[4]

Consistency: the same assumptions e.g. about asset values must be made clear from one year to the next. If a company changes its depreciation policy in the middle of the life of an asset, it will affect the depreciation charged and therefore profit (*see Unit 37*). The business must therefore be consistent in its application of accounting rules.

Prudence (conservatism): states that when a business draws up the accounts, it presents the worst possible case by valuing its profit at the lowest value e.g. a business reports a profit only when the profit has been earned (*see below*) but if it thinks a customer will

not pay (i.e. the business is doubtful of payment) then it will deduct the value of the money earned immediately. A business will also value its stock at the lowest value (usually the cost).

Question 5

Fill in the blanks with one of the phrases below:

When auditors compile a set of accounts, they must consider several issues which mean that the accounts represent a _____**(a)**_____ of the business, meaning the figures are accurate. For instance, according to the _____**(b)**_____ the business must write of the cost of goods sold only when the products are actually sold. A sale can be recognised only when the goods change hands and not when cash changes hands, an assumption which is covered by the _____**(c)**_____.

The auditors cannot change any of the accounting assumptions without first consulting the shareholders; this is to ensure _____**(d)**_____ of reporting from one year to the next. Sometimes a director will express his or her own opinion on e.g. the value of an asset; the auditor must ignore this, because of the need to show_____**(e)**_____ when drawing up accounts. Auditors must also be aware of _____**(f)**_____, so that the accounts represent matters of financial significance and not those which are trivial e.g. paper clips! Finally, the profit which is stated must be the most pessimistic picture, so as not to overvalue the business; this is done in accordance with the concept of _____**(g)**_____.

realisation principle   true and fair view
window dressing   stakeholders
conservatism/prudence   matching principle
objectivity   materiality   consistency

[4]

Accounting conventions

Over history, there have been several **conventions of accounting** which have been accepted by the accounting world as standard practice when drawing up accounts:

True and fair view

True and fair view – the auditors sign the financial report, by making this statement. Auditors are bound by this claim and there have been occasions in history where auditors have been held responsible for inaccurate information in the balance sheet.

Business entity – the business will always be seen as a separate entity from the wealth of the owners and any assets which belong to the business as separate from those of the owners. Any profit which is earned belongs to the owners, whose wealth is separate from that of the business. Hence the owner will have a business bank account and a personal bank account. In reality, however, some sole traders will purchase a car and use it for private means, whilst writing off the depreciation in order to reduce the tax bill for the business.

Going concern – the business could easily overvalue the assets if it intended to wind itself up (put itself up for sale). The convention of going concern assumes that the business will continue to exist and will not be sold. If it was for sale, then the owner would naturally want to value it as highly as possible so as to secure the maximum price.

Double entry – it is said that Sir Isaac Newton, famous for his laws in physics, produced a law for accountants to follow. This law stated 'for every possible transaction, there is an equal and opposite reaction in the balance sheet!' Double entry bookkeeping means that whatever the financial transaction which takes place, the balance sheet will always balance. The balance sheet is divided into two parts – assets (what the company owns) and liabilities (what the company owes) (*see Unit 36 Balance sheet for more detail*).

Consider the following examples:

a) Stock is bought for £3,000 using cash

Effect: Assets will rise by £3,000 by increasing stock, but cash will fall by £3,000, thereby creating no change to the overall value.

b) A business borrows £5,000 for one year

Effect: Liabilities will rise by £5,000, but assets will also rise by £5,000 because the money will be placed in the business's current account.

c) A business uses cash to pay off a supplier's bill of £4,500

Effect: Cash down £4,500 (assets) and creditors (liabilities) down by £4,500.

d) A business takes out an overdraft of £7,000 to pay a proposed dividend to shareholders

Effect: Liabilities increase by £7,000 (overdraft), and other liabilities decrease by £7,000 (dividend).

Question 6

Taking each transaction separately, express the following in double entry bookkeeping terms, showing as much detail as possible e.g. 'A business raises £10,000 from selling shares' should be represented by:

Assets (cash) up £10,000; liabilities (shareholders) up £10,000

a) Purchase £2,000 of components on credit   [2]

b) Buy a machine for £20,000, 25% with cash, the rest on credit (N.B. there are three changes to be made here)   [3]

c) Borrow £23,000 from the bank   [2]

d) Sell goods worth £5,000 for £7,000 cash (N.B. think carefully about profit and whether it is an asset or a liability)   [3]

How does finance (and accounting) link in with the rest of the business?

Referring back to the definition of finance, there are close links with other parts of a business which must be considered carefully.

Marketing

Advertising campaigns can be costly and budgets which are set by the business must be controlled. If a business fails to meet sales targets, then management must react in some way or other; if the business provides a detailed budget and compares this with the actual results, then action can be taken. Pricing, which is frequently used to gain a competitive advantage, depends on the calculation of average cost (how much the business pays to make and sell one unit) so that the business can make profit for its shareholders and undercut competition. New product development also requires financing and the business will need to consider finance on a long-term basis. Pharmaceutical companies, for example, budget for seven years ahead when developing ground-breaking cures and medicines.

Production

New machinery will require a source of finance to purchase it, or perhaps it will be rented (leased) from the supplier. Expansion in capacity also requires more stock to be purchased, which will in turn place pressure on cash flow.

Personnel

Employees will need to be assured that the business will pay their wages and that it can afford to increase wages in line with inflation. Training schemes also require finance, which will provide the employees with opportunities to develop their skills further.

Points for Revision

Key Terms

finance	anything which allows the business to operate
accounting	the process of recording, reporting and analysing financial information
financial accounting	information collected for the external user e.g. balance sheets
management accounting	information collected for managers to help with decision making
accounts	the actual record of financial information
annual report	the main method of communication with shareholders; required by law for all fully listed companies
auditor	normally an accountant who is responsible for ensuring an objective, true and fair view of the financial position of the business
accounting principles	rules and regulations governing how accounts are drawn up
accounting conventions	traditional ideas behind drawing up accounts

Definitions Question:
By referring to a business you know, choose any three of the above and explain their significance (your teacher may wish to help you with your choice).   [5] per definition

Summary Points:

1. Accounting and finance are very frequently seen as the most important part of a business in terms of analysing the performance objectively.

2. The annual report is a most important document which provides all the financial information which a shareholder or potential shareholder will require.

3. Stakeholders will look for different issues in a set of accounts.

4. There must be continual communication between finance/accounting departments and other areas of the business.

Mini Case Study

John and Flora Peters listened to their accountant, who was also the auditor, as he went through this year's accounts. They set up their boat hire business, Peter Hire, at the end of 1997 as a result of a competitor going out of business and selling off the assets cheaply. The competitor had tried to undercut its own rivals, but had not paid sufficient attention to its costs, resulting in the business being wound up. Once Peter Hire had been established, sales rocketed due to some magnificent sunny weather and an increase in the local tourist trade; so the business had to expand by purchasing 10 boats at a cost of £9,000 each; the purchase was financed by borrowing money. As profits grew, the business expanded by developing the mechanical side of the business and now operates a small, though highly successful, boat repair service.

The profit from last year was £36,000, which had been represented as a liability in the balance sheet: 'But we don't owe it to anyone, it's ours!' John exclaimed. He wanted to take all the money out of the business to spend on his house which was in need of repair. The accountant was trying to explain why he could not do such a thing – 'the money is not available, because profit is only a paper figure and the cash has already been reinvested into machinery for the boat repair business.'

1 Define: auditor, wound up, financed by.   [6]

2 Explain how the financing of boats by borrowing would have been presented in a double entry system.   [3]

3 What problems might the business have faced when opening the boat repair centre?   [4]

4 Why is profit seen as a liability in the accounts?   [3]

5 Explain the final sentence concerning the availability of the profit for John.   [4]

20

Maxi Case Study

Until 1997, the Halifax was the largest building society in Britain. Following a period of consultation with its customers, it decided to float the business on the stock exchange with a view to increasing its access to finance. The reason that customers were invited into the process of consultation was that by its very nature, the Halifax was a mutual society. This meant that when an investor opened an account, the investor became a 'member' of the Halifax and was therefore a part-owner. By deciding to convert the building society to a bank, the Halifax was required to turn the present customers into new shareholders.

This meant offering a certain number of shares, free of charge, to each customer who had held an account for a certain period of time before the flotation was announced. Each adult account holder was offered a certain number of shares according to various criteria stipulated by the Halifax; some customers were offered more shares than others. Typically a customer was offered 200 20-pence shares, although the market price was well over £7.00. Although the share price fluctuated, holding on to the shares for the next 18 months would have resulted in a capital gain.

At the beginning of 1999, following a very successful year when earnings per share grew by 9% and dividends grew by 19%, the bank announced that it was going to redistribute some of its profits back to the shareholders. In a letter to shareholders, the chairman announced 'We have more capital than we currently need and are unable to earn a full return on the surplus.' The idea behind this move was that by restructuring the ownership, the Halifax might be able to increase its return on capital. The proposal was that shares and cash would be handed out to shareholders, directly proportional to the amount of shares already owned. For every 40 shares already owned, the bank offered 37 shares plus 62 pence in cash per ordinary share. Giving back money to shareholders received a mixed reception from various shareholders and customers. Despite the large cash layout, the bank still had excess cash of £1.5 billion.

The pay-out followed a year of intense competition in the mortgage market, which had become less profitable due to lower prices as new companies entered the market. Although the Halifax's total market share stood at 11%, price competition meant it was becoming unprofitable. The Halifax had bought one or two other companies in an attempt to grow – Birmingham Midshires was a small building society whose shareholders received a healthy windfall when the Halifax bought it and Lex vehicle leasing was bought as part of the company's attempts to diversify; the diversified businesses of the Halifax had actually contributed 29% of the group's profit during 1998.

By early 1999, the business had 21 million customers, although not all customers were necessarily jumping for joy following the news; such a large pay-out, coupled with the admission that the business was unable to use the excess cash to generate a sufficient return, may well have dented investors' confidence in the company's ability to invest wisely.

1 Define: return on capital, price competition, windfall. [6]

2 a) Identify the various stakeholders mentioned in the case. [3]

b) Which other stakeholders might have been affected by the Halifax's decision to become a bank? Explain your reasons. [6]

3 What might the Halifax have considered when deciding on the number of shares offered to customers when it floated? [4]

4 By converting customers into shareholders before the restructuring, how might the business have needed to change its financial objectives? [5]

5 If a shareholder owned 400 shares before the restructuring, calculate

a) the number of extra shares receivable [1]

b) the extra value of shares and cash the shareholder would receive if the share price at the time of the restructuring was 875 pence and the shareholder sold them immediately. [2]

6 What might have been the financial consequences of purchasing the two businesses mentioned in the case study? [5]

7 Discuss why there might have been a degree of conflict between the interest of the shareholders and the interest of the customers, following the announcement to hand back £1.5 billion. [8]

Activity

Carry out some research on the offers made by banks and building societies – look for fixed rate schemes, low interest rate starters, cash back facilities. To what extent do the results of your findings support the contention that intense competition exists?

40

Cash flow and working capital

Learning objectives

Having read this unit, students will be able to

1 understand the significance of cash flow in a business as opposed to profit

2 build a cash flow statement with a view to identifying potential cash flow problems

3 understand the importance of working capital in making business decisions

Context

It is tempting to assume that the sole measure of business success is the profit it earns and that more profit means a better business. If a company suddenly received an order which would double its revenue and profit, it would apparently be the most foolhardy managing director who turned down the order. But it is not profit which pays wages or rent, buys materials, and pays dividends to shareholders; it is cash that fulfils these functions. If the said order were not paid for until eight months after the business bought its materials and hired new labour, then the business would need to find cash from somewhere if the order were to be satisfied. The accounting process which recognises profit when the goods change hands (*see previous unit*) provides no help if the cash is not available in the business. Prior to Christmas 1998 and well into the new year of 1999, a pottery business faced uncertainty over whether it would be allowed to continue trading. Stoke Potteries was unable to pay its workers for over six weeks because of a lack of cash. It was a lack of cash that eventually led to the closure of the factory.

Cash is the lifeline, or the petrol of the business; no matter how large the car, if there is no petrol to make it run, it won't go – the same goes for a company. If the car needs to travel faster it will need more petrol, and possibly more repairs and maintenance; if the business wishes to grow, it will require more cash.

Ideally, the cash will be generated within the business, usually from the sale of goods or services; otherwise it will have to be borrowed (*see Unit 40 Sources of finance*).

The importance of cash

Cash is the money which allows the business to operate; without cash, the business will cease, for a variety of reasons:

■ Without cash the business cannot pay its employees, who will look for work elsewhere

■ Suppliers will cease to provide materials

■ Banks will call in loans

■ Shareholders will withdraw their investment if no dividends are paid due to **cash flow** shortages

■ Landlords will evict businesses from rented property

■ Gas, electricity and water supplies will be cut off if the business fails to pay the bills

It is not the profit which pays the bills, but the cash. It is essential that a business has a sufficient amount of cash to enable the day-to-day costs of operating a business to be paid.

Positive and negative cash flow

If the business runs out of cash, it does not necessarily mean it will go 'bust'. A business will always aim to have a positive cash flow i.e. have money in the bank, although when this is not the case, the bank provides an **overdraft**. When a business starts, it will need help from the bank to buy materials, labour etc. without any revenue coming into the accounts. Even when it is operational, there will still be times when it requires an overdraft. The overdraft is an agreement that the business can use money from the bank which does not belong to the business itself. The bank will usually set a limit on the overdraft and will charge interest if the overdraft is used.

In Figure 34.1, cash flows in and out of the overdraft. If the business thinks it may need a bigger overdraft, then it must approach the bank for permission to withdraw more money. The authorised overdraft can then be extended if the bank deems it fit to do so; if the

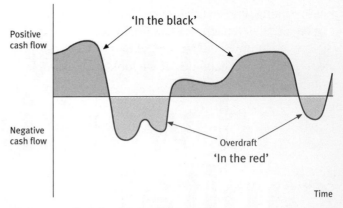

Figure 34.1   Cash flow in a business over time

business uses the unauthorised overdraft without permission, the interest rate rises significantly. Every business, at some stage in its life, relies on an overdraft as a form of lifeline for the future of the business. In fact, if you talk to any business people about finance, it is likely that they will have continual reliance on an overdraft.

Question 1

When a bank is approached by a business for an overdraft, what specific information will the bank manager require before making the decision to grant the request?   [6]

Working capital and its implication for cash flow

Working capital allows the business to operate on a day-to-day basis. Working capital therefore involves the money required to buy materials and components, pay for labour, pay the rent, pay for supplies of electricity etc. Cash is obviously required to purchase machinery, but the business must also invest money in the running of the business. A doubling of sales may not simply require a doubling of the machinery to produce that output, but also twice as much money tied up in stocks, debtors (because there will be twice the amount of customers, in terms of value). This will be partially offset by a doubling of creditors (which is advantageous because the business keeps the money in its own bank until it has to pay the creditor).

In accounting terms working capital (net current assets) can be calculated using the balance sheet (*see Unit 36*), by looking at how much money is tied up in current assets and current liabilities. If we look at an example from a set of accounts:

Stock   = £40,000
Debtors   = £30,000 +
Cash   = £10,000 +
_____
                   £80,000
Creditors = £50,000 –

Net current assets = £30,000

The business has £80,000 'tied up' in current assets, which is partially offset by the money tied up in creditors. This represents money which the business owes but is yet to pay, so there will be working capital of £30,000. As more money is tied up in working capital, it presents potential problems for cash flow, because the money is not actually earning anything for the business until the products are sold and cash is received i.e. when stock is turned into debtors, which is then turned into cash. The business can then pay its bills and reinvest the profit in more stock, or other assets. In the above example, only £10,000 in cash is available to pay bills. The working capital cycle is represented in Figure 34.2.

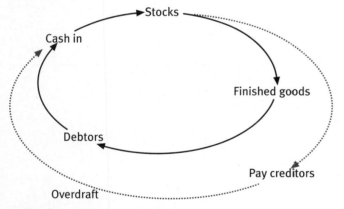

Figure 34.2   The working capital cycle

The business will always aim to achieve a fast turnover of stock, debtors and cash, meaning the quicker the business turns raw materials into finished goods, sells the goods and gets the customer to pay, the quicker the business can earn profit. In addition the less time it has money tied up in parts of the business which are not actually earning profit, the better.

The longer a product stays in storage, the less efficient the company; the longer the debtors take to pay, the less able the company is to reinvest the cash. Any attempt to minimise the working capital cycle is likely to result in a more efficient company.

Costs of holding too much cash

It is possible, however, to have too much cash in a business. If you were planning to go on holiday in July and it was only March, would you draw out from your savings the money you required as spending money immediately? Probably not. Ask yourself why.

If a business were to have too much cash the consequences might well be:

- **Loss of interest** – although there may be a token amount of interest earned on current accounts, it will be nowhere near the interest rate for longer-term accounts

- **Loss of purchasing power** – unless the rate of interest is more than the rate of inflation, the money held in a bank account will actually lose its purchasing power i.e. over a period of time the business will be able to buy less with the same amount of cash due to a continual increase in prices (inflation)

- **Opportunity costs** – shareholders do not invest money in a business for the business to store it in a bank account. Shareholders expect a business to take well managed risks with their money; if the money is in a bank account, the business is possibly risk-averse (i.e. unwilling to take risks) and the shareholder may remove the investment. Analysts in the City do tend to view businesses which pile up cash as less likely to make an acceptable return. Alternatively, the cash could have been used to purchase an additional machine or replace an old machine, which would increase the productive capacity of the business

Costs of holding too little cash

■ **Inability to meet creditors' demands** – when suppliers require cash payment for goods, lack of payment or consistent late payment could well result in a company losing its credit facility

■ **Need to borrow at expensive rates** – overdrafts, especially those which are unauthorised, are expensive in terms of interest. Insufficient cash will mean the business will come to rely on an overdraft (*see Figure 34.3*).

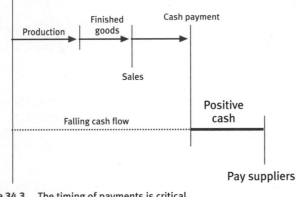

Figure 34.3   The timing of payments is critical

Causes of cash flow problems

■ **Overtrading** – if a business grows too quickly, then it will need to buy materials and machinery for a production level which is much higher than the cash which is coming in from sales. Such a fast rate of expansion can frequently lead to companies being wound up because of their inability to pay creditors

■ **Holding too much stock** – a business may well pile up stock, especially if it thinks prices have temporarily fallen to an unusually low level. Alternatively, a supplier may be winding up the business and selling off stock at a huge loss

■ **High borrowing (therefore high interest payments)** – when a business overtrades it frequently needs to borrow money to finance both fixed and working capital, because the cash from sales is insufficient to meet its expansion plans

■ **Allowing too many goods to be bought on credit** – this is frequently used as a method of promotion. Unfortunately, as credit periods lengthen it is possible to concentrate too much on sales as opposed to getting the cash in

■ **Businesses that rely on seasonal trade** – during the time that sales are very low, cash still needs to be spent on running the business. Such an outfit will then experience a sudden rush of cash flow during the period of sales

■ **High unemployment** – leading to lack of demand for products and less revenue and cash

---

Question 2

a) Draw the projected cash flow for a business that manufactures
 i) fireworks
 ii) Christmas crackers   [5]

b) Which product do you think has a more pronounced seasonal pattern?   [2]

Methods of improving cash flow

A controlled, manageable and sustainable level of growth is likely to create a positive cash flow – this is idealistic because a business is very unlikely to refuse orders because they are over the sales targets. However, if the business is growing, looking for further orders may not be wise, given the pressure on cash flow from **overtrading**.

Stock: the longer a product stays in storage, the less efficient the company; the longer the debtors take to pay, the less able the company is to reinvest the cash. A fast turnover of debtors can also be achieved by factoring the debtors (*see Unit 40 Sources of finance*).

Debtors: reducing the credit period given to customers. This cannot be done without close negotiation with customers, especially if the business has only a few major customers. The business may well have to offer a discount to encourage prompt payment. In such instances, it will need to balance profit with cash i.e. cash flow is ensured, although profit is reduced. A business must use careful **credit control** when it is considering giving credit to customers. Credit control involves the monitoring of a customer's credit rating as well as the decision making process at the outset to determine the length of credit appropriate for a particular customer

Creditors: increasing the time it takes to pay creditors requires understanding suppliers, and the business may well lose out on a discount which has been offered by the supplier for prompt payment

Dropping prices: although an obvious idea, this ought to generate greater revenue, although the credit terms will also be significant in this respect. Extra sales are of little value unless the money comes in.

Leasing as opposed to buying: when a business wants to keep cash within the business, it may choose to lease assets, thereby not needing to find the principal sum for outright purchase.

Subcontraction: instead of paying the work-force a regular weekly wage, the business may decide to contract out work to a company which will allow a generous credit period (e.g. three months)

Selling fixed or idle assets: only those assets which are earning money for a business should be kept. Sometimes a business will sell its headquarters and move into rented accommodation in order to improve cash flow

---

Question 3

Ice-It, an ice-cream manufacturer, invented a new product, Cream X, two years ago. Initially it sold well and the growth stage of the product life cycle meant the business made profit almost immediately, although the cash flow was the opposite story (*see Figure 34.4*). Recent attempts to revive the product have met with some success, although last week, the business decided to drop the new product altogether.

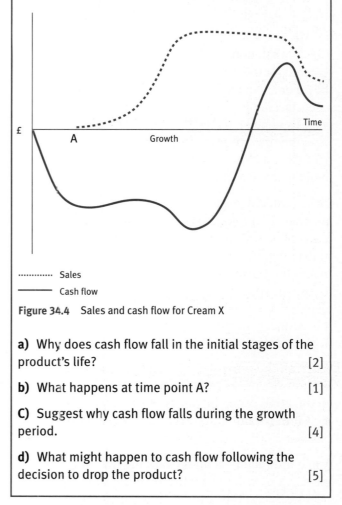

.... Sales
———— Cash flow

Figure 34.4   Sales and cash flow for Cream X

a) Why does cash flow fall in the initial stages of the product's life? [2]

b) What happens at time point A? [1]

C) Suggest why cash flow falls during the growth period. [4]

d) What might happen to cash flow following the decision to drop the product? [5]

Cash versus profit

Surprisingly a successful company, one that is expanding rapidly, may fall into the trap of failing to ensure it has enough cash or liquid assets.

In its desire to expand, any profits are quickly ploughed back into the business in the form of new machines and an extension to the factory, both fixed assets.

Yet, extra employees and more materials require cash. It would be of little use telling the work-force that unfortunately there is no money to pay wages because the business has bought a new machine. The business has the assets, but they are tied up in the machines and the factory extension, neither of which can be quickly converted into cash.

The only solution would be to borrow the cash required for the wages, which would be costly. If, on the other hand, the business kept a large amount of its assets in a liquid form to ensure that it could pay its wages and buy the raw materials and other day-to-day expenses, this would mean that there would be little left to invest in machines to make goods, which bring in the revenue to make a profit.

There is an old adage in business which says 'profit is a matter of opinion, cash is a matter of fact'. In terms of its use to the business, cash is fundamentally different to profit. Profit is what makes the business grow and is calculated according to a set of specific accounting rules. If the rules are changed, then the profit may change, even though the business may have spent the same amount of money and received the same revenue.

Cash, on the other hand, is the most liquid asset the business has at its disposal and can be used to pay all the costs of the business. It can also be seen as a measure of value in terms of the revenue of the business.

A major difficulty is understanding that different transactions will have differing effects on the levels of cash or liquidity and profit within a business.

Read 1–5, and then examine Table 1 below, which summarises the effect of each transaction on cash and profit separately:

1 If a local shop buys a new display unit (a fixed asset) with cash for £1,000, the liquidity within the business has fallen. There will be no immediate effect upon the level of profit made by the business. It is hoped that the new display unit will help to encourage impulse buying by its customers as a result of the goods being displayed more effectively, thus leading to a higher level of sales and therefore more profit. But the increase in profit does not happen straight away, nor is any increase guaranteed. Yet the fall in the level of cash within the business does happen, and straight away!

2 When a business raises money e.g. £10,000 either from extra shares or from an extra loan, the cash or liquidity of the business will increase by that amount (albeit temporarily, on the basis it is borrowed for a particular reason) although this will not be recognised in the profit and loss account as increasing revenue or profit, because both of these are capital items.

3 If a business sells products on credit for a profit of £3,000, the profit will be recognised, because the goods have changed hands, but the cash will not change until the goods have been paid for by the customer. The cash has yet to flow into the business.

4 When wages of £500 are paid, cash and profit are reduced by the same amount.

5 When a business makes an allowance for depreciation of £300 in the profit and loss account, cash will not flow out of the business, but the profit will fall. The extent to which this occurs will depend upon which method of calculating depreciation is used (*see Unit 37 Asset valuation*).

Table 1   Effect on cash and profit of different transactions

	Effect on cash	Effect on profit
1	−£1,000	none
2	£10,000	none
3	none	£3,000
4	−£500	−£500
5	none	−£300

Finally, when tax and dividends are calculated, the profit will fall because they are each separate costs which must be accounted for during a particular accounting period, although it will be some time after the accounting period that the business actually pays for those items.

If a business has a constant stream of orders, from reliable customers, then cash flow becomes much easier to manage. It also helps if there is a close link with suppliers when negotiating payment terms, but

Question 4

Quick-Grow plc has recently invested heavily in new plant and machinery for its range of gardening implements. It has received three large orders which meant overtime had to be paid and a new material supplier had to be found requiring payment within 30 days of each delivery, although the three large orders were sold primarily on long credit periods of 90 days. Extra storage was also required for the work-in-progress while the business awaited delivery of one particular component. All the necessary factors of production were assembled within two weeks of receiving the order and it took only three further weeks to complete.

The managing director was delighted with the new orders given that it would use the new capacity to good effect and the delivery had gone out on time to all three customers. Unfortunately, the bank manager had telephoned that morning to invite the MD in to discuss the mounting overdraft which the company had had to use.

Explain why the business has made a profit and yet is facing an overdraft.

[8]

the stream of regular cash payments is of prime concern to any business. If, however, the business faces irregular demand, or the pattern of orders fluctuates widely, or perhaps the business is highly seasonal, then there will be times when cash flow becomes a major concern.

It also becomes a major focus for the company's attention when there are several payment schedules e.g. customers require monthly delivery, and will pay in instalments, two months after delivery; materials will need to be bought in the month before production, and paid for with a 10% deposit and the rest one month after delivery. Overheads may be paid monthly or quarterly, or both, and the employees require regular monthly salary cheques. Hence the need for a format which will show the prediction of cash flow, to identify the times when cash flow will be negative so the bank might be approached to arrange an overdraft.

Cash flow forecasts

As the unit has explained, if the business can ensure there is sufficient cash flowing in to cover the day-to-day expenses of running the business then it is more likely to survive and prosper.

Therefore it is wise to plan ahead by preparing a **cash flow forecast**. This will provide a visual and easy-to-understand check of the cash flows in and out of the business. It should provide the opportunity to predict the times when there may be problems, where more cash is flowing out than is flowing in (negative cash flow).

Tim and Emma Elms were planning the launch of their new business venture, selling perfumes and after-shaves on a party plan basis.

The Smell-It Company was planning to start trading in the next few months and had been advised to provide the bank with a cash flow forecast (see Table 2):

Table 2

	Sept	Oct	Nov	Dec
Inflows				
Opening balance	0	4350	575	(2850)
Savings	2000	0	0	0
Bank loan	5000	0	0	0
Sales	0	500	2000	3000
Total inflows	7000	4850	2575	150
Outflows				
Expenses				
Purchases of stock	500	3000	3000	3000
Wages	2000	2000	2000	2000
Interest	0	275	275	275
Overheads	150	150	150	150
Total outflows	2650	5425	5425	5425
Closing balance	4350	575	(2850)	(5275)

Looking at the above there are several points of interest:

- Although sales are predicted to rise quickly, an insufficient amount of cash is generated to meet the major outflows, such as materials and wages.

- A visual representation of the figures enables the reader to assess when the main problem times are going to be and where remedies may be found. Perhaps it may be wise at an early stage of the business to pay themselves less or purchase less stock.

- It highlights how quickly a business can utilise cash, even when the initial amount appears to be sufficient.

- Ways of 'delaying' payment for stock (buying on trade credit) may help to reduce the outflows.

- It highlights that the start-up capital is insufficient.

- It may indicate that the business is not going to be viable – note the time of the year. If insufficient cash is generated during its best selling period, namely Christmas, it is quite likely that the lack of cash will worsen in periods of low sales.

Question 5

Using the information provided in the cash flow forecast in Table 2:

a) suggest with reasons whether Tim and Emma would be wise to launch the business. [5]

b) suggest whether the bank would be likely to provide a loan for Tim and Emma's proposed business. [5]

c) assume the sales figures had been badly underestimated and ought to be double all the sales figures quoted and that they had omitted to include a quarterly phone bill estimated at £50, to start at the beginning of September. Prepare a new cash flow forecast for the business. [10]

Question 6

Rate plc has just delivered an order for 20,000 packaging units, to be sold to Sony for its hi-fi products. The price of each unit was £6, with material cost of £2, labour of £1 and variable overheads of £1. In addition there was a design cost of £5,000, which is due in 30 days' time. The payment schedule for the costs and revenue is as follows:

Money received from Sony – 90 days from now
Money paid to suppliers   – 30 days from now
Money paid to labour   – end of the week
Variable overheads   – 60 days from now

The business is due to receive an initial payment of £10,000 from Sony at the end of the week.

a) Calculate the profit from the order. [2]

b) Calculate the cash flow for the order
   i)   at the end of the week
   ii) 30 days from now
   iii) 60 days from now
   iv) 90 days from now [8]

Question 7

The following information was extracted from a computer file for Spec-It, a manufacturer of glasses frames.

	Jan	Feb	Mar	Apr
Sales	30000	50000	60000	50000
Cash in from sales on credit	10000	12000	15000	25000
Cash sales	15000	25000	30000	25000
Materials	9600	12000	20000	24000

50% of sales were for cash, the rest on credit.

a) How many months' credit was given to customers? [1]

b) Calculate the amount of debtors for the end of April. [3]

c) If materials were bought on one month's credit, calculate how much was owing to suppliers at the end of April. [3]

d) Calculate the total sales value for the previous December. [2]

Points for Revision

Key Terms

cash flow	the amount of liquid assets (cash) moving in and out of the business
overdraft	when a business draws out more from the bank than it owns (both authorised, when the overdraft has been agreed, and unauthorised when it has not)
working capital	the finance required to run the business on a day-to-day basis
overtrading	rapid expansion which normally results in a strain on cash flow
credit control	the process of monitoring debtors to reduce pressure on cash flow
cash flow forecast	predicting likely movement of cash in and out of the business

Definitions Question:

By referring to a business you know, explain the importance of any three of the above terms (your teacher may wish to select the terms).   [5] per definition

Summary Points:

1   A business must be able to generate cash in order to operate.

2   Occasionally a business will sacrifice the pursuit of profit in favour of generating cash flow.

3   There are several factors which cause cash flow problems; many can be alleviated with careful attention to the components of the business's working capital.

4   A cash flow forecast is used to predict the cash position, with a view to approaching a bank for finance.

Mini Case Study

Hugh Peach set up Y2K computers in 1997 when he realised that the forecast impact of the millennium bug was more significant than the government was suggesting at the time. The problem of the Y2K bug, as it was called, concerned the conversion of the dates on computers from 99 (meaning 1999) to 00 (intending to mean 2000, although it was predicted that computer systems would read this as 1900!) The problems that were predicted to occur were expected to wreak havoc across the technological world. This prompted Hugh to create a piece of software which would solve the problem. The software would be inserted in a CD-ROM drive and would retail at a modest £100. Despite a cautious approach by potential customers in the first couple of months, he received a major order from a large county council, which ordered 400 of the CDs in one go (ordering one CD and loading it on to 400 computers was strictly against the law.)

Details of the costs were as follows:

Material costs: £5 per unit, bought during the month of production, for cash.

Labour costs: £40 per unit, paid one month after production.

Overheads: £3,000 per month, paid during the month of production, for this particular order.

Depreciation on Hugh's computer as a result of this order: £500.

The first delivery was to be made during July 1999, with subsequent deliveries of 100 per month. Payment was to be made in two equal credit instalments in September and November. Production was to be carried out during the same month as delivery i.e. goods were delivered immediately once a batch of 100 CDs had been produced.

1 Define the following terms: overheads, credit.   [4]

2 What is the advantage to Hugh of delivering immediately following production?   [4]

3 Calculate the profit that Hugh could earn from the county council order.   [3]

4 Using the following table, build a cash flow forecast for the order.   [8]

	July	August	September	October	November
Sales					
Cash in					
Materials					
Labour					
Overheads					
Cash out					
Opening balance	£3,000				
Surplus					
Closing balance					

5 What is the maximum level of overdraft required for this order?   [1]

20

Maxi Case Study

'How much?' asked Nick, in astonishment. 'Well over £10,000 above your present limit' came the calm answer from the bank manager. 'But I can't turn down a £20,000 order!' He was beginning to feel that running a business was not as exciting as he had originally thought as his mind went back to only six months before when he had started the business.

Nick Lindy and John Close began their business in late 1999, following an inspirational idea that was based on an observation made by Nick when he was on a skiing holiday in Scotland. Having spent three days hurtling down hillsides either on skis or on a sledge with his three-year-old son, he was putting the suitcases on to his roof-rack when he realised that the roof-rack was designed in a similar way to the sledge he had hired at a cost of £15 per day. Although the cost of hiring the sledge was much less than that of hiring skis, the sledges were probably manufactured at a cost of £40–£50, so the hiring business was making a great deal of money. With roof-racks retailing at £80 plus fitting he felt that there was an opportunity to sell a product to those people who wanted to go sledging whilst on holiday, but whose cars were too small for the sledging kit.

The two partners began a process of new product development by visiting various car dealers to gauge opinion on the new product; this allowed them to modify their original designs so that the manufacturing would be made easier.

Nick handled all the finance and marketing issues, so he was the first one to identify the need for long-term capital. So he set off to the bank, with a business plan in his briefcase, to persuade the bank to lend the business some money. The bank was interested in his ideas and granted them a loan of £10,000 to begin with, although it did make it clear that an overdraft facility would be needed as well, so this was set at a limit of £4,000. Although orders came in slowly in the first six months, this was to be expected given the seasonal nature of demand. The sudden change in their fortunes came when they received an order for 240 Slookies (the name was derived from sledge and roof-rack) from Parker and Slate, a motor car retailer which had heard of the products from a customer and wanted to supply the Slookies ready fitted.

Parker and Slate was willing to pay a price of £80 per unit, but would pay in full only once the order was complete. John estimated that it would take three months to manufacture the 240 Slookies, although payment was required for materials, labour and overheads well in advance of the cash being paid from Parker and Slate.

The materials would be bought during the month of production, although the business had negotiated one month's credit with the supplier. Labour had to be paid during the month of production and fixed costs had to be paid at the end of October. The Slookies were delivered in the month following production of each batch of 80 units and production was scheduled to begin in July. The order was profitable and with some casual labour, the business could just about meet the deadline. Before he accepted the order, Nick went to see their bank manager to ensure that they had not overlooked anything of significance. Looking at the size of the overdraft required, he was beginning to regret the visit.

'Don't worry,' the bank manager assured him. 'I think there may be one or two solutions to this.'

Table 3

	July	August	September	October	November
Production	80	80	80		
Cash in					£19,200
Materials @ £25 per unit		£2,000	£2,000	£2,000	
Labour @ £20 per unit	£1,600	£1,600	£1,600		
Fixed costs				£5,000	
Opening balance	£1,000	−£600	−£4,200	−£7,800	−£14,800
Surplus/deficit	−£1,600	−£3,600	−£3,600	−£7,000	£19,200
Closing balance	−£600	−£4,200	−£7,800	−£14,800	£4,400

1 Define: business plan, casual labour, surplus/deficit.   [6]

2 What problems might occur in a business where one person oversees marketing and production?   [4]

3 a) How much profit does this order earn for the business?   [3]

   b) Calculate by how much the overdraft required for this order exceeds the pre-arranged limit.   [1]

   c) What do the answers to a) and b) tell the business about the significance of cash and profit when taking decisions?   [4]

4 The bank manager proposes two solutions:

   a) Ask Parker and Slate for monthly payment, one month after each delivery

   b) Take out a short-term bank loan for the difference between the present overdraft and the required overdraft

   Analyse both solutions for The Slookie Company.   [12]

5 Discuss the possible stock control problems within The Slookie Company that might arise from seasonal production.   [10]

40

Profit and loss account

Learning objectives

Having read this unit, students will be able to

1 recognise and distinguish between the various sections of the profit and loss account

2 understand the importance of profit for the business and its stakeholders

3 remind themselves of the distinction between cash and profit

4 be able to analyse the key issues within a profit and loss account

Context

Businesses are always keen to show both prospective and existing shareholders that more profit has been made. Most company reports will within the first few pages present 'soundbites' referring to profitability in some form. Almost all annual reports will feature extracts from the profit and loss account. These extracts are quoted as an instant guide to the success or otherwise of the business.

The report and accounts of Unigate plc 1998 stated, 'Unigate has increased its profit for the seventh year in succession. Operating profit rose by 11.7 per cent to £138.9 million, and profit before tax was up by 13.0 per cent........ The Board is recommending a final dividend of 14.5p, raising the total dividend for the year to 22.0p a share.'

What is the significance of these figures? How are they calculated? The answer to these questions can be found by studying the profit and loss account.

Once the figures are understood, a useful insight into the business is gained. It will then be possible to comment on the performance of the business, to analyse the various sections of the account and to understand the factors that affect the figures in the P&L account.

What is profit?

- **Profit** is the return on the enterprise factor of production, a reward to the entrepreneur for his or her endeavours.

- Profit is one of the main reasons why individuals start a business.

- Profit is essential if a business is to thrive and prosper. It is essential for the growth of the business; it allows the business to purchase new machinery to compete in the market-place, to take advantage of any economic upturn or other favourable market conditions.

- Profit can be a source of income for investors in the business, for example shareholders or, indirectly, members of the public who subscribe to a pension fund. It can also be an additional source of income to the employees of a business who have a profit-sharing scheme and consequently have an interest in the level of profit made by the business.

- Profit is used as a measure of performance, as mentioned in the 'context' section of this unit. It can be used as a tool by the business to ascertain if management policies have been successful.

- Profit is used by prospective lenders to the business as a means of telling whether a potential loan will be paid back.

The numbers

The figures issued are normally for a particular period of time, the trading period, which is usually one year.

In its simplest format, profit is calculated by subtracting the costs of the business from the revenue (**turnover**) it receives. The difference is the profit. If, however, the level of sales is exceeded by costs then a loss is incurred.

Normally, the profit and loss account is prepared on an annual basis, though such accounts can be issued at more frequent intervals. Plcs issue an interim report (half-yearly). A study of company reports will show

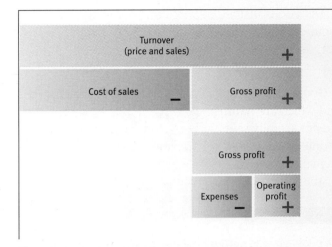

Figure 35.1 Gross profit and operating profit

that there are many ways to present these accounts, but there are certain aspects that are standard to all:

Turnover or sales revenue

This figure is the main source of income for the business; the value of the goods or services sold is obtained by multiplying the sales volume by the price of those goods. The value of the sales revenue will normally be the largest figure in the accounts. From then on that amount appears to get smaller and smaller!

Care has to be taken to ensure that this figure is realistic. If the amount is inflated for any reason, then a false picture will be given and consequently the level of profit will be inaccurate. The price that the goods are sold for may include taxes that the government of the day has imposed.

For example, VAT, excise duties, customs duties may have been 'added' to the price of the goods and therefore ought to be subtracted if a realistic value of sales is to be used (selling price minus taxes equals factor price). It is the price of the goods without the tax that is the value that businesses have to use when calculating the sales or turnover. If possible, have a look at the accounts of Tesco or Sainsbury; both provide figures with and without VAT.

There are other factors that have to be borne in mind when calculating the turnover:

1 Any goods that are returned under guarantee or not required for any reason ought not to be included because in reality the good has not been sold. A sale was made but has been subsequently cancelled.

2 Goods that are 'sold' on the basis of sale or return and which are returned, as with the previous example, are not actually sales and therefore ought not to be counted. This is a common practice for certain elements of the retail sector, which sell to private customers for special functions.

Question 1

A business has earned revenue of £67,000, although just before it sends the accounts off to the tax office, it notices two items which need to be dealt with:

1 £3,000 of goods returned by a customer due to an error (the wrong colour has been sent to the customer)

2 An extra £2,500 cash receipt which was paid on an invoice issued the year before.

How, if at all, do these items affect the sales revenue?

[4]

Cost of sales

This figure refers to the cost of producing the goods – all direct costs such as the raw materials that are required, the labour costs of those on the production lines and, in addition, any of the overheads that are directly related to the production process. These overheads are referred to as production overheads. Subtracting the **cost of sales** from the turnover will give the figure for the **gross profit**.

Plant-It Ltd
Profit and Loss Account year ending 31 December 1999

£	
Turnover	700,000
(minus/less)	
Cost of sales	250,000
Gross profit	450,000

Remembering that the P&L account represents the trading activity of the business within a stated period of time, it is important to ensure that there is no information that belongs to a previous trading period.

The cost of sales includes the cost of the stock that the business has purchased. There may be instances when stock that was purchased in the previous trading period is sold in the following year. This would give an inflated level of gross profit. The cost of the stock would have been counted in year 1 and the sales revenue would be counted in year 2, hardly an accurate portrayal of the business's activities. This situation can be avoided by a careful adjustment.

Supposing Plant-It Ltd, a retailer of pot plants, started the financial year with plants that it had purchased last year (1999) with a value of £52,000. During the present trading year (2000), it purchased additional stock valued at £308,000 and at the end of the year had stock left to the value of £110,000. Assessing the real value of the sales within the trading period (the year 2000) can be calculated as follows:

Cost of sales allowing for stock adjustments

Opening stock 1.1.00	£52,000
Stock purchases during 2000	£308,000
Goods available	£360,000
Less closing stock	£110,000
Cost of sales 31.12.00	£250,000

The figure of £250,000 gives a true picture as to the value of the cost of sales that ought to be included.

Similarly, it is important to understand that a true picture of what trade has taken place within the trading or account period will be gained only by being aware of what is and what is not counted.

Profit that is calculated for a given period of time must include the value of the sales that have occurred within the same period of time. Once a product has been delivered to the customer, it is counted as a sale regardless of whether payment has been received. However if a product has been manufactured but not sold it is not included. This should fit with the previous explanation of cost of sales and stock.

Further deductions (**expenses**) are made to cover the costs of the other overheads or fixed costs that are not directly involved with the production of the goods.

These will include such items as marketing expenses, administrative costs including the wages of the administration and marketing, electricity and depreciation. Whenever you look at a P&L account of a business, it is quite likely that all these items are listed under the umbrella term expenses. However, details of the above will normally be given within the notes to the accounts at the back of the company report.

Gross profit minus expenses equals the **operating profit** (*see Figure 35.1*).

Question 2

Which of the following costs will appear in the cost of sales and which in the expenses?
  i) advertising
  ii) packaging wrappers for each product
  iii) depreciation
  iv) raw materials   [4]

At this stage, consideration can be given to any other revenue the business may earn which has not been earned as the result of sales.

This may include:

Rent, interest and dividends

These items are collectively referred to as **non-operating income**. Rent may be earned from property owned by the business; interest earned from any cash held on deposit; and dividends from shares held in other companies.

The values of these non-operating income items are **added**. Any payments of interest are listed separately at this point (even though this is an overhead) and **subtracted**. Listing separately the interest paid is helpful when it comes to calculating the interest cover ratio. If it was just included amongst the other overheads such a calculation would be quite difficult (*see Unit 38 Ratio analysis*).

Now the P&L account will look like this:

Year ending 31 December 1999

£

Turnover	700,000
– cost of sales	250,000
Gross profit	450,000
– expenses	300,000
Operating profit	150,000
Rent	10,000
– interest	50,000
Profit before tax*	110,000

* You may also come across the terms Profit on Ordinary Activities before Tax, or Profit before Tax and exceptional items. These 'items' may be a reference to the sale of assets, the purchase of another company, anything that is unusual when compared to the day-to-day trading of the business. For example, Tesco will buy and sell food as part of its normal business operations. It may sell land, which is not part of its normal operations.

Profit before tax is also referred to as **net profit**.

There are further subtractions to be made from the business's accounts:

Corporation tax

This is a tax on the profits of companies and is paid as a proportion of profit before tax. The proportion varies, according to the size of the business. Once Corporation tax has been deducted, this is known as **profit after tax**. Look for this profit in any company report and you may find these terms which mean the same:

- **Profit for the financial year**
- **Profit attributable to the company**

The final deduction is the dividend that is paid to shareholders. The level of the dividends is determined by the board of directors who submit their decision to the shareholders at the Annual General Meeting which normally approves the decision of the directors. The directors have to perform a balancing act in terms of satisfying the shareholders by declaring a reasonable level of dividend, whilst ensuring there are sufficient funds for future investment.

Directors may avoid paying a dividend if an insufficient amount of profit has been earned. The last option is perfectly legal; there is no obligation to pay a dividend to shareholders. Interestingly it is possible to declare a dividend when the business has made a loss. The value of the dividend is determined by the business in the knowledge that it has to ensure that the shareholders are going to be satisfied with the return on their investment. Assuming the business has built up cash reserves from retained profits in previous years, it can utilise these reserves. This may be done to satisfy the shareholders.

Once these final deductions have been made, the business is left with **retained profit**, which the business can use for investment purposes. This final part of the P&L statement is sometimes referred to as the appropriation section as it highlights what has happened to the profit for the financial year.

This will leave the P&L account as follows:

Plant-It Ltd P&L account year ending 31.12.99

Turnover	£700,000
less cost of sales	£250,000
Gross profit	£450,000
less expenses	£300,000
Operating profit	£150,000
plus non-operating income	£ 10,000
less interest payable	£ 50,000
Profit before tax*	£110,000
less tax	£ 25,000
Profit after tax**	£ 85,000
less dividends	£ 15,000
Retained profit	£ 70,000

The difference between gross profit and retained profit may be quite substantial; much will depend upon the type of business and therefore the amount of expenses (overheads), the amount of non-operating income and the amount of tax paid.

*Although there are set rates of Corporation tax, the actual amount of tax paid is governed not only by the amount of profit, but also by the level of tax allowances that the business is able to claim.

**Profit after tax, or profit attributable to the company, or profit for the financial year.

Question 3

P&L account for Aquatics Ltd year ending August 1999

Turnover	£100,000
?	£?
Gross profit	£ 65,000
?	£ 40,000
Operating profit	£?

Fill in the blanks to complete the P&L account for Aquatics Ltd.

[4]

Question 4

Using the following information, construct a P&L account for Splash-It Ltd, a manufacturer of hose pipes and garden fountains.

	£
turnover	300,500
taxation	30,000
non-operating income	20,000
interest payable	5,000
dividends	10,000
expenses	75,000
cost of sales	100,000

[6]

Any retained profit that the business earns is transferred to the retained profit reserve in the balance sheet. All retained profit is expressed as a liability, because it belongs to the shareholders, whether it is in the form of cash or has already been used to buy stock or machinery.

Uses of the P&L account

The directors of the business need the information within the P&L in order to assess the success of the decisions that have been made in the past and to help them make the appropriate decisions for the future.

The P&L account, apart from being a statement on the performance of the business in itself, provides the basis to apply specific ratios to measure particular aspects of the business's performance. These ratios include: return on net assets, profit margin, interest cover (*for a detailed explanation of ratios see Unit 38*).

A business will always be keen to use the results from the P&L account, providing they are good results, to show the shareholders that the business is prospering. The shareholders will be able to assess how successful the directors have been in running the business and whether to vote in favour of the proposed dividend declared by the board of directors at the AGM. Prospective suppliers to the business may want to check whether there are likely to be any problems with payment. Using the P&L in conjunction with the balance sheet, this will be possible.

Similarly, any prospective provider of finance will want to judge whether the business is able to pay the interest payments on any agreed loan. By looking at the P&L, a prospective lender will be able to calculate this (*see Unit 38 Ratio analysis for an explanation of interest cover*).

To comply with a legal requirement, a copy of the P&L has to be filed with the Registrar of Companies (a requirement of the Companies Acts).

To comply with another legal requirement, the P&L is required by the Inland Revenue so it can calculate the amount of Corporation tax to be paid.

Question 5

Drive-It Ltd, a car hire business located near to Birmingham airport, issued the following P&L account for the year to 31 December 1999.

	£000
Turnover	240
Cost of sales	60
Gross profit	180
less	
Marketing	15
Salaries	60
Administration	15
Depreciation	50
Operating profit	40
Non-operating income	10
less interest payable	20
Net profit	30

a) If you were approached by the business to provide funds for its expansion, suggest what you would look at on the P&L account. Give reasons for your choice.   [5]

b) If you were a potential supplier to this business, what would be of interest to you in the P&L? Give reasons for your answer.   [3]

c) If as a potential shareholder in the business, you were told this was only the first year's trading for Drive-It, would you be impressed with the net profit obtained? Explain your answer.   [7]

d) In terms of the appropriation account, suggest with reasons whether there ought to be a dividend pay-out to the existing shareholders.   [4]

Question 6

Tip-It Ltd P&L account

£000	1998	1999
Turnover	120	150
Cost of sales	80	110
Gross profit	40	40
Expenses	20	22
Operating profit	20	18
Interest payable	5	5
Net profit	15	13
Tax	4	3
Profit for the financial year	11	10

Tip-It Ltd is a skip hire company based in the West Midlands. As Tip-It Ltd is still run by one family who own all the shares, no dividend is paid and any profit is ploughed back into the business.

a) Using the information provided, compare the performance of the company for the two years.   [5]

b) Suggest possible reasons for the changes in the figures for the two years.   [5]

Points for Revision

Key Terms

profit	the excess of revenue over costs; vital to ensure the business remains competitive and a vehicle for growth
turnover	main source of income; calculated by the number of units sold $\times$ price
cost of sales	direct costs, for example, raw materials and labour costs of production
gross profit	turnover less cost of sales i.e. the surplus of revenue over the cost of making the goods which were sold
expenses	fixed costs or overheads, not related to the productive process
operating profit	gross profit less expenses; the profit earned from trading
non-operating income	other sources of income, for example, rent and interest
net profit	profit before tax is deducted
profit after tax/ profit for the financial year/ profit attributable to the company	profit after tax and before payment of dividend
retained profit	profit after payment of dividend, which is reinvested in the following financial year

Definitions Question:

By referring to a business you know, explain the meaning and significance of any three of the above terms (your teacher may wish to select the terms).   [5] per definition

Summary Points:

1. The purpose of the P&L account is to provide a statement of the business's performance over a given period of time as a result of its trading.

2. The P&L can be used to calculate performance ratios.

3. The P&L gives an indication of the flows of money within the business.

Mini Case Study

Meg and Ryan Graydon own and run a thriving business in the heart of the Cotswolds. They live in a large house which serves as their home and their shop. Next door is their hotel which specialises in relaxing breaks for the discerning customer. The business became a limited company several years ago. Apart from themselves, there are several shareholders who have invested in the business as it has grown over the years.

On average, the hotel charges £105 per person per night and has an occupancy rate of 75% for the 36 twin rooms. Single occupancy is charged at twice the rate. The hotel is open for 50 weeks of the year. The labour costs per customer are £15 and the other variable costs are £10 per customer.

The overheads for the hotel are £120,000 per annum. Earlier in the year, Meg and Ryan sold a piece of land attached to their substantial garden for £30,000. A loan to refurbish several of the rooms in February meant that they had interest payments of £1,000 per month.

The agreed dividend payment would be 40% of profit. (For this case study assume Corporation tax is equivalent to 10% of profit.)

1 Construct a P&L account for the business, year ending 31 March 2000.	[10]
2 How might the profit and loss account help the business to take decisions?	[3]
3 What is the break-even number of customers?	[3]
4 How would becoming a limited company have helped Meg and Ryan?	[4]

20

Maxi Case Study

J N Nichols plc is more famous for Vimto than for anything else, although sales of the product account for only one third of the total revenue for the group of companies. In addition to Vimto, the business has three other divisions: Nichols Foods, Stock Pack and Cabana. The following information has been taken from extracts of the annual report, published during March 1999.

£m	Nichols Foods	Vimto	Cabana	Stock Pack
Sales revenue (1998)	34	24	8	7
Sales revenue (1997)	33	28	8	6
Operating profit (1998)	3.4	3.8	1.7	0.3
Profit margin	?	?	?	?
Operating profit (1997)	3.2	4.1	2	0.8
Profit margin	9.7%	14.6%	25.0%	13.3%

$$\text{Profit margin} = \frac{\text{operating profit}}{\text{sales revenue}}$$

Figure 35.2   Sales revenue by product

Summaries of each division

Nichols Foods: this part of the business operates in vending and retail markets. The vending market involves supplying ingredients to the operators of vending equipment. It aims to find long-term contracts with schools and colleges, as well as retailers, the latter of which are the smallest part of Nichols Foods. Last year it developed new products, such as Thick 'n' Creamy and other hot chocolate ranges. The business has invested in Information Technology in order to improve customer service levels and efficiency. Market conditions are extremely competitive and the business has had to invest heavily in sales and marketing activity.

Vimto: Vimto is the cash cow of the business, having been in existence for over 90 years. Sales of Vimto depend primarily on the weather. The poor summer of 1998 had a significant effect on sales revenue, despite price cuts and extra advertising expenditure. The advertising campaign which was created during 1998 centred on a cartoon character call Purple Ronnie (*see below*) which helped to bolster flagging sales. The company also sought to achieve a more efficient operation by reducing its cost of manufacture. Despite operating profit falling, the profit margin actually rose.

Stock Pack: the least profitable part of the group. It is involved with packing dried ingredients and supplying them to many of the UK's leading blue chip manufacturers; products such as Horlicks come under this category, supplied to Cadbury's. The company has worked hard to improve the efficiency of the business through automating part of the production process which has resulted in a reduction in the work-force of nearly 8%.

Cabana: soft drinks on draught; this product is sold to the leisure and catering market and the market share has increased since last year. Cabana also has an agreement with Barrs, ironically one of its competitors, which allows Nichols to manufacture, distribute and sell Barrs brands, including Irn Bru and Tizer.

During the year, the business closed its canning plant at Southampton due to the expiry of property leases. The canning line was incorporated into the factory at Haydock, Lancashire. This is the first time the entire division of Vimto has operated under one roof, which will potentially lead to substantial cost savings in the future. The following is a summary of the company's profit and loss statement, reported on 31.12.98:

Table 1

£000	Year ended 31.12.98	Year ended 31.12.97
Turnover	72966	75075
Gross profit	9131	19202
Operating profit	9203	10218
Exceptional item*	1440	
Profit before taxation	8105	10523
Profit for the financial year	5486	7256
Retained profit	2427	4257

*Sale of Southampton plant

1 Define: group of companies, blue chip. [4]

2 a) Calculate the dividends for both years and identify the percentage increase from 1997 to 1998. [4]

   b) Comment on the dividend payment in the light of the company's performance. [3]

3 Why would a company wish to manufacture, distribute and sell a competitor's drinks? [5]

4 a) J N Nichols plc made attempts to improve efficiency during 1998. Suggest ways of measuring efficiency. [3]

   b) Why will the closure of the canning plant lead to cost savings in the long run? [4]

5 a) Calculate the profit margin **(i)** for the business for 1997 and 1998 **(ii)** for the four divisions in 1998. [3]

   b) Suggest reasons for the change in profitability of the business from 1997 to 1998. [6]

6 Discuss the usefulness of the overall profit and loss account when assessing the performance and profitability of Nichols plc. Suggest additional information you may require in your assessment of performance and profitability. [8]

40

Balance sheet

Learning objectives

Having read this unit, students will be able to

1 recognise and distinguish between the various parts of the balance sheet

2 understand the significance of the balance sheet for a business and its stakeholders

3 appreciate the advantages and disadvantages of using a balance sheet to assess the financial position of the business

Context

Stakeholders of Marks and Spencer plc will want to examine the financial position of the company. Investors may want to know the value of the business or how much shareholders have invested, or perhaps how much profit the business has ploughed back into the company. Suppliers may wish to know whether the business has enough cash to pay their invoices. The bank will want to examine how much money it has borrowed and the value of its land and buildings as they may be needed to act as security in case the business wishes to take out a loan. Shareholders and potential shareholders may wish to examine the wealth of the business with a view to either keeping money invested in M and S shares, or buying more, or even selling some! All this information is found in a balance sheet, which is published twice yearly by public limited companies. Private companies have to send a copy of the balance sheet to Companies House, so this information is available to all stakeholders.

The balance sheet defined

The balance sheet represents a valuation of what the business owns (assets) and owes (liabilities) at any one time. In effect, it is a snapshot of the business's wealth, reported at the end of its financial year. As a business grows and makes profit, it will be worth more to shareholders. Liabilities represent the sources where business finds its finance, whereas the assets represent how its finances have been used.

Question 1

State which of the following are assets or liabilities for a computer manufacturer:

a) Plant and machinery used to manufacture the computers
b) An overdraft, taken out from Lloyds Bank
c) Shares which it owns in a microchip producer
d) The tax bill which the business has been sent to be paid next year
e) Dividends for the shareholders
f) Cash which it holds in a deposit account at the Alliance and Leicester
g) Shareholders' investment   [7]

The structure

At the start of every balance sheet there will be reference to a date which will immediately distinguish it from the profit and loss account. The title will state: Balance sheet for ABC plc as at 31/12/00, meaning that this balance was accurate on that particular date. The profit and loss, by contrast, refers to the entire year.

In the balance sheet, assets will then be grouped separately from liabilities.

Fixed assets

These are the parts of the business which it owns and means to keep.

Fixed assets divide into three parts:

■ Tangible fixed assets

e.g. land and buildings, plant and machinery. All capital equipment will be a fixed asset and in manufacturing industries, this part will represent the majority of the company's assets. In a service company e.g. an accountant's, the fixed assets will include office, as well as some office furniture. Some of these assets will depreciate over time, so an allowance will be made each year, in order to reduce the value of the asset over its useful life.

■ Intangible fixed assets

Patents are bought by the business as a means of protecting its investment in a new product (*see Unit 16 Product*). Patents are issued by the Patent Office and are designed either to protect a smaller company against a larger one, which might copy the invention and then produce at a lower cost, or to allow a business that spends a large proportion of its revenue on research to recoup some of the investment costs. Patents are particularly common in technological industries e.g. Dyson took out a patent on the bagless vacuum cleaner; pharmaceutical companies do the same to protect their discoveries. A business therefore owns a patent and will keep it for as long as it is able to, because different patents last for different lengths of time.

Goodwill

When one company buys another, it may pay more than the value of its assets e.g. when Nestlé bought Rowntree, the takeover was famous for the fact that Nestle paid £2.4 billion for a business the assets of which were worth only £400 million! The difference of £2 billion had to be accounted for in goodwill. Accounting goodwill therefore appears only when one business takes over another.

■ Financial fixed assets

Sometimes a business will use money to invest in government bonds, or perhaps shares in a supplier. These are meant to be kept as long-term investments and are therefore represented as fixed assets.

Question 2

Examine the following fixed assets and state whether each is tangible, intangible or financial:

a) a fleet of company vehicles for the sales reps at Heinz
b) money invested in a special savings account
c) shelving at Marks and Spencer   [3]

Question 3

Why might a business invest in
a) government bonds?
b) shares in a supplier?   [4]

Current assets

These represent the parts of the business that it owns but does not intend to keep i.e. will turn into cash as quickly as possible. **Current assets** allow the business to operate on a day-to-day basis and are short-term assets.

■ **Stock** – this includes raw materials, work-in-progress and finished goods. A business needs stock for production, but will wish to sell the stock as quickly as possible because holding stock costs the business money, without adding any value (*see Unit 28 Stock control*). In a service business, such as BT, this figure has very little relevance for the company, because it will be very small in relation to its fixed assets.

■ **Debtors** – these represent the customers who owe the business money. As with stock, the business will always encourage debtors to pay because debtors are effectively holding the company's money in their bank accounts. A typical credit period provided by companies will be 30, 60 or 90 days. A credit controller is sometimes employed by a business to manage the speed of payment of customers and to chase up payment when it is late.

■ **Cash** – the most liquid of assets; a business will need to keep cash flowing through the business, although holding too much cash can mean the business is not capitalising on opportunities.

The **structure of assets** in the balance sheet is organised in such a way as to demonstrate ascending order of liquidity. **Liquidity** means the ease with which an asset may be turned into cash. Fixed assets are the most difficult to turn into cash, although in reality, the business will not normally aim to do this. Stock will be sold eventually, although debtors represent stock which has been sold, the money for which is sitting in a customer's bank account.

Asset structure

Depending on the nature of the business, the relative amount of investment in fixed assets and current assets will vary. British Telecom will have very little money tied up in stock whereas it owns capital equipment ranging from telephone exchanges to the thousands of miles of wiring and pylons which cover the nation. A car dealer, on the other hand, is likely to have much more money tied up in stock (cars it is about to sell) than in land and buildings. Although the car dealer will need the land, the value of the cars which are on the premises is much greater, especially if the dealer sells cars of between one and two years of age as Motorhouse does.

Question 4

State the asset structure i.e. whether the business will have more money tied up in current assets or fixed assets, in the following circumstances:

a) a manufacturing company that has just sold its headquarters, in favour of renting property
b) a business, such as Hanson plc, which makes money by asset-stripping i.e. suddenly taking over a business, then selling off the parts at a profit
c) a stockbroker
d) a business which arranges credit terms for companies such as D.F.S which sell on interest-free credit
e) a fruit and vegetable farmer, just after the harvest has been collected, taken to market and paid for by the customer   [10]

Current liabilities

Current liabilities are the opposite of current assets i.e. amounts of money which the business owes and intends to pay within the next 12 months:

Overdraft – an arrangement with the bank to use some of the bank's cash on a temporary basis, when the company runs out of cash. An overdraft may therefore be needed due to late payment by a customer, or early payment to a supplier to take advantage of an early payment discount. The time deadline to pay an overdraft back to the bank will depend on the amount of notice already given by the bank. Officially the repayment deadline can be as short as 24 hours, although one working week tends to be more typical. A bank will call in an overdraft only if there is a risk that the bank may never recover the money from the business.

Short-term loan – used to finance short-term assets e.g. a car loan repayable within one year.

N.B. interest does not appear as a current liability, because there is no invoice or notice to pay; when the business owes the bank interest, the bank will simply deduct it from the cash balance or add it to the overdraft, normally without asking!

Trade creditors – these are suppliers who have provided the business with products, but the business has not yet paid. In the same way as debtors, the business will have credit terms stated by the supplier. If the business is to manage its cash flow, the ideal situation is to pay the suppliers after it has received money for the sale of its products, although this is a rare occurrence in reality.

Dividends – at the end of the year, a business will announce its final dividend, although when the balance sheet is put together it will not have paid the dividend out, so the final dividend will appear as a current liability. The interim dividend, which is announced after six months of trading, will already have been paid by the time the balance sheet is drawn up at the end of the year.

Taxation – when a business reports its profit, it must send its accounts away to the Inland Revenue who will calculate the corporate taxation which the company must pay, based on the amount of profit it has earned. This amount must then be paid, normally within the next 12 months.

Net current assets

This is calculated as current assets minus current liabilities. Another term used for this is working capital i.e. the money tied up in the business which is used for the day-to-day operations of the business. Too much money in net current assets implies the business is not being financially efficient i.e. is tying money up in assets which will not, on their own, earn money. Rather it is the *speed* with which the working capital is turned into cash and reinvested which determines productivity and profitability. Too little money in net current assets may imply the company could face cash flow problems now or in the near future. So by looking at the balance sheet it is possible to assess the financial shape the business is in.

Long-term liabilities

Long-term liabilities represent money which the business owes, but does not need to repay within the next 12 months. Long-term loans are a prime source of finance for the business and are normally owed to the bank.

Mortgage – normally used to purchase property, using the property as security in case the business cannot repay either the interest or the original (principal) sum.

Debenture – another source of long-term finance, issued only if a company is a plc. A private investor lends money to the business and receives interest on a long-term basis.

Net assets

Calculated by fixed assets plus net current assets minus long-term liabilities i.e. the total amount the business owns less the amount it owes. This does not include any part of the shareholder stake in the company. In effect, **net assets** are a form of net wealth.

Work out your own net wealth, or perhaps that of one of your parents. Add up everything they own: car, house, clothes, savings etc. and subtract everything they owe: mortgage, loans, tax bill, credit card bill. What is left represents their wealth i.e. how much they would be worth if all assets were turned instantly into cash and this cash was used to pay off the loans etc.

In the same way, the business would, theoretically, be left with some money if it turned all its assets into cash and used it to pay off the liabilities. The remainder would then belong to the shareholders and is represented in the balance sheet by the money they invested plus any profit which has been ploughed back, which also belongs to the shareholder.

Shareholders' funds

This represents the total amount which either the shareholders have invested (or have 'tied up') in the business through buying shares, reinvesting profits or other means:

- **Issued ordinary share capital:** the investment made by ordinary shareholders i.e. those with ownership rights. This will increase over time if the business issues more shares to investors when it wishes to raise more finance. This figure is different from authorised share capital, which is the amount the stock exchange has allowed the business to issue.

- **Preference share capital:** this differs from ordinary shares in two ways
    i)   the dividend is paid out before (i.e. in preference to ordinary shares) and is usually calculated by a fixed percentage on the investment made in each share

    ii) in the event of winding up a business, priority or 'preference' is given to these shareholders if there is enough money to pay the investment back to them. Usually there is very little left if the business has failed.

- **Retained profit reserve:** during the life of the business, it will hopefully earn profit, some of which will be reinvested (retained profit). It will be reinvested in making the value of assets larger, by buying more stocks or fixed assets; alternatively it could be used to reduce liabilities – paying off bank loans or creditors. However it is used, the extra amount ploughed back into the business will increase the net assets and to balance this the retained profit reserve will rise.

- **Revaluation reserve:** this is included in this section when property increases in value. This is particularly important when the majority of a business's assets are land and buildings, because historically such assets increase in value over time. Such an increase means the asset will be worth more, meaning that the net assets will increase, making the business worth more. As the business belongs to the shareholders, this section must also be increased by the same amount e.g. a business has a valuation of land and buildings of £400 million, which has been the value for five years. If a new valuation puts the land and buildings at £550 million, the land and buildings will now be entered as being worth £550 million in the fixed assets, which will make the net assets worth an extra £150 million. This represents the increase in property values, so the same amount is entered in the revaluation reserve, which therefore acts as a balancing item.

N.B. It can be tempting to assume that reserve is something which the business can draw upon when it needs finance. This is not the case. Retained profit reserve and revaluation reserve are both *balancing items* which mean the balance sheet will balance. They are set against other increases in values of net assets, due, respectively, to reinvested profit or an increase in assets' values. Seeing the reserve as a source of finance suggests the business can turn the extra value of the building into cash! Using retained profit reserve is also impossible; assuming the money has already been tied up in non-cash assets, it is no longer available.

Task

Check you understand where the figures in bold type come from.

Balance Sheet for Nimbus Ltd as at 31/11/99
(£000)

Fixed assets		90000
Current assets		
Stock	70000	
Debtors	3000	
Cash	35000	
		108000
Current liabilities		
Short-term loan	12000	
Creditors	27000	
Dividends payable	13000	
Tax payable	23000	
		75000
Net current assets		33000
Long-term liabilities		28000
Net assets		**95000**
Shareholders' funds		
Issued ordinary share capital		60000
Retained profit reserve		17000
Revaluation reserve		18000
		95000

Figure 36.1

Question 5

Without referring to the balance sheet above, copy the grid below and tick the relevant part of the balance sheet that items **a) – n)** appear in. Use fixed assets, current assets, current liabilities, long-term liabilities and shareholders' funds as your classifications. (Two items below do not appear in the balance sheet).

a) trade creditors
b) mortgage
c) stock sold
d) debtors
e) cash
f) dividends payable
g) retained profit reserve
h) overdraft
i) work-in-progress
j) land and buildings
k) shares in a competitor
l) finished goods
m) taxation payable
n) interim dividends   [14]

Stakeholders

Various stakeholders will have a specific interest in the balance sheet, although sometimes the balance sheet needs to be examined in conjunction with the profit and loss account, depending on what the stakeholder is wishing to discover.

■ **Present and potential shareholders** will look at how the business has invested its funds in the various assets of the business, to earn the best return e.g. shareholders will want to see their money tied up in productive, operating assets (fixed assets) and will not want to see too much tied up in current assets. Potential investors may also look at the breakdown of shareholders' funds, specifically the amount of profit reinvested, which demonstrates how high a value the business places on internal funds, making the cost of finance cheaper, and possibly leading to higher dividends.

■ **Banks** will be concerned with the present level of borrowing, both on a long- and short-term basis. This will be looked at in relation to shareholders' funds with a view to making a comparison between risk and non-risk capital. If the management of the company has approached a bank to apply for a loan, the bank will want to check that the business will be able to pay back the loan and that it does not have too many loans at present. It will also want to see whether the business has sufficient **collateral** to back the loan in event of non-repayment, so it will look at fixed assets. This, however, will tell it only of the approximate value and may not inform the bank how many of the fixed assets are already being used as collateral.

■ **Suppliers** will need to see if there is likely to be a problem with being paid. Current assets, particularly debtors and cash, will be considered, in addition to the amount of current liabilities. Too little money tied up in working capital may mean payment might be delayed, resulting in cash flow problems for the business.

■ **Directors** at the Annual General Meeting will be anxious to present the financial situation of the business in the best possible light. Ian Martin, Chairman of Unigate, referred to the balance sheet in his report to shareholders by mentioning the 'excellent results' being a 'reflection of investment'. Such a statement implies there will be interest in capital equipment and growth in net assets.

> **Question 6**
>
> In what way would a supplier view the balance sheet differently to a shareholder?   [4]

Format

The format of a balance sheet depends normally on whether the accounts are published i.e. whether the business is a plc. Such companies must produce a balance sheet in a vertical format, with assets at the top and liabilities at the bottom. The horizontal format is not used today, although it is a good starting point to understand the parts of the balance sheet.

Horizontal format

The following example demonstrates how a balance sheet can be built using the horizontal format.

The format is liabilities on the left and assets on the right. Liabilities tend to represent the places where the business sources its finance and the assets represent the uses of the finance (*see Figure 36.2*).

With this format, the shareholders' funds are seen as liabilities, in that the business is separate from the owners. It also shows clearly where money has been invested and where money has come from.

Liabilities		Assets	
Shareholders' funds	£60m	Fixed assets	£70m
Long-term liabilities	£40m	Current assets	£53m
Current liabilities	£23m		
Total liabilities	£123m	Total assets	£123m

Figure 36.2

Vertical format

The vertical format, which is the usual format for published accounts, provides a summary of the net wealth of the business and how the equivalent amount is represented within the shareholders' funds.

The balance sheet shown in Figure 36.2 is represented in Figure 36.3 using the vertical format:

Fixed assets		£70m
Current assets	£53m	
Current liabilities	£23m	
Net current assets		£30m
Long-term liabilities		£40m
Net assets		£60m
Shareholders' funds		£60m

Figure 36.3

By calculating the net assets, this gives one possible value of the business, which the horizontal format fails to provide at a glance.

Limitations of the balance sheet

Although the balance sheet does provide an insight into a company's finances, there are limitations to its use and effectiveness e.g. the valuations of its fixed assets, especially the tangible fixed assets, are highly subjective. Depreciation is estimated at the time of purchasing the machine and takes no account of sudden technological advances rendering machinery obsolete. The aim of depreciation is not to represent an accurate value of the fixed assets, which further detracts from the accuracy of the fixed asset figure.

Updating valuations of land can also be subjective, according to the individual valuer. In the mid-1990s, Sainsbury's suddenly had to write off £300 million from its assets (therefore its profit) due to a devaluation of its land and buildings which had occurred over a period of years, but had not been recognised as significant by the valuer.

Working capital changes on a day-by-day basis as the business sells stock, receives cash from its customers and pays bills out of its cash. Any conclusion about the amount tied up in working capital, based on one day's figures (as at the time when the balance sheet is drawn up), is likely to be inaccurate.

Some firms invest in shares, and the market value may rise and fall according to supply and demand for that share – such changes to the value of the investment can occur on a daily basis. The accurate value of the investment cannot be represented on the balance sheet because of these short-term fluctuations.

Window dressing – a firm may deliberately attempt to massage the figures on its balance sheet by window dressing the final accounts e.g. a loan may be paid back the day before the accounts are audited only to be taken out again two days later. Hence it could appear that borrowing is much less than it is in reality.

The inclusion of brands?

There has been considerable debate in the accounting world as to whether brand names should be included in fixed assets. After all, the existence of famous brand names is one of the main reasons why a company might be targeted for takeover. The investment a company makes in brands takes place over a number of years; some of the most famous brands are normally the oldest: Coca-Cola, the second most recognised brand in the world (next to McDonald's), is over 100 years old. Prolonged investment in the product leads to high expectation of future sales and profits. Such expectation leads predator companies to target businesses with famous brands, so the argument that brands make a company more valuable and therefore should be included in the balance sheet is a strong one. The opponents to this idea suggest that valuing a brand based on future sales is a subjective valuation and prone to inaccurate forecasts; to date, such opponents have won the argument, although this issue will remain. The next problem facing the accounting world is how to recognise the earning potential of a business's most valuable assets – its people.

Question 7

a) Argue the case for Liverpool Football Club including Michael Owen on its balance sheet. [4]

b) On what basis would players be valued? [6]

Points for Revision

Key Terms

fixed assets	how much the business owns and wishes to keep e.g. plant and machinery (which are tangible), patents (which are intangible) and shares in suppliers (which are financial fixed assets)
goodwill	when one company buys another and pays more than the value of the net assets of the target business, the difference is known as goodwill
patents	a method of protecting an invention against copying by other businesses
current assets	the business owns stock, debtors and cash, but wishes to turn them all into cash as quickly as possible and then reinvest the cash
asset structure	the extent to which the majority of a company's assets are made up of fixed or current assets
liquidity	the ability to convert assets into cash
current liabilities	the amounts of money the business owes and is due to pay within the next 12 months
long-term liabilities	the amount the business owes, but does not need to pay back within the next 12 months
net assets	a measure of the net wealth of the business; calculated by total assets less current liabilities less long-term liabilities
shareholders' funds	represents the amount of money which belongs to the shareholders; comprises issued ordinary shares, retained profit reserve, preference shares and revaluation reserve
reserves	the balancing item in the shareholders' funds; when a profit is made and reinvested or when land and buildings are increased in value due to market forces pushing the value of land up, then reserves are adjusted as a balancing item
collateral	assets used as security when borrowing money

Definitions Question:

By referring to a business you know, explain the meaning of any three of the above terms (your teacher may wish to help you with the choice).   [5] per definition

Summary Points:

1   The balance sheet is a method of summarising the company's wealth at any one time.

2   It is divided into sections, fixed and current assets, long-term and current liabilities and shareholders' funds.

3   There are two formats which can be used – horizontal and vertical.

4   The balance sheet is a record at a point in time which instantly becomes out of date, so conclusions drawn from the figures must be treated with suitable assumptions of accuracy.

Mini Case Study

Following a successful year, when Nimbus, a manufacturer of toys, recorded a record level of profit, the managing director, Petra Pligette, thought carefully about further expansion. It had been a good year and with another bumper Christmas just around the corner, it was likely that next year's results would be even better. Although the market was not too competitive, she could not be sure that new retailers would not enter the UK market. There were several American companies that had expressed interest in a joint venture with Nimbus, although Petra had resisted this idea, given the rather brash style of American marketing. Nimbus had always prided itself on letting the customer be the judge of its products without frequent, intensive advertising. The share price was rising, such that a takeover from one of these companies seemed unlikely. Even so, she had approached the bank and the shareholders with a view to raising £5 million to buy two new stores. The balance sheet she had in front of her was still unaudited and one or two alterations might still be required, but she felt confident she could persuade most of the 4,000 shareholders to invest.

Balance Sheet for Nimbus Ltd as at 31/11/99

(£000)

Fixed assets			90000
Current assets			
Stock	70000		
Debtors	3000		
Cash	35000		
		108000	
Current liabilities			
Short-term loan	12000		
Creditors	27000		
Dividends payable	13000		
Tax payable	23000		
		75000	
Net current assets			33000
Long-term liabilities			28000
Net assets			**95000**
Shareholders' funds			
Issued ordinary share capital			60000
Retained profit reserve			17000
Revaluation reserve			18000
			95000

1 Define: marketing, unaudited, retailers. [6]

2 a) Why might Petra prefer to go to the bank to borrow, than to persuade shareholders to invest? [2]

 b) What is the value of the business, according to the balance sheet? [1]

3 Examine the current assets of the business. Comment on the relative size of the stocks, debtors and cash, in the context of Nimbus and its chosen market. [5]

4 Using the balance sheet below calculate how the value of net assets would change if, *ceteris paribus*,

 i) dividends were paid with cash

 ii) the land and buildings were increased in value by £15,000 due to a surveyor's report. [6]

Maxi Case Study

EMI is a famous company which has been associated with both recording and publication of music for many years. Until 1998, it owned HMV record stores and took a decision at that time to sell the record shops. This had a significant effect on the balance sheet, which even allowing for the reduction in sales through HMV showed a drop in sales revenue.

During 1998, sales grew significantly in the United States which bolstered an otherwise lacklustre performance in other parts of the globe. Music sales are prone to regional fluctuations due to variations in the state of the economy within different countries. By selling its music in many countries, however, EMI reduces the risk of being reliant upon one major economy that could suffer from recession.

In Asia and Latin America, sales fell steeply as a direct result of the economic crises in those countries. It may be that EMI will cut off its links with Brazil because about half of the drop in operating profits was due to the drop in trade in Brazil. In response to the drop in profit, the business has focused on maintaining a tight control on costs and a high level of investment in new artists and recording contracts.

The balance sheet for 1997 and 1998 is contained in Table 1:

Table 1

Balance sheet as at		30/9/1998		30/9/1997	
Fixed assets (£million)					
Music copyrights		363.4		401.1	
Tangible		344.2		516.5	
			707.6		917.6
Current assets					
	Stocks	56		188.5	
	Debtors	858.7		882.8	
	Cash	309		179.2	
			1225		1257.3
Current liabilities					
short-term loan		919.8		726.4	
other creditors		1221.5		1282.6	
			2141.3		2009
Net current liabilities			916.3		751.7
Long-term liabilities			573.8		699.6
Net assets			697.7		451.9
Capital and reserves					
Issued share capital		110.2		110.1	
Reserves		587.5		341.8	
			697.7		451.9

Such artists as Smashing Pumpkins, Spice Girls and Beastie Boys represent some of its major contemporary revenue earners, each having albums which have sold over one million copies.

In addition, EMI is responsible for the *Now* series which regularly achieves sales of over one million units. Such a series is a stable product in terms of earning revenue and profit, which allows for the risks that EMI takes with new artists.

EMI achieves sales of over one million units with the *Now* series

Sales through the company's catalogue also represent part of the revenue and artists such as The Beatles, Frank Sinatra and The Rolling Stones all had contracts with EMI.

EMI is the world's leading music publisher and sales have grown by 10% over the last year due to major contributors such as The Verve, Robbie Williams and the soundtrack of *Titanic*. Despite this growth in publishing 1998 was not the best year for EMI and the forecast remains uncertain, so the best way (EMI claims) of facing this uncertainty is to cut costs and invest in new artists.

1 Define: state of the economy, investment. [4]

2 Explain the major changes to the balance sheet which the sale of HMV might have caused. [6]

3 Explain how the drop in sales revenue might affect individual figures on the balance sheet. [4]

4 Show how net assets have been calculated. [3]

5 Suggest why reserves increased by £245.7 million from 1997 to 1998. [2]

6 Explain why the asset structure of EMI might differ from a business which manufactures CD players, selling them to electrical retailers such as Dixons. [5]

7 a) Why is copyright such an important fixed asset for EMI? [3]

  b) What are the difficulties of valuing copyrights? [3]

8 Discuss the factors that EMI might have considered when deciding to sell HMV. [10]

Asset valuation

Learning objectives

Having read this unit, students will be able to

1 understand the importance of accurate asset values for accounting purposes

2 understand the purpose of depreciation and recognise the effect of depreciation on profit

3 appreciate the effect of closing stock valuation on profit and calculate stock values based on various assumptions

Context

When any stakeholder examines the annual report of a business, and in particular, the balance sheet, there will always be an expectation that the figures which are reported are accurate and demonstrate the 'true and fair' view of a business. However, a manufacturing business such as GKN, which manufactures a range of engineering and defence products, will have a great deal of money tied up in fixed assets which will account for the majority of its net assets. Some of the fixed assets will fall in value over time due to either age or perhaps use. Although GKN is not intending to sell the fixed assets it will still have to estimate a value for the balance sheet. If a business intends to own an asset for a number of years and realises that at the end of its life it will be worth less than the purchase price, it faces a problem of when to recognise such a cost. If it writes off the cost in one lump sum, this will mean a significant reduction in profit for that particular year. In order to present a more accurate level of profit, the business will reduce the value of the asset over its useful life; this process is known as depreciation.

Alternatively, a business such as Shell which buys millions of barrels of oil may purchase them at different prices, according to the change in market price over time. If this is so, then Shell will hold barrels of oil at different prices. Although Shell could use an average price of each barrel, it could also make assumptions about which barrels are kept at which prices. This, in turn, is related to the assumptions of the order in which the barrels are used.

Depreciation

Why do fixed assets depreciate?

There are various reasons why **fixed assets** suffer from **depreciation** or fall in value over their economic life:

■ Age

As a piece of machinery or a computer gets older, even if it is not being used, it will reduce in value. This is particularly true of cars which fall in value much more due to their age than the amount of miles travelled.

■ Usage

As a machine is used over and over again, it will become more expensive to maintain and less efficient. Its value is likely to fall due to the wear and tear on its parts.

■ Technology

Computers depreciate almost immediately after purchase. In 1996 a computer which was loaded with the ability to use a word processor, spreadsheets and databases, along with a printer, cost £1,400. By 1999, a computer with eight times the amount of memory, four times the amount of hard drive space and four times the processing speed cost £400 less! All this was due to the speed of technological development in the market for home computers.

■ Incorrect use by untrained operators

Highly specialised, technologically advanced machinery needs to be handled in the right manner; if this is not the case, then damage can occur to the machinery which reduces its life and therefore its value.

■ One-off occurrences

If a fire damages premises, or stock, or even machinery itself, this may cause the business to write off the value of its machine i.e. to zero.

■ Fixed economic life

A patent, when awarded to a product or business, is valid for an agreed length of time. The patent costs money, so the value of the patent is reduced in equal amounts over its life, after which the patent is no longer valid.

■ Obsolescence

If a machine manufactures a product which has become obsolescent (out-of-date) then the asset has no value for the business.

Which fixed assets?

The only fixed assets which depreciate are those whose value falls over time. The length of time during which an asset is useful is known as its **economic or useful life**. Examples of these are:

Machinery
Vehicles
Patents
Fixtures and fittings
Stocks (due to obsolescence)
Buildings (*see note*)
Land (*see note*)

Note: Historically, the value of land and buildings has increased. If a business owns a great number of fixed assets which are property-based, when the value of the land and buildings rises then there must be an allowance for this in the balance sheet (known as the revaluation reserve (*see Unit 36 Balance sheet*).)

As the population has grown, so has the demand for property, so it has been generally assumed that the land and buildings of particular businesses will increase in value over time, thereby not qualifying them to be included in depreciation. However, recent recessions have meant that property prices have periodically fallen.

The purpose of depreciation

It is tempting to conclude that depreciation is carried out in order to represent the value of the asset accurately in the balance sheet. However, given the fact that, by definition, the business will not intend to sell the fixed asset until its useful life is over, an accurate value serves little purpose.

A bank may wish to know the value of land and buildings with a view to establishing whether an asset can be secured against a loan, but the bank is likely to use its own independent valuation. This is not the main purpose of depreciation.

The matching principle concerns the matching of costs against revenue; in the same way the cost of using and operating the machinery should be matched against the time it is used. Depreciation is therefore an operating cost and is carried out in order to write off the **net cost** of a fixed asset over its useful life. The net cost is calculated as the historic cost (the original amount paid for the asset) minus the **residual value** (the expected saleable value).

As a business depreciates a fixed asset, it is effectively putting funds to one side, so that when the asset is worn out and needs replacing, there are funds available to finance the new fixed asset.

Terminology

Depreciation involves specific terminology:

economic life/useful life – this can be defined as the period of time during which the benefit of using the asset outweighs the cost of using it i.e. the profit which is earned is greater than the extra running costs due to using it

residual value – an estimate of the saleable value of the asset at the end of its life

historic cost – the original amount paid for the asset

Question 1

a) Replace the italicised terms with one from the list below, which is a clearer expression.

When a business *writes off the net cost of an asset over the period of its useful life*, it needs to think carefully about several issues e.g. whether the *asset which it means to keep* will perform as expected and have a long period of time when it is earning money for the company. When the business is estimating *the amount it expects to receive for the asset when it is sold*, it needs to collect various sources of information in order to make a well informed guess. Once it has calculated the *length of time the asset will be used* and the *difference between the original amount paid and the expected amount to be received from the asset* then it can calculate a depreciation expense. This can then be deducted from the *original cost of the asset* to calculate the *amount at which the business values its assets at a particular point in time*.

residual value   historic cost   economic life   net cost
depreciates an asset   fixed asset   net book value

[7]

b) What information might the business use in order to estimate the residual value and economic life? [6]

If the business did not depreciate its assets over a period of time, it would have to depreciate it in one lump sum. This would understate the profit in the particular time period when it was written off in one lump sum, and overstate it in the years when nothing was written off.

The only circumstance when a business can do this is for tax purposes. If a business moves into an Enterprise Zone, the government allows the business to write off the value of any capital investment over one year. The advantage of this is that the taxation bill for the year will be dramatically reduced. This may be important for a company relocating because there may be pressure on cash flow because of the move.

e.g. a business buys assets worth £800,000, to be written off over 10 years, in equal instalments of £80,000 per year:

Sales   £8,650,000
Gross profit   £4,000,000
Depreciation   £80,000
Other expenses   £2,720,000
Profit   £1,200,000
Tax @23%   £276,000
Profit after tax £924,000

If, on the other hand, the business is allowed to write off the entire value of the asset over one year, the new tax and profit position is this:

Sales   £8,650,000
Gross profit   £4,000,000
Depreciation   £800,000
Other expenses   £2,720,000
Profit   £480,000
Tax @23%   £110,400
Profit after tax £369,600

Although the profit after tax is less, the tax bill is less, meaning more cash will stay within the business.

The process of calculation

In order to calculate the depreciation expense for an asset, it is necessary to identify four pieces of information:

- The historic cost
- The residual value
- The useful/economic life
- The method of depreciation

Method

Although there are several methods of depreciation, this section will focus on the two most frequently used. These are known as **straight-line** depreciation and **declining balance**.

Straight-line

This method writes off the same amount of depreciation each year throughout the asset's useful life. The amount to be written off is calculated by:

$$\frac{\text{historic cost} - \text{residual value}}{\text{number of years}}$$

e.g. a machine is bought for £40,000 and is expected to be sold for £5,000 in seven years' time. The depreciation per year is therefore

$$\frac{£40,000 - £5,000}{5 \text{ years}} = £7,000 \text{ per year}$$

The graph of the value of the machinery over its useful life is represented by Figure 37.1. It is easy to see where straight-line depreciation gets its name.

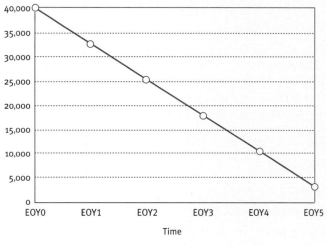

Figure 37.1 Straight-line depreciation

Question 2

A business buys an asset for £560,000 and intends to keep it for eight years, with an estimated residual value of £80,000.

Calculate
a) the depreciation expense for each year
b) the value of the machinery after the fifth year.
[4]

Question 3

The same business buys another asset for which it pays £100,000 and intends to write off £9,000 a year to a residual value of £19,000. How long does the business expect the asset's economic life to be? [3]

Declining (reducing) balance

This method writes off more of the asset's value in the early years of its life than in the later years. Declining balance is measured using a percentage (*see Key Terms for formula*). You will not be required to apply this formula for A level and if declining balance is required to be calculated, you will always be told the actual rate.

e.g. a business purchases an asset worth £40,000, with an expected residual value of £6,500, with a life of five years. This results in a percentage of just about 30%. This percentage is applied to the **net book value** at each point in the machine's life.

So depreciation in the first year will be:

30% × £40,000 = £12,000

Therefore net book value at the end of year 1 =

£40,000	historic cost
– £12,000	depreciation year 1
= £28,000	net book value end of year 1

The next year, the depreciation expense will be:

30% × £28,000 = £8,400

So net book value at the end of year 2 =

£28,000 (net book value at end of year 1)

– £8,400

= £19,600

If this process continues, the net book value will take the values as shown below:

Time	Net book value	Depreciation expense for year
EOY 0	40,000	
EOY 1	28,000	12,000
EOY 2	19,600	8,400
EOY 3	13,720	5,880
EOY 4	9,604	4,116
EOY 5	6,723	2,881.2

By putting the numbers into the formula, this produces an answer of about 30%. The actual answer is slightly different, but rounding the percentage to a whole number makes the calculations less problematic. This may result in the net book value not being exact (according to the precise percentage) although this does not matter given the nature and objective of depreciation.

i.e. in the final year, the depreciation charge has taken the net book value to £6,723, but if the business sells the asset for £6,500, the business will need to write off another £6,723 – £6,500 = £223 in the depreciation charge in the final year.

The final year's depreciation charge therefore ends up as

£2881.2 + £223 = £3104.20

The following is a graph of the net book value over time:

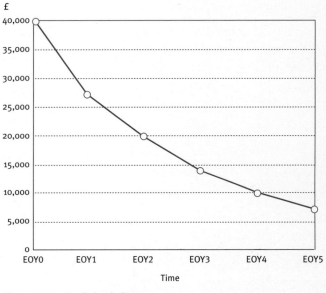

Figure 37.2   Declining balance

This is to allow for the fact that in the later years of an asset's life, the maintenance, repairs and operating costs of the machine are higher. Using declining balance allows the business to spread the total costs of using an asset (part of which is depreciation) more evenly over the asset's life.

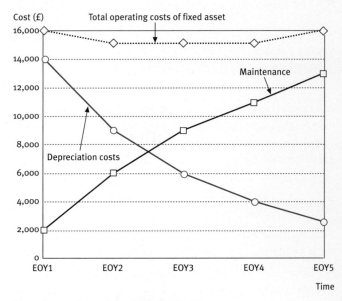

Figure 37.3   Total costs of using a machine

Question 4

A business purchases a motor vehicle for £10,000 and intends to depreciate it at 50% per annum. Fill in the following table.

Time	Net book value	Depreciation
EOY 1		
EOY 2		
EOY 3		

[6]

As time passes, the amount of depreciation deducted each year decreases, so if maintenance and repair costs increase, this means the running costs will be evenly spread over the asset's life.

Profit or loss on disposal

It is accepted that depreciation is an estimate, based on a prediction of economic life and residual value, and therefore occasionally businesses do make errors in this respect. They may have to sell the asset early or may need to make further investment in order, for example, to upgrade the technology. In most annual reports there is a section which describes the depreciation policy and to play safe, most PLCs will use a residual value of zero. However, if and when the business disposes of the asset and the residual value is not exactly the same as the market value i.e. the actual amount the business will receive if the asset is sold, then there must be a change to the reported profit by altering the depreciation charge.

Altering the depreciation charge is known as incurring a **profit or loss on disposal**. If the net book value is greater than the market value of an asset, then when the asset is sold, there will be a loss on disposal e.g. an asset worth £3,000 in the balance sheet is sold for £2,400, so a business would incur a loss of £600 following the disposal of the asset.

Alternatively, if the business owned an asset worth £25,000 and actually sold it for £28,000, the profit on disposal would be £3,000. This would be deducted from that year's depreciation charge, because it is a profit.

Question 5

An asset is bought for £200,000 and is intended to be kept for eight years, with a residual value of £8,000. If after five years, the business has to sell the asset for £70,000, it will need to adjust its depreciation charge for the fifth year. Work out the value of the machinery at the end of the fifth year, then calculate by how much the depreciation charge needs to be adjusted when the business sells it for £70,000. [4]

Selling an asset early

When a business sells an asset before the end of its useful life, and therefore before it has reached its residual value, it will need to write off the remaining depreciation in the final year e.g. an asset which has been bought for £100,000, with an expected life of 10 years and a residual value of zero, needs to be scrapped after the seventh year. Using straight-line depreciation, the value after seven years is calculated by:

$$\frac{£100,000 - 0}{10 \text{ years}} = £10,000 \text{ per annum}$$

After 7 years, total depreciation = £10,000 × 7 = £70,000, so net book value = £30,000 (£100,000 − £70,000)

If it is scrapped (for £0) then an extra £30,000 will need to be written off at the end of the seventh year, making the depreciation charge =

£10,000 + £30,000 = £40,000 for year 7

Question 6

An asset is depreciated by £25,000 per year from £300,000 to £50,000.

a) How long is the expected life? [2]

b) If the asset needs to be sold after six years for £20,000, calculate the amount that needs to be written off in the sixth year. [4]

Prolonging an asset's life

There may be occasions when an asset is not replaced – it may be because the business does not have the necessary finance in place, or it does not have the need for a new asset. Perhaps the asset has proved to be reliable and has been maintained carefully. If the net book value has been reduced to zero and the life is extended then effectively the business has 'free' use of the machine i.e. it can use the machine but will not be required to charge depreciation for the following years.

However, a business may recognise the fact that the asset will be kept beyond its economic life at a point before the economic life is complete e.g. if an asset is to be kept for eight years but after seven years, the business decides the life will be extended for a further two years, then the depreciation charge will change.

Worked example: A business recognises that an asset which has been bought for £100,000, with an expected life of 10 years and a residual value of zero, must be kept for two more years. It is now the end of the ninth year, so only £10,000 remains to be depreciated. According to the definition of depreciation (writing off the net cost of the asset over its useful life) then the £10,000 still remaining to be written off must be spread over two years, not one. Therefore £5,000 per year is written off.

Other provisions

Apart from the change in value of fixed assets or stock (see page 425), there are other parts of the balance sheet which may change in value. A frequent example is that of bad debts. A **bad debt** is when a business feels that the money which it is owed by customers (debtors) is unlikely to be paid. This is connected with the accounting convention of prudence, because even though there may be a small chance that the customer will eventually pay, realistically, the business will assume the money will never be paid. So it must allow for the loss in income by writing off the bad debt as an expense in the profit and loss account. This is usually entered in the section on sales and administration costs, because credit is used as a form of sales promotion.

e.g. Water-It sells fountains and sold a fountain to a company which installed it in its reception area. It is rumoured that the company is going into liquidation, although nothing has been confirmed. The invoice was sent out five months ago and is still to be paid. In this circumstance, Water-It will write off the price of the fountain under bad debts.

Question 7

A taxi company purchases a diesel vehicle to add to its fleet. The new car costs £25,000 and the vehicle is intended to last for four years, being depreciated on a straight-line basis to a residual value of £3,000.

a) Calculate the annual depreciation charge. [2]

b) Calculate the net book value after three years. [3]

c) After three years, the business realises the machine is so reliable it will keep it for a further two years, although the residual value will be reduced to £2,000. Calculate the new annual depreciation charge which it must write off each year. [2]

Points for Revision

Key Terms

depreciation	writing off the net cost of a fixed asset over its economic/useful life
fixed asset	an asset the business owns and intends to keep
net cost	historic cost minus residual value
residual value	the expected scrap value at the end of the fixed asset's useful life
economic/useful life	a period of time during which the machine can be used
straight-line	a method of depreciation which writes off equal amounts each year
declining/reducing balance	a method of depreciation which writes off more in the early years than in the late years; calculated by $(1 - \sqrt[n]{\dfrac{\text{Residual value}}{\text{Historic cost}}} \times \dfrac{100}{1})$ where n is useful life (years)
net book value	amount at which the business values its assets at a particular point in time
bad debt	writing off the value of a debtor, when the business thinks it is unlikely to be paid
profit/loss on disposal	accounts are adjusted if the residual (market) value is not the same as the book value

Definitions Question:
By referring to a business you know, explain the significance of any two of the above
(your teacher may wish to help you choose the terms).   [5] per definition

Summary Points:

1	Firms depreciate those fixed assets which fall in value over their lives.
2	This is done in accordance with the matching principle, whereby the cost of the assets is matched with the benefit it creates for the firm.
3	Depreciation is not a cash flow, rather a method of saving up for the next purchase of a fixed asset.

Mini Case Study

Bert Bacon purchased a computer for his small hotel in December 1999. Although he did not aim to compete with the major hotel chains such as Stakis and Jarvis, he found that customers did make direct comparisons between the quality of the product they provided and those provided by his own establishment. He could not compete with them on price due to the benefits of economies of scale achieved by the competition, although loyal customers of Bert's Hotel preferred the family atmosphere to the rather bland atmosphere of the larger hotels. He tended to attract businessmen who worked away from home on a regular basis. Bert felt that he could enhance his product by offering the use of a computer, so he installed three computers and a printer, at a total cost of £3,000, into an attic room and charged for the use of the computers by the hour. They were to be depreciated using a declining balance method at 40% per annum, for four years. Two years later, he realised that the machines needed upgrading with more memory and software which would cost a total of £400. This would increase the value of the computers by £400.

1 Draw up a table showing the annual depreciation and net book value of the computers predicted for the economic life *at the time of purchase*.   [6]

2 a) If the profit in the second year (before depreciation) was £35,000, calculate the profit after depreciation of the new equipment.   [2]

   b) Calculate the net book value of the computers after the investment in new memory and software.   [2]

   c) Based on your answers to a) and b), calculate the new depreciation expense for the third year.   [2]

3 If Bert decided to sell the computers for £400 after the third year, what would be the loss on disposal?   [2]

4 An alternative way of charging for the computer use might have been simply to add a nominal charge to the price of the hotel room. Outline the advantages and disadvantages of doing this.   [6]

20

Stock valuation

Although stock is an asset which is primarily associated with the balance sheet, any change in the value of stock could affect profit. In the profit and loss account, the cost of goods sold, or cost of sales, is calculated by:

Opening stock + Purchases – Closing stock

	£ million
e.g.	
Sales revenue	80
Opening stock	45
+ Purchases	16
– Closing stock	33
Cost of sales	28
Gross profit	52

If the business sells pork sausages and a food poisoning scare forces the business to destroy £10 million worth of sausages, then this will make the closing stock reduce to £23 million.

By substituting the £23 million for the £33 million, the cost of sales will now be

	£ million
Sales revenue	80
Opening stock	45
+ Purchases	16
– Closing stock	23
Cost of sales	38
Gross profit	42

Remember that the sales revenue has not changed, only the value of the stock. The effect of decreasing the value of stock is to increase the cost of sales, which therefore reduces profit.

Closing stock increases → cost of sales decreases → profit increases

Closing stock decreases → cost of sales increases → profit decreases

A short cut to this is therefore if closing stock increases, profit increases and the opposite is also true.

Question 8

A curtain manufacturer is about to report a gross profit of £47,000 – see accounts below.

Sales revenue		£112,000
Opening stock	£34,000	
Purchases	£49,000	
Closing stock	£18,000	
Cost of sales	£65,000	
Gross profit		£47,000

A fire destroys two-thirds of the closing stock and the business is forced to write off two-thirds of the value.

Explain how the accounts will be adjusted before the profit is announced. [3]

Lowest value of stock

The accounting principle of conservatism (*see Unit 33 Introduction to finance*) states that the business will report the lowest value of profit. Stock is therefore valued at the lower of cost or selling price. The lowest value will therefore report the lowest profit.

Usually, the cost is less than the selling price. However, if the selling price has to be reduced to a figure lower than cost, perhaps for marketing purposes, then any unsold goods must be valued at the selling price.

e.g. a market trader who has bought 300 suitcases for £10 each is forced to lower the price, having sold only 200. To sell the rest, he reduces the price to £8; the closing stock must then be reduced in value. If 100 units are held in closing stock, the value of the stock will be

$100 \times £8 = £800$

and *not*

$100 \times £10 = £1,000$

The reduction in the value of closing stock will reduce profit by the same amount i.e. £200.

Question 9

Frame-It buys in picture frames, paints them in a variety of wood stains and sells them on to furniture stores. The standard frame is bought from the manufacturer for £7 and the business then spends £3 per unit on painting and marketing, selling each one for £15.

a) What will be the value of its closing stock if the business buys in 300 frames and paints them, ready for sale? Explain your answers.   [2]

b) If the market price were forced down to £6 due to competition, how would this affect the closing stock valuation?   [4]

Assumption of stock flow

When a business purchases the same materials over a period of time, the price it pays is likely to change. This will affect the value of the closing stock as reported in the balance sheet, as well as operating profit.

e.g. the following stock information has been extracted from the accounts of Click-It Ltd, a lock manufacturer.

Opening stock 300 springs at £2 each
Week 1 purchased 100 springs at £2.10
Week 2 purchased 300 springs at £2.10

During the two weeks the business uses 500 springs.

What value should the business place on the 200 springs left at the end of week 2?

Assuming that the cost of the stock is lower than the selling price, the value of the closing stock at the end of the second week depends on the assumption of the flow of stock through the business. Three assumptions may be made:

■ **FIFO (first in first out)** – this means that the stock in the business at the start of the two weeks is assumed to have been used first. In the above example the stock which is left is the stock which has been purchased most recently
i.e. 200 × £2.10 = £420, which is the closing stock

■ **LIFO (last in first out)** – this assumes that the stock which is used first comes from the most recent purchases. Therefore the closing stock would be the original stock, which in this case is the opening stock – 200 × £2.00 = £400.

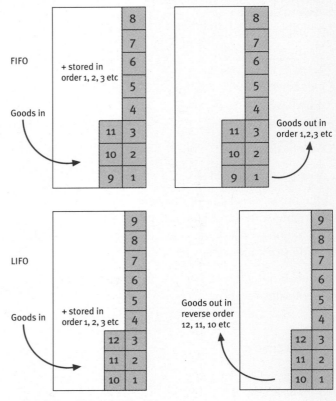

Figure 37.4   FIFO and LIFO

■ **AVCO (average cost)** – this takes the average value of all the stock which has been available for use:

Opening stock:	300 × £2	=	£600
Week 1	100 × £2.10	=	£210
Week 2	300 × £2.10	=	£630
			£1,440

Total value of goods = £1440/700 (number of springs) = £2.06. This is the average value of stock held.
200 × £2.06 = £412

Summaries of the stock valuations are
FIFO = £420
LIFO = £400
AVCO = £412

Question 10

Which of the above valuations will produce the greatest profit? Justify your choice.   [2]

Question 11

Flow-It manufactures plastic tubing. It purchases plastic pellets which it then moulds into tubing. The supplier of the pellets has put its prices up over the past three months. Purchasing patterns are as follows

Month 1 = 300 kg @ £4.00 per kg
Month 2 = 200 kg @ £4.12 per kg
Month 3 = 200 kg @ £4.15 per kg

Opening stock is 100 kg valued at £4 per kg.

The business has 200 kg left at the end of month 3.

Calculate closing stock using
a)   LIFO
b)   FIFO
c)   AVCO
d)   Which method would produce the highest reported profit?   [8]

Historically, in developed countries, there has been a continual increase in prices throughout most industries. This has tended to result in a higher value of closing stock if LIFO has been used (*see Questions 10/11*). Consequently, the Inland Revenue has made stock valuation using LIFO an illegal accounting process which clearly understates profit and therefore understates tax (assuming the cost of buying in stock is rising).

Profit versus cash

Of all the income and expenses within a profit and loss account, the only one which will never be a cash flow is depreciation. The expense which is calculated above is the allowance for writing off the net cost of an asset, not an expense, which means cash must leave the business when the accounts recognise the annual depreciation.

Similarly, the change in value of stock will affect profit, but there will be no effect on cash. The change in stock value arises either due to a change in market conditions or deterioration.

Points for Revision

Key Terms

LIFO   last in first out; assumes most recent stock purchased is the first to be sold

FIFO   first in first out; assumes stock sold first is the original stock bought

AVCO   average cost – uses a weighted average to value the stock

Summary Points:

1   Stock valuation refers to the process of placing a value on closing stock only.

2   The volume of stock does not change when changing the method of valuation.

3   When closing stock falls in value, profit falls by the same amount.

4   There are three methods of valuing stock – LIFO, FIFO and AVCO.

Mini Case Study

In response to suggestions by the weather forecasters, John Cowan bought paddling pools in three batches during the months of March and April in anticipation of a heat wave. He found a supplier who was willing to supply the pools in batches of 500 each, because John could collect them only in this volume, using his brother's transit van. The supplier sold him the first batch at a price of £9 per pool, although for some reason unknown to John, he put his prices up to £10 per pool for the second batch and £11 per pool in the final batch. The supplier was particularly persuasive that John should order enough to be able to satisfy the sudden increase in demand and that having sufficient stock was a prerequisite. May turned out to be one of the hottest months on record and John sold 600 pools from the back of his brother's van in the local market. However, the hot weather quickly subsided during June and sales reached only 200 units. July turned out to be the wettest on record, and he sold only 50 units.

1 Calculate the value of closing stock using
   a) LIFO
   b) FIFO
   c) AVCO
   at the end of July.   [6]

2 Having realised his stock valuation was optimistic and that he had far too many pools left unsold, he estimated that the selling price could be £6 for each of the remaining pools – what would be the effect on profit of the price drop, if previously he had used FIFO?   [3]

3 What market research could John have collected when considering the decision to sell paddling pools?   [5]

4 Discuss how John might have reacted to the increase in the cost of the pools over the three months.   [6]

20

Maxi Case Study

Live Suppliers established itself in Britain in the late 1990s by persuading one famous brand name supplier of jeans to use it as a wholesaler. The owners purchased some buildings in a run-down industrial estate and opened a warehouse. It was located reasonably close to several motorways in the Midlands and used this point to gain contracts with retailers. The business signed a contract five years ago to import and distribute jeans manufactured by an Italian designer – Fabio. Unfortunately the nature of the market meant that style changed quickly and Fabio's main target market, 16–24-year-olds, moved on to new styles the moment the jeans were released. All the famous brand names such as Wrangler and Pepe tried hard to produce innovative styles in the hope that the teenage market would accept the new style, triggering a sudden increase in sales. If the brand failed or the business was second in line to a new product, it would need some frantic marketing activity in order to generate sales. In addition, price cutting was usually undertaken.

The machinery which Live used packaged the jeans before they were dispatched to retailers. The machine was bought three years ago for £80,000 and was to be depreciated over 10 years to a residual value of zero. The business recently decided to update the machinery so Live could package them more securely and stick on the bar code, previously done by hand. The bar code was then scanned at the retailers at the point of sale. The improvement cost £12,000. This added £12,000 to the net book value of the machine at the time of investment. Live has worked out that the machine will not last for 10 years, given the amount of usage. The residual value will remain at zero, but the machine will last only eight years (i.e. a further five years). The business uses straight-line depreciation.

Live Suppliers was the first wholesaler to be used to distribute flared jeans. The first year's trading was extremely successful so the business ordered a large amount of jeans at the end of that year in anticipation of further sales. Its purchasing pattern was as follows:

Table 1

Opening stock		=	0 pairs
Month 1:	2500 pairs	@	£20 per pair
Month 2:	3600 pairs	@	£20.50 per pair
Month 3:	3000 pairs	@	£21 per pair
Month 4:	3000 pairs	@	£21.50 per pair

Each pair of jeans was sold for £35. Unfortunately the business was too focused on the one product and the competition produced the first version of bootleg jeans which meant Live was left with 5000 pairs which had to be sold off at a reduced price. Live approached several discount retailers with a view to selling the excess stock, and received an offer of £15 per pair. Although the business was reluctant to create the wrong image by selling to the discount trade, the extra costs of holding stock and the wasted space meant it had to sell them at any cost.

1 a) Calculate the new net book value following the update of the machine. [3]

b) Calculate the new depreciation charge following the business's decision to write off the machinery over the next five years. [2]

c) If the business decided to change the method of depreciation to declining balance at 40%, work out how profit would be affected during the next year in comparison with straight-line. [4]

d) Compare and contrast the two methods of depreciation. [6]

2 a) Assuming the business uses LIFO, calculate the valuation of stock at the end of the fourth month. [3]

b) How would this valuation change if the business used AVCO? [4]

c) Which of the two stock valuation methods would result in the highest reported profit? [1]

d) How does the offer of £15 per pair affect the valuation of stock?
Explain your answer. [4]

3 Discuss how useful an accurate balance sheet might be to Live Suppliers. [8]

35

Ratio analysis

Learning objectives

Having read this unit, students will be able to

1 appreciate the need for inter-firm, intra-firm and inter-year comparisons of financial statements

2 distinguish between various performance, liquidity, shareholder measures

3 draw conclusions from the calculations whilst recognising the limitations of ratio calculations

Context

The two previous units have been devoted to explaining the elements within financial statements, although the entire process of putting accounts together is aimed at providing an opportunity for stakeholders to interpret and analyse various aspects of a company's activities. Consider two companies, Denby Pottery and Airtours, whose accounts are summarised in Table 1:

Table 1

Both companies' accounts refer to y/e 30.9.98

	Sales revenue	Operating profit	Net assets
Denby Pottery	33.8 million	7.6 million	21 million
Airtours	£2.75 billion	102 million	166 million

(Figures have been rounded for ease of interpretation)

Evidently, Airtours is a larger business in respect of revenue and operating profit, although this does not necessarily make it a better company to invest in, nor a more efficient business. If a calculation is made to compare profit with revenue i.e. the amount of revenue which is turned into profit (operating profit/revenue) then Denby Pottery appears to be the more successful business. Ratio analysis helps stakeholders to judge a company's performance more accurately.

Comparison

Intra-firm – comparing individual figures between different businesses is meaningless unless the context of the size of the separate businesses is clearly stated. A small, specialised hardware shop is going to earn less revenue than B and Q, even though they both operate in the same market and aim their products at the same type of DIY customer. **Intra-firm comparison** therefore means comparing figures within the same business to remove the effect of size.

Inter-firm – looking at several businesses means that comparisons can be made between firms in the same industry, as they will be operating within the same business environment and facing the same trading conditions. **Inter-firm comparison** then allows a direct comparison to be made in terms of relative efficiency, profitability and shareholder performance.

Inter-industry – the above comparison extends to looking at different industries and comparing overall performance of companies in different sectors. This is particularly relevant for potential investors who may target particular industries especially when growth in profit and revenue is expected. Alternatively, a shareholder may wish to invest in a stable, blue-chip business which will earn steady returns. **Inter-industry comparison** allows the investor to make comparisons between two industries which conform to that specification e.g. banking and retailing are both blue-chip industries, with large, stable and famous companies.

Inter-year – financial statements are prepared at one point during the year; although the reference points for each statement are different, each set of accounts reports for only one year. Hence, businesses will provide five-year summaries in their accounts to demonstrate their financial performance over time. This **inter-year comparison** is far more significant in industries where the environment is changing in the following ways:

- in businesses where technological change has an impact on the business e.g. Psion plc

- if a business is sensitive to changes in the trade cycle e.g. McAlpine, the construction business

- when a business operates in different overseas markets which might be growing faster than its domestic market e.g. Unilever, which operates in 180 countries

Whichever reason is cited, comparison over time has an important role to play in the analysis of business performance.

Ratios defined and explained

Ratios can be used to analyse three separate issues in the operations of a business:

Performance, which encompasses profitability and productivity.

Liquidity, which refers to the ability of the business to generate cash for operating the business (for working capital and fixed capital) as and when required.

Shareholder, which concerns the variables that just the shareholders are likely to be interested in, such as dividends, profit for shareholders or the return each share has earned.

For the next section, ratios will be calculated from the balance sheet and profit and loss statement from particular sets of accounts. The business, Wall-Right plc, makes various types of wallpaper and faces strong competition from other companies. Its best-selling line is a market leader which is aimed at the luxury end of the market. Recently, the industry has been in recession which has had an effect on the business. The first ratio (for 1998) has been calculated with direct reference to the figures. You are encouraged to verify the second ratio (1999) by referring to the balance sheet and profit and loss statement below in order for you to be clear where the individual figures are found.

Table 2

Profit and Loss account for year ending 31/12/99 for Wall-Right plc:

	£ million	
	1999	1998
Sales revenue	19	20
Cost of sales	12	12
Gross profit	7	8
Marketing costs	1.5	1
Other operating costs	3.5	4
Operating profit	2	3
Interest payable	0.7	0.5
Profit before tax	1.3	2.5
Tax	0.2	0.5
Profit attributable to Wall-Right plc	1.1	2
Dividends	1.1	1
Retained profit	0	1

Balance sheet as at 31/12/99 for Wall-Right plc:

	1999	1998
Fixed assets	9	10
Current assets		
Stock	4.5	4
Debtors	4.5	3
Cash	1	1
Current liabilities		
Creditors	3.5	3
Other current liabilities	1.5	2
Net current assets	5	3
Long-term liabilities	5	5
Net assets	9	8
Capital employed		
Issued share capital 5m shares @£1	5	5
Retained profit reserve	3	3
	8	8
Average share price	£3.00	£5.00

Performance ratios

Return on net assets = $\frac{\text{operating profit}}{\text{net assets}}$

Otherwise known as primary efficiency ratio, this shows how well a business uses its assets to generate profit (a broad measure of performance). Operating profit is used in these performance ratios because the business has the most influence over that level of profit.

Wall-Right: $1998 = \frac{£3m}{£8m} = 37.5\%$; $1999 = 25\%$.

Description: for every £1 of net assets, the business has earned 25 pence (37.5 pence in 1998) of operating profit. Interpretation and analysis: a significant fall in performance, due possibly to the decline in sales revenue, forced on the company due to the recession. Such a conclusion requires further evidence – using one ratio to summarise and analyse a business's performance is insufficient.

Profit margin = $\frac{\text{operating profit}}{\text{sales revenue}}$

This is a measure of profitability because it shows how well the business controls its operating costs. Industry standards are frequently quoted here and individual results will vary significantly from business to business and industry to industry e.g. a profit margin in food retailing of 6% is exceptionally high, whereas a profit margin of 10% in a restaurant is exceptionally low – a bottle of wine in a restaurant which costs £10 is likely to have cost the restaurant £3–£4 to buy from the wine wholesalers.

Wall-Right: $1998 = \frac{£3m}{£20m} = 15\%$; $1999 = 10.5\%$.

Description: for every £1 of sales revenue, the business has earned 10.5 pence (15 pence) in operating profit. Interpretation and analysis: profitability has fallen, due to operating profit falling, possibly through a fall in sales revenue due to the recession.

A recession may also force the business to increase its spending on promotion, which will have the same downward effect on the margin.

Net asset turnover = $\dfrac{\text{sales revenue}}{\text{net assets}}$

This is a measure of how well the business uses its assets to create sales (a broad measure of productivity). A manufacturing company will have much more money tied up in assets – both fixed and current, so it must make these assets work to earn a profit, as opposed to e.g. a solicitor who will have very little tied up in assets, compared with sales.

Wall-Right: 1998 = $\dfrac{£20m}{£8m}$ = 2.5 times; 1999 = 2.375 times.

Description: for every £1 of net assets, the business has earned £2.375 (£2.50) of revenue.

Interpretation and analysis: Wall-Right has become less productive; although the net assets have remained the same, it is not earning as much sales revenue from their use.

The above three ratios can be combined in the following way:

Return on net assets = profit margin × net asset turnover

Or, put another way,

Performance = profitability × productivity

A business operates and makes profit by initially investing money in assets, which are then used to make and sell products, the revenue from which creates the profit. It is a continually revolving cycle (*see Figure 38.1*).

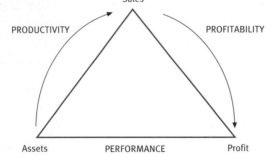

Figure 38.1 This diagram can be used to demonstrate the constituent parts of a business's performance i.e. productivity and profitability

---

Table 3

	Performance	=	profit margin	×	net asset turnover
1998	37.5%	=	15	×	2.5
1999	25%	=	10.5	×	2.375

Interpretation: the drop in performance is indeed due to a fall in both productivity and profitability.

Perhaps the two are linked – if the business cannot sell as much, it does not make as much and possibly loses out on purchasing economies of scale, thereby leading to higher costs, which reduces the profit margin.

Alternatively, it could be trying to sell products at a much cheaper price, which has reduced revenue, because either consumers are very short of spare income to spend on luxuries, or the product is price inelastic and a price reduction has led to a reduction in revenue.

A third interpretation is that extra marketing (marketing costs have increased by 50%) has not been targeted in the correct way, since sales have fallen.

Gross profit margin = $\dfrac{\text{Gross profit}}{\text{sales}}$

Although operating profit has been covered in detail, this is another ratio which examines the extent to which profit is earned from sales. Referring back to Unit 35 Profit and loss account may help you to understand the difference between operating and gross profit.

Wall-Right: 1998 = $\dfrac{£8m}{£20m}$ = 40%; 1999 = 37%.

Description: for every £1 of sales revenue, the business earned 37 pence (40 pence) of gross profit.

Interpretation and analysis: the fall in this ratio goes some way to explaining the fall in performance. The cost of sales is the same, but with a lower revenue.

Question 1

The Light Company manufactures different types of light shade which it sells to various specialist retailers. The market has grown by 20% in the last year. The information in Table 4 has been taken from its annual report.

Table 4

	31/1/00	31/1/99
Sales revenue	130000	100000
Gross profit	78000	55000
Operating profit	39000	33000

a) Calculate, for each year,

    (i) operating profit margin   [2]

    (ii) gross profit margin   [2]

b) Suggest reasons for the changes that happened in the business in the 12 months up to 31.1.2000.   [6]

c) In the analysis above, why is operating profit used to assess the performance of the business, as opposed to other profit calculations which appear later in the profit and loss account?   [3]

Question 2

Manchester United and Weetabix Ltd are two very different businesses in terms of size and activities. Only one-third of Manchester United's revenue comes from gate receipts.
Table 5 shows an extract from the 1998 accounts for both businesses:

Table 5

£m	Weetabix	Manchester Utd
Revenue	308	101
Profit	50	32
Net assets	205	81

a) The other two-thirds of Manchester United's revenue comes from other sources. Suggest what these two sources might be.   [2]

b) Calculate, for each company
    (i) return on net assets
    (ii) profit margin
    (iii) net asset turnover   [6]

c) Using the model explained in Figure 38.1, analyse and compare the performance of the two companies. State, with a reason, which company you would prefer to invest in.   [6]

Liquidity ratios

$$\text{Debtor days} = \frac{\text{debtors}}{\text{sales}} \div 365;$$

otherwise calculated by

$$\text{debtor turnover} = \frac{\text{sales}}{\text{debtors}}$$

e.g. sales = £400 million, debtors = £40 million; debtor turnover = 10 times i.e. debtors pay once every $\frac{365 \text{ days}}{10 \text{ times}}$ per year = 36.5 days

This figure will vary according to how the business uses credit to sell its products. If a furniture store, such as D.F.S, markets its products on a 'buy now, pay later' basis, then debtor days are likely to be over 100 (i.e. over three months). This is especially true when D.F.S advertises on a 'buy now, pay nothing for the first year' basis, as it frequently does.

A milk delivery business, on the other hand, will have debtor days of well under two weeks, since cash or cheque collections are made at the end of each week. Apart from the nature of the business the important factor to look for is whether this ratio is increasing or decreasing. An increase means the business is tying up more money in debtors (which may be as a result of expansion, using credit as a way of selling more units). A decrease may mean that the business is encouraging its customers to pay earlier; this may be done by offering a discount as an incentive.

Wall-Right: 1998 = $\frac{£3m}{£20m} \div 365 = 54.75$ days;

1999 = 86.44 days.
Description: debtors take on average 86.44 days (54.75 days) to settle their bills.
Interpretation and analysis: to tempt customers to buy more, the business might have extended its credit period. Alternatively, it may be concentrating so hard on maintaining sales volume that it may be forgetting to collect in the money owed by customers, or perhaps it has a large customer who is using this business to improve its own cash flow (keeping the cash in its own bank account, by delaying payment). This often happens when a small business has a large business as its main customer.

Creditor days = $\dfrac{\text{creditor}}{\text{purchases}} \div 365$

This ratio demonstrates the speed at which the business pays its suppliers and is therefore the opposite of debtor days. In an ideal world, the business sells its products and gets the cash in, then pays the suppliers! Comparison between creditor days and debtor days may reveal whether the business is facing potential cash flow problems. Purchases are used in the formula (as opposed to sales revenue) because creditors arise out of purchasing goods. As purchases are not available, it is possible to use cost of sales, which is the nearest thing to purchases in the profit and loss account.

> Wall-Right: 1998 = $\dfrac{£3m}{£12m} \div 365 = 91.25$ days;
>
> 1999 = 106 days.
> Description: the business is taking 106 days (91.25 days) to pay its bills.
> Interpretation and analysis: if cash flow is becoming less due to lower sales, then the business will try to put off paying some of its creditors, to ensure cash stays in the business.

Stock turnover = $\dfrac{\text{cost of sales}}{\text{stock}}$

This demonstrates the speed at which the business moves stock. This has been covered in more detail in Unit 28 Stock control. If stock is turned over more quickly, it might mean the business is holding a lower average amount and is perhaps working towards a just-in-time production system. Alternatively, it could be running stock down, especially if it is a business which needs the space for new product lines – calculating stock turnover in a furniture store at the end of December is not a suitable time for analysis of the business, because it will be running stock down in the sales, in preparation for new designs in the New Year.

> Wall-Right: 1998 = $\dfrac{£12m}{£4m} = 3$ times i.e. once every four months (120 days); 1999 = 2.67 (or once every 136 days). The time equivalent of the stock held in days, weeks, months etc. is found by the formula stock days = $\dfrac{365}{\text{stock turnover}}$.
> Description: the business holds enough stock to sell products for 136 days (120 days) without needing more stock.

Interpretation and analysis: As demand has fallen, the business may have insisted on producing the same amount, thereby taking longer to shift the stock. Perhaps it feels the effect of the recession will not last for long, or it has introduced new lines which are not selling. It could also be the case that the business is expecting a sudden surge in demand shortly after the end of the year, hence it will have stock-piled in anticipation of this sales increase. A build-up in stock also represents a significant cost in terms of holding and financing the stock as well as an opportunity cost of tying money up in assets which are unproductive (i.e. not doing anything).

Current ratio = $\dfrac{\text{current assets}}{\text{current liabilities}}$ (a broad measure of liquidity)

Consider the following scenario: all the current liability stakeholders – government (tax), shareholders (dividends), suppliers (creditors), banks (overdraft and short-term loan) – simultaneously call in their debts. This could be because they all think the business is about to go bust and so will be unlikely to repay the amounts owed. Although very unlikely to occur, the business will initially look for the finance in its current assets (i.e. its most liquid assets).

If there is enough money to cover the current liabilities, then the business ought to be able to pay its debts. This, of course, assumes all its debtors pay up straight away and that the business can sell all its stock.

There is no rule-of-thumb which exists for the correct value of this ratio; if the ratio increases over a period of time, then perhaps the business is tying up too much money in working capital, incurring opportunity costs; if the ratio is falling, either the business is running down its current assets on purpose (with a view to raising finance – *see Unit 40 Sources of finance*) or perhaps the business is increasing its current liabilities. Any attempt to earmark an appropriate level for the current ratio (and acid test ratio – *see below*) is dangerous and will result in an incorrect assessment of liquidity.

Most manufacturing businesses may have a current ratio anywhere between 1 and 2, whereas food retailers have current ratios as low as 0.6 (*see question 3*).

Wall-Right: 1998 = $\dfrac{£8m}{£5m}$ = 1.6 times; 1999 = 2 times.

Description: for every £1 of money tied up in current liabilities, the business owns £2 (£1.60) in current assets. Interpretation and analysis: in terms of the analysis of Wall-Right plc, this ratio adds very little. It has been established that there has been an increase in stock days and an increase in debtor days. Although the increase in creditor days suggests one might balance the other, the effect of the lack of sales has been more money tied up in working capital, suggesting the business is being unproductive with its financial resources.

Acid test ratio = $\dfrac{\text{current assets} - \text{stock}}{\text{current liabilities}}$

This is a more stringent test of liquidity which removes the effect of holding stock on the company's liquidity. The main difference between stock and debtors/cash is that stock is unsold and may be more difficult to turn into cash. Although a manufacturing business may well aim for a ratio of 1 (meaning all current liabilities can be met from debtors and cash) this could well be significantly less for companies which have debtor days of one week and stock which can be turned over in two weeks (meaning the stock can be turned into debtors relatively quickly) e.g. Dixons will be able to sell all its stock within three weeks of it arriving at the store and will generate cash immediately (from cash sales) or within a week, from credit sales. This will push the ratio to well below 0.5.

Wall-Right: 1998 = $\dfrac{£8m - £4m}{£5m}$ = 0.8; 1999 = 1.1.

Description: for every £1 of current liabilities, the business has £1.10 (£0.80) tied up in debtors and cash (or liquid assets).
Interpretation and analysis: the increase in acid test reflects the sudden increase in debtor days – money is being tied up with debtors for a longer period of time.

A balance must therefore be made between risk (having a lower current/acid test ratio) and return. As these ratios fall in value, it means the business is being more efficient with its finance and is possibly releasing money for other uses, thereby increasing the overall return.

Question 3

The following pieces of data have been taken from the company accounts of Tate and Lyle, a manufacturer of sugar and other sweetener products, and Somerfield, the food retailer.

Table 6

	Tate and Lyle	Somerfield
Current ratio	1.45	0.32
Acid test ratio	1.00	0.10

a) From the above figures comment on the liquidity of both companies and suggest reasons for the figures.   [6]

b) Explain why a supplier of Somerfield might not be worried about the size of the ratios.   [3]

Capital gearing = $\dfrac{\text{long-term liabilities}}{\text{shareholders' funds}} \left(\dfrac{\text{debt}}{\text{equity}} \right)$

This ratio measures the financial risk of the business. A business will rely on long-term finance from two sources – borrowing (long-term liabilities, or debt) and shareholders (equity or shareholders' funds, which will also include the retained profit ploughed back into the business).

This is an important ratio that a prospective lender will consider before lending the business money (*see Unit 40 Sources of finance*).

Debt/equity therefore measures the amount of risk capital (borrowed finance), compared with non-risk capital (shareholder finance).

No rule-of-thumb exists for this ratio. If the answer is 100%, this means that for every £1 of shareholder funds, the business has borrowed the same amount. Banks will look at this ratio carefully before granting a loan. Some companies have a policy of relying as little as possible on bank borrowing, whereas some can find themselves relying too much on the bank. At the height of its financial problems, Euro Disney had a gearing ratio of 1900%. This meant that to all intents and purposes, the banks owned the business.

Wall-Right: 1998 = $\frac{£5m}{£8m}$ = 62.5%; 1999 = 62.5%.

Description: for every £1 of shareholder funds, the banks have lent 62.5 pence.

Interpretation and analysis: there has been no change in gearing due to there being no extra borrowing and no change in shareholders' funds. Perhaps due to the recession, the banks are unwilling to lend the business any more money.

$$\text{Interest cover} = \frac{\text{operating profit}}{\text{net interest payable}}$$

This calculates the number of times a business can pay its interest from its operating profit. A business normally aims to have this as high as possible. A cover of 4 means one quarter of the profit is used to pay interest. A cover of 1 means all the profit goes to pay interest and less than one means interest must be paid partly from profit, but partly from other sources. In the 1980s, Chrysler, the American car-making business, had an interest cover of 0.1 i.e. it was paying out 10 times as much interest as it was earning in operating profit.

Wall-Right: 1998 = $\frac{£3m}{£0.5m}$ = 6 times; 1999 = 2.86 times.

Description: the business can pay its interest 2.86 times (6 times) from its profit.

Interpretation and analysis: a worrying reduction in this ratio as operating profit has fallen and interest payments have risen. Given that there seems to have been no extra borrowing, it is possible to conclude that the interest rate has risen on the borrowed money.

Question 4

The Lumberjack Company, which sells a variety of tree-felling equipment, has recently expanded to build some new stores in Scotland. The following information has been extracted from its accounts, published on 30.4.2000.

Table 7

£000s

	1999	2000
Operating profit	356	395
Interest payable	90	150
Long-term liabilities	950	1250
Shareholders' funds	3000	3100

a) (i) Calculate gearing and interest cover for the two years. [4]

(ii) Suggest possible reasons for the change in the two ratios in the past 12 months. [5]

b) Why might an increase in gearing be viewed in a positive way by the company's shareholders, even though it may mean, in the short run, lower dividends? [4]

c) Why would a bank be ill-advised to consider just gearing and interest cover before lending to a business? [4]

Shareholder ratios

The difference between this section and the liquidity and performance ratios is that shareholders can make direct comparison and do not necessarily need to allow for the nature and activities of the business.

$$\text{Return on capital employed} = \frac{\text{profit for the financial year the company}}{\text{capital employed}}$$

This demonstrates the amount earned by the business for the shareholders in relation to the shareholders' investment. In this case, capital employed actually means shareholders' funds and the profit attributable represents the amount earned by the company, before dividends.

Wall-Right: 1998 = $\frac{£2m}{£8m}$ = 25%; 1999 = 13.75%.

Description: for every £1 of shareholders' invested money, the business has earned 13.75 pence (25 pence) of profit.

Interpretation and analysis: the reduction in this return is due entirely to the reduction in profit.

$$\text{Earnings per share} = \frac{\text{profit for the financial year the company}}{\text{number of issued ordinary shares}}$$

This shows how much each share has earned in the year. The shareholder is unlikely to receive all this amount, because most companies will elect to pay shareholders a dividend. It is, however, a starting point for the earning potential of each share, both now and in the future.

Wall-Right: $1998 = \dfrac{£2m}{5 \text{ million shares}} = £0.40$; $1999 = £0.22$.
Description: each share has earned £0.22 profit (£0.40).
Interpretation and analysis: the reduction in earnings is due to the reduction in profit.

Dividend per share = $\dfrac{\text{total dividends}}{\text{number of issued shares}}$

This shows how much each share has earned in dividends and each shareholder will multiply the number of shares owned by dividend per share in order to calculate the total amount receivable.

Wall-Right: $1998 = \dfrac{£1m}{5 \text{ million shares}} = £0.20$; $1999 = £0.22$.
Description: each share has earned £0.22 (£0.20) in dividends during the year.
Interpretation and analysis: given the reduction in profit, the business has elected to pay an increase in dividends. This may be due to pressure from shareholders to pay a similar dividend as competitors, if these are increasing their dividend. It may also be an attempt to attract new investors if the business is intending to raise more finance in the future.

Dividend cover = $\dfrac{\text{earnings per share}}{\text{dividend per share}}$

This shows the ease with which a business can meet its dividend payments with this year's profits. As the dividend cover rises, the business will be able to pay dividends more easily from this year's profit and will also be aiming to reinvest a greater proportion of profits. Dividend cover can fall below 1 if the shareholders vote for this. It does mean, however, that the business needs to find finance to pay the dividends which cannot be met from this year's profits. Such an action is very much a short-term measure designed to persuade shareholders to keep their investment in the business and not sell their shares which may lead to a fall in their value.

Wall-Right: $1998 = \dfrac{£0.40}{£0.20} = 2$ times; $1999 = 1$ (once).
Description: the business can meet its dividends payment once (twice) from its profit.
Interpretation and analysis: the insistence of the business on increasing its dividend payment from a reduction in profit means the business has no money left for reinvestment this year. Any new investment will require funding from elsewhere.

Dividend yield = $\dfrac{\text{dividend per share}}{\text{market price per share}}$

This shows the percentage yield of the dividends in relation to the price of the share. This ratio changes regularly, as the shares are traded and the share price changes. Dividends stay the same once they have been announced for the financial year, therefore not much can be read into this ratio unless it is examined on a day-by-day basis over a period of time. On this basis, if the dividend yield increases, it normally means the share price has actually reduced.

Wall-Right: $1998 = \dfrac{£0.20}{£5.00} = 4\%$; $1999 = 8.8\%$.
Description: each share is earning a yield from the dividend of 8.8% (4%).
Interpretation and analysis: the dividend has been increased, but between last year and this year, the price has fallen significantly (40% of last year's value) implying that investors have been selling the share, probably because they believe the share will lose further value, or because the reduction in profit suggests the company is facing problems with the recession.

Price earnings ratio (PE) = $\dfrac{\text{market price per share}}{\text{earnings per share}}$

This shows the confidence which investors have in the future prospects of a particular business. If a PE ratio is 10, calculated from an example of a business with a share price of £4 and earnings per share of £0.40, when a share is bought, the new owner will be able to earn £0.40, assuming earnings stay the same in the future. In other words, it will take 10 years (× £0.40) to repay the investment. Of course, the investor hopes that the earnings will increase. Consequently, if a PE ratio is

20 times, it means investors are willing to pay 20 times the earnings, in order to own the share. Investors who invest in companies with a high PE ratio expect the share price and the business to grow in the future.

Wall-Right: 1998 = $\dfrac{£5.00}{£0.40}$ = 12.5 times; 1999 = 11.4 times.

Description: the market is willing to pay 11.4 times the earnings (12.5 times) in order to receive the profit for the financial year the business.

Interpretation and analysis: the halving of the share price, even though the earnings per share are just above half, has produced a fall in the PE ratio. The market feels that this company will continue to suffer during the recession.

Whether this ratio is high or low depends on the average for that particular industry sector and for the stock exchange as a whole. The PE ratio and dividend yield are quoted in the *Financial Times* each day as are the averages for the FTSE 100 and for each sector. Such ratios give a clear indication of the market's perception of future growth.

Question 5

Consider the following graph of earnings per share and dividends per share for File-It Ltd, a business which makes diaries for executives.

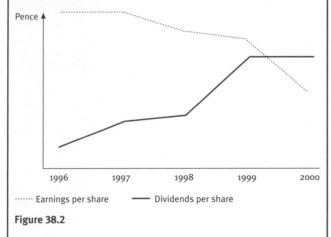

Figure 38.2

Explain the problems faced by the business in the above diagram and suggest possible remedies.   [8]

Question 6

Henry Osros, an investor, is considering a £20,000 investment in one of two companies:

1 WOW plc, a distribution business which has grown steadily over recent years.

2 The Local Eastland Bank, which has been established for 120 years and has just converted into a PLC.

Table 8

Average figures for 1999

	PE	Dividend yield
WOW plc	23	3%
Eastland	16	6%
FTSE 100	19	4%

Using the ratios,
a) Based on the information provided in Table 8, advise Henry on the benefits and potential problems of investing in either business.   [7]

b) What other factors should Henry consider before making the investment?   [5]

Activity

By referring to the website of any broadsheet newspaper, keep a record of the share price, dividend yield and price earnings ratio over a period of 10 days of six different companies, each within different industrial sectors. Compare the performance of the companies with the stock exchange average for the two ratios.

Try and suggest possible reasons for the changes that occur.

Limitations of ratios

Being able to calculate ratios is by no means the only method of analysing a set of accounts, because there are limitations to the use which ratios may serve:

■ No account is taken of changes in strategy or management over a period of time. Thus a business may have taken the decision to aim at the lower end of a particular market, meaning that profit margins may drop, but net asset turnover may rise.

- No account is taken of inflation over time, which can have an effect on the values within the accounts, thereby rendering analysis almost useless without some reference to the magnitude of inflation.

- No account is taken of external influences such as the trade cycle or a competitor's actions, which may cause a change to the ratios e.g. a competitor goes out of business, allowing the company to increase its price. This will be reflected through, amongst other things, an increase in profit margin, implying the business has been more efficient, which, in this case, is not strictly correct.

- Accounting rules and regulations may alter over time, meaning that the auditors may value assets in a different way, even though the assets are the same from one year to the next.

- Detailed knowledge of the business and how it operates is required before meaningful conclusions can be drawn.

- Both the balance sheet and profit and loss account have several inherent problems in terms of accuracy (*see Units 35 and 36*). The ratios and therefore the analysis that ensues always assume the figures within the financial statements are accurate. Once accuracy is lost, the analysis is meaningless.

- Several assumptions need to be made e.g. although debtor days give some guidance to potential cash flow problems, there are some assumptions which underlie this ratio:
  1 all customers pay the full amount owed i.e. none of the customers goes bust between signing an invoice and paying
  2 sales are constant throughout the year, which is impossible in any business
  3 the debtor figure is the average debtor figure for the year. This may not be the case e.g. if a major customer has just paid a large bill, then debtors will be unrealistically low compared with the average.

Ratios therefore provide a framework for identifying problems, rather than adding anything to the decision making process.

Question 7

Using a supply and demand diagram, show the likely consequences for the share price if the business declared a dividend that was a lot lower than expected. [4]

Points for Revision

Key Terms

intra-firm comparison	the comparison of figures within the same company and within the same year
inter-firm comparison	a comparison of two businesses, usually within the same industrial sector
inter-year comparison	examination of financial information over a period of time
inter-industry comparison	comparison of overall industries
performance ratio	examines the profitability, productivity and activity of a business
liquidity ratio	examines the parts of the business associated with either short-term or long-term finance
shareholder ratio	considers the information which shareholders might examine and analyse
profitability	the ability of a business to earn profit from revenue or assets

Definitions Question:
By referring to a business you know, explain the significance of any three of the above terms (your teacher may wish to select the terms).   [5] per definition

The following is a summary of the ratios and formulae for your reference when making calculations:

Return on net assets = operating profit/net assets

Profit margin = operating profit/sales revenue

Net asset turnover = sales revenue/net assets

Debtor days = debtors/sales/365

Creditor days = creditors/purchases/365

Stock turnover = cost of sales/stock

Current ratio = current assets/current liabilities

Acid-test ratio = current assets – stock/current liabilities

Capital gearing = long-term liabilities/shareholders' funds (debt/equity)

Interest cover = operating profit/net interest payable

Return on capital employed = profit for the financial year the company/capital employed

Earnings per share = profit for the financial year the company/number of issued ordinary shares

Dividend per share = total dividends/number of issued shares

Dividend cover = profit for the financial year the company or earnings per share/dividends per share

Dividend yield = dividend per share/market price per share

Price earnings ratio (PE) = market price per share/earnings per share

Summary Points:

1 Once accounts have been drawn up, then analysis of the business can take place.

2 Ratios will differ according to the nature and activities of the individual business.

3 Comparison must be made within the company and between other companies and industries as well as over a period of time.

4 Ratios fail to consider non-financial information, so they help to identify problem areas with a view to taking decisions.

Mini Case Study

Fab-Weld Ltd manufactures a range of iron and steel products to order. Staircases, iron gates and decorative plant pot holders earn the most money for Fab-Weld, because of the volume of orders, although the most profitable orders are for steel structures for the building of workshops and small factories. It purchases raw materials and employs a variety of sheet metal workers and welders to assemble the products. Due to the long lead time of manufacturing, the business has a large amount of work-in-progress stock and has to manage its liquidity carefully.

Recently, the business has struggled to maintain a full order book and has been forced to reduce its prices. With sales revenue under pressure, cash flow has also become another concern for the business. The turnover of products sold has gradually fallen, leading to an increase in stock days. In addition, the previous financial director seemed more obsessed with his own career than his job, and the newly appointed financial director has mentioned the worrying increase in debtor days, since the standard period of credit is 90 days. In 1999, the business earned operating profit of £630,000 from revenue of £3,400,000. Despite revenue falling by only 2% during 2000, operating profit had decreased by £40,000, which resulted in a lower profit margin. Shareholders were clearly concerned about how the business was going to turn the situation round.

The following five-year profile has been taken from the set of accounts from 2000.

Table 9

	1996	1997	1998	1999	2000
Sales revenue	£2.3m	£2.5m	£3.1m	£3.4m	?
Stock days	65	68	68	79	102
Debtor days	60	59	73	75	110

1 State and justify your choice of three ratios that the shareholders may consider when analysing Fab-Weld's use of their investment.   [5]

2 Explain why cash flow is important for a business such as Fab-Weld.   [3]

3 a) Calculate revenue for 2000 and the profit margin for 1999 and 2000.   [5]

   b) Explain why there is a difference in the two profit margins.   [4]

4 By using all the numerical information available, analyse the problems facing the business and suggest possible solutions.   [8]

25

Maxi Case Study

MFI is a group of companies associated primarily with furniture retailing, although it also manufactures kitchens and bedroom furniture, as well as building and leasing property. The retailing business sells a range of kitchen furniture throughout its 186 stores in Britain. The products are displayed in the store, but are sold as a flat pack, which the buyer must then assemble. Its main brand is Hygena; although the business does sell a variety of different furniture products, kitchens are regarded as the firm's core products and during 1998 MFI focused carefully on developing the markets for these core products. This was done by

1 targeted advertising

2 brand support

3 new product development

4 a focus on sales and distribution

Some products were dropped which fell in the category of not being able to be 'home delivered economically'. This meant a fall in the product range from 12,000 lines to 5,000 lines as less profitable product lines were discontinued. This meant that one-off costs of redundancy and stock write-offs cost the business £20 million during 1998, although the cost savings were likely to increase profit by £25 million per year in the future.

MFI also moved towards a home delivery service which was increasingly demanded by customers. It then became possible to remove the branch warehouses altogether, replacing them with Home Delivery Centres which would hold all the stock. Now, when a product is ordered, instead of the customer picking it up at the branch warehouse, it is delivered directly to the customer's home. This has allowed the business to save costs by reducing warehouse space and staff, which has more than offset the extra costs of home delivery. Despite that, 1998 was a difficult year with a rise in interest rates which affected consumer confidence, resulting in sales which were a good deal lower than expected.

Profit and loss account for year ending 25/4/98

£ million	1998	1997
Turnover	894.8	845.6
Operating profit*	65.4	75
Net interest payable	(5)	(4.7)
Profit before tax	60.4	70.3
Profit after tax	43	48.5
Dividends	(29.3)	(28.5)
Retained profit	13.7	20

* includes profit on disposal of fixed asset of 5.1 million

Balance sheet as at 25/4/98

		1998		1997
Fixed assets		357.8		309.1
Current assets				
Stocks	93.9		96.5	
Debtors	70.9		75.6	
Cash	38.2		24.2	
		203		196.3
Current liabilities		293.5		275.7
Net current assets		(90.5)		(79.4)
Long-term liabilities		(27.2)		(6.5)
Net assets		**240.1**		**223.2**
Capital employed				
Share capital		59.5		59.1
Reserves		180.6		164.1
		240.1		**223.2**

The manufacturing business Hygena is the lowest cost producer of kitchens and bedrooms in Europe and in 1998 MFI invested well over £30 million in redesigning the production process to create space for further manufacturing projects which have since allowed MFI to broaden its core product range.

1 Define: new product development, stock write-offs.   [4]

2 Calculate the increase in the level of gearing from 1997 to 1998. Outline the evidence in the text which explains the increase in gearing.   [4]

3 How will the profit on disposal of fixed assets have been calculated?   [2]

4 Explain how the focus on the market (numbered 1–4 in the case study) might have contributed to the success of MFI's core products during 1998.   [6]

5 a) Calculate, for both years:
  i) stock days
  ii) debtor days
  iii) current ratio   [3]

  b) Comment on the liquidity of the business from 1997 to 1998.   [5]

6 Using the three ratios outlined in Figure 38.1, explain how the performance has changed between 1997 and 1998.   [5]

7 Calculate two ratios which the shareholders of MFI might be interested in. Comment on the results you find.   [4]

8 Discuss whether the businesses under the control of MFI have a logical connection.   [12]

45

Investment appraisal

Learning objectives

Having read this unit, students will be able to

1 understand the nature of the decisions which can be made using investment appraisal

2 identify and use the various techniques for assessing investments, drawing conclusions from the answers

3 appreciate the assumptions which underlie the calculations

Context

When a business makes an investment, this usually refers to the purchase of capital goods such as plant and equipment (machines). It is important for any business to be able to decide whether a particular investment is going to be 'worthwhile'. It is also important to be able to compare potential investment plans assuming it is not possible to undertake all such projects in one go. When Bass built its canning plant in Burton-on-Trent, it invested significant levels of capital in modern machinery, in addition to several redundancies. When assessing whether to carry out this investment Bass would have balanced the initial costs against the benefits of faster production. Several criteria can be used to judge whether a long-term investment is worth carrying out. The business may consider how quickly the investment is recouped (payback)/assess the profitability of the investment (annual rate of return). Bass would also have considered the effect of redundancies on the work-force and perhaps the need for training to use the new machinery.

Types of investment

The **investment appraisal** techniques considered in this unit all relate to long-term investment i.e. investment which lasts for more than one year e.g.

- **plant and machinery** – buying new, technologically advanced machinery

- **land and buildings** – new factories and warehouse space for expansion

- **redundancies** – when becoming more capital-intensive

- **marketing** – when spending a significant amount on long-term brand building

- **patents** – when a company spends money protecting its inventions

- **an entire company** – acquisition of a competitor or a supplier

All the above result in some form of benefit. This benefit is achieved in one of two ways: either the business will increase its revenue (perhaps with an advertising campaign) or it will reduce its costs (when employing less labour due to new machinery).

How is the investment assessed?

Payback

One method of measuring the success of any proposed investment is to calculate how quickly the cost of the investment can be recouped. The quicker the **payback** period, the better.

Table 1

	Project A	Project B
Cash flow		
End of Year (EOY) 0	– 40,000	– 40,000
EOY 1	20,000	40,000
EOY 2	30,000	30,000
EOY 3	40,000	20,000

Cash flow means revenue – operating costs, assuming all transactions are in cash. This does not include the investment cost. End of year means that the cash flows come into the business by the end of the year.

Payback is the amount of time that it takes for the investment to be repaid. In Project A, the investment is £40,000. £20,000 comes in during the first year and £30,000 during the second year. So by the end of the second year, £50,000 has come in, and payback has been achieved by EOY2. If an accurate payback period is required (i.e. to the nearest month), it must be assumed that the cash flows are constant throughout the year. In this case, after EOY1, the business needs a further £20,000 to achieve the payback of £40,000 (initial investment). Due to the fact that £30,000 comes in during year 2, the business will reach payback in

$$12 \text{ months} \times \frac{£20,000 \text{ (initial investment)}}{£30,000 \text{ (total received in year 2)}}$$

Therefore payback is achieved in 1 year and 8 months.

The payback for Project B is exactly 1 year.

Question 1

For the following two projects, calculate the payback period. Recommend which project to choose.   [5]

Cash flow (£000)

	Project A	Project B
EOY 0	– 100	– 100
EOY 1	20	35
EOY 2	25	35
EOY 3	35	30
EOY 4	25	15
EOY 5	25	10

Question 2

Calculate the payback for an investment costing £100,000, which earns cash flows of:

Year 1: £10,000
Year 2: £20,000
Year 3: £50,000
Year 4: £60,000
Year 5: £60,000   [3]

Complicated cash flows?

Table 2

	Cash flow	Cumulative cash flow
EOY 0	– 29,700	– 29,700
EOY 1	11,300	– 18,400
EOY 2	12,900	– 5,500
EOY 3	15,200	9,700
EOY 4	10,400	20,100
EOY 5	5,100	25,200

In the above example, the numbers are more complicated, so using a cumulative cash flow may be easier. Here the payback will be by the end of year 3 i.e. when the cumulative cash flow is positive.

Timing of cash flows

In Table 3, both projects have the same payback, but in different ways. If a business is attempting to decide between the two projects, it may choose B on the grounds that the earlier cash flows (in B, the greatest cash flows) occur in year 1, which is arguably easier to forecast and therefore more accurate. The fact that more is coming in earlier could be significant to the liquidity of the business.

Table 3

	Project A	Project B
EOY 0	– 12,000	– 12,000
EOY 1	4,000	6,000
EOY 2	4,000	3,000
EOY 3	4,000	3,000
EOY 4	4,000	3,000
EOY 5	4,000	3,000

In addition, no account is taken of any cash inflows after the payback period.

Although according to the payback method, projects have the same payback, the cash flows after the payback make Project A more attractive. So, taking into account all the cash inflows over the life of the investment, in other words the cash inflows after the payback period, Project A is a much better option. It is therefore important to realise that the payback method

is only one guide to which is the best investment option to undertake. As it is clear to see, there is no consideration of the profitability of each of the options proposed.

Another weakness of the payback method is its failure to take account of the value of money over time.

■ Advantages of payback

a) It is simple to use
b) It is easy to understand
c) It is an appropriate method to use if there is concern over liquidity problems
d) It is a useful initial 'test' as to the validity of an investment
e) It is a valuable assessment of the risk involved (the shorter the payback the less risk involved)

■ Disadvantages of payback

a) Payback fails to take into account any of the cash inflows after the payback period
b) It takes no account of the value of money over time
c) It does not consider the profitability of the investment

There is therefore a need to find a method of calculating a more realistic value for the likely return on the proposed investment.

Annual average rate of return (AARoR)

otherwise known as
Accounting rate of return (ARR)
Average rate of return (ARR)

N.B. The following technique may be called any of the above.

Measuring profitability as a rate of return on an investment is a simple method of assessing different investment proposals. In its simplest form it is calculated by finding the percentage of the investment that the profit gained represents. There are several steps to this calculation, demonstrated by the following example.

Cash flow		
	EOY 0	(£20,000)
	EOY 1	£10,000
	EOY 2	£12,000
	EOY 3	£13,000

Step 1: Calculate total cash flow

Total cash inflow	£35,000

Step 2: Calculate profit

– cost of investment	£20,000
Profit for 3 years	= £15,000

Step 3: Calculate average profit by dividing by number of years

$$\frac{\text{Total profit}}{\text{Number of years}} = \frac{£15,000}{3}$$

Average profit = £ 5,000

Step 4: Divide average profit by initial investment

$$\frac{\text{Average profit}}{\text{Initial investment}} = \frac{£ 5,000}{£20,000}$$

AARoR = 25%

It is this average profit that is then divided by the value of the investment to give a return figure.

Whether this rate of return is an acceptable level will depend upon the targets set by the individual business.

This technique also avoids the danger of just selecting the investment which yields the highest cash inflow without taking into consideration the percentage return on the investment (see Table 4).

Table 4

Cash flow

	Project A	Project B
EOY 0	– 10,000	– 18,000
EOY 1	3,000	6,000
EOY 2	6,000	9,000
EOY 3	7,000	12,000
Total cash inflow	16,000	27,000
Total profit (minus investment)	6,000	9,000
Average profit	2,000	3,000
AARoR	20%	16.7%

It is of interest to note that the total cash inflow, the amount of profit and the average annual profit were higher for Project B. But the **annual average rate of return** is higher for Project A.

Question 3

Using the information contained in Table 5, calculate the AARoR, showing all your working for both projects. [6]

Table 5

Cash flow (£000)

	Project A	Project B
EOY 0	– 100	– 100
EOY 1	20	35
EOY 2	25	35
EOY 3	35	30
EOY 4	25	15
EOY 5	25	10

■ Advantages of AARoR

a) It takes into consideration all cash flows throughout the life of the investment

b) It gives an indication of both the cash flows and the profitability of the investment

■ Disadvantages of AARoR

a) It takes no account of when the cash flows occur

b) It takes no account of the consequences of time upon the value of money

Question 4

A manufacturer of assembly equipment has to decide whether to invest in one of two projects. The first is to purchase a new factory to house its packaging machines which are always in high demand. The alternative is to manufacture and market a machine that checks the weight of packaged products – a completely new idea for the business and the market. The costs and cash flows for each option are given overleaf.

(£000)	New factory	New machine
Investment cost	− 500	− 100
Cash flows EOY 1	80	30
EOY 2	130	30
EOY 3	180	40
EOY 4	280	50
EOY 5	350	60

a) Calculate the average rate of return for both options (show your working). [6]

b) Calculate payback for both options. [4]

c) Which option would you choose and why? (Include any other information you would like before making a final decision). [10]

Net present value

This method takes into account the value of money over time and is therefore a more realistic appraisal method.

It concentrates on the timing of cash flows and allows an estimation as to the likelihood of the investment being profitable.

Try to think about lending a friend £5 and being paid back in one year's time; would you be able to buy the same amount of goods with the £5? The amount that could have been earned if the money was put into a bank rather than spent on buying a new machine is another important consideration and ought to help you to understand the concept of **net present value**.

If £100 cash was placed in a bank account which yielded interest of 10% per annum which is compounded, the account would be thus:

Table 6
Year 1 £100 @ 10% = £110
Year 2 £110 @ 10% = £121
Year 3 £121 @ 10% = £133
Year 2 £133 @ 10% = £146

According to Table 6, £100 today is worth £146 in four years' time. Conversely, £146 in four years' time is worth £100 today. Therefore, although an investment may have a cash inflow of £150 in four years' time, it is actually only worth just over £100 at today's value. The cash is 'converted' into today's values by discounting the future inflows.

Opportunity cost

When choosing an investment (e.g. in a new machine, known as X), a business will consider alternative uses for the capital. The most simple is putting the money in a bank at e.g. 10% per annum. This recalls the definition of opportunity cost i.e. if the business invests in machine X, it cannot deposit the money in the bank and therefore earns no interest from the bank. Net present value compares the return from machine X with the potential interest gained from the bank.

In order to make the comparison, a discount rate is required, which is based on the opportunity cost (here, the interest rate).

If machine X is expected to last only one year and return £9,400, but costs £8,300 to purchase, should the business put the money in the bank if the interest rate is 11%?

The target amount the business needs is £9,400, so how much must it invest in order to take out £9,400 in one year's time?

Let us call the amount required in the bank £y.

£y × 1.11 (increasing the deposit by 11%) = £9,400

$$£y = \frac{9,400}{1.11} = £8,468.$$

So the business must invest £8,468 now in the bank if the interest rate is 11%. However, the machine costs only £8,300, so if the business gets £9,400 in year 1, the return from the machine is greater than 11%.

With a machine which lasts longer than one year, the calculation becomes more complicated and requires a table of discount factors (which are always supplied in examinations).

$\frac{9,400}{1.11}$ which can otherwise be written as $9,400 \times \frac{1}{1.11}$

$$\frac{1}{1.11} = 0.901 \ (\textit{see Table 7 for more information}).$$

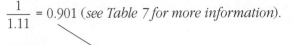

Table 7

Discount rate

Year	6.00%	7.00%	8.00%	9.00%	10.00%	11.00%	12.00%	13.00%	14.00%	15.00%
1	0.943	0.935	0.926	0.917	0.909	0.901	0.893	0.885	0.877	0.870
2	0.890	0.873	0.857	0.842	0.826	0.812	0.797	0.783	0.769	0.756
3	0.840	0.816	0.794	0.772	0.751	0.731	0.712	0.693	0.675	0.658
4	0.792	0.763	0.735	0.708	0.683	0.659	0.636	0.613	0.592	0.572
5	0.747	0.713	0.681	0.650	0.621	0.593	0.567	0.543	0.519	0.497
6	0.705	0.666	0.630	0.596	0.564	0.535	0.507	0.480	0.456	0.432
7	0.665	0.623	0.583	0.547	0.513	0.482	0.452	0.425	0.400	0.376
8	0.627	0.582	0.540	0.502	0.467	0.434	0.404	0.376	0.351	0.327
9	0.592	0.544	0.500	0.460	0.424	0.391	0.361	0.333	0.308	0.284
10	0.558	0.508	0.463	0.422	0.386	0.352	0.322	0.295	0.270	0.247

Once the discount rate has been chosen, it is possible to calculate the net present value (NPV) which is calculated by adding all the **Discounted Cash Flows (DCFs)**. When this process is applied to several years of an investment, the calculations are set out as follows:

Table 8

Year	Cash flow	Discount factor	Discounted cash flow (cash flow × discount factor)
		10%	(DCF)
0	(5,000)	1	(5,000)
1	1,000	0,909	909
2	1,000	0.826	826
3	1,000	0.751	751
4	1,000	0.683	683
5	1,000	0.621	621
6	1,000	0.564	564
7	1,000	0.513	513
8	1,000	0.467	467

Net present value £334

The NPV is calculated by adding the DCFs for each year and then subtracting the initial cost of the investment. It is interesting to note that, at first glance, the investment appears worthwhile. A net present value simply means that in comparison with the discount rate, the return of the project is greater (than 10%) and on financial grounds is worthwhile.

Question 5

Calculate the net present value for Schemes A and B, showing all your working. Use a discount factor of 6%. [6]

Net cash flow (£000)

	Scheme A	Scheme B
EOY 0	– 100	– 100
EOY 1	20	35
EOY 2	25	35
EOY 3	35	30
EOY 4	25	15
EOY 5	25	10

Question 6

Woof-It, a manufacturer of dog collars, is considering the purchase of a new machine to produce a range of new leather collars. The machine will cost £42,000 and will result in the following cash flows:

(£000)

EOY 1	15
EOY 2	14
EOY 3	12
EOY 4	11
EOY 5	8
EOY 6	7

The above figures were seen as being slightly optimistic by the local firm of accountants, which suggested that it was more likely that sales would cease after four years. As a consequence, the machine could be sold for £10,000.

Calculate the NPV for both the optimistic and pessimistic options (assume a discount factor of 8%). [6]

Factors affecting the choice of discount rate

- **Opportunity cost** – the alternative investment choice. The business must earn more than the 'next best alternative'.

- **Cost of capital** – if the business needs to raise finance, the return on the project must exceed the cost of finance. Otherwise, no profit will be made.

- **Manager's objectives** – Lord Weinstock of GEC used to state that all investment projects should make a return of 20% – this was apparently not based on any scientific decision making process.

- **Risk** – as projects become riskier, the required return increases; this is then reflected in the discount rate (being higher).

- **Returns on net assets of the business** – any investment ought to earn a return which is consistent with the return on net assets for the business.

- **Time length of investment** – the longer the investment's life, the higher the discount factor.

- **Previous similar projects** – if the business has performed this type of investment before, it has a method of comparison for deciding on the appropriate discount factor.

Two final assumptions need bearing in mind – that the discount rate remains appropriate for the entire investment because if the interest rate is changed in the middle of an investment, this cannot be reflected in the calculations at the outset e.g. between July 1998 and February 1999, the interest rate changed five times. The business can forecast an investment with several possible interest rates and change them accordingly – this is known as sensitivity analysis.

- ## Advantages of discounted cash flow

  a) It takes into account the value of money over time
  b) All cash flows are taken into consideration, unlike payback
  c) It is more scientific than the other techniques

- ## Disadvantages of discounted cash flow

  a) It is more difficult to calculate
  b) The selection of the discount factor is crucial to the NPV, but it is to some extent guesswork what percentage is used

All three together?

Payback, net present value and annual average rate of return (ARRoR) can be used to decide which investment option ought to be undertaken. Using just one appraisal technique could be misleading e.g. a business which considers two projects involving the same initial cost may find the results conflict with each other. One may have higher cash flows early on in the project but which deteriorate quickly, whereas the other may have constant steady cash flows which produce a higher profit. Clearly the first will have a quicker payback, but the second will have a better AARoR. The final decision, in these cases, will depend on the business's objectives.

Question 7

a) A business which manufactures soft drinks is considering three projects
   A several new labour-saving machines
   B a new marketing campaign
   C buying a small packaging business

   Using Table 9, calculate:
   i)   Payback   [4]
   ii) AARoR   [6]
   iii) Net present value at 10%   [6]

b) Advise the business as to the best option, on financial grounds only.   [5]

c) Suggest the non-financial factors that would influence your final decision.   [5]

Table 9

Net cash flow (£000)

	Project A	Project B	Project C
EOY 0	– 100	– 100	– 100
EOY 1	30	35	10
EOY 2	32	35	30
EOY 3	35	30	40
EOY 4	25	15	30
EOY 5	10	10	25

Internal rate of return

Sometimes calculating the net present value does not give us enough information. Specifically, it does not tell the business the exact rate of return which the project is earning (taking into account the time value of money). The **internal rate of return** allows this figure to be calculated. This is done by calculating two net present value figures using two discount factors – one which produces a positive net present value and one which produces a negative net present value. This allows the business to find out the discount factor which creates a net present value of zero. Referring back to the net present value calculations earlier in this unit, the answer tells the business how the return of the project compares with the discount factor which is being applied. If the NPV is positive, the return is higher than the discount rate and if the answer is negative the return is lower. If, then, the net present value is exactly zero, the discount factor which is applied is, in fact, the internal rate of return of the actual project.

The way of finding an approximation to the internal rate of return is by plotting the two net present values against the two discount rates.

e.g. Project R is assessed at 10% and 15%, producing the following results:

Plotting these two figures results in:

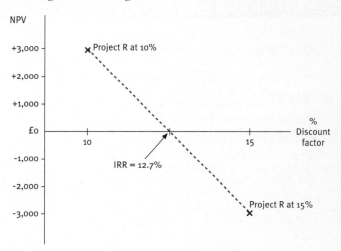

Figure 39.1   Internal rate of return

The internal rate of return is approximately 12.7%. This means the business can ascertain whether the project is financially viable. If it finds a return which is better than 12.7%, with the same level of risk, it will not undertake Project R.

Table 10				
	10%		15%	
Cash flow	Discount factor	DCF	Discount factor	DCF
– 50000	1	– 50000	1	– 50000
20000	0.91	18200	0.86	17200
20000	0.83	16600	0.75	15000
15000	0.75	11250	0.65	9750
10000	0.68	6800	0.57	5700
	NPV	2850	NPV	– 2350

Points for Revision

Key Terms

investment appraisal	an attempt to assess the financial feasibility of an investment option
payback	the time it takes to recover the cost of an investment
annual average rate of return (ARRoR)	an investment appraisal technique which measures the average annual rate of return as a percentage of the cost of the investment
net present value (NPV)	the present value of the future cash inflows, after subtracting the initial cost of the investment
Discounted Cash Flow (DCF)	an appraisal technique to calculate the NPV, allowing for the opportunity cost of the investment
internal rate of return	the discount rate at which the net present value equals zero – i.e. the return of the project when adjusted for the time value of money

Definitions Question:
By referring to a business you know, explain the significance of any two of the above terms (your teacher may wish to help you choose).   [5] per definition

Summary Points:

1   A business uses investment appraisal to assess the financial viability of long-term investments.

2   The application of the various investment appraisal techniques is an attempt to assess the risk involved.

3   There are several assumptions involved within investment appraisal e.g. accuracy of cash flow, discount factors and the ability of the business to finance the investment.

Mini Case Study

Shift-It Ltd, a transport services business located near Stockport in Cheshire, is facing some intense competition from nearby companies and is wondering how best to deal with the problem. In an attempt to maintain its share of the market, the business has to decide between two plans put forward by the fleet manager.

The first option is to purchase a new low loader vehicle capable of transporting very heavy and bulky loads. This vehicle would cost £85,000. The transport manager has indicated that the low loader would bring in receipts of £600 per day and would be used on average three days a week, for 48 weeks a year. Tax, insurance and fuel are estimated to cost £65,400 a year. The estimated life of the low loader is seven years.

The second option is to purchase a fleet of five removal vans in an attempt to widen the customer base of the business. This option would cost £150,000 and the estimated cash inflows are £32,000 per annum. The expected life of these vehicles is only five years at the most.

1 Calculate the payback period for both options.   [4]

2 Define and calculate the average annual rate of return (ARRoR) for both options.   [6]

3 Using your answers to questions 1 and 2, suggest which option, if any, Shift-It ought to pursue.   [2]

4 Discuss the other factors which the business might consider before making a final decision.   [8]

                                                                                              20

Maxi Case Study

KALO Ltd manufactures the frames on to which caravans are fitted. The frames are made of either steel or aluminium. The latter is a lighter material and therefore earns the business more in terms of sales revenue, because it means that the caravan weight is lighter. Caravan owners prefer aluminium frames because their cars do not have to be as powerful to tow them. Therefore caravan manufacturers are keen to use aluminium frames because they mean more sales. Unfortunately, demand has outstripped capacity at KALO's factory and in order to be able to capitalise on the growing market, the board of directors has been faced with two choices.

Option 1 concerns investing in new machinery, which would allow it to increase output to satisfy the growing demand. The new machinery would be imported from Germany and would cost £6 million, although with the prospect of a fluctuating £:euro exchange rate, forecasting the cost of replacement parts will be difficult. Despite this, the business has made an attempt to forecast the new sales levels and costs as follows:

	Volume	Price	Variable costs	Fixed costs
EOY 1	6,000	£1,200	£700	£900,000
EOY 2	8,000	£1,200	£700	£900,000
EOY 3	9,000	£1,250	£730	£950,000
EOY 4	10,000	£1,250	£730	£950,000
EOY 5	10,000	£1,300	£770	£980,000

Option 2 is to take over one of its competitors, The Alum Co., for a proposed price of £5 million. It is a small business that has built up a small but incredibly loyal group of customers who purchase regularly. Owning The Alum Co. would allow KALO to market itself to new customers, so it could increase its output and possibly widen its product range. However, The Alum Co. has not made any significant capital investment for some years and its machinery is old, outdated and unreliable. KALO would have to make a £1 million capital investment immediately and then £800,000 next year to update the factory fully. Its owners are approaching retirement and have built up the business over a period of 30 years, with a loyal work-force of 12 employees. In an attempt to assess the investment, KALO's accountant has prepared the following cash flow estimates:

	Net cash inflows (not including investment)
EOY 0	
EOY 1	2,000,000
EOY 2	2,300,000
EOY 3	2,300,000
EOY 4	2,500,000
EOY5	2,600,000

Although profitability is an important issue with KALO, the board was a little concerned about the effect on working capital of both investments. The new machinery would mean an increase in output and therefore more investment in stock. Although buying Alum would place less strain on cash flow, KALO was much less sure of the accuracy of the cash flows. The loyal customers of Alum could easily take their business elsewhere, unless KALO took significant steps to retain their loyalty.

When assessing investments, KALO has a policy of using the cost of capital (presently 8%) for the discount rate although the financial director has argued that the level of risk is different in the two options and that the discount rate should be different for the two.

1 Draw up a table of cash flows for the investment in Alum. [6]

2 For both options:

  a) calculate the payback period

  b) calculate the annual average rate of return [6]

  c) comment on the usefulness of these two investment appraisal techniques for KALO. [2]

3 Suggest various ways that KALO might attempt to persuade Alum's loyal customers to continue buying from them after the takeover. [4]

4 **a)** Calculate the net present value of buying the new machinery (Option 1). [4]

  b) By calculating the net present value of the investment in Alum, state the maximum amount that KALO should pay for Alum. How does this figure compare with the agreed price of £5 million? [4]

5 Suggest a reason for choosing **a)** the cost of capital **b)** the level of risk as the basis for the discount rate. [4]

6 Discuss the non-financial information which the board should consider before making a decision on which option to choose. [10]

                                                40

Sources of finance

Learning objectives

Having read this unit, students will be able to

1   identify the various financial needs of a business

2   describe the various sources of finance which a business can use

3   evaluate the most appropriate source of finance within a given business situation

Context

Whenever we go shopping we need to pay for the goods we buy. A large proportion of purchases is paid for using cash. But there are alternative ways of paying for the products required. Cash cards (such as Barclays Connect card), which draw on funds from a current account, are now widely used and readily accepted by the majority of shops. For many, especially at Christmas time, a credit card is used to 'buy now and pay later'. For the family car, the traditional source of finance has been a loan from either the bank or a finance company, and buying a house normally involves a mortgage.

But how does a company gain finance for its expenditure? Heinz will need to raise finance to purchase fixed assets such as a new giant mixing bowl used for making the soups, as well as running the business on a day-to-day basis to pay the wages of the employees who produce the various soups and cans of baked beans. They will need money to buy all the ingredients for their range of products produced.

Finance defined

Finance is very simple to define: it is anything which allows the business to operate. A business therefore needs finance for two areas:

- to purchase or use capital equipment which is either to replace outdated machinery or expand present machinery, known as fixed assets
- to run the business on a day-to-day basis – buying materials, paying labour etc., known as working capital. (*This is dealt with in more detail in Unit 34 Cash flow and working capital*)

Classification of sources

Finance is categorised according to
a) the length of time it is required for
b) whether it is generated internally or found externally

Short-term finance – tends to be limited to up to three years, although if you look at any company report, it usually refers to a period of just one year due to the accounting rules which determine current liabilities

Long-term finance – anything over three years. The length of time refers to the period for which the finance is borrowed

Internal source – the finance comes from within the business

External source – the finance is borrowed from a financial institution

---

Question 1

Consider the following requirements for finance and state whether they are short- or long-term:
a) a car
b) stock
c) a new machine, with an expected life of eight years
d) moving to a new location
e) paying wages
f) paying dividends
g) repairing a broken machine

h) taking advantage of cheaper materials due to a supplier being wound up
i) tiding the business over until a major debtor has paid   [6]

Internal sources

■ Retained profit

This is the profit which is left after all costs have been deducted. One definition of profit is the amount by which the business grows; if a business has made retained profit of £1 million, then this will be reinvested in the business in one of two ways. Either it will be used to make assets larger or it will be used to make liabilities smaller. Either way, the net assets (one measure of the wealth of the business) will increase.

One of the main advantages of using any profit retained by the business is that it is a cheap source of finance as there is no interest to pay or any need to repay the amount involved. But the opportunity cost of using the profit must be taken into account when deciding how to use it.

■ Depreciation

Having read Unit 37, you will hopefully understand that depreciation is not a cash cost and can therefore be used as a source of finance.

e.g.

Sales revenue	£100m
Operating costs	£ 80m#
Operating profit	£ 20m
Profit after tax	£ 12m
Dividends	£ 8m
Retained profit	£ 4m

includes a depreciation charge of £6m.

Assume all transactions are for cash – this has some realism attached to it, because eventually all the costs will be paid in cash and all the revenue will be received in cash, even though at the time of reporting the profit, some money may still be owed to creditors and some may be owed by debtors.

However, because of the nature of depreciation, the charge of £6 million will not actually leave the business in cash. It will stay in the business, because the asset has already been bought and paid for.

In addition to the amount of retained profit the company has made, the business will also be able to use depreciation, so in the above example the total amount of internal finance is £4m + £6m = £10m.

This also assumes this money is available. It is likely that as the business received money from customers, it will have reinvested the profit already. After all, a business would be treated with considerable suspicion by its shareholders if it waited until reporting profit at the end of the year before it spent any of it!

Question 2

A business makes a retained profit of £340 million in a year. It owns assets of £800 million, which depreciate at 15% per year.

a) How much finance is available to the company during the year? State your assumptions.   [3]

b) Why might this figure not be available at the end of the year, when the profit is reported?   [2]

■ **Working capital**

The current assets of stock and debtors, along with the current liabilities of creditors, can be used as a source of finance. Remembering that finance is defined as anything which allows the business to operate, a supplier who gives the business credit is effectively providing a source of finance. The business can use the stock that has been delivered, but does not need to pay for it immediately.

For example a supplier offers trade credit of one month on £36,000 of stock, meaning the business has the stock to work on yet the £36,000 remains in its bank account for one month. If this credit facility is extended by one month, the business is effectively keeping the cash for a further month, rather than paying the supplier.

Alternatively, if a business reduces its average level of stock by either turning stock over more quickly (with the same delivery pattern) or selling off stock and not replacing it, this will release money into the business e.g. stock is £30 million and represents two months' sales; if stock were to be reduced to one month's sales i.e. £15 million, the business would release £15 million of cash, which it would not reinvest in stock.

The final method of squeezing **working capital** is achieved by reducing debtors. If debtors are encouraged to pay one month earlier, this will release money into the business. (*This is covered in more detail under debt factoring, later in this unit.*)

e.g. Debtors = £60m Payment terms = 3 months

Sales revenue = £20m per month.

If debtors pay one month earlier (i.e. every two months), then there will be only £40 million tied up in debtors (£60m – £20m), releasing £20 million. Such a reduction is likely to be achieved only if there is an incentive for customers to pay early, such as a discount on the original price.

Question 3

Trade-Now Ltd is a wholesaler which imports clothes and sells them to market stall holders. It holds enough stock for two months of selling products, has debtors on two months of credit and has an agreement with suppliers to pay one month after receiving delivery of a particular batch of clothes.

An extract from its balance sheet shows the following details:
Stock = £450,000; Debtors = £600,000;
Creditors = £225,000

a) Assuming stock, debtors and creditors are the only items in working capital, calculate how much the business has tied up in working capital.   [2]

b) Calculate how much Trade-Now would generate by squeezing working capital in the following ways:
   i)   stock is reduced to one month of sales
   ii) debtors are reduced to one month of sales
  iii) suppliers are paid two months after delivery.
    [3]

c) Calculate the new level of working capital, following all three of the above changes.   [4]

■ Dividends

Due to the fact that a business is not under any legal obligation to pay dividends, it may decide, if it wishes to maximise the amount of finance available from profit, to reduce or even postpone dividends. Shareholders will have to be persuaded this is in their interest and the management will need to produce an argument which claims that the short-term reduction in dividends will be more than made up by the long-term increase in profit, due to the investment being made with the savings made by the reduction in dividends.

External sources – short-term

■ Bank overdraft

This is probably the most commonly used form of finance – a business takes out more from the bank than it has invested there. The bank will set a limit for the overdraft facility, allowing the business to draw on its current account up to a set limit. Interest is paid on the actual amount that is overdrawn at any given time, calculated on a daily basis. The overdraft is used to allow the business to operate during times when cash flow is negative and can act as a lifeline when a business is facing cash flow problems (*see Unit 34 Cash flow and working capital*). Interest is charged on a two-tier basis – authorised, which is agreed between the business and the bank, and unauthorised, whereby the business draws out more than the authorised amount. At this point, the interest rate increases sharply.

■ Bank loan

Unlike an overdraft, a bank loan is for a fixed amount, for a fixed period of time. Hence there is not the same degree of flexibility.

The majority of loans will be secured loans. As the size and duration of the loan increases, some form of security such as a fixed asset, otherwise known as collateral, will be required by the lender, to ensure that in the event of the money not being paid back, the lender will be able to recoup the value of the outstanding loan by selling the asset that has been used to secure the loan.

By offering security for a loan, there is less risk involved on the part of the lender and consequently, the loan is easier to obtain. The business taking out the loan, knowing the repayments are for a fixed amount and for a fixed period of time, is able to plan more easily. This sort of finance is used to purchase assets such as machines, vehicles and factory extensions. Most businesses are able to negotiate with the bank as to the rate of interest to be paid.

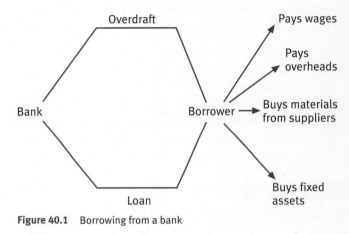

Figure 40.1   Borrowing from a bank

Question 4

Bass-It is a small family business which sells fishing tackle throughout the country.

a) How can an overdraft help this business?   [3]

b) When is this business more likely to require a bank loan rather than an overdraft?   [5]

■ Hire purchase

This type of finance derives its name from the ownership rights during the period in which finance is provided. The business hires the asset while it is paying for it, then once payments are complete, the business owns the asset. Rather than having to find a lump sum to pay for the item up-front, the business provides a small deposit or initial payment which is followed by regular payments including interest until the amount 'borrowed' has been repaid. Unlike paying for the capital equipment with a bank loan or with internally generated finance, the ownership is not gained until the last repayment has been made (it cannot therefore be counted as an asset on the business's balance sheet).

The actual finance is provided by a finance house which specialises in hire purchase agreements. When a business enters into a hire purchase agreement, the finance house will pay the supplier of the equipment immediately and then receive repayments from the business buying the equipment (*see Figure 40.2*).

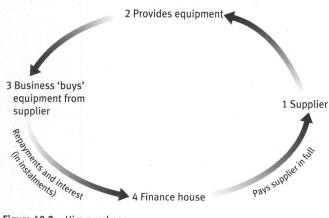

Figure 40.2   Hire purchase

This is a comparatively safe method of providing finance because the equipment belongs to the finance house until all the instalments have been made. If the business using hire purchase to buy equipment fails to meet the instalment schedule then it would have to hand over the item that had been purchased to the finance house. This may be the area of uncertainty for the finance house, coupled with the degree to which the equipment may have depreciated, thus affecting its resale value. This form of finance is more likely to be used by a smaller business which wants to spread the cost of purchasing capital equipment over a period of time.

Question 5

Pete Jones Ltd buys motor-bikes directly from Suzuki on hire purchase and then uses the bikes for people who are preparing to take their test. He has been a regular customer of Suzuki for eight years and a reliable payer. Recent cash flow problems have meant that he is unable to place a deposit on the eight bikes he ordered last month and Suzuki has refused to supply them, because the finance house will not provide the money.

a) Describe the action that Pete Jones might take in these circumstances.   [5]

b) What information might a finance house wish to discover before granting the hire purchase agreement?   [5]

■ Trade credit

Many businesses provide trade credit to customers as a method of promotion and use trade credit as a source of finance. The actual period of trade credit offered may even be used as a means of gaining a competitive advantage. However, many suppliers will try to encourage buyers to pay promptly by offering a discount. There may also be a penalty in the form of a higher price if the account is not settled within the agreed time. In addition the supplier may reduce the credit period in the future if payments are not made on time.

Trade credit is very helpful to businesses if they can sell the products before they have to pay for the materials used. For the business offering a trade discount, the opposite is true; the provision of trade credit relies on selling more goods to compensate for the later payment. (The supplier may also have bought the goods from another supplier using the same type of finance.)

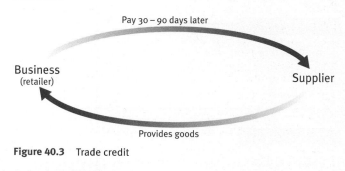

Figure 40.3   Trade credit

Question 6

Why is it in the interest of a business to offer a prompt payment discount to its customer?   [3]

■ Debt factoring

To any business, being owed money can be a problem. Goods or services will have been provided and costs will have been incurred, but revenue has not been received. As a consequence the business may run into cash flow problems and consequently have to borrow money itself until its debtors pay.

A factoring company can alleviate this potential problem by providing finance against the value of any unpaid invoices (this is the document that provides the proof that the business is owed money from the sale of goods).

The factoring company will 'buy' or take over the debts, paying the business up to approximately 80% of the total value of the debt. The factoring company will then attempt to chase up the unpaid invoices and if successful will pay the remaining 20% of the debt to the business minus a service charge, which is normally 1–1.5% of revenue.

Although this may appear an expensive form of finance, having access to 80% of debts initially is preferable to no funds at all or at best funds coming in at some indeterminable time in the future.

Unfortunately, the factoring company is usually very selective as to which business it will 'assist'. Factoring companies tend to trade with the larger businesses which have a turnover of at least £250,000 and which in turn trade with a few large businesses rather than a lot of small businesses. This is because it is considered easier to collect on the unpaid invoices more easily and incur fewer expenses in doing so.

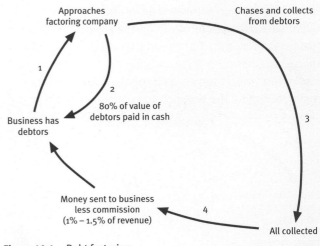

Figure 40.4   Debt factoring

Question 7

Suggest a reason why a business using debt factoring could be viewed as a strength rather than a weakness.
[4]

Question 8

Cash-It Ltd has experienced one or two problems recently with late payers. It has invited a debt factoring company – Boys-round and Bros (BRAB) to take over its debtors. BRAB charge 1.5% of revenue and Cash-It has debtor days of 130. Initially BRAB will advance 80% of the amount owed and deduct the charge once the remainder has been collected.

a) If revenue is £700,000, calculate the amount of revenue owed by customers, if debtor days are 130. [3]

b) How much will Cash-It receive in total from BRAB? [2]

c) What would happen if £50,000 of debts are unrecoverable? [3]

■ Leasing

Leasing has become a more popular source of finance in recent years. Car retailers frequently offer this facility to fleet managers and more recently to individual customers. Customers will pay a regular amount to the car retailer over two to three years; after which, the customer has the option of purchasing the car, or starting a new leasing agreement. This method allows businesses to use machines, equipment and vehicles that it may not otherwise be able to afford to buy outright. Nor is the business committing itself to a large expenditure that would take a long time to repay if a loan was undertaken. This is another method of finance that allows the business to spread the cost over an agreed period of time. Leasing agreements are more flexible both in time and rental payments.

Finally, one of the major advantages of leasing is that the equipment can be changed if, due to technological advances, it becomes obsolete. Some leasing agreements allow the business to benefit from free maintenance.

One of the advantages is that the monthly or quarterly leasing payment can be used as an expense to reduce a tax bill i.e. more expenses mean less profit, which means less tax. Depreciation does not always carry this advantage (*see Unit 37 Asset valuation*).

A disadvantage is that the asset leased belongs to the leasing business and therefore cannot be classed as an asset of the lessee.

Regular fixed amount paid

2/3 years

CAR RETAILER — Customer

Car for 2/3 years

Not owned by customer – but option to buy at end of lease period

Figure 40.5 Leasing

Question 9

What are the main differences between a leasing and a hire purchase agreement? [4]

Question 10

Copy-It Ltd is a small, privately-run business which provides a photocopying service. It owns two machines and is considering adding another, by either leasing or buying. Leasing would cost £150 per quarter and the contract would last for five years. On top of the leasing payment, the business must pay £0.08 pence per copy. There is an option to upgrade after four years to a newer model, although the payments per month would be renegotiated.

Alternatively, the business could purchase it outright at a cost of £3,000 which would probably last for five years. The estimated total number of call-outs for maintenance and servicing would be 50 during the six years, at a cost of £50 per call-out, although the first eight call-outs would fall within the guarantee period. The money to purchase the machine would be borrowed on a one-year loan at an interest rate of 11%.

a) What is a guarantee period? [2]

b) Compare the cost of leasing with the cost of purchasing if the business makes 10,000 copies over the six years, then advise the company on the best method of financing the new photocopier. [6]

c) What other factors might the business consider when deciding whether or not to lease or buy? [4]

External sources – long-term

■ Share capital

This type of finance is one of the major sources available to limited companies (*see Unit 3 Types of business*). It is a popular form of finance because usually it does not have to be repaid, although raising money through shares is probably more expensive than borrowing. Shareholders, depending on the type of shares held, will have voting rights and a share of the profit every year in the form of a dividend. Once issued by the business, the shares can be bought and sold privately (in the case of private limited companies) and via the stock exchange (for public limited companies). Several types of shares can be issued by the business:

i) Ordinary shares (or equities)

These are the most commonly issued. Although this type of share provides a voting right, it is the riskiest type because shareholders are the last to be paid and will receive a dividend only

a) if the business makes a profit
b) at the discretion of the director

It is well worth finding a prospectus of a company that is about to 'go public' to see the amounts of finance that can be raised.

Ordinary shares can be sold either by a public issue with the issuing business fixing the price of the shares or by tender, where a minimum price is fixed and potential buyers bid for the shares; the business accepts the highest bids. The latter may be viewed as a more realistic reflection of the market price and avoids the business trying to guess the appropriate price to charge.

ii) Preference shares

This is another type of share but without voting rights, although holders receive a fixed rate of return once the dividend has been declared. Although less risk is involved for the holder of this type of share, the potential to gain so much in dividends if the business does well is not so significant.

A business is able to issue more shares after its initial issue when 'going public'. If further finance is required a 'rights issue' can be made. Those who already own shares in a business are given the 'right' to purchase additional shares at a reduced rate. This is often used to gain extra finance quite cheaply and is carried out by offering shares to current shareholders as a proportion of their present holding. As a further incentive, the price is usually discounted.

Question 11

Why might a rights issue be a cheaper method of raising share capital than a new issue?   [4]

Question 12

Float-It plc intends to carry out a 2 for 5 rights issue. There are presently 10 million shares issued, with a market price of £4 per share. The discount for each share will be 15%.

a) Calculate the number of shares issued in the rights issue and the amount of money raised.   [4]

b) Explain what might happen to the share price following the rights issue.   [4]

A smaller business wanting to raise capital by going public but unwilling to be a fully listed company is able to gain a listing on the Alternative Investment Market (AMI). This is often seen as a half-way house before gaining a full listing on the stock exchange. The advantage is that the cost of gaining a listing is much smaller than a full-blown quotation on the main stock exchange.

■ Mortgage

This is a form of borrowing which is used when a business buys property and secures the loan against the property.

Much of the finance for business mortgages comes from pension funds and insurance companies apart from building societies. The loans may be for anything between 10 and 30 years, depending upon the individual business's circumstances.

■ Debentures

This is a specific type of loan where the holder of the debenture is a creditor of the company (though unlike a shareholder, not an owner). Debenture stock is issued only when a business has floated on the stock exchange.

Throughout the period of the debenture the business will pay a fixed rate of interest regardless of the performance of the business. Debenture holders have priority in terms of payment before any shareholders. The holder of a debenture will have a certificate stating when the loan is to be repaid, known as the maturity date. The holder of the debenture is unable to get money returned until the maturity date is reached; however it is possible to sell the debenture to someone else.

Returns to debenture holders do not always take the form of interest. Wimbledon lawn tennis club last sold debentures in 1994, each for £19,625, which also entitled the owner to a seat at the championships for five years. This debenture can be sold on to other members if the owner requires the cash before the five years is complete; this type of debenture therefore does not pay interest, rather a free seat for 10 weeks of tennis!

■ Venture capital

This is capital made available by venture capital companies (such as 3i). This source tends to be for the innovative business that wishes to invest in a new product or is perceived to be too high a risk by the traditional providers of finance. Consequently, venture capitalists require a higher return and a quicker return and normally like to plan an 'escape route' if the investment fails to produce a quick enough return. In an attempt to lessen the risk involved, many of the venture capital companies provide a range of advice services featuring financial, recruitment and managerial expertise. They even offer competitions to innovative businesses in an attempt to build their share of this often lucrative market.

Question 13

At the end of 1998, 3i repeated a successful competition for businesses involved in the technology sector. This second competition, named the 3i Technology Catapult, concentrated solely upon the science industries. The idea was to allow young businesses the opportunity to win up to £1 million to move their business forward. A spokesman for 3i said in the first 6 months of 1998 3i had already invested in 91 technology businesses. One of the previous winners of 3i's competition was The Cropland Company which developed a mobile phone data-communication and vehicle tracking system. There is, however, a tendency for venture capitalists to concentrate on the provision of loans for well over £100,000.

Discuss whether this competition was sufficient incentive for a business to approach 3i for capital.

[6]

The Longbridge Rover plant

Tokyo. Nissan had already accumulated debts of over £12 billion and as a consequence was having difficulty in obtaining finance through the normal channels.

Similar schemes, offering grants for areas of high unemployment, are available from the European Union. The Prince's Trust is another organisation that provides capital to would-be entrepreneurs to enable them to set up their own businesses.

Question 14

Why do you think Nissan was experiencing difficulties in obtaining finance through the normal channels?

[4]

■ Government (central and local) grants

A range of grants and loans can be obtained from the government. For those businesses that require assistance to start, there is the Business Start-Up Scheme, whereby, usually through local TECs (Training and Enterprise Councils) grants are available for employing people who had been unemployed. These grants are payable until the business is fully operative, usually after a year.

Often the area of the country, governed by the amount of unemployment and the status given (Assisted Area, Enterprise Zone), would determine the type and amount of grant or financial assistance made available. Much of the help would be in the form of subsidised rent or investment grants.

Car manufacturers are quite frequently the beneficiaries of large aid packages from the government which is keen to ensure that such a large employer within a given area should not either go elsewhere or even close down. BMW was keen to seek the help of the government in order to undertake a major reinvestment at the Rover plant at Longbridge (*see Unit 57 Government intervention*).

At the beginning of 1999, Nissan was in talks with the government, hoping for a regional aid package to help it because of the financial crisis of the parent company in

Factors affecting sources of finance

Many factors must be taken into consideration when a business is selecting the most appropriate source of finance. Assuming the business has satisfied itself that the cost of obtaining the finance will be less than the expected profit generated from the finance (otherwise known as economic value added), the main considerations are:

■ Objectives of the business

A business may be reluctant to borrow because of the risks involved. Such an objective is frequently seen as a sign of weakness and share prices have been known to fall accordingly. The reason is because a business that refuses to borrow may be refusing to take risks and therefore may not be able to generate sufficient returns to keep shareholders interested in the business. On the other hand a business may change existing debt in the form of an overdraft to purchasing stock with trade credit because it is keen to reduce its reliance on the bank.

■ Costs

Calculating the amount of interest to be paid is a major factor but not the only cost that has to be considered: any administrative charges or service charges need careful attention as they can be substantial. 'Going public' (changing status from a private limited company to a public limited company) incurs high administrative costs. Even finance that has been raised internally has a cost, albeit an opportunity cost (i.e. the potential return from other uses of finance).

■ Time

How long the finance is required for will greatly influence the type used. If finance is required for only a very short period of time in order to supplement working capital, then an overdraft will suffice. But if there is a long-term need, a mortgage will be more appropriate. Naturally, the amount of time allowed before the finance is repaid will also affect the cost.

■ Legal status of the business

The type of business, whether it is a plc or a sole trader, will automatically open or close certain avenues of finance. Legal status will usually give an indication of the business's ability to repay the loan. A large plc would probably have no difficulty in meeting the repayments on a loan as it would be able to gain the advantages of economies of scale and thus would be spreading the cost of the loan over many units of production. Status will also give a prospective lender an indication of the assets that could be sold to cover the value of the loan if for some reason the business was unable to meet repayments.

Of course it is quite possible that some very large partnerships would be able to gain finance easily regardless of their status e.g. Lloyds of London, the insurance house.

■ Financial situation of the business

The health of the business is an important factor; lenders are more willing to lend to a business that is well established and with a known 'track record' i.e. a business that the lender has traded with before and is therefore confident is creditworthy. Newly established businesses usually find it harder to gain finance and as a consequence have to pay more for the privilege.

■ Interest rates

If a business is highly geared, interest rates will exert a greater effect on the choice and cost of finance. In addition, as interest rates fall, the stock market usually rises as investors move money from banks to the stock market. This makes shares much more attractive as a source of finance.

In addition to the above, it is important to note that in many instances the effect that a particular source of finance has upon the business will be an important factor in itself.

■ Economic climate

This is related to interest rates. When the economy is growing, profit grows due to a growth in demand, which in turn leads to greater reinvestment and growth. Interest rates are likely to be lower and consumer and business confidence, whilst difficult to measure accurately, is likely to be at its highest during a boom, therefore investment will take place. In addition, during growth, investors move their money from banks and government bonds into shares. This means there is more willingness to buy shares, so raising equity becomes easier.

■ Implications for the business

All businesses have to be conscious of the fact that obtaining finance will have repercussions on the financial statements, namely the balance sheet and the profit and loss account (*see Units 35 and 36*).

Any increase in current liabilities – short-term loans, overdrafts or creditors – may mean a reduction in the amount of working capital. But it may not be quite that simple. Much will depend on what the finance is to be used for.

Supposing a local shop, having obtained an overdraft, used the additional cash to purchase new stock:

Current assets		Current liabilities
Stock	£1000	–
New stock	£ 500	£500 (overdraft)

The net current assets or working capital has not changed (still £1,000).

Some sources of finance do have a significant effect on the business. If the business issues shares, this could have an immediate effect on the gearing of the business (*see Unit 38 Ratio analysis*). Assuming the long-term liabilities remain the same there will be a reduction in the gearing ratio which in turn ought to make it easier for the business to obtain finance from the bank. The gearing ratio is one of the main indicators that a prospective lender will consider (along with the interest cover.) If the gearing ratio is too high then a business will find it difficult to obtain additional finance.

Taking on additional finance without altering the amount of the shareholders' funds will increase the gearing ratio.

For example:

K L Smith Ltd, a manufacturer of locks, has long-term liabilities of £100,000 and shareholder funds of £1,000,000. In an attempt to modernise its machinery the company wishes to increase its borrowing. A new loan is obtained for £400,000.

Before new loan:

	Long-term liabilities	Shareholders' funds
	£100,000	£1,000,000
Gearing ratio is therefore	10%	

After new loan:

	£500,000	£1,000,000
Gearing ratio is therefore	50%	

As a consequence, any further loan would create more risk for K L Smith Ltd. Obtaining finance by issuing shares can have an effect upon the gearing of the business. Increasing the equity of the business has the advantage of reducing the gearing and therefore obtaining finance more easily in the future, remembering that the issue of the shares is a source of finance itself. However there are sources of finance that are available that will not affect the gearing of the business. Leasing, which could be viewed as a long-term 'loan', does not affect the gearing because it is a rental and is therefore not considered to be a form of borrowing.

Obtaining any additional loans will affect the interest cover. As the extra loan is taken on, the total amount of interest the business will be paying increases. On the assumption that the level of profit, especially in the short run, is the same, the interest cover will decrease.

The interest cover gives an indication to the prospective lender of how easily the business will be able to pay the interest. It is quite possible that in the long run, if the loan has been put to good use, the level of profit will increase and thus increase the interest cover.

There are other elements of the balance sheet that are affected by the utilisation of loan finance. By simply using a trade credit facility, a business may avoid using its own cash and at the same time increase the level of its stock, thus the level of current assets has increased (though current liabilities will have increased as well; but the trade credit has enabled the business to appear to have plenty of cash and as a consequence has no immediate liquidity problems).

Points for Revision

Key Terms

external finance	finance raised from outside the business e.g. loans
internal finance	finance raised within the business e.g. profit
short-term finance	finance that is needed and raised for between 0 and 3 years
long-term finance	finance that is raised for longer than 3 years
fixed capital	assets which the business intends to keep, requiring long-term finance
working capital	assets which the business intends to sell or change, normally requiring short-term capital

Summary of sources of finance

Internal	**External**	
	Short-term	*Long-term*
Own savings	Bank overdraft	Bank loan
Profit	Bank loan	Hire purchase
Sale of assets	Hire purchase	Leasing
Depreciation	Trade credit	Mortgage
	Debt factoring	Debentures
	Leasing	Venture capital
		Government loans/grants
		Share capital
		Ordinary shares
		Preference shares

Definitions Question:

By referring to a business you know, explain the significance of any two of the above terms (your teacher may wish to help you choose the terms).   [5] per definition

Summary Points:

1. Finance is defined as anything which allows the business to operate.

2. Finance can be divided into two types – long- and short-term, according to the time period it is required for.

3. Finance can be raised either internally or externally; internal finance is the least expensive.

4. The choice of finance depends on a variety of factors, although primarily the use of the finance will be considered.

Mini Case Study

Short-It Ltd specialises in maintaining a variety of household appliances on site (i.e. at people's homes), such as dishwashers, fridges and washing machines. It is located in an industrial park near Newcastle, but wishes to open a retail outlet in Carlisle, where it feels there is room for growth. In addition to providing the same service, the outlet will allow customers to identify the business more easily. It will have a shop front and it will be in a position to sell recognised brand names in the shop. The expansion in its product portfolio will hopefully improve its profit.

The capital cost of the new outlet is £150,000, in addition to £50,000 required for new stocks of maintenance equipment as well as the finished products it will sell.

Extracts from its balance sheet and profit and loss account which were put together on 30/4/2000 are as follows:

Table 1

Long-term liabilities	= £180,000
Retained profit	= £ 50,000
Sales revenue	= £650,000
Shareholders' funds	= £200,000
Depreciation	= £ 30,000

There are 20 shareholders of this business, eight of whom make up the management team who have decided that expansion is required. Of the remaining 12 shareholders, eight have demonstrated opposition to what seems to them to be a foolhardy and unresearched expansion plan.

---

1 Referring to Table 1:

   a) identify which items can be found in the profit and loss account and which can be found in the balance sheet.   [2]

   b) How much money can be raised through internal sources? State your assumptions clearly.   [4]

   c) Calculate the present gearing level of Short-It Ltd.   [3]

2 Explain the significance of the eight shareholders who have opposed the expansion.   [5]

3 Based on all the information available, discuss the various sources of finance available for expansion.   [6]

                                                                                        20

Maxi Case Study

Although Yates' Wine Lodge is a well established restaurant and pub chain, it has also expanded the number of product concepts in recent years. In addition to the wine lodges, the business also owns and runs outlets under the names of the Blob Shop, Ha! Ha! Bar and Canteens and Watling Street Inns. Part of its growth has been due to the business becoming a fully listed company on the stock exchange in 1994. Prior to 1994 the business had a quotation on the stock exchange under rule 535; this meant that it was still a plc, but had restricted access to finance. Under rule 535, the rules of disclosure of information were less stringent than with a full quotation, which was attractive to the business at the time.

At that time, there were two or three institutional investors owning about 10% of the equity, with about 75% of the equity being owned by 36 family members. However, only one member of the family was actively involved with the business! The share price was particularly vulnerable to any member of the family selling shares, which would have pushed the price of the share downwards, so there was a need to dilute the influence that any one member of the family could exert in this respect.

The industry was also shrinking because there were too many pubs and the average consumption of alcoholic drinks was falling, although drinkers were moving up-market. The company therefore concentrated on developing a product concept that generated high-volume sales. To achieve this, certain locations became crucial and Yates researched the market potential very carefully and realised there was a tremendous opportunity for growth in the sector. The majority of its outlets were based in the north of England although it did feel there was potential for expansion in the south as well. One other factor influencing the flotation was that there was a bull market in shares in 1994 and the business was more likely to succeed in this respect.

The business decided on a 'placing' as the most appropriate way to gain a listing. A placing is when a business invites certain dealers to trade in the shares, meaning the company can control the amount being traded, ensuring control is kept with the family. For the placing to occur successfully, Yates needed a track record; a return on capital was required at a certain level, with a trend of increasing, sustainable earning in terms of profit and revenue as well as expertise in the business and a forward development plan. One of the selling points to the dealers was that the business was easy to conceptualise. Preparation was all-important, so it brought in a non-executive director who was a main director in a company in the FTSE 100, adding to the expertise of the business. This was also to add weight to its credibility if the business attempted to persuade investors on the stock exchange that it was worth investing in.

The process of the placing was as follows:

1 Consult the family and agree on a standstill i.e. not to sell shares for up to one year after the flotation – this ensures an orderly after-market.

2 Consult senior employees to ensure they were behind the idea of a flotation.

3 Prepare prospectus, which included previous and projected returns.

			Flotation	Actual results				
	1992	1993	1994	1995	1996	1997	1998	1999
Return on net assets	10.2	11.9	11.9	11.9	14.3	14.3	16.5	17.3

4   Check of due diligence to ensure that everything on the prospectus stood up to the test of whether it could be verified.

5   Pre-marketing: visiting likely institutional investors for placing. This is followed by the brokers ringing the fund managers to assess where the price should be placed.

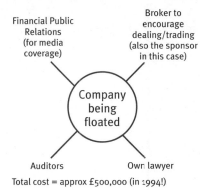

Total cost = approx £500,000 (in 1994!)

Figure 40.6   The players involved in going public

The pricing of any share issue is crucial – if it is too high, then shares will not trade at a premium (i.e. increase in price the moment trading begins). If it is too low the business loses out on gaining greater capital. To calculate the price, the brokers used the forecast price earnings ratio for the business which was 18.9 times, with a quoted placing price of 140 pence.

When the flotation actually took place, the share rose to 165 pence on the first day of trading, representing a premium of 17.5%.

Since the flotation, the business has been able to fulfil its expansion plans – in the end the business raised about £7 million although the final costs of the flotation were £500,000. Now that being a PLC is a way of life, the directors have two intense periods of the year – interim results and final results, where they have to travel to the City, giving presentations to various analysts.

1   Define: PLC, prospectus, interim results.   [6]

2   Calculate the earnings per share at the time of flotation.   [2]

3   What is the role of a non-executive director?   [3]

4   What problems might the business have faced if all the senior management was engrossed in going public?   [5]

5   Explain why the cost of raising equity is greater than the cost of borrowing.   [6]

6   Imagine you were responsible for explaining the issues of gaining a full quotation on the stock exchange to the family members who were not involved with the business. Prepare a presentation which outlines these issues and which is designed to persuade them that, despite the risks, the flotation will be beneficial in the long term.   [8]

7   Discuss the advantages and disadvantages of running a family-owned firm.   [10]

Cost classification

Learning objectives

Having read this unit, students will be able to

1 classify costs into fixed and variable

2 represent these costs in calculations and understand how unit cost varies as output changes

3 recognise how different businesses have different cost structures

Context

Staples, the office equipment retailer, is a business that has achieved significant growth due to careful cost control. Famous for its low prices, it has also paid close attention to its costs in order to make a profit. The costs of this business divide conveniently into two, fixed and variable. Fixed costs will have to be paid whether the business sells a million products a week or just 100. Variable costs, on the other hand, will be the costs of buying the office equipment from the manufacturer. The extent to which the total costs of a business are made up of either fixed or variable has significant implications for the decisions the company makes; such implications are considered in Units 17 (Pricing), 42 (Break-even), 43 (Contribution).

Fixed costs

These are costs that the business must pay, regardless of the amount of output produced in the short run. Within the scope of Business Studies, the definition of short run means **capacity** is fixed i.e. there is a maximum level of output which a business can produce within a particular time period e.g. a week, month, quarter or year with its present capital equipment. **Fixed costs** are therefore **period** or **time costs** which are accounted for each accounting period e.g. rent is usually charged for a year, given that the contract signed will specify the amount per square foot per year.

These costs must be expressed as a lump sum, because the lump sum will not change as output increases.

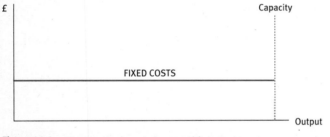

Figure 41.1   Fixed costs do not change with output

Variable costs

A business will also incur costs depending on how many units it makes. A business which makes toys will need to buy a variety of plastic components as well as materials such as glue, nuts, screws, bolts to assemble the toy. The more units it makes, the higher will be the total cost of these parts. So these costs will increase and decrease in direct proportion to output i.e. according to increases and decreases in output and are known as variable or direct costs. By definition, they are known as **product costs**, because they can be easily allocated to the manufacture or production of a particular product. It is assumed that as output changes variable costs per unit will stay the same. This means that **variable costs** as a total will increase in a straight line.

Confusion arises over costs such as repairs and maintenance. These costs are not fixed in that as output increases, machinery will be used more frequently and

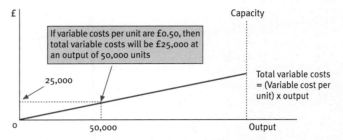

Figure 41.2   Variable costs change with output

Question 1

List the costs incurred when running a car and divide these into fixed and variable costs.   [5]

Question 2

Classify the following costs according to whether they are fixed or variable:
a) Marketing costs
b) Manager's salary
c) Materials
d) Depreciation
e) Labour
f) Rent
g) Interest payments
f) Maintenance   [8]

more repairs and maintenance will be required. However, these costs will not increase in direct proportion. They are therefore known as **semi-variable costs** and are represented diagrammatically in Figure 41.3:

Figure 41.3   Semi-variable costs change, but not in direct proportion to output

Labour?

It is tempting to classify labour as a variable cost, although this needs some consideration. In a manufacturing business, if output is easy to predict e.g. the manufacture of pre-packed Christmas puddings, it is possible to calculate the labour cost per unit, and therefore treat labour as a variable cost. Similarly, if a salesman is paid on a commission-only basis, then these costs will be incurred only when a sale has taken place – again a variable cost. Consider labour in an airline company; the business is hardly likely to increase the number of employees when more seats are sold on a particular flight. A bank is also unlikely to increase the number of accounts clerks and product managers when new customers open bank accounts.

Whether labour is treated as a fixed cost or a variable cost will depend on the nature of the business or the industry. In exam questions the assumption as to how labour costs are treated will usually be clearly stated.

Total costs

Total costs are the sum of variable costs and fixed costs at different levels of output.

Total costs = fixed costs + variable costs

These will increase as output increases. Diagrammatically:

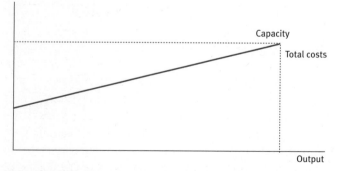

Figure 41.4   Total costs increase as output increases

Question 3

Ink-It Ltd, a manufacturer of writing equipment, has fixed costs of £100,000 per month and variable costs of £2 per unit. Capacity is 200,000 units. Copy and fill in the table below.

Output	0	50000	100000	150000	200000
Total variable costs					
Total costs					[6]

Question 4

Write-It, a retailer of writing products, has total costs of £500,000 per annum and fixed costs represent half this amount at an output level of 100,000 units.

a) What is the variable cost per unit?   [2]

b) What would the fixed costs be if the output level was half this amount?   [2]

Short versus long run

So far the analysis has been confined to the short run, in that the capacity (*labelled in Figures 41.1 to 41.4*) has been fixed. If sales continue to grow, eventually capacity will be reached which means that to satisfy demand, the business must purchase new assets to create greater capacity.

There will be two separate effects on costs:

- an increase in fixed costs – rent, depreciation etc. increase with the purchase of e.g. new machinery. This will result in fixed costs increasing across the entire output range, not just the increase in capacity (*see Figure 41.5*).

- a reduction in variable costs per unit. The business may use better machinery as a result of increasing capacity, which may mean less wastage, or quicker production time, both of which may result in a fall in variable costs. The variable costs line would therefore become less steep.

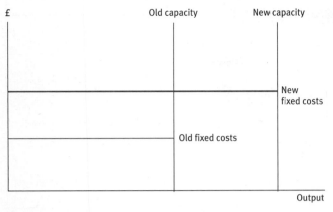

Figure 41.5   As capacity is increased, so fixed costs increase

Fixed asset or fixed cost?

It is important to note the difference between fixed costs and fixed assets. If Hertz, the hire car company, expands and buys more fixed assets in the form of motor vehicles, fixed costs will increase as a consequence, because there will be more insurance, depreciation and road tax. The increase in fixed costs is not the same as an increase in fixed assets – the assets represent the physical ability of the business to make more units of output (in the case of Hertz, earn more revenue by selling more hire contracts) and are represented on the balance sheet (*see Unit 36*).

Question 5

Store-It and Co. makes plastic storage boxes. Recent changes in market demand have prompted the decision to expand and buy an extra machine which allows it to produce an extra 30,000 units of output. Fixed costs increase from £250,000 to £300,000. Variable costs, however, fall from £9 per unit to £8 per unit.

If capacity output before the expansion was 120,000, draw, on the same graph paper,
a) fixed costs before and after   [2]
b) total costs lines before and after the expansion
                                                                    [2]
c) (i) At what level of output do the total costs lines
         cross?   [1]
    (ii) What does this signify for the business?   [3]
d) Briefly explain one reason for each of the changes in variable and fixed costs following the purchase of new machinery.   [4]

Unit costs

Although total costs increase as output increases, **unit costs** tend to do the opposite. This is because the same amount of fixed costs are spread over more units, thereby reducing the amount of fixed costs each unit needs to cover e.g. if fixed costs are £20,000 and only one unit is made, that particular unit will have a fixed cost of £20,000. If the business makes two units, each unit will have a fixed cost of £10,000 each. If output increases to 20,000 units, fixed cost per unit will be only £1. To calculate the unit cost (otherwise known as average cost), use the following formula

$$\text{unit costs} = \frac{\text{total costs (at a particular level of output)}}{\text{output}}$$

$$= \frac{\text{fixed costs} + \text{variable costs}}{\text{output}}$$

Using the figures for Question 3, but this time calculating unit costs, produces the graph in Figure 41.6. Check you can calculate the unit costs at the different levels.

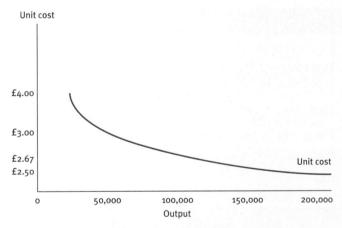

Figure 41.6   As output increases, unit cost falls

The issue of falling unit costs with rising output represents one of the major justifications for mass production; the ability of a business to make as many products as possible has implications for profitability, pricing, competitive advantage and productivity. Although this is straightforward in terms of calculations, the reduction in unit cost as output gets larger remains a key objective for most businesses. This reduction in unit cost as output rises is referred to as **economies of scale**, and is dealt with in more detail in Unit 4. There is a limit, however, to the gain that can be made. Heinemann, a publisher, tends to use a sales figure of 20,000 as a standard level to achieve. After this point, the reduction in unit cost is insignificant when compared with the reduction in unit cost before this level of output.

Question 6

Cater-It manufactures plastic trays at a variable cost of £2 each. Fixed costs are £150,000 per annum.

a) Calculate the unit cost for the following levels of output:

(i) 20,000 **(ii)** 40,000 **(iii)** 60,000 **(iv)** 80,000, using the following format: [8]

Output	20,000	40,000	60,000	80,000
Variable costs				
Fixed costs				
Total costs				
Unit costs				

b) Compare the percentage reduction in unit cost as output increases by 20,000, by copying out the table below and filling in the three spaces for percentage reduction in unit cost. What conclusions might you draw from this comparison?

output increase	20000 to 40000	40000 to 60000	60000 to 80000
% reduction in unit cost			

[6]

Cost structure

Depending on the nature of the individual business or industry, costs will accrue in different ways. In certain businesses, fixed costs will take up a significantly higher proportion of total costs at all levels of output. Such companies have negligible variable costs.

Alternatively, a business might have very low fixed costs and a steep variable costs line. The relative size of both variable and fixed costs is known as the **cost structure**. This has significant implications for pricing, break-even and contribution, all of which are dealt with in other units. The relationship between fixed costs and total costs is referred to as operational or operating gearing, not to be confused with capital gearing (*see Unit 38 Ratio analysis*).

Operating gearing $= \dfrac{\text{fixed costs}}{\text{total costs}}$ at a particular level of output

At zero output, this percentage will be 100% i.e. total costs are the same as fixed costs, because as there is zero output, the variable costs are zero. As output increases, the answer to this calculation reduces.

Question 7

Consider the following businesses and comment on their probable cost structure (i.e. whether a significant part of their total costs will be fixed or variable, at capacity output).
a) A hotel
b) A builder
c) A supermarket
d) A one person business that makes watches to order
e) An independent school (fee-paying)   [10]

Question 8

Gear-It Ltd, a supplier of gear boxes to a tractor manufacturer, has fixed costs of £4 per unit and variable costs of £2 per unit at an output level of 30,000 units per month (which is capacity).

Calculate operating gearing at
a) 20% of capacity
b) 50% of capacity
c) Capacity   [6]

Points for Revision

Key Terms

fixed costs	costs which remain the same as output changes in the short run
period/time costs	costs which can be attributed to a particular time period
product costs	costs which can be allocated to a particular unit of output
variable costs	costs which change in direct proportion to output, otherwise known as direct costs
total costs	the sum of variable costs and fixed costs at a particular level of output
unit cost (average cost)	$\dfrac{\text{total costs}}{\text{output}}$
cost structure	the relationship between fixed costs, variable costs and total costs
semi-variable costs	costs which change as output changes, but not in direct proportion (sometimes known as indirect costs) e.g. maintenance costs
capacity	the maximum level of output available using company's own assets
economies of scale	the reduction in unit costs as output increases
operating/ operational gearing	$\dfrac{\text{fixed costs}}{\text{total costs}}$ – a method of measuring cost structure

Definitions Question:
By referring to a business you know, explain the importance of any three of the above terms (your teacher may wish to select the terms). [5] per definition

Summary Points:

1. Costs can be classified into fixed, variable and semi-variable. The total costs of a business vary as output changes and are calculated by the sum of all costs.

2. A business's costs move from the short run to the long run by increasing its capacity. As a result, fixed costs will increase.

3. Unit cost will decrease as output increases, due to spreading fixed costs over a higher level of output.

4. The cost structure of a business depends on the nature of its activities and has implications for pricing and break-even.

Mini Case Study

Jenny Brief looked at the accountant's figures carefully. There seemed to be no way of getting round the fact that the business she had started three years ago was experiencing significant financial problems. She had qualified as a design engineer in 1996 and, having worked for a company which was a competitor to Filofax, recognised a gap in the market for high-quality, imitation leather briefcases. Market research had confirmed this gap and she had bought some machinery and rented a small factory in a local industrial estate. Initially orders had been healthy and she had managed to create a positive cash flow.

Recently, however, demand had fallen due to a series of foreign competitors flooding the market and consequently, output had to be decreased. This had forced the unit costs of each briefcase to rise, forcing the business into a loss-making position.

Variable costs per unit were £15, with fixed costs of £15 per unit at an output level of 500 (which represented two-thirds of capacity and the output level during the first two years). Last year, however, output dropped to 300 per month. At the present price of £38, it was still a little more expensive than the competitor's products although of higher quality, but it was not making any profit. She was unsure whether to drop the price to generate more volume or to embark on an aggressive advertising campaign in order to increase sales.

1 Define: positive cash flow, variable costs. [2]

2 a) Calculate the capacity of the business. [1]

   b) Calculate the loss the business is incurring at 300 units of output. [3]

3 a) Calculate and plot the unit cost at 200, 300, 400 and 500 units of output. [7]

   b) Plot the price on the graph (a horizontal straight line) and determine the level of output required for the company to break even. [2]

4 Considering all the information available, advise Jenny as to the best way of ensuring the business begins to earn a profit. [5]

20

Maxi Case Study

Andrew Westwood sighed inwardly; he had been in the board meeting for well over four hours and at the present rate of progress it seemed he would still be there in four hours' time. It had begun well when the entire board had agreed to a new marketing campaign to relaunch a product which was in its decline stage. Launching a new product would be too costly, agreed the board, and there was insufficient evidence from market research to suggest that the market could absorb yet another new product. But problems had arisen about the decision over the new machinery which the business was proposing to purchase and which would close an area of the factory. The business, The Pine Factor, manufactured furniture, partly by hand, partly by machine. It also imported some of its cheaper products from Romania because the labour costs were much lower and therefore the business could cater for a range of market segments and make some profit on all products.

Several members of the board fell into the category of what Andrew described as 'the good old days brigade'. They had sat on the board for 10 years having risen through the ranks of middle management and Andrew was fairly sure that their arrival on the board had been the culmination of their careers. Since then they had contributed very little to discussion, except when it concerned radical change, at which point they dug their heels in and refused to accept anything which might endanger their position of authority. The area of the factory which was due to close was run by one of these awkward directors and his like-minded colleagues closed ranks to defend his job. The new machinery would have meant the possible loss of 15 jobs. The employees would be given the option of being retrained for other work in the factory, although their salaries would probably fall. The new machinery would also reduce the amount of craftsmanship required.

Andrew despaired at the attitude of the directors; investment was needed and quickly; competition was intense and modern machinery would allow the business to cut prices. In addition, the machinery would improve quality on their main product line, known as The Ambassador Range, which was sold as one product, incorporating a wardrobe, a bed and two chests of drawers, for £1,200. Variable costs at the moment are £700 and fixed costs are £8,000 per month. The business was selling at capacity output, which was 25 Ranges per month, although the new machinery would allow the level of output to increase to 40, which Andrew was confident the business could sell given the level of demand. With the machinery, the variable costs would fall to £550, although the fixed costs would rise to £11,000 per month.

Although the machinery was going to cost £350,000, plus the redundancy costs, it would allow the business to reduce the price of the range to £1,100 which would mean it could be advertised as the cheapest in the region. The other directors were convinced that the economy was due for a recession, although Andrew did not share their doom and gloom. Even if they were right, argued Andrew, he wanted the business to be prepared for the recovery which would certainly bring more sales.

Despite all these apparently convincing factors, the 'good old days brigade' had flatly refused to accept the change. As Andrew looked round at the weary faces of the boardroom and then at his watch, he thought it was going to be a long night!

1 Define: decline stage, market research, middle management. [6]

2 a) Copy the table below and fill in the empty cells:

	Output	0	15	20	25	30	35	40
Old machinery								
Variable costs								
Fixed costs								
Total costs								
Unit costs								
New machinery								
Variable costs								
Fixed costs								
Total costs								
Unit costs								

  b) Draw the total costs line for both the new and old machinery on the same graph. [8]

3 a) What level of output is required to make the new machinery more profitable than the old machinery? [1]

  b) To what extent are the figures above realistic? [4]

4 Advise the company whether it should invest in the new machinery, taking all the information into account. [8]

5 After the meeting Andrew Westwood was quoted as saying: 'The only way this company is going to survive over the next few years is if we recruit management from outside the company who are young and willing to introduce a fresh, new way of thinking.'

Discuss the extent to which you agree with the principles of such a statement, in the context of business survival. [8]

35

Break-even

Learning objectives

Having read this unit, students will be able to

1. appreciate the nature of the relationship between costs, revenue and output

2. perform calculations and draw graphs using the break-even model

3. understand the limitations of the break-even model

Context

In the early part of the life of a business, profit will not necessarily be the primary objective. Famous companies such as McDonald's will need to earn a profit to satisfy shareholders, but newer, less well established businesses will certainly not have profit on their mind in their first few months of operation.

When Sir Richard Branson began his business life, selling advertising space in a magazine, his first objective was to break even, that is, to ensure that the revenue earned covered the costs of producing the magazine. Businesses which make a profit during their first year are rare, given the various pressures on a new business (*see Unit 2*). The maxi case study in that unit is one case in point. Covering costs with revenue has important implications for pricing, output and costs (both fixed and variable).

Revenue

The previous unit dealt solely with the issue of costs. By adding the **revenue** line, it is possible to identify the point at which the business will **break even**. In this case, revenue is calculated as

quantity × selling price

and represents the income that is earned by a business from selling its products.

To represent this diagrammatically, assume Simon's Shelving company has capacity of 1,000 shelves per month and sells each shelf for £40. The revenue line at zero output will be at the origin and at capacity will be

£40 × 1,000 = £40,000

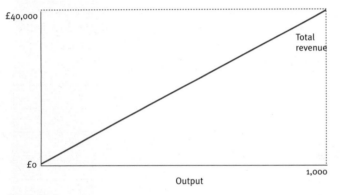

Figure 42.1   Total revenue

Note that only two points of reference are required for drawing this line; these are 0 and capacity output. This is because the relationship between revenue and output is one which produces a straight line when plotted on a graph.

Supposing that the above business had fixed costs of £10,000 per month and variable costs of £15 per unit.

At zero output, total costs would be £10,000 (just the fixed costs).

At capacity output, total costs would be

£10,000 + (£15 × 1,000) = £10,000 + £15,000 = £25,000 per month

Superimposing this on to Figure 42.1 would result in the diagram above right.

Notice that break-even is calculated in units. In this case, break-even point is 400 shelves per month. The

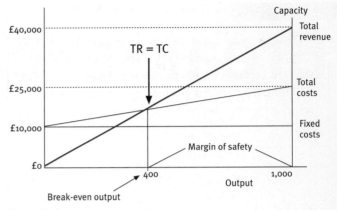

Figure 42.2   Break-even chart

business can also compare its present level of output with the break-even output to ascertain the difference. This is known as the **margin of safety**.

Margin of safety = actual output – break-even output. If it is assumed that the business is producing at capacity, its margin of safety is therefore

1,000 – 400 = 600 shelves

This measures the amount by which output can fall without the business making a loss.

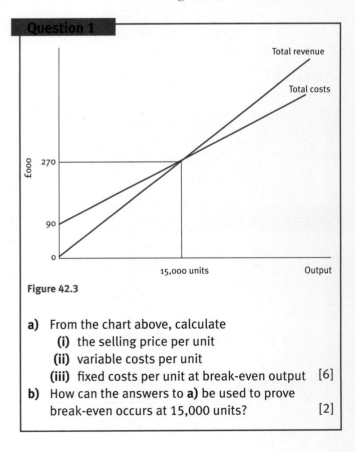

Question 1

Figure 42.3

a) From the chart above, calculate
   (i) the selling price per unit
   (ii) variable costs per unit
   (iii) fixed costs per unit at break-even output   [6]
b) How can the answers to **a)** be used to prove break-even occurs at 15,000 units?   [2]

Question 2

Porthill Ltd manufactures jacuzzis at a variable cost of £250 per unit, with a capacity of 20 per month. Fixed costs are £6,000 per month and the business charges £750 for each finished product. By drawing the break-even chart, show the break-even point and the margin of safety.   [5]

It is also possible to use the diagram to calculate profit or loss at various levels of output. Using the original example, Simon knows that his business must produce 400 shelves to break even. If he is producing 1,000 units the business will be making profit, but how much? By the same token, if output dropped to 800, 600, 400 or 200 units, what would be the profit? Clearly, the most important point in terms of his business surviving is 400 units. On the diagram any level of output to the right of 400 shelves means the business will make a profit and any output level to the left of 400 shelves means a loss.

The actual profit or loss can be ascertained by examining the vertical distance between the total cost and total revenue lines at particular levels of output. Referring to the diagram above will allow you to estimate profit at various levels of output. This examination will hopefully demonstrate one problem of using the charts. If any of the lines is incorrectly plotted, even by the smallest error, the calculations will become much more difficult to perform accurately. Indeed, it will be easier to calculate the level of profit using just the numbers.

Calculation of profit

Profit is the surplus of revenue over cost and is therefore calculated as

Total revenue – total costs

= (quantity × price) – (variable cost per unit × quantity) – fixed cost

Examination of profit will have shown different levels of profit or loss depending on the level of output. The following table shows how this profit will alter:

Table 1

Output	Revenue £	Fixed costs £	Variable costs £	Total costs £	Profit £
0	0	10000	0	10000	–10000
200	8000	10000	3000	13000	–5000
400	16000	10000	6000	16000	0
600	24000	10000	9000	19000	5000
800	32000	10000	12000	22000	10000
1000	40000	10000	15000	25000	15000

It is a good idea to check these calculations for yourself by putting various levels of output into the formula. If the level of profit is plotted against the level of output, it produces what is known as a **profit–volume** chart and is another version of break-even which focuses on profit. You will note that at zero output, the loss is the same as fixed costs, and at 400 units of output, break-even is achieved.

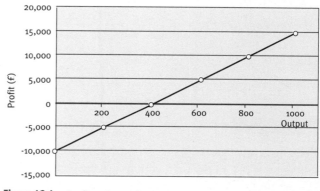

Figure 42.4   Profit–volume chart

Question 3

a) Using the data provided in Question 2 (Porthill Ltd) show that break-even is achieved at 12 units, by calculating the profit at 12 units of output.   [4]

b) Calculate the various levels of profit at 0, 5, 10, 15 and 20 jacuzzis per month. Based on your result, draw a profit–volume chart and use it to estimate profit at 8 and 18 units of output. Verify your estimations using calculations (total revenue – total costs).

You could build a simple spreadsheet to calculate the answers, using Table 1 as the format.   [10]

Loss of accuracy

If a business has a capacity of 1 million units per annum and break-even output of 763,793 units, this will be impossible to demonstrate to this level of accuracy on a piece of normal graph paper! Using a formula is a quicker and usually more reliable method of calculation. To ascertain the formula, consider the profit equation:

Total revenue = total costs

At break-even output:

Total revenue – total costs = 0 i.e. profit is zero.

Therefore total revenue = total costs

Price × quantity = (variable cost per unit × quantity) + fixed costs

Rearranging this makes

(Price × quantity) – (variable cost per unit × quantity) = fixed costs

Quantity (price – variable cost per unit) = fixed cost

so break-even quantity = $\dfrac{\text{fixed costs}}{\text{price – variable cost per unit}}$

Using Simon's Shelving as an example,

Break-even = $\dfrac{\pounds10,000}{\pounds40 - \pounds15} = \dfrac{10,000}{25}$ = 400 units.

Question 4

A business has fixed costs of £700,000 per annum. Its selling price is £35 per unit, with a variable cost of £15 per unit. Calculate the break-even point, margin of safety and profit if the business produces 48,000 units.   [5]

Changing the formula using contribution

Price and variable cost have one thing in common – both are multiplied by output in the calculation of profit. The difference between the two i.e. price minus variable cost per unit is known as **contribution**. This is because as every unit is made and sold, a business pays the variable cost and receives the revenue. The difference is used to pay initially for the fixed costs, then, once they have all been paid for, the difference contributes to profit (*see Unit 43*).

The break-even formula takes on a slightly simpler look now:

$$\dfrac{\text{fixed costs}}{\text{contribution per unit}}$$

The calculation for profit also becomes a little easier, by rearranging the formula of total revenue – total costs, profit becomes:

(Contribution × output) – fixed costs.

The break-even formula can be further manipulated if the business does aim to make a profit e.g. a business makes teddy bears at a variable cost of £5 and fixed costs of £8,000 per week. The selling price is £9, so the break-even point is

$\dfrac{\pounds8,000}{\pounds9 - \pounds5}$ = 2,000 bears.

If the business wanted to earn a profit of £3,000, this means that contribution must be £8,000 + £3,000 in order to cover the fixed costs and meet the profit target. Think of the contribution as a steady stream of income into the business, initially going to pay for fixed costs; once the fixed costs have been met, then any more contribution goes towards profit.

Figure 42.5   Break-even using contribution

Once the stream of contribution has filled the fixed cost bucket, it then goes towards filling the profit trough. Naturally, the business will normally wish the profit trough to be as large as possible.

The formula of $\dfrac{\text{fixed costs}}{\text{contribution}}$ now becomes

$\dfrac{\text{fixed costs + profit}}{\text{contribution}}$ when establishing the quantity required for a target level.

In the above example: $\dfrac{(\pounds8,000 + \pounds3,000)}{\pounds4}$ = 2,750.

By putting this answer into the formula of

contribution × output – fixed costs
= £4   ×   2,750   –   £8,000   = £3,000

proving the **target profit** formula to be correct.

Question 5

A business produces pens and sells them for £2 each. Variable costs are £0.75 and fixed costs are £5,000 per week.

a) Calculate break-even output. [2]

b) If the business wishes to earn a profit of £4,000, calculate how many units it must make and sell. [3]

c) Assuming it produces this amount, what is the margin of safety? [1]

Question 6

In each of the following circumstances, complete the row of figures for each business.

Present output	Price	VC	Fixed costs	Break-even point	Profit	Margin of safety
a) 30,000	£8	£6	£12,000	?	?	?
b) ?	£10	£5	£18,000	?	£7,000	?
c) 600,000	?	£8	£900,000	600,000	?	?
d) ?	£25	£15	?	200,000	£500,000	?

[12]

the café has reached break-even, it still has to use half its revenue to pay the variable costs.

Question 7

Chuggy is a small private limited company which makes aprons and overalls. At present its production is housed in old premises with little modern machinery and is rather labour-intensive. As orders have risen, production has been stretched to cope, and the company is considering investing in more modern machinery. This will reduce variable costs by cutting out much manual labour but will increase fixed costs because of the fixed overheads associated with the new machinery.

The price of the most popular apron is £8 and current volume is 20,000 units per month.
Other costs are as follows:

	Old machinery	New machinery
Fixed costs allocated	£20,000	£45,000
Variable cost per toy	£6.00	£4.50

a) Calculate break-even on each basis. [4]

b) Calculate profit at 20,000 units. [4]

c) Advise the company whether or not to buy the new machinery. State your reasons clearly. [5]

Cost structure

Consider two businesses:

1 Hotel

With high fixed costs and negligible variable costs, break-even will take a longer time to reach. Once the break-even point has been reached, more or less all the revenue will contribute to profit e.g. variable costs of a hotel room are unlikely to be more than £10 per person per night and many hotels charge between £60 and £100.

2 Café selling all-day breakfasts

This business will face higher variable costs in relation to its price e.g. for an all-day breakfast, the variable cost will be about £2.00, with a price of £4.00. Once

Assumptions

Like any model, there are several assumptions which limit the usefulness of the said technique.

■ One product and one selling price

Frequently a business may sell the same product to different customers at different prices e.g. if a customer buys in bulk then the unit price will be less than if the customer purchases individual units.

■ Straight-line variable and fixed costs

Such an assumption means semi-variable costs are assumed to be directly proportional to output i.e. they increase in direct proportion to output

■ All output which is made is sold

If this does not happen, the business will either experience a build-up in stock (if output is greater than sales) or will need to run down its stock (if sales are greater than output). The stock level used (in the case of the latter) could have been produced at a different variable or fixed cost per unit.

■ The production process is assumed to be sufficiently flexible to allow break-even point to be achieved

If break-even point is 368 and the business produces only in 100s, then the business will need to decide whether to produce 300 or 400. Either way, the precise break-even point will not be achieved.

■ The model is static

Any change in any of three factors affecting break-even (price, variable costs or fixed costs) will result in the diagram needing to be redrawn and the calculations repeated with different numbers.

Points for Revision

Key Terms

break-even	the level of output at which revenue equals total costs; calculated by $\dfrac{\text{fixed costs}}{\text{contribution}}$
revenue	the value of goods or services produced and sold by the business
margin of safety	the amount by which output can be reduced without the business making a loss
profit–volume	a chart to demonstrate the relationship between profit and output
target profit	when a business aims to make a profit, this calculates the number of units required to achieved that level of profit. Formula: $\dfrac{\text{(fixed costs + target profit)}}{\text{contribution}}$
contribution	the difference between selling price and variable costs

Definitions Question:
By referring to a business you know, explain the importance of any three of the above terms (your teacher may wish to select the terms). [5] per definition

Summary Points:

1   Break-even point is measured in units and depends on price, variable costs, fixed costs.

2   An alternative diagrammatic representation is the profit–volume chart.

3   A more accurate method of discovering break-even point and profit is using formulae.

4   Break-even helps a company set its price and control its costs, but there are several assumptions which limit its usefulness in real-life situations.

Mini Case Study

Severnhill & Sons Ltd produces string. It is working at full capacity and hardly keeping up with demand – the management believes it could increase orders by 10% without changing the price. The current capacity on the single shift per day basis is 100,000 balls of string per week. It sells to wholesalers at a price of 60p per ball and the current cost structure per ball is as follows:

Materials	22p
Direct labour	10p
Variable overheads	2p
Fixed overheads	15p

Severnhill is evaluating two options to increase capacity:

Option A: By working overtime, it could increase output by 10% with only a £1,000 per week rise in fixed costs. However, the average direct labour cost for the whole production amount would rise to 11p per ball.

Option B: The sales director proposed moving to a two-shift basis. This would almost double capacity with only a £2,000 per week increase in fixed costs, but shift allowances would mean that direct labour per ball would rise by 20%. The extra output produced would reduce material cost by 2p per ball. He said that recent market research had shown that demand for the string was highly price elastic and he proposed an across-the-board price reduction of 10% which he hoped would increase sales by 40%.

1 Define: cost structure, highly price elastic. [4]

2 Calculate the current break-even point, margin of safety and profit per week. [3]

3 Calculate the new break-even point, margin of safety and potential profit of each of the two options outlined. [6]

4 Compare each of the two options with the present situation and recommend to the board the most appropriate option – A, B or staying the same. [7]

20

Maxi Case Study

Bushrow pre-school play centre is contemplating expanding its service to cater for parents who want to leave their children for an afternoon session. At the moment children stay only for the morning and the manager of the play centre feels there is an opportunity to earn more revenue. In particular, Mrs Swaywood, the manager, is hoping to attract parents who both work full-time, given that their income may be higher and there will certainly be demand for such a service. Mrs Swaywood is a registered nursery nurse, who has operated from the existing premises for 10 years. Unfortunately, offering this expanded service would necessitate the play centre moving to different premises as the present venue, the local church hall, is used by the Women's Guild most afternoons. The church charges £150 for five mornings a week.

All four of her present staff would be prepared to work the additional afternoon session, but would require an additional 50 pence per hour for working all day.

At present the staff are paid £3 an hour for the 3-hour session. The afternoon session would also be for 3 hours. The increase in pay would then take their wages above the level required by the minimum wage legislation. There would be the need to take on one additional member of staff on a full-time basis. The cost per child, to provide a drink, disposables, play materials and biscuits is 80 pence per session.

The rent for the new premises would be £200 per week, but would enable the play centre to take a maximum of 40 children for each session. Each child is charged £2 per hour (£6 per session).

Mrs Swaywood's latest estimate of the number of children per session, based on the present levels, is 30 children.

There are concerns about the reliability of the staff although they have all said they are willing to work both sessions. To comply with local authority bye-laws, the play centre must have at least one member of staff for every eight children. If she can avoid using herself for this it would ensure that the meeting and greeting of the parents, the marketing, the ordering of materials and keeping the books can be done within the opening hours of the play centre. Mrs Swaywood prefers to step in to cover only as a short-term solution for unexpected absences of her staff and only for a day, otherwise she would get behind with all her other essential tasks.

1 Define: revenue, minimum wage legislation.   [4]

2 Calculate: [4]

   a) the break-even number of children for a morning session at the Church Hall   [3]

   b) the break-even number of children per day at the new premises   [3]

3 If the actual number of children attending remains at 30 at both sessions, calculate the
   margin of safety and the profit per day at the new premises.   [4]

4 **a)** Mrs Swaywood is keen to fill the play centre with 40 children at both sessions and
   intends to achieve this by lowering the price per day in the hope that more children will
   be enrolled. What is the difference in the break-even number of children if the price is
   reduced to £9.00 per day?   [2]

   b) Draw a break-even chart for your answer to **a)**.   [5]

   c) Calculate the price elasticity of demand if the reduction in price leads to full capacity
   (40 children) being reached.   [2]

5 Comment on how the legal environment may restrict Mrs Swaywood's plans.   [5]

6 Discuss the appropriateness of the break-even model as an aid to making the decision
   to move.   [8]

                                                                                                  40

Contribution

Learning objectives

Having read this unit, students will be able to

1 understand the principles behind marginal cost

2 appreciate the significance of contribution for business decision making

3 distinguish between contribution and profit

Context

Following recent dramatic price cuts by various cross-Channel ferry companies and Eurotunnel, there have been questions asked about the wisdom behind such a move, and whether it is in the interest of shareholders to do this. The companies face a problem of over-capacity (too many firms providing the same product) and therefore a problem of capacity utilisation. Each journey on one of the ferries' coaches is instantly 'perishable'. This means that any unfilled place is lost revenue; unlike a manufacturer who can put the product into stock and sell it the next day or week, once a journey has taken place and a seat has not been filled, this revenue and profit can never be recovered. Consequently, Stena P & O and other businesses must concentrate on ensuring maximum use of capacity is achieved. The main way to encourage customers to buy products is by reducing prices. This can result in a business charging an amount that does not cover its unit cost. However, this does not necessarily matter, as long as the extra revenue of the extra place sold covers the extra cost of the journey. This is known as the marginal cost. The marginal cost of a journey from Dover to Calais is almost zero – no more than the minute amount of wear and tear of sitting on a seat for two hours, so prices can be reduced to a very low point and still cover the costs of providing the extra journey; the difference between the extra revenue and extra cost in these cases is known as contribution.

Marginal cost

Marginal cost is defined as the addition to total costs of producing an extra unit or extra units of output.

$$\text{Marginal cost} = \frac{\text{increase (or decrease) in total costs}}{\text{change in output}}$$

In the short run, this is just the variable cost i.e. the extra materials, labour and variable overheads required to produce the extra unit.

Marginal cost can, however, include fixed costs e.g. when a business is approached to produce a batch of extra products according to a specific design, then in addition to the extra materials, labour etc. required, it may need to invest in a specific design template which is used only for the extra order.

Contribution redefined

In Unit 42, contribution was defined as selling price less variable costs (or direct costs), which is the correct formula when the only extra costs are variable costs. However, a more precise formula is

Contribution per unit =
selling price – marginal cost per unit

Total contribution = sales revenue – marginal costs

e.g. selling price = £40; variable cost = £32; volume = 10,000 units

Contribution per unit = £40 – £32 = £8

Total contribution = (£40 × 10,000) – (£32 × 10,000) = £80,000

or (£40 – £32) × 10,000 is the quickest method of calculating total contribution

i.e. (selling price – variable cost) × contribution

This calculation may include some extra fixed costs only if they are associated with the extra products being made e.g. if the business in the above example suddenly discovered that an extra design template was required costing a one-off £15,000 regardless of the volume produced, then contribution would be:

(£40 – £32) × 10,000 – £15,000 = £65,000

Application of contribution

Contribution is used in four specific circumstances of decision making:

■ Special order
■ Dropping a product
■ Product mixes
■ Make or buy

Special order – the financial factors

In many businesses, especially those that deal with a small number of customers buying a large amount of products e.g. the oil industry selling to various retailers of petro-chemical products, prices are negotiated regularly. When a present customer requires an extra order, it may wish to pay a lower price than usual. The business will consider the marginal costs of the extra units for the **special order** and set a price based on that.

e.g. a business produces shelving units with a variable cost of £10 per unit and fixed costs of £8,000 per month. Present output is 500 units per month and the usual selling price is £30. It has been approached by a potential customer who is willing to pay £20 per unit for an order of 100 units.

Here, the business will not consider the fact that unit cost at 500 units is

$$\frac{£8,000}{500} \text{ units} = £16 + £10 \text{ (variable costs per unit)} = £26$$

nor that it will decrease to

$$\frac{£8,000}{600} = £13.33 + £10 = £23.33$$

but rather that the selling price for the special order is £20 and that the marginal cost is £10, so the contribution per unit for the extra 100 units is

£20 – £10 = £10, multiplied by 100 units = £1,000

This is £1,000 extra contribution. A quick calculation of profit for the present output at 500 units will tell you that the business is already making a profit of

[(£30 – £10) × 500] – £8,000 = £2,000 so the extra order will mean the business earns a new profit of £3,000.

Even if the business were making a loss, then any extra contribution would help to pay for the fixed costs which have not already been covered and then adds to profit.

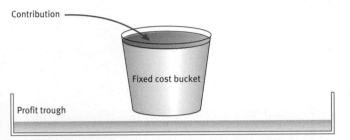

Figure 43.1 The extra contribution puts more into the bucket

In the above diagram, fixed costs have not been fully covered i.e. the business has not yet reached break-even point. Even though the selling price of the special order may be priced below the usual amount, any contribution which is made will take the business closer to break-even point, or even beyond it, putting some money into the profit trough!

Question 1

Screen Ltd sells computer screens for £100 each, with a variable cost of £60. Fixed costs are £11,000 per month at an output level of 350. An extra order has been received from Meg-Chip plc for 150 screens at a price of £70 each.
Calculate the contribution from this extra order.

[3]

Question 2

Grove Ltd makes fans for cooling hot air. Revenue last year was £740,000, variable costs were £14 per unit and fixed costs were £360,000 at an output level of 20,000 units. It has been approached by RBL plc for a special order of 3,000 units per annum, at a selling price of £20.

a) Calculate the present selling price.   [2]

b) Calculate contribution from the new order and therefore the new level of total profit if the business takes on the RBL order.   [5]

Question 3

A business sells 5,000 units per month at a selling price of £5 per unit. The unit cost at this level of output is £4 (half variable and half fixed). The business is approached for a special order of 500 units at a price of £3. Calculate contribution and the new level of profit if the business does take on the extra order.   [4]

Question 4

A business sells 20,000 units that it produces at a unit cost of £53, although the market is so competitive that it can charge only a price of £49. Fixed costs are £30 per unit at this level of output. The business is approached for an extra one-off order of 5,000 units at a price of only £43. Even though the business is presently making a loss, using contribution, show that the business becomes profitable with this extra order.   [5]

Occasionally, there may be some fixed costs incurred that specifically relate to a special order. This is usually the case when a specialised design is required for a product. In such cases, the extra fixed costs must be included in the marginal costs of the extra order and deducted from the extra revenue.

Question 5

A car radio manufacturer is approached by a major car manufacturer to design and produce 1,000 radios on a trial basis for one of its new models. The variable cost of each radio is estimated to be £25, and there will be a fixed design cost of £15,000. The radios will be bought for £40 each.

a) Calculate the total contribution from this extra order.   [3]

b) What other factors might persuade the business to take on this extra order?   [5]

And the non-financial factors?

The financial criteria for accepting an extra order (or not) can sometimes be outweighed by other factors which the business will consider.

■ Business objectives

The business may have made market share one of its primary objectives, above that of profit. In this case, the order may be accepted to gain a foothold in the market in the hope that either the business can reduce its costs through e.g. purchasing economies of scale as it gets larger or the customer accepts an increase in price if the business delivers promptly at the required level of quality.

■ Capacity

In order to deliver promptly, the business will need to have the capacity available in its own plant. Occasionally, if capacity is not available, it may have to postpone its usual order, thereby delivering late to its present customers. Or it could subcontract the extra order to another manufacturer in order to deliver to the customers on time.

■ Reputation

If a small, unknown exhaust pipe manufacturer is approached by Toyota for a five-year contract, even though it may not be initially profitable, the spin-off due to the prestige of supplying Toyota can be used in the company's marketing.

■ Use of capacity

A business may aim to use its capacity efficiently or may aim to provide continual work for its employees, especially if it is a non-profit making organisation.

■ Reaction of present customers

If loyal customers hear of a price reduction for a special order, they may also demand a price reduction.

■ Future sales

Special orders may lead to further sales in the future, especially if the customer's business is growing

■ Cash flow

Despite the attractiveness of special orders, the customer may not be able to pay on time, which will result in cash flow problems for the business.

■ Customer in competition

If the customer persuades the business to supply goods at a deeply discounted price, there is always a threat that the customer might set up in competition to the business.

■ Flexibility

The one-off design costs which are sometimes incurred may be used to widen its product range or to find new customers.

Question 6

Pot-It Ltd, which manufactures high-quality pottery, is making a profit on one of its many lines of £4,000 per month at the present output of 15,000 units. The variable cost per unit is £14 and total fixed costs are £30,000. The business has been approached by a major discount retailer, Cheap-Pot, for an order of 2,000 units at a price of £14.80.

a) Calculate the present price being charged. [4]

b) Calculate break-even output. [2]

c) Advise the business, considering financial and non-financial factors, on whether it should accept the order. [8]

■ Dropping or discontinuing a product

Contribution can be used to ascertain whether a product should be kept on or discontinued e.g.

Product	A	B	C
Selling price	£15	£10	£12
Variable cost	£9	£7	£6
Contribution	£6	£3	£6
Quantity	4000	5000	1500
Total contribution	£24000	£15000	£9000
Fixed costs	£12000	£12000	£12000
Profit	£12000	£3000	–£3000

Assume fixed costs are spread equally across the three products. In the above example product C is making a loss of £3000. What would happen to the company's profits if it decided to drop product C? It is tempting to assume that if C was dropped, then the profit would increase by £3000 (i.e. the amount which product C is losing at the moment) meaning a total profit of £15,000. Remembering that the fixed costs must still be paid in full, products A and B must now cover the fixed costs at £18,000 per product.

Product	A	B
Quantity	4000	5000
Total contribution	£24000	£15000
Fixed costs	£18000	£18000
Profit	£6000	–£3000

Therefore profit for the business is now only £3,000. It is no coincidence that the difference in profit before and after dropping C is £9,000, which is the contribution from product C. Financially speaking, if a product is making a contribution, then it should not be discontinued.

Question 7

Whidgys manufactures three types of metal trays which it sells to restaurants and catering establishments for £10, £25 and £15 respectively. Fixed costs for the business are £54,000 and are spread equally between the three trays. During last year, it sold 5,000 of A, 3,000 of B and 7,000 of C. Information on variable costs is as follows:

Costs per unit	A	B	C
material	£3.00	£7.00	£5.00
labour	£4.00	£10.00	£5.00

a) Calculate the contribution and profit for each product and for the company as a whole. [7]

b) The managing director decides to discontinue product A. Do you agree with this decision on financial grounds? [3]

c) What other factors might the managing director consider when deciding whether or not to discontinue product A? [3]

Contribution or profit

The example and question above demonstrate the fundamental difference between contribution and profit. Contribution is easier to calculate than profit, because it is easier to allocate variable costs to a particular product. Material costs can be calculated according to the materials used in the manufacturing process and the same is true for labour if it is a variable cost. Fixed costs tend to apply to the entire company, so are more difficult to apportion to one product. This makes the calculation of profit more subjective depending on the way fixed costs are allocated. Contribution is therefore a more accurate measurement of a product's financial performance. Profit (contribution – fixed costs) can provide an indication of the entire business and its financial performance, but not individual products.

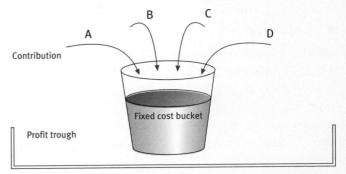

Figure 43.2   A business will use contribution to assess whether to continue a product on financial grounds

As long as the product is making a flow of contribution into the business, it should be continued. The only time it may be dropped is if there is insufficient capacity and another product is making greater contribution (see Product mix). The business will therefore decide to drop the product based on the flow of contribution.

Product mix

A business will consider contribution when deciding on the **product mix** – producing the products which earn the greatest total contribution; looking not just at contribution per unit, but also at the volume produced and sold. It has been assumed so far that there is no restriction on the amount of products which can be made in a particular business. But there could well be restrictions on the number of machines a business can run, the materials available or the level of skill required. If there is a restriction on the number of materials which a business can source (find a supplier for) and this restriction prevents it from producing the required amount, then contribution can help with the decision making process.

e.g. Oralelle, a French perfume manufacturer, produces two products, Fraîche and Gageac, both of which require special oil which is in short supply, with only 60,000 grams available. Fraîche requires 2g per unit produced and Gageac requires 5g per unit produced.

Fraîche and Gageac make a contribution of £12 and £20 respectively, with sales of 10,000 each. Clearly, Gageac is making the most contribution, so resources must be concentrated on Gageac. But there are only 60,000g available and the company needs $10,000 \times 5$ for Gageac and $10,000 \times 2$ for Fraîche, making a total of 70,000g.

In this circumstance, the business must calculate the contribution per unit of **limiting factor** (the special oil)

$$= \frac{\text{contribution per unit}}{\text{amount of materials required per unit}}$$

For Fraîche: $\frac{£12}{2g}$ = £6 per gram. In effect, this means that for every gram used, the business earns a contribution of £6. In other words it is a form of return.

For Gageac: $\frac{£20}{5g}$ = £4 per gram.

The priority therefore goes to product Fraîche:

$10,000 \times 2g = 20,000g$ used, leaving 40,000 remaining.

This means $\frac{40,000}{5g}$ = 8,000 of Gageac can be made.

Therefore the contribution will be

$(10,000 \times £12) + (8,000 \times £20) = £280,000$

If, however, the business had concentrated on Gageac first, producing 10,000 units and using 50,000g, this would have produced less contribution:

$(10,000 \times £20) + (5,000 \times £12) = £260,000$

N.B. 5,000 is the maximum amount of Fraîche which can be produced because only 10,000g remain

Therefore when there is a limiting factor, the business needs to calculate the contribution per unit of limiting factor. Where there is no restriction in this respect, the business takes the decision on the product mix by looking at total contribution made by each product.

Question 8

The Smelly Shop is a business specialising in making and selling products to retailers of aromatherapy products. The process of production requires an extremely rare oil known as Starcol, found in Tibet.

Product	W	X	Y
Price	£10	£9	£12
Variable costs	£4	£5	£6
Demand per week	70	50	80
Materials per unit (g)	4	5	8

a) By calculating the contribution, list the products in order of priority for production. [4]

b) Starcol is in short supply, with only 730 grams available each week. Show that the new order of priority for production, given the shortage of materials, is W, X, Y. [6]

c) Show that with a material restriction of 730 grams, the weekly profit earned by The Smelly Shop is £770. [5]

Make or buy

Not all businesses will manufacture their entire output by themselves. Occasionally, given the right circumstances, a business may invite another business to do the manufacturing for it i.e. contract out the process of making the products. This is otherwise known as **subcontracting**. The main reason for the business doing this is when another company is more efficient, and therefore can produce the product at a lower unit cost than the business itself, or perhaps has specialist knowledge and equipment. This will ultimately lead to a higher contribution than with the business manufacturing the product 'in-house' i.e. using its own machinery. There are other reasons why a business will subcontract, apart from the immediate financial benefit.

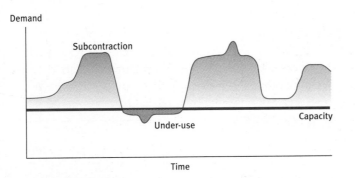

Figure 43.3 Fluctuating demand makes it difficult to find the correct level of capacity

In Figure 43.3, demand fluctuates widely over time. In such circumstances, the business may decide to work at a capacity level of the dark, straight line, and subcontract the work to others whenever demand outstrips capacity. That way, the business uses its capacity constantly, achieving economies of scale, but does rely on capacity being available at the subcontracting factory. This saves the business from having to expand capacity for an occasional order.

There could simply be a special one-off order (*see Special order above*) which takes the business above its capacity level. In order to maintain its commitment to present customers, a business may well decide to subcontract the extra work.

Specialist skills or equipment may be required. This is particularly useful, for example, when a business that manufactures computers needs packaging equipment. The expertise of the computer firm is unlikely to encompass the packaging function, so subcontracting becomes necessary.

Advantages of subcontracting

■ It allows the business to concentrate on its core activity, leaving peripheral activities to others

■ The business can concentrate on marketing, not manufacturing

■ Quality may be better if the work is done by a specialised business

Disadvantages of subcontracting

■ It may well reduce the profit margin if the business is forced to pay more when e.g. it needs an order to be dealt with quickly

■ The business does not have as much control over the way it is made and may feel at the mercy of the subcontractor

■ Frequently employees have a negative reaction to subcontracted work, because it may mean that they will be no longer needed if work is subcontracted out to another business

Points for Revision

Key Terms

marginal cost	addition to total costs of making extra units/an extra unit
special order	when a business receives an order for products in addition to normal levels of production
subcontracting	when a business contracts out the production of some units of output to another business
product mix	the combination of products which a business produces
limiting factor	when a business is restricted in its production by one or more factors of production

Definitions Question:

By referring to a business you know, explain the significance of any three of the above terms (your teacher may wish to choose the terms).   [5] per definition

Summary Points:

1 Contribution (sales revenue minus marginal costs) has many applications which help businesses make better decisions.

2 Companies assess the financial outcome of a special order by calculating the contribution.

3 A business will cease producing a product on financial grounds only if it fails to make sufficient contribution.

4 Contribution can help to decide a product mix, especially when there is a limiting factor of production.

Mini Case Study

Smooth-It Ltd manufactures a range of beauty products aimed at the 18–24-year-old unisex market. The products are sold individually, although at special times during the year, normally Christmas and Valentine's Day, it presents the entire range in a special gift pack, which helps to sell more of the poorer selling lines. At the moment, the product mix is rather unbalanced, with two cash cows but with no product that is growing, nor with any being researched and developed. Financial details of the products are as follows:

Product	Body lotion	Shampoo	Shower gel	Gift pack
Selling price	£3	£3.50	£2.50	£9
Variable costs	£1.50	£2	£1.50	£5.50
Volume sold per annum	50000	120000	130000	30000
Fixed costs per annum	80000	80000	80000	40000

The profitability of each product had been scrutinised by the board at the latest meeting, after which the managing director had said quite bluntly 'I don't know why we bother producing body lotion, it seems obvious to me that we need to stop its production.' The financial director groaned inwardly. 'Is this managing director ever going to understand contribution?' she thought to herself. Only yesterday she had spent an hour with the managing director on the virtues of calculating contribution and not profit, and now she would have to do it again! As she stood up to say her piece, the telephone rang …

1 List the factors that the business might have considered when deciding its product mix.

[3]

2 (i) Calculate contribution and profit for all three products and for Smooth-It as a company.   [5]

 (ii) Calculate the break-even level of output for body lotion.   [2]

(iii) Advise the business, based on (i) and (ii) above, and any other information you feel is relevant, whether to drop the body lotion.   [3]

3 You receive this memo from the financial director:

Dear Kev,

The board meeting yesterday was cut short due to a phone call from the bank; I was about to explain the merits of contribution to the MD but she asked that I prepare a presentation for the next meeting (this Thursday). I have just remembered that I will be away that day, so please prepare a three-minute presentation, with a brief report to hand round to the board, on the significance of contribution in a business like ours.

Carry out the instructions of the financial director.   [12]

25

Maxi Case Study

Charles Linners was facing a difficult decision; he had taken over his father's family firm and had immediately stated his commitment to carrying out the company objectives. The objectives were:

- To earn as high a gross profit margin as possible
- To employ as few people as possible
- To subcontract as much work as possible
- To focus in-house on developing new products for health care

The business, Texipak, is based in America and is responsible for providing products which are concerned with health care. Its main product, contributing over 70% of sales revenue, known as the 'Pharbreathe', is a device which aids breathing for those who have had operations on the throat and nose. The company is therefore in a niche market, although sales have grown over recent years as technological advancement in surgery has meant more treatment for those with respiratory problems.

In order to improve the profit margin, Charles is looking carefully at subcontracting the production of Pharbreathe, which is presently carried out on site. The figures, however, are not convincing:

Direct costs per box of 20 Pharbreathes, manufactured in-house:

Materials	$ 1.25
Labour	$ 0.65
Total	$ 1.90

It was estimated that Texipak would be able to be reduce its overheads by only $6,000 per annum if Pharbreathe was subcontracted. The subcontractor, Stealth Substances, had offered a price of $2.40 per box of 20. Presently, 30,000 boxes were sold to various health care organisations, at a price of $10 each.

Pharbreathe has been manufactured in-house for seven years, although there have been some staffing problems with a rather high level of labour turnover. The work-force involved in Pharbreathe is employed as casual labour to reduce costs. Ironically this has caused extra costs given the nature of the business: every time a new member of staff joins the business, he/she needs overalls, cleaning equipment and training. Casual staff are not the most reliable and Charles presently spends the first 30 minutes of the day pacing up and down the factory floor, uncertain as to whether all the casual labour have turned up. The company could also lease out the second warehouse it uses because it would no longer be needed if subcontracting took place.

However, in-house manufacture means the company can monitor all quality very closely in order to ensure the product meets various quality standards e.g. ISO 900. Texipak's buyer was also concerned that the company might lose discounts on its materials if it stopped purchasing for Pharbreathe. Consequently, Charles was intending to visit the material suppliers to inform them of the new arrangement to ensure they realised the volume of purchasing would be the same, despite it originating from two companies. Stealth was a reliable company, and was likely to react favourably to the new arrangement, although no agreement has been made for the delivery charges in terms of who was to pick up the bill. The other issue which seems to be most obvious to Charles is that Texipak is not a manufacturing business – its expertise lay elsewhere (see company objectives). Selling off the machinery and tooling for Pharbreathe would mean that Charles could focus the group into a niche area of expertise.

1 Define: gross margin, labour turnover.   [4]

2 Explain why the business 'wants to employ as few people as possible'.   [6]

3 a) Explain one reason for the difference between the direct cost of manufacturing in-house and the offer made by Stealth to manufacture Pharbreathe for Texipak.   [2]

    b) Calculate the contribution per unit for both in-house and subcontracting.   [2]

    c) Taking into account the volume sold and the saving in overheads due to subcontracting, calculate the net gain/loss of subcontracting Pharbreathe to Stealth.   [4]

4 What are the advantages and disadvantages of casual labour for Texipak?   [4]

5 Evaluate the non-financial issues facing Texipak when making the decision whether or not to subcontract to Stealth Substances in order to achieve Texipak's objectives.   [8]

30

Cost allocation

Learning objectives

Having read this unit, students will be able to

1 identify the importance and problems of allocating fixed overheads

2 understand the difference between full costing and absorption costing

3 recognise a cost statement when they encounter one

Context

C & A, the department store, incurs a variety of costs, some of which are easy to allocate to particular parts of the business, whilst others are not. Material costs and the salaries/wages paid to staff employed in the stores can easily be matched against the revenue from a particular store. It is easy, therefore, to calculate the contribution which each store, or, indeed, each department makes towards the company's fixed costs. However, there are many costs which the business must pay for, but which cannot be easily allocated, such as marketing costs for the company as a whole. How much should, for example, the Manchester branch of C & A pay towards this marketing cost? After all, some of the marketing may have helped the Shrewsbury store to increase its sales of children's clothes. The important point to make is that earning a contribution is not always sufficient to judge the performance of a particular part of C & A. This is because the total of all the separate contributions from all the stores must meet those costs which cannot be allocated easily; consequently the performance of a particular department will be determined in part by contribution, but also by profit.

C & A in more detail

Revenue is earned by each department, be it menswear or ladies fashion, children's or teenagers'. The material and labour costs can easily be apportioned to those departments as can the depreciation on the fixtures and fittings, although there are store-wide costs which must be accounted for (which are not linked to any particular department). These are telephone costs, rent, administration costs (including managerial salaries, canteen costs, heating and lighting and insurance).

In addition, there are costs which are spent on the company as a whole. These range from costs of running headquarters, board of directors' salaries, dividends to shareholders, interest on borrowed money, all marketing costs such as research and advertising, and distribution costs. On top of this, the business will be expected to make a profit for reinvestment. Each individual department, once it has covered its direct or variable costs, must contribute enough money to pay not only for the fixed costs for the store, but also to contribute to the company-wide costs and the profit for shareholders.

The main purpose of allocating costs such as those above is to make the managers of individual parts of a company aware of the extra costs *they* must account for. The process of cost allocation is highly subjective and depending on the method chosen can turn a profitable part of the business into a loss making part, by a stroke of a pen or computer key. The main category of costs tends to be fixed overheads i.e. independent of output (fixed) and difficult to allocate to a particular unit of output (overheads).

Cost, revenue and profit centres

In order to identify clearly those parts of the business to which revenue and costs can be allocated, the business can be divided into different 'centres' for which cost and revenue can be both identified and allocated.

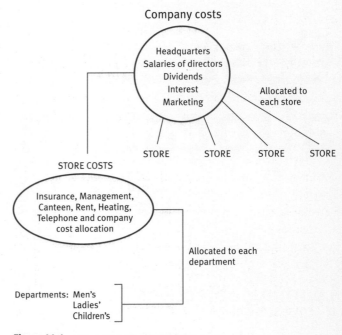

Figure 44.1 Allocation of costs at C & A

Question 1

When a new McDonald's restaurant is opened, the owner will have to pay a proportion of its revenue to McDonald's headquarters.

What costs will McDonald's have to account for which are not incurred by individual restaurants? [4]

■ Cost centres

These are parts of an organisation to which costs can be allocated and which do not earn any revenue e.g. in a town council, each department will have a budget determined normally by central government and then by the finance department of the council. Each department incurs costs and must work within a budget which will limit the amount it can spend.

■ Revenue centres

Parts of an organisation to which revenue can easily be allocated, but which do not spend a great deal of costs e.g. a courier for a travel agent's will earn revenue for changing currency at the port, hiring cars, booking trips, although the costs will be only his/her wages.

Profit centres

These are parts of an organisation to which both revenue and cost can be easily allocated and so profit targets are easy to set e.g. a product manager will have sales targets and a cost budget for his or her sales-force for commission and training; consequently the manager will be given a profit target.

Costs which are allocated to certain areas of the business may be referred to as **standard costs**, because they are used for making decisions and are therefore calculated based on a close observation of the business. Such costs are also used in budgeting (*see Unit 45*) as they are calculated using all the information available to make a forecast of the costs involved.

Investment centres

These are parts of the business responsible for a significant amount of capital investment e.g. a research department.

Methods of allocating cost

Full costing

This takes the overheads of the business and divides them between the various cost centres according to one criterion. This is not a particularly technical method of allocating costs, but it achieves the objective. Overheads, which may consist of 10 or 15 separate costs, are lumped together as a total, then allocated into cost centres.

e.g. a business has overheads of £100,000 per month which consist of:

Rent	£ 30,000
Store costs	£ 10,000
Managerial salaries	£ 42,000
Office costs	£ 6,000
Depreciation	£ 12,000
TOTAL	£100,000

Full costing takes the £100,000 and allocates it to cost centres using one criterion. As long as the business applies the criterion correctly and consistently, it does not really matter which criterion is used, given the subjective nature of this technique.

Several criteria can be demonstrated, using the following example.

Product	A	B	C
Revenue	£200,000	£150,000	£150,000
Material costs	£80,000	£50,000	£70,000
Labour costs	£50,000	£40,000	£30,000
Contribution	£70,000	£60,000	£50,000
Total contribution	= £180,000		
Fixed overheads	= £100,000		
Profit	= £80,000		

Criterion 1: equally

This would mean $\frac{£100000}{3}$ = £33,333 would be allocated to A, B and C. N.B. this would mean £99,999 and not £100,000 would be allocated, but the subjective nature of this method means it does not matter at all which product has to account for the extra £1!

Criterion 2: revenue

The calculation for each product would be:

A

$$\frac{£200,000}{£500,000} \times £100,000 = £40,000$$

B

$$\frac{£150,000}{£500,000} \times £100,000 = £30,000$$

C would have the same amount allocated as B due to the product earning the same revenue.

From the original example,

	A	B	C
Contribution	£70,000	£60,000	£50,000
Fixed costs	£40,000	£30,000	£30,000
Profit	£30,000	£30,000	£20,000

giving a total profit of £80,000.

Criterion 3: contribution

Product A: $\dfrac{£70,000}{£180,000} \times £100,000$

(i.e. the proportion of total contribution earned by product A, multiplied by fixed costs)

Product B: $\dfrac{£60,000}{£180,000} \times £100,000$

Product C: $\dfrac{£50,000}{£180,000} \times £100,000$

Contribution	£70,000	£60,000	£50,000
Fixed costs	£38,889	£33,333	£27,778
Profit	£31,111	£26,667	£22,222

Although the total profit is the same, the individual products earn different profit levels.

Question 2

Using the above example, allocate the fixed costs according to the following criteria

a) direct labour   [4]

b) direct materials   [4]

c) Why might direct labour be more appropriate than direct materials when allocating fixed costs in a labour-intensive business?   [3]

Question 3

Tread-It make a range of four different types of shoes, which will be known as products C, D, E and F. Details of the costs and revenues are as follows:

Product	C	D	E	F
Selling price	£35	£39	£29	£50
Volume per month	4,500	5,000	4,000	2,000

Fixed costs are £180,000 per month.

a) Calculate the total monthly revenue for each product and for Tread-It as a whole.   [4]

b) Allocate fixed costs according to revenue for each product.   [4]

c) When might the criterion of using volume be inappropriate when allocating fixed costs?   [2]

Absorption costing

This is a more scientific approach to allocating costs that recognises the fact that using one criterion is too simplistic. Consider the breakdown of costs used in the above example:

Rent	£30,000
Store costs	£10,000
Managerial salaries	£42,000
Office costs	£ 6,000
Depreciation	£12,000

The factors which cause rent to increase, such as the floor space available, will be different from the factors which make insurance premiums increase e.g. value of property. These will be different again from why office costs increase. Different elements of the total fixed overheads will therefore change according to different reasons. If these reasons are isolated and applied to each different fixed overhead, then the allocation to each profit centre will be more accurate.

Suggested methods for allocation are as follows:

Rent	Floor space
Store costs	Material costs
Managerial salaries	Revenue
Office costs	1% of work carried out for each department
Depreciation	Value of machinery

Question 4

For the above fixed costs, explain why the suggested methods of allocation are appropriate for the associated fixed costs when allocating the costs to a particular profit centre (or product, in this case).

    [10]

Whilst it is acknowledged that the above criteria for particular fixed costs will go some way to achieving the objective, it must be remembered that it is also impossible to allocate fixed costs accurately. Even though floor area is probably the most appropriate method to allocate rent, there may be part of the floor area which is common to several cost or profit centres. This means that whatever criterion is used, there will never be one perfect solution to the problem of allocating overheads accurately.

Cost statements

In an attempt to summarise the information which has been collected and calculated, businesses use cost statements. These take two forms – contribution and total cost statements.

The contribution statement for Fire-It, a supplier of various bottles of gas:

Product	4.5kg bottle	7.5kg bottle	13kg bottle	Total
Sales revenue	22500	25200	52250	99950
Variable cost	12000	14700	30000	56700
Total contribution (revenue – variable cost)	10500	10500	22250	43250

To produce a total cost statement, the allocation of fixed costs is written in underneath contribution and then profit is calculated. In addition, the total contribution etc. can be calculated by adding the horizontal row:

Product	4.5kg bottle	7.5kg bottle	13kg bottle	Total
Sales revenue	22500	25200	52250	99950
Variable cost	12000	14700	30000	56700
Total contribution	10500	10500	22250	43250
Fixed costs	8000	7000	10000	25000
(Contribution – fixed costs)				
Profit	2500	3500	12250	18250

Play-It, a manufacturer of dolls, has three main product lines: Penny, Pat and Muttley the dog. The company is unsure how to deal with its fixed overheads and has collected the following information:

Rent	£45,000
Administration	£35,000
Fuel and power	£20,000
Accounting costs	£ 6,000
Marketing costs	£24,000
Canteen costs	£14,000
Depreciation	£10,000
Interest	£12,000

Information on the three products is

	Penny	Pat	Muttley
Selling price	£12	£14	£8
Material costs	£4	£5	£3
Labour costs	£3	£5	£3
Contribution	£5	£4	£2

The business sells 20,000 of Penny and Pat, but only 10,000 units of Muttley.

Other information provided is:

Number of employees	3	2	2
Value of machinery	£40,000	£30,000	£30,000
Floor space (m²)	120,000	15,000	9,000
Value of capital	£80,000	£80,000	£40,000

The assets have been financed by a loan.

a) Identify appropriate criteria for allocating the separate fixed costs to each product. Justify your choice. [8]

b) Allocate fixed costs according to your own criteria and produce a total cost statement, showing revenue, variable costs and total fixed costs for each product. [12]

c) Why might absorption costing be less appropriate than full costing, even though the technique is more scientific? [5]

Consideration of costing approaches

Clearly there are several criteria of allocation which can be used to achieve the same objective of allocating overheads. Some criteria are more appropriate than others in certain circumstances e.g. if contribution is a more accurate reflection of performance than revenue, then contribution should be used. This is because a more successful product ought to account for more of the fixed costs.

The allocation criterion tends to be a subjective judgement based on the opinions of those involved in the decision. This can mean that by changing the criterion of allocation, a profit centre, which was previously earning no profit, can become profitable with no change to its efficiency.

Points for Revision

Key Terms

allocated fixed costs	total fixed costs are divided according to certain criteria and are allocated to individual products/cost centres
overheads	costs which cannot easily be associated with a particular unit of output or product
cost centre	part of the business which generates costs
revenue centre	part of the business which generates revenue
profit centre	part of the business which generates both profit and revenue
full costing	allocating fixed costs as a lump sum, using one criterion
absorption costing	dividing fixed costs into separate parts and allocating each one according to a separate criterion
standard costs	costs used either in the allocation process or in budgeting

Definitions Question:
By referring to a business you know, explain the significance of any two of the above terms (your teacher may help you choose the terms).   [5] per definition

Summary Points:

1   Overheads need to be allocated to cost and profit centres in order to make managers more accountable for costs which are not necessarily connected to their own area of operation.

2   Allocating overheads is subjective and can lead to a profit making part of the business showing a loss.

Mini Case Study

Kirkland and Co. make specialised bowls for bowling greens, made from ivory substitute. There are three types of bowl – the Straight, the Corner and the Curler – which are sold in sets of three plus a jack. Following an increase in the number of old age pensioners, the business has had to increase its capacity to meet a growing demand. It has also recognised that there are opportunities to sell a wider range of products to this market, starting with products which seem to be complementary to the demand for bowls. These range from scoring cards, cases and specialist cloths impregnated with chemical to dry the bowls when wet without damaging the finish.

The cost structure of a set of each is as follows:

		Straight	Corner	Curler
Selling price per set		£20.00	£30.00	£41.00
Materials	(£2/kg)	3kg	4kg	4.5kg
Direct labour	(£4/hour)	2 hours	3.5 hours	5 hours
Machine time	(£3/hour)	50 mins	1 hour	1 hour 40 mins

Demand for each of the products is 5,000 sets per month and fixed costs amount to £60,000. The managers must ensure that the product for which they are responsible earns a contribution to the fixed costs, although to make them more accountable to the bottom line, the financial director has suggested that fixed costs should be allocated fairly.

1 Define: demands, complementary products.   [4]

2 a) Calculate total variable costs for each product and then allocate the fixed costs using total variable costs as the criterion.   [7]

  b) How useful are your calculations in a) to Kirkland?   [3]

3 To what extent can complementary products improve a firm's performance?   [6]

20

Maxi Case Study

Bounce-It Ltd is based in Surrey and hires out bouncy castles for children's parties. It was set up 10 years ago by James Dobbs who previously worked in a toy shop and was made redundant.

During his time there, he worked in all the departments of the toy store, but was intrigued to observe the gradual increase in the number of people coming into the store wishing to hire bouncy castles. The nearest supplier was 40 miles away and whilst the store obviously did not sell them, he felt that with some thoughtful marketing, he could make a success of such a business, if the opportunity arose. His redundancy money was used as start-up capital and he arranged an overdraft with the bank just in case he needed funds for his own use – he was by no means certain that the business could provide him with enough to live on in the first year or so.

While he was still working, he hired out just one product, the Bouncer, which he advertised for hire throughout his local town, using both radio and newspapers. Demand was encouraging for the first year and the business quickly repaid its start-up capital. Results for the first year were as follows:

Demand	80 days of hire	at £70 per day
Travel costs	£5 per hire	
Cleaning costs	£15 per hire	
Fixed costs	£40 per hire (including his own labour)	

1 Calculate the break-even level of hiring days.   [2]

James soon realised that to make enough money to live on, he would have to expand. He therefore bought two more bouncy castles; one was known as the Grand Castle, for larger parties, but he also bought the Little Jumper, which was designed to be used in small back gardens. The success of the Little Jumper was very encouraging. It became clear that the contribution pricing policy was appropriate and that there was an untapped market for small parties of children. Indeed, the design of the Jumper meant that it could be erected inside as well as outside, which allowed him to earn revenue throughout the year and therefore avoid the problem of being a seasonal business.

Despite all three products earning a contribution, James was unclear whether they were earning enough to pay for each product's overheads. The business as a whole was profitable, but each product earned different amounts of contribution and therefore spreading fixed costs equally was probably not the most accurate method of allocation. The Little Jumper was used the most, although the Bouncer earned the most revenue and the Grand Castle earned the largest contribution margin (contribution/sales revenue). James felt that the most appropriate method for allocation was the number of days hired and decided to apply this criterion to allocating the fixed costs.

Details of the three products during the second year of operation were as follows:

	Bouncer	Grand Castle	Little Jumper
Demand	80 days of hire	50 days of hire	170 days of hire
Price	£70	£110	£40
Travel costs	£5 per hire	£10	£5
Cleaning costs	£15 per hire	£20	£10
Fixed costs	£12,000		
Consisting of:			
Own labour	£10,000		
Depreciation	£ 600		
Advertising	£ 1,000		
Insurance	£ 400		

Other information that is available to help James's decision is in Table 1:

Table 1

Value of asset	Bouncer	Grand Castle	Little Jumper
	£2,000	£3,000	£1,000

2 Define: start-up capital, contribution pricing, seasonal business.   [6]

3 Allocate fixed costs to each product, using a full costing approach with volume sold as the criterion for allocation.   [5]

4 Discuss the appropriateness of using volume to allocate fixed costs under a full costing approach in this case.   [8]

5 Calculate total contribution for each product and using the allocation calculated in question 4, the profit for each product and the company as a whole for the second year.   [4]

6 **a)** Identify the most appropriate criterion for each separate fixed cost and justify your choice.   [6]

   b) Allocate the fixed costs using the criteria in **a)** above. Produce a statement which shows revenue, contribution, allocated fixed costs and profit.   [9]

40

Budgeting

Learning objectives

Having read this unit, students will be able to

1 understand the nature and significance of a budget to a business

2 perform simple calculations to build a budget and to analyse the variances (difference between budget and actual results)

3 draw conclusions from the calculations

4 identify the limitations in the calculation and usage of variances

Context

After Christmas, adverts for the summer holidays appear on our TV screens. Planning for this annual event requires careful thought and enough money to pay for it all.

Many families will decide on a budget for their holiday and then select the resort and accommodation accordingly. The budget will be based on the amount of money that the family knows it is capable of saving, which in turn will be determined by the income expected for the coming year. Industry operates in a very similar manner. Any planned expenditure will be based on the amount of revenue and a 'shopping list' of what needs to be bought. Sometimes, at the end of a holiday, when all the spending money has gone, someone will ask 'Where did it all go?' or perhaps, 'Did we spend as much as we originally planned?' Budgeting and variance analysis help us to solve some of these issues.

What is a budget?

A budget is a plan of the relevant costs and revenues in order to achieve the objectives of the business for the coming financial year.

All businesses have a company **budget** which includes all the activities of the business but has been formulated on the basis of a sales forecast. All businesses are ultimately reliant on the sales of goods or services for revenue to pay for the costs incurred within the business. Setting a budget provides the business with:

- a basis for control; clearly laid out objectives are related to the budget. Targets may be set for the production department (the majority of car assembly plants have large boards within the plant showing the target and actual output levels for all employees to see).

- a basis for measurement of success or failure with the usage of **variance** to undertake the measurements. It will enable the management to see easily whether targets are being adhered to and, if not, allow for early corrective procedures to be implemented.

- a basis for co-ordination between departments within a business. Once a budget for sales has been set, this will have repercussions on the production department.

- a simple tool for all employees to see and strive for and therefore acts as a possible incentive.

- the opportunity to manage by exception – looking for the areas where the business has not performed as expected, pinpointing problems and attempting to solve them.

There are many types of budgets that a business can utilise:

Sales revenue budget
Cash flow budget (*see Unit 34*)
Capital expenditure budget
Current expenditure budget
P&L budget

The problems of budgets

Managements need to be flexible with regard to the budget; there are dangers that the budget might be adhered to in a rigid manner, regardless of a change in circumstances; not paying the employees for the last week of the year because the business is about to go over budget would not be a sensible option!

If the budget is used as a tool to motivate the workforce, failing to meet the budget may lead to demotivation of the workers. Similarly, if the budget is seen as not being attainable, the workers will not be motivated; on the contrary, they will be frustrated by such a target.

Setting a realistic budget may be very difficult, especially in a volatile market. This in turn may mean the budget as a tool for control is rendered inoperative.

For example:

Floss-It, a manufacturer of tooth cleansers, set a sales budget as follows:

£000	1999	2000
Sales revenue	250	275

Given that fast-moving consumer goods are involved, it is appropriate that the marketing budget increases by a similar amount. This is realistic given the competitive nature of the market and the fact that these products require constant marketing.

If, however, the product was in a different market, for example, an industrial product, the marketing budget would not necessarily reflect the sales budget so closely. Industrial goods do not require the same degree of advertising. Using the sales budget to set other related budgets could be seen as an obvious approach, to mirror planned sales. But there are dangers in setting budgets in this manner. Although budgets are planned levels of sales, costs etc. they are based on information collected (past sales) or objectives to be attained; there are many variables, though, that can upset the best laid plans (the economic environment, externalities such as the weather, world events, changes in legislation). None of these can be predicted with any degree of accuracy, yet all will greatly impinge on the outcome or actual level of sales, costs etc.

As a consequence, businesses often prepare more than one budget, one optimistic, the other, pessimistic.

Alternatively, a business may set its budget to be in line

with its major competitors, though this requires a lot of information that may not be readily available.

Question 1

Suggest two factors that might appear on the news that would support
a) an optimistic budget
b) a pessimistic budget   [4]

Question 2

You have been asked to advise a business that sells computer accessories which needs to set a sales budget. State all the information the business would need to try and collect in order to build an accurate budget.   [4]

The process of setting budgets

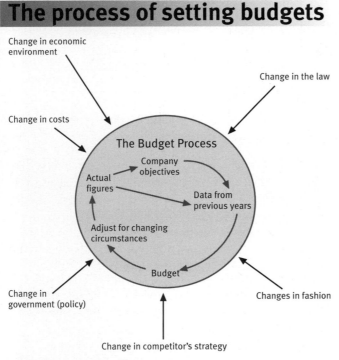

Figure 45.1   Changing circumstances

The process is usually governed by the objectives of the business. Using existing information of past records (desk research), forecasts are made that are in turn used to set the budget for the coming financial year. A monitoring of the budget ought to take place throughout the year, either monthly or weekly, depending upon the product and the nature of the budget. Alterations can be made if, for example, the government of the day introduces tax changes in its own annual Budget. At the end of the year, the actual figures can be considered and the difference between the planned and actual figures calculated. This information in turn becomes part of the databank of figures for the following year.

Calculations

Gloss-It, a producer of cosmetics which include a range of lipsticks supplied to major chain stores throughout the UK, set its sales budget for the forthcoming year at 48,000 units per month. Each unit is sold to the retailer for £1.50. The sales revenue budget would be as follows:

(Sales revenue = price × sales)

Table 1

Sales revenue budget for 2001

Sales	Jan	Feb	Mar	Apr	May	Jun
£ 000	72	72	72	72	72	72
	Jul	Aug	Sep	Oct	Nov	Dec
	72	72	72	72	72	72

Therefore the annual sales budget would be
£72,000 × 12 = £864,000

(Or 48,000 × 12 = 576,000 × £1.50 = £864,000)

As a consequence of setting the sales budget, Gloss-It is able to gauge the production costs of the 576,000 lipsticks.

Gloss-It is then able to fix a budget for the production costs using the following costs:

Direct costs
Materials per unit   30p
Labour per unit   10p
Overheads per unit   80p
Total cost per unit   £1.20p

The production budget can be calculated as follows:

For the year and therefore for 576,000 lipsticks,

Direct costs

Materials	30p × 576,000	= 172,800
Labour	10p × 576,000	= 57,600
Overheads	80p × 576,000	= 460,800
Total cost	£1.20p × 576,000	= 691,200

So, using the sales budget and assuming the costs given, the production budget will be £691,000.

Question 3

Calculate the production budget for Gloss-It if labour costs increased to 15p and materials to 40p. [4]

Once the budgets have been calculated, they can be used as a basis of control and measuring success or failure as stated previously.

Once the period of the budget is complete a comparison can be made between the budget and the actual figures.

For example, a business selling sports T-shirts (Giles Sports) produced the following figures:

Table 2

	Budget	Actual
Selling price	£12	£13
Sales volume	3,000	3,200
Material costs per unit	£5	£4.80
Labour costs per unit	£3.50	£3.55
Fixed costs	£10,000	£10,200
Sales revenue	£36,000	£41,600
Material costs	£15,000	£15,360
Labour costs	£10,500	£11,360
Fixed costs	£10,000	£10,200
Profit	£500	£4,680

It is possible to calculate the differences between the two sets of figures and put forward suggestions as to the reasons for the discrepancy.

Variance

Once the business has the actual figures to compare with the budget, it is necessary to be able to calculate the difference between the two sets of figures in order to assess the performance of either the business as a whole or the particular department involved. The assessment is carried out with reference to how well the business has actually performed in comparison with how it was expected to perform. The **variance** is the difference between the planned level and the actual level.

If a business had a budget of £5,000 for sales in a particular month and the actual sales were £5,500; the variance would be:

£5,500 − £5,000 = £500.

This variance can be expressed as a percentage and is calculated as follows:

$$\frac{\text{variance}}{\text{budget}} = \frac{£500}{£5,000} = 10\% \text{ of the budget.}$$

Question 4

Using the figures in Table 2, calculate the variance for the sales revenue budget. [4]

If the actual sales revenue figure is greater than the budget sales revenue figure, this is referred to as a **positive variance** (or favourable).

If the actual sales figure is below the sales budget figure, this is referred to as a **negative variance** (or adverse).

For the example above, the actual sales figures were £500 greater than the budget and so is a positive variance.

But great care needs to be taken with regard to what the figures represent. A higher level of sales is obviously good news and is rightly referred to as a positive variance. If the actual figure was higher than the budget for costs, then it would be inappropriate to refer to this as positive, despite the figure being higher.

A more accurate guide to whether the variance is positive or negative is the effect the variance has on the company in terms of profit. For example, if Gloss-It had budgeted for labour costs of £5 per hour per employee, but the actual figure was £5.50p per hour, although the actual figure is higher, this would have a negative effect upon the company.

Consequently, a positive variance would include:
a) higher sales figures
b) lower costs

whereas a negative variance would include:

a) lower sales figures

b) higher costs

Using the information in Table 2, calculate the variance for the production costs and state whether the variance is positive or negative.   [6]

It is important to be able to understand why such variances may and do occur. As shown in Figure 45.1, there are many factors that affect budgets. Any changes in any of the items shown in Figure 45.1 can have considerable consequences for either the sales revenue or the production costs of a business.

The sales revenue has increased by £200 (200 extra sales × £1 increase in selling price). This may be due to one order placed by a school travelling abroad on a combined hockey and soccer tour of Spain and wanting a set of distinctive T-shirts. Such an order could not have reasonably been predicted and consequently did not appear in the sales budget.

Question 6

With reference to Table 2, suggest the likely consequences for Giles Sports if there was a large advertising campaign by a major competitor (JJB Sports).   [3]

There are several reasons for the variance in the production costs; one might be that by selling more T-shirts, more materials would be required which enabled the retailer to gain a better discount for buying in bulk and as a consequence the material cost (the actual T-shirt) has fallen 20p per T-shirt.

These are included in Table 3 below.

Table 3

Reasons for the variance in production costs:

 i) Economies of scale – bulk buying

 ii) Alternative, cheaper materials can be used in producing the T-shirts.

 iii) An alternative, cheaper supplier of materials used.

 iv) A change in the production process which yields greater efficiency – reducing unit costs.

Question 7

Given the following sales budget for Fizz-It, a producer of children's flavoured mini drinks, suggest what pieces of information would have been considered by the business before deciding upon these figures.   [4]

Sales	Jan	Feb	Mar	Apr	May	Jun
£000	90	110	150	180	210	290
	Jul	Aug	Sep	Oct	Nov	Dec
	310	300	250	240	230	250

Question 8

Prepare a marketing budget for 2001 for Gloss-It, given the following information (*see Table 1 for the sales budget*):

After an initial advertising campaign which is planned to start in November 2000, it is intended to continue the promotion throughout the year 2001. The company has planned to spend £10,000 per month for a magazine advert feature which will last for two months, starting in January 2001. This will be followed by a sales promotion which will cost 25p per lipstick sold. The sales promotion will be run from April to June inclusive. Finally, as an attempt to encourage sales during the run-up to Christmas, display bins will be provided for all the chain stores that sell Gloss-It products. The cost of this is estimated to be only £6,000 and will be paid for in November.   [5]

Question 9

Using the information provided for Gloss-It,

	Budget	Actual
Materials per unit	30p	35p
Labour costs per unit	10p	9p
Overheads per unit	80p	80p
Total costs per unit	£1.20p	£1.24p

Suggest reasons for the variances for each of the above costs (remember to relate your answer to the type of product).   [8]

The calculation of variances can help a business to pinpoint problems. But all those costs which are directly related to sales volume will change if the budget for volume is different from the actual volume.

e.g.

	Budget	Actual	Variance
Sales volume	1,200	1,500	+300
Selling price	£10	£9	
Sales revenue	£12,000	£13,500	1,500
Material cost	£6,000	£7,500	−1,500
Labour cost	£2,000	£2,500	−500
Contribution	£4,000	£3,500	−500
Fixed cost	£2,000	£2,000	0
Profit	£2,000	£1,500	−500

In the above example, revenue has changed partly due to the increase in volume (probably caused by the reduction in price). However, although the material cost variance is negative, this does not necessarily mean there is a problem for the business because, as volume increases, so does the material cost. Notice that the fixed costs have not changed between actual and budget; this is entirely within the definition of fixed costs in that they do not change as output changes. The same idea applies to labour costs. It is therefore necessary to isolate the effect of a volume change on the actual results so that further analysis can be made.

e.g. a business which makes squash balls forecasts the following budget:

	Budget	Actual
Sales volume	10,000	9,000
Selling price	£6	£6.10
Variable cost per unit	£3	£3.20
Fixed cost	£20,000	£19,000

By calculating the budget, actual and variance figures, the result will be:

	Budget	Actual	Variance
Sales revenue	60,000	54,900	(5,100)
Variable costs	30,000	28,800	1,200
Fixed cost	20,000	19,000	1,000
Profit	10,000	7,100	(2,900)

The variable costs variance is positive, but how much of this has been due to the fact that the business has sold less?

The way this is dealt with is by the use of a **flexed** or **flexible budget** which takes into account the volume changes by asking: What would the budget have looked like had the volume been correct in the first place? i.e. in the above example, if the budgeted volume had been 9,000 units, what would the budget have looked like?

The answer is provided below. The same calculations have been performed but with a volume of 9,000 to create the flexed budget. This demonstrates the budget that the business would have built had the volume been estimated correctly. If this is compared with the actual results, a new variance can be calculated, known as the flexed or flexible variance:

	Flexed budget	Actual	Flexed variance
Sales revenue	54,000	54,900	900
Variable costs	27,000	28,800	−1,800
Fixed cost	20,000	19,000	1,000
Profit	7,000	7,100	100

The changes contained in the flexed variance are represented by changes other than the volume of goods sold i.e. the effect of the volume change has now been isolated.

Volume variance is the amount by which profit has changed due to the change in volume: this is reflected by the difference in the flexed variance and original variance in the profit figure reading.

The original profit variance was (£2,900), but the flexed variance was £100. So, having taken volume into account, the profit was £100 higher than expected, but without volume being accounted for, profit was £2,900 less, therefore the difference between (£2,900) and £100 is £3,000. This is a negative variance due to the drop in volume.

Closer detail

The sales revenue flexed variance shows that profit has risen by £900 due to factors other than the volume. In effect, there is only one other factor which can influence revenue apart from volume and that is price.

The figure of £900 can be found using a formula:

difference between budget and actual price × volume sold

Substituting the figures gives:

£6.10 – £6 × 9,000 = £900 – this is a positive variance because the price has risen.

Exactly the same formula can be applied to the variable costs, substituting the change in variable costs for the change in prices:

£3.20 – £3.00 × 9,000 = (£1,800) – this time it is a negative variance.

There is also a fixed cost variance of £1,000 (positive).

Question 10

The following information refers to the budget of Pen-It, a manufacturer of cheap biros, for one of their more exclusive products.

	Budget	Actual
Volume	3000	3200
Sales revenue	10500	11840
Variable cost	3750	3840
Fixed cost	2000	2000
Profit	4750	6000

a) Calculate
  (i) the budget and actual selling price
  (ii) the budget and actual variable cost per unit
                                                      [4]

b) Using your answer to a) draw up a flexed budget, using the actual volume sold.   [3]

c) Compare the actual results with the flexed budget by calculating a flexed variance.   [3]

d) Check the answers to the flexed variance for sales revenue and variable costs by substituting the relevant numbers into the formulae in the above section.   [4]

If sufficient figures are provided, it then becomes possible to divide the variance for variable costs into more detail.

Whether the budget figures can be compared to the actual figures depends upon three factors:

■ volume

■ material cost per unit

■ number of units of materials used in the production process.

The change in volume can be dealt with by the flexed budget, so there is a need to analyse the change in profit due to the second and third factors. If a business

which makes door handles planned on producing 2,000 handles, using an average of 2 kg of brass per unit (at a cost of £3 per kg) the budgeted material cost would be:

2,000 × 2 kg × £3 = £12,000.

Supposing the actual figures were as follows:

volume sold = 2,500
kg of brass used = 4,800
cost per kg = £3.40

The actual cost would be: 4,800 × £3.40 = £16,320.

A significant part of the increase from £12,000 to £16,320 is due to volume. This increased by 25% from 2,000 to 2,500, so increasing the budgeted material cost by 25%:

£12,000 × 1.25 = £15,000. Despite this, there is still a difference of

£15,000 – £16,320 = –£1,320, which is a negative variance.

This is therefore due either to the usage or efficiency of material being different from the budgeted usage, or to the material cost of each unit changing, or to both.

Both variances can be calculated using formulae:

material usage variance = difference in usage × budgeted cost per unit of materials

The budgeted usage in this case must be calculated at the new volume, otherwise the calculation would apply to different levels of output which would produce the wrong answer.

New budgeted volume = 2,500 × 2 kg = 5000 kg. So putting this into the formula =

(5000 kg – 4800 kg) × £3 = £600, which is a positive variance because the actual amount used is less than the budgeted amount used. This means profit has fallen by £600 due to an increase in the efficiency of using materials.

The material cost variance = difference in cost × actual usage

(£3.40 – £3.00) × 4,800 = £1,920 – this is a negative variance because the actual cost is greater than the budget cost.

Summarising the two produces: material usage   £600
                                 material cost   (£1920)
                                                  ─────────
                                                  (£1320)

(£1320) is the original figure calculated above. The purpose of these calculations is therefore to pinpoint the fact that the improvement in efficiency of usage did not offset the considerable increase in the cost of materials.

The same figures can be applied to labour costs, substituting hours for materials used.

Question 11

a) Calculate the material usage and cost variances for the following results:

	Budget	Actual
Volume sold	10000	9000
Material cost per kg	£5	£5.10
Use per unit of output	3 kg	3.5 kg
Total usage	30000 kg	31500

[6]

b) Calculate the labour usage and cost variances for the following results:

	Budget	Actual
Volume sold	10000	9000
Labour cost per hour	£6	£5.90
Use of labour per unit	2 hours	2 hours 15 minutes
Total usage	20000 hours	19000 hours

[6]

Hint: don't forget that when calculating usage variances, it is vital that the budgeted usage of materials and labour is calculated at the new volume of sales.

Once the calculations have been done for the above question, it is important to spend some time analysing the variances and it is possible to look at the figures with a view to explaining why the changes occurred. These are summarised in Table 4.

Whilst the table is not designed to provide an exhaustive list, it is possible to look at the figures and produce a plausible set of reasons why the changes occurred. The calculation of variances is then designed to analyse the extent of each change in terms of its effect on profit.

Table 4

Change	Suggested reasons
Volume sold falls	Extra competition, increase in material and labour costs may have forced business to raise its price
Material cost rises	Reduction in volume may have meant business loses economies of scale, supplier may have increased price due to its own cost pressures
Material usage rises	New production technique, inexperienced employees making too many errors, more material in product, leading to higher quality, perhaps being reflected in higher prices mentioned above
Labour hourly rate falls	Employer has pushed wages down as part of cost control programme, pay may be linked to productivity and wastage may have to be paid for by employees
Labour usage per unit increases	Quality has increased, new design so takes longer to make, less experienced employees being trained

Question 12

The figures below relate to Top-It, a hat producer which uses felt to make the majority of its products:

	Budget	Actual
Volume	20000	22000
Selling price	£15	£14
Material cost per metre	£1.50	£1.80
Material used per hat produced	2 metres	2.2 metres
Labour cost per hour	£8	£8.50

a) Calculate budget and actual contribution. [3]

b) Calculate the variance between the two figures. [2]

c) Using the actual volume, calculate a flexed budget and a flexed variance. [4]

d) Calculate the cost and usage variations for both labour and materials. [6]

e) Comment on your last answer, suggesting reasons for each of the variances. [5]

Points for Revision

Key Terms

budget	a figure that represents the planned level of expenditure or planned level of sales
variance	difference between the planned (budgeted) and actual level of costs or sales
positive variance	when the actual level of sales is higher than the budgeted level or where costs are less than the budgeted level
negative variance	when the actual level of sales is less than the budgeted level or where the costs are greater than the budgeted level
flexed or flexible budget	takes into consideration any changes in, for example, the volume of sales and consequently shows what the budget would have been

Definitions Question:
With reference to a firm or firms of which you have direct knowledge or experience, explain the importance of any two of the above key terms (your teacher may wish to select the terms).   [5] per definition

Summary Points:

1   A budget is a level of planned expenditure or sales, not a forecast.

2   Variance is a method of measuring the difference between the budget and the actual level of sales or costs etc.

3   There are limits to the usage of variances, governed by the reliability of the figures used.

4   Budgeting is a tool that can be used to assist the business with monitoring its performance.

Mini Case Study

Play-It Ltd is a distributor of CD players, selling mainly to specialist retailers of TVs, video recorders and sound entertainment systems.

The following document was submitted by the sales manager to his sales team at their annual review meeting held at the Prince of Wales Hotel, Southport.

	1998		1999		2000	
	B	A	B	A	B	A
£000						
Sales revenue	180	183.6	190	185	200	190
Sales promotion costs	9	9.3	9.5	9.25	10	9.6
Distribution costs	10	10	11	12	12	12.5

(B = Budget A = Actual)

Before the meeting, the sales manager for north-west England had checked the population trends using the CSO Regional Trends HMSO publication and noted with interest that Liverpool, Manchester, Salford and Merseyside had all experienced a fall in population between 1981 and 1994. He assumed that trend had continued and decided to bear this in mind when looking at the sales figures for these areas. He had also consulted his *Marketing Pocket Book* for 1999, which showed that the percentage of adults owning personal CDs had increased to nearly 10%.

1 a) Calculate the % variance for i) 1999 ii) 2000 for: sales revenue, sales promotion and distribution costs (for each answer, state whether the variance is positive or negative).   [6]

2 Suggest reasons why the variances for the sales promotion and the distribution are so different when compared to the sales revenue.   [6]

3 What may be the problems for the sales manager and his team having heard the sales director state that he considered the results for the north-west area were 'very poor'? [3]

4 State, with reasons, whether the sales manager is right to be concerned about losing his job due to his team's poor performance.   [10]

25

Maxi Case Study

Charlie's Chairs began life in late 1997 in East Lancashire, when the founder, Charles Stone, made a small chair for his younger brother's birthday. To personalise the chair, he engraved his brother's name into the seat. Although his brother was only three years old at the time, he insisted on taking it to nursery with him the following day and within three hours of his return home, Charlie had received orders for a further nine chairs. All the chairs were given the same design, although each had a different name! This did not matter, because as the names were hand carved, it was not really possible to benefit from economies of scale in this respect, although buying a bulk load of wood did mean that materials were a little cheaper.

He began by selling to nurseries and play schools, although by the end of the second year he realised that in order to earn sufficient profit, he would have to expand his business further. This required a business plan and a budget in order to persuade the bank manager to lend Charles money to buy a lathe for the wood. The budget would also allow him to have a target to aim at in terms of both sales and profit, which would mean a tighter focus on costs. The other reason was that it would allow Charles to identify the problem areas of the business (negative variances) with a view to solving them.

He therefore sat down with his accountant, Peter Smith, and built a profit budget for the following 12 months for the main product, children's personalised stools. The budget continued with the following information:

Selling price	£25
Sales volume	2,000
Material cost per metre of (2" by 1") wood	£4
Labour cost per hour	£7
Amount of metres of wood per chair	3
Amount of time spent per chair	1 hour
Fixed costs	£6,000

The year began with the business finding three new retail chains willing to stock the product. This meant that capacity was reached so new machinery had to be bought; Charlie was able to find space in his warehouse for the machine, although he could not persuade the supplier (who was reliable) to increase the number of deliveries. As a result, Charles had to take larger-sized deliveries into his warehouse, in order to stock the products for production.

By the end of the year, sales had increased by nearly 50%, although Charles was a little disappointed not to see a corresponding increase in profit; in fact, the business had made less profit than before the output had increased. He had taken a little more care over some of the products because the turning machine had become unreliable. His supplier had also increased the cost of wood, though with reliable delivery Charles was able to meet the retailers' deadlines which was a primary objective (despite the increase in cost). He looked harder at the figures – no matter how hard he tried to understand, he could not see where the problem lay. It was clear to him that there were areas of the business which were reducing profit, but he could not fathom which they were. His accountant informed him that he would need to calculate some variances, so as to be able to identify and analyse the problem areas.

End of year results were:

Revenue   £ 50,600
Labour costs   £ 14,058
Material costs £ 27,740
Fixed costs   £ 7,000
Profit   £ 1,802

Additional information: volume sold = 2,200; actual usage per stool = 3 metres of wood; actual usage of labour per stool = 54 minutes.

1 Identify the evidence in the article as to the reason(s) why Charles made a budget. [3]

2 Calculate the variance in profit between the actual and budget figures. [2]

3 Calculate the following:

   a) the actual amount paid per metre of wood [1]

   b) the actual amount paid per unit of labour [1]

   c) the labour cost variance [2]

   d) the labour usage variance [2]

   e) the material cost variance [2]

   f) the material usage variance [2]

   g) the fixed cost variance [1]

4 Calculate the actual selling price and, using the formula, prove the sales price variance is (£4,400). [4]

5 Using the variances in questions 3 and 4 above, analyse the effects of the change in profit between budget and actual figures. [8]

6 Discuss the usefulness of the budgeting process for Charlie's Chairs in the context of the case study. [8]

36

'Friday afternoon'

End of section test

1 Company 1 has variable costs of £30 per unit, selling price of £50 per unit and fixed costs of £10,000. Present output is 720 units.
   a) Calculate break-even output. [2]
   b) Calculate margin of safety of the company. [1]
2 Company 2 produces 8,000 units per month, with total fixed costs of £36,000. The selling price is £15 and variable costs are £5 per unit.
   a) Calculate the unit cost of 8,000 units. [2]
   b) How many units would Company 2 need to make in order to earn £16,000 profit? [3]
   c) If sales for Company 2 drop to 6,000 units, calculate the new level of profit. [3]
3 Define and give an example of
   a) fixed costs
   b) variable costs
   c) short run [6]
4 Apart from the financial statements for a company, state two other pieces of information that are given in the annual report. [2]
5 The following information has been extracted from an annual report:

Fixed assets	£30m
Stock	£13m
Debtors	£6m
Overdraft	£3m
Net assets	£38m
Retained profit reserve	£14m

   a) Briefly define the six terms. [2]
   b) Which ones might be used to value the business? [1]
6 The profit and loss account for the same annual report showed the following figures:

Sales revenue		?? (i)
Cost of sales	£14m	
Gross profit		£26m
Expenses	£8m	
Operating profit		?? (ii)
Interest	£4m	
Profit before tax		?? (iii)
Tax	£3m	
Profit after tax		£11m
Interim dividends	£2m	
Final dividends		£3m
Retained profit		?? (iv)

   a) Define the terms underlined in the profit and loss account [6]
   b) Fill in the blanks i) to iv). [4]
   c) Calculate three of the following ratios using the profit and loss and balance sheet above and comment briefly on each answer.
   Profit margin
   Net asset turnover
   Interest cover
   Debtor days
   Stock turnover $3 \times [3]$

7 Explain how an acid test ratio can help a business. [2]

8 Company X has been offered a contract for 3,000 toy bears at a selling price of £9 each. Their usual selling price is £12 and the variable cost per bear is £6. The company has a fixed cost of £8,000 although the extra order will add a further £5,000 to fixed costs. Calculate the contribution if Company X accepted the extra order. [4]

9 The following information has been extracted from the management accounts of Company Y:

	Budget	Actual	Variance
Sales revenue	£118,000	£130,000	
Material costs	£72,000	£75,000	
Labour costs	£34,000	£33,000	
Contribution	£12,000	£22,000	£10,000
Fixed costs	£8,000	£10,000	
Profit	£4,000	£12,000	£8,000

a) Calculate the variance for each of the above. [4]
b) Explain one reason why labour costs might have fallen despite an increase in sales revenue. [2]

10 a) Briefly explain two reasons why profit might be different from cash. [4]
b) How can a cash flow forecast help a business? [2]

11 Explain three of the following sources of finance:
rights issue
debentures
mortgage
debt factoring
hire purchase 3 × [2]

12 Company Z invests £35,000 in a new machine, which it expects to last for 4 years. The cash savings are forecast to be:
EOY 1 £13,000
EOY 2 £15,000
EOY 3 £7,000
EOY 4 £6,000
a) Calculate the payback period for this investment. [2]
b) Calculate the average annual rate of return. [3]

13 Define the following terms:
a) marginal cost
b) economies of scale
c) variable cost
d) total revenue
e) overheads 5 × [2]

14 A business produces 40,000 units per month (capacity output of 60,000 units) with an average cost of £20. Variable cost is £14 per unit.
a) What is the total fixed cost? [2]
b) What is the average cost if output increased to 50,000 units and variable costs reduced to £12? [3]

85

'Friday afternoon' 1

Toys R U is a manufacturer of children's games. It has three main lines – A, B and C.

	A	B	C
Selling price	£10	£12	£9
Variable cost per unit	£6	£4	£6
Fixed costs per unit (at present output)	£6	£5	£2
Output	20,000	13,000	15,000

a) Calculate the fixed costs for A, B and C and for the business as a whole. [2]
b) Calculate break-even for Products A, B and C. [3]
c) Calculate the margin of safety for Product B. Explain how this calculation helps the business. [3]
d) The managing director has looked at the table and has recommended that Product A should be discontinued. You are the product manager of A and you may well be made redundant if this happens; provide financial and non-financial information to persuade the managing director to keep Product A. [6]
e) A new customer has been found for Product B, and wishes to order 3,000 units but will pay a price of only £7. Using financial and non-financial reasons, explain why you would

   i) accept the order
   ii) reject the order   [6]
f) Reallocate the fixed costs to the three products, using revenue as the basis for allocation.   [5]

                                          25

'Friday afternoon' 2

Barge-It Ltd is a canal cruise hire business based on the Staffordshire–Worcestershire Canal just outside the village of Penkridge. The owners, Vickie and Edward Winters, are considering how best to achieve their objective of expansion, to ensure that they remain competitive with some of their main rivals such as Rakeseasons, a national chain that advertises heavily in the press and on television.

There are two canal cruise companies within about 10 miles of their headquarters in Penkridge which are both for sale. Both these companies, for differing reasons, have expressed a preference to sell to a local company rather than to a national chain.

Having visited both sites, Vickie and Edward were undecided whether to put a bid in for either company. They were advised to look carefully at the accounts of both companies that were for sale.

The following information was made available to Vickie and Edward:

Trading and P&L Account for the year ending 31 December 1999

	Whitelines Ltd £	Brewood Barges £
Turnover	160,000	280,000
Cost of sales	100,000	200,000
Gross profit	60,000	80,000
Expenses		
Marketing	15,000	8,000
Clerical costs	20,000	22,000
Net profit	25,000	50,000

1 By calculating gross profit margin and net profit margin, comment on the performance of the two companies.   [6]

2 Why should Vickie and Edward be aware of the limitations of using the ratios you have used?   [4]

3 What other information would you want before advising Vickie and Edward which of the two companies to buy?   [5]

                                          15

'Friday afternoon' 3

The Cup-It company is a manufacturer of crockery. At the beginning of 2000 it purchased a machine for making a new design of teapot which cost the business £200,000, and was expected to have a useful life of four years.

1 Produce a table of the annual depreciation cost and the year-end book values, assuming a residual value of £20,000.   [4]

2 How would the depreciation charge alter if, separately,
  (i) after two years, the business realised the net book value would be £12,000?
  (ii) once the asset had been purchased, the useful economic life was recognised as being five years, not four?   [6]

3 What would be the difference to the depreciation charge in years 1 and 2 if the business used declining balance at 40% as opposed to straight-line depreciation?   [5]

                                          15

Maxi Case Study

Diamment is an American firm which makes personal care products. Originally a private company, owned by the Edwards family, Diamment became a quoted company on the Dow Jones four years ago, but with the family keeping two-thirds of the shares. Since then, the business has progressed well by expanding through earning profit.

At the present time the company has sales of $12 million per annum. The cost of bought-in materials and components amounts to 50% of sales value, labour costs a further 20% and sales/admin. 8% of sales value. The other large operating expense is production costs. The current profit margin is 7%. The firm had taken out a term loan of $750,000 some 18 months previously to cover expansion, and was worried because the cost of borrowing charged by the bank last year had been 12% and looked like staying at that level.

The year-end accounts showed that they took 2 months' credit on purchases, the same terms that they allowed customers, and that stocks represented 1 month's purchases. Provision for tax of 33.3%, one-third of profit, had been made and dividends of 40% of profit after tax were recommended for the full year (an interim of $75,000 had been paid). This left a retained profit for the year of $300,000.

Fixed assets amounted to $4 million. This included a minority stake in a raw material supplier which it had bought for $600,000, plant and machinery at a net book value of $1.5 million, fixtures & fittings (including vehicles) with an NBV of $400,000 and land and buildings which had cost $500,000, and which had recently been revalued at $1.5 million.

The company had been launched on the Alternative Investment Market by issuing 8 million 25p shares. The current market price had now reached 160p, and total retained profits stood at $1.15 million. In order to cope with the expansion it was planning, it had taken out an overdraft facility for the first time just before the end of the year, which stood at $225,000. Assume that there is no cash in hand.

The expansion referred to is 25% increase of production and sales in the coming year. It will not need to increase fixed assets, but materials, labour, production costs and sales/admin. are reckoned to go up in proportion to sales. Stock levels and debtor/creditor terms will remain in the same ratio to sales and it can be assumed that tax and dividend percentages will be unchanged.

Assuming that production and sales are level through the year, that all production is sold at the end of the month, and that all costs other than materials are paid for in the month in which they are incurred:

1 Construct a monthly cash flow forecast for the next 6 months on the basis of the 25% increase. Assume interest on your monthly overdraft total is added at 12% p.a. Work to the nearest $000. Ignore dividends and tax.   [12]

2 The bank has agreed an overdraft ceiling of $300,000. How would you recommend Diamment to react to this?   [3]

3 Discuss in detail the options open to the firm if it wishes to raise a further $1m to cover a major mechanisation of the factory.   [10]

4 Reconstruct the Balance Sheet and Profit and Loss Statement for last year in vertical format.   [20]

5 Using the financial statements prepared in question 4, calculate any five of the following ratios on performance and liquidity. Comment on the results.
Return on net assets
Asset turnover
Current ratio
Acid test ratio
Earnings per share
Dividends per share
Dividend yield (gross)
Return on equity
Dividend cover
Price earnings ratio $5 \times [4]$

6 a) Diamment is considering a further plan to mechanise production at the higher level of sales planned for the year.
There are two basic options:
   i) A relatively unsophisticated machine costing $250,000. This will reduce labour costs by 5% but increase production and admin. costs (including interest charges) by $6,000 per month. It expects the machine to be worth $50,000 at the end of its anticipated 6-year life.
   ii) A more complex machine costing $1 million.
   This will reduce labour costs by 25% but increase other costs by $40,000 per month. It is expected to last 8 years but have no residual value except a negligible scrap value.
Assuming that the same savings are made each year, calculate payback, AAROR, NPV (assume a discount factor of 12%).   [15]

   b) Prepare a presentation as to which option the business should select.   [20]

    <u>100</u>

People in organisations

Introduction to people

Learning objectives

Having read this unit, students will be able to

1 distinguish between personnel and human resource management

2 understand the significance of the work-force plan

3 identify the signs of low morale within an organisation

Context

If you were to take away the people from any organisation, be it your own school, the corner shop or a local manufacturing company, what would be left? The answer is a few buildings and not much else! Who would invent products, make them, sell them, distribute profits, raise money and so on?

In almost every company report there is a reference made to the quality of the people within the organisation. 'The most important asset is our people' is a phrase frequently used by chairpeople to recognise the role that people have to play in an organisation. If you examine the reasons why businesses fail, one of the most frequent internal factors is that the people in the organisation are not motivated, or perhaps simply do not care about the future of the business. This is not necessarily true of all business, but there is common agreement across all businesses that if the people within the business are hard-working, keen to succeed, well skilled and well motivated, the business is much more likely to be successful than if the organisation is full of unwilling, uncooperative, uncaring people.

Just the full-time work-force?

An assumption is frequently made that the only people in a business worth spending time on are those who are employed on a full-time basis. However, as the organisation has become a combination of managers, shopfloor workers, full-time, part-time, temporary, permanent, across skills which are functional (marketing, production etc.) and skills that are cross-functional (computers and IT), the word 'people' has come to represent anyone who works in an organisation. It is particularly important to remember that managers are also human beings and react to the same stimuli and motivation measures as anyone else.

Currently, the work-force of any company comprises fewer full-time or **core employees** and more **peripheral employees** who are either part-time or employed to perform a one-off task for the business.

Question 1

What might be the consequences of an organisation concentrating only on its full-time employees?   [4]

Human resource management (HRM) is never the first department to be created when a business is started. As businesses grow, more people need to be recruited, trained and promoted; indeed, some may need to be dismissed if they do not meet the organisation's requirements. Such is the importance of people within an organisation that specific departments have evolved as businesses have become larger in order to monitor and motivate people. In addition to the recruitment function mentioned above, these departments involve themselves in dealing with unions and ensuring the morale of the work-force engenders growing productivity.

Personnel or Human Resource Management?

In recent years there has been a shift away from the term Personnel towards Human Resource Management.

Personnel:

The **personnel** department has traditionally been the part of the business responsible for recruitment, training, discipline and morale of the work-force. Experienced personnel staff will often say that they are the social conscience of the organisation, reminding senior management of its social responsibilities.

However, this function is sometimes seen as a fairly straightforward administrative task which does not really perform the role of motivating employees and developing the individual.

HRM

Although this term is frequently confused with Personnel, HRM has followed the modern management method of the Japanese (who have tended not to have a personnel department) in developing the individual as a vehicle to helping the business grow. Such a role exists to assist the other functional areas e.g. a product manager oversees a brand manager and is primarily responsible for his/her welfare, career, tasks etc. If mistakes are made it is likely to reflect on the product manager's results, so managers are encouraged to assume responsibility for developing the individual as opposed to leaving the personnel department to do it.

In addition, personnel used to consist of several different areas – training, recruitment, dismissal, wages etc. and there was very little linkage between the various areas. HRM is also seen as a subset of the function of personnel which is carried out in addition to the usual personnel tasks, with the division of hard and soft tasks.

Soft HRM: these are the tasks which cover how people are managed and are mainly subjective and difficult to measure accurately

- developing an organisational culture which helps to achieve the company's objectives

- motivating employees to work to their best ability

- providing support and training, so as to develop the individual

Hard HRM: these concern the more quantitative side i.e. the hard side can be assessed objectively and from the basis of the work-force or manpower plan

- analysing current and future needs for employees

- assessing whether there is likely to be a future supply of employees

- predicting labour turnover

HRM therefore aims to incorporate the individual's objectives with those of the company, so that, for example, a particular individual can receive specific training according to his/her individual needs. Such training requirements are also linked to the objectives of the organisation.

Work-force (Manpower) planning

The work-force plan, or manpower planning, is one of the main areas of responsibility of HRM. The **work-force plan** is needed by the organisation so that the correct number of employees is recruited (now and in the future) at the appropriate level of skill and that they are trained to do the job which helps the organisation achieve its own objectives.

There is therefore a crucial relationship between the work-force plan and the objectives of the organisation e.g. if a business aims to penetrate new markets, with new products, then the business must have the expertise to target markets effectively and produce to the anticipated level of demand. Sometimes a business will anticipate growth in demand and employ the necessary employees even before demand has increased, just so that the lead time is reduced to a minimum when demand increases.

Question 2

Shropshire Dairies, a milk and food delivery company, has just seen one of its competitors go out of business and anticipates a sudden increase in demand in the short term as customers seek another supplier. The work-force plan needs to be altered to allow for this sudden increase in demand.

a) What information might Shropshire Dairies seek when changing its work-force plan?   [4]

b) If the business wishes to build sales of Christmas hampers over the next three years, what longer-term adjustments might be required to the work-force plan?   [4]

Factors affecting the work-force plan

As the title suggests, there will be a planning process involved. This planning process must take into account the following factors:

Supply of labour

Whether or not a business finds employees depends primarily on whether sufficient labour is being supplied. The supply of labour depends on many factors; some are economic, such as the wage rate, and some are technical, such as the skill level. Any business seeking to locate in a new area will look carefully at the local labour market for the appropriate supply of labour when it comes to selecting the location of its investment. The supply of labour will tend to depend on:

- **Population** – the demographic structure will certainly affect the supply of labour; if there is an ageing population, with few school leavers, then there may not be as much labour to choose from, leading to higher wages (*see Figure 47.1*).

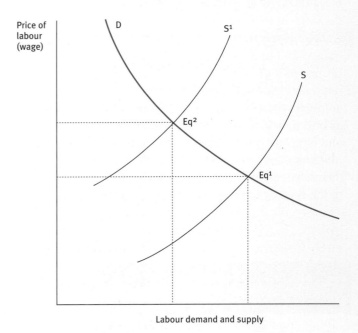

Figure 47.1   Demographic trends

When the ship building plant at Ravenscraig in Scotland closed down in the early 1990s, there was a sudden increase in the availability of local labour; Samsung – one of the large Korean Chaebols (industrial giants) – decided to locate there, because of a local labour force willing and ready to work. The work-force plan was formulated with relative ease.

■ **Social factors** – if the social environment is suspicious of a new business, because it might take away trade from a local, respected employer to whom local society is loyal, there will be further difficulty in encouraging people to work.

■ **Competition** – if local competition is intense, this will push up wages and encourage employees to trade one company against another. This is sometimes the case with financial companies in the city, where a talented young financier may be head-hunted by a competitor.

■ **Customer demand** – as markets change due to customer demand, so do the requirements of the labour force. If there is an emphasis on extra customer service or after sales service as a car dealer, then the appropriate personnel needs to be targeted. This is particularly difficult to plan for if demand changes quickly, such as the new demand for after sales computer advice.

Question 3

Reduce your insurance bills by up to £50!

Such is the claim by Alliance Direct, the insurance arm of the Alliance and Leicester. There has been a sudden recent growth in direct insurance i.e. cutting out the middleman in order to save costs and identifying low-risk customers to whom companies offer the cheapest insurance. Direct Line was one of the first to do this, but a glance at the Insurance section in Yellow Pages shows a vast number of companies now offer this service. This has meant a change in the structure of the industry, away from insurance agents, who acted as middlemen, towards telesales teams, who receive inquiries from customers and quote the cheapest possible level.

Discuss how such a change in structure and customer demand might affect the work-force plan for a company like Alliance and Leicester, which previously operated as a bank and has just begun to offer home insurance, sold over the telephone.   [8]

■ **Trading environment** – if the economy is booming, then more people will have jobs, so skilled employees will be more difficult to find. This problem is made worse by the fact that demand for products will be rising and demand for labour will also be rising.

■ **Skill levels** – certain businesses require certain skill levels which are specific to a particular industry e.g. AOL, the American Internet server, will employ only those people who are either computer-literate (regarding e-mail and the Internet) or can be trained in such a skill to solve the problems of customers.

■ **Technology** – as the demand for higher technology continues, so does the demand for skilled employees.

The State

The government may pass new regulations concerning length of contracts or National Insurance contributions. This will then determine how many the company can afford to either keep on the payroll or move to employment on a casual basis (thereby removing the need to pay NICs). The minimum wage will also affect the manpower plan because it could well mean that profit will be reduced, unless the numbers of people or hours of labour hired are reduced.

Finance

The HRM department will need to work closely with the finance department in order to build a budget for employment over a particular time period. This is particularly important if the business is labour-intensive.

Question 4

How might stakeholders have a role in the formulation of the work-force plan?   [6]

Signs of poor morale

If the Personnel or HRM department does not do its job properly, there may be evidence of low morale as follows:

- **Decreasing productivity** – output per person is very likely to fall; a reduction in productivity is probably the most worrying sign to a business, because it means unit costs will rise and profitability will be affected

- **Absenteeism** – employees telephone in, claiming to be ill and possibly claiming sick pay, because they actively do not want to come to work

- **Industrial action** – any form of stoppage e.g. down tools, work-to-rule, sabotage will be a sign that morale is low

- **Increasing defect rate** – as workers take less pride in their work because they find it boring, quality will fall causing the defect rate to increase and the number of corrections to rise

- **Accidents** – employees will take less care over procedural rules regarding health and safety

- **Lateness** – lack of willingness to get to work on time or even early is normally a sign that employees simply do not value promptness as important. Think about individuals who are motivated arriving at their desk 30 minutes early

- **Militant work-force** – as depicted by the amount of complaints and unwillingness to change or adapt to new working practices

- **Frequent union representation to management** – at the Ford Motor Company during the 1980s there was a representation via the shop steward several times a day over some extremely trivial issues e.g. there was one incident when a shop steward at the Halewood plant in Liverpool reported to the senior foreman that there was a revolt on the shop floor, when it turned out to be a piece of metal protruding from a machine. Neither the metal workers nor the welders were willing to take a hacksaw and remove it – it was not their job to do so! Job demarcation is also more prevalent during times of low morale

- **Low suggestion rates** – despite an attempt by managers to invite suggestions, this will not be received in a positive light unless employees feel their suggestions are being listened to

- **Widespread rumours** – all organisations have some form of grapevine which transmits messages informally; use of this grapevine can lead to all sorts of rumours, from managing directors leaving, to potential strikes, to takeover bids

- **Increasing labour turnover** – this is measured by:

$$\frac{\text{number of full-time equivalent work-force leaving}}{\text{average number of full-time equivalent work-force on the staff}}$$

e.g. if the number of employees who left in one year was 15, in a business of 120, **labour turnover** would be:

$$\frac{15}{120} \times 100 = 12.5\%.$$

Question 5

Quiche-It, a food packaging business based in Bristol, has employed an annual average of 56 people over the past two years, 40 of whom are full-time. During 1998, four full-time employees left and this increased to seven during 1999. The company treats two part-time workers as equivalent to one full-time worker.

a) Why would Quiche-It employ part-time employees?   [2]

b) Calculate labour turnover in 1998 and 1999.   [4]

c) Suggest two reasons why labour turnover has increased.   [4]

What are the main issues facing the HRM department?

As a way of summarising the remainder of this section, the following are the issues which the HRM department will need to consider on both a short- and long-term basis:

1 The structure of the business – whether it should be a tall, rigid business with many layers of management or a flat business with a larger number of subordinates for managers to look after

2 The effectiveness of communication both internally and externally

3 The precise factors which determine the level of motivation of each individual; some individuals prefer financial incentives only, others prefer money plus a variety of other ways to make them work harder

4 The recruitment, training and dismissal of employees

5 The leadership style of certain managers and the importance of management as opposed to leadership

6 The extent to which a business forms its groups and how well employees work in groups as opposed to individually

7 The need to react to change and to create change

Points for Revision

Key Terms

core employees	those who have an important task, vital to the business; usually highly skilled
peripheral workers	those who are sometimes subcontracted in to do a one-off task, or those employees who are ancillary or non-essential
Human Resource Management	a subset of personnel, which concentrates on using the resource of people to achieve company and individual objectives
personnel	the function of recruiting, training and dismissing work-force
work-force/ manpower plan	the process of planning for the correct number of employees with the appropriate skill level in the short and long term
labour turnover	the rate at which people leave the business

Definitions Question:
By referring to a business you know, explain the significance of any three of the above terms (your teacher may wish to help you choose the terms).   [5] per definition

Summary Points:

1 HRM or Personnel has the responsibility of getting the best out of the people within the business.

2 A significant role for HRM is to develop the work-force plan in tandem with the company's objectives.

3 There are many signs of low morale in the business, all of which add cost without adding value.

Mini Case Study

Metro makes and sells a range of car accessories from seat belts to car shampoo which are distributed through car retailers such as Halfords as well as general retail stores such as Argos. The HRM director, Elly Smoothe, was going through the work-force plan for the year 2000–2001 building in short- and long-term requirements. The company was about to make some redundancies in production due to a sudden fall in profit although was investing in more marketing personnel with a view to capturing back some market share lost to foreign competition. Her role in charge of HRM had many parts to it and she occasionally panicked at the level of responsibility with which she was entrusted; not only had she to devise a recruitment and training procedure, decide who to promote and how much to pay employees, but she was charged with ensuring the highest level of motivation, since the company made a clear statement that its staff were 'highly motivated and well trained' in its report to shareholders.

1 Define: distributed, recruitment.   [4]

2 Identify the evidence in the above case to suggest the work-force plan must be built in accordance with the company's objectives.   [6]

3 Briefly explain two measures that Elly could use to assess whether the employees were motivated.   [4]

4 What might be the effect of the change in personnel at the company, planned by Elly Smoothe?   [6]

                                                                                          20

Maxi Case Study

Hypercare plc is a business that serves a variety of markets within the health care industry. The business employs 21,000 people, 1,000 of whom work at the headquarters in Kent involved in marketing, manufacturing and administration. The business is structured as three separate divisions, with directors who have responsibility for their particular function across all the divisions i.e. the marketing director is responsible for marketing in all three divisions. Each director has a manager who is responsible for running a particular function e.g. marketing, within each division and the director delegates most of the decision making on a day-to-day basis to the individual managers.

```
                          Headquarters
                               |
     ┌─────────────┬───────────┴───────────┬─────────────┐
Portal Provider   Domestic Chemist   International Business   Manufacturing
```

Domestic chemists – the retailing arm of Hypercare plc. Last year market share rose by 3%, because a small competitor had gone out of business and Hypercare had filled the gap it left in the market.

International business – large chemists located in hypermarkets around mid and southern Europe. Although its gross margin increased by only 0.1% during 1999, the like-for-like sales increased by 15%. The growth fuelled further expansion and the business was intending to employ a further 100 people in this division during 2000.

Manufacturing – the company makes 60% of the products it sells under its own brand name, and profit has fallen resulting in proposed job losses of 400 people.

Further cuts of 200 administration personnel are expected in an attempt to reduce costs.

The business is attempting to add a fourth, pioneering division. Dixons the retailer began a 'portal' in 1999. This acts as an information gateway and permits free access to the World Wide Web, allowing products to be sold across the Internet. Hypercare will need to arrange a joint venture with a network browser in order to make the division cost-effective. This will hopefully mean that users can browse for longer, allowing Hypercare to charge higher advertising rates.

Two issues remain a concern for managing director Simona Boot. The first is the level of labour turnover. Data for recent years is provided below:

	1997	1998	1999	2000 (forecast)
Number leaving	510	700	840	?
Total employees	17000	19300	21000	?

The increase in labour turnover is placing unnecessary strain on the company's costs and the managing director has employed a new Human Resource Management Director, John Prentice, to reduce the labour turnover; the target of 3% has been set for 2000, although John feels this is rather ambitious, given the inherent problem of labour turnover already within the business.

The other problem arose at the first board meeting attended by John, when the marketing and production directors belittled his task, suggesting that it was their job to hire and fire as well as manage the level of motivation within their own areas. The managing director produced the labour turnover figures and insisted that John had a clear, well defined task and that he should be given as much support as possible to achieve this objective.

1 Define: delegation, like-for-like sales.   [4]

2 **a)** Calculate the percentage increase in the number of employees from 1997 to 1999.
                                                                                                 [1]

   b) How would the business have been affected by the increase in employees?   [4]

3 **a)** Calculate the labour turnover for 1997–1999 and the target number of employees leaving if the labour turnover target is met for 2000.   [6]

   b) Suggest two possible reasons for the change in labour turnover over the period 1997 to 1999.   [4]

4 How might the expansion in **a)** the international division and **b)** the portal division affect the work-force plan?   [4]

5 Suggest possible reasons why the marketing and production directors were suspicious of John Prentice.   [4]

6 Discuss the likely effect on the manufacturing division of 400 redundancies.   [8]

                                                                                           $\overline{35}$

Organisational structures

Learning objectives

Having read this unit, students will be able to

1 understand the different types of organisational structures

2 be aware of the implications for the performance of the business with regard to span of control, communication, levels of hierarchy and delegation

3 appraise the appropriateness of different structures for different business situations

Context

Consider the management structure at your school or college and write down who you think is responsible to whom. Start with the Headteacher or Principal and add the other staff as you deem appropriate. When you begin a new job, if you are ambitious for promotion, you will ask about the number of management levels in the business; you may also ask about the number of people you will be responsible for and who you are answerable to. All these questions can be answered by looking at the organisational structure within the business. Most structures have a logical format and are easy to understand, but what about the structure of your school? Who is at the top of the organisation? – if you say the Headteacher, you will be incorrect because of the role of governors; who has authority over whom? Do Heads of Year have more power than Heads of Department? Do Heads of Sport have more power than the Head of Drama? Understanding the organisational structure is therefore crucial in establishing lines of communication and levels of responsibility.

Task

Try to draw the structure of your school, then compare it with the structure of a business you know. What do you notice about the main differences?

What is an organisational structure?

It is the way in which a business is organised and the consideration of its internal workings in an attempt to find an efficient operational practice.

With a small family business, there will probably be little need for a formal structure or a set procedure for communication or chain of command (who is responsible to whom). The organisation is small enough to cope with an *ad hoc* procedure. However, as the business grows in size and the number of personnel increases there is a need to ensure that the objectives of the business are achieved. Once the common goal or consensus of the small group is lost, then defined procedures need to be in place to ensure that if any conflict arises there is someone who has the ultimate responsibility to make the necessary decision.

For the very large organisations e.g. BP there will be a need to break down the organisation into manageable departments or groups; these may be based on individual brands that are produced, such as retail petrol, chemicals or a sales area, although such groups may have conflicting interests and goals. It is essential that the business establishes tight control to ensure its objectives are achieved. But in order for the whole organisation to be manageable there may well be the need to delegate some responsibility to employees.

Finding the correct structure will require careful attention to the ability of the business to control and communicate with its employees for the benefit of the organisation as a whole.

Throughout the 1980s the accepted rigid **organisational structure** had to be dismantled to cope with the great pace of change facing businesses.

A brief history of organisational structure

Henri Fayol (*see Unit 52 Leadership and Management*) advocated a strict, rigid structure to ensure tight management control and clearly defined responsibility. However, as businesses became larger and the number of levels of hierarchy had to be increased, the organisational structure became very bureaucratic i.e. there were employees whose job was simply to ensure that the correct procedures were applied. This meant that organisations became inflexible, resistant to change and were normally top-heavy i.e. had too many managers. One of the reasons General Motors was overtaken by the Japanese during the 1960s was because of its monolithic organisational structure.

Question 1

IBM made a name for itself 30 years ago with large mainframe computers. Such was its success that as its organisational structure became more complicated and less flexible it became more inward-looking. The smaller, more flexible companies paid more attention to changing customer needs and were more adaptable than IBM. Compaq, the American computer manufacturer, now sells more computers than IBM. Due to inflexibility, IBM posted a pre-tax loss of £4.5 billion in 1991 – the biggest in corporate history. In response, it divided the business into 12 distinct parts, known as strategic business units (SBUs), each of which had responsibility for generating profit.

a) Why was it wrong of IBM to sit back and glory in its own success?   [4]

b) Why might the SBUs create more profit than the old structure?   [3]

c) To what extent do you think the problems caused in the 1960s were due to the organisational structure?   [3]

Since then, organisations have gradually reduced the number of levels of management (hierarchy), normally removing middle managers from the structure. The move from tall, rigid structures to flatter, wider structures has been primarily due to the need to be able to adapt to change more quickly and to be able to disseminate information more efficiently throughout the business.

Types of organisational structures

Theodore D. Weinshall, quoted in C.B. Handy's *Understanding Organizations* (Oxford University Press, 1993), put forward various management structures which were related to the size of the business.

■ Entrepreneurial

This structure is applicable to small businesses where the Managing Director is the central figure.

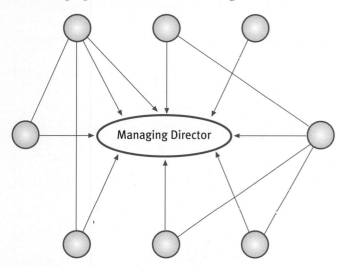

Figure 48.1 Informal structure centralised

■ Product

This type of structure is operated as if it is a separate company with its own production, finance, sales and research departments each serving a particular product. Although there is a degree of duplication within the business, operating in this manner may be advantageous. The needs of the particular product are unique and may be better understood by people who are very familiar with the product in question (when compared with a marketing executive who is an expert in marketing but not necessarily an expert in the actual product). Brand managers for the various chocolate bars would be in a much better position to decide how best to market the product than a marketing expert who would market all the brands of chocolate.

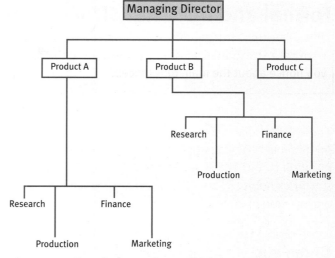

Figure 48.2 Formal structure decentralised

■ Area

Concentrating the organisation on a particular geographical area instead of on a product will mean operating in a similar manner and may allow regional differences to be catered for in a more informed and sympathetic manner e.g. a multinational company such as Unilever which needs to accommodate cultural, religious and social differences.

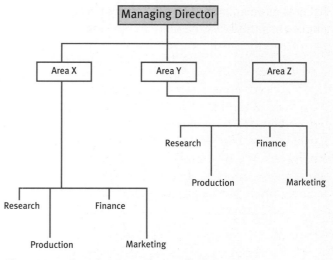

Figure 48.3 Formal structure decentralised

Each of the above three structures has distinct advantages and disadvantages that will be explained as the unit progresses and new terms are introduced. There is a multiplicity of terms related to organisational structures, each considering a different aspect of the business.

Formal and informal structures

Organistic and mechanistic

These terms relate to the type of organisation and focus on different characteristics of how the business in question is run. The shape of the two organisational structures helps to show the manner in which the organisation operates.

Organistic

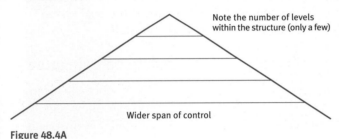

Note the number of levels within the structure (only a few)

Wider span of control

Figure 48.4A

From Figure 48.4A it can be seen that the structure is horizontal. **Organistic structure** is more flexible and as a result is more able to cope with change. This is an important attribute in the modern business world. Because of the small number of levels within the organisation there are fewer barriers to effective communication *(see Unit 51)*.

Mechanistic

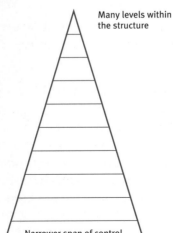

Many levels within the structure

Narrower span of control

Figure 48.4B

Figure 48.4B illustrates clearly that here there are many more levels within the organisation. Communication can become ponderous and highly formalised. The civil service and the armed forces, which are bedevilled with layers, epitomise **mechanistic structure**. Such organisations are frequently highly **bureaucratic** and machine-like in their ability to respond to change and the manner in which they perform even the most mundane of tasks. Given the number of layers within this type of organisation, there are many barriers to communication.

Matrix structure

In a bid to become more flexible, more responsive, 'faster' organisations, traditional rules governing organisational structure have undergone a sea change. Companies have progressed towards a matrix approach. This works in the following way. Imagine BT is developing the next piece of telecommunications equipment, a recording device built into mobile phones. These phones are then marketed to business executives who want to dictate messages while they are driving. The process of creating such a product, from the concept board (where the idea is first generated) to the launch, is one for which BT would use a **matrix structure**. Given the nature of the design process, there will be members of each function of the business involved at several stages.

Stage	Activity
1	Marketing discusses the idea with customers
2	Marketing reports to design
3	Design develops three prototypes to test on customers
4	Customers reject two, but accept third
5	Design reports to production subcontractors who say they cannot produce to that specification
6	Redesign of prototype
7	Marketing retest and it is still accepted
8	Production says it can be produced, but finance says it will be priced too high

The list goes on and on until the product meets all the criteria and only then can a launch take place. To avoid this problem, a project team will be selected across the range of functions within a business e.g. representatives from marketing, sales, finance, personnel, design, engineering, production will be in a project team whose brief is to launch the new product within a certain time frame.

This will ensure there is cross-fertilisation of ideas and the inter-functional communication will be much quicker. Toyota adopted this approach when launching the Lexus and it took only four years to get the product to market. Contrast that with Ford, who took well over seven years to launch the Mondeo.

Delegation

Delegation refers to the extent to which a superior passes work down the hierarchy to his/her subordinate. Managers consider delegation only when the number of tasks or the actual size of the job is too great for one individual to carry out effectively. Most people tend to be unwilling to delegate, because their own performance will depend on someone else carrying out work for them. As more work is delegated, there is a trade-off between trust and control.

Delegation leads to increased trust and decreased control. This means that the level of trust placed by the superior in the subordinate increases, but the level of control held by the superior decreases as the task is passed down.

The superior then becomes responsible for the subordinate carrying out the work, whereas the subordinate becomes accountable to the superior if mistakes are made.

The amount of work that is delegated will depend on:

- **the nature of the employee** – with a talented, ambitious subordinate, willing to take on extra work, the superior will be more willing to delegate responsibilities

- **the leadership style of the superior** – if the superior's usual style is democratic, then there will be plenty of opportunities for the subordinate to get involved in the discussion and actively seek to take on work

- **the workload of the superior** – as the superior becomes busier it will mean more must be delegated, although this is usually one of the initial problems with extra work. If a manager has achieved promotion entirely through his own work, then there will be an automatic reluctance to delegate tasks. Alternatively, if the manager has been promoted for managing a team effectively, then more delegation will take place

- **the skill level of the superior** – if an accountant has been asked to develop a system which will keep records more effectively and has no experience of computer packages which will do this for the business, someone may need to be hired temporarily from outside the business to install the hardware and train staff

- **the nature of the task to be delegated** – a manager will try to keep a close eye on the essential tasks for which he/she is responsible and may then delegate the less essential tasks to subordinates

Levels of hierarchy

This is the number of levels of authority within a particular business. When British Leyland was at its nadir, there were 56 **levels of hierarchy**, from the chief executive to the cleaner. At the same time at Toyota, there were seven levels of hierarchy, including the president and the cleaner!

As the number of levels of hierarchy increases, the business will face several consequences:

The business will lack flexibility; it will take a long time for information to feed through to the lower levels; in the same way, any suggestion from the shopfloor will need to pass through many levels before it reaches the decision maker. In the 1930s Max Weber saw this structure as an important characteristic of future organisations, given that it provided clear promotion prospects and a salary which reflected responsibility attached to each level. However, when he was writing his ideas, organisations did not need to be flexible and adaptable. Since then, Charles Handy and Tom Peters have both dismantled the thinking behind his work

The business will reach 'message overload'; the middle manager especially will become bearer of news and will act as a go-between/mediator between junior management/shopfloor and senior managers/directors. This is one of the reasons why middle managers lost their jobs during the change in structure which occurred during the 1980s and 1990s

A 'them and us' attitude will be generated; the distance from the top of the organisation chart to the bottom may mean that shopfloor workers rarely get to see or hear the managing director; in addition, the managers never get round to talking to the workers on the shopfloor to hear their views and listen to their opinions. This may be due to the fact that it might have been seen as circumventing other managerial positions

---

Question 2

Nick David runs DTP (David Travel Promotion) which arranges adventure holidays in Scandinavia. He runs the company single-handedly, but has a P.A. to help him out with administration.

He has two directors – one for marketing, Archie Jones, and one for finance and logistics, Katie Peters. Archie has a small team of four assistants who travel the country making demonstrations to schools and also act as liaison officers when schools decide to book a holiday with DTP. On the finance side Katie has two full-time clerks who monitor cash flow and run the sales ledger and a part-time computer expert who has helped the company install computers into the office. On the logistics side, Katie oversees six different 'trip organisers', each of whom has an assistant who works primarily as a courier during the holiday season, but who also helps with marketing when there's time.

Draw the organisational chart and comment on the potential problems that it may reveal.   [8]

Too few levels of hierarchy will result in:

Lack of promotion prospects; the army has 15 levels so there is plenty for officers and cadets to aim at. As organisations become flatter, a more subtle method of promotion through responsibility, but not through extra levels of hierarchy, is required to retain talented staff

Wider spans of control; managers are usually responsible for more people, resulting in little guidance for the subordinate. The superior is also usually overworked due to the sheer number of people that have to be dealt with.

Each of the structures referred to above will have differing characteristics such as span of control, levels of hierarchy, chains of command, lines of communication and may be considered as centralised or decentralised.

Span of control

This refers to the number of people who are directly responsible to a manager. Research was carried out in Ohio on 610 companies all with at least 100 employees to discover typical spans at control. The finding of the research was that the size of the organisation influenced the **span of control** (*see Table 1*).

Table 1

Size of company (employees)	Typical span of control
Less than 1500	5
1500–3000	8
Over 3000	9

The implication of a larger span of control is the difficulty of overseeing too many employees, both in terms of control and ensuring sufficient attention is given to them in order that they have a sense of belonging and recognition. However, a larger span of control can encourage more delegation and therefore a greater sense of responsibility.

In addition, there may be pressure on subordinates to perform if they are left to their own devices in a large span of control, whereas subordinates may suffer from too much interference when there is only a small span of control. The latter may also lack the opportunity to be creative, because they must conform with the wishes of the immediate superior.

Factors that affect the appropriate span of control

a) The skill, experience, and training of the employees or subordinates – more experience means employees can be left to get on with their own jobs without the need for close supervision

b) The degree of similarity of tasks that have been delegated – if there are 20 tasks to delegate, all of which are similar, then the explanation to all the subordinates can be done at the same time, thus reducing the amount of time spent delegating

c) The rate of change within and outside the organisation – if the business needs to change, it will need a structure which is more responsive

d) Communication techniques and the amount of personal contact that is necessary to perform the required tasks

f) The ability of the superior or manager

g) The level of hierarchy involved – if the level within the hierarchy is high then there will be a smaller span of control

Question 3

Comment on the likely span of control for a large business which has just opened a new factory and employed 90 employees who are about to start their induction course.   [5]

Chain of command

This refers to the way authority and responsibility pass up and down the organisation i.e. by referring to an organisational chart, it is possible to see which individual managers are responsible for or accountable to others. In traditional organisations, the **chain of command** is seen as the backbone of the organisational structure in that it demonstrates who has authority over whom as well as the usual **lines of communication**. However, the chain of command is more difficult to discern in organisations which have a matrix structure, because the structure is ever-changing according to the projects which need to be carried out.

Centralised and decentralised

These terms are concerned with where the control lies and the degree of authority that is passed on to others. The entrepreneurial structure (*Figure 48.1*) described by Weinshall is highly **centralised**, whereas the structure based on an area (*Figure 48.3*) is decentralised. The authority has been handed out from the centre in order for the business to flourish. The key is not the actual location of the organisation but the movement of authority away from a person or particular post.

As the amount of delegation and utilisation of structures based on either product or area increases, the degree of decentralisation increases. Similarly, the more authority that is delegated to the various levels of the organisation the more decentralised the organisation is. However it is quite usual for organisations that are focused on an area or a product to maintain some parts of the business centrally.

The main advantages of decentralisation are:

– It allows subordinates to take responsibility and develop their own ideas without having to refer back to higher levels within the organisation. This in turn may be a source of motivation for those to whom responsibility has been delegated
– It prevents the highest levels of management from having too much of a burden in terms of responsibility and workloads
– It provides a more flexible approach bearing in mind the individualistic characteristics of a given product or sales region

The main disadvantages are:

– Lack of control, which could be significant if the decentralisation leads to a divergence of objectives
– Effective communication may be hampered and add to the costs of the business
– Slower decision making may also add to the costs of the business
– It may be out of touch with specific product or area needs

The main advantages of centralisation are:

– It encourages responsibility in top management
– It allows local knowledge to prevail
– Decisions will be quicker in many instances

The main disadvantages are:

– Too much responsibility and work may fall on management
– A lack of flexibility and ability to change
– It prevents subordinates from taking responsibility and therefore being motivated

The factors that determine the degree of centralisation or decentralisation are:

- The objectives of the business
- The need for co-ordination
- The growth history of the business
- The entrepreneur's charisma
- The skill of the employees
- The geographical spread of the business (multinationals)

Line and staff

Although management is a phrase which covers a multiplicity of functions, there are two broad types of managers within any organisation:

Line managers

These managers have responsibility for a function within the business and are therefore responsible for a task which has to be performed e.g. marketing. Tasks are delegated down the 'line' so that the overall marketing function can be carried out, although each level of the hierarchy tends to have contact with only one level up and/or down. Delegation passes along the chain of command which is likely to be structured in the following way:

Marketing director
Product manager
Brand manager
Assistant brand manager

Staff managers

These managers have responsibility for a task which applies at all levels of the business e.g. personnel. In such a case, the personnel function will be involved at all levels of the hierarchy.

Question 4

Suggest whether the following are line or staff managers:
  i)   Tesco store manager
  ii) Tesco store bakery manager
  iii) Tesco staff recruitment manager   [3]

The role of organisational charts

The main purpose of organisational charts is to provide a visual representation of the business which enables management to see easily the main lines of communication.

By drawing the organisational chart for a particular business it will be possible:

- to demonstrate to employees the promotion prospects within the business. Employees can see the company hierarchy and the step up the ladder

- to show employees their immediate superior, to provide a clear line of communication

- to show employees where their role fits in the entire business

- to demonstrate who to pass information to, given a particular problem
- to highlight potential problems in terms of over-burdened managers through excess span of control, too many levels of hierarchy
- to help rationalise departmental organisation

The alternative organisation

Charles Handy has written at length about the future of work and the way he thinks organisations will be shaped in years to come. One interesting application of this is 'The Shamrock Organisation' which is explained in *The Age of Unreason* (Arrow Books, 1995). Named after the small flower which has three leaves, the organisation of the next century is seen as comprising three specific parts:

1 The core

These are the decision makers; they commit themselves to the job as a way of life and sacrifice their own private lives, sometimes their marriages, for the sake of their career in the core. They are rewarded with high salaries and German cars. They are expensive to hire and as a consequence there are fewer of them. Most successful organisations that have tripled their turnover will have halved their professional core; whether it is known as restructuring, or downsizing, the results are the same. There will seldom be more than four layers of seniority so promotion usually occurs by the age of 40. Promotion is an inadequate way of motivating beyond this age, so the organisation must look to other methods of motivating (*see Unit 50 Non-financial motivation*).

2 The contractual fringe

A recent and growing trend has been to subcontract out all non-essential parts of production; this includes the manufacture and sometimes the fitting of nuts and bolts, canteen services, cleaning services, training and repairs/maintenance. Car companies have been outsourcing metal fabrication and even painting. A recent survey by Coopers, the accounting firm, established that 65% of companies that outsourced performed better than those that did not. Toyota and BMW (which outsource 75% of their production) have performed better than Ford (50%) which, in turn, has performed better than General Motors (25%). The shamrock therefore puts the non-essential staff functions out to contract.

3 The flexible labour force

Whilst still essential to the organisation, these people are committed to the job rather than the career. In recent times the labour force has included more and more part-time workers, usually women, who seek to fit work around their other responsibilities. As organisations have sought longer opening hours, operating even for 24 hours a day, this has brought extra demands for a flexible labour force.

(A fourth, rather questionable part of this organisation is the customer. Much more time is spent travelling to and from the supermarket, whereas we used to send the order to the grocer who would make it up and have it delivered at no extra cost! Banks now get customers to fill in deposit slips when paying in money and fast-food restaurants now ask customers to clear away their own trays! Money is extracted from a hole in the wall and we have been pouring our own petrol for years! Under a label of customer preference, organisations have saved labour costs significantly by allowing customers to choose for themselves.)

Question 5

To what extent do you agree that the customer should be seen as part of the organisation?   [4]

Points for Revision

Key Terms

organisational structure	the way the organisation is put together in terms of personnel and positions
formal organisation	the structure of relationships between different levels as stipulated by the organisation
informal organisation	the non-official structure where nothing is sanctioned by authority
organistic structure	flexible organisation, able to respond to change, few levels of hierarchy, horizontal communication
mechanistic structure	bureaucratic, inflexible, rigid, many levels of hierarchy, vertical communication
bureaucratic	an approach to work which concentrates more on red tape/defined procedures, than it does on the actual task in hand
matrix structure	modern, highly flexible, business organised into project teams
delegation	the extent to which authority and responsibility are passed to the subordinate
span of control	the number of people a person is responsible for
levels of hierarchy	the number of layers of authority
chain of command	the direction of authority within a business
centralisation	the extent to which the business is controlled from headquarters
line managers	responsible for one function of the business
staff managers	responsible for a task which affects all levels of the business
line of communication	formal route that different types of communication can take

Definitions Question:
With reference to a firm or firms of which you have direct knowledge or experience, explain the importance of any three of the above terms (your teacher may wish to select the terms).   [5] per definition

Summary Points:

1   There are many different types of structure, each being defined by the levels of hierarchy, span of control and degree of centralisation.

2   Delegation plays an important role in non-financial motivation and is determined by several factors.

3   The ability of the organisation to respond to external change will depend significantly on the structure.

Mini Case Study

Andy Wild has been called in to help Mr Patel, the owner of a babywear manufacturer. His company, Chandel's Babywear, produces a wide range of baby clothes for a variety of retailers throughout the country. Mr Patel employs over 100 people, many on a part-time basis. He has had difficulty with some of his staff who he feels may have not had the opportunity to take on responsibility and are often late or absent. There are others whom he considers are in need of greater supervision because the standard of their work and their productivity are often low.

Mr Patel does not want to lose any more staff, as his labour turnover is high enough already. He has already spent his budget on recruitment for the year and there are still four months of the financial year remaining.

Andy Wild has asked to see the company organisational chart and has been amazed at what he has seen. It is quite clear that there are some problems that need his attention.

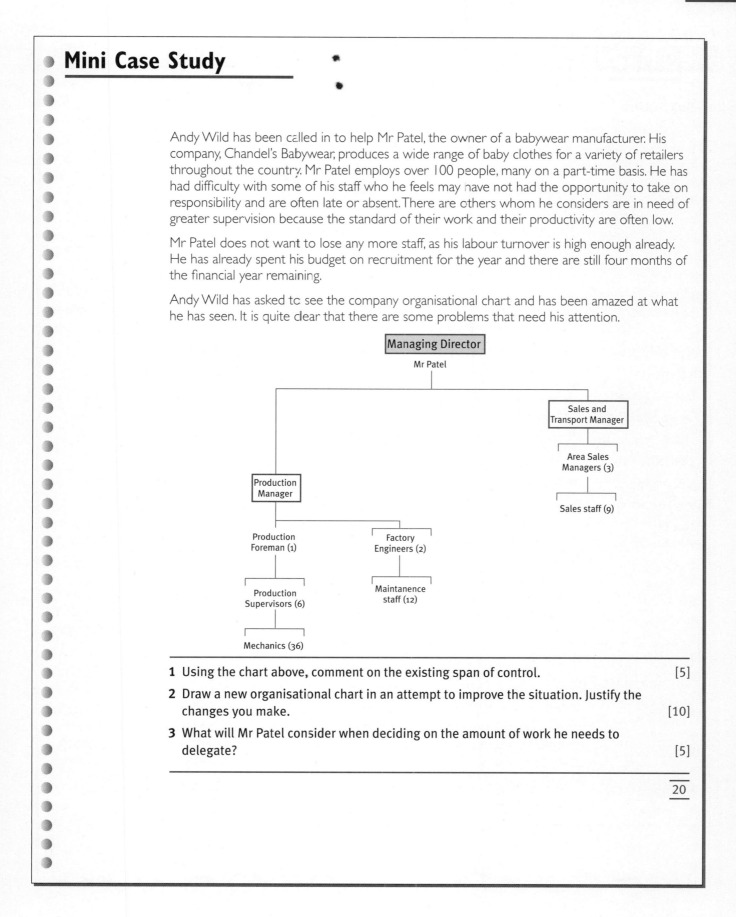

1 Using the chart above, comment on the existing span of control.   [5]

2 Draw a new organisational chart in an attempt to improve the situation. Justify the
   changes you make.   [10]

3 What will Mr Patel consider when deciding on the amount of work he needs to
   delegate?   [5]

                                                                                       20

Maxi Case Study

Semco is a small engineering company in the outskirts of Sao Paulo, Brazil, manufacturing dishwashers, whisks and other mechanical products. Its chairman, Ricardo Semler, took over the business from his father and immediately tried to transform it into a modern organisation. One of the main changes was in its organisational structure. Despite several attempts to prune top management, Semler observed that this part of the company continued to be top-heavy.

The problem, according to Semler, was the pyramid structure. Employees on lower levels of the pyramid with some aspiration and ambition would never have all their ambitions realised because there were fewer jobs at the top than at the bottom. Their opinions were never sought and no one actually explained the company's decisions to them. The lucky few who did reach the top sometimes found that there was no further progression and rapidly got bored with the job. As new management levels were created, complicated and confusing structures failed to achieve the goals of the business.

Despite using job rotation within the company, the pyramid structure was seen as claustrophobic and restricted advancement because promotion was too limited by the structure. The solution was therefore based on something more fluid – a circle! Semler decided there would be three concentric circles, with six Counsellors, as they were to be called, responsible for strategy in the innermost circle. The second circle would have between seven and 10 business unit leaders, known as Partners. The last, immense circle, would hold everyone else from cleaners to operators to salesmen, all of whom would be known as Associates. Within this last circle, there would be several triangles each enclosing a single person known as a Co-ordinator. These people would be the first level of management – marketing, sales, engineering, quality – all of whom had some leadership responsibility.

Even though the number of levels was reduced to four, this did not mean the salaries were the same; these continued to be paid according to the level of responsibility and leadership which was required within a particular job. The main effect was to reduce the number of bosses by removing the levels of hierarchy which meant that those who did not qualify to be Co-ordinators were left with no title or authority, but they did receive the same pay level. Even though Co-ordinators were paid at different rates, when it came to decision making in their weekly meeting with the Partner, they operated on a one person, one vote system.

Inevitably people left and some were dismissed and others went back to their old jobs. The decision as to who was the Co-ordinator and who went back to their old jobs was left to the factory committees that were part of the democratic process. However, the primary objective was to shorten the path people had to follow to get decisions made or complaints heard. A lot of skill and talent was lost, but it was a price the business was willing to pay.

Such a change is sometimes difficult to understand from outside the business, so whenever a promotion was made, Semco issued blank business cards and invited a title which signalled externally what the job entailed; despite the enticement to write anything from Procurement manager to 'First Pharaoh in charge of Royal Suppliers', most people wrote their names!

The organisational chart is therefore seen only as the birth certificate of the business; thereafter it is not normally something which accurately correlates proven competence and position. Semler's view is that power and respect are almost impossible to achieve by position and title, therefore position and title count for very little in modern businesses, except to communicate externally to those businesses which are still traditional, what the individual actually does.

1 Define: bureaucratic structure, job rotation, communicate externally.   [6]

2 Outline the reasons why Ricardo Semler opposed traditional organisational structure so strongly.   [6]

3 a) What was the main objective of the change in structure?   [2]

   b) What advantages would result in achieving this objective?   [5]

4 Draw the new organisational chart for Semco, following the restructuring.   [6]

5 Discuss whether you agree that the change in structure would actually address some of the criticisms Semler held of traditional organisational structures.   [10]

                                                                                            35

Financial motivation

Learning objectives

Having read this unit, students will be able to

1 demonstrate an awareness of the importance of financial measures used to motivate employees

2 understand the financial methods used to motivate the work-force

3 understand the role of financial incentives in motivating the work-force

Context

Imagine that your teacher, in desperation to make you work harder for the forthcoming A level, had suddenly offered you money in return for work. What sum of money (in a lump sum) would you require to make you work harder? £50, £100 or perhaps a four or five figure sum – such is the pain of extra academic work! Despite sounding initially attractive, for how long will this financial reward continue to push you to greater heights – a week? a month? even for a whole term? Sometimes, in industry, extra payment is given for extra work, although a bonus once given becomes expected. So if financial rewards are expected and have been promised, not paying the extra amount may well result in a slump in productivity.

Crispin Odey, who runs a pension fund in the city, earned £36 million in 1997; is it likely that he will be motivated to work for the £40 million mark, given that he openly admitted that he struggles to spend more than £50,000 a year?

Scientific management

Frederick Taylor, in his book *The Principles of Scientific Management* (Harper, 1911), stated that it was money that motivated individuals to work harder. He carried out research at an American company called the Bethlehem Steel Works, with a man called Alfred Schmidt. Schmidt's job was to move pig iron. By examining the job closely with a stopwatch and redesigning it so that Schmidt could work more productively, he managed to increase the amount of pig iron moved in a day from 12.5 tons to 47 tons, with no obvious increase in effort. As a result Schmidt received a doubling of his salary – (he was chosen for the experiment because he had made it abundantly clear that the doubling of his salary was of prime importance to him.) Taylor went on to work closely with Henry Ford who had pioneered specialisation within the car industry; the division of labour was essential to Taylor's work because it meant that each person could perform the job very efficiently.

Coupled with this was a much higher wage attached to the increase in output; indeed, some people could earn $5 dollars a day, which almost sanctified Henry Ford as one of the most influential industrialists of the twentieth century. Taylor followed the assumption of 'economic man' laid down by Adam Smith 150 years earlier in that man is rational-logical and will seek to maximise economic gain at all costs. The other stipulation in his work was that it was the responsibility of management to train the work-force, organise jobs and employ a wage system which rewarded the extra output. Workers were seen as lacking direction and initiative given that most trades and skills had been handed down through generations without question. Taylor's critics said that his ideas took no account of the human side of work – the need for interesting, challenging work, the need for responsibility and recognition (*all these are covered in more detail in Unit 50 Non-financial motivation*).

Work study

Taylor used a system called Work Study which concerns close examination of a particular task, with a view to redesigning the job to make it more efficient. The first stage uses time and motion studies (otherwise known as method study), whereby operators and assemblers are observed at work and all the movements and tasks are recorded in detail, including the time taken and the amount of distance travelled within each job. If there are several people doing the same job, each worker is given a rating according to how hard he or she is deemed to be working. Following the redesign of the job, a basic time is calculated, based on the amount of time it is expected to take the average worker. Targets can then be set for each individual, according to his/her rating i.e. an employee with a higher rating can be given a higher than average target, with a suitable pay award attached.

Methods of payment

Time-based payment – wage and salary

The most common form of payment is based on a time period e.g. an hourly rate, or an annual **salary**. Payment that is quoted in hours and paid on a weekly basis is known as a **wage** and a salary is a payment that is quoted annually and normally paid monthly. Pay rates tend to be quoted gross of taxation when advertised in job centres and newspapers. The principle behind the payments is as follows:

■ Wages

The employee is paid to turn up i.e. once the employee has 'clocked in', earning begins. It then becomes the responsibility of the management to use the resources of that employee in a sensible, productive way.

An employee of Virgin Megastore, for example, will be expected to carry out various tasks, having been trained in a variety of functions. Wages are paid by employers when there is a possibility of a change in the number of hours required from week to week. Perhaps if there is a sudden downturn in demand, the business will not require as many hours to be worked. However, if the employee has signed a contract stipulating a certain number of hours, then the employee is under a legal obligation to offer that number of hours as a minimum.

Critics of the minimum wage say the extra wage per hour is likely to be cancelled out by companies demanding fewer hours from their employees. Alternatively, if demand increases, the business will need to offer **overtime**.

Clocking in

Overtime is paid at a multiple of the normal rate e.g. time and a half meaning the normal rate increased by 50% for the extra hours worked.

e.g. the standard working week for a carpenter at a wardrobe manufacturer is 40 hours at a wage of £6 per hour. Overtime is offered for eight hours, at time and a half, therefore the total amount earned will be:

40 hours × £6   =   £240
+
8 hours × £9   =   £72

$$= \frac{£312}{48 \text{ hours}} = £6.50 \text{ per hour}$$

The reason overtime normally commands a higher rate is that the employee is in no way obliged or expected to accept overtime if the employee has completed 40 hours during the week.

Question 1

Simon Luigi works as a welder. His normal weekly wage is £300 for 40 hours' work and he has been offered 12 hours of overtime over the Easter Bank Holiday period at 'double time'.

a) Calculate the normal hourly rate.   [1]

b) Calculate the total amount earned if he accepts the overtime.   [1]

c) If he accepts the overtime, what will be the average rate per hour for the entire week?   [2]

d) Why might Simon refuse the overtime, despite the significant increase in pay?   [4]

e) How might the business decide on the overtime rate?   [4]

■ Salaries

Salaries tend to be paid for those jobs which do not stipulate hours; rather the employee is paid to carry out a role within the business e.g. purchasing manager or teacher of a subject/age group. The salary is meant to represent the going rate for that function and because it is expressed in annual terms, there is likely to be more security in receiving a salary due to there being a contract associated with the salary. A teacher will be paid to teach pupils, but may also be requested to coach a sport, or be a form tutor. He/she will not receive any extra money for this, but will be expected to carry out these jobs in addition to the teaching. Marking and preparation also take up time, for which the teacher will receive no extra income.

Question 2

Which of the following jobs are more likely to be paid by salary or wages? Give your reasons.
a) a chip fryer at McDonald's
b) an assembly worker who fits bumpers on to cars
c) a milkman
d) a Member of Parliament
e) a coach driver
f) a solicitor   [12]

Fee income

This is paid on a one-off basis, normally for a service which is provided over a specific period of time, for a specific job e.g. solicitors will charge for work which is carried out when a client wishes to move house. The **fee** relates to the amount of time spent by the solicitor in addition to expenses and a profit margin. If the solicitor wishes to earn more, he/she must find more clients, each of whom will pay a similar fee income for the same service. Sometimes companies will hold training seminars by hiring the services of a training company e.g. for training on the use of a computer. The trainer will then be paid on a daily (fee) basis. The income is less reliable, because it depends on finding the work in the first place; given the choice, people will use fee income as a form of topping up total income. Charles Handy, the business writer, has predicted that in the near future there will be a retirement age of 50 and these people will then hire themselves out to companies on a consultancy basis, earning fees for their services as peripheral employees.

Performance-related pay (PRP)

This comes in several forms and is based on the principle that if money is used as an incentive to work harder then, given the right circumstances, it will cause the desired effect and output will increase, hopefully more than the increase in pay, leading to an increase in productivity.

The second reason behind **PRP** is that as organisations have become 'flatter' (*see Unit 48 Organisational structures*) the option to reward through promotion has been less easy. PRP becomes one answer to solving this problem.

Companies also make substantial savings in salary costs. Many companies still provide an additional increment in salary for each year of service completed (in addition to the annual pay award that takes into consideration the rate of inflation, often referred to as a cost of living increase). PRP scales have removed these seniority-based pay awards, although the inflationary adjustment has been retained.

The main argument in favour is to be able to reward someone who is just avoiding being sacked because of a minimal work-rate at a lower rate than someone who is keen to get on in the business. In addition, The Peter Principle may apply (whereby someone who is good at their job is promoted into a job he/she cannot do) so PRP allows more earnings without the burden of promotion.

PRP has become commonplace in many industries, including the public sector where the National Health Service and the Civil Service have linked pay awards to improvements in productivity. Such pay awards should not, however, be linked to **appraisal** reviews.

■ Piece rates (Bonus systems)

This means that employees are paid according to the amount they produce. This was the basis for the pay system implemented by Taylor in all his work. In these cases, employees were paid according to how many units were produced (*see Figure 49.1*).

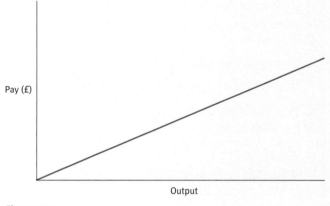

Figure 49.1

In the above case, if the employee produces nothing, then nothing will be earned. Such a system depends not just on the employee, but also on factors such as the reliability of suppliers and machines. Late delivery and unreliable machinery mean that the employee is unable to earn anything.

In response to this, a basic salary can be offered which guards against the uncertainty of being able to produce the required output. The basic can then be set at a subsistence level – enough to allow the employee to pay for basics such as food and shelter, and the **bonus** can be targeted at providing discretionary income (*see Figure 49.2*).

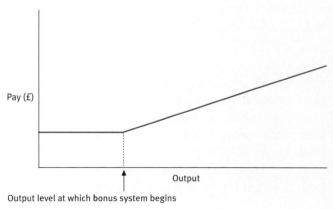

Output level at which bonus system begins

Figure 49.2

Bash-It manufactures bolts. It pays its employees a basic salary of £6,000 per annum, with a bonus system of £20 per 1,000 bolts. It is considering changing the system to paying a basic of £5,000 plus a bonus of £30 per 1,000 bolts.

a) If the company presently manufactures 150,000 bolts per employee per annum, what is the labour cost per person

    i) before the change in the payments system? [2]

    ii) after the change in the payments system?   [2]

b) Why might the business impose such a change on the work-force?   [3]

c) What might be a typical reaction by the employees to the change in the payments system?   [3]

If the business is concerned to keep output at a reasonably constant level, then a third alternative might be offered (*see Figure 49.3*).

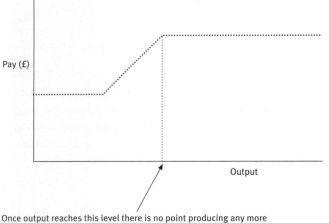

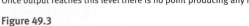
Once output reaches this level there is no point producing any more

Figure 49.3

This system provides an incentive to the employee, but also puts some form of control on the output produced. The business may not want a sudden increase in output close to Christmas, for example, due to employees working harder for the festive season. The extreme of this method is an agreement to pay a bonus once a certain level of output has been achieved (*see Figure 49.4*).

This will mean that the factory produces a fixed amount, assuming always that the employees are

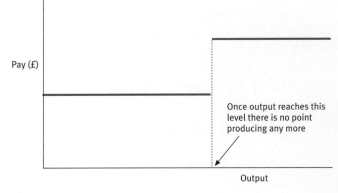
Once output reaches this level there is no point producing any more

Figure 49.4

motivated towards the financial rewards attached to the extra output. This type of agreement, which is much more popular with the unions because it provides a more stable form of income and can be shared amongst the entire factory, is known as Measured Day Work.

■ Commission

This is the equivalent of a piece rate system for the sales-force, given that it will not be responsible for manufacturing, but for the revenue which is earned. Some companies pay only commission to their employees with a view to driving them to work harder. People who work as sales-force are trained to have some form of 'hunger' for the money which could be earned. Industries which use commission are those that use salespeople as the main way of earning revenue e.g. retailers would not use commission because the vast majority of employees are not directly involved with sales. Double glazing 'reps', financial advisers and insurance agents, travel agents, even the Betterware door-to-door sales-force are paid on a commission basis. Commission is normally paid with a basic salary, and has the same type of structure as Figure 49.2.

Seal-It, a double glazing firm, pays its sales-force on a commission-only basis of 15% of sales. Glass-It, a company of approximately the same size and in the same industry, pays a basic salary of £500 per month, plus a commission rate of 12%.

Mrs Slick, a successful salesperson who wants to earn as much as possible, has been offered a job by both companies.

a) If the average amount of revenue per employee earned by each company is
  i) £13,000
  ii) £20,000
  which method of payment will earn Mrs Slick the most pay?   [6]

b) What other factors would Mrs Slick take into account before deciding which business to work for?   [8]

One of the main problems with PRP is administering the programme accurately. Individual schemes are notoriously difficult to monitor because someone or something needs to check the entire output of one individual. Commission systems are appropriate in this case, given that revenue, as shown by the invoice, is unquestionable. However, when there are 250 people producing products independently, accurate measurement is almost impossible. When the individual scheme is not based on output i.e. is decided by appraisal, then this will also be difficult to monitor because of a) the time-consuming nature of appraisals, b) the subjective nature of measurement.

One solution to this is a group performance measure, where the team receives a bonus based on output of the team; this can also be applied to quality circles made up of the team if they produce an idea which reduces costs. This therefore provides an incentive for quality circles to meet more regularly and take their discussion more seriously. Again, however, this requires greater monitoring and means that harder-working individuals may have to 'carry' the lazy ones within the team.

Company-wide performance solves the problem of the accuracy of measurement posed by the above schemes. The only way of doing this is to allow the employees to share in the profit of the business.

■ Profit-related pay

Whilst commission and piece rates provide attractive prospects for those wishing to earn large amounts of money, they both tend to engender a selfish approach to work. A more successful method of encouraging company or group commitment to increased income is by using a profit-related pay system. This has the extra advantage of including all employees in an effort either to increase revenue or control costs in both the short and the long run.

It works by the business allocating up to 15% of its pre-tax profit to employees. This obviously has an effect on the amount that shareholders receive, so in order to approve this, shareholders, assuming the dividend pay-out is important to them, need to feel that the hand-out to the employees is likely to result in more profit in the long run. An alternative to this is to distribute profit in the form of shares. This will dilute existing shareholding percentages, but not to any significant extent, given that the amount of shares handed out is usually less than 10% of the total.

Unfortunately, many employees do not fully understand the value of this method of payment and as a consequence prefer to receive their reward in the normal way i.e. money. Furthermore, calculating the value of PRP is not easy and may not relate to the amount of effort put in by the employee. Nevertheless, it has the advantage of involving the employee to a greater extent because higher profits bring higher returns in the form of dividends.

■ Employee share ownership programmes (ESOPs)

This is where employees share profits through **SAYE** (Save As You Earn) schemes whereby employees build up savings which are invested in shares of the business. John Lewis, the department store, finds this approach particularly effective given that it boosts wages by 15–20% and means that employees have a secondary stake in the success of the business.

NFC (National Freight Corporation) found this effective, given that 82% of their shares are owned by employees, their families and ex-employees. Employees therefore act like owners in their dealings with customers. In addition to the shareholding, 15% of pre-tax profits are distributed to employees; employees therefore have the best of both worlds.

Question 5

To what extent might a profit-related pay scheme cause **a)** conflict **b)** harmony between employees and shareholders?   [6]

What factors will determine whether performance-related pay will work?

- **Cost structures** – if the business is labour-intensive, improvements in productivity will affect profit much more than if the business is capital-intensive. Handing out a little more pre-tax profit will also reduce the amount of tax the business has to pay.

- **Type of product and market** – if a product is constantly changing and therefore the manufacturing process is changing, more time will need to be spent on training to adapt. If demand is unstable, and work flow is therefore inconsistent, employees rarely have the opportunity to add a bonus to the wages on a consistent basis.

- **Quantity, as opposed to quality, of output required** – one of the major drawbacks of PRP is that it can focus entirely on quantity, which means quality may be sacrificed. PRP then becomes a short-term incentive, because if quality drops, customers will, over a period of time, take their trade elsewhere.

- **Labour relations** – management will not attempt to introduce a payments system which either reduces overall pay for some members of the work-force or discriminates against the less skilful. Unions will be swift to object to such a system and may take industrial action as a result.

- **Capability of personnel and administration staff** – such systems are complicated to administer and need a tight control on figures; skilled staff will be needed to ensure there are no problems matching individuals' output with appropriate pay.

- **Attitude of the employee** – much of the desired effect of these systems depends on whether employees are motivated by money and nothing else. An observation of PRP is that the quality of working life actually falls as people compete with each other on the shopfloor and the drive for quantity at the expense of craftsmanship means less pride is taken in the work done. Alternatively, it can mean that an incentive scheme makes the employee feel valued by the organisation.

Despite the above conditions incentive schemes have not always worked. Alfred Kohn wrote in the *Harvard Business Review* that incentive systems are inappropriate for western industries for six reasons:

1 Pay does not motivate; if pay is halved, this will demotivate, but if pay is doubled, the effort does not double

2 Frederick Herzberg (*see Unit 50 Non-financial motivation*) said that a reward once given becomes a right, so removal of a bonus may be seen as a punishment

3 Rewards destroy co-operation between employees as there is competition to achieve them. They also encourage creeping to the boss!

4 Managers may use rewards rather than actually addressing problems; it is arguably easier to increase the amount of money in the pay packet than to discuss problems, provide support and deal with awkward personalities

5 Rewards encourage people to aim to produce a certain quantity and therefore do not encourage creativity and ideas

6 Employees concentrate only on the reward and not on the job itself

Fringe benefits

Money is not the only way to reward employees using financial benefits. In addition to the salary/wage/bonus/commission etc. an employer can add on financial 'extras' which are non-monetary, but which will result in greater wealth in the short or long run or will improve the standard of living for the employee.

Company car – as an alternative to purchasing a motor vehicle, the employee is rewarded with a particular model of car according to the responsibility level held by the employee. Some employees have no use for a car e.g. if they work and live in central London, so a cash alternative can be taken.

Paid holidays – a typical professional job will have a certain number of holidays written into the contract, normally 25–30 days. This means employees will be paid, even though they are not at work.

Sick pay – an employee needs to have some security when away from work through illness; the more generous schemes will pay someone for between six and 12 months if they are off sick, on full pay. This is in addition to the statutory sick pay they will receive.

Subsidised meals – having an on-site canteen where the company subsidises meals means employees spend less on lunch than if they had to leave the building and purchase food at a profit-making establishment.

Medical insurance – although this does not improve the wealth of the individual, it means that injuries, which may well be sustained at work, can be treated much more quickly than if the employee has to wait for the NHS.

Pensions – some companies will make contributions to a pensions scheme on behalf of the employee, in addition to the contributions the employee makes. This will contribute to the employee's long-term wealth at the expense of short-term wealth.

Does money motivate?

This question has been researched endlessly by various writers on motivation, none of whom have produced an all-embracing, conclusive answer. It is certainly the case that financial rewards are desired by most people and that as human beings, we desire to purchase material goods as well as save for the future. Both these needs are satisfied by money. However, this does not explain the vast amount of voluntary work that goes on in charities, churches and clubs which goes unpaid. Nor does it prove that money actually makes people work harder. The theorists who have examined the effect of paying people more have come up with two ideas:

1 Money allows people to purchase what they need to achieve a basic standard of living, although companies use money to drive employees to higher standards of living.
2 Money itself will not cause someone to work harder in the long term; rather it is the non-financial factors which achieve this.

Points for Revision

Key Terms

scientific management	theory whereby management is responsible for making the task easier and quicker to perform
F W Taylor	the founder of scientific management
work study	a method of examining a particular task and identifying the separate sub-parts with a view to making the task more efficient
wage	time-based payment, quoted by the hour, paid weekly
salary	time-based payment, quoted annually, paid monthly
overtime	an incentive to work more hours, paid as a multiple of normal wage
fee	a one-off payment for a specific job
performance-related pay (PRP)	pay which is related to output, sales, or profit
appraisal	a one-to-one interview between employer and employee which covers job satisfaction, career progression and overall performance
ESOP	employees are given shares as an incentive to take a greater interest in the company's financial performance
bonus	normally paid as a result of extra output or profit
SAYE	Save As You Earn, whereby employees save part of their wages to buy shares at a discounted price
commission	a percentage of revenue paid usually to sales-force
fringe benefits	financial extras, which are non-monetary, but which increase employee's standard of living

Definitions Question:
By referring to a business you know, explain the importance of any three of the above (your teacher may wish to help you choose the terms).   [5] per definition

Summary Points:

1 There is conflicting evidence as to whether money is a motivator.

2 Companies use a variety of methods to motivate using money; some are time-based, others are performance-based.

3 Companies also use non-financial rewards as an incentive to attract and retain employees.

4 The assumption that money motivates ignores other factors which affect employees' motivation.

Mini Case Study

Scot-Lec operates in a fiercely competitive market, selling consumer durables. The main competition comes from Dixons, which also owns Curry's as well as Comet. Normally these companies locate their business on retail warehousing land, in out-of-town retail parks. All these companies offer similar prices and promotional offers. The ability of the salesperson to convince potential customers is therefore a very important factor in achieving revenue. In order to motivate the staff, Scot-Lec pays a basic salary of £9,000 plus a commission rate of 10% on sales over £150 per day (measured over a 24-day month). This can cause conflict between staff as sometimes a particular staff member can do all the work on a customer who may then leave the shop to consider the purchase, returning on a day when that member of staff is away!

Carol Peters had just finished her monthly appraisal with the manager and was close to tears. That month she had been so close to achieving what would have been the only sale of that day with four customers, all of whom would have spent an average of £1,000 each. As a result, she had failed to reach her target of sales by £500 that month and had been given a verbal warning. She would much rather receive a salary of £10,500 and be given a target of sales for the year – the short-term nature of the commission system was divisive amongst the staff and was affecting her standard of living.

---

1 Define: retail warehousing, sales promotion. [4]

2 Calculate the amount of sales revenue that Carol had earned during the month in question. [2]

3 What would her income have been during the month in question had she achieved the extra sales of £4,000? [3]

4 Had the business altered the salary to £10,500 per annum, what target of annual sales would have been stipulated for the business to be no worse off than before in terms of labour costs? [5]

5 Discuss the usefulness of an appraisal when assessing the performance of a Scot-Lec employee in the above context. [6]

20

Maxi Case Study

Combined Insurance Company of America (C.I.C.A.) was started in the 1930s by W. Clement-Stone who went on to become a self-made millionaire, writing several books on motivation and the desire for success. He began his salesman's career selling newspapers in a restaurant. Having been thrown out twice by the owner, he insisted on returning and eventually the bemused diners bought newspapers from him until he had run out. He persisted because he had no other use for the papers and his livelihood (at least for the next day) depended on him selling them. Despite this being a simple message, he used it as a basis to motivate and inspire thousands of insurance salesmen.

The business sold accident hospital policies i.e. the insured could claim only if an accident caused them to be hospitalised overnight. Once the insured had held a hospital policy for six months, he or she could then purchase 'full cover' which paid out even if the insured was not hospitalised, but lost days at work. The company spent no money on corporate advertising, preferring to concentrate its resources on a generous commission system. The motivation of the sales-force worked on a very straightforward system in that all were conditioned to aim for goals in terms of material goods. Phrases such as 'achieve your goals and strive for the top' were regularly thrust at the sales-force at monthly meetings. Every morning each team met to decide on its goals for that day, such was the pressure to achieve. The entire organisation was dedicated to achieving sales revenue in three ways

1   new policies, which cost £25 and paid a commission of 60%

2   additional policies adding on to an old policy, costing £30, paying a commission of 40%

3   collecting in money from existing policies at an average of £40 per customer, at a commission rate of 15%

In addition, every two months, the company offered prizes for hitting sales target within the first three days of each week, and at the bi-annual conference, the high achievers were paraded in front of the entire company. The reason behind all this inspiration was that the nature of the job itself was inherently unpleasant. The standard target was five new sales per day and at a success rate of 1 in 7, this would mean finding 35 people who were willing to receive the hard-sell demonstrations. Rejection became an unpleasant though necessary part of the job. Sales reps were relatively unpopular individuals because they had to be pushy; no sales meant no commission and therefore no income. It was perfectly possible to earn over £200 per day, but equally possible to earn £10 per day, which, after petrol and subsistence costs, amounted to a loss of £10, for 10 hours' work. There was therefore a high turnover of labour, with a loyal core that continued to succeed and be paraded as the high achievers.

One particular salesman, Michael Cowper from Cheshire, used to earn colossal amounts; on one day he visited 13 customers, only one of whom refused to renew the policy. Of the rest, two-thirds renewed their policies and added full cover and half of them provided a referral for other potential customers, leading to new sales for each referral. Michael did not have a mortgage and did not care what people thought about him – the job was not pleasant, far from it, but his goal was high income. On the same day another salesman, Samuel Fry, had a terrible time – he had been insulted by several car mechanics as his back was turned and his company had been openly ridiculed by them for its lack of pay-out following a claim one of the mechanics had made. He felt there was more to working life than this and his family would need providing for, but he would never be given responsibility because promotion was going to be given to the person with the best results in the team, and he was the worst performer!

1 Define motivation as applied to the above company.   [3]

2 To what extent does the system of payment relate to the work of F.W. Taylor?   [6]

3 Why might commission-only not always produce the best long-term results for the business?   [4]

4 What were the non-financial methods of motivation which the business used to motivate the sales-force?   [3]

5 A visiting management consultant advised the business to pay a basic rate of pay, but CICA argued that this would not be cost-effective. What arguments might it have used in defence of the commission-only system?   [5]

6 Calculate the amount that Michael Cowper earned during the day described in the case study.   [6]

7 Discuss the extent to which financial measures are the most effective method of motivation for a business such as C.I.C.A.   [8]

35

Non-financial motivation

Learning objectives

Having read this unit, students will be able to

1 identify the various non-financial measures which a business might use to motivate its employees

2 associate theories with various writers on motivation

3 recognise the application of theories in various business situations

Context

If you ask a nurse employed in the National Health Service whether he or she would like a pay rise, the answer is obvious. Ask the same nurses whether the pay rise would increase their output (output in this type of job is difficult to measure, but the number of patients for whom a nurse is responsible or the number of tasks completed within a given period of time may suffice) and the answer would be less predictable. More money may enhance the living standards of employees, but it does little in many instances to drive them to higher levels of productivity. Nursing is a caring profession, and as such the level of pay is not the main factor that drives nurses to perform their role to a higher standard or treat more patients.

What is it that spurs them on day after day? Treating patients who are often abusive, dealing with traumatised relatives and with very seriously ill people – providing these nurses with more money would not achieve any increase in their motivation. Rather, it is a non-financial part of the job which goes a long way to motivating people.

The difference between morale and motivation

Morale tends to refer to the feeling of the group or the employees as a whole; morale within an organisation may be low, but one or two individuals, perhaps who have just been promoted or are keen to earn promotion, may well be motivated. **Motivation** therefore relates to the individual as opposed to the group. Having said that, managers are likely to pay attention to the morale of the work-force only if this will have a significant effect on the company as a whole.

So what does motivate?

This is a question which has preoccupied countless business writers and gurus over the past 100 years. Some have insisted that money is the only motivator, which has contributed to the success of specialisation through the payment of piece rates. However, as specialisation became more significant to improve productivity, the actual content of a particular job became all the more tedious and repetitive. In turn, this made the unions more active and industrial action and disputes became commonplace during the early part of the 20th century. At the time, managers could not understand this – at the Ford Motor Company, operators were paid the magical $5 per day and still there was high labour turnover. It therefore became quite clear that there were non-financial issues which had to be considered. Since then, writers have been hard at work producing all sorts of theories, some of which are included here.

F. W. Taylor – *Principles of Scientific Management*

Taylor was mentioned in the previous unit, because the main thrust of his work was that man was motivated and driven solely by money. The main criticism of his work was that it failed to recognise the social side of work i.e. the need for people to work together or the quality and content of the job as significant. The principle that it was up to the managers to decide how the job was to be carried out, and it was the employees' job to listen and comply, was vigorously challenged by other writers. They believed that the employees themselves could design the job just as well and that managers did not need to provide financial rewards as a way of recognising good work.

Elton Mayo

Mayo started from the viewpoint that employees were more motivated by non-financial factors, contrary to the findings of Taylor. His initial ideas were based on the principle that the working environment was of significance to the motivation of workers. He began his experiments at Western Electric's Hawthorne plant in Chicago during the 1920s and they lasted for over five years. He tested his hypothesis that working conditions greatly influenced the productivity of the work-force and found that productivity did increase as the working environment was changed.

He selected two groups and altered the lighting conditions within the factory for one of the groups. As a consequence the output increased for the group which had had the lighting enhanced. However, the output of the control group also increased!

Mayo altered other elements of the two teams' working environment and on every occasion output increased. The number of rest breaks was changed, the length of the breaks, the lunch break was paid for, the weekly hours worked were reduced, even when the rest breaks were taken away, output still increased. The only occasion when output fell was after the number of breaks was increased and the workers complained that their work patterns were disrupted.

Throughout the experiments the workers were consulted on a regular basis and as a result they felt they were important to the company and their self-esteem was greatly enhanced. The rate of absenteeism fell dramatically as well (which helped to boost output). The fact that Mayo undertook 20,000 interviews goes a long way to explaining why the work-force felt important.

Recognition and a sense of involvement were the key factors that motivated the work-force, regardless of working conditions.

Following this study, the issue of involving workers in discussing their tasks was known as the **Hawthorne Effect**.

Question 2

Derek Skinner and his supervisor, Sue Bream, were discussing the workstation he had inherited from the recently retired Albert Carp. Sue had just taken on the role of supervisor and was keen to hear the views of her charges. Derek was uncertain about this; Sue's predecessor had simply issued orders and he initially viewed her approach with some suspicion. Albert had been renowned for sloppy workmanship and for never tidying his workstation; in addition the station was close to the boiler which meant extreme temperatures during the winter when the boiler was on full. Derek was hoping for a pay rise as a result of the conversation given that his output was 30% higher than that of Albert.

How can Sue use the work of **a)** Taylor or **b)** Mayo with a view to motivating Derek?   [6]

Abraham Maslow – Hierarchy of needs

Maslow identified the reasons why people work and set them out in a **hierarchy of needs** distinguishing between lower and higher order needs. Lower order needs are those that do not actually cause motivation, but mean that employees avoid stress or discomfort in their lives. Higher order needs are those that do drive employees to greater levels of achievement whereas lower order needs are concerned with the basic economic needs of man, which today are considered to be an employee's right and as a consequence are not viewed as being motivators. Higher order needs satisfy the intellectual needs of the employees.

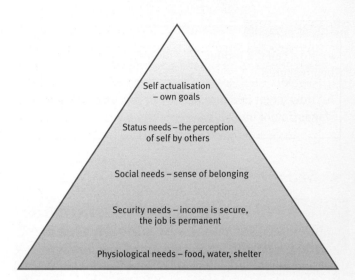

Figure 50.1   Maslow's hierarchy of needs

How are these achieved?

- **Physiological needs** – money. There is no substitute for this in terms of purchasing power. Employees need to be able to survive as human beings and protect their dependants in the same way.

- **Security needs** – having a large amount of money for a short period of time is less preferable (according to Maslow) than having less money per week, but as a payment which is guaranteed. Salespeople on commission-only pay structures may well prefer to receive a basic salary with no commission, because it provides some security. A contract also provides security – employees will prefer to have long-term contracts. Pensions are also important in this respect because an employee can retire and enjoy his/her savings through a pension scheme.

- **Social needs** – individuals are naturally social animals who like to mix with others, working with people in an office or in a team on the shopfloor or on a board of directors. People like to identify with a group because it allows for affiliation and direction (*see Unit 53 People in groups*).

- **Status** – people like to be seen by others as achieving progression, power and responsibility; this can be applied to society as a whole e.g. the phrase 'Keeping up with the Joneses' refers to some members of society who thrive on status symbols like a big house or smart holiday destinations. In the same way, managers can use status to motivate individuals although the symbols of status may be slightly different. Company cars, personal parking space, size of desk, having an office to yourself, having a secretary, an impressive job title, can all be used as symbols of status and power in this respect.

- **Self-actualisation** – this goes beyond the need to be recognised by others. It concentrates on more intellectual needs such as achieving promotion for themselves, or achieving a higher level of growth in the share price.

The main principle behind this hierarchy is that the lower order needs must be satisfied before the managers can use the higher order needs to motivate employees e.g. no matter how much team spirit is involved in the work-place, if the wage fails to allow the individual to meet basic physiological needs, then he/she will not be driven by the need for social affiliation. In addition, the management must be aware that workers will be at different levels of the hierarchy and so will require differing methods to motivate them.

Question 3

Verphail Gupta left the office of his manager, anxious about the future. He had just been promoted to a job that sounded impressive and one which his family and friends would be proud to hear about. Unfortunately, the company still refused to give him more than a three-month contract, so he still could not purchase a house because the bank required more security for a mortgage. He had also failed to organise a pension; despite the increase in salary which would arise from the promotion he was still worried about the future.

Explain how his manager should use Maslow's hierarchy of needs in order to put Verphail's mind at ease. [6]

Frederick Herzberg

Herzberg wrote 'One more time: how do you motivate employees?' *HBR* Vol. 46, No. 1, 1959 following interviews with over 200 engineers and accountants based in Pittsburgh about what they considered were the positive and negative aspects of their work or what satisfied them and dissatisfied them about their work.

The factors that were seen as positive and therefore could be seen as **motivators** were: recognition, achievement, a sense of responsibility and the actual nature of the job.

The factors that caused the most concern, which Herzberg named the **hygiene** factors, were all related to the working environment. They were the administration and bureaucracy of the business, the working conditions, the wages or salary, concern over job security and the way in which their posts were seen by others within the organisation i.e. the status of the job. The relationship with their peer group was another hygiene factor.

Table 1

Motivators

Achievement
Nature of the work
Recognition
Responsibility

Hygiene factors

Company policy and bureaucracy
Working conditions
Salary
Job security
Status
Relationship with peers

Table 1 is a summary of the two distinct groups of factors that influence workers. The motivators are the factors that actually motivate the workers whilst the hygiene factors do not motivate but can lead to worker dissatisfaction and possibly low morale within the business. However if the hygiene factors are addressed, although in the words of Herzberg 'pain will have been avoided', the motivation of the work-force will not have been enhanced. The enhancement of motivation can be achieved only by attending to the motivators.

Herzberg used the above to suggest how a knowledge of the motivators and hygiene factors could be used within the business environment. It is of interest to note that the motivators are related to the higher order needs of the individual (*see Maslow*). The motivators are all related to the specific job, whereas the hygiene factors are lower order, economic factors or human needs of the individual and are related to the working environment.

In an attempt to provide clear recommendations to the managers of the companies he visited, he recommended three ways of changing the job which were designed to improve the quality of working life (q.w.l.).

Applying the thoughts of Herzberg introduces the concepts of job enrichment, job enlargement and job rotation.

Job enrichment, not to be confused with job enlargement (which is merely giving the employee more to do of a similar nature), is concerned with providing a wider range of tasks. The wider range is often referred to as vertical enrichment as the additional tasks ought to be of a higher order, involving more responsibility and allowing for more achievement which in turn can be recognised by the business. Herzberg suggested that job enrichment should encompass the following:

- Less supervision (to provide a sense of responsibility)

- Allowing employees to be responsible for a whole process of production or a complete unit of production where possible (to provide a greater sense of achievement)

- Ensuring that there are meetings with management or immediate superiors (to provide a sense of involvement and recognition)

Job rotation provides the opportunity for the work-force to experience a variety of tasks and as a consequence eliminates to a degree the likelihood of boredom. It also provides an opportunity to experience job enrichment and the possibility of being involved in the whole process of production, which in turn may enhance the opportunities for gaining a sense of achievement.

Question 4

The Power Company manufactures various heaters, drills and electronic products. The work-force is used to being paid enough to maintain a satisfactory standard of living and is provided with a canteen and gym for use during the lunch hour and after work. Absenteeism has always been a problem, as has the number of products that have been returned by customers. The chairman, Andrew Pook, worried about the returns by customers, invited a management consultant to look at the business to provide an objective assessment of where things might be improved. The main issue which arose from the consultant's report was that there was not much variety in the task which each of the 20 employees had to perform and consequently they were all very bored with the work. There was also a flat structure to the organisation that prevented promotion.

a) What are the two signs of low morale which are mentioned in the above case?   [2]

b) Describe how the two signs may affect the business.   [4]

c) How might the work of Herzberg help Andrew Pook to solve the problem in the Power Company?   [6]

Douglas McGregor

The author of *The Human Side of Enterprise* (McGraw-Hill, 1960), he followed the thoughts of Maslow regarding levels of needs, developing these in terms of how managers could benefit from this knowledge. He submitted that the method used by managers to motivate employees depended entirely on the manager's perception of the employees. He divided this into two views of workers and managers:

Theory X and **Theory Y**.

The former concentrated upon the traditional Tayloristic view of man as lacking direction and being motivated only by money.

Consequently management is responsible for the organisation of the business to ensure the economic goals of the business are achieved. Workers are perceived as being lazy, distrustful of management and unwilling to work. Management would be responsible for directing and controlling the work-force to achieve the objectives of the business. Money is used as the main motivator, along with threats of reprisal, sacking, demotion etc. If management were not present the work-force would not be prepared to change and would lack a sense of direction. Finally, management is responsible for rewarding and punishing the work-force.

According to theory Y, people are not innately passive or lacking in direction, nor are they necessarily resistant to change. If these attributes exist it is because of the organisation. All workers within an organisation have the capacity to take on responsibility, be trained to undertake new and varied tasks and be motivated for the benefit of the organisation and themselves. It is the task of management to ensure that the procedures within the business are such that these attributes are allowed to be developed.

Question 5

Donald Adams looked at the notice-board in his works canteen. The managing director of the small engineering company had retired and had been replaced by Thomas Round. Mr Round had moved from a rival business and was famous (in the locality) for encouraging worker involvement and delegating responsibility. This was in contrast to the approach taken by his predecessor, who had issued orders, paid bonuses according to output and been dictatorial with any workers not complying with the many rules and regulations of the business. Donald discussed the change with Valerie who was sorry to see Mr Round coming to the business. Valerie liked the piece-work agreement and enjoyed the security of being told what to do; Donald, on the other hand, craved more responsibility and resented the continual orders – he was looking forward to his future under the new boss.

a) What will be the consequences of a theory X manager trying to motivate a work-force that is interested in taking on more responsibility?   [4]

b) What will be the consequences of a theory Y manager trying to motivate a work-force that is lazy and not interested in work?   [4]

Victor Vroom

In contrast with the other theorists in this unit, Vroom was concerned with the factors that affect the strength of motivation. He developed a formula:

$$M = f (V \times E)$$

M = the degree or strength of motivation

f = a function of (i.e. depends on)

V = **valence**, or the attractiveness or importance of the reward to the individual

E = expectation, or the extent to which the reward is perceived to be achievable.

He therefore stated that strength of motivation depended both on whether the reward was attractive and whether the reward was expected. For instance, if your parents were to offer you £10,000 if you achieved a grade A in your Business Studies A level, you might feel that the reward was attractive, but that the goal was way out of your reach!

Alternatively, if your parents offered you £10 for a grade D, then the target is relatively easy to achieve (high expectation) although the attractiveness of the reward is not particularly exciting!

Tom Peters and Robert Waterman – *In Search of Excellence* (Harper and Row, 1982)

Their work is covered in more detail in Unit 55 Managing change. Two of the main criteria for excellence which they cited were:

Productivity through people – by treating rank and file as a source of quality

Allowing autonomy and decision-making powers to be held on the shopfloor (known as a loose-tight policy). This meant that managers could allow decoration e.g. plant pots, pictures etc., a change in the working day i.e. factors that did not actually make people work harder but which satisfied what they wanted from the 'trimmings' of work. The tight side is required when it comes to unpopular reforms e.g. a change in overtime.

In his book *Thriving on Chaos* (Guild Publishing, 1987), Peters listed 45 objectives for all managers if they wished to run successful, adaptable businesses. He made specific reference to employees in nine of the objectives:

- Applaud champions
- Involve all personnel in all functions
- Organise teams in as many areas of the business as possible
- Invest in human capital as much as hardware
- Provide financial incentives for all
- Guarantee continuous employment for all
- Ensure that front-line people know they are heroes
- Encourage participation
- Share information with everyone

Rosabeth Moss Kanter – Empowerment

Although she wrote several books on change (*see Unit 55*) the issue of empowering an individual has been a preoccupation in Moss Kanter's work. **Empowerment** of an individual simply means delegating authority to someone else, as opposed to managers holding on to the decision making process. In January 1979, she wrote an article in the *Harvard Business Review* on 'Power Failure in Management Circuits' which identified the organisational factors which affect the individuals who have the authority to influence others i.e. her writing was more about management motivation than anything else. She focused primarily on front-line supervisors – those who at times were actually powerless, given that the middle and senior managers took all the decisions and the junior managers did as they were told! This, in turn, led to resistance to change and a conservative approach to management. Her key message was that by empowering others, 'a leader does not decrease his/her power; instead, he may increase it, especially if the whole organisation performs better'.

Activity

Write out the names of the theories mentioned above along with the underlying principles of the theories. Try to establish where one theorist has said the same thing as another, even though it has been given a different title.

Points for Revision

Key Terms

morale	refers to how willing the employees (as one body) are to work i.e. how content they are with work
motivation	from the word motive, why people behave in a certain way
Hawthorne Effect (Mayo)	employees will respond positively to management paying attention to them
hierarchy of needs (Maslow)	managers using higher order needs to motivate e.g. status symbols, will need to be sure that lower order needs (e.g. realistic pay levels) are already in place
two-factor theory	developed by Herzberg; managers must be aware of factors that do not motivate and those that do
motivators (two-factor theory, Herzberg)	factors that motivate – achievement, recognition, advancement, growth, promotion
hygiene (two-factor theory, Herzberg)	factors that by themselves do not motivate, but their absence causes dissatisfaction – payment, working conditions, supervision
Theory X (McGregor)	managers assume workers are lazy, distrustful of management and motivated only by money
Theory Y (McGregor)	managers treat workers with more respect, allow them to take on responsibility and trust them to do the job well
valence (Vroom)	the degree to which the reward is important or attractive
empowerment (Moss Kanter)	giving managers and shopfloor workers the power to take their own decisions

Definitions Question:
By referring to a business you know, explain any three of the above (your teacher may wish to help you choose the terms).   [5] per definition

Summary Points:

1. There has been a wide range of theorists who have commented and written about motivation.

2. Several of the theorists have said broadly the same thing, but used different titles for their writing.

3. The influence of non-financial motivation is significant in certain circumstances, although financial motivation must never be neglected if non-financial motivation is to have the desired effect.

Mini Case Study

Jamie Vernon was puzzled; he had moved from his job in Saudi Arabia where he had employed Indian nationals who used to send the majority of their wages back to Delhi and Bombay. They had not bothered about the number of hours or the nature of the work and were certainly not keen to take on responsibility unless it meant extra pay. He had therefore developed a piece-rate system that allowed the employees to maximise their wages.

The new company had faced a loss in productivity and Jamie's first decision was to introduce the piece-rate system, although looking at the first month's productivity figures, he could not believe that productivity had fallen. 'What do these people want?' he asked the personnel manager. 'The old system' was her reply. She continued, 'The previous managing director had regular meetings with the work-force, asked for their opinions, inviting criticism and recognising the high achievers – they are all keen to take on responsibility and to share views with management. By way of contrast you have completely ignored them and the other managers; I have had people coming to me every day, but you have not allowed me to take any decisions!' James was beginning to see where the problems lay – he would need to take a more involved approach in the business and perhaps listen to the employees in greater detail.

1 Explain how the work of
   McGregor
   Herzberg
   Taylor
   Maslow
   Mayo
   might be applied to the above case.   [15]

2 Stating your reasons, which of the above theorists has the most useful message for
   James?   [5]

   ───────
   20

Maxi Case Study

In 1993 when Leyland Trucks came into existence, there were significant pressures to perform well. The business was formerly known as DAF Trucks, although DAF had gone into receivership and the business was purchased through a management buy-out, from the receivers.

Formerly part of British Leyland the company had to begin by changing the culture of its work-place; British Leyland was the old government-owned company which gained notoriety in the 1970s for poor levels of quality and enormous amounts of working days lost due to militant unions. The issue of collective bargaining remained, although the old confrontational style has since been replaced by something which is altogether different. This has allowed the work-force to be involved in every decision on the shopfloor – from introducing fish tanks to changing the vacation days.

The first change introduced followed a survey carried out by a team of consultants revealing that employees were looking for more responsibility in their work, in terms of assessing quality and introducing ideas for a change in the work-flow. The most radical change was that managers were faced with the introduction of a character assessment which was difficult for most managers to face. Rather than taking the form of an appraisal it was a straightforward attempt to improve the managers' performance and help them think about the way they carried out their job.

The employees who had been used to following orders were suddenly asked to generate their own ideas about production and the tasks they carried out. These changes were based on the idea of recognising contributions of workers, by handing out certificates of achievement. Small gifts were used as a reward and every sensible suggestion was rewarded with a £1 shopping voucher and a thank you letter from the management; as a result there is now an average of 20 suggestions per worker per year. This new approach has resulted in the following changes:

1 Litter bins were suspended on the production line near each lorry cab. Stewart Pierce, the personnel director, stated that it was a worker-generated idea based on the fact that the cab became cluttered with rubbish during the production process and contractors had to be employed to clean it at the end of the line. Now rubbish is binned during production.

2 The assembly of the Isuzu trucks also involved the employees who were asked to look at the problem and the shopfloor teams devised their own plan. The result was a reduction in work-in-progress of nearly £200,000.

3 'Zigzagging' where teams move between two parallel production lines.

Prior to these changes, technical engineers were the people who used to implement such alterations; the managers have learnt to trust the people on the shopfloor who are obviously the experts on the system. Even clocking on and off has been abandoned, given that an integral part of the new system is trust. The improvement in communications is not just due to the new teamwork structure – the production line is also stopped for two hours per month for the chief executive to discuss issues with the employees.

The improvements have been wide-ranging; the break-even figure has been reduced from 11,500 vehicles to 6,000 vehicles, although some of this reduction has been helped by the change to lean production. Accidents have fallen from 96 in 1989, to two in the past three years! There were 28 defects per vehicle in 1989 which have since been reduced to five, with smaller, less significant defects being observed.

The company's managing director, John Oliver, has stated that at no point in time was this seen as a cost-cutting exercise; ironically, as the company has focused less on cost saving, the actual benefit has been greater – this is entirely due, he says, to employees and management working together.

Source: *Financial Times* 9/7/1997

1 Define: management buy-out, receivers, collective bargaining.   [6]

2 Why was it difficult for managers to face criticism from their peers?   [4]

3 Discuss the extent to which theories on motivation can be applied to the changes
   implemented by Leyland Trucks.   [10]

4 Explain why the changes made will have led to a reduction in break-even point.   [5]

5 Discuss how the improvements that were made following the changes might affect
   other parts of the business.   [10]

                                                                                                                        35

Communication

Learning objectives

Having read this unit, students will be able to

1 identify the various types and channels of communication

2 be able to recognise and select an appropriate communicational medium

3 be aware of the barriers to effective communication and be capable of suggesting remedies for these barriers

4 understand the significance of communication for motivation and leadership

Context

If you stand on railway platforms, or listen to the pilot speaking to you over the public address system on your flight to Florida, you may agree that there are many occasions when you are unable to hear what is being said to you. This can be most alarming if you are on a strange platform, or sitting on a train, not quite sure if it is going where you want to go. Note also the reaction of your fellow passengers who thought the announcer said Stafford or Stratford; there is an element of 'No, he said Stretford' which culminates in a breakdown in communication and ultimately chaos. Similarly, imagine a tired businessman who has checked in at a hotel late at night and needs to leave very early the next morning to catch a plane to Canada in order to clinch a contract worth over £4 million. He gives his room number and requests an early alarm call for 5 a.m. and would like a breakfast of cereals, toast and coffee and a taxi to the airport at 5.45 a.m. Relying upon the hotel staff to pass such a message on by word of mouth alone would be highly dangerous! As the message is passed from the reception desk to the night porter and then on to the kitchen night staff and finally to the early morning porter, there is a very high chance that it will get distorted. The resulting error could mean a missed plane and a lucrative contract lost.

What is communication?

In simple terms, it is the transmission of information from one person to another. There are various components to what constitutes communication (*see Figure 51.1*).

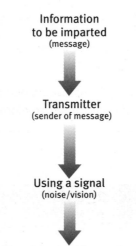

Figure 51.1   Components of communication

There has to be some form of signal that is received if communication is to take place.

Effective communication is achieved when the desired action has taken place.

Question 1

Using Figure 51.1 as a guide, suggest who the transmitter is, who the receiver is and what the signal is for:

Woof-It, a manufacturer of dog food, advertises on TV its latest food for dogs sold in a packet.   [3]

Types of communication

Several types or forms of communication can be used; all are influenced by the message, the sender and the receiver:

One-way and two-way
Formal and informal
Open and closed
Vertical and horizontal

One- and two-way communication

One-way

This is a very simple form of communication (*see Figure 51.2*).

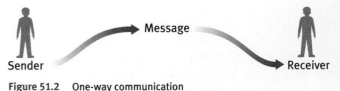

Figure 51.2   One-way communication

The advantages of one-way communication are that it is quick and therefore cheap when compared to two-way communication. There are no pressures upon the sender as a reply is not required. However, this type of communication may suffer from a low degree of accuracy as there is no opportunity to check what has been written or said. It can, as a consequence, be a cause of frustration to the receiver.

Two-way

(*See Figure 51.3.*)

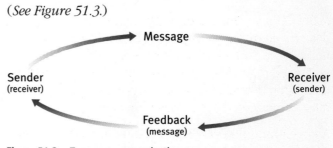

Figure 51.3   Two-way communication

This form of communication is more time-consuming and provides the receiver with an opportunity to question what has been said or written. As a consequence the information is more likely to be understood because clarification is possible. This ability to gain feedback ensures that this is more accurate than one-way communication.

Question 2

When would it be appropriate for a business to use one-way rather than two-way communication?   [4]

Formal and informal communication

One method to help distinguish between these two types is the environment in which the information is being imparted.

Formal

There are set procedures for the information in terms of the media to be used, the style of language and the presentation. For example, many businesses have house rules for how the telephone is to be answered and how letters are written. Communicating through the managerial hierarchy is also an example of **formal communication**; when the process of appraisal takes place to assess the performance of an employee, this will be done usually by the immediate superior. This is a typical illustration of the formal approach, as there will be a pro forma (pre-printed form to be filled in by the employee) followed by an interview which is conducted in a prescribed manner by the superior involved (*see Unit 54*). School reports are another example of formal communication.

Many of these procedures or house rules are determined by the management. Some documentation needs to be formalised; legal papers need to comply with fixed rules if they are to be valid; items such as ownership of land and Certificates of Incorporation must be presented in a standard manner.

A large proportion of the information has to be written in order for records to be kept and to ensure accuracy of the information to be imparted.

Question 3

Make a list of information for which a business would need to use a method of communication which is formal. [4]

Informal

When meeting friends in the local disco, the style will be **informal** as no particular rules have to be complied with. There is no planned agenda, the information passed is of relevance because the people involved are friends, not because of the position they hold. Most importantly, the information is rarely written down, it is mostly spoken. There is an assumption that the information is given because it will be of interest to that particular person.

Question 4

a) Which is the most reliable, formal or informal communication? (State why.) [6]

b) Suggest the factors that would determine whether the communication was formal or informal. [5]

Open and closed communication

These types refer to the language that is used in the communication process.

Open

Open communication has to be universally understood to be effective and assumes no specialist knowledge is required. Stating that there is a new bar of chocolate for sale will be easily understood by any member of the public. Great care has to be taken to ensure the public does understand the message of the advert, which in turn requires careful thought for the selection of the language used.

Closed

The language used may well be understood only by those within the business or a particular group of people. For example, unless you are a golfer, the terms birdie, eagle and albatross may mean very little to you other than that they appear to be connected to flying creatures! This **closed communication** is appropriate when in golfing circles but not in general conversation. A student and a teacher may refer to GCSEs, AS levels, OCR and an A level grade of N, but much of this would not be understood by a person who has very little to do with education.

Question 5

Indicate which type of communication (open or closed) is being used in the following examples:

i) Virgin Airlines booking slots for its planes to land at Gatwick airport
ii) Asda ordering stock from Heinz
iii) Two computer technicians holding a conversation at work [3]

Vertical and horizontal communication

(*See Figures 51.4 and 51.5.*)

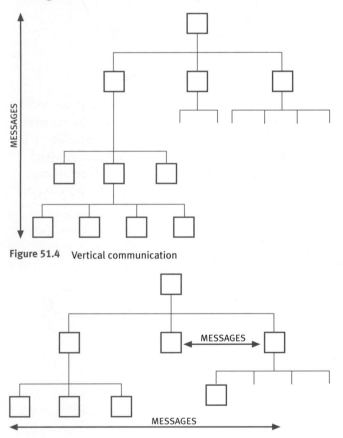

Figure 51.4 Vertical communication

Figure 51.5 Horizontal communication

These terms are sometimes referred to within channels of communication. A look at a typical organisational chart of a business shows the lines of communication which are most used.

Vertical

The vertical channels or lines of communication are usually used when information or instructions are handed down from the management to the shopfloor (or from employers to employees) and when information or suggestions are passed upwards to ensure the management is kept informed as to what is happening and whether its wishes are being implemented. Valuable information can be passed to the management from the employees that may well influence the decision making process.The employees have an opportunity to state their view of the business which ensures management is kept in touch with the feelings of the employees. **Vertical communication** provides a channel for feedback for both employers and employees and at the same time ensures that there is a sense of involvement within the business which aids the motivational process (*see Unit 50 Non-financial motivation*).

Horizontal (or lateral)

This is when communication takes place between personnel on the same level within the organisation. Two employees within the sales team of the marketing department discussing the best way of meeting their sales targets or two directors deciding whether to purchase a new machine are suitable examples. **Horizontal communication** can be very beneficial when trying to appreciate the views and priorities of other departments within an organisation.

Question 6

State which types of communication are being used for each of the following:

e.g.

A tennis coach addressing 30 children on the basics of the backhand – Formal, one-way, closed.

a) Teacher discussing the general issues of education with a group of parents.
b) A business advertising a radical programme of price cuts.
c) Two adults talking about their time together at school.
d) A Board meeting of a business discussing a report prepared by the finance department on the viability of an investment proposal. [12]

Communication networks

There is no set route for communication within a business. The route, or **network** as it is normally referred to, shows the path of information around the business. Networks will exist where the size of the business precludes an informal system of communication, which is possible if there are only one or two people involved.

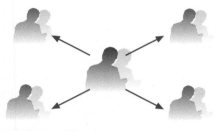

Central figure – Managing Director
Headquarters – or regional officers

Figure 51.6A   Communication networks: the wheel

See Figure 51.6A – the 'Wheel'. The central person (or head office) in the wheel is seen as the leader and as such is in a good position to be able to have an overview of the department or business. All communication goes through the leader, enabling contact with all regions or personnel within a department. The wheel network tends to be associated with vertical communication.

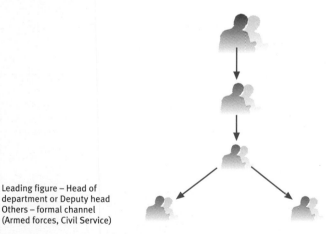

Leading figure – Head of
department or Deputy head
Others – formal channel
(Armed forces, Civil Service)

Figure 51.6B   Communication networks: the chain

See Figure 51.6B – the 'Chain' is best represented by a large, highly formalised organisation such as the civil service or the armed forces. Information is passed up and down, each person receiving the information and then in turn passing it on to the next person in the chain.

This has the possible advantage of allowing the person at the top of the organisation to have an overview of the information that needs to be passed down.

The problem with this network is the effect it has on the people at the bottom who rarely have the opportunity to communicate directly with those at the top of the hierarchy of the business and thus may be demotivated and somewhat left out.

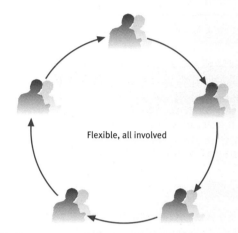

Flexible, all involved

Figure 51.6C   Communication networks: the circle

See Figure 51.6C – the 'Circle' is a restricted network as communication takes place between only two people or departments at any one time. Communication on a wider scale takes a lot longer, as it has to be passed around the group from one to another stage by stage. This particular network is appropriate for those on the same level of business.

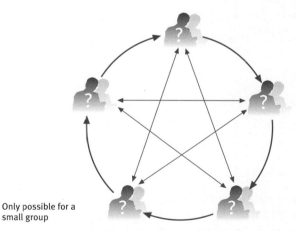

Only possible for a
small group

Figure 51.6D   Communication networks: all-channel

See Figure 51.6D – the 'All-channel' network, unlike the others considered, has no set channels and is therefore more appropriate for smaller groups that do not require a highly organised or formalised system of communication. The flexibility of this network allows it to be used as required, enabling all personnel to contribute to solving a problem or developing a new product. It is not a particularly fast network because there is no set procedure to ensure all participants receive the information to be imparted. It is also susceptible to a dominant personality taking control but at the same time its flexibility allows for different leaders to be used, depending on the task in hand.

Question 7

a) Suggest which of the networks are more likely to be associated with particularly large groups, stating your reasons.   [6]

b) Which networks would be quicker to make a decision, if an emergency solution was required?   [4]

Question 8

How would you decide which network was the most appropriate for a particular business?   [7]

Communication media

Spoken (or oral)

e.g. face-to-face, telephone, radio, public address, video-links

Written

e.g. notice, letter, newspaper, magazine, report, book, fax, e-mail, ISDN.

■ Spoken

The spoken word is by far the most used and can take place face-to-face or between people who are many thousands of miles apart. It is much more personal and has the advantage of providing additional signals such as facial expression and other body language that can be used by both the sender and the receiver to aid the understanding of the information to be imparted. In addition, face-to-face may encourage discussion which

in turn may generate ideas and enhance team spirit. It conversely has the disadvantage of not permitting the sender to hide his/her true feelings about the message to be given. The telephone is quite useful when compared with face-to-face communication if the message being sent or received is difficult for whatever reason!

The telephone provides convenience to a business and is a very cheap method of communication, due to the amount of time saved by not having to meet people who may be miles away.

The more people to be addressed at any one time, the more likely a public address system is to be used; though with the development of pagers, three-way lines on phones and other such techniques, there are now fewer examples of this. Public announcements are still made at airports, football matches and within businesses, to contact a particular person who could be anywhere in the building. Apart from pagers reducing the need for the last example cited, even small businesses such as restaurants are using alternatives to the public address system. In the United States, it is commonplace in restaurants to call customers to their table by using a device which pulsates when summoned; putting such a device in your pocket will mean the summons is a subtle way of communicating as opposed to the nuisance or embarrassment of a mobile phone ringing.

■ Written

The written word enables the information to be read several times to ensure it is understood. It can be stored and referred to at a later date, thus providing a useful record of what has been agreed or of what was required by a customer. There is a variety of written forms of communication that are used in business, ranging from a memo which may consist of just a few words, informing employees of a change in the holiday arrangements or how they should claim for their petrol expenses, to a company report to be issued to shareholders.

Reports are of interest as many students will be required to produce such a document for their coursework. Reports tend to be formal in their format and usually are laid out using some or all of the following sections:

Title
Terms of reference/Objectives
Introductory comments
Data collected
Implications for the business
Conclusions
Recommendations/Proposals
Appendices

All forms of the written word are more expensive than the spoken word, not only in terms of producing but in terms of absorbing. Which type of written communication is used will depend upon the nature of the information to be communicated and the number of people who are required to receive it. According to Sir John Harvey-Jones, former chairman of ICI, presenter of a TV series on business and successful author, 'Written words are notoriously difficult to use as a method of communication, since there are few of us who can write clearly and concisely. Moreover, written words are seldom personal.' (*Managing to Survive*, Penguin, 1993). (*See also the use of Information Technology in Unit 25 Technology*).

Question 9

a) Produce a summary of the main advantages and disadvantages of three written and three oral communication media.   [12]

b) There are many factors that influence the medium used to impart information:

i) the message to be imparted – the seriousness of the message will affect the medium because of the accuracy that is required in conjunction with how urgent the message is. If a member of the family has suddenly been taken ill, there will be a sense of urgency coupled with a desire to ensure that the message is received. Whereas a message to a friend who has been away from school, concerning the homework to be attempted, often seems to lack the same degree of urgency and accuracy!

ii) the status of the sender and the receiver – information that has to be given to a prospective customer will use language that is appropriate.

iii) the context/environment – whether the situation is formal or informal will affect the medium and the vocabulary that is used

iv) the medium to be used – this is not a mistake, as the type of information to be imparted affects the medium to be used so too does the medium used affect the message that is imparted and how it is imparted. Some things are best said face-to-face rather than relying upon a fax or e-mail.

Use the answer to **a)** to suggest the most appropriate media to use for the following:

1) A Ltd company wishes to inform its employees of forthcoming redundancies.

2) A business needs to inform customers who have purchased a particular model of kettle that it ought to be returned to the retailer for a safety check.   [6]

Barriers to effective communication

According to Shannon and Weaver's theory of communication, there are three distinct areas that are the cause of ineffective communication.

■ Technical

This is concerned with the physical ability to receive the message. The receiver must be capable of hearing and seeing the information to be imparted. If for any reason the message cannot be read or the voice cannot be heard, as suggested at the railway station, then effective communication has not taken place.

■ Semantic

This is concerned with the understanding of the message. Assuming the message has been heard or seen, the receiver must understand the language used or the symbols seen before the communication is complete.

■ Effectiveness

Finally, assuming the message has overcome the first two hurdles, communication is only truly complete when the appropriate action or response is made by the receiver.

The technical problems are relatively easy to identify and solve.

The semantic problems are relatively easy to identify, but are harder to solve.

What is important to those in business is that they are aware of the problems and can therefore take the appropriate actions to either avoid or remedy them.

Question 10

Suggest, using Shannon and Weaver's categories, which type of problem the following represent:

i) Inability of a passenger to read the TV monitor at a railway station, because the screen has condensation on it.   [3]

ii) Your business studies lesson being conducted in a foreign language.   [3]

iii) An employee has failed to comply with a new work rota that had been given out by hand to the person and signed as being understood.   [3]

iv) An inspector at the local bus station has been asked to take a look at a new female driver.
Explain your answer.   [3]

There are further barriers to effective communication:

These further barriers can be easily divided into those related to

a) the people involved
b) the organisation

The skills of the people involved, namely the sender and the receiver, are the key to the effectiveness of any communication. The sender's choice of words bearing in mind the message and the person who is to receive the message is crucial. The timing of the communication and the medium chosen by the sender will also influence how the message is received.

If the bell has gone to signal the end of a lesson and you are asked whether you understand a complicated mathematical formula, it may be quite likely that you indicate that you do! The same may be true within a business; not hearing the phone ring a couple of minutes before the end of the day is commonplace.

The views and perception of the receiver will also be important in determining the effectiveness of the communication. Much will depend upon past events; a manager who has proved to be honest when negotiating with employees is more likely to gain a favourable hearing than one who was less truthful. Similarly, trying to convince an elderly female customer to try the latest fashion in clothes may be a lot harder than persuading a teenager who will be only too keen to listen and absorb the message given.

The type and efficiency of the organisation will impinge upon the effectiveness of communication; the larger the organisation, the more opportunities there are for a breakdown in communication.

The type of business is significant; if a noisy industrial process is undertaken, this will present more problems for effective communication than a quiet factory or office.

Points for Revision

Key Terms

vertical communication	communication between different levels within the business
horizontal communication	communication between people on the same level of the business
formal	utilising set procedures and channels for communication
informal	no set or authorised procedure or channel for communication
open communication	using language that is understood by all
closed communication	using language that is understood only by those who need to know
networks	different channels or patterns of communication

Definitions Question:
With reference to a firm or firms of which you have direct knowledge or experience, explain the importance of any three of the above key terms (your teacher may wish to select the terms).   [5] per definition

Summary Points:

1   For communication to take place there needs to be a sender and a receiver.

2   There are several forms of communication e.g. formal and informal.

3   Barriers to communication exist that reduce the effectiveness of communication.

4   There are many examples of communication media which are vehicles for transmitting and receiving information.

Mini Case Study

Mr Newton ran a successful franchise business, cleaning carpets and lounge suites. He advertised on a regular basis in his local newspaper which highlighted the virtues of his service to potential customers. His telephone number was always included in the advert to enable people either to ring with enquiries or to book his services.

Unfortunately, there had been a growing number of problems with the advertisements. Either the wrong telephone number was published or the printing was slightly smudged, making the telephone number difficult to read. In addition, his telephone answering machine was proving unreliable and as a result he was starting to lose orders. When customers were able to leave a message, it was often cut short for some unknown reason.

His friend had suggested he invest in a fax machine as it would print out the customer's requirements or enquiries, unlike the telephone.

1 Using Shannon and Weaver's model, suggest what type of communication problems Mr Newton is facing.   [2]

2 Suggest the main barriers to effective communication that affected the use of the telephone apart from the points made in your answer to question 1.   [3]

3 Would you recommend that Mr Newton invested in a fax machine? Justify your answer.   [6]

4 What other media could Mr Newton use to ensure that potential customers are not lost? Explain your suggestions.   [5]

5 Throughout his working day, suggest the types of communication he is most likely to use.   [4]

20

Maxi Case Study

Black and Decker, the manufacturer of household electrical tools such as drills and saws, has been keen to improve communications between the various divisions within the company.

One of the major difficulties facing any business the size of Black and Decker is coping with the inevitable barriers to effective communication due to the number of tiers within the organisation. The simple and speedy exchange of ideas and comments within the organisation tends to be reduced to a snail's pace as information is passed from department to department and from division to division. Unfortunately, as the pace of communication slows down so does the ability of the business to respond quickly to any changes in the market, whether from consumer requests or competitor actions. In addition, the lead time for new products has been hindered by the communicational problems.

Black and Decker's European division has taken drastic action to alleviate the problems by altering its organisational structure. At its large plant at Spennymoor in Durham, which employs around 2,000 people, every attempt has been made to break down the functional barriers between the different departments such as marketing, production and research.

There was a realisation that the design, production and marketing of products produced by Black and Decker was a process that impinged on many different departments and as a consequence, it was preferable to appoint someone who could be responsible for the process as a whole. Appointing one person, Bob Bowlam, as technology director for the consumer product division, enabled him to have an overview and link different departments who previously tended to be rather insular. Because Mr Bowlam was dealing with the design of new products and at the same time considering the needs of the consumer and how the production workers would be best able to produce the goods, it was easier to ensure all the departments were involved as one and not as separate entities.

He was also able to use his awareness of new production techniques to the advantage of the business because he was able to see how these could be used for the production of consumer and industrial products. A case in point was his knowledge of a new welding technique that could be used in design and production in many parts of the business. If the research department had discovered it, it would not necessarily be aware of a potential application for it in the design department. Such a technique would allow the design department to consider smaller gauge materials, thus providing a greater variety of designs at probably lower cost.

At the Spennymoor factory changes to the structure of the business were made to 'democratise' the decision making process. The normal channels of communication whereby the shopfloor operatives reported to their immediate superiors, historically their supervisors or quality control personnel, were radically altered. The new communicational channels encouraged discussions between teams of workers who were responsible for the production of specific items. Two or three members of each production team met to share ideas, discuss problems and consider solutions. 'Coaches' were appointed to act as a link with the production teams and the management. The business structure has therefore become a lot flatter than was the case before implementation of the changes.

Black and Decker also gave its vice-president the task of linking the various units of the business world-wide to ensure they were aware of one another's activities rather than to allow them to operate in isolation. By doing this the business ensured that information that would be beneficial to all was communicated as a matter of course.

1 Define: barriers to effective communication, organisational structure, communication channels.   [6]

2 Why might lead times slowing down be a problem?   [3]

3 Suggest how the change to democratic decision making might improve communication within the business.   [3]

4 How has communication improved at Black and Decker as a result of the new structure?   [3]

5 Suggest whether you think as a result of the changes, there has been a change in the type of communication network that operates at Black and Decker.   [3]

6 Would making the organisational structure more horizontal improve communication? [4]

7 Discuss the implications for the type of media used as a result of the changes made at Black and Decker.   [8]

30

Leadership and management

Learning objectives

Having read this unit, students will be able to

1. understand the different styles of leadership

2. demonstrate the consequences and appropriateness of various styles of leadership

3. understand the role of management and how it differs from leadership

'Leaders do the right thing; management do things right' Walter Bennis

Context

Looking through the business section of any newspaper, you will find references to a variety of chairpeople and managing directors. Alternatively, the back pages may well refer to football managers and the front pages to military leaders, politicians or royalty. Most people who regularly make the national newspapers do so because they are leaders; they have become leaders either because they have been born into a family which has inherited leadership or because they have become leaders through their personality, character and beliefs. Leaders provide a vital focal point for any organisation and when a business or organisation fails it can be due to ineffective leadership. The word lead is an Anglo-Saxon word meaning road, or way, whereas the word management is different – this comes from the Latin word *manus*, or hand, in the context of handling a sword, ship or horse. Nowadays it tends to be closely linked to any resource a business uses. Management, therefore, is something different from leadership. Everyone needs to be able to manage at some time during life: managing cash, managing people, managing time, managing change, managing shareholders, the list is endless. This unit will therefore consider leadership and management separately, then make a comparison between the two.

Leadership

What is leadership?

Providing a clear definition of leadership is impossible. There are so many examples of good leadership and even more ways of describing it. One of the tasks set for you at the end of this unit is to define leadership in 25 words, although you will find this very difficult to do. The reason is that leadership involves a process which includes the leader, those who are led and the situation in which leadership is present.

The trait theory

The debate over whether leaders are born or made has caused several management writers to produce tomes of research, none of which has produced a satisfactory conclusion. What is certain, however, in the minds of such writers is that in order to be a leader it is necessary to display certain personal qualities. These will vary from person to person and there is not one particular characteristic which, on its own, makes a person a leader. However, by describing the following famous leaders in terms of their personality, it is possible to draw together a series of words which describe a leader's character:

- Mother Teresa
- Mahatma Gandhi
- Moses
- Margaret Thatcher
- Bill Gates

Qualities such as vision, judgement, commitment, knowledge, will-power, energy and drive, ambition, sensitivity to others, communication skills, strongly held personal beliefs – all these descriptions, and many others, show that the **trait theory** (the belief that leaders develop from their own personal qualities) can be substantiated by considering leaders past and present.

Question 1

Write down the names of five leaders that you would rate as the five most influential individuals in history. List their personal qualities. Is there a common quality which you think is most appropriate to leadership?

[8]

Question 2

In 1998, Malcolm Walker, Chief Executive of Iceland, the frozen food retailer, made a statement that his company was going to concentrate on pure foods and shun genetically modified foods. One year later, when GM foods received very bad publicity and caught the big retailers out, Iceland's sales had risen by 10% against the competition.

To what extent does this decision illustrate the trait theory?

[4]

The situation theory

Definition: leadership is a function of the situation or context in which potential leaders find themselves. Although leaders need certain personal qualities, they must also be allowed to lead in a context which is appropriate for their qualities to come through. It is frequently asserted that neither Hitler nor Winston Churchill would have made their mark in history were it not for the situation in which they rose to power. The **situation theory** therefore contradicts the contention that leaders have natural qualities; rather it is the situation in which leaders find themselves that determines their success as a leader. J.M. Barrie's story *The Admirable Crichton* concerns an aristocratic family that becomes shipwrecked on an island in the middle of the ocean. The butler, who is far more expert at survival and more resourceful takes over as head of the family and manages them back to safety. Once back home, the roles are reversed to their original states, and the butler takes up his position as head of the servants, with the family back in charge. You may be able to think of people you know – captain of sports, school prefect, leader of an orchestra, who become leader in certain contexts, although do not presume to be leader in everything they do i.e. leadership comes to the fore in certain situations.

Leadership styles

Given the characteristics and situation in which leaders operate, there is another dimension to leadership which is the style adopted. Some leaders prefer to lead on their own, with no reference to others in terms of consultation and involvement, while at the other extreme, leaders prefer to step back from the responsibility of taking decisions and leave it up to the group being led. Each style of leadership can have significant repercussions on whether individual, group or task needs are satisfied.

Autocratic – a dominant leader who decides by him/herself, without consultation with others. Decisions are therefore taken based on the experience and wisdom of one individual and tend to be less popular than if there were some form of group consensus. Education analogy – the teacher walks into the classroom and informs you of the subject matter and exercises which you will be studying in a particular lesson.

Democratic – a leader who actively encourages the sharing of ideas amongst the group and asks the group for their opinions. Whilst not everyone's opinion will be satisfied, at least there will have been a chance to air views, which arguably makes employees feel they are involved in the decision making process. Education analogy – the teacher, probably going through revision of a subject, will ask you what you would like to revise, taking a vote to find the most demanded topic.

Laissez-faire – literally translated as 'leave to do', this style of leadership is more like abdication of leadership than anything else. Here the leader has almost no influence on the group which decides everything. Education analogy – the teacher announces (at the beginning of the sixth form) that it is up to the students to organise themselves. You are then given a) the specifications (syllabus) b) books c) the exam date and you are told to visit the teacher if you require help with anything (*see Figure 52.1*).

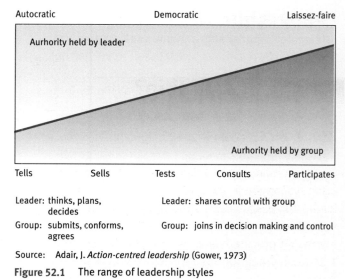

Source: Adair, J. *Action-centred leadership* (Gower, 1973)

Figure 52.1 The range of leadership styles

Question 3

In each of the following examples, explain why each person described fits a particular leadership style:

Alan Sugar, the man responsible for rescuing Tottenham Hotspur from the brink of liquidation, made his name as a pioneer of the home computer. He identified the need for home computers in the early 1980s and had several very successful years, including a flotation. He was described in several articles and by several business commentators as dictatorial, aggressive and determined. He insisted that all decisions went through his office and he never let anyone else take responsibility for a decision unless he had been briefed beforehand. Following several years of unimpressive performance, he tried to buy back all the shares single-handedly, so as to regain control of his company.

Richard Branson was also a product of the 1980s, starting business selling advertising space in a magazine. The size of his business grew quickly and he was keen to identify growth markets, making the Virgin name synonymous with something new and exciting. The business spread across an enormous range of diverse products – vodka, radio, financial products, cola, rail travel, to name but a few. He has always claimed that open discussion with employees and a thoughtful, motivated management team have been the key to his success. While he still likes to have his finger on the pulse, so to speak, he does also delegate responsibility and allows talent to come through. His recent venture into rail travel has not been as successful as other products under the Virgin banner and he has had to take responsibility for this.

Ricardo Semler (see Maxi Case Study, Unit 48 Organisational Structures)

Ricardo Semler (*see Maxi Case Study, Unit 48 Organisational Structures*) followed in his father's footsteps but wanted to generate a business environment with a difference; one where the employees had the tightest control over their work-place. Hiring and firing of employees, wage levels and other major decisions were left to the factory committees to take. Although he admits that there are some employees who abuse this privilege, he has developed this culture to such an extent that most see the benefits and act in accordance with the wishes of the group. His main goal in the business (as described by himself) is to 'get people to decide things for themselves'.   3 × [4]

An alternative style of leadership is one which emphasises concern for the needs of workers beyond the immediate working environment. The word **paternalistic** means fatherly i.e. the leader will try to engender family spirit and a sense of belonging. This is achieved by provision of additional facilities such as housing, social and sporting clubs as well as paying profit-related bonuses and actively showing interest in the work-force and individual career development.

Consequences of the above styles

Autocratic

- Work-force is not encouraged to think for itself
- Emphasis is more on quantity than quality
- The leader is detached
- Decisions are made on the opinions of one person
- Leader insists on every decision going through him/her
- Group not responsible for actions
- Decisions can be made quickly without the series of meetings and discussions associated with democratic leadership
- Emphasis on decision taking rather than decision making
- Uses one-way communication with consequently no opportunity for feedback

Democratic

- Opinions listened to, although not always considered in the final decision
- Slower decision making process
- Group actively involved in all aspects of the business and encouraged to take responsibility for decisions made
- Two-way communication is the norm

Laissez-faire

- Every member's opinions taken into account when making decisions
- Very difficult to arrive at a consensus, so decisions take a long time to be made, but usually encompass all views; often a compromise rather than the best option results
- Numerous discussions and deliberations which add unnecessary costs to a business

Factors affecting leadership style

- **Preference of leader in terms of personal characteristics** – the leader may be a person who likes to feel in control, leading to an autocratic style

- **History of the business** – a family business may well be more autocratic, although equally likely, it could take a paternalistic approach to management and consult employees

- **The job/task which needs to be performed** – the more complicated a task, the greater the direction which is needed

- **The attitude of the work-force** – some employees may not be interested in taking part in the decision making process

■ Markets in which the business operates

– a fast changing market may need quick decisions to be made, whereas a highly technical market may need shared experience in developing new products

There have been many individual management writers who have commented on the significance of leadership, most of whom have produced theories which are similar to the above, although have different terminology associated with them:

Adair – Action-centred leadership

John Adair, in his book *Understanding Motivation* (Gower, 1990), set out his theory using the following diagram:

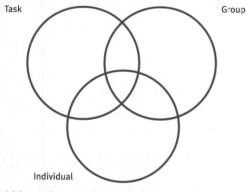

Source: Adair, J. *Action-centred leadership* (Gower, 1973)

Figure 52.2

He stated that 'Leadership is about teamwork in that teams need to have leaders and leaders tend to create teams.'

Any group therefore shares three areas of need:
1 the need to accomplish a task
2 the need to be seen and maintained as a cohesive unit
3 the need to satisfy an individual's needs within that group

If the leader fails to achieve/take account of all three simultaneously, then the failure to achieve one will affect the other two. In the above diagram, place a coin over one of the circles, which will block out some of the other two circles e.g. if the group fails to achieve its task, or even does not get set a clear task, then this will lower group cohesion as the group will ask 'Why have we been created?' and it will lower individual satisfaction, because of the lack of direction. He also created a 50-50 rule, which stated that 50% of motivation comes from within an individual and 50% comes from the leader.

Walter Bennis

Bennis identified four key abilities in a study of 90 American public figures; these are the management of:
1 attention – by creating a vision that others can believe in and adopt as their own; this provides a link between the short term and the long term. He cites Martin Luther King and Lee Iacocca of Chrysler as two exponents of this
2 communication – the ability to communicate ideas to those being led is of paramount importance. Many chief executives now place a high value on the company's long-term vision, which must be shared by all employees
3 trust – perhaps one of the main reasons why Richard Branson commands such respect within his empire is because the employees of Virgin feel that he can be trusted to be true to his word
4 self – if the individual has persistence, commitment and is willing to take risks and learn from mistakes, then future leadership will be effective. One of the most frequent problems of leadership is early success. The example of Sir Clive Sinclair inventing the pocket calculator and then failing dramatically when he thought he was a visionary businessman – with the Sinclair C5, described by Richard Stilgoe, a songwriter, as the electric bedroom slipper – is a case in point (*see Unit 11 Introduction to marketing*)

Likert

Rennis Likert was a believer in participative management. So much so that some of his critics commented on the unrealistic assumption that group discussion was the only way forward. He sent detailed questionnaires to various US companies and then made a profile of four different and progressive leadership styles, relating each one to performance.

1 Exploitative authoritarian – essentially management by fear, communication is one-way (top–down) with superiors and subordinates a long way apart

2 Benevolent authoritarian – management by carrot rather than by stick; any information which flows upwards is likely to be only what the management wishes to hear. All policy decisions are taken at the top, with minor unimportant ones delegated

3 Consultative – there is communication both ways and management does attempt to discuss matters with employees, but major decisions are still taken at the top

4 Participative management – sets challenging goals for the work-force and works closely with teams of workers

Blake and Mouton

They devised a matrix of management styles, contrasting those that demonstrated a concern primarily for production, or the task/product, with those that gave priority to people. Some managers had concern for both and the extent of the balance determined how they acted in certain situations (*see Figure 52.3*).

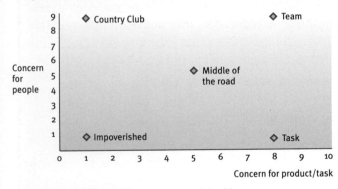

Figure 52.3   Blake and Mouton managerial grid

Examine the following situations and plot where you think each leadership style appears on the Blake and Mouton Grid:

a) a dictatorial headmistress obsessed with league tables at the expense of everything else in the school. She expected staff to come in at all hours for no extra money, stating that 'they should want to get good results for their charges'

b) the captain of a rugby team who felt that as a captain he would be liked as an individual. He went out of his way to buy his team drinks and seemed much more concerned about being seen to be a good chap, rather than talking to his team about tactics

c) a groundsman who had been on a supervisory studies course to perfect his management skills. He showed equal concern for both the people who worked for him and for getting the job done, although he did not always like to push himself for the sake of the organisation. He was occasionally late for work and never stayed a minute after 5.00 p.m.

d) the manager who took over his father's company, intent on living off the profits; he cared only for himself, which was why it was likely that the business would fail within six months

[8]

Mini Case Study

James Eason looked proudly at the profit statement which had just come back from the auditors: a 20% increase in profit despite only a 13% increase in sales. 'That cost-cutting exercise has worked wonders to our bottom-line of profit,' he thought to himself. Following a poor year when strong competition had forced the business to look for new products, James was sure he had turned the business round. He had employed two new managers: Jane Invent was hired to develop new products, and Malcolm Motivator was hired to drive the work-force to increase productivity. James was famous for trying to discuss issues with other managers, then ignoring their advice and going ahead regardless. Despite an in-depth research programme on changing customer wants which highlighted how outdated their products were, James ignored the messages until profit was affected.

The employees immediately took to the idea of teamwork introduced by Malcolm; they had been longing to get involved with decision making. In actual fact, the business had cut costs due to decisions made by the work-force, as opposed to decisions from James himself.

Malcolm was hired because James's threats to sack lazy workers had resulted in an increase in labour turnover to 15% in one year; Malcolm had pointed out some fundamental flaws in James's management style, although James had been quick to defend his own actions, stating that employees require firm, decisive leadership.

1 Explain how Jane Invent might be helped by a team approach to new product development. [4]

2 With reference to the ideas on leadership developed in the unit,

  a) Comment on the approach to leadership taken by James. [6]

  b) Discuss whether an alternative style might be appropriate in this case. [10]

20

Mini Case Study

John Hars, the managing director of Chip-It, a food packaging company, stared in exasperation and disbelief at the third report of 4,000 words which had just arrived on his desk. He had an in-tray jammed with the minutes of several committees and a meeting with the new chairman to discuss the recent change in company policy. Earlier that year John had attended a lecture on participative management which had been given by Tom Peters, the management writer. Peters had expounded the virtues of a democratic approach to management from getting involved on the shopfloor to having worker-directors.

On his return, Hars had invited employees to volunteer for discussion groups and he had set up several committees to look at

Efficiency at work
Health and safety at work
Employee involvement

The chairman was particularly keen to encourage this approach, although John was now beginning to have his doubts. There seemed to be endless minutes to write up, factory committees shooting up out of nowhere, each publishing agendas and minutes. Profit was down for the year and some quick decisions had to be made; new machinery, bought last year, was unproductive and he suspected redundancies were needed along with a reorganisation of the shopfloor to make the machinery more productive. The business also had to take a decision on whether to take on four extra customers, one of which was a blue-chip food manufacturer, making breakfast cereals. The constant committees, reports and minutes were beginning to make the business slow to react to change and were also increasing costs without the corresponding increase in sales. Despite that, he reflected, at least the employees have stopped grumbling and do seem happy with working here – labour turnover was at only 2%.

1 What are the advantages of setting up committees to solve problems?   [4]

2 Explain the style of leadership, with reference to theorists, adopted by John Hars in this
   case.   [6]

3 Discuss whether the company might benefit from a change in leadership style.   [10]

                                                                                    20

By examining the material in both case studies above, discuss why certain leadership styles are appropriate in some cases, but not in others. [10]

Management

It is important to distinguish between the functions of management and the role of a leader. It is perfectly possible to observe leaders who are ineffective managers and managers who are ineffective leaders.

What is management?

In a similar way to leadership, it is almost impossible to define management. As you read through this section, try to meet the same challenge that was set about leadership i.e. describe the meaning of management in fewer than 25 words. Robert Heller, the editor of *Management Today*, once said any attempt to define management is doomed to failure because 'Any definition must be right, because almost any definition must fit something so amorphous and shifting.' He was referring to the way that a manager's role is continually evolving and changing.

What do managers do?

Before considering the nature and function of a manager, it is necessary to provide a context. Think about the way your day is structured; you may well begin thinking about your day by setting the alarm the previous evening, having done some homework which is due in the following morning. You will have packed your sports kit, having had it washed beforehand because you have a fixture to attend tomorrow afternoon. Without giving it a moment's thought, you will have been involved in a process of planning and organising even before the day has begun. Once the day has begun, as a school prefect, you may have had to deal with some awkward

individuals in the dinner queue and possibly then planned a rota of something or other. At the end of the match you get together with the team and discuss where things went wrong in the 6–0 thrashing you received from a local rival.

All the above points to a day full of management responsibility. The focus of management is not just your own life, but those for whom you have responsibility.

As early as 1910 Henri Fayol identified five particular elements of management as:

- **Planning** – this will involve the process of forecasting; based on the forecast of e.g. sales revenue, the manager must build a work-force plan to assess how many employees will be needed to meet sales targets

- **Organising** – money, people and functions will need to be organised in order to meet sales targets

- **Command** – this will involve maintaining activity through various methods of motivation. If the resources that are co-ordinated are unproductive, then management will be unable to achieve the company's objectives

- **Controlling** – this involves checking performance against previous yardsticks such as sales revenue, profit and productivity

- **Co-ordinating** – on its own this is meaningless; co-ordination involves all the other four in the pursuit of the organisation's objectives

Using the description of the typical day of a sixth former, highlight where Fayol's elements fit into the day. [5]

Fayol believed that a manager produced his best performance not just by leadership qualities, but also by his knowledge of the business and by the ability to instil a sense of purpose in his employees. From his experience in industry, he built up 14 principles of management:

Management according to Fayol

1. Division of labour
2. Authority to carry out the job
3. Discipline in the employees
4. Unity of command – one boss per employee
5. Unity of direction
6. Appropriate pay for effort
7. Subordinate individual interest to group
8. Centralisation
9. Scalar chain (need for hierarchy)
10. Social order
11. Equal treatment of employees
12. Stability of tenure for employees
13. Initiative of thought
14. *Esprit de corps*

Management according to Drucker

Peter Drucker is probably the most influential writer on management in the twentieth century. His main work, *The Practice of Management* (Harper and Row, 1954), provided the framework on which many other writers hung their own ideas. His idea on what made a manager was very similar to Fayol's:

■ Setting objectives
■ Organising activities and people to achieve the objectives
■ Motivating (through pay, promotion etc.) and constantly communicating with subordinates
■ Establishing measurements (yardsticks) i.e. methods by which people and managers can assess their own performance
■ Developing people, including him/herself

This further role of developing people meant that managers not only work to achieve the organisation's objectives, but also help the people within the organisation to achieve their own objectives and careers.

The key link in all of this is management by objectives which became the hallmark of success.

Management by objectives: although this was developed nearly 50 years ago, it is a firmly held belief that the pursuit of objectives forms the basis for all management. Most companies will state their objectives clearly and some may well have them emblazoned across the factory walls (*see Unit 7 Objectives and strategy*). Drucker based this theory on work he carried out at General Electric; each manager was in charge of a profit centre and given two targets to achieve – 7% profit margin and 20% return on net assets (*see Unit 38 Ratio and analysis*). Failure to achieve these annually meant you lost your job! His thinking centred on the principle that a business survived based on profit and corporate goals should be built according to this and nothing else. This clearly brought criticism for not taking into account the theories on motivation.

Handy

Charles Handy has written several books on management and how the role of the manager is now distinct from what it has been perceived to be throughout history, by managers and writers alike. In *The Age of Unreason* (Arrow Books, 1995) he cited three particular concepts which organisations had to face up to if they were to survive into the new millennium. In some ways he developed the ideas which were created by Fayol and Drucker and in others he stated that a radical change was required in the way in which managers perceived their role in organisations.

The Shamrock Business: the way that organisations are structured is ever-changing. One interpretation (*developed in greater detail in Unit 48 Organisational structures*) is the organisation that has three parts – the core of managers, the flexible employees and the contracted-out services and manufacture. The number of core managers is decreasing, so there is an expectation that those remaining will need to be more flexible and responsive to change, both internal and external. Individual training will become more commonplace as managers seek to expand their skills to adapt.

The Triple I: competitive business will need to use three areas to guarantee any chance of success. I3 = AV, where AV means added value and the I3 stands for intelligence, information and ideas. The old adage that large amounts of land, assets and market presence were sufficient for business success has to all intents and purposes disappeared. There will still be mundane jobs to organise for management to oversee – letters to be opened, visitors catered for, meetings arranged etc. and these jobs will never be automated, but there must be sufficient added value in order to pay for these extras.

The Inverted Doughnut: see Figure 52.4.
A doughnut is round with a hole in the middle. The inverted doughnut has the solid part in the middle with space outside. The analogy is that there will always be a part of any job which is clearly defined, which is the heart or the core of the doughnut. These may well be written down in a contract, but a job of importance means that the individual is expected to develop the function and improve on that which went before i.e. to

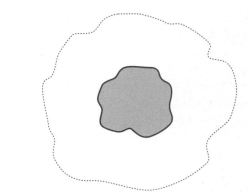

Figure 52.4   The inverted doughnut

show responsible initiative to move outside the core. Unfortunately, it is not defined in any way, except for the need to add value.

Points for Revision

Key Terms

trait theory	leaders arise from personal charisma and character rather than any formal training
situation theory	leaders arise in particular situations and thrive given certain external/internal conditions
autocratic leadership	where decisions are taken by one person at the top of the hierarchy
democratic leadership	where decisions are taken at the top, but following close consultation with the rest of the group
laissez-faire	decisions are taken by the group
MBO	management by objectives – the setting of clear goals is used to direct the activity and performance of managers
paternalistic	fatherly form of leadership, showing concern for work-force beyond the working environment

Definitions Question:
By referring to a business you know, explain the significance of any three of the above terms (your teacher may wish to help you to choose the terms).   [5] per definition

Summary Points:

1   There are various styles of leadership, some of which are more appropriate than others in certain contexts.

2   Management is fundamentally different from leadership.

3   There have been many writers on both management and leadership, all of whom have stated broadly the same theme.

> Activity and presentation: and finally, having read through the unit, try to summarise the meaning of the words management and leadership in fewer than 25 words each.

Maxi Case Study

Japan

The main role of a Japanese executive is to focus on human resources. At Toyota, the role of the manager is to motivate, train and educate each individual to achieve his or her own potential. From this, company performance ought to improve. The emphasis is on the team approach and decisions are designed to reflect a consensus; a Japanese manager must have patience – the idea is that in contrast to the USA, where managers will tell others what to do, in Japan, they will drop a hint. Although the consensus takes longer to build, once the decision has been made, everyone is behind it. However, there is change ahead; the recession of the late 1990s has forced people to move jobs and companies to restructure through voluntary retirement. Two new skills are being required of Japanese managers – English as a spoken language and computer literacy. The foundations of Japanese companies – life-time employment, promotion through seniority and single-company unions – are disappearing as companies need to be more flexible. Toshiba is one company that responded to the changes early on in the recession; whilst the consensus approach used to be used, with final and ultimate responsibility lying with the president, Toshiba has begun to devolve the authority to take long-term investment decisions to the directors who are each in charge of one of four major groups within the business.

Germany

Germany's managers are steeped in tradition. Given the deep and prolonged recession that has forced unemployment up to four million people, German managers are going to need new ideas and managers who are sufficiently courageous to implement them. The tradition has been that German managers have not been encouraged to think as individuals or be flexible. Emphasis on technical expertise has been at the expense of personal charisma. As markets are breaking up and becoming more segmented, future managers will need to know not only about specific areas but how that knowledge fits into the whole picture – there is therefore no need for managers with limited scope. Teamwork, presently a dirty word in a country where respect is given only to title and position, will be the new phrase. Training at VW is designed to make managers broader-based and able to lead a team. One German executive described the role of managers as being a mix of entrepreneur and intrapreneur – the latter being a person who introduces fresh ideas and a willingness to take risks into a traditionally risk-averse corporate culture.

1 Define: long-term investment decisions, single-company unions, training.   [6]

2 To what extent do you think that the democratic approach lower down the company contradicts the autocratic approach of most company presidents in Japan?   [4]

3 Compare and contrast the future expectations of managers in Japan and Germany.   [10]

4 How far do you agree that leadership and management are shown to be similar issues in the above case?   [10]

30

People
in groups

Learning objectives

Having read this unit, students will be able to

1 identify the importance of groups in industry

2 understand how managers must attempt to meet the needs of the groups

3 identify the functions of trade unions

4 understand the various actions that unions can take and the various methods of resolving conflict in the work-place

Context

What constitutes a group? Is it a queue of people waiting for a bus, some people having a drink together, a crowd of angry workers on strike, a team of runners, a staffroom of teachers? All the above do constitute a group, although some are created by external forces and would not normally group themselves voluntarily, whereas others come together of their own accord.

If you consider the way you behave and react when speaking to a teacher on a one-to-one basis and compare it to how a particular class reacts to the same teacher, you will notice some differences. If you have been taught by the same teacher at two different times during your years at school, the way the teacher responded to and treated the first class may have been radically different from the second class. In the same way you may well have behaved differently in one group of students than in another. The group in which you are placed for lessons will therefore have a significant influence on the way you behave in the group as opposed to when you are on your own. Crowds of football hooligans may well be mild-mannered, co-operative, family-loving people during the week, but their behaviour takes a radical turn for the worst when they join together wearing football shirts and meet on the terraces.

What is a group?

At any one time, most of us will be a member of five or more different groups, some of which will be created by the business/organisation, some of which will be created voluntarily e.g. the class you are in for Business Studies, the tutor group, the sports team, the church congregation.

E.H. Schein defined a group as a collection of individuals who:

a) interact with each other
b) are psychologically aware of each other
c) perceive themselves as a group

Question 1

Which of the following constitutes a group according to the definition by Schein?

a) Theatre audience
b) Group of fair-haired girls between the age of 17 and 22
c) Football team
d) Board of directors
e) Employees who regularly meet in the pub after work
f) An amateur dramatic society   [6]

Another definition of a group is a collection of individuals whose existence (as a collection) is rewarding to the individual or enables them to avoid punishments. This definition is particularly appropriate in education; a group of rowdy school children who misbehave when the teacher turns away are using the existence and nature of the group to express their rebelliousness. On their own they would certainly not attempt such behaviour.

The group therefore allows this individual to 'hide' and express feelings without fear of individual punishment. In this case, the group does not have to share one common goal, but there is a common characteristic.

Groups at work

Formal groups

Formal groups have been consciously created to achieve the organisation's goals e.g. getting work done, creating ideas, liaising between management and work-force; the group is therefore defined by the functions or tasks assigned to it.

They have a formal structure, are task-orientated, and members form a group when they develop inter-dependence.

Therefore a formal group has:

- a definable membership
- group consciousness
- a sense of shared purpose
- inter-dependence
- interaction
- an ability to work as one

In other words:

- Relationships are functional
- Group exists to work on a task
- Leadership is chosen on skill/trait
- Groups are frequently temporary because they are set up to perform a particular task; once the task is complete, the group disbands

Informal groups

Informal groups provide social and interpersonal relationships and support to each member of the group. Anyone not conforming to the informal norms faces disapproval. Control depends on whether the individual receives satisfaction and support from the group.

The coal-mines provide an interesting case study in the importance of the informal group; coal-mines are dark, cold and dangerous. The miners had previously coped with this by forming close, tight-knit groups. Groups were informal, and therefore the workers chose each other and knew each other. If there was an accident which affected the livelihood of a miner, the other members of the group used to regard it as their responsibility to look after the family of the dead miner.

As coal became more expensive to collect, the technology was developed which relocated miners to larger areas in the mine, so that group cohesion was reduced as communication could not take place as easily. Their jobs isolated them further given that close collaboration and intra-group trust was required when getting coal out of the mine i.e. the jobs had become much more specialised.

Thus the groups had to disband due to mass production technology. Where adjustments were not made to substitute a new social arrangement for the old ones, morale, productivity and mental health suffered.

Factors which determine whether a group is successful

The effective group or team is one that achieves its goals in the most efficient way; and is keen to take on more challenging tasks if and when required to do so.

Communication within the group – are ideas expressed clearly in the correct language? If there is discussion with the individuals on a democratic basis this will ensure close communication because everyone should be invited to put forward opinions.

Cohesiveness – a group is more likely to be cohesive depending on group proximity, maybe the similarity of work or perhaps the personalities.

Atmosphere – if this has been created as a friendly, relaxed atmosphere then this will make the members of the group feel more involved and more a part of the group.

The ability to satisfy all the needs of the group – within every group there is a task need, a group need and individual needs and the ability of the leader to satisfy all these will result in greater productivity: easier said than done!

Even though team spirit and teamwork are often seen as the catchphrases for pulling people together this is rather difficult to conceive given that people go to work on their own, build their career on their own and seek financial rewards on their own. It is therefore not always easy or obvious to create teams at work. The following question provides two cases in point.

Question 2

How might the business try to develop effective teams from these employees?

a) machines have been designed for an operative which can isolate the operative from anyone else

b) the sales team of a particular business is likely to cover the market area, will be responsible for its own sales and, by its very nature, tends to spend most days in the car visiting customers

[6]

Question 3

The Volvo plant at Kalmar is famous for building teams in car assembly; the old way of manufacturing a motor car was done according to the style of Ford, in his work with F.W. Taylor at the beginning of the century. Volvo saw this as demeaning and counter-productive to the importance of meaningful work, despite the fact that the claims of Volvo contradicted the real proof that specialisation improved productivity.

Instead of one man doing one job, a team of workers, with an engineer, was trained to produce an entire motor car, from start to finish even though the training took longer than for one job and the productivity of the car plant did not change significantly.

Despite the change having little effect on productivity, why might Volvo have insisted on its implementation?

[6]

Question 4

In contrast to Volvo, General Motors attempted to assess whether teams could be implemented on its own production line. The typical amount of time it was estimated to take to build a car within the group was eight hours per person; although the initial attempts took 13 or 14 hours, the team managed to reduce this to just under two hours per person. Some team members decided they preferred the assembly line approach. GM explained this away as characterising the type of person who had developed a style and rhythm of work and did not want to change. The operators could not actually cope with a multiplicity of tasks. GM saw the main problem as an organisational one; supplying 15,000 parts to teams of 5–10 employees was almost impossible, especially when the business was trying to implement just-in-time management. Changing the job due to new products or new investment was the major cause of not being able to train the work-force.

Explain what you think were the main reasons why teamwork might not have worked at GM.   [6]

Problems for managers

Group norms

There will be **group norms**, or standards, on a variety of issues.

The extent to which the individual conforms to the group depends on:

- desire for affiliation/need to avoid displeasure
- conformity with the group view
- the individual's own insecurity to stand alone
- the extent to which the individual believes in the goals of the group

Consider the employee at Ford who wore a 30 years of service badge, and walked out on strike with the rest of the work-force. The error made by the manager who judged the employee was to correlate the performance of the individual with the performance of the group. In the above case, there were two different agendas which the managers had not addressed. Businesses will therefore go to considerable lengths to engender team spirit in order to allow a group to build its own set of values and norms. Management training weekends, as tried by William Hague in an attempt to reunite the Conservative Party following its dramatic 1997 election defeat, are aimed at building teams.

Robert Bales examined the importance of committees and consultative groups in business activity in 1952. The groups had the following common characteristics:
1 they were small in number
2 there was to be no formal leader before the study
3 each task was a small problem which the group really wanted to solve

He reached the following conclusions:

- Members of a group contribute more when the group is small
- Remarks tend to be addressed to one or two individuals, with a pecking order of the highest contribution being addressed to the next highest individual
- High contributors initiate ideas
- The apparent formal leader (who evolved during the study) becomes disliked and the informal leaders tend to be liked

Robert Tannenbaum and Warren Schmidt discussed the need to conform to group norms in their article 'How to choose a leadership pattern' (*Harvard Business Review*, January 1973). They looked at the power of the group as an instrument of control over its members. The more attractive the group is to the members, the more likely the members are to change their views in order for the individual to be accepted by the group.

An individual who does not conform will be rejected and is more likely to be rejected by the group on issues which are of significance e.g. rugby players will be less impressed by a star player on the field who refuses to sing rowdy songs and drink beer after every match. However, if the star player does not wear a gum-shield, this may not be significant to group cohesion and group identity, so the player will not be rejected.

The same applies to groups of students on issues such as smoking etc. In return, the group provides comfort, protection and support in fear of adversity for the individual. Such an issue is relevant primarily when work-force clashes with management, but can refer to a director clashing with a chief executive.

There will also be roles within the group which are well defined e.g. the comedian, the drinker, the pacifier, the sounding board, the aggressor, the sage. Disturbing the group's structure can therefore be extremely damaging.

The Hawthorne Effect Part 2

(see Unit 50 for Part 1)

Elton Mayo's investigations into productivity and working conditions revealed an important fact about group cohesion. By discussing work with employees in detail, it was revealed that employees gained enormously from the feeling that they were part of a team of individuals and as such they took immense pride in the performance of individuals and of the team.

Output, and therefore productivity, was affected by the imposition of the group norm. The group established its standard level of output and produced what it considered the proper amount of work. To the observers at the Hawthorne plant it became apparent very quickly that each individual could produce a much larger amount if left to his/her own devices; this seemed illogical to the observer given that a piece-rate system had been imposed, so by conforming to the group, the employees were giving up their right to earn a larger pay-cheque.

In the employees' eyes, an increase in production would mean the business would raise the basic piece work level of output, thereby removing the initial incentive for higher output.

Mayo's work therefore provided the following conclusions:

1 Work is a group activity

2 Employees have certain ingrained attitudes and their effectiveness is conditioned by social factors both in and out of the work-place

3 Informal groups within the work-place exert strong controls over the habits and attitudes of the individual, to the extent that the individual will subordinate his/her own goals to that of the group

4 Group collaboration must be planned for and developed. If this is achieved, disruptions and stoppages can be kept to a minimum. Productivity can therefore be improved by ensuring that the informal groups are led towards achieving this. Therefore organising teamwork and developing co-operation should become an obsession of management

Further proof

In 1917 the first-ever study took place on group behaviour by the Industrial Fatigue Research Board, examining monotony in the working cycle. This included observing women wrapping soap, men fitting wheels on cars and people folding handkerchiefs, all jobs which were the result of the drive for specialisation. The social conditions of work were found to have significant consequences on output; boredom was less common when employees were allowed to work in groups.

Employer–employee relations

Many of the disputes that occur between employers and employees are related to employee rights. Legislation in recent years has been adding to the rights of the employee. Apart from the rights concerned with the contract of employment (*see Unit 54 Recruitment and contracts*), additional rights have been granted to a variety of groups of employees. Legislation on race relations, sex discrimination, equality of pay, disability rights and union membership has featured in the statute book. Yet a large proportion of disputes between employers and employees centres on dismissal.

Historically employees have attempted to protect themselves by joining a **trade union**. To prevent exploitation by the management, employees would rely on their union to fight for their rights. However, during the 1960s and 1970s, the power of the unions led to many disruptions, culminating in the 'winter of discontent' in 1974–75. As a result of close collaboration between the Labour government and the unions, an agreement was made (the Social Compact) to work together over 'beer and sandwiches at number 10'.

Margaret Thatcher was determined to reduce the power of the unions, which had held the country to ransom for so many years. A range of legislation was passed between 1980 and 1982 and after a significant amount of conflict between the government and employers (designed to be the main beneficiaries of the legislation), on the one hand, and unions, on the other, industrial peace resumed. The number of days lost to industrial action fell to their lowest levels for decades and continuous production enabled British manufacturers to compete on a more equal footing.

Structure of unions

Shop steward – the lowest rank of the union, a **shop steward** is elected by the union members at the work-place and expected to represent members at a local level. This post is unpaid

Regional/branch officer – may work exclusively for the union and will be called in to resolve disputes which are either too important for the shop steward to deal with or involve too many people

Executive – involved with policy and strategy of the union

Types of unions

Traditionally there were four distinct types or categories of unions:

■ General

There is no particular group of workers classified by industry or skill but the union would represent workers from all sorts of industries with skilled and unskilled members. The Transport and General Workers' Union (TGWU) used to be one of the largest unions along with the General Municipal Workers and Allied Trades Union, now known as the GMB.

■ Industrial

Workers employed within a particular industry would join the respective union such as the National Union of Mineworkers.

■ Craft

Employees who had a common skill regardless of the place of employment. Equity, the actors' union, is a good example of this.

■ White collar

Employees who were skilled and worked in an office environment as opposed to the shopfloor would join this type of union.

Examples are the National Union of Teachers (NUT) and National Association of Local Government Officers (NALGO).

However today's working environment has blurred many of the old categories and in conjunction with the rapid fall in union membership throughout the 1990s has led to fewer but larger unions of a more general nature. The majority of the craft unions have ceased to exist or have amalgamated with others to ensure the concept of **collective bargaining** (*see below*) survives.

The role of trade unions

To negotiate on behalf of their members for
 i) better pay
 ii) improved working conditions
 iii) employment rights
 iv) job descriptions
 v) grievance procedures
 vi) redundancy packages

Many of these roles or functions are undertaken through the process of 'collective bargaining' which entails representing all the members and speaking as one voice with the employers and thereby negotiating from a position of strength.

Collective bargaining can take place at either plant, area or national level.

Question 5

Mark Iron, an employee at the local engineering plant, has been confronted by the regional union officer about his reluctance to join the union. Why might Mark not want to join a union?   [3]

Strong or weak unions

The degree of strength that any particular union has depends on several factors:

1 The size of the membership. The larger the membership of a union, the more power it has at the negotiating table.

2 The degree of militancy within the union. There may be a tendency for employers to take more notice of militant unions to avoid what may be perceived as inevitable industrial action taking place.

3 The level of unemployment within the economy. When unemployment is low, and labour is more likely to be scarce, the union is in a better position to negotiate a favourable settlement.

4 The charisma of the union leader. There have been several examples of renowned leaders who have exerted strength as a consequence of their personality, for example, miners' leader Arthur Scargill.

5 The success rate of any disputes in the past. The rail workers' unions, ASLEF and NUR, gained several successes throughout the 1980s and as a result, may be seen as being in a stronger negotiating position, learning from their previous record.

6 The success of any tribunal hearing. If the union has gained success in the past, there is the opportunity to use this experience for the next dispute.

Employer associations

In the same way that employees have a representative voice with their trade union, employers have Employers' Associations. The aim of these is to represent the employer at either local, regional or national level, in the collective bargaining process.

Management of a particular business will tend to use its Employers' Association if the local collective bargaining process has not resulted in a solution to the conflict. In the same way that all unions are affiliated to the Trades Union Congress (TUC), Employers' Associations are affiliated to the CBI (Confederation of British Industry). The body acts at a national level, advising and criticising the government by representing the opinions and concerns of individual employers.

Single union deal

One of the problems that has affected industrial relations in this country has been the number of unions that the employer has had to negotiate with. Some of the industrial disputes of the 1970s involving the newspaper industry meant negotiating with lots of unions and sections of unions which in the newspaper industry are called 'chapels'. Any agreement with one union may not have been agreed with another and consequently, a vast amount of time was taken up negotiating a settlement acceptable to all rather than, for example, getting on with managing the business in order to survive in a competitive market.

Consequently, many places of employment during the 1980s entered into a **single union agreement**. Such an agreement simplifies negotiations considerably. It reduces the amount of time spent on negotiations and reduces the amount of conflict that used to exist in multi-union businesses. The union in question has benefited because any employee wanting to join the union would join the one that has the agreement at that place of work. Toyota agreed to a single union deal when it decided to locate at Burnaston, near Derby.

Task

Find out the name of the single union with which Toyota made the agreement.

Industrial action

When the process of negotiation between unions and their employers breaks down, the former may resort to **industrial action** in an attempt to 'persuade' the employer to reach an agreement.

The unions may take any of the following measures:

■ Work-to-rule

This is where union members are not permitted to do anything which is outside the job description as written into their contract e.g. if employees at a food manufacturing company are concerned about a dirty machine, then legitimately they can stop work, but not do anything about it. The contract will be connected with food manufacturing, not cleaning the machines. That job is for the machine cleaner! Such stoppages were very frequent in the mid-1970s when job demarcation (strict definition of each job) was frequently raised in disputes.

■ Go-slow

Employees purposely take their time, perhaps if they are being paid overtime or are concerned not to work too hard, in case they run out of work and some employees have to be laid off. The other more straightforward reason is to disrupt production.

■ Sit-in

The work-force turns up to work, but does nothing. This prevents the employer from hiring extra labour to come in and do the work.

■ Down tools

Employees simply stop what they are doing, whilst the production line continues, thereby forcing management to stop the line and address the problem.

■ Overtime ban

The union stipulates that members cannot accept overtime. This means that income levels will suffer for the employee; unions may use this at a time when extra output is particularly important, perhaps when an extra order has come in to the business from a prestigious client.

■ Industrial sabotage

Employees would deliberately damage the product in some way that would hinder the performance of the business. This might involve anything from ensuring the machinery did not work properly to damaging the finished product. Johnson and Johnson once had to recall all its baby foods following reports that an employee had deliberately put glass in the mixture which went into the pots of food.

■ Strikes

Although strikes are the main way that union action hits the headlines, they are the last form of industrial action a union will consider. Strike action will occur only after protracted negotiation with all concerned. When an employee goes on strike, it means, apart from a token amount of strike pay, there will be no other form of income. Some employees resist strike action, at the risk of being ostracised by the local community (and being known as 'a scab'). Recently strike action has been less frequent due to Mrs Thatcher's reforms on union action, but also because of the growing realisation of the need to co-operate at the work-place.

Employers' action

In the same way that unions can prevent disruption to the company, employers are able to take action in a dispute in an attempt to persuade the union to 'see their point of view', using the following measures:

- **Withdrawal of overtime** – as opposed to an overtime ban, this is where the employer does not allow an extra pay rate for overtime.

- **Lock-outs** – the employer may well refuse to let the work-force in. The Liverpool dockers were locked out of the docks because they had refused to implement new working practices and accept new manning levels. Such action can lead to an extremely antagonistic attitude for a long time into the future and employers always need to think very carefully before doing this. Bilton pottery in Stoke also forced a lock-out on its employees; having called in the administrators to rescue the business there was no pay for the employees over the Christmas period and no work was done.

- **Short-term contracts** – in order to build some insecurity and therefore fear into the minds of employees, it is possible to change all contracts to include a short-term notice requirement and short-term renewal. Contracts as short as one week (where the contract is renewed each week) have been used in the building industry. This also means that redundancy payments can be saved when a contract is severed.

■ **Alter working practices** – in exchange for either higher pay or shorter hours, many employers have insisted on more flexible working practices.

Resolving disputes through industrial democracy

If no agreement can be struck between the two parties, there is the facility to use a neutral third party in an attempt to find some common ground.

Works councils

All companies in the European Union employing over 1,000 workers, with at least 150 or more of them in at least two member states, were to set up an employer–employee consultative committee by the end of 1999. Prior to September 1999, companies could decide the format of this committee, but from then on the EU laid down rigid guidelines for the formation of these committees, known as **works councils**. Works councils are most significant in Germany's manufacturing industry, with an average size of 25 members. Works councils are simply another form of **industrial democracy**, allowing employees into the decision making process.

Companies within the UK were exempt because it had opted out of the Social Chapter (*see Unit 61 International trade and the EU*). There are some companies, according to the TUC, which have voluntarily formed such committees.

Worker directors are employees invited to sit on the board of directors, although with no change in salary. This can be seen as a way of avoiding unions, especially if the workers' views are not listened to carefully. However, there have been some successful examples. British Steel has insisted on having worker directors ever since the miners' strike of 1984; such a presence means that employees are represented at the very highest level of decision making.

ESOP (Employee Share Ownership Programme)

By including employees in sharing profit, through extra dividends, or by allowing them to benefit from an increase in the share price, the intention of ESOPs is to encourage employees to have the same objectives as employers, thereby minimising the risk of conflict. (*ESOPs are also covered in Unit 49 Financial motivation*).

Work groups/teams – these are included in more detail in the first part of this unit.

ACAS (Advisory, Conciliation and Arbitration Service)

When employers and employees cannot come to any agreement or perhaps refuse to discuss the matter further, it is possible to call in **ACAS** whose role is to bring the two parties together and try to reach some half-way point where the two sides agree.

ACAS therefore has the following duties and powers:

■ to reduce the chance of conflict occurring
■ to seek out-of-court settlements for unfair dismissal cases to be heard at industrial tribunals
■ to promote the improvement of industrial relations

The name of the service explains exactly what it does:

Advisory – advising unions and employers on procedure and legislative matters

Conciliation – bringing about the settlement with or without the parties' consent

Arbitration – acting as a go-between in an attempt to mediate a settlement

Industrial tribunals

Industrial tribunals are an informal way of settling claims of unfair dismissal (*see Unit 54 Recruitment and contracts*). They were started in the 1960s and the majority of disputes are settled in this way. The panel consists of three: an employer representative, an employee representative and a chairperson (legally trained). The employee can represent him/herself but may need help from the union if the employer has hired a lawyer.

Pendulum arbitration

Sometimes managers and unions are unable to come to a mutual agreement. This is usually over an issue such as a pay increase. In such a circumstance, ACAS may be called in as 'pendulum arbitrators'. When this happens, the management and unions will have come to an impasse because neither is willing to compromise any more. For example, the management may be willing to pay only a 4% pay increase but the unions might be insisting on an 9% increase. By using pendulum arbitration, both parties must abide by the decision of ACAS, regardless of whether they agree with the decision.

ACAS will then investigate the issue of a pay increase and will decide the figure which is the most appropriate for the individual business. If it decides that the appropriate pay increase is 6%, then the management's offer, being closest to the ACAS figure, is adopted i.e. the pay increase awarded is 4%. This does mean that the union loses out by a considerable margin, although ACAS might judge the appropriate pay increase to be 7%, in which case, the union would be granted their pay rise of 9%. Both parties are therefore encouraged to compromise as much as possible before the issue goes to pendulum arbitration.

Question 7

'That's the third time I have had to explain my behaviour in the past two months!' exclaimed Lisa as she was recovering from her meeting with Helen Holmes, the Personnel Director. Holmes had made reference to her lateness and her poor quality of work and had threatened her with dismissal if her overall approach to work did not improve. Her supervisor shrugged her shoulders. 'I'm not sure you can do anything about it; Holmes has always been like that – you've just got to make sure you don't get on the wrong side of her.' Lisa felt she had been treated unfairly, so she went to find Peter Price, the shop steward, in order to seek his advice.

What extra information might Peter Price need to make a realistic case to the management against Holmes about unfair treatment?   [6]

Points for Revision

Key Terms

formal group	a group which has been brought together to perform a task for the business
informal group	a group which is created voluntarily, due mainly to social factors
group norms	standards set by the group, which are usually different to the standards of the individual
shop steward	the lowest-ranking union official, elected by the members, employed by a business
trade union	a collective organisation that represents the work-force at the work-place
employers' association	the employer's equivalent of a union, created to protect employers against union action
single union deal	designed to reduce the amount of negotiation between management and unions; one union only represents the work-force
industrial action	employees take some form of action to disrupt the working process
collective bargaining	unions and employers discuss issues and arrive at an agreement, compromising their objectives where appropriate
industrial tribunal	place where most disputes over unfair dismissal are settled
industrial democracy	any attempt to involve the work-force in the decision making process
ACAS	a government-run organisation created to bring together management and unions when they cannot agree and to find a solution
works council	another form of team which discusses issues at work

Definitions Question:
With reference to a business you know, choose any three of the above terms and explain their significance (your teacher may wish to help you choose the terms).

[5] per definition

Summary Points:

1. The importance of the group must not be underestimated by managers.

2. Groups of employees will subordinate their own objectives in order to satisfy those of the group.

3. Unions are the main example of how groups influence decision making at work.

4. There are various forms of industrial action, although a business will try to prevent this through industrial democracy.

Mini Case Study

As the mechanics of Deliver-It, a distribution company, picked up their wage packet on Friday afternoon, they wondered how long it would be before their pay was increased to the appropriate level. The management had been locked in a dispute with the TGWU (Transport and General Workers' Union) for the past three days and they seemed to be no nearer a solution. The dispute had begun when the mechanics responsible for repairing lorries had staged a down tools, following a disagreement over wage levels. They felt they were as important a part of the distribution business as the drivers and should be paid at the same rate. They accepted that overtime was less likely to be offered to them and that the lorry drivers had to work unsociable hours, but they still felt that they had a case. In addition, the lorry drivers received a bonus for prompt delivery which of course did not apply to the mechanics. The mechanics felt that there was little they could do to get their point across which did not involve further disruption. One mechanic, Mike Mender, had been working in Germany where he had been a member of the works council in a similar company and had been impressed with the ground they had covered in discussions and the number of industrial disputes that had been solved without any stoppages being caused.

1 What other forms of industrial action might the mechanics take if management does not agree to their wage demands?   [3]

2 Make a case for management to refuse the mechanics the same rate of pay as the drivers.   [8]

3 How might a performance-related pay system be applied to the mechanics?   [5]

4 What issues might a works council discuss at Deliver-It?   [4]

20

Maxi Case Study

In June 1999, junior doctors delivered an ultimatum to the government regarding their industrial dispute that had been simmering for some time. The doctors, who are not noted for their industrial militancy had voted to undertake industrial action if the government failed to respond to their request for negotiations on 'out-of-hours' pay. The huge number of hours that a junior doctor was expected to work had been recognised by all who had any connection with the health service. Many people were aware that there were too many occasions when lives were put at risk because a tired doctor was on call for the third successive day, having had virtually no sleep for the three days.

The result was that 30,000 junior doctors voted in favour of industrial action at their annual conference. This was the first time doctors had got close to such action since 1975 when doctors suspended normal duties and operated emergency cover only because of a dispute over new contracts. The 1999 dispute had the full support of the BMA and all other ranks in the hierarchy of doctors. The result of a survey conducted prior to the vote revealed that 95% were in favour of industrial action. With regard to the type of action to be taken, 79% were in favour of a work-to-rule.

The threat of industrial action, as reported at the time, was thought likely to be carried out during the winter of 1999 and to lead to chaos in the National Health Service. This would be at the very time when it might already be facing severe problems with millennium celebrations that would create additional work due to over-indulgence on New Year's Eve, notwithstanding any problems related to the millennium computer bug. The junior doctors had indicated the proposed work-to-rule would mean that much of the essential clerical work would not be undertaken. However, the chairman of the BMA's junior doctors committee stated that they wanted the dispute settled before the end of the millennium.

The dispute had been fuelled by grievances over pay arrangements during the run-up to the millennium period; the junior doctors' pay for working weekends and bank holidays was half their normal £8 an hour. The chairman suggested that doctors would be better off cleaning the wards than being responsible for them, because the cleaners were paid £6 an hour. The Health Secretary stated that he was willing to consider changing the structure of junior doctors' pay to accommodate some of their demands.

1 Explain: stakeholders, industrial militancy, work-to-rule.   [6]

2 Assume you are a member of the junior doctors' negotiating team; suggest an
   argument for an increase in pay.   [5]

3 Would you advise the doctors to take industrial action? Explain your answer.   [5]

4 To what extent would any pay rise improve the motivation of the junior doctors? [8]

5 Evaluate the other possible forms of industrial action junior doctors might have
   considered.   [8]

6 Argue either for or against industrial action 'at any cost'.   [8]

40

Recruitment and contracts

Learning objectives

Having read this unit, students will be able to

1 understand the various types and stages of recruitment

2 demonstrate an understanding of the legal requirements related to recruitment and employment

3 evaluate selection procedures and make recommendations for improvements

4 understand the purpose of and differences between on- and off-the-job training

5 be aware of the different ways in which employees may be dismissed

Context

Selecting the right person for the job is becoming more important; getting the wrong person for a particular job may prove expensive. Having invested heavily in the recruitment process and the training of the successful applicants only to discover they are not suitable and are surplus to requirements will take many man hours, which have to be paid for, yet may not have resulted in any return on the investment. The NHS, for example, spends significant amounts of money training nurses, many of whom leave to work in the private sector. Many job advertisements are vague, selection processes are hasty – no wonder mistakes are made. A clear understanding of what the job entails and the qualities or skills that are required are the minimum points that need to be stressed clearly.

The recruitment process

Every business will, at some time, require labour to perform a particular role. How that need is assessed will depend on the type of business and the product or service involved. Businesses that are capital-intensive will require fewer units of labour than others that are more labour-intensive.

Once the need has been recognised the actual recruitment procedure starts.

What is the job?

One of the first tasks is to decide what the job is. What will the person be required to do?

Some large businesses have a personnel department that will analyse the job requirements (job analysis) in an attempt to ensure the right person is appointed. This information is then used to formulate a **job description**.

For example:

Title of the job	Legal secretary
Name of the business	Batters and Pickers
Where	Birmingham, New Street
Indication of the job requirements	Working with the Litigation solicitor
Details of the job	Administrative support to fee earner
	Dealing with clients' initial inquiries by phone and in person
	Preparing legal documentation
	Preparing bills for clients
Working conditions	Open plan office
	Hours, minimum of 37
	25 days' holiday plus statutory Bank Holidays
	Salary monthly (by negotiation) depending on experience
	The company operates an annual appraisal scheme

Figure 54.1   An example of a job description

Question 1

Prepare a job description for *one* of the following:
 i) Trainee electrician
 ii) Shop assistant
 iii) Sales representative for a FMCG
 iv) Computer programmer   [5]

Having prepared the job description, the business can decide what type of person is required to undertake the job in question. To do this a **person profile** or **person specification** is drawn up.

Required qualifications	
Experience	
Personal characteristics	Punctual
	Able to use initiative
	Able to work under pressure

One of the first decisions that has to be made once the job description and person profile have been determined is whether it is possible to recruit from within the business or whether there is a need to go outside.

Internal

Internal recruitment can mean offering an existing employee the job in question, or perhaps offering it to a certain group of employees by inviting their applications. Keeping the job within a specific boundary of employees is known as ring-fencing.

This can either be a change in job in an attempt to find the most efficient way of using the existing work-force or a promotion to those that the business is keen to keep. In the latter case, promotion and consequently more responsibility may act as a form of motivation to the employee concerned (*see Unit 50 Non-financial motivation*).

Advantages of selecting internal candidates

Appointing an internal candidate is obviously a lot cheaper as money is not required to advertise the position. Nor is there a need to spend hours sifting through application forms and interviewing candidates. Further savings may be made because less will need to be spent on the training process, as the internal appointee will be aware of many of the procedures that are unique to the business.

Another big advantage is that the business is well aware of the strengths and weaknesses of the internal appointee and therefore there is less risk involved than if an external candidate is appointed. The latter may have impressed at interview but may be disappointing once appointed.

However, there may be a danger of jealousy from other internal candidates who felt they ought to have been approached. This is often why many businesses appoint from outside the business. In addition, appointing from within may mean a lack of objectivity resulting in the appointing of sympathetic or like-minded staff who will not therefore bring new ideas to the business.

External

The majority of jobs are advertised in the press, either in the local newspaper or in the national papers, depending on the type of job to be advertised. The more specialist posts may be advertised in a specialist magazine or trade journal. There are other **external methods of recruiting**. If the business is keen to employ young people then it may attend careers fairs or visit universities or use the local authority careers advisory service to promote the vacancy. Using these methods ought to ensure there is a wider potential field of candidates for the post.

Alternatively, the local job centres or employment and advertising agencies could be used for a wide range of vacancies. For the top professional posts, apart from the employment or recruitment agencies, executive agencies 'headhunt' suitable candidates. Headhunting is where a person is suggested to a business based on reputation, or has the particular experience that is required. The person is approached by the agency to sound him/her out with regard to the job in question. Using headhunters allows the business to keep the fact

INTERNATIONAL MARKETING MANAGER

c£50,000 + BONUS + CAR + BENEFITS
HOME COUNTIES OR PARIS

If you're looking for a unique opportunity to establish and build a European business working within a market leading £multibillion international plc – then this is for you.

Take up this pivotal role, and you'll be tasked with the development and launch of a premium product range as manager of both the marketing and R&D teams. From day one, you'll have responsibility for all elements of the marketing mix including strategy development, research and new product development, the launch plan and cost-effective communications/promotional programmes.

To meet this challenge, you must be a blue chip FMCG trained marketeer who's fluent in French and English – and who ideally has business-to-business and pan-European marketing experience.

Interested? Then please send your full CV, with current salary details, to Mike Stephenson quoting reference R9013 to the address below. All CVs will be opened and forwarded to the client without any review or selection process. Please name any companies to which you do not wish to apply.

R A A   S p r a g u e   G i b b o n s
Advertising People

Church Court
North View | Soundwell
Bristol BS16 4NQ

Fax: 0117 956 9562
E-mail: call@raa.co.uk
Web: www.raa.co.uk

Figure 54.2   An example of a job advertisement

that there is a post to be filled under wraps for a range of reasons (it may not want to damage its prospects within the business if other applicants do not materialise).

Question 2

Suggest which type of recruitment would be most suitable for the following:

a) An executive for a top FMCG company
b) Post of foreman at the local builders
c) Graduate entry to a firm of accountants
d) Train driver   [4]

Application forms

With all job advertisements, there will be a telephone number or an address or e-mail address to obtain more details about the job and an application form.

For many jobs today the selection procedure is much more 'scientific' and as a result much more care is taken over the questions on the application form. By having an application form time is saved when sorting out the replies. The initial stage will be to ensure the applicants have met the requirements for the post and therefore only a few of the responses on the application form will need to be scrutinised initially. If applicants were asked just to write in, many hours might be wasted reading all the letters to ascertain the key facts for the first sorting stage of the selection process. In addition, or alternatively, a curriculum vitae (CV) may be requested.

The most obvious details that are required of an applicant are:

Personal details	Name, age, sex, address
Qualifications and experience	GCSEs, GNVQs, A levels, degrees
	Previous jobs
Names of referees	Previous employer, existing employer, headteacher

Some businesses will require applicants to write (not word process) a letter of application stating why they are interested in the advertised job.

Question 3

Why do some businesses insist on the letter of application being handwritten? [3]

It is becoming more common for additional forms to be sent out alongside the application forms. These additional forms contain questions on personality, intelligence or aptitude. These test questions may be used at a later stage of the recruitment process, usually at the interview, as a more reliable objective assessment of the applicant. There is much debate as to the reliability of interviews and assessment testing, without any concrete evidence as to which is the most effective method of selection.

Apart from the ability of a selection procedure to ensure the best candidate for the post is obtained, consideration of the costs involved is important.

The most modern method of applying for a job is to respond to a vacancy that appears on the Internet. Applicants can surf the net for appropriate jobs and send a completed application form while at work and with their present employer none the wiser. An American company, Cisco Systems, a telecoms equipment company, stated that over 50% of its job applications are from the net. Some American companies are even conducting their initial interviews online.

Interviews

The interview is probably the most used and the most efficient method of gathering information about the candidate. However, it is the interpretation of this information and how it is imparted that is the difficult aspect of any interview.

Although most people will have experienced an interview, few have experience of how to conduct one in an appropriate manner. If the interview is to be a success, there are several important aspects to be taken into consideration.

The number of people on the interview panel is something that is often overlooked and yet is crucial in terms of ascertaining the required information from the candidates. If there are too many interviewers, the candidate (interviewee) will feel intimidated and not know who to look at when replying! However, more than one interviewer provides the opportunity to have different perspectives and reduces the likelihood of too much subjectivity in the selection process. There is no correct number of interviewers but an awareness of the advantages and disadvantages is helpful.

It is important that candidates are put at ease to ensure they are able to provide the information that is necessary. That is why many interviews start with a simple question, often about the journey.

The most important factor to consider when conducting interviews is to ensure that the right questions are asked to enable the required information to be obtained. It is also important to remember that it is an interview and not an interrogation! The correct use of open and closed questions will be essential if the required information about the candidate is to be successfully gathered.

A simple closed question is to gather facts such as: Have you used a spreadsheet? This type of question (closed) requires a brief answer, which is often just a 'yes' or 'no'. An open question, such as: What do you think about the use of spreadsheets as a method of displaying information? will require an opinion from the candidate and therefore much more detail.

According to Tom Peters, in *Thriving on Chaos* (Guild Publishing, 1987), Hewlett-Packard subject their applicants to as many as 12 interviews assuming they pass the initial screening test!

Tom Peters is a firm believer in investing heavily in people as much as machinery and therefore considers time spent on interviews is well spent.

When conducting an interview it is important to remember the following:

a) Size of interview panel

b) Establish what information is required

c) Put the candidate at ease by starting gently

d) Have the right balance of open and closed questions

e) Ensure sufficient time is available (but not too long, it ought not to be an ordeal)

f) Give the candidate the opportunity to ask questions

Question 4

Suggest which of the following jobs would possibly involve the use of an aptitude test, an intelligence test, or a personality test as well as an interview:

  i) A doctor for a local health centre

 ii) A fireman

iii) A shop assistant

 iv) A garage mechanic   [4]

Question 5

Table 1

		Low				High
Energy and drive	General level of work output, ability to stay with a problem, persistence, enthusiasm, motivation	1	2	3	4	5
Work discipline	General efficiency, ability to plan, control, and monitor work and time, ability to set objectives and standards	1	2	3	4	5
Decision making	Quality of judgement on personnel & technical matters, willingness and ability to take decisions	1	2	3	4	5
Intellectual effectiveness	Analytical ability, speed of thinking, creativity	1	2	3	4	5
Relationships	Sociability, ability to work individually & in teams, extent of guidance & support needed from boss, ability to delegate	1	2	3	4	5
Flexibility	Ability to adapt to new and different people, technology & environments, responsiveness to change	1	2	3	4	5
Emotional stability	Ability to work under pressure, response to setbacks and failure	1	2	3	4	5

Using the information in Table 1, suggest the difficulties of assessing the items listed in column A.   [6]

Many businesses are now using recruitment agencies to find the right calibre of candidate for any given job. Aztech Computer Recruitment aims to provide permanent and contract personnel for the computer industry. It has a large database of both clients and potential candidates, performs the task of sifting through applicants for given jobs and will check CVs before submitting names to the business for interview. The agency will act as an intermediary between the two parties for such matters as salary packages.

Appointment

One of the first steps is to define employment; this is when a person supplies his or her labour for payment. To ensure the person is employed rather than working for another as contractor, control tests can be applied. These are referred to as the control, integration and the multiple or economic reality tests (*see Unit 58*).

Upon appointment the employee, under the Employment Rights Act of 1996, must receive not later than two months after commencement of employment, a written statement of the terms of employment or **contract of employment**.

This document must state:

Title of the job
Place of work
Rate of pay
Timing of payment
Hours of work
Holidays
Entitlements such as sick pay, holiday pay, pension rights
Length of notice by both parties

It is of interest to note that the actual duties to be performed do not have to be stated. Often the information collected to build a job description is used to form the basis of the contract of employment.

Itemised pay slip

If the business employs more than 20 people, under the Employment Rights Act 1996, employees have the right to an itemised pay slip. The statement must show:

gross pay
deductions (and type of)
net pay
method of payment

Again, if more than 20 are employed, the contract of employment must also show the disciplinary and grievance procedures. If there are fewer than 20 employees, the contract of employment need only show to whom the employee can go if there are problems.

The legal requirements for short-term contracts are not as detailed and will be dealt with in Unit 58 Legal environment.

Induction

To ensure that new employees settle in quickly and smoothly, many businesses operate a programme of familiarisation. The 'ways' of the business are explained and training for the particular post will commence. **Induction** is concerned with details about the business whereas training is related to skills that are required to perform a particular job.

Training

Training ought not to be seen as applicable only to those who are just starting their working life or who have recently joined the business. Investing in employees is essential if the business is to get the best out of its investment in the recruitment process.

Tom Peters asks the question, 'What have you done today to enhance (or at least insure against the decline of) the relative overall useful-skill level of your work-force *vis-à-vis* competitors?'

IBM has always invested heavily in the training of its work-force to good effect; Sainsbury's and Marks and Spencer also have a good reputation for training.

Training is a process that helps to improve the performance of an employee in a given area of the business. In today's competitive industrial markets, training can help employees to cope with technological developments, with ever-changing consumer needs, environmental and legal changes; in fact any kind of change. An adaptable work-force is a prerequisite in today's business environment.

Any good training programme should firstly assess the needs of its work-force. Once this has been done, a suitable programme to meet these needs can be established and delivered at an appropriate time. Care should be taken to ensure that feedback is gained in order to assess whether the training has met the needs of both the recipients and the business.

Types of training

Types of training will normally depend on the needs of the employer and the employee. Many businesses draw up a training contract which is an agreed document laying out the needs of the employee or the aim of the training and the action to be taken (*see Table 2*).

Training can be organised and operated:

On-the-job or **Off-the-job**

The chosen method or combination of methods will again depend upon the particular circumstances of the business in question.

Table 2

Training Contract

Joe Want	Superior
Tim Tomm	Trainee
Emma Elm	Training Manager

Aim or purpose of training

Tim Tomm will:

- familiarise himself with the departmental handbook to ensure the health and safety procedures are known and understood
- attend the induction course organised by Emma Elm every Monday for 4 weeks
- be able to undertake the opportunities that arise throughout the normal working day to practise the skills learnt every Monday

Joe Want will:

- ensure that Tim has access to the distribution computer terminal to allow the necessary practice to take place
- provide a minimum of one hour a day to explain the tasks that are undertaken by the employees who report to Joe

On-the-job training

There is a variety of methods or vehicles for **on-the-job training**, all of which use the work-place as the training venue:

a) Observing or learning by watching others – this is sometimes referred to as work shadowing. Watching an experienced worker is a useful way of learning the job though the new employee may pick up bad habits as well.

b) Mentoring – this is where a new employee will be assigned to an experienced worker not to learn how to perform the job but to gain personal support. The mentor is not an immediate superior, thereby ensuring the employee can talk openly about problems and discuss any concerns frankly. The mentoring usually takes place on a regular basis.

c) Coaching – this is one of the mainstays of on-the-job training. Demonstrating the technique to the trainee and then allowing him or her to practise is appropriate for many jobs which require a certain skill. Frequently, the coaching is undertaken by an experienced worker who is assigned to a trainee by the management.

Training is not just for new employees or trainees and therefore there are other forms of on-the-job training:

d) Secondment or attachment – this may involve the employee widening his/her skills by visiting other departments or learning other skills. Such training may also be used to increase awareness and understanding of other departments' problems and concerns.

e) Action learning – this involves employees undertaking special assignments, usually outside their own department or even company. This is a further attempt to widen their experiences.

Off-the-job training

For this type of training, the venue tends to be away from the actual place of work. The most common type of **off-the-job training** is courses, which can vary in length from hours to months or even, in some cases, years. There is a variety of names that are used for such courses e.g. seminars, workshops.

These courses can be either 'in-house' or run by an external agency. Courses run in-house can be tailored to meet the specific needs of both the business and the individual concerned. They can be timed to suit the needs of all concerned and being in-house ought to be cheaper than external courses.

Induction courses are an example of in-house training, as are courses run by the personnel department. Many of the larger businesses have their own training centres to which staff are sent. However, there is a move towards subcontracting training rather than staying in-house. Prior to privatisation BT employed several thousand employees in training roles. This has subsequently been reduced to fewer than 50 who are responsible for booking the courses with outside agencies.

For external courses, agencies such as TECs and local colleges of higher education may be used, especially for day release courses. Some businesses encourage their staff to join a sandwich course where they will spend a term or two at college, followed by a placement in business to put into practice some of the theory learnt. In a few cases, a business will sponsor an employee through university either for a first degree or for an MBA.

A comparatively new trend is distance learning courses; the original format of these was pioneered by the Open University using television, but to some extent this has been superseded by the use of CDs.

Another recent trend is to send executives, though not solely management, on adventure training courses designed to enhance leadership and group skills. Employees are sent off to a remote part of the country to fend for themselves, build rafts to cross rivers and cope with life out of doors.

Question 6

Suggest the advantages and disadvantages of
a) shadowing
b) coaching [6]

Question 7

State and justify whether you would use on-the-job or off-the-job training for the following:
  i) A new employee who has just left school
 ii) A recently appointed marketing director
iii) An experienced and highly skilled employee who has gained promotion to a supervisory post within the company.
Justify your answers. [6]

Appraisal

In recent years, more businesses have been successfully using an **appraisal** system as a method of assessing employee performance and raising standards.

The performance of any organisation is determined by the performance of the individuals within that organisation; consequently, improving the effectiveness of the individual improves the effectiveness of the organisation.

A typical appraisal system will assess the appraisee (the person being appraised) using predetermined criteria. At Ishida Europe, employees' performance is measured in two ways – by assessing their achievement of agreed targets and by rating them against a series of 'attributes' and 'skills' (*see Figure 54.3*).

Attributes include:

Commitment, flexibility, teamwork, initiative and awareness.

Skills include:

Knowledge, judgement, planning, negotiation and management.

Each of these categories is measured by the appraiser (the person who is responsible for the appraisal) and the results are reported back to the appraisee. These will then be discussed with a view to improving where necessary and then setting new targets for the next appraisal period. It is hoped that such a system will ensure that all employees are being constantly monitored for the benefit of the organisation and the individual employees (*see Figure 54.3*).

The latter will have the opportunity to discuss their achievements and training needs and any career aspirations. Any problems or weaknesses are then addressed by matching these problems with the appropriate training. This discussion may well be an obvious source of motivation as the employee is being given the opportunity to have any achievements noted and a sense of involvement, both considered to be important motivators.

Some businesses also use the appraisal system to assess the effectiveness of their recruitment policy.

Cost of training

Much depends on the skills to be imparted and the number of people to be trained, but the main costs consist of:

Resource materials for the employees
Trainers' fees or salaries
Administrative costs of the training department
Loss of production while aiding the employee during the induction period
Cost of any external examinations

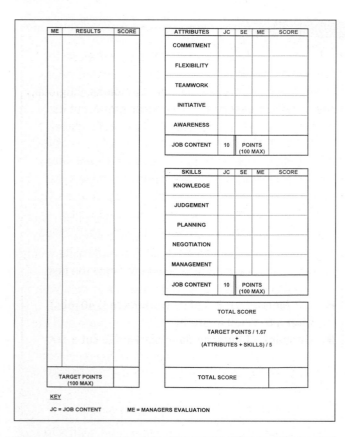

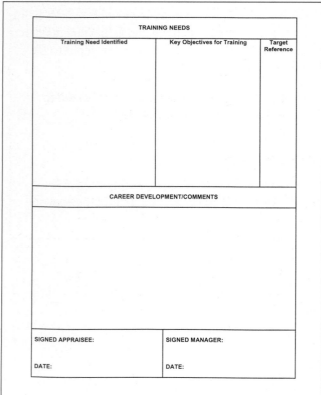

Figure 54.3   Ishida appraisal forms

Ending employment

Most of the rights assigned to employees are contained in the Employment Rights Act of 1996. These mostly pertain to employees who have been continuously employed for a given period of time.

Dismissal

The area of unfair dismissal is often the cause of disputes within a company. An employee is protected from unfair dismissal only if he or she has been employed by that company for a minimum period of two years. After that period an employee may not be dismissed without notice. There are exceptions to this: a worker may not be dismissed without notice if the reason itself is unfair e.g. joining a trade union and being dismissed for it would be deemed to be unfair. Similarly, regardless of the length of employment, an employee may not be dismissed for becoming pregnant.

Legitimate reasons for dismissal (known in this case as fair dismissal) include:

i) misconduct e.g. theft of products
ii) lack of ability e.g. unable to perform the required tasks
iii) redundancy
iv) a statutory restriction which prevents the employee continuing.

In addition the burden of proof is on the employer to show that he or she has acted reasonably in dismissing the employee. In the event of a dispute over whether the dismissal was reasonable, the employee may seek recourse to an industrial tribunal. If the decision of the tribunal is disputed it is possible to appeal to the Employment Appeal Tribunal.

Redundancy

Redundancy occurs when:

i) the employer ceases trading
ii) the employer ceases trading in the present location
iii) there is insufficient work for the employee, due to a fall in demand or an end to the demand for the product in which the employee is involved.

If redundancy occurs, the onus is on the employer to compensate the employee by way of redundancy payments.

The amount due to the employee is calculated by taking the number of years' service into account as well as the rate of pay at the time of the redundancy.

Termination by notice

If the employee has a contract for a given period i.e. a short-term contract or to complete a particular task, the contract is considered to be at an end when the time has elapsed or the work is completed.

However, for normal employment contracts which do not stipulate a given period of time, there is a duty to give notice of termination. For many, the length of time required for giving notice is often stipulated within the contract of employment. To avoid conflict, case law states that reasonable notice must be given if no such time is stated within the contract of employment.

There is a sliding scale of notice; as the duration of employment increases, the minimum period of notice increases. For example, even after only one month of continuous employment, an employee is entitled to a minimum of one week's notice. The maximum period of notice is 12 weeks. This does not prevent a longer period of notice being used as long as it is stipulated within the contract of employment.

Employees do not have to give the same amount of notice; the statutory period of notice is one week regardless of the length of continuous employment.

Question 8

Beginning in late 1998, the financial services sector (banking, insurance, stockbroking) underwent some radical restructuring over the next 12 months. Citigroup, the world's largest financial services group, cut its work-force by 10,400 employees (6% of the global work-force). The restructuring cost the business $900 million which was written off in one lump sum during 1999. As a result, the business hoped to save $680 million in 1999 and $975 million in 2000. At the same time, the following companies announced similar plans, having been hit by tough market conditions:

- Meryll Lynch eliminated 3,400 jobs (5% of its work-force) after losing $164 million in the last quarter of 1998
- J. P. Morgan cut 5% of its work-force (740 jobs) after a 61% fall in profits
- Germany's Deutsche Bank planned to cut 5,500 jobs having taken over Banker's Trust which lost $488 million dollars in the last quarter of 1998
- Barings, the company made infamous by Nick Leeson, laid off 1,200 employees

Most of these employees were well qualified, highly specialised, committed and ambitious people who were made redundant due entirely to factors outside their control.

Source: *America Today*, 15/12/98

a) Calculate the gain which Citigroup expected to make as a result of the redundancies.   [1]

b) Are there any non-financial costs when redundancy takes place?   [3]

c) Discuss how the companies mentioned above might have managed the difficult situation of making redundancies.   [8]

Points for Revision

Key Terms

job description	a summary of the main job details
person profile/ person specification	the main characteristics and requirements to enable a person to undertake the job
internal sources of employment	employing and promoting existing employees
external sources of employment	employing someone from outside the business
contract of employment	legally required document stating details such as pay, entitlements and conditions
induction	introducing a knowledge of the company and the way in which it operates
on-the-job training	training that takes place at the place of work and concentrates on the skills necessary to perform a given task
off-the-job training	training that takes place away from the place of work and which is frequently run by an outside agency
appraisal	a method of assessing employees' performance
redundancy	the process of dismissing an employee due to lack of work available

Definitions Question:
With reference to a business or businesses of which you have direct knowledge or experience, define any three of the above terms (your teacher may choose three for you).   [5] per definition

Summary Points:

1   Recruitment involves a variety of techniques to ensure the right candidate is selected for a given job.

2   Training is important if a business is to gain maximum efficiency from this valuable resource of labour. The training can be on-the-job or off-the-job.

3   Appraisal is now an integral part of assessing the performance of employees.

4   Redundancy procedures are defined by law to protect employees against unfair dismissal.

Mini Case Study

Byte-It is a relatively new business which writes software packages for major companies. As the business is expanding rapidly, it needs to take on more staff on a regular basis since it started trading only three years ago.

It is concerned about recruitment problems. It has noted the number of businesses in the United States that are trying to reduce the time and therefore the costs of their recruitment programmes. The owner, Miss Hickman, was keen to utilise the technology that she was already using as an integral part of the business. She placed the job vacancies on the website of the company. By providing an application form with the advertisement, prospective candidates could reply by e-mail and this would then be sifted by her and her colleagues.

Once she had eliminated those candidates who were not suitable, she had the bright idea of attempting to gain publicity for her business by conducting the interviews using a video conference facility. She was convinced this would be a much more cost-effective way of recruiting the people she needed and it would attract the right type of applicants, those who were interested and surfed the Internet.

1 Define: video conference facility.   [2]

2 What information would Miss Hickman have to put on her website to ensure applicants would have enough details to pursue an application?   [4]

3 Many businesses insist on a letter of application that is handwritten; suggest if it would be a disadvantage not having this option.   [3]

4 Miss Hickman suggested this method of recruitment would be cheaper than the traditional methods of recruitment; suggest how this may be true.   [5]

5 Discuss the likely limitations of Miss Hickman's method of recruitment.   [6]

20

Maxi Case Study

Business Link Sandwell (BLS) is based in the West Midlands. It is a locally funded advisory service for businesses in the catchment area of Sandwell. Its aim is to operate for the benefit of the local business community, providing advice and starting initiatives for training and improving the performances of businesses. It has continually stated that people are the most important asset a business has. However, of more significance is its view that not enough importance is given to the needs and aspirations of employees by many businesses.

Even when a business is aware that expenditure on training and development can enhance productivity and quality of goods, there is a degree of reluctance to undertake or finance such training. This is particularly true, according to BLS, when there is a shortage of IT specialists or engineers. At BLS, they have set out to show the value of staff development. Starting from the premise that all good managers require a programme of continual training to cope with the ever-changing business environment that they face, BLS introduced a Management Development programme.

The programme starts by taking a detailed look at the performance of the business in question and noting the plans that it has for the future. These are then considered in the light of the skills of the managers of the business. A programme of action is then agreed between BLS and the company. For many businesses, this programme will mean sending managers out to specific training courses, though not exclusively; in-house training via workshops is an option as well.

Since the Management Development programme was launched in 1998, it has been brought to the attention of many businesses in the local area that many of their managers receive far less training than their European counterparts. Only 24% of UK managers are graduates, compared with 50% in France and Germany and 85% in the USA and Japan. Perhaps of more concern is the fact that only 2% of West Midland company directors have had any training as directors. Its biggest success to date has been its ability to get businesses to undertake an audit of their performance, plans and managerial skills. From the initial scheme that asked the participating companies to answer questions on various aspects of management skills, BLS found, using the audit programme Enabler 2000, that there were some alarming gaps in certain important skills (26 skills or competencies were put into six categories, all of which were considered to be vital for survival in the modern world of competitive business). The main gaps were:

Leadership skills
Motivating others
Delivering customer satisfaction
Interpersonal sensitivity

The gaps would then be the skills that would require a training programme to be implemented. For example, managers portraying a lack of interpersonal sensitivity may be operating as autocratic leaders and therefore require skills in team building and delegation.

BLS then utilises its many contacts throughout the region to put into place the appropriate training to 'correct' these difficulties or gaps.

Critics or sceptics ask how it is possible to measure the value of the training programmes that have been used by BLS, or they suggest that spending large amounts on training can be wasted because of the danger that the recently trained will move to another company. BLS replies by stating that once trained, the managers feel that their company is taking a genuine interest in them and are therefore more likely to stay, which is in itself cost-effective as the expensive recruitment process is avoided.

One final step in the training programme is to ensure that once trained the managers are allowed to put into practice what has been learned. The ethos of the business has to be flexibility and a willingness to change.

1 Define: asset, productivity, in-house training, autocratic leaders.   [8]
2 Why is it that for IT businesses there is a tendency to make training a low priority?   [4]
3 Suggest the consequences of UK businesses spending far less on training than their main rivals in France, Germany, USA and Japan.   [5]
4 Comment on the main gaps in the managers' skills, as found from the results of the initial survey.   [8]
5 Evaluate the benefits to a business of training its managerial staff (consider the financial and non-financial factors).   [15]

40

Managing change

Learning objectives

Having read this unit, students will be able to

1   identify the meaning of change in a modern business

2   understand why acceptance of change is one of the crucial yardsticks for success

3   appreciate some of the ways that business can manage change effectively

Context

In 1998, the Teletubbies and the yo-yo dominated the market for children's fads. In 1999, Beanie Babies and Furbies looked set to break records of demand. Although children's fads, by definition, do not last, the industry must be able to change quickly.

The computer industry has become a role model for change; Amstrad's computer software dominated the home computer market in the 1980s, with Microsoft's Windows 95 and 98 dominating in the 1990s. The speed of technological change means that within two months, investment in the newest home computer technology is redundant.

Mobile phones grew in popularity in the 1980s, although they were bulky, unreliable and very expensive; since then the cost of using a mobile has been dramatically reduced and the service has become much more reliable, with smaller, pocket-sized telephones.

No skill is more important than the corporate capacity to change. 'If you aren't reorganising pretty substantially every 6 to 12 months, then you are probably out of step with the times.'
Tom Peters, *Thriving on Chaos* (Guild Publishing, 1987)

What is change?

Change is anything which causes us to alter our working or private lives; in commercial terms, it is anything which causes the business to alter its process of operation or perhaps which causes its profit to change. Change is divided into two types:

■ Scientific and technical change

New production processes and technological advancement have made a significant impact on the way businesses carry out their day-to-day activities. New discoveries in genetics have allowed sheep to be cloned; quantities of data, similar to the size of all Shakespeare's works, can be passed down telephone wires in a matter of seconds; and the amount of technological capacity on a Nintendo Gameboy is greater than the technology which controlled the American Defense missile system in the 1960s.

Question 1

A major problem of scientific and technical change has been controlling the rate of change; what is sometimes desirable from one point of view is not so from another. Consider the following in terms of benefits and problems of the change in question
a) automating a production process
b) air travel
c) electronic music   [6]

■ Organisational change

There have been several attempts to describe organisational change in terms of altering the structure, all of which refer to the same thing. The most significant change in this respect is the change from tall, rigid structures (mechanistic), to flatter, 'leaner' structures (organistic).

Rather than celebrating their size, larger companies have been trying to imitate smaller rivals. This has been done by shrinking headquarters, removing layers of management and subdividing the business into smaller, more manageable units. This has involved two significant alterations in the way an organisation operates:

a) removal of most of middle management – this has meant that the job it used to do has been either taken on by the remaining managers or delegated to the level below
b) power and responsibility has been passed further down the hierarchy, inviting rank and file workers to take part in the decision making process. This has been difficult for two types of employees:
(i) senior executives who are used to taking all the decisions themselves and who are also accustomed to unquestioning acceptance by the staff
(ii) front-line (factory workers) who have been used to being told what to do and who find the idea of being responsible for their own work contradictory to their work philosophy

How is change created?

Internally

■ A business may decide that its objectives need to alter e.g. change in emphasis from survival to growth, perhaps with a business that has survived its first two years and is now looking to create profit.

■ New appointments and resignations, particularly at the top end of the business, may introduce new perspectives and energy.

■ Staff's skills, backgrounds and experiences change along with their own needs from the job they are doing.

■ R and D may invent and innovate products and processes which the market wants.

■ Financial pressures may demand cost-cutting through redundancies or financial growth may mean the business can invest in more capital equipment.

Externally

■ The customer base may change. Customers have different requirements and therefore purchase from competitors e.g. petrol stations now have to compete with the large retailers, because customers have taken their trade away from the petro-chemical companies.

- Society changes its attitudes and values – customers are far more aware of 'green issues' and base more of their purchasing decisions on this new awareness.

- Globalisation – as markets in far-flung foreign countries have developed quickly, so has the need to capitalise on the growth of that country e.g. China and the capital investment which has been made over the past 10 years. Globalisation makes knowledge more important – as the price of communication falls (it will soon be cheaper to telephone Delhi from London, than to phone Manchester) this will allow contact and therefore competition between the cheap hands of the east and brains of the west. So the only way to create a competitive advantage is to produce new ideas.

- Cultural and social changes within the domestic economy – this is particularly relevant for companies which sell products to the 16–24 age bracket where fashion changes and tolerance of certain issues becomes more widespread e.g. 25 years ago, any advert with any sexual connotation was frowned on, whereas it is more acceptable to advertise in such a way now.

- Competition – in highly competitive markets, when one company initiates a change the others must do so immediately or risk losing market share.

- Technological change – this has been one of the most significant factors affecting change both for companies and for consumers. The way a business orders goods from suppliers and the method of paying for goods through credit cards has changed beyond recognition after 15 years.
  Companies are inventing new, faster methods of communicating with customers. Through the Internet, shopping at home will soon become a popular method of purchasing products. The market for computer products for the home has grown from the days when people bought computers to play computer games to the present day, when a computer is now seen as a necessary part of life.

- New management techniques are published – every year there are several new executive publications which claim to have found a new way of running a business; most are phrases which mean the same thing, but are expressed differently e.g. re-engineering, restructuring, bench marking, delayering, downsizing, zero-basing. Some companies will deliberately pick up on the next management fad and try to implement it in their own business.

- The government makes political or economic changes e.g. deregulation and privatisation of buses or the railways, or perhaps introduces a new law on pollution control.

- Economic trends also affect a business both in terms of the domestic economy e.g. through interest rate changes, or perhaps international economies e.g. the Asian crisis, which had a significant effect on any company that had assets – cash, shares or buildings – in any Far Eastern/south-east Asian economies. A more significant effect is on those companies which traded with those economies.

Proactive change

Some companies deliberately initiate change and accept change as a necessary part of survival. In recent years, companies carrying out **proactive change** have been called 'fast companies'. Although this can be viewed by the cynics as another example of corporate jargon which means nothing, others view fast companies as a vital part of industrial growth. An example of a fast company is Reebok which has successfully converted the sports shoe into a fashion accessory, or perhaps Virgin which uses its brand name to move into markets where it thinks it can gain a competitive edge.

Major telecommunications firms have an important role to play in developing 'fast companies' in this respect because the way a business relates to customers and suppliers is changing rapidly due to computers and highly efficient telecommunications systems.

Question 2

Statement 1: Bill Gates has become the world's richest man by anticipating change.
Statement 2: Bill Gates simply had to follow the market trends and invent products quickly; he made his billions by following the market.
To what extent do you agree with either of the above statements? [8]

Reactive change

Reactive change occurs when the firm waits for evidence that change has become unavoidable and reluctantly joins in; the problem at Marks and Spencer during 1998/1999 has been described as being due to the business relying on its traditional relationships with suppliers and customers.

Question 3

Traditional companies have been compared with east European companies before the revolutions of the early 1990s: controlled from the centre and over-manned. The spread of information technology allowed companies to bypass middle managers (whose job was frequently to collect and control information). The pace of innovation and fickleness of consumer taste was rendering long-range planning impossible and poorer countries were beginning to compete, forcing larger companies to slash labour costs and replace employees with either machines or more efficient production processes.

a) Identify the changes which have taken place in recent years.   [4]

b) What problems might traditional companies face in effecting the changes?   [8]

Why is change a problem?

Whatever the cause of the change, individuals and companies react in a certain way to the necessity to alter part or all of the way they carry out day-to-day activities. Human beings are creatures of stability; regardless of the attraction of being different, most individuals go through a state of change early on in their lives and relish the stability as they get older. In *As You Like It*, Shakespeare depicts the seven ages of man which reflect the inevitability of change, but does not address the need for stability. Companies go through similar stages of their lives; once the profits start rolling in, and the business has established its own way of operating, why change it, if it works? Any threat to that stability is therefore treated with suspicion.

The threat comes in several forms:

■ Employees may end up financially worse off

This occurs either through redundancy or a change in location of the business, forcing employees to move to a more expensive area.

■ The job becomes more complicated and technical

There is sometimes a fear of technological change because of the likelihood that it will make employees look incompetent and mean they cannot do their job properly e.g. a secretary who has used a typewriter and duplicating machine for years, but suddenly has to learn how to use a computer and printer, may be concerned at not being able to use the new technology.

■ Uncertainty

Rumours of change, doubts over the effects of a particular deal struck by one company e.g. a potential takeover may mean that the stability of tenure is lost. Maslow (*see Unit 50*) commented on the importance of security as a need which employers must satisfy.

■ Change in status

The introduction of new machinery may mean that a group of people who have worked together are split up, losing their group affiliation. At Semco, employees were invited to grade their immediate superiors, awarding them marks for the way they did their job! They then decided that subordinates should actually elect their new superior. Both are cases of the need continually to change the status and social standing of the individual for the improvement of the organisation.

■ Attitude of self and group

Rosabeth Moss Kanter wrote about change in *The Change Masters* (Simon & Schuster, 1985) by developing 10 blocks or barriers to change that managers were guilty of erecting when they wanted to defend their position. These ranged from regarding any new idea with suspicion to making decisions in secret! Managers who are sitting comfortably at the top of the hierarchy, biding time until their pension is payable, will be unwilling to see a new, modernising chairman, aged 34, coming into the business and shaking it up by removing senior executives (which is usually the first thing that shareholders request!).

Is resistance to change always a bad thing?

1 It will ensure that the issue is discussed and that all those who are likely to be affected by the change will have a chance to put forward their opinions.
2 It forces managers to make the situation clear for all concerned and therefore brings any doubts to the fore.
3 It allows those affected to use their expertise and knowledge in determining the details e.g. automation may be seen as blindingly obvious for senior management, but if it will result in lower quality, or perhaps a need to change another part of the working process, the ideas of the shopfloor worker become the most valid. When companies censor criticism and state that they do not want their decision questioned, it is usually being made for the wrong reasons.

How can change be managed effectively?

Management must be absolutely clear on its objectives – once change has been decided on, there must be the usual trait theory leadership to see the change through to the end. When Sir John Egan initiated quality circles at Jaguar in the early 1980s, he met with some significant criticism. Only once some success had been achieved with quality circles could he then show the resisters that the change was for the better, demonstrating the necessary judgement for the idea to be accepted.

Attitude to change – that innovation and change are a necessary part of business is worth building into the minds of everyone in the business, either from the moment the business starts or from when new employees join. This means the recruitment process (*see Unit 54*) must look out for individuals who will accept and encourage innovation. In addition, there needs to be a part of the training programme that educates employees to generate ideas.

Trust – the willingness to accept change is based on trust. A trusting work-force is likely to be one which is positive about work and one where there is good morale. If a conscious effort is made to build up morale in the weeks before change is announced, this will help to ease the situation.

Planning – this needs to be done in phases so that a clear timetable can be seen by all concerned. By permanently reminding stakeholders of change, acceptance of the change will become easier.

Training – if employees are given special training, then the organisation will be seen as making a commitment to the change in terms of real preparation for its staff. If employees feel that they will benefit from the change in terms of their career, they are more likely to accept it.

Communication – this must be open and thorough. The timing of the communication is also important; it could be argued that the earlier the change can be introduced in the minds of those who will be most affected, the less resistant they will be as their minds adjust to the new ideas. However, it could mean that there is greater resistance if those affected decide to resist – they have longer to prepare arguments against the change.

Participation – where possible, change must involve discussions with all staff affected so that they can design their own part of the change process. When Semco had to make redundancies, it was the factory committee that decided who was to be made redundant, following discussions which involved the entire work-force.

Compromise – if the essential strategy of change is not affected it is possible to use symbolic compromise over the smaller details e.g. the timing of breaks. This can be seen as a way of understanding the employees' concerns; if the management is seen to be understanding, the hope is that the employees will agree to the change.

Points for Revision

Key Terms

scientific and technical change	caused by discoveries in research and technological advances
organisational change	where the business as a whole restructures
internal change	generated within the business itself
external change	generated by external forces
proactive change	where the change is anticipated by the business and can be used to force other companies to adapt
reactive change	where the business assesses others and changes because competitors have done so; the business is responding to change rather than initiating it

Definitions Question:
By referring to a business you know, explain the significance of three of the above terms (your teacher may wish to help you choose the terms).   [5] per definition

Summary Points:

1 Change is a necessary part of modern business.

2 The ability of a business to identify the forces of change and to anticipate change will frequently determine its success.

3 Managing change requires a commitment towards participation for employees and clear communication to all stakeholders.

Mini Case Study

Asea Brown Bovery is a large business which operates in the power industry e.g. robotics, power distribution and power transmission. Chief Executive Percy Barnevik has reorganised the business along the following lines: eight business segments, each with a director in charge (each segment serving one of the markets the company operates in).

The eight segments are then broken down into a total of 1,300 independent companies, which are further divided into 5,000 profit centres. Within each profit centre, 10 people work as a multi-functional team. Despite this total there are only three management layers. Such reorganisation has taken place since Barnevik took control of the business. When buying another company, Barnevik applies what he calls the 30% rule, which means he aims to reduce 30% of head office costs per year in the first three years. He reduced the head office staff from 2,000 to 200 at ABB by stating to the staff that 'they had three months to find a job in one of the operating divisions.' In an interview with the *Harvard Business Review*, he said, 'You can't postpone tough decisions by studying them to death and you can't permit a honeymoon of small changes over a year or two. A long series of changes prolongs the pain. We would rather be roughly correct and fast, than exactly correct and slow.'

1 Define: profit centre, management layers.   [4]

2 What is the reasoning behind splitting the business according to its market segments as opposed to its production facilities?   [4]

3 What problem might Barnevik face when applying the 30% rule?   [4]

4 Discuss how the statement at the end of the case study might help managers to effect change.   [8]

                                                                                    20

Maxi Case Study

To: A. Student

From: Mr. M. Director

Re: Changing World of Work

Dear Andy,

We have just commissioned this report from McKinsey, the management consultant group. I would appreciate your comments.

Michael

The Changing World of Work

Introduction

Charles Handy states that having a typical 9–5 job for 47 weeks a year, for 47 years is becoming untenable. This equates to about 100,000 hours; what is much more likely is that working lives will last for 50,000 hours, according to one of four options:

1 a series of full-time jobs, with different skills being required along the way, after a lengthy study period and possible intermittent study periods in order to change skills: 25 years × 45 hours × 45 weeks = 50,000 hours

2 a full-time job which stops at 50 as younger, more energetic individuals come through the organisation and the 50 pluses work on a fee basis. See 1 for calculations.

3 a part-time contract, working 25 hours a week for 45 weeks, or perhaps working 45 hours a week for 25 weeks (a temporary contract), both for 45 years. 25 hours × 45 weeks × 45 years (part-time) or 45 hours × 25 weeks × 45 years (temporary) = 50,000 hours

4 work for 10 years, then take 10 years out to raise a family, then return to work – this option is already used by women, though increasingly is becoming attractive to men who want a change in their lifestyle. See 1 for calculations.

In addition to these, however, are multiple other factors effecting a change in work patterns.

Work at home or on the move

Working at home has evolved due mainly to the change in technology (allowing tele-working to take place) which has allowed work to be done in the comfort of home, or even on the move. Although fax machines have been used for over 20 years, electronic mail has become a more popular and quicker form of communicating messages. Companies have encouraged employees to work at home by the simple provision of a computer and a modem, costing not much more than £1,000. Laptops have become standard issue for those who need to use a computer as part of their job. Such laptops can be linked to the electronic mail system using a mobile telephone, which increases the speed at which information is passed from one user to another. Hotels have responded to this new work pattern by installing 'business centres' which are specifically targeted at the working, mobile manager and charging high prices for them. Fax machines, Internet access and desk space are hired out to managers at premium rates. Video conferencing has also meant that there is much less need for travel to and from work.

Home-working can save organisations vast amounts of money through allowing them to reduce the size of the office space. It also allows a dual life at home, although the reality of working at home does mean there are more interruptions from children and the 9–5 structure disappears.

Hot-desking

The days when managers had their own space are slowly disappearing. By encouraging home-working, employees probably need to be in the office for only two days a week. Hot-desking simply means that employees can sit at a desk and immediately have their work to hand by logging on to the company computer network system.

The need for flexibility

There is a continual call from industry to be able to employ 'flexible' employees; what this means is that hiring and firing is now cheaper than it ever used to be for those employees with less experience.

Negating the advantage of flexibility is the insecurity which is built into work, through either part-time or temporary contracts, however lucrative the rate of pay.

Managers type, secretaries add value

Managers have broadened their skill levels so that there is less need for secretarial staff. Semco redeployed secretaries into the business because they were adding costs, but not adding value.

Longer opening hours for retailers

It is rare to find a retail park where the shops do not stay open until 8 p.m. from Monday to Saturday. Some retailers have actually begun 24-hour opening! This results in the work-force being made up of many more part-time workers than full-time employees. Sunday trading has also contributed to significant strains on family life.

Conclusion

Taken to its extreme, a business will no longer have premises, just a logo and employees working at home i.e. it will become what is known as a 'virtual organisation'.

Either

Summarise the above in the form of a presentation, giving your opinions as to its effect on a company of which you have direct experience.   [30]

Or

Answer the following questions:

1 Define: tele-working, manager.   [4]

2 Highlight the three most important changes facing the work-force as described in the above case. Justify your choice.   [6]

3 Evaluate the most important reasons causing the change from 100,000 hours to 50,000 hours in a typical working life.   [10]

4 Discuss the likely effects on a business of becoming a 'virtual organisation'.   [10]

                                                                                                        30

'Friday afternoon'

End of section test

1 List the items that ought to be included in a job description. [5]
2 What is the difference between internal and external recruitment? [4]
3 What is the purpose of a CV (curriculum vitae)? [2]
4 List two advantages of interviews as a method of selecting candidates for a given job. [4]
5 What information ought to appear on an itemised pay slip? [4]
6 What is the purpose of a contract of employment? [3]
7 Explain the purpose of training. [4]
8 Make a list of the different types of on-the-job training. [5]
9 State the minimum length of employment which provides employees with protection against unfair dismissal. [1]
10 How is appraisal of benefit to an employee? [2]
11 How did Schein define groups? [3]
12 Explain what is meant by a formal group. [4]
13 State the factors necessary for a group to be successful. [3]
14 Give an example for each of the following types of unions:
   i) craft ii) industrial iii) general iv) white collar [4]
15 List the main functions of a trade union. [5]
16 What determines the strength of a union? [4]

17 What is the equivalent of the TUC for employers? [1]
18 Explain how having a single union agreement will be of benefit to: the employers, the employees. [4]
19 Imagine negotiations have broken down; make a list of the possible types of industrial action that could be used. [5]
20 To avoid industrial action, which bodies are available to help reach a settlement? [3]
21 Describe the differences between salaries and wages. [4]
22 Explain what is meant by the term 'piece rate'. [2]
23 Is commission a good method to motivate a sales-force? [5]
24 What is profit-related pay? [3]
25 List the main factors that will determine whether performance-related pay will work. [4]
26 Why might incentive schemes fail to work? [4]
27 What is scientific management? [2]
28 Who founded the school of scientific management? [1]
29 What are fringe benefits? [3]
30 How has the government made fringe benefits less attractive? [2]
31 List three leadership styles. [3]
32 What are the main factors that influence the style of leadership? [4]

33 According to Adair, what is action-centred leadership? [3]

34 Draw a Blake and Mouton leadership style matrix. [4]

35 According to Fayol, what are the five elements of management? [5]

36 Explain the term 'management by objectives'. [2]

37 Either draw and label, or explain, the 'inverted doughnut'. [3]

38 Explain the difference between the trait theory and situation theory of leadership. [4]

39 Suggest a well known 'leader' and state what style of leadership he or she uses. [3]

40 Select any writer on leadership and state his or her main findings. [3]

41 What is communication? [2]

42 What is the main difference between one- and two-way communication? [2]

43 Give two examples of formal and informal communication which could take place within a business. [4]

44 When would it be appropriate to use closed communication? [2]

45 Draw a diagram to show vertical and horizontal communication. [3]

46 Which communication network tends to be associated with vertical communication? [1]

47 Draw a chain network and suggest an example of such a network. [4]

48 Write out the list of headings that ought to appear in a report. [5]

49 According to Shannon and Weaver, what are the three barriers to hinder effective communication? [3]

50 Apart from Shannon and Weaver's barriers, what other factors may hinder effective communication? [5]

51 Weinshall put forward three basic types of organisational structures; draw any two. [4]

52 What are the main characteristics of a mechanistic organisation? [3]

53 Explain the benefits of a matrix structure. [4]

54 Why is delegation necessary in a large organisation? [2]

55 Why is communication harder in an organisation with many levels of hierarchy? [4]

56 List the factors that affect the size of the span of control. [5]

57 What are the main advantages of decentralisation? [3]

58 Explain the differences between line and staff managers. [4]

59 Why is an organistic structure better for motivation? [4]

60 Draw an organisational structure to show a large span of control. [2]

200

'Friday afternoon' 1

The manager of a country club just outside Southampton was trying to persuade staff at their monthly meeting that she would ensure it would be worth their while working on New Year's Eve. However, many of the staff had already made the point that a new millennium does not arrive very often and they wanted to be free to enjoy the celebrations on what promised to be a very special occasion.

Unfortunately, Helen Todd, the manager of the country club, was responsible not only for the staff at the club but in addition for the task of organising the club's New Year's Eve bonanza! The £125 tickets had already been sold out for months and the 200 guests were to be wined and dined from 8.30 till 2 a.m.

Helen had calculated that a full complement of staff would be required to operate the function suite, as many of the guests had booked into the hotel of the club as well and that too was fully booked. However, to date, she had persuaded only about half the staff to work, having offered them five times their normal rate of £4 an hour. The hotel manager was not prepared to lend Helen staff as he himself had only just enough staff who had agreed much earlier to work for £20 an hour.

With little time to organise extra staff from outside, Helen was determined to ensure the right number would be available for the big night. She decided to offer an additional £5 an hour to the function staff, though was conscious that the kitchen staff had already settled for £20 an hour; this did not include the chefs who had negotiated their own deal a few weeks earlier. Her deputy, Harry, had not seen anything like this before; 'staff refusing to work for five times the normal rate!' He suggested offering the staff a couple of days off and a free ticket to see *Cats* in London.

Helen had another idea; she decided to get the staff together and explain the problem that she and the business faced, hoping that getting them involved would make them feel that they mattered.

1 Assuming that the number of function staff is 25, calculate the additional labour cost for New Year's Eve.   [3]

2 Suggest which theory of motivation Harry is relying on to win over the staff. Explain your choice.   [4]

3 What are the likely problems that Helen will incur if the staff accept her additional offers of pay?   [3]

4 How would you describe the offer of tickets to see *Cats* as a form of 'payment'?   [2]

5 Has Helen given sufficient attention to the non-financial methods of motivation that may lead to more staff being prepared to work on the big night?   [8]

_____

20

'Friday afternoon' 2

Eddy Shah, famous in more recent times for *Today* newspaper (before it was closed down), gained fame and a certain degree of notoriety in the early 1980s for standing up to the unions.

One of the most famous industrial battles of the 1980s took place in Warrington, Merseyside during 1983. Although some time ago, it created an unprecedented change in the relationship between businesses and unions and began the steady decline in the massive union power and influence which until then had gone unchallenged. Shah, who ran a newspaper business at the time, stood up to the power of the unions, risking his business, reputation and at times his own personal safety.

He began his media experience working as a floor manager in charge of a studio at Granada TV. Here he developed the important communication skills which are such a significant part of leadership. Dealing with actors ranging from the *Coronation Street* team to Laurence Olivier, along with a variety of camera men,

props organisers, technicians and programme managers, meant that decisions had to be made swiftly and correctly!

He left the TV industry and began his own newspaper company employing a team of journalists and subcontracting the printing. Gradually the finance was saved to buy his own printing works. As the business grew the unions began to pay attention to the influence of the company and insisted that all members of the work-force had to join a union. In effect, the NGA, the typesetters' union, was asking for union recognition in the work-place by insisting that everyone joined the union; the business as a whole did not need this, so in typical democratic style, Eddy Shah held a ballot as a method of gauging the response.

In those days, unions ruled by fear; despite Margaret Thatcher's radical union-busting techniques, very few employers were brave enough to instigate them because of the fear of reprisal from the union. The ballot also revealed that many people wanted to join the union, which Eddy Shah promptly allowed. The ballot revealed that five employees did not want to join the union and the union's response was to tell Eddy Shah that he was to sack the five workers and they would then inform him whom to replace them with! He refused to comply with these commands which was the catalyst for the ensuing struggle.

On July 4, 1983, six union members within his company went on strike and for the next six months, he was faced with between 100 and 10,000 pickets outside his printing press at Warrington. Shah's response was to go into work with his staff, in order to make a clear statement that he was going to dig his heels in. The union then closed down Fleet Street (the headquarters of the nation's newspapers) and arranged buses and taxis to travel up the motorway to picket the printing press. The NGA fuelled the problem by inviting local support; Eddy Shah described the union movement as one which was run like a religion.

After some very serious threats one night, the police, through the timely intervention of Margaret Thatcher, came to the company's rescue. A court order was issued on the NGA and its assets were frozen. At the same time, Andrew Neil, then the editor of *The Sunday Times,* wrote an article supporting Shah which the unions refused to print, because they were beginning to realise that the events at Warrington represented a microcosm of feeling within the country; eventually, the union was fined £1.25 million.

Following this event, Eddy Shah expressed several views on leadership:

1 Leadership is about persistence, dedication and commitment – reference to any of the famous leaders in history lends proof to this idea.
2 Democratic leadership is about the person at the top of the business being clever!
3 Any manager who takes the organisation away from its core business will lose the company money.
4 The situation which leaders find themselves in depends on the skill and appropriateness of their ability to lead.
5 The leader of a business must allow total and free communication between all employees and management.
6 The ability to listen and learn means the leader gets better at understanding the business, but this does not necessarily create better leadership.

His final viewpoint was based on the characteristics which make leaders – he believes very much in the need for charisma in that any leader must lead using ideally their heads, but usually their hearts!

1 Define: communication skills, strike. [4]

2 Outline the evidence in the text which can be related to the theories contained in the unit on leadership (state the theory). [9]

3 Why might a business put financial implications as a secondary objective? [5]

4 To what extent do you believe that leaders are born, not made? [12]

–––––
30

Maxi Case Study

Dig-It Ltd was set up in the early 1990s to supply major retailers with a range of gardening equipment. Initially the company concentrated on spades and forks and for eight or nine years, the company grew slowly, selling its products at a slightly more expensive price than its competitors, although this was compensated by the life-time guarantee. By 1999, sales had been the same for three years in succession, so the managing director looked carefully at two options. The first was to reorganise the production process in order to achieve greater efficiency. The second was to introduce some new products. Initially, the business considered more gardening tools although quickly realised that the growth area was that of power tools. Black and Decker and Bosch were the main competitors. However, the company reckoned it had a strong enough understanding of the market as well as a reputation for quality for the business to succeed in this area of diversification. The owner, Robin Lewis, had discussed this with one or two marketing staff and was convinced that there was room for them in the market-place.

He had also been worrying about falling levels of productivity and was therefore looking at reorganising the factory into product areas as opposed to one long production line. With this in mind he commissioned a production adviser to examine the possibility of reorganising the factory to produce the old products alongside the newer power tools. This would require training and new machinery.

The work-force was very suspicious that something was going on when the team of advisers spent four days studying the employees at work, huddling in corners of the factory with plans and clipboards. Rumours abounded that they were from a rival company looking to take Dig-It over; other employees thought they were hired by management to identify lazy workers with a view to making them redundant. Jaia Jones, the Personnel Director, was astonished to hear of the plans. The shop steward had walked into her office demanding an explanation for the action of the visitors, but she had not actually been told about them, so she excused herself and marched up to Robin's office.

'This is no time to think about trying to implement such a radical change,' she exploded, having heard of Robin's plan. 'During this year alone we have had eight people leave us out of a total work-force of 40. Morale is at its lowest at the moment and any talk of change will create more problems. Thank goodness we have been able to replace those employees.'

Robin suddenly realised that Jaia had a clear understanding of the state of the work-force and was rather embarrassed that he had not discussed the issue with her before. She went on to highlight several points of concern:

1 The jobs that they do are very dull; the process of production is highly specialised so there is very little variation in their daily routine.

2 They are also isolated from each other given the flow production system.

3 Productivity, measured by output per employee, had fallen and this trend was set to continue if nothing was done to resolve the issue.

Robin suggested that they should introduce a payments by results system which would help to increase output. Present output, for the factory as a whole, was 7,200 units (a combination of both forks and spades per week). Each employee was paid a basic wage of £7 per hour, regardless of output. Robin proposed that this was reduced to £6.80 per hour, but with a bonus of 80p per worker per unit made after 170 units, up to a maximum of 200 units per worker. 'I think our employees will be more than happy with that deal; it will allow them to earn up to £16 more per week if they produce 200 units per employee.'

Jaia pointed out that it must be a group-based agreement which could be achieved by dividing the production line into small teams. Robin also wanted to hire a new product manager to be responsible for the new product. He was keen to keep control of the product, in terms of the decisions made about it, given that the new power tools were his idea.

Although Jaia pointed out that an external appointment would be better for the business, Robin was adamant that he was going to promote one of the junior production managers, to give him experience of marketing.

As the meeting came to a close, Jaia was wondering why she had bothered to share her opinion. She didn't think Robin was really listening, although he was trying to show interest in her ideas while not paying much attention to them. As she turned to go, she muttered, 'I can't see why you are viewing the two issues of new products and reorganisation of the factory as separate issues – why not use the reorganisation as a way of introducing the new product?' Now there's an interesting idea, thought Robin!

1 Define:
  a) reorganise
  b) redundant
  c) personnel director
  d) shop steward
  e) output   [10]

2 Describe and explain the communication barriers which appear to exist at Dig-it Ltd.   [6]

3 How would you classify Robin's style of leadership? Comment on its appropriateness in this case.   [8]

4 a) Calculate the level of labour turnover in the company.   [2]

  b) Discuss how motivation theories might help Jaia and Robin to solve the problem of falling productivity.   [12]

5 Demonstrate how Robin can make his claim of £16 extra pay per worker per week under the new system.   [5]

6 Calculate a) the old labour cost per unit
            b) the new labour cost per unit
   at (i) 180 units
      (ii) 200 units   [6]

7 Analyse the likely reaction of the work-force to the new pay offer.   [8]

8 Explain what information would have been required by the personnel department in order to adapt the work-force plan for the introduction of the new product.   [5]

9 Explain how the company might carry out the training programme.   [4]

10 How might the understanding of the management of change help the business to reorganise the factory? [6]

11 Present the case for:
  a) Jaia
  b) Robin

for the appointment of the new product manager responsible for power tools. [8]

80

Business environment

Government intervention

Learning objectives

Having read this unit, students will be able to

1 identify the main economic objectives adopted by the government when attempting to manage the economy

2 understand the main economic policies a government may use to manage the economy and their possible impact on businesses

3 understand the causes of the trade cycle and assess the impact on a business of the various stages within the trade cycle

Context

BMW employees greeted with tremendous relief the news that the company was to receive a £200 million grant from the British government in order to keep the Longbridge plant open. It meant their jobs were secure for the medium term and the wealth of the locality was assured. Anyone who has worked in the coal industry or the shipbuilding industry will tell you a different story of uneconomic coal-mines and communities being destroyed by the refusal of governments to fund industry.

When the Chancellor of the Exchequer takes out his battered red briefcase on Budget Day, every business holds its breath to see if he is going to be cruel or kind to its own industry. Whatever decision he takes, there will always be some winners and some losers. It is the government's aim to ensure that there are more winners than losers, otherwise it will not be re-elected!

The role of government

For a business to thrive and gain an international reputation, it needs an economic environment which will allow it to prosper. The responsibility for creating such an environment lies with the government. How the government creates that environment tends to depend not just on its economic ideals, but on its political ideals; the government of China under Deng Xiao Ping remained staunchly Communist, and yet encouraged capitalism and paved the way for double-digit economic growth during the 1990s.

The role of the government as provider encompasses many areas:

- finance for companies trying to set up, as well as greatly needed subsidies to enable struggling businesses to survive

- jobs for people who have been unemployed – Labour's 'New Deal' was aimed primarily at the longer-term unemployed, which worked by giving employers money to assist with the cost of training and employing new people

- marketing support overseas, to encourage other foreign companies and governments to purchase products from the domestic businesses

- assets which the company can use and expertise which can help to guide companies through difficult times

- education and training for young people so that they can be equipped to deal with the world of work

The government also acts as a consumer by purchasing goods and services from and for a variety of different people and firms. The government purchases:

- skills from teachers, doctors and nurses

- catering services in order to run school kitchens

- advisory services from qualified and experienced people on issues such as the BSE link with CJD

- administrative staff for the three levels of government – local, regional and central – to allow civil servants to perform their tasks on behalf of government

The extent to which government intervenes in the level of economic activity will depend largely on the political party in power at the time. At one extreme is a **planned economy**, where the government takes more or less all the economic decisions, such as what to make, where to make it, how many to make and where to sell it. Such a system is no longer seen in the vast majority of countries in the world. The nearest and most recent example of planned economies were those in the old east European Communist states, led primarily by the USSR (the old version of Russia). Despite government control, there was about 5% of private business, usually in the agricultural sector.

The opposite extreme to the planned economy is a **market economy**, where there is almost no government intervention; this is a theoretical extreme because all countries will have some form of ruling body, mostly with a state parliament.

All economies therefore combine private sector business with state intervention to form a **mixed economy**. The private sector businesses provide the majority of the goods and services and the state provides those goods and services that the private sector is not able or willing to provide. Examples of the latter are often referred to as **merit goods** such as health services, libraries and social services as well as **public goods** such as street lighting.

Question 1

On your next journey to school, look out for examples of government activity. Summarise how the government activity has had a direct impact on your journey to school.   [6]

The government therefore has three functions, which would not otherwise be carried out by private sector institutions:

1   To create a legal environment which is fair and just and balances the needs of all those in the economy – individuals and businesses

2   To enhance the social environment to eradicate areas of poverty, racism and sexism and to encourage people to work as hard as possible, with rewards that match the skill and effort used in work. Included in this is to create a society where people are free from danger

3   To create an economic environment which encourages businesses to aim for profit and allows them to earn without exploiting others or harming the environment

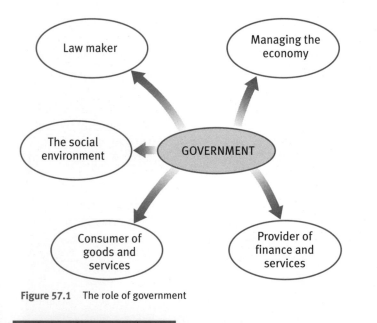

Figure 57.1   The role of government

Discussion Question

Why would the private sector be unwilling to carry out numbers 1 and 2 of the above?

Managing the economy

One of the major roles for any government is the effective management of an economy. Different governments will place different emphases on their economic objectives.

There are four economic objectives:

- Economic growth
- Stable prices
- Full employment
- Balance of payments surplus

- Economic growth – this is the increase in the level of **gross domestic product (GDP)** within an economy. During 1999, Britain's GDP was £848 billion – having grown at about 1% during the previous year. **Economic growth** leads to prosperity and wealth for most of the country's population. Employment levels rise, incomes rise, profits rise, investment rises. The opposite is the case during a period when the economy contracts (otherwise known as a **recession**).

- Stable prices (or zero inflation). Before 1900, inflation was non-existent – now it is a way of life. The problem with rising prices is that they cause lack of competitiveness in overseas markets, as well as wages that are difficult to control. The Conservative government of 1979–1997 pursued low inflation as its main economic objective (*see Unit 59*).

- Full employment – if every member of the working population had a job, there would be plenty of wealth, less crime and greater prosperity. It would also mean that people were using their talents – i.e. the obligation of the government to make the most of its human capital is of paramount importance. This was a policy that was pursued by successive Labour governments, since the Labour Party was born in the 1920s. Tony Blair's approach, known as the Third Way, comes somewhere between the pursuit of low inflation and the pursuit of low unemployment (*see Unit 59*).

- Balance of payments surplus – this means that the total value of exports is greater than the total value of imports. If we import more than we export, then money is constantly leaving the country to go into another country's bank account and to contribute to that country's wealth. Maintaining the balance of payments in surplus has been a challenge which virtually no government has been able to achieve consistently, except for the time when Britain discovered oil in the North Sea (*see Unit 61*).

Question 2

Why might a reduction in economic growth be seen as advantageous to a business that manufactures necessities?   [6]

Question 3

Suggest the circumstances when the government's insistence on achieving its economic objectives might mean it has to subordinate its objective to create a fairer society. When might the two objectives be compatible?   [6]

How does the government achieve these economic objectives?

The government uses a variety of economic policies in order to achieve these objectives:

Monetary policy – this involves using the **interest rate** and the **money supply**. The interest rate is the cost of borrowing and the money supply is the stock of money in the economy. A government may encourage a reduction in interest rates to make borrowing cheaper and therefore encourage investment. Alternatively, it could print more money, which would hopefully lead to greater wealth per capita, but unless it is matched by extra output, may well lead to inflation. The hyper-inflation in Germany in the 1920s was due to excessive printing of money.

Fiscal policy – governments raise money through taxation and then redistribute it through their expenditure plans. **Fiscal policy** is about setting the taxation rate at a level which encourages business activity, but also ensuring there is enough money for the government to distribute into the economy. Taxation comes in two forms

a) **direct taxation** e.g. income tax (the tax on personal income) or corporation tax (the tax on profits). A rise in direct taxation will cause less money to be earned and so will reduce disposable income (money earned after deductions for taxation, National Insurance and pensions)

b) **indirect taxation** e.g. VAT and excise duty. As opposed to a taxation on income, indirect taxation is a tax on expenditure.

Sometimes the government raises less than it wishes to spend, in which case it creates what is known as the **public sector net cash requirement** (or PSNCR). This is, in effect, the deficit of expenditure over income for an entire economy and the government finances the PSNCR by issuing government bonds, or gilt-edged securities. These are bought by companies, private individuals and foreign governments. A gilt is a promise to repay a sum of money, with a fixed term and a fixed

level of interest. This also affects the value of the pound. By needing to borrow money, this raises the interest rate, which raises the pound, making exports more difficult to sell.

An alternative to reducing taxation within fiscal policy is to increase the taxation allowance. This means a person or business can earn more money before tax is levied. The result is the same as a tax decrease, but the way it is achieved is slightly different.

Where taxpayers' money is spent

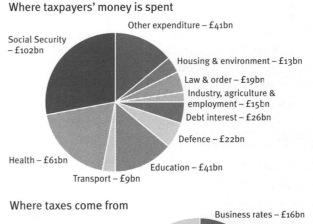

Where taxes come from

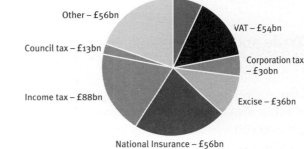

Source: Budget 99, issued by HM Treasury

Figure 57.2   Income and expenditure for the government

Keynes – the use of the term 'Keynesian' refers to the type of economic policy used to solve unemployment. It is named after the economist John Maynard Keynes, who wrote a ground breaking book in the 1930s. His ideas were based on government intervention in managing the economy in an attempt to increase the level of employment. To achieve this, a government should attempt to influence aggregate demand by spending money.

Exchange rate policy – this is concerned with influencing the level of international trade of an economy. By manipulating the **exchange rate**, the government can either help or hinder companies trying to export products to the rest of the world. Alternatively it can make imports cheaper or more expensive:

exchange rate stronger = exports more expensive and imports cheaper

exchange rate weaker = exports less expensive, imports more expensive

There are two ways the government can achieve this; the first is by direct intervention on the foreign exchange market by buying or selling pounds. The government holds large stocks of foreign currency for the purpose of buying pounds. By selling foreign currency, it may be able to increase the demand for pounds sufficiently to increase the value. This will require expenditure of a large sum – probably in the £ billions.

The second way it can intervene is to change interest rates. This is dealt with in more detail in Unit 60. Raising the interest rate can lead to a stronger pound and reducing the interest rate to a weaker pound.

Trade policies – in addition to influencing the exchange rate, governments try hard to generate a climate which favours the domestic economy, without restricting the choice of its consumers. An import tax (tariff) is sometimes imposed on certain products, as are quotas (limits on the volume of imports). Both are designed to limit the flood of cheaper, and therefore more competitive, foreign goods on to the market. Another method is subsidies, whereby the government pays money to a company for each unit of output. This means the company can charge a much lower price, because it makes up the difference with the government payment.

Supply-side policy – this was created during the years when Margaret Thatcher was in office. For many years, economists had argued that the only way to achieve full employment and economic prosperity was for the government to intervene and spend money. That is, it was the government's job to generate demand by spending money. **Supply-side economics** adopts the point of view that if the government can create an environment, which means businesses and

individuals can prosper, then the attraction of opportunities, profit and wealth will, through the natural forces of supply and demand, be an enticement for people to work harder and firms to set themselves up or invest.

The constituents of the supply-side approach are as follows:

- Reduce direct taxation so that individuals have more money at their disposal and companies have more money to reinvest and pay to shareholders

- Reduce interest rates to encourage borrowing

- Offer government subsidies to encourage small businesses to start, such as the enterprise allowance scheme

- Privatisation – force inefficient parts of the state system to become more efficient and invite competition into markets that previously were monopolistic (one company)

- Actively encourage entrepreneurial activity and material wealth

---

Question 4

One of the criticisms of privatisation is that companies profit from being in a monopolistic situation e.g. BT makes £111 profit per second.
To what extent does this level of profit provide an argument against privatisation? [4]

Recent trends

Both the Conservative government elected in 1979 and the more recently elected Labour government have taken a similar approach to managing the economy. Although Gordon Brown, the Labour Chancellor, opted out of deciding interest rates, both governments have used interest rates as a careful control mechanism to ensure economic growth is achieved at a sustainable level. They have also acted to reduce direct taxation rates, but, in order to maintain a balanced budget, have been forced to increase indirect taxation.

In the **Budget** of 1999, Chancellor Gordon Brown made the following changes (among others):

⇒ A 1% reduction in the basic rate of income tax (the amount that most working people pay) from 23% to 22%, to be introduced in April 2000
⇒ A new 10 pence rate of income tax for the first £1,500 of taxable income
⇒ The national minimum wage of £3.20 per hour for students and £3.60 per hour for everyone else
⇒ A guarantee of a minimum income of £200 per week for a full-time earner, by supplementing the minimum wage with tax credits
⇒ A reduction to £100 in vehicle excise duty (the tax disc) for small cars and an increase in the tax on diesel fuel
⇒ A new 10 pence corporation tax rate for small businesses
⇒ Research and development tax credit to encourage small businesses to invest in R and D
⇒ An extra £40 billion for education and health

Taking each of the above in turn, state whether the Budget measures would affect the following businesses:

a) The Marriott hotels in London – an up-market hotel chain that caters mainly for tourists and conference delegates, charging upwards of £80 per person per night
b) JCB – the excavator manufacturing business
c) Van den Bergh – one of the major manufacturers of margarine. Van den Bergh will probably have manufactured almost all the brands available in the supermarket
d) A local plumber that has just set up in business

4 × [5]

Can all economic objectives be achieved?

It is almost impossible, in a well developed economy with a significant amount of private sector wealth, to be able to satisfy all four objectives.

e.g. if a government tries to reduce unemployment it can reduce interest rates, reduce tax rates or spend

money. All are intended to create growth, but ultimately the result will be higher prices due to extra demand (*see Unit 59*).

Alternatively, the government might try to keep the pound low to encourage export growth. This may then make imports more expensive, so the costs of companies that import will rise, or the costs of goods going straight to the retailer will rise, which may result in inflation.

The trade cycle (or business cycle)

The **trade cycle** is the pattern of growth and contraction within an economy. It is measured by the change in Gross Domestic Product from one quarter to the next. The term 'cycle' refers to the fact that particular rates of growth or contraction will occur regularly and sometimes these periods can be predicted.

Typically the trade cycle will resemble the following:

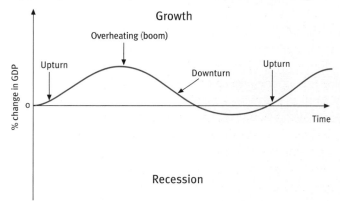

Figure 57.3   The trade cycle has several stages

Although the term recession is used frequently in the media as a term which refers to economic downturn, there is a precise definition:

Recession is said to occur when the economy has two successive quarters of negative growth in GDP. Put a simpler way, if the economy gets smaller for two successive quarters, then it is said to be in recession.

In Table 1, the recession will be recognised as occurring only during Qtr 2 of year 2. However, given that in year 1 growth was 0.2% and in year 2, growth was –0.2%, the effects of economic contraction will

Table 1

	Year 1				Year 2			
	Qtr 1	Qtr 2	Qtr 3	Qtr 4	Qtr 1	Qtr 2	Qtr 3	Qtr 4
Change in GDP (%)	0.2	0.1	–0.1	0	–0.1	–0.2	0	0.1

have been felt by many individuals and companies earlier than when the recession is officially recorded. In these circumstances it is more likely that only the government, in the form of the Chancellor of the Exchequer, will conform to the textbook definition, whilst everyone else will not!

Why does the level of GDP fluctuate?

This is a question that has fuelled considerable debate over the past 60 or 70 years. There are many cases of external 'shocks' (for want of a better word) to an economy that can cause fluctuations. It is generally understood that a government has particular responsibility for the trade cycle within an economy and has the responsibility to ensure it does not move from growth into recession.

The cause and effect of changes in the trade cycle

Although there are several explanations of the change in economic activity over a period of years, the recent trend has been towards managing the trade cycle carefully to achieve long-term sustainable growth.

All governments aim to achieve economic growth, because it leads to greater wealth and prosperity. Despite this being a common goal, there is a variety of ways that the government can influence economic growth. The following is a step-by-step process, which the economy will go through from growth to recession and back again.

1 Assume to begin with that the economy is growing. The growth in GDP will mean higher profits are being earned, more investment is taking place and wages are increasing, probably faster than the rate of inflation. The extra wages, dividends and profit are likely to lead to higher spending which normally leads to higher prices.

2 The higher prices mean an increase in inflation, which governments will try hard to avoid, so at this point the government will intervene with measures to halt the rate of growth. It will use either interest rates (monetary policy), or taxation rates and government spending (fiscal policy) to reduce the rate of growth, by reducing spending (through a reduction in disposable income).

3 The reduction in income will mean a reduction in demand by consumers and possibly a reduction in investment by companies. This is more likely to affect products which are income-elastic i.e. sensitive to changes in income.

4 As demand falls, revenue and profit fall, so businesses will aim to cut costs with a view to maintaining profitability. This may involve laying off some employees, which will increase the level of unemployment. This may be felt more acutely at the local or regional level if a major employer has to lay off a sizeable proportion of the work-force.

5 The increase in unemployment will further reduce demand; this is not just because consumers have less money, but the fear of unemployment for those remaining in work may mean that they defer expenditure until a later date. At this point, the economy is likely to be moving towards a recession; at the very least, the rate of growth will be falling.

6 This process will continue, with business failures and further redundancies, until the government steps in to remedy the situation. This will take the opposite form to the measures taken in step 2 i.e. interest rates or tax rates will decrease, or government expenditure will increase.

7 These expansionary measures will hopefully encourage consumers to spend more money, leading to an increase in demand, more employment, which further increases demand and greater investment. This will continue until the government judges that growth has become excessive, and so the brakes will be applied and the cycle will return to step 1.

Task

Summarise the above in a flow chart.

The outdated boom and recession

Since Britain left the Exchange Rate Mechanism in 1992, government policy on managing economic growth has altered. There is a more acceptable half-way house between the boom and bust economies of the 1960–1980 period. During those years, the economy lurched from growth to recession (*described above*) which meant that forecasting was difficult to carry out and it prevented long-term investment, particularly for the major multinational businesses.

The change in policy was towards longer-term sustainable growth. A growth rate of 4% or 5% in Britain was great when it was here, but it usually led to a deep and prolonged recession (1990/1991). The government therefore decided that by keeping control of inflation, mainly by using interest rates, it could achieve growth rates of 2–3%, which is a level that can be sustained. Since then, it has focused on various economic measures, all of which have the capacity to indicate inflationary pressures. When the evidence has been sufficiently convincing the government, and latterly the Monetary Policy Committee (MPC) of the Bank of England, has altered interest rates to ensure the economy does not overheat. Similarly, when there is possible evidence that the economy is slowing down, then interest rates have been reduced to inject extra spending into the economy.

Effects of a recession on business

Stock levels – a recession means less demand, which reduces the requirement for business to hold stock. A recession is also likely to be caused by higher interest rates, which means the cost of financing stock is greater. This leads to businesses trying to cut down on levels of stock to save costs. A business will obviously not decrease stock until either the interest rate has risen, or demand has fallen. There is therefore a time lag between the onset of the recession and the decision to drop the level of stock. Alternatively, stock is built up if there is anticipation of recovery. In the

Bank of England's agent report on 1,700 businesses in the country in May 1999, there was a feeling of optimism in the business world, and so stocks, having been run down the year before when recession loomed, were being built up to meet the anticipated increase in demand.

Investment – the capital expenditure of a company is likely to reduce as companies aim for productivity improvements as opposed to new machinery. Finance becomes more expensive and there is less demand, so investment in assets is saved until the cost of borrowing falls and there is proof of extra demand.

Cash flow and profit – lack of demand will result in less profit and probably less cash, although the short-term cash situation may improve if prices are dropped to stimulate demand. Some companies rely on a high turnover in order to achieve economies of scale. Although the reduction in cost due to economies of scale is offset by the reduction in price, the maintenance of volumes ensures work is available. Companies also look hard at costs and may need to make people redundant; this not only reduces profit through the effect on redundancy payments, but there is also a cash outflow with redundancy payments.

Big-ticket items – consumers will tend to cut back on the so-called big-ticket items, which tend to be consumer durables such as cars and houses. The car industry suffers when there is a recession, and house prices also remain static or fall during a recession.

Question 6

Nigella Trotman runs an electronics company in the Midlands. It supplies a variety of electrical goods manufacturers such as Sony and LG. Recent government action has led Nigella to believe that there will soon be a recession and her company may well suffer as a result of the downturn in economic activity.

a) Explain two pieces of economic evidence that might suggest a recession is looming. [4]

b) How will Nigella's company be affected by the recession? [6]

How might a business try to survive a recession?

When there is a recession, the squeeze on incomes, lack of demand and a drop in confidence levels are likely to cause firms to implement a contingency plan. The plan is likely to include some, if not all, of the following business principles:

1 Ensure total customer satisfaction – by doing this, consumers, who may be looking for an excuse to cut back on their own expenditure, may continue to purchase.

2 Focus on the core business (otherwise known as zero-basing) – a diversified business may be one which spreads its risk, but it also means entering markets which are unknown. Frequently companies will sell off the diversified parts and concentrate on what they know best – their core.

3 Explain the situation to all employees, calling for attempts to increase productivity – by losing demand and therefore losing opportunity for economies of scale, the business will need to pay close attention to costs.

4 Accept a period of losses – if a company has a generous bank and shareholders that understand the turmoil within the industry caused by lack of demand, then this will increase the chance of survival. Naturally, smaller or less efficient companies do not always get through a recession.

5 Keep a watchful eye on consumers/companies which have been given credit so that they continue to pay the bills.

6 Find new markets for the same products. This will mean the company might be able to maintain sales or possibly increase them, without spending money on new product development.

7 A business will always aim to cut back during a recession, or even when profit needs to increase, otherwise known as **retrenchment**. This might take the form of rationalisation (cutting back on employees), or freezing recruitment (to reduce hiring and training costs as well as labour costs). Retrenchment can also involve closing a part of the business down – perhaps a factory which is unprofitable or a product which is failing to make a contribution. At all times, ethical considerations are of paramount importance to the long-term well-being of the business.

What opportunities does economic growth create?

Profit – the extra demand which is characteristic of a period of growth will generate more sales and profit. Sometimes companies will need to pay close attention to their cash flow, because overtrading can lead to liquidity problems.

Risk taking – when demand grows and profit grows with it, companies will feel more comfortable when taking risky decisions. When opportunities arise to diversify, expansion will seem more attractive and the level of optimism within the economy will be high.

Economies of scale – growth in demand can also lead to economies of scale as businesses achieve a greater level of capacity utilisation. This will help them to be more competitive and achieve even more sales.

Dividends and higher share price – the extra profits are likely to lead to extra dividend payments. Extra profit also means more finance is available for expansion, and the prospect of growth and dividends is likely to increase the share price of a publicly quoted company.

More employment – as the economy expands, the demand for labour increases and as a consequence the level of unemployment falls. There may be a time lag involved in order to match the skills required with the skills of those who are seeking employment, but the extra wages being paid will mean extra income being distributed around the economy, leading to further increases in wealth.

Points for Revision

Key Terms

planned economy	when the government takes all the economic and business decisions
market economy	the private sector takes all the decisions
mixed economy	when a combination of government intervention and private sector influence is employed to take decisions in the economy
merit goods	goods that are not always provided by the private sector and are considered important
public goods	goods that are available to all without direct cost
gross domestic product	the value of goods and services produced in an economy within a particular time period
economic growth	an increase in the value of GDP
recession	two successive quarters of negative growth in GDP i.e. the economy contracts
monetary policy	the use of interest rates and the money supply to regulate economic activity
interest rate	the cost of borrowing
money supply	the stock of money in an economy
fiscal policy	the use of taxation and government expenditure
government expenditure	the amount of money spent by the government in a year
direct taxation	payment made to the government based on a direct proportion of earnings e.g. income tax
indirect taxation	payment made to the government based on expenditure e.g. excise duty on petrol
public sector net cash requirement	the amount government has to borrow to finance the difference between taxation income and government spending
exchange rate	the value of one currency in terms of another
supply-side economics	the process of creating an environment which encourages trade
Budget	the forecast for the coming economic period
trade cycle	the repeating pattern of growth and recession over time
retrenchment	cutting back on labour, productive capacity or other assets with a view to saving costs

Definitions Question:
By referring to a business you know, choose three of the above terms and explain their significance (your teacher may wish to help you choose the terms).   [5] per definition

Summary Points:

1.   A government uses a range of economic policies in order to achieve its economic objectives.

2.   Each decision by the government will have an impact, whether direct or indirect, on businesses.

3.   Businesses will be affected, in different ways, by the trade cycle.

Mini Case Study

The North Yarlet Advertiser is a free newspaper that is distributed to every household in North Yarlet and the surrounding small towns and villages in Devon. The target readership totals 65,000 people and the paper is essentially an advertising medium, principally for businesses in the area, although the revenue from private classified adverts has grown in recent years as the circulation has increased.

The paper was initially restricted to Yarlet itself, which has a population of only 40,000, and although advertising revenue from the businesses meant the paper could break even, the margin of safety was very small. By increasing the circulation, more businesses have been willing to advertise in the paper, which has increased revenue and profit (although profit has increased by a greater percentage than revenue). The majority of private customers put adverts in for household products such as fridges, freezers and vacuum cleaners, although there is also a major section on cars. There is a broad range of businesses that advertise in the newspaper, although the majority are small, usually traders and craftsmen such as plumbers, electricians and builders.

1 Define: advertising medium, margin of safety.   [4]

2 Explain why profit has risen by a greater percentage than revenue.   [4]

3 Briefly explain the marketing problems for The North Yarlet Advertiser, given that it has two customers – readers and advertisers.   [4]

4 Discuss the effect on the company of a period of economic growth.   [8]

                                                                                      20

Maxi Case Study

Park-Lane Chairs Ltd is a manufacturer of high-quality furniture, although its main speciality is reclining chairs. The business began at the end of the 1970s when two friends, Edward Park and James Lane, rented a smallholding on the outskirts of London. Edward was the marketing man who travelled around the country drumming up orders while James put his craftsman skills to work, producing the chairs using a small amount of machinery, although the small factory was labour-intensive. On one of his journeys, Edward came across a small company which made tables and chairs aimed at the same target market as Park-Lane's products. The company had been put up for sale in 1990 due to loss of orders in the recession, although Edward noted that the management had failed to address falling productivity and poor morale in the work-place. Quality had fallen and with the high level of income elasticity in the product (estimated at about 1.9) sales had plummeted during the recession.

Edward subsequently bought the company and mechanised it to produce a higher level of output, which resulted in a much higher level of productivity. As the economy grew, further opportunities arose. The level of retained profit was enough to persuade Edward that further expansion was necessary, so Park-Lane Chairs Ltd began making bedroom furniture, and although the market was less income-elastic, there was still a danger of sales falling during a recession.

The windfall pay-outs by the building societies during 1998 caused a mini-boom which pushed the company's sales to a record level. Shortly afterwards, however, the economy went from boom to recession as interest rates rose. The worry about recession and how it might affect Park-Lane Chairs were at the front of his mind when he attended a seminar given by a government minister, Dudley Parkhurst, on the government and its attitude to business.

In it, the government minister outlined plans to aim for long-term sustainable growth. Edward questioned him on support for small businesses during a recession which he suggested was one of the biggest problem areas a small company has to face. Although Parkhurst sounded supportive, Edward dismissed it as another political soundbite which meant nothing. He sensed that the only reason why the minister had arranged the seminar was to promote the government's stand on unemployment by encouraging employers to sign up to the New Deal.

1 Define: liquidation, management, quality. [6]

2 Why might 'long-term sustainable growth' be attractive to Park-Lane Chairs Ltd? [3]

3 Explain the significance of income elasticity of 1.9 in this case; what might the company be able to do in order to reduce the level of income elasticity on its reclining chairs? [5]

4 a) Consider how Park-Lane chairs might be affected by a recession. [5]

b) One of the ways a government can combat a recession is by reducing interest rates. Outline two other ways a government might create growth. [4]

c) For each example of government action outlined in your answer to **b)**, suggest how Park-Lane Chairs might be affected. [4]

d) Discuss how the company itself might react to the problems created by a recession by offering possible solutions to the problems. [8]

Legal environment

Learning objectives

Having read this unit, students will be able to

1 identify legislation that protects the individual as a consumer and as an employee

2 identify legislation related to competition between businesses

3 understand the impact of legislation upon a business and how a business might react to legislation

Context

All businesses are faced with the task of operating within the law. There are many different examples of legislation that have to be complied with if a business is to run smoothly. The range of laws covers most areas of a business, from establishing the business, how employees are recruited, conditions at work, how an employee may be dismissed, how products can be advertised and sold and how it may compete with other businesses.

Some of this legislation has been covered in other units and therefore this unit concentrates on how the law affects a business with regard to individuals, who are either employees or consumers, and the behaviour of a business within a given market.

A business may be affected by different sources of law:

- Government passing Acts of Parliament
- Case law (previous decisions made by judges that are then used to determine the outcome of future cases)
- European law (being a member of the European Union, Britain is affected by laws on competition, health and safety and, under the Social Charter, industrial relations)

Protecting the individual

Legislation designed to protect the individual from discrimination includes:

Sex Discrimination Act 1975

This Act states that it is illegal to discriminate against a person on the basis of gender or marital status.

The intention of the legislation was to prevent discrimination during the recruiting process. The wording of advertisements had to refer to sales staff rather than salesman and the interview procedure would be required to eliminate bias against women.

The consequence of the legislation was that it was easier for women, and especially married women, to seek and gain employment.

To enforce the legislation, the Equal Opportunities Commission was established. The role of this body was to promote equal opportunities and investigate complaints of discrimination. It can also help present cases to an industrial tribunal, which will hear a case of alleged discrimination.

Race Relations Act 1976

This Act stipulates that it is unlawful to discriminate against a person on the grounds of race.

The Act is enforced by the Commission for Racial Equality. The Race Relations Code of Practice is available to help employers with their recruiting procedures e.g. ensuring that adverts for posts are not placed in journals that would exclude particular ethnic minorities from being able to apply. There also needs to be a statement that indicates that the business is an equal opportunity employer and that applications will be welcome from anyone regardless of nationality, race or colour.

Disability Discrimination Act 1995

Employers have traditionally fought shy of employing people who are disabled. The additional costs of providing facilities and access to enable them to perform the job required have meant that many disabled people have not been able to gain employment.

The Act states that it is unlawful to discriminate against a person on the basis of disability.

It is also a requirement of the Act to take reasonable steps to ensure that difficulties for the disabled are eliminated.

Data Protection Act 1984

The Act defines data as 'information recorded in a form in which it can be processed and used'. The Act allows access to data held on an individual by that particular individual e.g. any credit card enquiries or balance requests on telephone bank accounts require passwords and forms of individual identification. The individual is entitled to have any information corrected that is inaccurate. This means the companies need to record data carefully and must also operate secure systems which manage the information accurately.

Health and Safety at Work Act 1974 and 1996

In attempting to improve the standard of safety of employees, the legislation concentrates on protective clothing, sufficient safety equipment and the establishment of a written policy, for a business that employs five or more people, on health and safety of which all employees are to be made aware.

The Act expects the employer to take 'reasonable care' of the health and safety of employees at work.

If there is trade union representation at the place of work, a union representative is allowed by right to inspect the working environment.

A safety officer should be appointed in an attempt to have someone who is not part of the management of the business to ensure safety standards are adhered to.

Under the Act, there is an obligation on employees to ensure they take 'reasonable care' of their own safety while at work.

To ensure the law is enforced, the Health and Safety Executive is responsible for inspecting work premises. Inspectors have right of entry to check that the appropriate policies are in place and are being adhered to. The major problem facing the Executive is the number of works premises that exist – many businesses have probably never been inspected.

The cost of implementing the safety policy of the business falls on that business, adding to its costs. Nevertheless, the existence of the legislation may prevent some accidents and therefore fewer days are lost through accidents and health-related problems.

Task 1

Make a list of all the Health and Safety issues that are relevant to a building site. Try to ascertain all the improvements that have been made in recent years. Although these improvements have resulted in increased costs for the building company, suggest how the company may have actually saved money in the long term.

European law with regard to Health and Safety concentrates on working hours and is spelt out in the Social Chapter. There are also specific references to procedures for lifting weights at work and what employers ought to provide for employees who use computer terminals.

Vicarious liability

In some circumstances an individual may be liable for the actions of others. Although the particular individual has done no wrong, he/she may be held responsible for the actions of those with whom there is a business relationship such as a partnership or employer. This liability usually only applies in torts and not in criminal law. The relationship between employer and employee is probably the best example to consider.

There are two conditions that determine whether there is **vicarious liability**:

i) The employee must be acting for the employer as part of the employment contract.

ii) The tort must have been committed during the normal course of employment.

It is important to realise that the employee must be acting with the authority of the employer. If a tort is committed against the wishes of the employer then there may not be vicarious liability on the part of the employer. Though careless actions and disobedience by an employee are not always acceptable excuses for

avoiding liability, case law is used to decide the limits of liability.

Under normal circumstances, when a person uses a contractor, that person is not vicariously liable for the actions of the contractor.

The willingness of employers to let their employees view the eclipse of the sun on August 11, 1999 was of interest:

Firms are warned of eclipse liability

BY SIMON DE BRUXELLES

EMPLOYERS who fail to warn staff of the dangers of looking directly at the Sun during next month's eclipse could be liable if their sight is damaged during work hours, the CBI said yesterday.

Companies are being advised to cover themselves by sending memos and putting warnings on noticeboards.

Sue Boyd, southwest regional director for the Confederation of British Industry, said: "Employers are responsible for their employees while they are on the premises and going about their duties. An employer could be put in a difficult position if a member of staff damaged their eyesight while at work. There is a possibility of the employer being liable and open to litigation.

"Employers have a tight line to walk, they don't want to be Scrooges, making members of staff miss this once-in-a-lifetime event, but they have to make sure they don't leave themself open to lawsuits."

Mrs Boyd's area covers Cornwall and south Devon, which will experience Britain's first total eclipse since 1927 at 11.11am of August 11. Most employees will be given the chance to go outside to watch, and some businesses will close down for an hour or more.

Across the rest of the country the eclipse will be only partial but staring at the uncovered part of the Sun for even a few seconds could cause permanent eye damage. The public are being advised to view it with special glasses or by reflecting the image on to a card.

Question 1

Using the information in the article, discuss whether there would be a case for vicarious liability.   [5]

Question 2

Emily Blount is the owner of a shop-fitting business and employs three staff on a full-time basis. Her business has won the contract to fit out a chain of restaurants in Lancashire. While working at one of the restaurants, Charlie spills his beer over one of the new pictures that was about to be hung on the wall. There is a company policy of not drinking alcohol during working hours. Is Emily vicariously liable?   [4]

Dismissal

The majority of the statutory rights related to dismissal apply only if employees have been *continuously* employed for a given period of time. Under the Employment Rights Act 1996 the given period of continuous employment for protection from unfair dismissal is two years.

(Details of the rules on unfair dismissal are given in Unit 54 Recruitment and contracts.)

It is possible for an employee to appeal to an industrial tribunal. Any complaint must be taken to a tribunal within three months of the dismissal. Having informed the employer, details of the particular case are sent to the Advisory, Conciliation and Arbitration Service who attempt to settle the case through mediation before the tribunal is involved.

If ACAS is unable to settle the dispute the case will be heard by a tribunal, where a decision will be reached. The tribunal has the power to decide that the employee must be:

Reinstated
Re-engaged (given another job)
Compensated (compensation is calculated in a similar manner to redundancy payments, where the length of employment is used)
Either side in the case has the right to appeal against the decision of the tribunal. This appeal is heard by the Employment Appeal Tribunal.

Consumer protection

It has always been the 'rule' that the buyer ought to be careful when buying anything. The expression 'let the buyer beware' (*caveat emptor*) still holds true today; nevertheless, successive governments have sought to protect the consumer in a variety of ways.

The legislation is designed to protect the consumer from exploitation by a business. The consumer has become more conscious of the law, due in part to the wealth of programmes on television that provide information.

Protection of the consumer falls under the umbrella of the Director-General of Fair Trading. The **Office of Fair Trading** was established under the Fair Trading Act 1973 and is responsible for overseeing the welfare of consumers, introducing codes of practice that business can follow and acting whenever there are signs of persistent offenders who are failing to comply with the legislation.

Sale of Goods Act 1979 and 1994

Whenever a purchase is made by a consumer a contract has been made between the consumer and the seller of the product. The Sale of Goods Act lays down particular terms for the contract:

- The goods must be reasonably fit for the purpose for which they were intended
- The goods must be of a satisfactory quality (merchantable quality)
- Goods bought must be of an equal standard to those displayed or shown by sample

If the seller fails to comply with the above regardless of who is responsible for the fault in the product, the buyer is entitled to damages or may be able to reject the goods.

Weights and Measures Act 1963 and 1985

These Acts were introduced to avoid goods being sold underweight or below volume. Local Trading Standards Officers were made responsible for scrutinising businesses.

Trade Descriptions Act 1968

To prevent consumers being misled by adverts, packaging and promotional material such as 'sale' signs, this Act states that any product must fit any claim made for it in an advert. The rules on labels were tightened to prevent false claims about the contents or ingredients.

Changes were made to the rules about sales. A business can claim a genuine 'sale' only if the products were sold at the advertised higher price for at least 28 days within the last six months.

Unsolicited Goods Act 1971

This is an attempt to prevent companies delivering products to consumers who have not ordered anything and then attempting to gain payment for the goods. The Act stipulates that the consumer does not have to pay for such products and is under no obligation to return them. If the goods have not been claimed by the company responsible for delivering them within six months of delivery, the consumer may keep them.

Consumer Protection Act 1987

This Act originated from the European Community in 1985. It is concerned with the safety of products. If consumers are injured as a result of using a particular product they are able to take legal action and claim damages. If a consumer was injured as a result of using a faulty lawnmower, the manufacturer would be liable for any damage or injury sustained.

Additions to what can be stated about the price of products reinforced the Trades Descriptions Act.

Question 3

Vickie Finch purchased an electric toaster from a retailer not far from her home. Within a week, the toaster stopped working and she took it back to the shop where it had been purchased. Unfortunately, the shop, although sympathetic, suggested that Vickie contact the manufacturer. Advise Vickie as to her rights.   [5]

Although the majority of the legislation puts an additional burden on the business either as an employer or as a producer, any extra costs incurred may be beneficial in the long run as there are likely to be fewer 'returns' of products due to poor quality and possibly a more productive work-force if working conditions are safe and conducive to production.

The legislation, especially Acts related to consumer protection, may require a business to employ staff to operate an extended personnel department to cater for customer complaints. The behaviour of companies in the market-place has also required the attention of the legislature. Companies that attempt to dominate the market using their monopolistic power are kept in check by the existence of various Acts affecting the level of influence a company can exert on a particular market.

Competition legislation

If a particular market is very competitive, the chances are that the consumer is treated well by the businesses trying to win their trade.

However, if a business is the dominant player within a market it is quite possible that the consumer will not be treated so well. Although to a degree this supposition is a generalisation, a company with a **monopoly** is in a much better position to influence the market. Governments since the Second World War have attempted to control the power of monopolistic businesses.

Today, the **Competition Commission**, formerly the Monopolies and Mergers Commission, is responsible for the control of companies in an attempt to encourage competition and ensure companies act in the public interest. The role and the power of the then Monopolies Commission has grown substantially from its birth in 1948 to the present day.

Several Acts have amended its role and authority to deal with companies that were not acting in the public interest.

The public interest encompasses:
- promoting effective competition
- promoting the interests of consumers in terms of choice and prices
- promoting the reduction of prices through competition

It is considered more prudent to prevent a business becoming a monopoly and consequently the Commission is able to scrutinise proposed mergers and decide whether the newly merged business will be in the public interest.

The Fair Trading Act of 1973 extended the Commission to include mergers. The Act stated that any merger that would lead to a combined business with 25% of the national market, or a significant part of a regional market, would be investigated by the Monopolies and Mergers Commission.

The findings of the investigations are passed on to the Office of Fair Trading which in turn reports to the government for the final decision as to whether the merger should be allowed to go ahead.

BskyB's recent attempt to join forces with Manchester United was a case that was investigated. An agreement was made between BskyB and the football club for over £600 million but after the Department of Trade and Industry's initial enquiry, the Department intimated that the merger would be subject to a full enquiry by the Commission; consequently, the merger was terminated.

The Office of Fair Trading was asked to investigate the large accounting firms over allegations of uncompetitive practices by accountants working, ironically, on mergers and acquisitions. John Bridgeman, the Director-General of Fair Trading, received a written request for an investigation from The London Investment Bankers Association (Liba). Liba's complaint followed closely after the merger between Price Waterhouse and Coopers & Lybrand.

The supermarkets were investigated due to their dominant position in the market; the top five supermarkets account for nearly 80% of the grocery trade. The Office of Fair Trading's report indicated that the supermarkets were guilty of not passing on to the consumer the huge benefits which they derived from bulk buying.

Contrary to the Office of Fair Trading report was the decision of the European Court that supermarkets could not pass on savings in the costs of purchasing designer label clothing and footwear, that had been sold in their outlets. The supermarkets had sold Levi jeans and Nike sportswear for a fraction of the 'normal' retail price, having imported the items from the 'grey market' (unofficial suppliers from Asia and America). The supermarkets had claimed that their purchasing strategy had enabled the consumer to benefit from lower prices. The Court declared that branded goods purchased outside the European Union could not be sold in Europe without the permission of the manufacturer.

Restrictive practices

Several Acts to curb **restrictive practices** have been passed over the years. The first, in 1956, introduced the Restrictive Practices Court and was the first attempt to control the behaviour of companies that abused their power within the market.

Restrictive practices include:

- Price agreements or price fixing – the manufacturer determines the price at which a product must be sold. The retailer is given no choice in the matter and failure to comply usually means the manufacturer refuses to continue to supply the product.

- Market sharing – this is an agreement where each company takes a particular part of the market. This allows a few companies to dominate the market and prevent others entering.

If agreements are made between companies for either price fixing or market sharing this is described as an example of a 'cartel'. The Competition Acts of 1980 and 1998 were introduced to enable anti-competitive practices to be investigated by the Monopolies and Mergers Commission (now the Competition Commission). In 1998 more powers were added to restrict cartels and introduce stronger penalties.

In addition to the powers of the Competition Commission, EU rules are even stricter. Heavy fines (as a percentage of the offending company's turnover) can be used against companies that abuse their power.

Although there appear to be plenty of safeguards in existence to protect the public from the power of dominant companies, much of the policing of their behaviour is self-inflicted. Losing the goodwill of customers, or damaging a reputation, is not what any major business relishes. Nor does a business want to run the risk of a full investigation by the Competition Commission. These concerns appear to act as sufficient deterrent for a large proportion of businesses.

Question 4
Explain how a cartel may be against the public interest. [4]

Tests for employment

It is important to ascertain whether or not a person has a contract of employment, because the rights of an individual may be affected when it comes to dismissal in terms of whether the individual is entitled to redundancy or perhaps a claim for unfair dismissal. An employee has protection under the law with regard to unfair dismissal which is not afforded to a contractor, i.e. someone who has been employed to carry out a specific task, on a short-term basis.

If there are disputes over employment, the law provides 'tests' that can be applied to ascertain whether an individual is an employee or a contractor. The tests are referred to as:

- the control test
- the multiple test
- the integration test

Control test

An employee can be told not only what tasks to do but how such tasks should be undertaken, whereas a contractor is contracted to perform a given task, but is at liberty to decide how the task is completed. If the description of the task or the method in which the task is to be carried out is clearly stated, then there is said to be a degree of 'control' over the employee, by the employer. The degree of control varies from industry to industry e.g. a teacher will be employed to teach a certain number of lessons per week – exactly how these lessons are executed tends to be up to the individual concerned. An assembly worker on a production line is likely to have much less freedom.

Multiple test

Noting who is reponsible for tax deductions, how the person is paid, who provides working clothes and equipment can be used to gauge a person's working status. It is more likely that a person who pays their own income tax and National Insurance, decides their working hours and provides all the equipment necessary to complete a task is a contractor.

Integration test

The extent to which a person 'belongs' to a business may provide evidence as to whether a person is a contractor or an employee. This may be done by ascertaining whether a person is an integral part of the business or just performing a task and remaining 'outside' the business. Being integral to the business can vary from involvement in a works sport team or works outing, to being part of the formal group at work.

No one 'test' in isolation will be sufficient to decide if a person is an employee or a contractor, but applying all three 'tests' ought to provide an answer.

Points for Revision

Key Terms

monopoly either a single producer in a given market or a firm that has a dominant share of a given market

restrictive practices actions by a company or group of companies that increase the price of a product or restrict the choice of the consumer

Competition Commission a body responsible for ensuring that companies do not act against the public interest

Office of Fair Trading established under the Fair Trading Act 1973 to oversee the operation of companies within the existing legislation

vicarious liability when an individual is liable for the actions of others

Definitions Question:
With reference to a firm or firms of which you have direct knowledge or experience, explain the importance of any three of the above terms (your teacher may wish to select the terms).   [5] per definition

Summary Points:

1 Legislation exists to protect the individual as an employee and as a consumer.

2 Legislation exists to restrict the power of dominant firms.

3 Businesses are faced with complying with laws from a range of sources – Acts, case law and European law.

Mini Case Study

Southall rail crash company is fined £1.5m

GREAT Western Trains was fined a record £1.5 million at the Old Bailey yesterday for jeopardising safety and putting passengers at risk in the Southall rail crash which killed seven people.

The company was guilty of a "dereliction of duty" in connection with the disaster in West London in which 150 were injured and millions of pounds of damage was caused in September 1997, the court was told.

"Those who travel on highspeed trains are entitled to expect the highest standard of care from those who run them. Great Western Trains failed to meet that standard and in my judgment they failed to meet it by a greater extent than they have been prepared to admit," Mr Justice Scott Baker said.

He said the fine imposed was not intended to "nor can it, reflect the value of the lives lost or the injuries sustained in this disaster. It is, however, intended to reflect public concern at the offence."

The judge renewed his criticism of Richard George, the company's chief executive, for not attending the court hearing. "I am surprised that neither Mr George – who it is said is in personal charge of safety at GWT – nor any other director of the company came to court to express personally remorse for GWT's breach of the Health and Safety Act and to allay any impression of complacency that may have been conveyed to the victims, their families and the public." But he accepted defence submissions that the company "does very much regret its responsibility for the disaster".

After the sentence, Jenny Bacon, director-general of the Health and Safety Executive, said: "This prosecution and record fine sends a vital message to the railway industry – safety must come first."

A spokesman for Great Western Trains said: "We have stated our extreme regret at the loss of lives and injury in this appalling tragedy. While working within the rules, we have accepted there was a serious breach of the health and safety laws."

---

1 What were the likely Health and Safety issues in this case?   [4]

2 What other legislation may have been relevant for this case?   [3]

3 Would there be a case to answer for vicarious liability?   [5]

4 To what extent does the message 'safety must come first' represent a conflict of interest for the directors of Great Western Trains?   [8]

20

Maxi Case Study

Nick and Christine Gillis owned an aquatics centre just outside Wigan, selling both freshwater and tropical fish and aquatic materials.

They had started the business nearly 10 years ago, when they rented a site about two minutes' walk from the nearest housing estate. As the interest in pond and tropical fish grew, Nick started to make, by request, fish tanks. Customers came to the centre with specific measurements and other requirements which he was able to satisfy, usually within one week. Having established a niche in the market, Nick and Christine started to advertise the 'tailored' fish tanks. Such was the success of this side of the business that they employed a full-time assistant to take over the task of making the tanks and installing the electrical heating units to accompany the tanks that were to be used for tropical fish.

John Butler had been working for the business for almost 20 months when, under pressure to produce the orders on time, he started to take several short cuts in the assembly process. At first there were no complaints about the standard of his workmanship, but things came to a head when a customer returned to the shop protesting loudly that the tank he had bought leaked and insisted on having his money back.

Christine was reluctant to give the customer his money, suggesting that the tank was tested before leaving the aquatic centre. Nick was also against accepting that the tank was faulty as none had been returned before. He did however suspect that John had been cutting corners, especially having noticed how quickly he had managed to finish some jobs that used to take Nick several more hours to complete. Nick gave John a warning as to the standard of his work, saying that he did not want any more complaints from customers, or else! Unfortunately, within a week of this warning, another customer, Mrs Singh, returned to the centre in a terrible rage. Her tank had leaked and the electrical heating element did not appear to have been insulated properly and had electrocuted her fish.

Nick was keen to ensure the reputation of the aquatic centre was not ruined, having built up a considerable amount of goodwill for the business. He was not, however, prepared to pay for the loss of the fish that had not been bought from him. He told Mrs Singh that although the electrical units were assembled at the centre, the actual heating elements were bought from a supplier and that she would have to contact the supplier herself. Nick did offer to replace the tank, fearing he would not be in a strong position if Mrs Singh took the matter further. After Mrs Singh had left the centre, threatening legal action, Nick told John he was sacked because he had not been doing his job properly, even after a warning. John threatened to take Nick to court, shouting that he had to work in cramped conditions, without the proper tools and with no clear instructions as to how to undertake what could be quite a perilous job, dealing with glass, water and electrical equipment.

It had not been a good day for Nick and Christine.

1 Define: niche, goodwill.   [4]

2 What Health and Safety issues are addressed in the case?   [6]

3 **a)** State whether you think John's dismissal is fair.   [6]

   b) What would you advise John to do under the circumstances?   [4]

4 Advise Mrs Singh on her rights.   [10]

                                                                                     ___
                                                                                     30

Inflation and unemployment

Learning objectives

Having read this unit, students will be able to

1 demonstrate an understanding of the different causes of inflation

2 demonstrate an awareness of the likely implications for a business of particular levels of inflation and the effect on business of attempts by the government to reduce inflation

3 identify different causes and costs of unemployment

4 understand the likely implications for business of unemployment and the action a government might take to reduce unemployment

Context – Inflation

'When I was a lad, we could go to the cinema on the bus, get a bag of chips on the way home with a bottle of pop, and still have change from two shillings (10 pence).' Such are the apparently extravagant claims of elderly relatives who find the concept of rising prices difficult to deal with. The change in the price of goods has been of concern to us only since the Second World War. Before then, inflation was virtually non-existent. Nowadays, many stakeholders watch inflation very closely. Next time you are negotiating pocket money or an allowance, you may need to consult the press for details of inflation. You might find that the amount of money you have been given is not able to purchase as many products; using the argument that inflation is at 3% and your allowance has not been increased to reflect this will surely persuade your parents to part with extra cash!

Inflation defined

The rate of **inflation** is one of those economic vital statistics that is regularly quoted and analysed by the press, television reports, economists and politicians. This is because it determines the way the government attempts to achieve its economic objectives and affects our personal wealth. Inflation is defined as the rise in the general level of prices. If, for example, inflation is 4%, then this means prices *in general* are rising at 4%. Some may be rising at more or less than 4%, some prices may even be falling. The result of inflation is that **purchasing power** (the amount which money can buy) is reduced i.e. more money is required to purchase the same product. If inflation falls from 7% to 3%, this does not mean that prices are falling, rather that prices are rising less quickly than before.

The history of inflation

Inflation is a phenomenon that has been of concern only since the Second World War. Before then, prices were more or less stable; indeed, during the world depression at the start of the 1930s, there was widespread deflation (when prices fall). The pursuit of stable prices has always been one of the government's main objectives although this has not always been achieved. In recent years, most western economies and, indeed, most developed economies have experienced single-digit inflation. This is a far cry from the mid-1970s when inflation peaked at around 24%, which, in itself, is insignificant compared with the **hyper inflation** experienced in some of the developing countries such as Russia where inflation regularly tops 1000%. Nothing compares with Germany during the inter-war period. Money lost its value 500,000,000,000 times in the space of just two years! Table 1 demonstrates the effect that inflation had on prices and incomes in Britain over the 50 years from 1947 to 1997.

Between 1947 and 1997 prices rose by an annual average of 6.3%, so the amount that could have been bought with £1 in 1947 needed £21.50 in 1997!

Table 1

	June 1947	June 1997
Prices		
pint of milk	2p	35p
pint of beer	7p	£1.65
1lb bar of chocolate	7p	79p
The Observer	1p	£1.00
Single record	24p	£3.99
6-bedroom Wimbledon house	£7,250	£775,000
Road tax	£1	£145
Incomes		
Doctor	£2,000	£46,450
Annual single old age pension	£67.60	£3,247.40
Primary school head teacher	£660	£31,000
Male manual worker	£312	£15,600
Prime Minister	£10,000	£100,000

Source: *Daily Telegraph*, August 1997

Question 1

a) Calculate the rate of increase in income of the male manual worker and compare it with that of the Prime Minister. Give one possible reason for the difference in the increase. [6]

b) Perform the same comparison between road tax and a bar of chocolate; explain one possible reason for the difference in the increase. [6]

Methods of measurement

RPI

The most frequently quoted inflation figure is the RPI or retail price index. This is measured by the Central Statistical Office and published each month, and quotes the change in retail prices of a typical 'basket' of consumer goods and services over the previous 12 months. Data is collected all the time from a variety of different retail outlets in different locations across the country with a wide range of products. The price changes are then 'weighted' according to their relative importance within the basket and a weighted average (*see Unit 14 Methods of summarising data*) is calculated. Another term of reference of this index is the **'headline' rate of inflation** i.e. one that is used as a starting point to examine the state of inflation at a particular time.

RPIX

One of the problems with the headline rate is that it takes account of mortgages. The difficulty with this is that mortgages are influenced by the interest rate or base rate, as set by the Bank of England Monetary Policy Committee (MPC). The problem here is that the MPC will use interest rates to regulate inflation (*see Unit 60 Interest rates*). If inflation is rising and the MPC increases base rates, this is very likely to mean mortgage rates rise, which will make the RPI rise. The paradox is that inflation rises in the short term in an attempt to reduce inflation in the long term!

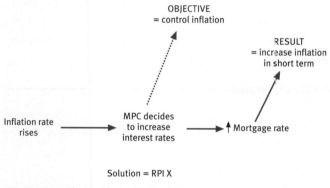

Figure 59.1   The problem with the RPI

The solution is therefore to use a measure that calculates inflation, excluding the effect of mortgages, known as the RPIX. An alternative reference to the RPIX is the **underlying rate of inflation**. This is used as the main measure of effectiveness in the control of inflation.

Problems with measurement

Even though the RPIX gives a more accurate measure, the actual rate of inflation published each month, be it the RPI or RPIX, is not really a representative measure of the change in prices facing an individual household.

■ Local differences in prices will mean that the rate of inflation in London may well be different to that of Birmingham

■ The spending patterns of each household also differ on a regional basis so in this respect the weighting will be inaccurate

■ The weighting is applied from a base year, so it could be that expenditure patterns change, although the weighting does not

Despite the above, RPIX is a useful measure of the general level of price rises. Another measure which is used to assess whether there is inflationary pressure within an economy is the PPI, the producers' price index, which measures the change in prices which retailers are paying for goods bought from producers. In theory and frequently in practice, if the PPI rises, there will be a time lag, and then the RPI will rise.

Question 2

Explain why an increase in the PPI might not lead to an increase in the RPI.   [4]

Causes of inflation

There are three main causes of inflation:

■ Demand pull

Demand pull occurs when there is an increase in the general level of demand in the economy. This might be caused by a reduction in mortgage rates or a reduction in taxation or perhaps a windfall payout by a building society or insurance company going public. The result is that the general level of demand rises faster than the increase in goods being supplied. The traditional way of describing this method is 'too much money chasing too few goods'.

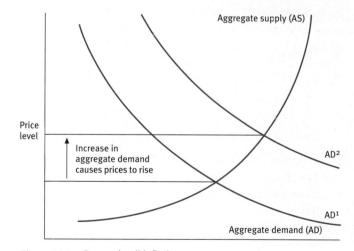

Figure 59.2   Demand pull inflation

■ Cost push

The increase in prices that is being felt in an economy is due to pressure on costs. It might be the material suppliers who are putting prices up due to a change in the prices of commodities. Commodities are goods such as oil, copper and gold that are traded on open markets. The price alters according to supply and demand e.g. if there is likely to be a shortage of oil, the prospect of a reduction in supply on the market will push the price up. Another reason might be a rise in wage rates being paid in one particular industry that employs a significant number of people. Unions may use these wage increases as a benchmark for their own negotiations, meaning wage costs may rise above inflation, leading to producers having to pass on the price rises to the customer.

■ Money supply

It was not until the 1960s that a third cause was suggested. For years before then, economists argued over the cause of inflation, because if the cause is identified correctly, then the remedy will be more effective. It was the monetarists, led by Milton Friedman, who offered a third, more simple reason in that if there is insufficient money in the economy, then there will not be the pressure for extra demand or extra costs. Therefore if the money supply can be controlled, inflation will also be controlled.

Effect of inflation on business

■ An increase in uncertainty – if it is possible
to predict the change in prices accurately, then this makes for more accurate forecasting of sales profit and production levels. Given that within any forecast there are many potential variables, inflation simply adds in another variable to make forecasting less accurate. If it were known that inflation would be 1 or 2%, or even 0% (stable prices), forecasting would be easier. As inflation rises the fluctuation in inflation rates also changes e.g. in Brazil, where inflation rates have fluctuated from 100–1000% within weeks, forecasting is impossible. In the western world e.g. in France, where inflation is usually less than 2%, forecasting becomes more reliable.

■ Reduction in investment – the effect of
unreliable forecasting is that investment is postponed or cancelled, because inflation means more chance of making a mistake. Therefore multinational companies will look for a stable level of prices, among other factors, when making the decision to invest in production facilities abroad.

■ Labour force bargains for higher wages
– if inflation is e.g. 6% then for the work-force to end up with greater purchasing power, the wage increase in the **annual pay round** must be more than 6%. The concept of **real wages** refers to the increase in purchasing power that a particular wage increase provides.

COMPANY				
Inflation = 6%	Wage rise = 8%	Real wage rise = 2%	🙂	Result
Inflation = 6%	Wage rise = 3%	Real wage rise = –3%	🙁	Result

Figure 59.3 Employees will always look for real wage increases

In the above example, both sets of employees will receive more money following the wage increase. The difference is that in company 2, the employees will not have the same purchasing power when compared to the previous year.

■ Wage–price spiral – once the work-force is
awarded a real wage increase, this will be expected from year to year and industrial action may result if such a pay increase is refused. If companies continue to pay at levels greater than inflation, this will result in a level of income which increases faster than prices increase, leading to more goods being demanded. This in turn will lead to an increase in prices, hence inflation rises. The rise in inflation is then allowed for in the next year of pay bargaining to ensure that real wages are paid. If the process continues, then this results in a **wage–price spiral**. As prices and wages (literally) spiral out of control, it is then up to the government to step in with measures that will reduce spending (e.g. tax increases) or it is up to the company to refuse the pay award.

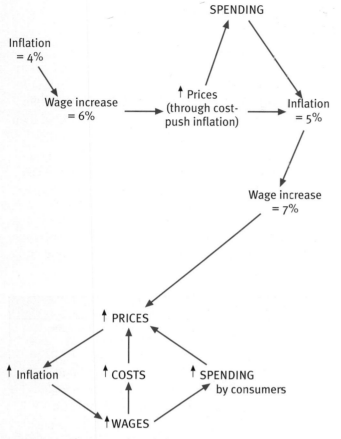

Figure 59.4 The wage–price spiral

- **Predictions on spending and wage increases will be based on the expected rate of inflation** – so if inflation is at 4%, but is expected to be at 6% by next year, there may be pressure to award a wage increase which will be a real wage based on next year's inflation, not this year's, accelerating the problem of a wage–price spiral.

- **Lack of competitiveness** – if inflation becomes built in to the pricing and wage bargaining process, this will ultimately make the economy's products less competitive for two reasons: a) inflation will increase the prices b) the expectation of further price increases may well mean that customers do not wish to enter long-term contracts because of the instability caused by uncontrolled inflation.

- **Inaccurate accounts** – price inflation can also lead to property inflation which may mean that companies try to revalue their fixed assets,

especially property companies where land values affect the rent they charge to their tenants. Inflation can distort accounts, leading to less reliable values of assets, but also it becomes less easy to make conclusions about the rate of growth of a business if prices are rising rapidly. Businesses may be tempted to overvalue their assets using the pretext of inflation. This valuation may in turn give a false perception of the business that may be considering a loan.

- **Reduction in profit margins** – for those companies operating in highly competitive markets, passing on cost increases to customers may mean that customers opt for a foreign supplier that is not facing the problems of inflation. This therefore means that in order to keep customers loyal, the business will have to absorb the cost increases, leading to lower profit margins. It is also difficult to predict prices, because companies may lose market share to competitors if their prices are not in line with the competition.

- **Liquidity preference** – as prices rise, and the value of money falls, a business will prefer to owe money to suppliers than be owed it by customers. Hence a business will put off paying its suppliers until the last minute, because the amount owed will stay the same but the purchasing power will reduce. If, for example, a business waits for 90 days to pay a bill and inflation is 16% per year, this means the value of the money owed drops by 4% over the three months. The business can, in the meantime, put the money into a deposit account and earn interest. Conversely, it will try to get its customers to pay as soon as possible, with a view to reinvesting the cash. Companies such as retailers that have very low debtor days and high creditor days are the prime beneficiaries in these circumstances. In addition, as the value of stocks and debtors rise, there will be greater need for cash to finance working capital.

- **Exchange rates** – purchasing power is reduced for companies who buy abroad, although the exchange rate may alter to reflect these differences in rates of inflation.

How do governments deal with inflation?

This has been dealt with in more detail in Unit 57 Government intervention. By way of a reminder, there are three ways the government can try to deal with inflation:

- **Monetary policy** = increasing the interest rate in order to make borrowing more expensive for companies and mortgages more expensive for individuals. This will mean there is a reduction in discretionary income and therefore a reduction in spending, which tends to reduce inflation.

- **Fiscal policy** = increasing the taxation rate, either direct or indirect. This will reduce income or make goods more expensive in the short term with a view to reducing demand.

- **Exchange rate policy** = intervening on the foreign currency market in order to make imports cheaper will help reduce costs of businesses that import. This will hopefully lead to a reduction in inflation as the cost savings are passed on to the customer in the form of lower prices.

Deflation

At the end of 1998, there was considerable concern in the retail sector that deflation might take a grip on the British economy, and possibly on the world economy. It appeared that consumers were holding back on their expenditure just before Christmas, in the hope that prices would fall after Christmas in the sales. Although special sales occur every year shortly after Christmas, the effect on pre-Christmas shopping levels was more than usually pronounced.

The threat of deflation has been exemplified by certain input costs falling (i.e. those used in the manufacturing process) such as

- Electricity
- Telephone
- Gas

The cost of high technology products has also been falling sharply in recent times. The reduction in costs has allowed companies to be more competitive, although certain manufacturers have insisted on holding their price levels and earning higher profit margins. Deflation is covered in greater detail in the Maxi Case Study.

Context – Unemployment

The prospect of watching television all day, every day would fill some people with sheer delight. Following the soaps in detail, listening to Kilroy and having the time to watch all the films you have ever wanted to has its attractions. However, being unemployed is not all about watching television; those who are unemployed have feelings of desperation because they have a talent which is not being recognised or used. They want to work hard and are willing to put in long hours, although no one will pay them for it. In addition, their families need providing for, but there is only a low level of income from the state and continual accusations that those on the dole are scroungers who don't want to work anyway – watching television all day is little consolation in this context.

Unemployment defined

Unemployment is the percentage of the working population that is out of work and is measured by the number of people who sign on the dole to receive unemployment benefit.

There are five types of unemployment:

Structural unemployment

This occurs when the demand for labour is less than the supply following a change in the structure of the economy when a particular industry runs down. The coal industry is a particularly good case in point. After the Second World War there were approximately 750,000 people employed in the mines. Today the number is closer to 15,000. This has been made worse because many of the coal-mines were the sole source of income in villages in Yorkshire, Nottinghamshire, Derbyshire and south Wales. The films *Brassed Off* and *The Full Monty* were set in such places, where redundant workers had to find alternative sources of income.

Cyclical unemployment

Caused by a reduction of demand in the economy as a whole, this results from a downturn in economic activity and is normally rectified by government action (*see Unit 57 Government intervention*).

Frictional unemployment

In an economy, it is accepted that some people will be between jobs. Either they are retraining, or they have deliberately resigned well before the new job begins to have time to look for houses, schools etc.

Seasonal unemployment

Some industries have seasonal demand, such as the hotel industry in Britain, which runs from March to October. During the winter months, hoteliers and those associated with the trade take their holidays. Ski resorts hire people for six to eight months of the year, but they are then without work for the non-ski season. Many of them come to work in Britain's hotels, because the holiday season follows on from the ski season.

Classical unemployment

This can be caused by the wage level in the particular job being too high when compared with the amount of people looking for work. This leads companies to lay off employees because the wage level is too high. One of the recent criticisms of the minimum wage is that it might cause unemployment (*see below*).

Question 3

Outline the causes of unemployment in the following situations:
a) the change of emphasis from manufacturing to services
b) poor weather in Britain during the summer causing seaside hotels to cut back on their labour requirements
c) excessive interest rates used to keep the pound high, resulting in a recession for the entire country
d) employees demanding real wages that are above the amount which firms can afford

[4]

The minimum wage

Part of the Labour Party's 1997 manifesto was to introduce a **minimum wage** in an attempt to increase the standard of living for many of the lowest-paid workers in the economy. The main aim of introducing the national minimum wage was to tackle the level of poverty and to provide an incentive for work. By raising the wage it was hoped the differential between unemployment benefits and the minimum wage would be increased, which would be a greater incentive for people to work and would increase the standard of living for those already in work.

The minimum wage of £3.60 per hour was implemented in April 1999. The rate of £3.60 was for all employees over the age of 22 and £3.20 for those aged between 18 and 21, the latter being referred to as the 'development rate'.

The government considered the development rate was essential because many employees in this category required training and were therefore less productive. Paying such employees £3.60 would have added too heavily to the costs of business.

The immediate effect of its introduction was an increase in pay for several thousand employees.

However, there were instances when employees saw no increase in their pay at all. Some employers were unable, or in some instances, unwilling to implement the new legislation, and simply cut the number of hours that their employees were allowed to work. Consequently, although employers had complied with the legislation, employees did not take home the intended additional income.

There were also some employees who found that not only did they not receive the additional pay, but that they were made redundant.

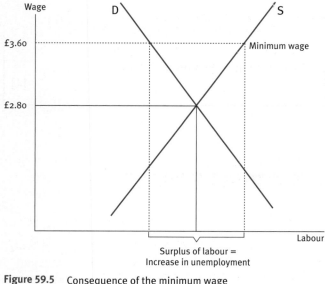

Figure 59.5 Consequence of the minimum wage

The theoretical consequences

According to economic theory, introduction of the minimum wage would mean there was an increase in the number of people willing to work whilst there was a reduction in the number of employers wishing to hire labour.

The excess supply over the demand for labour results in an increase in the level of unemployment. In reality the consequences have depended upon the type of industry, the level of wages prior to the legislation and the flexibility of the employer's profit margins, allowing for the opportunity to absorb the increase in wages.

The groups that benefit the most, according to the Low Pay Commission, are listed in Figure 59.6. An alternative way of classifying those who benefit from the minimum wage is shown in Figure 59.7.

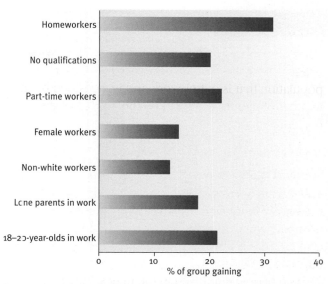

Source: Low Pay Commission Report, HMSO, June 1998

Figure 59.6 Groups gaining from the national minimum wage

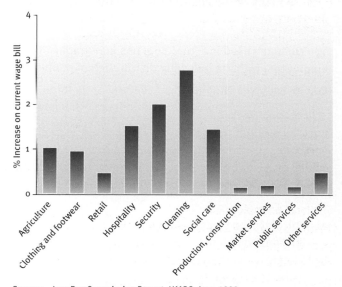

Source: Low Pay Commission Report, HMSO, June 1998

Figure 59.7 Effect of minimum wage

One other important implication of the minimum wage is the differential. By increasing the lowest level of wages, employees who are paid more than the bottom rung of employees will wish to see the difference in pay, otherwise known as the wage differential, maintained. Because the pay system should reflect skill, responsibility and seniority, this will cause a ratchet effect as wages increase all the way up the pay scale of people paid on an hourly basis (see Figure 59.8).

This shows that the differentials between each grade have been maintained and therefore there will be a significant increase in labour costs.

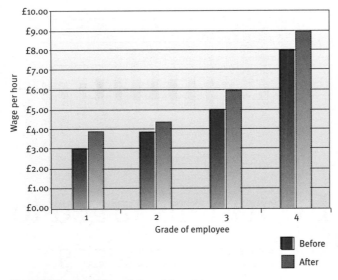

Figure 59.8   Pay differentials and the minimum wage

Question 4

The company used in Figure 59.8 has four grades of employees, with the following distribution of people:

Employee type	Number of employees	before minimum wage	after minimum wage
Grade 1	10	£2.80	£3.60
Grade 2	8	£3.60	£4.40
Grade 3	8	£5.00	£5.80
Grade 4	5	£8.00	£8.80

a) Calculate the wage cost before and after the introduction of minimum wage.   [3]
b) Suggest how the business might deal with the increase in wage costs.   [3]

Question 5

Munch-It, a local restaurant, is faced with the problem of how best to deal with the introduction of the national minimum wage. Although there are 20 employees, all but two of them work part-time. In terms of calculating wage costs, there is an equivalent of 11 full-time employees. The owner, Deborah Brown, has calculated the present wage bill assuming a 45-hour week at a wage rate of £3.

Assuming she will comply with the increase in wages due to the minimum wage but does not want to increase her total wage bill:

a) Calculate her existing wage bill.   [3]

b) Suggest how many hours her employees can be employed without increasing the total wage bill once the minimum wage has been implemented.   [2]

c) What other factors should Deborah consider before deciding her staffing requirements and hours staff should work?   [5]

The costs of unemployment

■ **Costs to the taxpayer** – if unemployment rises, the taxpayer must pay for the extra unemployment benefits that must be provided. This reduces the amount of money available in government finances to pay for all the other goods and services that the government either provides or consumes. Hence there is a smaller slice of the cake to allocate. The second issue to bear in mind is that the cake is also smaller, because fewer people are actually contributing to government through the tax system. In times of unemployment, government finance is therefore much tighter than when employment is high.

■ **Cost to local communities** – if a community relies on one industry or company, which is forced to close down, it has been suggested that being unemployed may lead to boredom and possibly an increase in the level of crime and vandalism.

■ **Costs to the unemployed** – not only is there a cost in terms of lost income, which has a serious impact on the quality of life of someone who has been made redundant, but there is also another hidden cost. There is the stigma of being made unemployed, which can be extremely upsetting to the person who loses the job and sometimes to his or her dependants. It can be seen as a failure and having to 'sign on' can be insulting to some people with high values. There is also a feeling of helplessness when a person is able and willing to work, not to say talented, but who is unable to find a job.

■ **Costs to the economy** – output is lost in that money is not spent on purchasing and the unemployment benefit which is paid does not result in any return output being produced. This incurs an opportunity cost in that government finances for industrial expansion will be restricted.

Characteristics of the UK job market

The UK job market displays some individual characteristics:

1 Easy hiring and firing; one of the attractions to foreign multinational companies is the ease with which employees can be hired and fired in Britain compared with other places in the EU. This is one of the reasons which has led to a number of foreign firms locating in Britain.

2 Elastic hours – there is a great deal of shift-work and overtime paid to UK workers, whereas other countries tend to have a more rigid contract The main advantage for the firms is that if a sudden order comes in to the business, it can meet the demand by employing people for more hours, as opposed to taking on a new employee. This does mean that extra money can be earned, although employers may use this as an excuse for paying slightly lower wages. It also means that employees may come to expect overtime.

3 Nearly a quarter of the working population is in some form of part-time job. Some are employed in two or three jobs. The vast majority of part-time employees are women, although there is a growing contingent of men who have to take on part-time work.

4 Wages are cheaper, as are non-wage costs, such as National Insurance and pension contributions (NICS). In Italy, Austria, France, Belgium, Spain, Germany and Portugal, non-wage labour costs were more than double the rate in Britain (*see Figure 59.9*).

5 There has been a reduction in union power in this country, which has led to less bargaining power at the work-place, further encouragement for firms to locate in Britain.

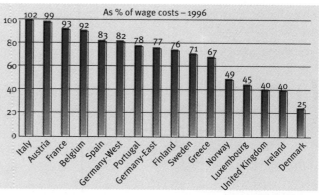

As % of wage costs – 1996

Italy 102, Austria 99, France 93, Belgium 92, Spain 83, Germany-West 82, Portugal 78, Germany-East 77, Finland 76, Sweden 71, Greece 67, Norway 49, Luxembourg 45, United Kingdom 40, Ireland 40, Denmark 25

EU nations urged to copy Britain's flexible economy

Source: Daily Telegraph, February 1998

Figure 59.9

Question 6

What are the consequences of such a high percentage of non-wage costs in relation to the wage rate for

a) Pirelli, the Italian tyre manufacturer? [3]

b) Pirelli's employees? [3]

---

6 Short-term contracts – in certain sectors of the economy the number of core workers has been reduced and replaced by contract workers. As a consequence the number of people now on short-term contracts is rapidly increasing.

7 Taking on new staff is certainly more expensive than offering the same employees more hours. Hence there is a tendency to keep the same people with more hours, rather than employing new people. This is one of reasons that the UK has a relatively high rate of unemployment, even during times of economic growth.

8 Flexibility – this is a word used to describe employees who co-operate and are willing to accept change. In reality, flexibility means lower unit costs, which can be passed on to consumers in lower prices. Flexibility in many instances therefore ends up meaning lower wages, higher productivity and overtime at modest rates!

Effect of unemployment on business

- **Loss of skill** – businesses lose talent when they create redundancies and there is the hidden cost of the level of creativity and output that could have been earned by keeping the employee at the business.

- **Loss of earnings** – unemployment can mean a loss of output and therefore loss of sales revenue, especially if there is a surprise order that the business does not have the capacity to produce.

- **Cash flow problems due to redundancies** – although a business will shed labour in order to save costs in the long run, the process of making people redundant involves redundancy payments. The level of redundancy is determined by law, although an employee's contract may have a more generous redundancy package.

- **Wage costs kept low** – some less scrupulous employers may use the fear of unemployment to drive down wages and force the remaining employees to accept a cut in wages, despite the obvious detrimental effect on morale and motivation.

- **Less government expenditure** – an increase in unemployment will lead to less money paid into the government coffer and more money paid out in dole. This will mean there is less money to redirect into helping industry.

Government action aimed at reducing unemployment

Introduction of the minimum wage – although the above section does suggest that this might worsen the level of unemployment.

Protectionism – a government might seek to subsidise a company to minimise the effect of foreign competition or penalise a competitor.

The 'New Deal' – the Labour government has introduced a financial incentive to employers who take on additional employees. They are paid £60 per week for the first six months of employment. This is a form of subsidy to encourage firms to take on the long-term unemployed.

Training and Enterprise Councils (TECs) – these were created to foster training as a way of making a company more productive.

Opting out of the Social Chapter – one of the directives in the Maastricht Treaty was a restriction on the number of hours in the working week. The argument for opting out is that restricting the maximum number of hours an employee can work may mean that instead of offering more overtime, a business has to employ another person which is usually more expensive than offering overtime, due to training and hiring costs.

Points for Revision

Key Terms

inflation	an increase in the general level of prices
hyper inflation	when prices double or treble in the space of a year
purchasing power	the amount of goods and services which money can buy
headline rate of inflation	the actual rate of inflation as measured by the Retail Price Index
underlying rate of inflation	the rate of inflation, excluding the effect of mortgage costs, measured using RPIX
demand pull	inflation caused by too much demand in the economy, in relation to the supply of goods and services
cost push	inflation caused by costs of inputs rising, forcing businesses to raise their own prices
money supply	inflation is caused by an increase in the money supply, allowing extra demand or extra costs to be met with higher prices
real wages	the actual wage increase minus the rate of inflation
wage–price spiral	when wages and prices increase out of control
annual pay round	the regular (annual) process of bargaining for a pay increase, usually based on inflation
structural unemployment	due to the decline in an entire industry
cyclical unemployment	caused by a fall in the level of demand in the economy
seasonal unemployment	caused by industries which do not operate throughout the year
frictional unemployment	caused by people changing jobs and the time lag between leaving one job and starting another
classical unemployment	when employees bargain for wages which are too high for the business to afford
minimum wage	a legal requirement for companies to pay a minimum wage

Definitions Question:
By referring to a business you know, explain three of the above (your teacher may wish to help you choose the terms).   [5] per definition

Summary Points:

1   Inflation reduces the purchasing power of money and is measured using RPI and RPIX.

2   Inflation causes uncertainty in investment and can result in lack of growth and in recession.

3   The economic policies that are undertaken to solve inflation may have detrimental effects on a wide range of businesses.

4   There are several causes of unemployment which require different policies to try and eradicate them; each policy has repercussions on businesses.

Mini Case Study – Inflation

Quik-frames

Quik-Frames is a London-based business, which specialises in manufacturing a range of photograph frames that it supplies to photograph developers in the high street. A typical frame costs just under £20 to produce, and the business uses a cost-based pricing policy:

Table 2

Cost of production	(per unit)
Materials	£8
Labour	£6
Fixed costs	£5
	£19

Price = £25

It has been aware that recent orders have been lost because of more competitive pricing. The rate of inflation for last year was 4% and although it meant that the financial director, James Lanyon, would have to award the work-force a 6% increase in the annual pay round, he did not think this would affect him too badly. More significant was the amount of time the retailers were taking to pay him; he honoured his invoices on time and kept his creditor days to 30. Unfortunately, the retailers were taking up to 90 days to pay their bills to Quik-Frames; that was putting strain on its cash flow and recently it had been forced to borrow on an overdraft. This was made worse by the MPC raising interest rates in an attempt to curb inflation.

1 Define: annual pay round, creditor days.   [4]

2 Comment on the pricing policy of the business and justify an alternative which might
   be more appropriate.   [5]

3 a) What is the real wage increase awarded to the employees?   [1]

   b) How might the company be affected if it continues to award such increases in pay?   [4]

4 How might Quik-Frames be affected by an increase in interest rates?   [6]

                                                                                                 20

Mini Case Study – Unemployment

Following a spate of building society conversions to banks, which added to the competitive pressure within the banking sector, Barclays announced it was shedding 6,000 jobs in May 1999 in an attempt to cut costs. It was hoped that annual costs of £200 million would be saved as a result of the job cuts. Although the initial costs would be in excess of £400 million to cover redundancy packages, the long-term savings were considered essential in its fight to remain competitive.

The bank tried to assure its customers that only 5% of the job cuts would be from branch staff to ensure that a personal service could be maintained. Barclays Chairman Sir Peter Middleton added that customers would have a wider range of channels that could be used to conduct their banking business. For some customers, however, using the 'hole in the wall' cash machines for making cash withdrawals would not be quite the same when compared to dealing with people. Barclays was not the only bank to introduce a programme of job cuts in order to remain competitive; HSBC and National Westminster had undertaken a similar exercise that year.

On hearing the announcement by the Barclays chairman, a major shareholder pointed out that without these job losses, there was a serious danger that a lot more jobs would be lost in the near future.

1 How would the job cuts help Barclays to remain competitive?   [4]

2 Suggest what type of unemployment the case refers to. Explain your answer.   [3]

3 Why will the government be faced with both an increase in expenditure and a loss of revenue as a result of the redundancies announced?   [5]

4 Discuss whether the point made by the shareholder is likely to be correct.   [8]

20

Maxi Case Study

At the end of the second millennium, one of the major fears facing British industry was not one of rising inflation. Precisely the opposite – it was the threat of deflation, in other words a reduction in the level of prices. This threatened to destabilise the economy, forcing employees to accept lower wages and making consumers put off their purchases, knowing that cheaper deals were round the corner. The following article highlights the real problems which deflation can cause:

Sting in the tail for new breed of bargain hunters

THE CONSUMER

Falling prices appear, at first sight, to be unadulterated good news for consumers, and there is every sign that in the years ahead they could enjoy value for money as never before.

Several important deflationary forces are at work that make the consumer king. Global competition is one of the most important arbiters of prices. There is now a critical mass of developing countries with low labour costs that are substantial exporters to the rest of the world. This is bearing down on prices. Traditional retailers are having to compete with bargains on the Internet. Electronic commerce is set to grow exponentially and prices will drop even further.

With the coming of the single currency to Europe, consumers will be able to compare prices across borders and be far less willing to pay over the odds. In the single market, a German car dealer charging 10 per cent more than his French counterpart will soon be deserted by his customers.

Even outside the euro zone, British producers are likely to come under greater scrutiny as consumers compare prices across the Channel. Why should cars, compact discs, shoes or a meal be so much more expensive than they are a ferry or train ride away?

Growing discontent about the prices consumers are asked to swallow is putting unprecedented pressure on retailers and producers to be more competitive and is reinforcing deflation. Price sensitivity is, in itself, a by-product of the low inflation of the 1990s. Employers have pointed to relatively low headline inflation rates to keep annual pay settlements low.

Employees with little or no increase in their salaries each year have been less and less prepared to accept higher prices on the high street.

Time and again the new canny breed of consumer has played chicken with retailers and won. When retailers tried to put up prices, sales went down. As soon as prices were cut again, shoppers returned.

Yesterday's new shop prices index from the British Retail Consortium showed that the 200 most commonly purchased items have fallen in price by nearly 1 per cent over the past year – proof, as the BRC put it, that inflation is not coming from the high street. Perceptions remain quite different. At the launch of the index, one reporter expressed reluctance to write a story about falling prices because he said he would be bombarded by calls from angry readers.

Despite low inflation and deflation in some cases, consumers want even better value.

This is where there is danger. Zero inflation is relatively healthy. Isolated examples of falling prices that reflect technological change or more efficient production are also good news. But falling prices across an economy are hazardous. There comes a point where companies cannot find any more efficiency gains and will simply go out of business. Suddenly, the powerful consumer is out of a job, his income drastically cut. Economy-wide deflation, however superficially attractive, has to be avoided.

JANET BUSH

1 Define zero inflation.   [2]

2 Outline and explain the main reasons for deflation which are highlighted in the
article.   [8]

3 Explain what is meant by the section which begins 'Price sensitivity is, in itself, ... ' and
ends '... on the high street'.   [5]

4 Explain the likely long-term effect of deflation.   [5]

5 Discuss the effect that deflation might have on shareholders.   [10]

                                                                                                30

Interest rates

Learning objectives

Having read this unit, students will be able to

1 understand why interest rates change

2 demonstrate the likely consequences of a change in the rate of interest upon a range of companies

3 discuss how a given company is likely to react to a change in interest rates

4 understand the relationship between the rate of interest and the exchange rate

Context

When evidence of the state of the economy is announced on the television or in the papers, the headline is frequently followed by speculation about the level of interest rates.

This is because the interest rate plays a key role in determining the level of growth; this was highlighted in Unit 57 Government intervention. It is easy to grasp the effect of interest rates on those people and firms with money in the bank, but the repercussions of interest rate fluctuations are much wider. The effect can be felt by those companies that import and export, those private individuals and businesses that have invested money in property as well as companies with high stock levels. It can also affect the decision on whether a business ought to expand and even the performance of a company on the stock market.

What is an interest rate?

The interest rate is the cost of borrowing. Although people who save money in a bank or building society watch interest rates closely, the interest rates which are more significant are those that the banks charge to borrowers. This rate is much higher than the rate paid on money deposited in the bank because it is one of the bank's main sources of revenue and profit.

Task

Arrange an interview with a building society and a bank to see if there is any comparison to be made between the rates each one charges on loans and overdrafts as well as the rates it pays to account holders.

The difference between the rates paid to lenders and to borrowers can be significant. In 1999, the Lloyds TSB classic account paid a rate of 0.5% per annum before tax, whereas the overdraft charge was 1.45% per month.

Question 1

David Nunn had kept a clean record with the bank, maintaining a positive bank balance for the first 10 months of the year, although some major purchases – a car and a holiday to Australia for his family – had meant he had gone overdrawn in November and December.

£	Jan to Oct (10 months)	Nov	Dec
Average monthly balance	8000	−2000	−3000
Interest	33.33	?	?

Assuming the interest rates were those for Lloyds TSB stated above:

a) Show that the total interest earned was £33.33 for the first 10 months. [3]

b) Calculate the interest cost for November and December and the net interest payable or receivable for the entire year. [5]

Who sets the interest rate?

Although financial institutions can control the amount they pay to investors, the minimum amount they can charge to borrowers is determined by the **base rate**. This used to be set by the government, in particular, by the Chancellor of the Exchequer, although the Labour government of 1997 broke with tradition and set up the Monetary Policy Committee at the Bank of England, which now has control over the setting of the base rate. The base rate therefore represents the minimum amount that a bank can charge when lending money. Most lending institutions charge a premium over and above the base rates e.g. in June 1999, base rate was 5%, although mortgages cost 7% to 8% per annum with credit card interest rates at about 18% and authorised overdrafts at 1.5% per month!

Why do interest rates change?

The basic economic relationship between the demand for money and the interest rate is shown in Figure 60.1:

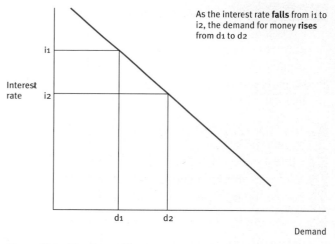

Figure 60.1   The demand for money

By changing the interest rates, the demand for money will alter, which will affect the overall level of consumer and capital expenditure within an economy. The interest rate has always been an economic tool that has been used to regulate economic activity. The cycle of economic activity is considered in greater detail in Unit 57 Government intervention. By way of a summary, the following factors may cause interest rates to change:

- a fall in the rate of growth, or a move from recession to boom – too much growth 'overheats' the economy
- if inflation becomes too high, meaning prices and costs become difficult to control
- if the pound becomes too strong, preventing companies from exporting at a profit
- if there is a stock market crash, interest rates may be reduced to encourage spending
- when investment needs to be encouraged

How are businesses affected by a change in interest rates?

If interest rates rise, a business will be less willing to borrow. This is because the cost of servicing the debt (paying interest) will become more expensive. This will have an effect on other parts of the business:

- The business may postpone or cancel major investment projects, preferring to aim for improvements in productivity because the cost of borrowing would be too high in relation to the expected return on the investment. The alternative may be to subcontract to other companies with spare capacity. Instead, too much growth, i.e. when the economy overheats, might lead to an increase in interest rates.

- The business will be more concerned to reduce its overall level of borrowing. This is because higher interest rates will increase costs and reduce profit. This reduction in retained profit means a fall in internal finance available for expansion.

- Short-term borrowing will also become more expensive, so businesses will need to concentrate on managing cash flow carefully. They may well try to reduce debtor days and increase creditor days to generate cash more quickly. They may also try to reduce levels of stock because stock represents money tied up in assets that are not productive. If the business has funded the purchase of stock with an overdraft, then running down the stock will not only release cash but will also reduce the cost of financing the stock. This can be done either by

reducing the rate of production, or by reducing the price with a view to increasing sales. The success of a price reduction will then depend on the price elasticity of demand as to whether the excess stock is sold.

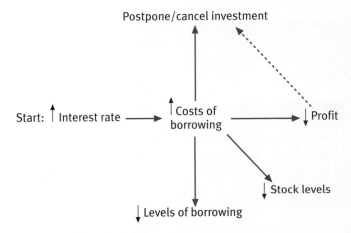

Figure 60.2   The effect of interest rates on borrowing

Question 2

Suggest how the following might react to an increase in the rate of interest:

a) a consumer with an overdraft
b) a business considering the purchase of three photocopiers using a bank loan over three years
c) a consumer buying a house
d) a heavy manufacturing company with high gearing
e) a consumer earning just under the average wage, who has three children and who makes purchases with a credit card   [10]

Question 3

A warehouse business has a gearing of 36%, with shareholder funds valued at £400,000. The operating profit figure is £60,000 and interest rates are 9%.

a) Calculate the amount of long-term borrowing, using the gearing ratio provided in Unit 38.   [3]

b) Calculate the interest payable and hence the interest cover ratio.   [3]

c) If the interest rate rose to 10%, what would be the increase in interest payable?   [2]

d) How would your answer to c) change if the company's gearing was 95%?   [4]

Question 3 highlights the significance of **gearing** when interest rates change. The forecast of interest rates is therefore a very important factor which businesses will consider when taking the decision to borrow.

Effect of interest rates on customers

The extent to which customers are affected by a change in interest rates will depend primarily on whether the customer is a **net saver** or a **net borrower**. A net saver is a household that has more money in the bank than money it has borrowed. In Britain it is seen as normal practice to purchase property as soon as the repayments can be afforded; this is done with the help of a mortgage (a loan for the purchase of houses). As a consequence, a large proportion of the working population are net borrowers.

A fall in interest rates will mean that customers with mortgages are likely to experience a reduction in the monthly payments made to the bank. Although the amount borrowed remains the same, the cost of borrowing will decrease. This will mean that there is extra money available to spend on non-mortgage items (i.e. everything apart from a mortgage). Hence there is an increase in **discretionary income** – the income that a person has to spend on non-essentials or luxuries. This may result in an increase in demand for such products. The term non-essential or luxury depends on the individual customer. Some will use the extra money to buy big-ticket items such as a hi-fi system or a holiday, although others will perhaps buy more food or will trade up – buy the same type of food, but a more expensive brand i.e. there will be some brand substitution. Others may simply decide to defer spending and save the money.

Effect of interest rates on asset values

The effect on asset values can be more significant for larger companies, because they will own assets worth

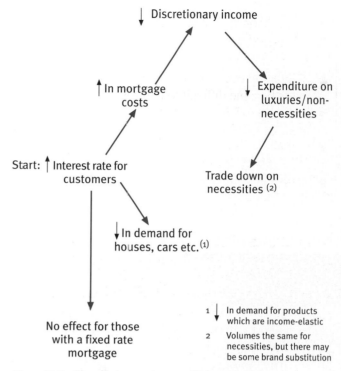

Figure 60.3 The effect on customers of interest rates

billions of pounds, so the fluctuation in asset values will be greater in money terms. As the value of assets falls, the collateral that a business can use to secure a loan will decrease in value, reducing the ability to borrow. When lenders – banks and building societies – are faced with this problem they can lend at higher rates, which increase the risk of non-payment. Alternatively, if a customer gets into financial difficulty over paying interest, the bank may well decide to cut its losses by repossessing the house (taking over ownership) and selling the house on behalf of the owner, although the value of the house may well be lower than the amount that was originally lent.

Such was the problem of falling asset values that the Prudential sold its estate agency business for 1 penny in the 1990s, in order to stem the tide of losses created by its property-selling arm.

This problem becomes more significant in economies where the majority of households do take out a mortgage. The debt burden in Germany, for example, is much lighter than that in Britain because the German population is less concerned about buying a house, preferring to rent. Therefore the impact of an interest rate change is much greater in Britain than in Germany.

If interest rates rise and less discretionary income is available, people will concentrate on paying their mortgage above all else. Successive interest rate rises can have a punishing effect on discretionary income, to the extent that some consumers may well have to default on their mortgage (i.e. not be able to pay the mortgage). This means the house owner must sell the house in order to pay off the mortgage, although on occasions the value of the house is less than the mortgage level, leading to the problem of **negative equity**

Negative equity: this refers to the reduction in the value of an asset on which a mortgage or loan is secured. The reduction is so great that the value would fail to meet the mortgage which was loaned in the first place. This reduction in asset values is normally due to higher interest rates which reduce the demand for houses and consequently force down the prices of houses. The house owner is left with a problem – the interest rates will be high, causing large expenses each month, and the only way to avoid this is to sell the property, but the value of the property will not meet the mortgage.

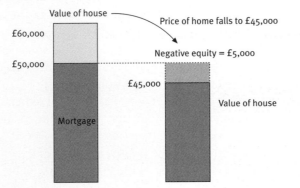

Figure 60.4   The nightmare of negative equity

With negative equity, the lender (i.e. the bank) will not receive the original amount it lent, so it must reduce its profit level. During the recession of the early 1990s the Abbey National had to write off over £500 million in losses due to falling house prices.

The following example illustrates the problem of rising interest rates and its effect on a house owner.

Mr Smith bought a house for £60,000, with a mortgage of £50,000. The interest rate of 6% seemed easy to meet when he was earning £1200 per month because it took up only one quarter of his monthly disposable income (gross income minus tax and pensions deductions). During the next two years, interest rates gradually rose to 10%, although his pay stayed the same. Costs of other items on his weekly shopping list rose with inflation and very soon he found the interest payments of £500 difficult to meet. He decided to sell the house, but the property market in his part of the country had been hit by higher interest rates and the estate agents advised Mr Smith, that the most he could hope for was £45,000. Mr Smith was therefore caught in the 'negative equity trap' and had to face considerable cutbacks in his personal expenditure to pay for the mortgage and other necessities.

Effect of interest rates on international trade

A fall in interest rates will, *ceteris paribus*, lead to a fall in the value of the pound. This is because a reduction in interest rates will make investment in UK financial institutions relatively less attractive.

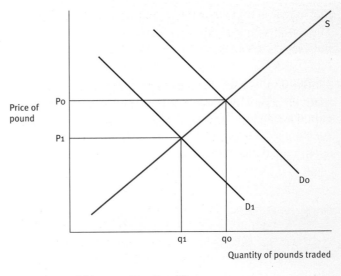

Do – D1 due to a fall in demand for money in UK financial institutions

The value of the pound therefore falls from Po – P1

Figure 60.5   Effect of a reduction in interest rates on the pound

This will exert an influence on companies that both export and import. The reaction to this problem is dealt with in more detail in Unit 61 International trade. However, by way of a summary of the effect on the pound, see Table 1.

Table 1

Interest rates	Demand for sterling	Price of sterling	Imports	Exports
Rise	Rises	Rises	Cheaper	More expensive
Fall	Falls	Falls	More expensive	Cheaper

Question 4

A large international steel company based in south Wales which manufactures and sells 45% of its output in Britain has just received the news that interest rates are to increase for the third time in a year. This will increase its total costs by 1%, and with a profit margin of only 4%, this has significant implications for the future. The business is labour-intensive, with a vast amount of reclaimed land and the threat of competition from abroad.

How might the business react to such a change in the interest rate?   [6]

But investors do not always behave in a logical, rational manner. For example, when the interest rate was cut in November 1998, theoretically the stock market should have risen. However, with so much uncertainty in the market at the time, the city viewed the cut in rates as an indication that the Bank expected further bad news and that the economic outlook was weak. The FTSE 100 fell by 141 points! Investors moved their money into 'defensive' shares – those that are relatively safe, such as supermarkets and utilities.

Figure 60.6   Effect of a reduction in interest rates on shares

Effect of interest rates on the stock market

If interest rates rise, this makes investing in the bank relatively more attractive, so there is usually a shift of capital into banks. Investors will take the view that the bank is reasonably safe, and will move their money accordingly. This will mean that shares are sold, pushing the price of shares downwards. As a consequence, it will become less easy to raise money through the stock market because of the fall in share prices. So with higher interest rates, profit will fall due to extra costs, borrowing will become less attractive due to higher cost and raising money through shares will become less attractive due to falling share prices – no wonder businesses prefer interest rates to be low!

Fixed rates

In recent years, lenders have begun to offer fixed rate terms. This means that for a period of time, sometimes for the entire term of the loan, but more usually for about 3–5 years, the rate is fixed. The main advantage of this is that the borrower is able to plan the cost of borrowing carefully and will not be affected by the periodic change in interest rates. The institutions choose the fixed rate by forecasting future rates and comparing them with the average level of interest in recent times e.g. the decision on the level of a fixed rate for 5 years will depend initially on the average rate of interest over the past 5 years. During the latter part of the twentieth century, interest rates gradually fell, so anyone who took out a fixed rate loan at that time is likely to have paid more than if the agreement had been based on a variable rate.

Summary

The extent to which interest rates will affect a particular company will depend on

a) The product it produces

b) The present level of gearing and interest cover

c) The nature of the business activity e.g. service or heavy manufacturing

d) The extent it relies on borrowing for expansion (connected to **b**)

e) Its reliance on overseas market for sales and sourcing imports

---

Question 5

To what extent will the following companies be affected by a fall in interest rates?
BP Amoco
Next
Boots the Chemists
W.H. Smith
A local newsagent   [10]

Points for Revision

Key Terms

base rate   the rate of interest set by the Bank of England Monetary Policy Committee, which is the minimum that lending institutions are allowed to use

net saver   a person or household that has more money in the bank than borrowed from the bank

net borrower   a person or household that has borrowed more than it has on deposit in the bank

gearing   the relationship between debt and equity, calculated by $\dfrac{debt}{equity}$

discretionary income the money left over once necessities such as food and mortgage have been paid for

negative equity   when the value of a property falls to a level below the amount of the mortgage borrowed to purchase it

Definitions Question:
By referring to a business you know, explain the significance of any three of the above terms (your teacher may wish to help you choose the terms).   [5] per definition

Summary Points:

1   Interest rates are one of most frequently used tools to regulate the level of economic activity.

2   A change in interest rates can affect a company's expansion plans, costs, profit and customers.

3   The extent to which a business is affected by interest rate changes will depend on a variety of factors.

Mini Case Study

The Med Bank provides loans for holiday companies wishing to raise money in order to build hotels and leisure complexes on the shores of the Mediterranean Sea. Initially it provides long-term loans in order to fund the cost of actually building the complexes although it also provides overdrafts so that working capital can be funded. One such company which has borrowed money from the bank is Sunny Villas; it identified an attractive part of the southern Sicilian coast-line which it wanted to develop into a series of villas to own and manage itself, renting them out to holiday-makers. Property prices were particularly cheap in that part of Europe, so the business borrowed £250,000 (750 million lire) to finance the purchase of the land and the actual construction. Unfortunately, the planning process in Sicily was very difficult to arrange and immediately the project had to be put back, even though Sunny Villas had hired the labour and purchased all the building materials in advance, in order to take advantage of cheaper materials through bulk-buying. When planning permission finally arrived, it was informed that only two of the three developments were allowed. This left the business with a large amount of stock that it had to hold until it could find a buyer. The stock was valued at £45,000 and the business was paying a 10% interest charge on the borrowed money, which decreased to 9% three-quarters of the way through the first year. Thankfully, the company found a buyer one year after it bought the materials.

Unfortunately, the recession in the Italian economy meant property prices fell and Sunny Villas was rather concerned that Med Bank would force it to sell up due to the possibility of negative equity.

1 Define: bulk-buying, long-term loan.	[4]
2 Calculate the cost of financing the stock that was not required.	[4]
3 What might be the reaction of Med Bank to the threat of negative equity?	[4]
4 Discuss how Sunny Villas might be affected by a fall in interest rates.	[8]

20

Maxi Case Study

Jim Terry set up The Brogue Company in late 1987 when he was made redundant after the stock market crash. He had made a great deal of money during the boom years of the mid-1980s and had invested it wisely in government bonds. At the time, there were opportunities for designer models in the shoe market aimed primarily at the fashion-conscious Yuppie market. Jim hired several craftsmen to manufacture the product by hand, selling at a significant premium, distributing by using a sales-force that focused primarily on the City. The sales-force arranged 'shoe fitting parties' after work which were an excuse for a drink and a chat between colleagues, and as the drinks flowed, so did the sales of new shoes! While making plenty of money on the designer label side, he began to import shoes from the Far East which were cheaper, although machine-made. These were aimed at socio-economic groups C1 to E. Although he felt the company had a market niche in the hand-made side which he exploited to the full, sales levels depended on the level of economic growth. He was pleased he made this decision during the recession of the early 1990s as the sales of hand-made shoes fell, but the mass-produced shoes ensured that there was enough profit and cash for the business to continue trading.

The results for the year ending 30 September 2000 had just been prepared and Jim was thinking about the future. In the past three years, the economy had gradually become overheated and inflationary pressures had meant interest rates had risen. Unfortunately the increase was so negligible (one quarter of one per cent) that further growth was expected, so Jim was rather concerned about the prospect of further interest rate rises.

His concern centred on a proposed expansion to the present factory, which would cost a further £2 million, given that he proposed to borrow the money. The expansion would allow him to increase the volume he sold of the mass-produced items because he would begin to manufacture the products, as well as continuing the importing of shoes. Recently the mass-produced shoes had become more profitable and were contributing a larger amount of revenue and profit than the hand-made shoes.

Table 2

	Percentage of sales	
	1995	2002 (forecast)
Mass-produced shoes	40%	62%
Hand-made shoes	60%	38%
	Percentage of profit	
Mass-produced shoes	25%	48%
Hand-made shoes	75%	52%

Borrowing the money would increase his present gearing, although the bank had intimated it would be happy for gearing to increase assuming the business continued to make a profit margin of 10%.

The following information was taken from The Brogue Company's accounts on 30/9/2000.

Sales revenue   £76 million
Operating profit   £ 9 million
Shareholders' funds £32 million

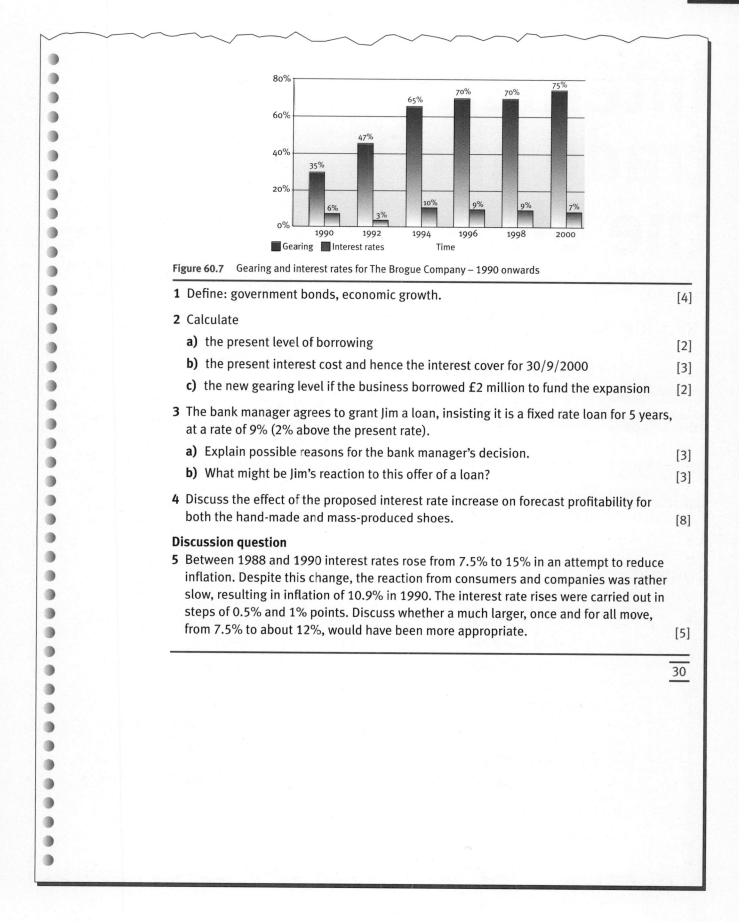

Figure 60.7 Gearing and interest rates for The Brogue Company – 1990 onwards

1 Define: government bonds, economic growth. [4]

2 Calculate

  a) the present level of borrowing [2]

  b) the present interest cost and hence the interest cover for 30/9/2000 [3]

  c) the new gearing level if the business borrowed £2 million to fund the expansion [2]

3 The bank manager agrees to grant Jim a loan, insisting it is a fixed rate loan for 5 years, at a rate of 9% (2% above the present rate).

  a) Explain possible reasons for the bank manager's decision. [3]

  b) What might be Jim's reaction to this offer of a loan? [3]

4 Discuss the effect of the proposed interest rate increase on forecast profitability for both the hand-made and mass-produced shoes. [8]

Discussion question

5 Between 1988 and 1990 interest rates rose from 7.5% to 15% in an attempt to reduce inflation. Despite this change, the reaction from consumers and companies was rather slow, resulting in inflation of 10.9% in 1990. The interest rate rises were carried out in steps of 0.5% and 1% points. Discuss whether a much larger, once and for all move, from 7.5% to about 12%, would have been more appropriate. [5]

30

International trade and the EU

Learning objectives

Having read this unit, students will be able to

1 understand the factors that affect exchange rates

2 demonstrate an awareness of policies that a government may pursue to influence the exchange rate

3 understand the effects of a change in exchange rates on a business

4 understand the role of the EU and how it affects business

Context

The only time some people are concerned about the exchange rate and international trade is prior to their annual summer holiday abroad.

Visiting the travel agency or the local currency exchange bureau sparks an interest in how many pesetas or dollars will be gained for each pound.

At the same time, consideration may be given to the amount of currency that is to be purchased for holiday pocket money. Each pound that is exchanged for foreign currency is money leaving this country to be spent abroad. On return from holiday, souvenirs and presents for relatives mean that foreign goods have been bought. Every one of the millions of tourists who travel abroad each year is part of international trade and has an effect on the value of currencies throughout the world.

Reasons for international trade

A quick glance around any home will clearly illustrate one of the reasons for international trade. Choice is an important factor for consumers and if that means purchasing products that are manufactured abroad there is little concern for the long-term consequences of their actions.

But one of the opportunity costs of having more choice and access to goods and services from abroad is that it may mean a UK business cannot compete and will go out of business and, as a consequence, there will be a loss of jobs in the UK. Many products are no longer produced in this country, due to competition from abroad forcing the closure of whole industries. Shipbuilding, the motorbike industry, coal-mining, steel and, to some extent, the car industry have all succumbed to pressure from international competition.

Globalisation has also contributed to the growth in international trade. As companies have sought to expand their operations around the world in an attempt to increase their world market share and to take advantage of new markets, trade has prospered.

Improved communication and transportation have reduced the barriers to international trade, further enhancing the amount of business around the world.

As more firms from different countries have been attempting to remain competitive or improve their competitiveness, productive units have been established throughout the world, either taking advantage of cheaper labour costs or circumventing government attempts to restrict trade by the imposition of taxes on goods being brought into their particular country. Whatever the reason, more trade has been taking and is continuing to take place on an international basis.

The terms

Exports – goods or services that are produced in a country and sold abroad e.g. goods manufactured in the UK sold to USA = UK *exports* to the USA and USA *imports* from the UK.

Goods made in A sold in B

Country A   Country B

Payment for goods

Country A exports van to B
Country B imports van from A

Figure 61.1   Exports and imports

(Some of the main UK exports are machines, manufactured goods, chemicals, tourism and food and drink.)

Imports – goods purchased from abroad e.g. goods made in China and purchased in the UK.
(The majority of UK imports are raw materials, manufactured goods, food and clothing.)

Visible trade – this refers to all goods; the trade in cars, furniture, pottery, electrical equipment are all **visibles**.

Invisible trade – this refers to all services; the trade in tourism, insurance, transport are all **invisibles**.

Balance of trade – this measures the difference between exports and imports for visibles. For the past few decades, the UK **balance of trade** has been in deficit as other trading nations have become more competitive.

Invisible balance – the difference between exports and imports for invisibles. Traditionally, the invisible balance has been in surplus.

Balance of payments – this measures the difference between the exports and imports for both visibles and invisibles. In 1999 there was a record deficit for the **balance of payments**.

Balance of trade

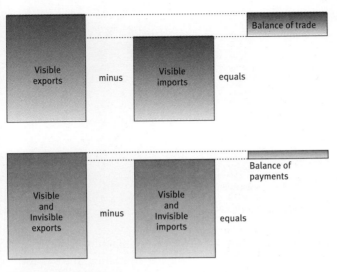

Balance of payments

Figure 61.2   Balance of trade and balance of payments

Surplus – when the value of exports exceeds the value of imports, there is a **surplus**.

Deficit – when the value of imports is greater than the value of exports there is a **deficit**.

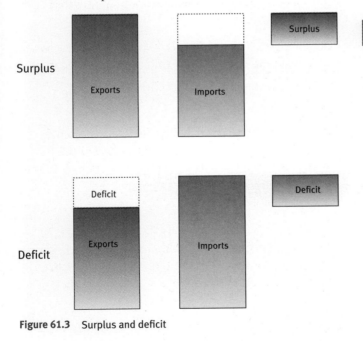

Figure 61.3   Surplus and deficit

Question 1

Classify each of the following in terms of export or import; visible or invisible:

For example:

Wedgwood pottery sold in USA = Visible export

a)   BMW sold in the UK

b)   Korean ship bought by British cruise line company

c)   British family having a holiday in Spain

d)   A machine made in the West Midlands sold to a business in Japan

e)   A British advertising agency working for a Malaysian company   [5]

Trade between nations is recorded to enable government to assess the economic performance of its country and to enable it to take any action that may be considered necessary. The figures are reported regularly in the media as one of several economic indicators used to judge the state of the economy and the performance of the government of the day. The current account or the balance of payments is featured on the news and measures the difference between the total exports and imports of a country.

Factors affecting trade

Several factors affect the amount of trade that takes place and whether a customer buys a British or a foreign product or service.

- Improved communications have enabled customers to purchase products from anywhere in the world. IT facilities such as the Internet have no national boundaries so customers are free to order products from whichever business offers the right package.

- Technology has improved the ease with which products can be transported and at the same time has reduced the price of many, therefore making more goods accessible to more people.

- The intensity of competition has led to a rapid improvement in the quality of products and the price at which they are sold is constantly being eroded by cost-cutting innovations. The combination of these two factors has meant that more customers are willing and able to purchase more goods.

■ Many businesses unable to compete on price have found other ways to entice the customer; speed of delivery has become much more important as all businesses are keen to reduce the lead time for their own products. Buying in components from abroad can be risky in terms of prompt delivery and therefore any guarantee of a fixed delivery date can provide a competitive edge.

■ All businesses attempt to improve their efficiency in order to compete in an international market. Reducing the unit cost of production can be achieved by gaining the benefits of economies of scale and therefore there is a greater determination to sell more products.

■ The attitude of a country's government can affect the amount of trade that takes place. If a country is keen to protect its own manufacturers from competition from abroad, it can impose sanctions to reduce the amount of imports. This can be done in a variety of ways.

Tariffs

These are taxes on goods being imported into the country. By adding a tax to the price of the product it is hoped that the price will be increased sufficiently to reduce demand for it and at the same time possibly increase demand for the home-produced alternative (*see Figure 61.4*).

Member countries of the EU operate a Common External Tariff with imports from non-members. The EU fixes the rate of the tariff that all member countries use for particular goods coming from non-member countries.

Quotas

A government can restrict the amount of goods that may be imported, either by volume or value. During the 1980s the British government introduced a quota on the number of Japanese cars that could be imported into the UK.

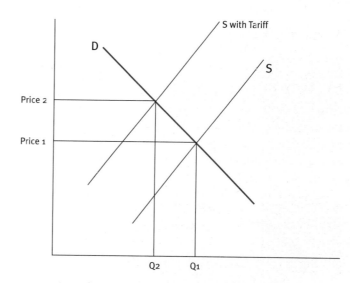

Demand falls from Q1 to Q2 as the price of the product increases after the introduction of the tariff

Figure 61.4   Consequences of imposing a tariff

The United States operates several quotas for products from abroad in an attempt to protect its own industries.

Embargoes

Governments may impose a total ban on the import of certain goods. Many countries operate an embargo on pornography and illicit drugs on social, rather than economic, grounds.

The use of such tactics is referred to as **protectionism** and is used throughout the world in an attempt either to protect employment, new industries and strategic industries or to address a serious balance of payments deficit.

Exchange rates

The **exchange rate** is a significant factor that affects the ability of a business to sell its products. Manipulating the value of a currency can affect the price of both imports and exports and therefore have a significant effect on trade.

An exchange rate is the value of one currency in terms of another. The most frequently quoted exchange rates for pounds sterling are the dollar (American), the mark (Germany) and the yen (Japan).

In addition, since 1999, the value of the pound has also been given in terms of the euro.

Whenever there is a demand for a product or service from another country there is a need to buy the currency of that country. If there is a significant increase in the demand for UK goods, there would be an increase in the demand for pounds. This in turn may increase the value of pounds and consequently the exchange rate will change.

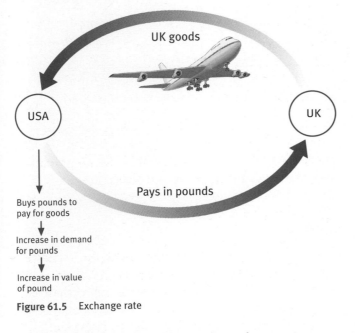

Figure 61.5   Exchange rate

(*The consequences of changes to the exchange rate are dealt with in detail later in this unit.*)

Causes of changes in the exchange rate

The exchange rate is determined by supply and demand. Anything which influences these two market forces will affect the value of the exchange rate.

- If demand is high in comparison to supply, the value of the currency will increase. If demand falls in relation to supply, its value will fall. So it is important to understand the factors that affect the demand and supply for any given currency.

- The amount of trade that is taking place – if demand is high for the products of a country, there will be a high demand for its currency.

- The amount of imports that are being bought – if import levels are high there will be a need to sell pounds (sterling) to buy foreign currencies.

- The level of interest rates within a country – investors from abroad will be attracted to invest in UK banks if the rate of interest increases in relation to other countries. This investment will increase the demand for pounds and therefore increase the value of the pound. This form of investment is often referred to as 'hot money'.

- Speculation – on occasion, no actual change either in interest rates or economic news is needed to alter the value of the exchange rate. The mere prospect of change can be enough. Speculation about the Monetary Policy Committee's decision on base rates is frequently a reason for a change in the value of the pound.

- Any economic news that may be about to be announced – for example, a projection that the economy is suffering from an increase in inflation may mean that speculators realise that the government may take deflationary measures such as increasing interest rates. This speculation alone will increase the value of the pound.

- Government economic policy – the government may decide to implement an economic policy to affect either directly or indirectly the value of the pound. It may decide deliberately to buy pounds on the foreign exchange market (a market for buying and selling international currencies) in order to make the pound stronger (higher in value). Alternatively the government may impose a tariff on a particular product in an attempt to influence the quantity demanded which will in turn affect the demand for particular foreign currencies.

Question 2

If there was a fall in the rate of interest, what would be the likely consequences on the value of the pound?

[4]

Consequences of changes in the exchange rate

Being aware of the causes of the change in currency rates is most important to a business if it is to survive and prosper in the world market. Noting the cause may help predict the likely consequence of a change.

A simple illustration (*see Figure 61.6*):

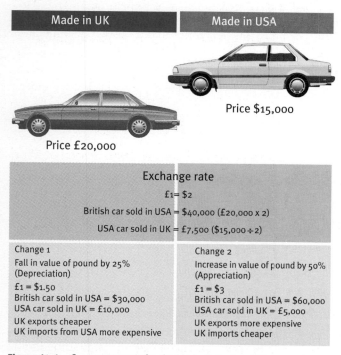

Made in UK

Made in USA

Price $15,000

Price £20,000

Exchange rate

£1 = $2

British car sold in USA = $40,000 (£20,000 x 2)

USA car sold in UK = £7,500 ($15,000 ÷ 2)

Change 1	**Change 2**
Fall in value of pound by 25% (Depreciation)	Increase in value of pound by 50% (Appreciation)
£1 = $1.50	£1 = $3
British car sold in USA = $30,000	British car sold in USA = $60,000
USA car sold in UK = £10,000	USA car sold in UK = £5,000
UK exports cheaper	UK exports more expensive
UK imports from USA more expensive	UK imports cheaper

Figure 61.6   Consequences of a change in the value of the pound

How much the demand for either exports or imports will change depends on the extent to which price is the main factor in determining whether the product or service is purchased. It will also depend on the elasticity of the product. An inelastic product will not be affected as much as an elastic product (*see Unit 18 Elasticity*).

If a business is aware of the likely consequences of a change in the value of a currency, it is more able to respond in an appropriate manner. For change 2 in Figure 61.6, the UK manufacturer, in an attempt to compensate for the increase in the cost of buying a car from the UK, may decide to reduce the price to lessen the effect of the change in the value of the pound. Whether the manufacturer is able to do this will depend on the profit margin prior to the change and the break-even level of sales.

Alternatively the manufacturer may increase expenditure on the marketing of the car to create or maintain demand for it. The manufacturer may ultimately decide that there is little possibility of compensating for the change in price.

As a result of the change in value of the pound the manufacturer may seek alternative markets where a more favourable exchange rate exists. For change 2, the effect on the business appears to be more favourable, yet there are areas of concern that need addressing. According to Figure 61.6, a 25% fall in the value of the pound ought to result in an increase in the demand for UK cars in the USA. The UK car manufacturer may be faced with an upsurge in demand that it is unable to handle. If the fall in the value of the pound is predicted then the business may wish to stockpile some cars to enable the increased demand to be met. Facing an increase in demand that it is unable to meet may lead to a loss of goodwill and a reputation for not meeting delivery times. Diverting stock to the USA from countries where the value of currency is not so favourable is another alternative.

Unfortunately, predicting the change in the value of currencies and the likely response of demand is never that simple. Furthermore the unpredictability of exchange rates can in itself be a cause for concern as purchasers of expensive products may not be prepared to risk buying them in advance only to discover the 'price' has increased as a result of a change in the value of the currency. This uncertainty is a serious obstacle to potential exporters and a problem that tests the ingenuity of marketing experts.

Question 3

a) If there was an increase in the value of the pound in relation to the yen, suggest the likely consequences for imports of Japanese video equipment.   [3]

b) If the increase in the value of the pound was from 175 yen to 190 yen and the price elasticity for video equipment was 1.5, explain what the change in the level of imports would be.   [4]

Question 4

Suggest how Thomsons, the travel company, would be affected by an increase in the value of the pound.

[8]

Changes in the value of a currency affect not only sellers of products but also purchasers. Many businesses in this country rely on foreign suppliers for vital components. Any change in the exchange rate may mean either an increase or decrease in the cost of purchasing these components. Much will depend on the value of these components, the finished product to be sold and where it is to be sold. Nevertheless, a business needs to consider carefully its strategy for such occasions. Using suppliers from different countries may not be possible or desirable as the reliability of the supplier may be much more important than the cost of the components.

Question 5

SS Canes plc manufactures hand-crafted wooden walking sticks. 60% of its output is exported to America, and it imports all of the wood from Scandinavia. The wood accounts for 30% of its costs and the business sells its canes at a 25% mark-up.

Discuss how a fluctuation in the exchange rate might affect SS Canes.

[4]

European Union

The background

Although trading within an international market brings its problems, there are ways of enhancing trade. Belonging to a trading union is one such way that has prospered over the years. The UK had traditionally traded with the members of the Commonwealth and fought shy of joining any European union until 1973.

The Treaty of Rome, 1957, had laid the foundations for the European Economic Community (EEC) which started with six member countries. The philosophy was to establish a **free trade** market between member countries making it easier for them to trade with one another. Previously, individual countries operated a series of tariff barriers that greatly restricted trade between them.

'The Common Market' was a trading union where there was free trade between member countries and the use of a common external tariff for trading nations outside the EEC. The intention was that not only were products and services to be free of tariffs and other barriers to trade, but also there was to be free movement of labour and finance within the Community. Belonging to such a union meant that businesses were able to gain free access to a much larger market. But it also meant that other European countries would have access to the UK market.

This was seen as a positive incentive to join because it forced many British businesses to strive for greater efficiency in order to compete in a wider market.

Disadvantages of joining included an increased cost for much of the UK's food imports from around the world as the common external tariff would have to be imposed. It was argued at the time when the debate over entry was in full swing that this would increase the retail price index considerably. Such an increase in the cost of living was seen as a major cause for concern.

The Maastricht Treaty of European Union was agreed in 1991. This treaty saw the creation of the European Union (EU), which encouraged not only economic union but also political and social union. Trading in Europe would never be the same again.

Question 6

Why was the issue of having to pay more for much of our imported food considered to be such a disadvantage?

[5]

The Social Chapter

This is part of the Maastricht treaty and is intended to bring into line the member states' approach to the rights of employees with regard to equality for all, minimum wage, working hours (the **working time directive** which restricts the number of hours an employee may work), industrial relations and trade union membership. Much of the above prevented the UK signing the treaty when the Conservative government was in office until 1997.

European Union established

By 1995 there were 15 member countries with more applying to join. The organisation and the bodies established can be seen in Figure 61.7:

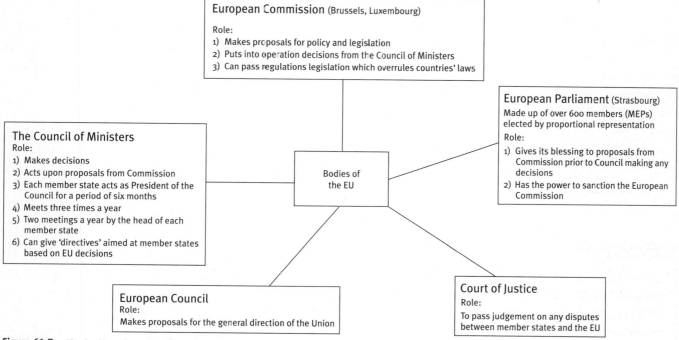

European Commission (Brussels, Luxembourg)

Role:
1) Makes proposals for policy and legislation
2) Puts into operation decisions from the Council of Ministers
3) Can pass regulations legislation which overrules countries' laws

European Parliament (Strasbourg)
Made up of over 600 members (MEPs) elected by proportional representation
Role:
1) Gives its blessing to proposals from Commission prior to Council making any decisions
2) Has the power to sanction the European Commission

The Council of Ministers
Role:
1) Makes decisions
2) Acts upon proposals from Commission
3) Each member state acts as President of the Council for a period of six months
4) Meets three times a year
5) Two meetings a year by the head of each member state
6) Can give 'directives' aimed at member states based on EU decisions

Bodies of the EU

European Council
Role:
Makes proposals for the general direction of the Union

Court of Justice
Role:
To pass judgement on any disputes between member states and the EU

Figure 61.7   The bodies of the European Union

In order for the Union to work effectively and for trade to take place without the problems of varying currencies and without barriers, the 'single market' has been the goal for all concerned within the Union.

There are nearly 370 million potential customers within the European Union and ensuring free access for all to trade required a goal of a common exchange rate and monetary union to co-ordinate economic policy.

Exchange Rate Mechanism (ERM)

This was an attempt to combine the currencies of the member states to form the European Monetary System (EMS) operating along the lines of having one exchange rate that each country fixes in an attempt to avoid fluctuations and therefore uncertainty and speculation with currencies. There was an allowance to move or float the individual currencies within a tight band to avoid any loss of certainty of value. However, severe difficulties with supporting these fixed currency values

quickly brought the ERM into disrepute and it was abandoned in the late 1990s.

Single currency

An alternative attempt to enhance trade was to introduce the European Currency Unit (ECU) as a single currency for member states. From January 1, 1999, prices had to be shown in the currency of the member state and in ECUs, otherwise referred to as the euro. By the year 2002 it was hoped to have the euro as the currency for all member states, replacing their individual currencies.

The cost of introducing these actual and proposed changes carried serious implications for member states.

Question 7

Suggest some of the likely costs a retailer would incur when complying with the requirement to show the price of its products in euros as well as the currency of that country.   [5]

The importance of international marketing

The natural progression for a business that has captured a large proportion of its domestic market is to look abroad. This is significant when the domestic market is static, but the business is trying to achieve further growth.

The advantages of international marketing are as follows:

- By producing more products a business is able to reduce unit cost by gaining the benefits of economies of scale.

- The expansion of the European market and the decline in trade barriers has exposed many businesses to the forces of competition. The need to be price-competitive along with producing a quality product delivered on time is now essential if the business is to survive in the world market. Companies that do this effectively have a clearly defined **pan-European strategy** e.g. Evian, the manufacturer of bottled mineral water, sells its product under the same brand name throughout Europe. The advertising and logo have the same theme and the product must conform to the same European standards of quality. However, the price which is charged does vary significantly from country to country due to the different market and economic environments.

- Finding markets abroad may be essential if a business is to compete with other companies from abroad also intent on expanding their customer base into the domestic market.

- By finding and developing additional markets abroad, businesses are able to spread the risk of reliance on one country for the sale of its products. By selling to several countries, recession in one country is cushioned by the buoyant level of sales in another.

BAT is an obvious example of a business that has looked for new markets abroad. Faced with a decline in sales in Europe due in part to a long-running campaign to reduce the amount of advertising tobacco companies could undertake, BAT targeted the Far East, with the emphasis on China. BOC has also looked to new markets abroad in order to increase sales. The Chairman of BOC, David John, stated that Asia and Latin America were the markets of the future.

Problems?

The product or service to be sold must be marketed in an appropriate manner; businesses will encounter problems selling goods abroad if they have not researched their markets carefully. Using the wrong name for the product (*see Unit 20 Promotion*), using the wrong distributor or targeting the wrong customer are all factors for concern.

There are different laws to comply with; countries have different rules with regard to health and safety, the environmental impact of products and advertising standards.

Care needs to be taken with religious, ethnic and cultural differences if a business is to be successful in a new market. It is therefore essential that effective marketing is undertaken if inroads into international markets are to be achieved.

Globalisation

In spite of the problems of trading abroad, many businesses have established themselves in countries around the world.

Globalisation refers to the growth of international trade; buying cheaper imported components and finding new markets for exports. It also refers to businesses that invest in production units abroad.

Given the reasons for the growth in international trade, building a manufacturing unit in or near to the foreign market helps reduce the costs of distribution and therefore improve the competitiveness of the product. The ultimate in globalised products is Coca-Cola, which has nearly half the world market for carbonated drinks. There are Coca-Cola plants throughout the world.

Many businesses claim to be global; GEC actually states in its 1999 Summary Financial Statement, 'We are global', writ large across two pages. GEC has several companies across America, Africa, Asia and Australasia, as well as companies in Europe. Apart from the obvious reasons for expansion that have already been referred to, satisfying the continual pressure from shareholders to maintain or increase profit is a major explanation for the pace of globalisation.

Points for Revision

Key Terms

visibles	the trade in goods from one country to another e.g. buying a motorbike from Suzuki
invisibles	the trade in services from one country to another e.g. Naomi Campbell modelling abroad
balance of trade	the value of exports minus the value of imports for visibles
balance of payments	the value of exports minus the value of imports for all trade between one country and the rest of the world
surplus	where the value of exports is greater that the value of imports
deficit	where the value of imports is greater than the value of exports
protectionism	when government deliberately ensures that domestic industries are allowed to prosper
exchange rate	the value of one currency in terms of another
single market	a goal which would mean free access for all to purchase products and services without barriers
working time directive	restricts the number of hours an employee is permitted to work in a week
free trade	where there are no restrictions on the movement of goods and services between countries
pan-European strategy	a long-term plan which helps to ensure effective marketing within Europe
globalisation	increase in international trade and ownership of production units abroad

Definitions Question:
By referring to a business you know, explain the significance of any three of the above terms (your teacher may wish to choose the terms).   [5] per definition

Summary Points:

1   Businesses are faced with an ever-increasing world market that provides both opportunities and threats.

3   There are several factors, including action by the government, that may alter the value of the exchange rate.

2   Businesses may be affected in a variety of ways by the value of the exchange rate.

Mini Case Study

From 1998 onwards the value of the pound steadily rose to such an extent that many manufacturers were unable to compete in the international market. With the rising pound manufacturers were unable to sell their products at a competitive price and as a consequence were having to lay off workers as export orders dried up.

There was also concern over the threat of inflation returning to dampen economic progress. The Bank of England had been handed the job of fixing the rate of interest by the new Labour Chancellor, Gordon Brown. The Governor of the Bank of England and the first Chairman of the Monetary Policy Committee had ruled that interest rates needed to be high in order to eliminate any fear of excessive borrowing fuelling inflation. But the effects on the exchange rate are now well documented. Even a series of small cuts in 1999 leading to one of the lowest rates for years could not inspire exporting manufacturers as they continued to shed jobs at an alarming rate. BOC, Delta, Diageo, Coats Viyella, Shell Haven, Siemans and Rover all announced large job losses.

Profit margins had already been slashed in an attempt to remain competitive, but were not enough to counter the large price differential created by the value of the pound.

Unfortunately that was not the end of the bad news; many UK manufacturers, in another bid to remain competitive, were starting to look abroad for cheap suppliers of what used to be UK-produced components. By the start of the year 2000 there was no real light at the end of the dark tunnel for British manufacturers as they continued to be pounded by the pound.

1 Explain the relationship between the rate of interest and the value of the pound.   [3]

2 With the aid of a numerical example of your own, show how the increase in the value of the pound affects the price of UK exports.   [3]

3 With evidence from the case, suggest what is likely to happen to the balance of trade as a result of the high value of the pound.   [4]

4 With reference to the article, suggest why UK companies were seeking to buy components from abroad.   [4]

5 Coats Viyella is a manufacturer of materials for the fashion industry. Suggest how it might respond to an increase in exchange rates.   [6]

20

Maxi Case Study

Whether Britain joins the European Monetary Union or not in the near future, the euro appears to be here to stay. Doug McWilliams of the Centre for Economic and Business Research suggested that the majority of international businesses would be dealing and thinking in euros from now on. A Labour MP, Giles Radice, claimed that British businesses were losing out heavily because they were not having the benefits of low interest rates and exchange rate certainty.

But others indicated that there were serious pitfalls in joining the 'euro train'; the European Research Group reported that there were only small savings to be made, but initial costs of converting to the euro were huge. The problems encountered when Britain joined the Exchange Rate Mechanism for a short while led to a large increase in unemployment and a large number of bankruptcies.

All was not well with those forming 'Euroland'; of the 11 countries that agreed to use the euro, many still showed large variations in the price of standard products sold throughout Europe. Allowing for variations in taxes that were on the table to be eradicated, prices still differed beyond the ideal for such a union.

It is the intention of member consumers to ensure that the euro price of a standard product is the same throughout member states. Even if Britain adopted the euro immediately, the British Retail Consortium indicated that its members would need at least three years to be in a position to operate on a euro basis. Having all the notes and coins printed and minted is easy; ensuring there are the facilities to use such a currency is a different matter. Not joining EMU has attracted much criticism; one issue is that the pound may be viewed as a fluctuating currency and the euro will be seen as a stable currency with all the associated advantages for one and disadvantages for the other. Having a stable currency may eradicate many of the currency speculators who earn their living investing other people's money on the assumption that financial gains can be made. This may lead to a shift in how much of the City's money is invested; the chances are that not all of it would be invested in British businesses which had a less certain future.

One final thought; if the final barrier to free trade is dismantled and businesses can therefore compete only on their own costs, will there be a spate of European mergers in an attempt to gain the benefits of economies of scale?

Adapted from 'Life with the Euro', *The Sunday Times* 3/1/1999

1 Define: unemployment, stable currency.   [4]

2 Suggest why it may take a considerable amount of time to ensure British retailers will be ready to use the euro.   [6]

3 What are the main advantages of having a stable currency for customers in Britain?   [5]

4 Why does the case suggest that many of Britain's businesses have a less certain future?   [5]

5 Evaluate the importance of joining the European Monetary Union for two companies of your choice.   [10]

30

Business ethics

Learning objectives

Having read this unit, students will be able to

1. appreciate how morality may affect the decision making process

2. discuss how a business may react to changes in ethical factors

Context

Reading any newspaper will provide ample examples of ethical issues. One such topical issue was the war in Kosovo. Shares in British Aerospace, Britain's top defence company, rose 410p at the start of the bombing to 464p. Shareholders might have been delighted at the rise in the value of their shares and the 400,000 employees in the British defence industry may feel more secure in their jobs, but at what cost to those on the receiving end of the military hardware that British Aerospace manufactures?

The ethical dilemma is obvious; the 'solution' is not so straightforward. There is no right answer, but businesses need to be aware that they have a responsibility to consider such matters when taking decisions.

BAT, the world's second largest international tobacco company, states: 'We have long considered that the choice to smoke or not is one exclusively for adults. We do not want children to smoke and we actively support programmes to prevent and reduce under-age smoking. ... We agree with public health authorities that it is proper not to smoke for prolonged periods around young children, but public smoking is a social issue, which can be resolved by having sensible regard for other people' (BAT Annual Review 1998).

The issue of ethics has, in recent years, become of prime importance to businesses and reflects the growing sense of social responsibility which a business faces.

Ethics defined

Ethics may be defined as a set of social principles that govern or influence how we behave.

Business ethics are the principles that influence the decision making process. There may be several occasions when decisions are made by a business which do not improve the profitability of the company. On the contrary, such decisions may even add to the costs that the business incurs. These decisions have been made in the light of ethical considerations such as the aim of ensuring the environment is not damaged or catering for the needs of its employees beyond legal requirements by providing crèche facilities.

Some businesses refer to a sense of social responsibility; providing special seating areas for the disabled at sporting venues and other places of entertainment is a typical example.

Marks and Spencer actually referred to 'ethical trading' in its Annual Review and Summary Financial Statement 1999:

'Agreeing good working standards has always been important to our partnership with suppliers. This presents more of a challenge now that our global supply base has become so vast and complex. But we are determined to do what we can. So we have joined the Ethical Trading Initiative and are enforcing a set of Global Sourcing Principles. These cover areas such as work-force rights, accurate labelling of country of origin and environmental responsibility.'

Social responsibility or ethical behaviour goes beyond complying with the law. Marks and Spencer provides audio tapes of its Annual Review for the visually impaired. There are instances of businesses that have not broken any laws being perceived as acting in an unethical manner. The behaviour of British Airways towards one of its rivals, Virgin Airlines, has been described as unethical.

Is it 'right' or ethical for a large company to delay paying a small company in an attempt to improve its cash flow, even at the risk of jeopardising the existence of the smaller company? Of course there is no right answer but the question of ethics is something that ought to be a part of any business's decision making.

Question 1

Highest paid directors at privatised companies

	Salary at privatisation	Salary, bonus & benefits, 1994	Salary, bonus & benefits, 1997–98
British Gas	50,000	492,602	427,245
British Telecom	94,000	663,000	1,101,000
Eastern	62,270	296,000	376,000
East Midlands	62,270	331,712	458,000
London	75,950	201,145	180,000
Manweb	62,270	240,509	487,345
Midlands	67,500	231,802	358,000
Northern	86,800	210,000	123,000
Norweb	62,270	215,274	238,400
Seeboard	65,100	184,000	407,000
Southern	62,270	258,000	297,148
Swalec	65,375	203,420	325,000
SWEB	70,525	213,000	269,000
Yorkshire	62,270	211,354	255,400
National Power	185,000	374,886	546,285
PowerGen	103,075	350,393	458,000
National Grid	N/A	330,000	355,000
Anglian	53,750	169,000	286,967
Northumbrian	54,800	135,000	175,000
North West	100,000	338,000	229,366
Severn Trent	75,250	224,200	239,800
Southern Water	100,000	169,000	487,345
South West (Pennon)	70,000	130,000	198,000
Thames	150,000	247,000	277,000
Welsh	59,125	139,000	325,000
Wessex	72,563	166,000	206,000
Yorkshire	54,825	156,000	298,000

Source *The Sunday Times*, 25/7/99

Are these pay awards for directors of privatised companies ethical? (Justify your answer)   [6]

Question 2

What are the ethical issues involved for the following?
a)   Trading with dictatorships
b)   Building new roads
c)   Banning fox hunting
d)   Manchester United not participating in the FA Cup
e)   Organ donations restricted to only certain types of recipients   [15]

The benefits of being ethical

Good publicity

For some companies their stance on issues such as the environment has been one of the reasons why people choose to be their customers. The Body Shop is the classic example of a business whose stance on the environment and not testing its products on animals has contributed to much of its success. In her book *Body and Soul* (Ebury Press, 1991), Anita Roddick states:

'In a society in which politicians no longer lead by example, ethical conduct is unfashionable, and the media does not give people real information on what is happening in the world, what fascinates me is the concept of turning our shops into centres of education.'

Much progress has been made since her book was published. Companies have realised there are benefits to taking a more ethical approach. Coca-Cola received much praise for the way in which it handled the difficult crisis that started in Belgium where a bottling plant allegedly used a poor batch of carbon dioxide to carbonate drinks. This was compounded by the contamination of cans in Dunkirk, France due to fungicide that was used to treat shipping pallets but had contaminated the surface of the cans. Coca-Cola responded swiftly by withdrawing all cans of Coke from the countries affected. The company could have spent a lot less telling the consumer it was an isolated incident and that there was no further risk to the health of its customers.

Additional sales and therefore profits

Consumers who are concerned about recycling or other environmental issues may make a conscious decision to purchase products from a company that actively supports such practices. As a consequence sales may increase.

A more content work-force

A company that provides additional facilities for the well-being of its employees may be 'rewarded' with a more productive work-force. In addition, the turnover of employees may be lower, saving the company the expense of recruitment and training of new staff.

The costs of being, or not being, ethical

The costs of being or not being ethical can be considered under two headings:
a) Costs specific to the company
b) Costs specific to the environment

Costs specific to the company

- **Bad publicity**
  Newspapers in the second half of 1999 were full of articles about the price of buying cars in Britain compared to prices on the continent. Knowing that a Rover 400 series could be bought for £10,995 in the UK and the same car could be purchased for £7,048 in France did little for the image of car manufacturers in the eyes of the British consumer. Trying to convince consumers that the manufacturers were acting in an ethical manner with regard to pricing policies proved difficult. The fact that the Competition Commission saw fit to investigate such practices might suggest that the consumer was being exploited.

  The car manufacturers featured again in 1999 after a series of 'recalls'. A company will announce a recall of a particular model of car if a fault has been found that could cause problems for the customer if not dealt with.

  A recall was announced for the Rolls-Royce Silver Seraph and the Bentley Arnage because of a fault with the heated seats. Ford recalled three out of every four new Focus cars to fix an electrical fault. The publicity for such recalls tends to be negative because the company is admitting a fault has occurred. It might be argued that at least the company is admitting to this and therefore deserves praise for doing so. Such recalls can however be very expensive.

- **Increased costs**
  The costs to the business of being ethical will vary depending on the product and the particular set of circumstances. They are also difficult to measure. The actual cost to a theatre of installing a lift to enable disabled people to visit can be measured. However the net cost is harder to assess. The number of additional customers that use the theatre as a result of the lift being installed may reduce or even cover the cost of the lift. There may also be some positive publicity from the expenditure.

- **Loss of profit**
  Any additional costs incurred may lead to a fall in the level of profits which may not be viewed favourably by the shareholders. The value of the company's shares may also fall as a result of the lower profits.

Costs specific to the environment

■ **Actions from pressure groups**

Groups such as Greenpeace, Friends of the Earth and the trade unions may bring negative publicity for the company by highlighting what the **pressure groups** deem to be a negative externality. This is a social cost incurred as a result of a particular business activity. A haulage company encouraging its lorry drivers to take a short cut through a small village creates additional noise pollution and will probably damage the roads as well. The savings achieved are benefits for the company, but the 'damage' is to areas outside the business. The **negative externalities** are the knock-on effects of the actions of the company.

Conclusion

It is difficult to assess whether a business is genuinely concerned about ethical issues or is just intent on avoiding bad publicity and is therefore paying only lip-service to such matters. What does matter is that there is a degree of common sense applied to the implementation of ethical issues. A judgement as to what is practical and profitable, both in the short and long term, has to be considered.

Making a North Sea oil rig safe for both the employees who have to work on it and the environment is almost impossible. The cost of gaining small increases in the degree of safety may render the rig too expensive to operate. The alternative is such a large increase in the cost of petrol that the consumer would not be prepared to foot the bill. Both options may lead to a loss of jobs for the rig workers. Such decisions have to be weighed against the risk of loss of life and of environmental damage.

Ask employees at a British Nuclear Fuels Limited plant whether they would prefer a job or to reduce the risk of contamination to zero.

Many companies have issued a code of ethics or a voluntary code of practice in an attempt to show they are taking seriously responsibility for their employees, customers and society as a whole.

Question 3

Should hospitals employ additional security guards to improve the safety of doctors and nurses on duty at the expense of medical facilities for the patients?

[5]

Points for Revision

Key Terms

ethics	set of social principles influencing behaviour
business ethics	social principles that ought to influence the decision making process of a business
negative externalities	the social costs of a business activity, for example, pollution
pressure groups	groups with a particular viewpoint that they wish a business to adopt; for example, Greenpeace or Friends of the Earth

Definitions Question:
With reference to a firm or firms of which you have direct knowledge or experience, explain the importance of any two of the above terms (your teacher may wish to select the terms). [5] per definition

Summary Points:

1   Ethics is concerned with a set of principles which may influence the decision making process.

2   More companies are attempting to show they have a social conscience.

3   There are benefits and costs for a business that operates in an ethical manner.

Mini Case Study

Consumers appear to be determined to have their cake and eat it. More supermarkets are selling vegetables that are fairly uniform in size, shape and colour in order to please their customers. To satisfy the customer, supermarkets have put pressure on farmers to produce more vegetables of a perfect colour and shape at a price the customer is willing to pay. This has required the use of pesticides, herbicides and various other agrochemicals.

The consequences for the bird population have been dramatic:

SONGBIRDS UNDER THREAT
The downward trend is all too obvious in these estimated populations from the British Trust for Ornithology

Skylark MINUS 60% 1972 – 7.72m 1996 – 3.09m

Willow warbler MINUS 23% 1972 – 6.06m 1996 – 4.67m

Linnet MINUS 41% 1972 – 1.56m 1996 – 925,000

Song thrush MINUS 52% 1972 – 3.62m 1996 – 1.74m

Lapwing MINUS 42% 1972 – 588,000 1996 – 341,000

Yellowhammer MINUS 60% 1972 – 4.4m 1996 – 1.76m

Blackbird MINUS 33% 1972 – 12.54m 1996 – 8.4m

Tree sparrow MINUS 87% 1972 – 650,000 1996 – 84,500

Corn bunting MINUS 74% 1972 – 114,000 1996 – 30,000

Providing the food that is required is the aim of all concerned from the farmer and the National Farmers' Union, the agrochemical industry and the supermarkets; none however puts much emphasis on the real price that has to be paid in order to achieve the aim.

It is not just the birds which suffer. Anglian Water spends many millions of pounds filtering the nitrate fertilisers and pesticides out of the water supply.

In order to meet such high expectations in terms of yields, farmers quickly eradicated the hedgerows to plant more crops and take full advantage of the subsidies that were readily available under the European Union's Common Agricultural Policy. The bird population did not stand a chance; there were no places left for nesting and what they ate would probably kill them. Members of BTO (British Trust for Ornithology) and the RSPB (Royal Society for the Protection of Birds) have produced figures and voiced their concern over the dramatic fall in the population of birds in Britain.

There are alternatives, but these require the farmer to be as determined to help the survival of the birds as to produce large yields. While the farmer continues to receive healthy subsidies for growing crops and the more that are grown, the larger the subsidy, then the bird population will continue to decline. Losing the hedgerows and the birds is the 'price' of cheap food. It ought not to be forgotten who pays for the subsidy!

The questions that remain to be answered are whether the customer is prepared to pay more for the food that is required; is the farmer prepared to reduce yields to allow for the hedges to be replaced and the use of alternative methods of controlling pests to be tried?

Adapted from an article, 'Where have all the flyers gone?'
The Sunday Times Magazine, 25/7/1999

1 Suggest the actions within the case that could be considered unethical.	[4]
2 Give two examples of pressure groups referred to in the case.	[2]
3 To what extent does the farmer face an ethical dilemma?	[6]
4 Present an argument in favour of banning the use of insecticides and pesticides.	[8]

20

Maxi Case Study

Severn Trent is a major supplier of water and waste services throughout the UK and Europe. It takes pride in proclaiming that environmental leadership and commercial success can go hand in hand. In the Annual Report for 1999, Severn Trent states:

'Throughout the 1990s we have increasingly understood that running water and waste management services profitably for the long term can only be sustainable by securing a balance between economic, environmental and social issues. For us, an evolving environmental agenda is a developing and growing business agenda. Environmental leadership lies at the heart of our business strategy'.

The report adds:

'Environmental leadership is important to the company in one further respect; it will enable us to articulate a series of values – the ethics by which we do business – to our key stakeholder groups, particularly our employees.'

To this end, Severn Trent has introduced a series of measures which it considers are meeting the needs of its customers and its caring philosophy. The measures include duty of care, a packaging directive and a new initiative for pollution control. Severn Trent provides several examples of its record in terms of achieving its environmental leadership mission. It has installed a special treatment process for Cadbury's Bristol factory that manufactures Crunchie, Picnic and Double Decker. The process enables Cadbury to extract water from a local borehole and discharge its waste water into the River Avon without producing any effluent or chemicals. The system meets with the approval of the Environment Agency, a 'watchdog' for pollution. The new process helps reduce the costs incurred by Cadbury.

Biffa Waste Services, part of Severn Trent plc, introduced the 'Bottleback' scheme. This is a scheme where Biffa collects bottles from pubs and clubs, restaurants and other outlets selling bottled drinks throughout the country. Due to the size of the operation, it is possible to gain the benefits of economies of scale and thus make such a scheme economically viable. It is hoped that the Bottleback scheme will provide nearly one-third of all recycled glass in the country. Another element of the company's environmental leadership mission is its community affairs programme. Severn Trent states:

'We recognise that we have an important role to play in these communities in helping make a real difference to the quality of life for the local people. Furthermore by investing in the community, we are investing in our future.'

The company lists addressing issues such as homelessness, deprivation, developing environmental awareness, providing environmental awards and raising money for self-help water schemes in developing countries.

Several pages of the Annual Report are dedicated to the various schemes that it has either initiated or actively supports. Meanwhile, Ofwat regulator Ian Byatt was about to announce imposed price cuts for the water companies for the five-year price review. The share price of these companies had already started to fall as a result of the impending announcement. An estimate by a writer for *The Sunday Times* indicated that Severn Trent could expect to have to cut its prices by as much as 15%. Such a price cut was contrary to the submission to Ofwat by the water companies which were asking for permission to increase prices in order to undertake a large programme of investment.

1 Define: business strategy, economies of scale, investment.   [6]

2 Suggest how the installation of the special treatment process at Cadbury's has helped reduce costs.   [4]

3 Using the evidence in the case, discuss whether the environmental leadership programme will mirror 'the ethics by which we do business'.   [6]

4 To what extent is it more important that everyone can afford to pay for the water they use, regardless of the lack of profit the water companies are able to make?   [6]

5 Discuss the ethical issues Ofwat may take into consideration before deciding whether to insist that the water companies reduce their prices?   [8]

30

'Friday afternoon'

End of section test

1 Define the following: quota, tariff. [4]
2 What is meant by a balance of trade surplus? [2]
3 What is the Common External Tariff? [3]
4 Who determines the rate of interest in the UK? [1]
5 What is globalisation? [4]
6 Draw a diagram to show the trade cycle. [3]
7 What is the main weapon used for monetary policy? [1]
8 When would a surplus budget be used by the Chancellor? [3]
9 What type of economic weapons would a Keynesian use? [2]
10 Name two causes of inflation. [2]
11 Draw a diagram to show the consequences of the introduction of the minimum wage. [4]
12 What is meant by the term seasonal unemployment? [3]
13 Give an example of a legal right for an employee. [2]
14 What type of budget is most likely to be used to tackle unemployment? [1]
15 What is hot money? [3]
16 Why would a business incur additional costs if the rate of interest was increased? [4]
17 Give three examples of legislation to protect the consumer. [3]
18 What is the name of the body that has replaced the Monopolies and Mergers Commission? [1]
19 What is the name of the body that acts as a mediator? [1]
20 What is the role of the Council of Ministers? [3

50

'Friday afternoon' 1

The marketing executives representing Nicky Clarke, the celebrity hairdresser, had discussed the issues long into the night.

Sales were vital to the success of his company and publicity would gain attention for the product. However, there was some concern as to how far the adverts ought to go in terms of decency. Furthermore, if the adverts were not considered acceptable by the Advertising Standards Authority, a lot of money would have been wasted on a campaign that few would ever see.

Several adverts had been the subject of investigations by the ASA. The Irn-Bru advert in which a cow is pictured saying 'When I'm a burger, I want to be washed down with Irn-Bru' had caused problems and, according to ASA figures, 589 complaints had been received.

The previous advertising campaign for Nicky Clarke's shampoo had featured a naked couple in the shower and, as a result of the advert, 131 complaints had been made to the ASA. Although the complaints were not upheld by the ASA, the question of decency had been raised.

The dilemma facing the executives was whether to repeat this type of advert or take a 'safer' option and not risk any ethical debate about moral standards. The fact that the advert had been a success in terms of gaining publicity for the shampoo was also important.

Should moral principles come before profitability? This was the question that faced the marketing executives.

1 Why were the executives concerned about the standard of decency? [3]

2 Explain what was meant by 'a lot of money would have been wasted on a campaign'. [6]

3 Are there any other ethical issues that the executives ought to consider before deciding on their next advertising campaign? [4]

4 Suggest whether the next advertising campaign for the shampoo ought to concentrate on gaining publicity and sales regardless of moral concerns. [7]

_____
20

'Friday afternoon' 2

1 Suggest how an increase in interest rates 'would damage consumer and business confidence'. [6]

2 Explain what is meant by 'inflation in the high street turned negative'. [3]

3 Why is the value of the euro so important to the member countries? [3]

4 How would knowing that the pound had fallen half a penny against the euro be of interest to a British cosmetics company intent on selling its products in Europe? [8]

_____
20

Euro at three-month high against sterling

BY LEA PATERSON AND ALASDAIR MURRAY

THE euro continued its remarkable turnround on the foreign exchanges yesterday, climbing to a three-month high against the pound and making further headway against the dollar.

Sterling's latest bout of euro weakness came despite hints from the Bank of England's Monetary Policy Committee (MPC) that UK interest rates were set to stay on hold at 5 per cent.

Minutes of the last MPC meeting, released yesterday, revealed the committee voted unanimously to leave rates unchanged and did not discuss further rate cuts.

According to the minutes, the committee also discussed the virtues of reversing the June rate cut, although it decided against such a move amid fears it would damage consumer and business confidence.

Growth in the UK economy is recovering steadily and inflation is set to remain benign, the committee said, a picture reinforced by data out yesterday.

According to figures from the Office for National Statistics (ONS), inflation in the high street turned negative in June, suggesting retailers are tempting customers back into the shops by cutting prices.

Retail sales volumes were flat, the ONS said, but revisions to historical data took the year-on-year growth rate to a healthy 3.8 per cent.

The growing perception that UK interest rates will not fall further bolstered the pound against the dollar, but was not sufficient to stop sterling slipping against the euro.

The pound closed in London at 66.73p to the euro, down half a pence from Tuesday's close. Against the dollar, sterling ended at $1.5738.

The euro racked up further gains against the dollar, climbing a cent to reach $1.0535, its highest level in more than a month. The single currency has risen by 4 per cent against the greenback so far this week.

The euro's two-day rally, sparked by signs of economic recovery in Germany, has left many in the market confident that the currency will now avoid the ignominy of falling to parity with the dollar.

A Reuters poll yesterday found that the number of economists expecting the euro to avoid parity had doubled in the past two weeks with two thirds now believing its recent rally would be maintained.

However, the medium-term picture remains more clouded, with some analysts cautioning that forward indications of improved European growth still had to be turned into reality.

Maxi Case Study

DD (Delicate Deliveries) is a private limited company which specialises in the distribution of fragile products such as chinaware and computers. It was established originally as a family business and transported almost anything to anywhere. More recently and after some salutary lessons about the consequences of running a business when the economy is in recession, the business has become a limited company and has found a market niche delivering fragile goods to and from Europe.

Jonathan Taylor, one of the major shareholders and a founder of the business, had decided he wanted to ensure the business was strong enough to cope with any change in the business cycle or government economic policy. The government had just announced a surplus budget in an attempt to deflate the economy, which was showing signs of an excessive increase in the level of demand. In addition, the Monetary Policy Committee had increased the rate of interest by one percentage point, the largest increase for several years. Another shareholder and the finance director of DD, Stephanie Fisher, was not pleased at the prospect of having to maintain the amount of business as a result of the economic announcements.

'We will have difficulties both at home and abroad. The cost of our British customers' products will increase due to the tight budget and therefore there will be fewer products for us to transport.' 'It is not all gloom,' suggested Jonathan, 'the increase in interest rates will mean more products will need transporting to Britain.'

Sheila, the marketing manager, was more concerned about the recent negative publicity one of their major customers had received after an article appeared in a Sunday newspaper about the 'sweatshop' factories that were used to assemble some of the components for computers that DD transported. She thought it would be difficult to continue trading with a company that was reported as being uncaring and paying its workers such low wages. Jonathan was not too worried and reminded Sheila that by keeping assembly costs down, the computers were cheaper and therefore sales were buoyant. High sales meant more computers to be transported by DD.

Stephanie had more immediate problems to contend with. One of DD's customers, Stoke Chinaware, had written a formal letter of complaint insisting on a full reimbursement for a consignment of pottery that had been damaged in transit. The driver had insisted the crates had arrived in good order and that it was the fork lift driver unloading the goods who had been responsible for the damage. Stephanie did not want to lose a valuable customer that had provided approximately 20 per cent of turnover last year. Nor did she want to spend money on an expensive court case or pay significantly higher insurance premiums to cover the cost of the damaged goods.

Sheila thought that because of all the recent events, now would be a good time for a new marketing campaign abroad to bring in extra business, perhaps even to diversify a little.

1 Define: market niche, assembly costs, turnover. [6]
2 Suggest why the cost of British goods may increase as a result of the surplus budget. [4]

3 Explain why an increase in interest rates may lead to an increase in the amount of goods that will need transporting into Britain. [6]
4 To what extent does the newspaper article present an ethical dilemma for DD? [8]
5 What are the legal rights for DD following the letter from one of its customers regarding the damaged goods? [6]

30

Ramsbotham brewery

Ramsbotham brewery – Episode 1

The Company

Ramsbotham Brewery is a Lancashire-based private limited company which was founded by Percy Arkwright in 1920. He brewed traditional ales and sold them to local public houses; growth was slow, though he built up a loyal consumer base. His son Harry Arkwright took on the business in 1960 and made a commitment to invest in more modern technology, though he continued to sell the same product range while expanding to pubs in the rest of the region. Harry Arkwright is about to retire and the business is to be run by his two sons, Jason and Darren, who have been serving their apprenticeship over a period of years and are ambitious to make the company grow. At a recent meeting of shareholders, there was concern that due to changes in both the market and the increasing range of products, the company was losing opportunities and, as a business, was not investing for growth: the shareholders emphasised the need for a change in objectives with a focus on expansion.

They also criticised the directors for the low levels of retained profit over the past four or five years which have stayed the same despite the following two points:
1 the company sells a product which is seen as high quality commanding a premium price
2 since 1991, the removal of regulations in the brewing industry had allowed the company to increase its volume to 90% of capacity though this was not typical of the industry as a whole (*see Table 1.1*).

The machinery in the brewery was installed when Harry Arkwright took over and maintenance costs have increased markedly in recent years. Indeed, none of the work-force is trained to repair the machinery so every time there is a problem (normally one a week) a technician has to be called in.

The company uses a labour-intensive process of brewing and has ignored changes in technology that have been adopted by large brewers in the industry; most of the 40-strong work-force are over 50 years of age and have been working at the company for an average of 27 years. They are loyal to the company and the owner, and still brew the ale and put it into barrels in the same way they have always done. The lack of retained profit has prevented the company from finding the funds to reinvest and Harry Arkwright refuses to use a bank as a source of finance. Approximately 10% of output is sent to a local bottle manufacturer to fill the bottles with ale. The size of each production run is particularly small (due to Ramsbotham's small share of the bottled ale market) and the peculiar design of the bottle that Harry Arkwright has insisted on (based on the original product from 1920) takes a long lead time to set up; the result is a relatively high cost to Ramsbotham for each bottle. The ales (both in barrels and bottles) are transported to each pub by the company's own fleet of lorries which are also ageing (all bought in 1970) and are designed only for carrying beer.

The Market

The company sells its output to a specific market niche – men who are over 50. Its customers are extremely loyal to the product as it is familiar to them (even the logo and colouring on the pumps is the same as it was 50 years ago). Customers frequent small, back-street pubs (old ale houses) which means the market is static and small. The shareholders have also been concerned that there have been some dramatic changes in the brewing industry over the past five years:

- Government regulation (through the work of the then Monopolies Commission) has restricted the number of pubs that an individual brewer may own

- There has been a growth in the number of free trade pubs (those which have no obligation to buy from one particular brewer)

- Pubs such as The Big Steak Pub and Brewer's Fayre (known as 'pubcos') have also grown in number because of their attraction for families and those customers who wish to eat out

Trends in purchasing have also altered:

- More people drink at home (purchasing products from off-licences); families use the pubcos more frequently; more imported bottled beer is sold (at a premium price)

- There is a general problem of over-capacity in the market (*see Table 1.1*)

Darren has noticed that 'soft' alcoholic drinks (otherwise known as 'alcopops') have been met with a positive response from the market. All of them seem to be expensive in relation to other drinks of the same alcoholic content, yet each product is differentiated with attractive, colourful packaging and lively advertising. He proposes that the company researches the possibility of introducing an alcoholic blackcurrant drink (Product X) to the market.

Appendix 1

Table 1.1 – UK beer production

	1990	1991	1992	1993	1995	2000
Million barrels	36	35	34	33	32	30
Excess capacity (%)	24	17	18	17	20	25
UK beer consumption	38.5	38	36	34.5	34.5	n/a
Ramsbotham's capacity 250 barrels per week (1 barrel = 36 gallons, 1 gallon = 8 pints)						

Source: S.G. Warburg, Datastream, adapted from *Financial Times* 9/2/95

Table 1.2 – Purchasing characteristics

Per cent of population	Sex			Age				Social grade			
	All adults	Male	Female	18–24	25–34	35–49	50+	AB	C1	C2	DE
Any alcoholic drink	63	74	53	73	66	67	56	73	67	62	52
Any beer	40	62	20	58	49	43	30	41	41	44	36
Vermouth (e.g. Cinzano)	2	1	3	3	1	3	2	3	2	2	1
Wine	30	28	32	23	32	36	28	49	36	24	15
Present customers		100					100			70	30

Source: *Marketing Pocket Book 1999*, NTC Publications

Postscript: An article in *Sunday Business* said:

'A report out by Mintel ..... people who are most likely to view alcopops (such as Product X) as an alternative to beer are single men aged 18–24, living in the south, Yorkshire and the north east.'

1 Explain the relevance of the following terms: retained profit, labour-intensive, lead time   [6]

2 Outline the likely effect of the government regulation reducing the number of outlets a brewery can own, on

   a) the consumer

   b) the producer

   c) the retailer   [9]

3 Why are economies of scale important to a firm like Ramsbotham?   [6]

4 Jason has read that price elasticity for the ale is 2. He wants to reduce the price by 10% in an attempt to remain competitive and as the main part of a promotional campaign.

   a) Calculate the effect on volume and revenue if the company follows Jason's idea. Assume a 50-week year.   [3]

   b) Suggest why Jason might be incorrect to assume a price elasticity of 2.   [6]

5 Using the data in Appendix 1 and relevant information from the text, identify an appropriate segment of the market for Product X. Explain your choice.   [7]

6 Bearing in mind the requests of the shareholders, as a marketing consultant, suggest appropriate marketing objectives that the company could follow.   [5]

7 Outline the market research required so that the company can put into effect a marketing strategy which will meet the new objectives of the company.   [5]

8 How would knowledge of the Boston matrix help the company in its implementation of the marketing strategy?   [6]

9 How might distribution of the product alter with the introduction of Product X?   [7]

60

Presentation

You have been hired by the company as marketing consultant for Product X. Write a report to the directors explaining the marketing strategy you would recommend to the company. Your report should contain the following headings: market segments, objectives, research, marketing plan (elements of the marketing mix). Make sure you justify your recommendations.

30

Ramsbotham brewery – Episode 2

The Forecast

Following consultation with one or two shareholders about the proposed venture into producing a product aimed at a younger age group, Jason undertook a market research campaign which confirmed to him that there was definitely a market niche to be exploited for Product X. He was quite clear that growth of the company should be the prime objective, though he was not quite sure how to achieve it.

The brothers asked a friend of theirs, Tarquin Carruthers, to forecast long-term cash flows in order to assess the potential of Product X. Tarquin estimated that the total cost of the machinery required to produce X was £480,000 and that £70,000 must be added to this cost in order to fund an effective marketing campaign (the results of his work can be seen in Table 2.1). The brewery has some old buildings at the side of the present factory where the old stables used to house the cart-horses during the war and the new production plant will be sited there, though the lead time to redecorate the building and install the new machinery will be six months, once the decision to go ahead has been taken.

Darren looked at the figures and was immediately convinced that such a venture was worthwhile, though Jason was a little more sceptical.

Jason agreed that the figures produced by Tarquin were realistic, but he was concerned about cash flow during the first six months. There would undoubtedly be teething problems with production and possibly a cautious public, given that the diversification into a new market was the most significant change in the company's history. Sales to begin with would be rather slow, and would begin only in the seventh month – an estimation of the sales pattern can be seen in Table 2.2. Materials will arrive for production in the same month as the product is sold; material costs are 40% of sales value, on one month's credit.

Labour costs are estimated to be £15,000 per annum per person and only two people would be needed to operate the machinery, though the company will need to spend £3,600 on a training course for the two employees in the first month of production (month 7). Fixed costs for the new plant are estimated to be £10,000 per month.

The Finance

Clearly the new venture would improve the company's profitability, though the success of the entire operation will depend on a meeting with the bank manager, for which the family is preparing. Looking through their recent accounting statements (*see Table 2.3*) there seem to be few alternatives; the present business has not been profitable and despite the lack of profit, the shareholders have awarded themselves a large dividend, because of their increasing reliance on dividends for their income; Darren has just decided to buy an expensive house and feels justified in this approach. Although their father is reluctant for the company to borrow, Jason sees it as the only possibility left. Initially, the company's gearing will increase and interest cover will fall, though if the operation is successful in financial terms, the gearing should decrease over time.

Appendix 2

Table 2.1 (£000)

Net operating cash flows for Product X:

EOY1	95
EOY2	200
EOY3	250
EOY4	310
EOY5	300

> NB. The capital outlay for this project occurs at EOY 0.

Although the new plant will be owned for considerably longer, Tarquin feels that a forecast beyond five years will be too inaccurate to use.

Discount factors @ 10%

Years hence	0	1	2	3	4	5
Value of £1	1	0.909	0.826	0.751	0.683	0.621

Table 2.2 (£000)

Projected sales revenue for Product X (price = £1):

Month	7	8	9	10	11	12
Sales revenue	15	30	38	48	50	65

Table 2.3

Balance sheet for Ramsbotham Brewery Ltd as at 31/12/99

(£000)

Fixed assets		
Land and buildings (includes revaluation)	435	
Plant and machinery	60	
Vehicles	10	
		505

Current assets		
Stocks	35	
Debtors	65	
	100	
Current liabilities		
Creditors	5	
Overdraft	50	
	55	
Net current assets		45
Net assets		**550**
Shareholder funds		
Share capital	150	
Reserves	400	
Capital employed		**550**

Profit and Loss Account for Ramsbotham Brewery Ltd for year ending 31/12/99

Sales revenue		**900**
Cost of sales	700	
Gross profit		**200**
Depreciation	35	
Maintenance*	50	
Other overheads	80	
Operating profit		**35**
Interest	5	
Profit before tax		**30**
Tax	8	
Profit after tax		**22**
Dividends	42	
Retained profit		**(20)**

(*includes technician charges for repairing old machinery)

1 Define: profitability, cash flow, gearing. [6]

2 a) Explain how shareholders can receive a dividend of £42,000 when the company has made a post-tax profit of only £22,000. [3]

   b) Apart from the level of profit, what factors affect the dividend payment made by companies? [4]

3 a) Explain the purpose of depreciation. [3]

   b) Depreciation is to be treated on a straight-line basis for the investment in the new plant; the residual value is expected to be £50,000 after 10 years. Calculate the effect on profit during the first year of ownership if the company used declining balance at 20% instead of straight-line depreciation.   [4]

4 Explain the last sentence in the case study which begins 'Initially, the company's gearing will....'   [5]

5 Using the balance sheet and profit and loss account, calculate three ratios which you would use to persuade the bank manager to lend money to the company. Justify your choice and evaluate the usefulness of the ratios you have chosen for Ramsbotham Brewery.   [9]

6 Using Table 2.1, calculate the net present value (at a discount rate of 10%), payback and average annual rate of return for the new investment. Assume cash flows occur at the end of each year.   [7]

7 a)   Using the information available, prepare an operating cash flow forecast for the first six months of producing the new product (i.e. months 7–12). Show that the operating cash flow for the first six months is £50,000. Assume marketing costs (£70,000) have been paid out by the time production begins and that the opening cash balance is zero.   [10]

b)   What is the value of creditors resulting from the production of Product X at the end of month 12?   [2]

8 a)   Using your answers to 5, 6 and 7 a), write a report to the bank manager justifying why the bank should lend the company £550,000 for Product X.   [12]

b)   What other information would the bank manager wish to discover before granting the company the loan?   [5]

9 If the bank decides not to lend the money, suggest alternative sources that can be used.   [10]

―――
80

Ramsbotham brewery – Episode 3

The Schedule

Following approval of finance from the company's bank, the brothers set about arranging for the new machinery to be purchased, delivered and installed. They also put an advertisement in the press for two new employees who would operate the production line. The brothers were very concerned about the time it would take to install the machinery, given that the old buildings in which the machinery was to be housed needed some renovation before installation. The fixed costs of £10,000 per month were to begin at the start of the month. In order to use their time efficiently the brothers hired the services of production engineer Colin Mackintosh (another friend from school), who asked Jason and Darren to list the activities required and their estimated length of time. The information is in Table 3.1.

The Stock

The original line was still fully operational, though it was inefficient. Colin had suggested the company should aim to reduce stock, because this would save money. Using the projected sales volume in Appendix 3 he prepared a stock chart for the first eight weeks of operation. The pattern of usage is shown in Figure 1.

Figure 1

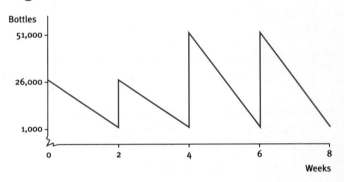

Originally the company had intended to use the present supplier of bottles who was used to delivering every two weeks. In an effort to reduce the level of stock, Ramsbotham asked for weekly delivery, though the supplier flatly refused, muttering something about impossible delivery schedules.

In the adverts in Bottles Weekly, a trade magazine for glass manufacturers, Jason found a new local, small supplier; an initial telephone call had confirmed that the supplier was keen to find new business and was able to supply on a weekly basis. The cost per bottle would be 30 pence and the supplier was willing to sign a contract to meet the first two months' sales (*shown in Appendix 3*).

Colin Mackintosh also recommended that the company should try to reduce its buffer stock to half of the present level though Darren felt this was too low, given that they had no idea how accurate their sales forecasts were likely to be.

Appendix 3

Table 3.1

Activity	Duration	Previous activity
A	5 days	–
B	4	A
C	5	A
D	3	A
E	2	B
F	7	D, E
G	3	C
H	5	G
J	8	G
K	2	F, H
L	3	J

1 Assuming salaries and training costs of the two employees are £18,500 for the first year and material costs are 40% of sales value:

   a) In which month will break-even occur, if at all? [4]

   b) Why is labour treated as a fixed cost in this case? [3]

2 What problems and benefits might the firm face when changing suppliers? [8]

3 **a)** Using the information in Diagram 1, draw a new stock chart, showing the levels of stock if a delivery was made once a week. Assume the same level of demand and a reduction in buffer stock of 50%. [5]

   b) From your diagram, establish the average level of stock for
   (i) the first four weeks
   (ii) the second four weeks [2]

   c) Interest rates are expected to be 10% until week 4, after which they will rise to 12%. Using your answers to **3 a)** and **b)**, calculate the cost of financing the stock for the eight-week period. Assume a 50-week year. [5]

   d) How useful is just-in-time stock management to Ramsbotham? [5]

   e) Explain the factors which affect the level of buffer stock set by the company. [5]

4 Quality control has not been particularly good in the old plant. How might a quality control system be implemented and what are the benefits to the company of producing zero defects? [10]

5 **a)**
   (i) Using Table 3.1, draw the network for the project. [9]
   (ii) From the network calculate the earliest start time and latest finish time of each activity. [4]

   b) State the minimum duration and critical path of the project. [2]

   c) Part of the installation requires two types of skill, known as 1 and 2. Draw a Gantt chart for the requirement of the skill level, given a maximum number of 12 units of labour available per day at the required level of skill.

Activity	Skill required	Number of men required
A	1	3
B	2	5
C	1	2
D	2	4
E	2	3

[6]

   d) Why would a delay of just one day be of more concern to Ramsbotham's for activity G when compared to activity D? [2]

                                                                    70

Ramsbotham brewery – Episode 4

The People

'Not another one,' thought Darren as the employee left his office. This had been the third resignation in as many weeks, bringing the total number of employees leaving in the year to six. Since the introduction of the new line of alcopops, the employees had faced problems coping with the new machinery and new working practices which had been introduced by Darren. He had anticipated that there would be some resistance to the change made and as a consequence had put up a notice informing workers that any opposition to the new machinery would result in them being sacked – certainly no-one could accuse him of poor communication skills, he thought to himself! He had actually discussed the most appropriate form of effective communication with his life-time friend, Sujith, who ran a clothing company up the road. Sujith had described his own sewing machinists as people who needed to be told what to do. 'They require strong leadership. If they see me being forceful and dictatorial, I reckon they will respect me more.' Darren agreed with this point of view because he felt that any questioning of his authority represented a sign of weakness and he also did not want to disrupt the production of what seemed to be a successful product launch with seemingly endless and pointless discussions on the new machinery. He was sure that the work-force would see the wisdom behind expansion and a more modern approach.

Jason, on the other hand, while on a search for some new computers, had visited a Japanese manufacturer and was interested to hear of the philosophy adopted by that company over involving employees in the decision making process. He observed a team of 'members', as the employees were called, sitting around a table during working hours discussing how to reorganise their part of the production line. The objective was to increase productivity. Such an approach, he was told, was carried out by the majority of the work-force of 45 employees, in groups of 8–10.

When Jason returned with his news, he was greeted with derision by Darren who claimed that the ageing work-force at Ramsbotham's would never accept such an alternative approach. Jason's immediate proposal was to make redundant those who were resistant to introducing such an approach and to hire a new, younger and more flexible work-force. Another alternative, proposed by Darren, was to put the entire work-force on shorter contracts and use part-time labour as a way of ensuring flexibility.

Jason had spoken with the younger employees who had been receptive to the idea of group discussions, although several of the older members were just interested in money. Jason had remembered reading about various motivation theories at night school and was pleased that they concurred with his own experience at Ramsbotham's.

The Future

What he could not remember from his work at night school related to the actions of the present government in controlling the economy. In an attempt to gain votes, the government had embarked on an ambitious expenditure programme to generate economic growth; Jason was unsure how this expenditure would affect sales of the new product. The other issue that concerned him was the integration of Britain into Europe and whether the business would be affected by Britain adopting the euro. He had read that interest rates would need to be the same for all countries within the single European currency trading bloc, and they had just been reduced to 3% for those countries, despite being well above that in Britain.

1 Define: effective communication, redundant, flexible work-force. [9]

2 Analyse the evidence in the case study which suggests there may be resistance to change within the organisation. [8]

3 Which motivation theories are appropriate for describing the employees' attitude to work? To what extent can these theories help Darren improve motivation at the business? [10]

4 Comment on the leadership style adopted by Darren: in what ways might an alternative approach to leadership improve the situation? [6]

5 Calculate labour turnover for the year. [2]

6 In addition to labour turnover, briefly explain *three* signs of low morale in a business. [3]

7 Analyse how the business might be affected by
   a) extra government expenditure [6]
   b) Britain joining the single currency [6]

$$\frac{}{50}$$

Index